Software Engineering

Modern Approaches

SECOND EDITION

Eric J. Braude
Boston University, Metropolitan College

Michael E. Bernstein
Boston University, Metropolitan College

WILEY

JOHN WILEY & SONS, INC.

Executive Editor	Beth Lang Golub
Editor	Jonathan Shipley
Assistant Editor	Georgia King
Editorial Assistant	Mike Berlin
Marketing Manager	Christopher Ruel
Designer	RDC Publishing Group Sdn Bhd
Production Manager	Janis Soo
Assistant Production Editor	Yee Lyn Song

Cover Credit: © Hulton Archive/Getty Images

This book was set in 10/12 Point Weiss by Thomson Digital, and printed and bound by R.R. Donnelley. The cover was printed by R.R. Donnelley.

This book is printed on acid free paper. ∞

Library of Congress Cataloging-in-Publication Data

Braude, Eric J.
  Software engineering : modern approaches / Eric J. Braude, Michael E. Bernstein. — 2nd ed.
    p. cm.
  Includes bibliographical references and index.
  ISBN 978-0-471-69208-9 (cloth)
 1. Software engineering. 2. Object-oriented programming (Computer science) I. Bernstein, Michael E. II. Title.
  QA76.758.B74 2011
  005.1—dc22

                                       2009051247

Printed in the United States of America

10 9 8 7 6 5 4 3 2 1

For Judy (Eric J. Braude)
To Bambi, Garrett and Reid,
for all their love and support (Michael E. Bernstein)

Brief Contents

Contents

Preface

Much of the modern world runs on software. As a result, software engineers are entrusted with significant responsibility. Although it is a biomedical engineer, for example, who designs health monitoring systems, it is a software engineer who creates its actual control functions. A marketing professional develops ways to reach customers online but it is a software engineer who makes the system a reality.

Today's software engineer must be able to participate in more than one kind of software process, work in agile teams, deal with customers, express requirements clearly, create modular designs, utilize legacy and open source projects, monitor quality, incorporate security, and apply many types of tests.

THE ISSUE OF SCALE

A software application consists of tens, hundreds, even thousands of classes. This is very different from managing three or four of them, and results in the dragon of complexity suggested by this book's cover. As also suggested there, however, this dragon can be subdued. Indeed, to deal with numerous and complex classes, software engineers have at their disposal a wide variety of tools and techniques. These range from the waterfall process to agile methodologies, from highly integrated tool suites to refactoring and loosely coupled tool sets. Underlying this variety is continuing research into reliable approaches, and an acknowledgment of the fact that one size does not fit all projects.

THIS EDITION COMPARED WITH THE FIRST

The first edition of this book emphasized the object-oriented approach, which has subsequently become widespread. It was also designed to help student teams carry out hands-on term projects through theory, examples, case studies, and practical steps. Object-orientation and hands-on continue to be major features of this edition. However, we have widened the scope of the first edition, especially by including extensive coverage of agile methods and refactoring, together with deeper coverage of quality and software design.

Readers of the first edition made extensive use of the complete video game case study—an example that they could follow "from soup to nuts" but which was significantly more comprehensive than a toy. This edition retains and updates that case study, but it adds the exploration of a simpler example on one hand (a DVD rental store) and large, real, open source case studies on the other. In particular, to provide students a feeling for the scope and complexity of real-world applications, this book leads them through selected requirements, design, implementation, and maintenance of the Eclipse and OpenOffice open source projects. The size, complexity, and transparency of these projects provide students a window into software engineering on a realistic scale.

Every book on software engineering faces a dilemma: how to reconcile the organization of the *topics* with the organization of actual software project *phases*. An organization of chapters into process/project management/requirements analysis/design/implementation/test/maintenance is straightforward but is liable to be misinterpreted as promoting the waterfall development process at the expense others. Our approach has been to use this organization in the seven parts of the book but to demonstrate throughout that each phase typically belongs to a cycle rather than to a single waterfall sequence. In particular, our approach integrates agile methodologies consistently.

This edition also introduces somewhat advanced influential ideas, including model-driven architectures and aspect-oriented programming. Nowadays, formal methods are mandated by government agencies for the highest levels of security, and this book aims to educate readers in their possibilities. Due to print space limitations, some of this material is to be found in the online extension of this book.

In summary, specific features of this edition compared with the first are as follows:

- A sharpening and standardization of the material from the first edition

- A strong agile thread throughout, including a chapter on agility alone and one devoted to refactoring.

- A separate chapter on quality in six of the book's seven parts

- Real-world case studies, taken from the Eclipse and OpenOffice open source projects

- Greatly expanded coverage of software design and design patterns

- New chapters on advanced, influential software engineering ideas

- An organization of many of the book's seven parts as follows:

  - Principles

  - Details

  - Quality

  - Advanced Methods

HOW INSTRUCTORS CAN USE THIS BOOK

This book has been designed to accommodate multiple approaches to the learning and teaching of software engineering. Most instructors teach the fundamentals of software process, project management, requirements analysis, design, testing, implementation, and maintenance. Beyond this common ground, however, instructors employ a wide variety of styles and emphases. The following are major approaches, together with the sequence of chapters that support each of them.

A. *Process emphasis*, concentrating on how applications are developed
   All of Parts I through IV; and Chapters 15, 22, and 25 (the remaining principles and introduction chapters)

B. *Design emphasis*, which teaches software engineering primarily as a design activity
   Principles and introduction: Chapters 1, 3, 7, and 10; all of Part V; and Chapters 22 and 25 (principles and introduction)

C. *Programming and agile emphasis*, which emphasizes software engineering as a code-oriented activity that satisfies requirements, emphasizing agile approaches
   Principles and introduction: Chapters 1, 3, 7, 10, and 15; all of Part VI; and Chapters 25 and 26

D. *Two-semester course*, which enables the instructor to cover most topics and assign a substantial hands-on project

D_1. All of the chapters in the book, either in sequence from beginning to end
or

D_2. In two passes as follows:

   (i) Principles and introduction chapters in the first semester: Chapters 1, 3, 7, 15, 22, and 25
   (ii) The remaining chapters in the second semester

E.   *Emphasis on a hands-on projects and case studies*, which relies mostly on an active team or individual project as the vehicle for learning theory and principles
Principles and introduction chapters: Chapters 1, 3, 7, 15, 22, 25, and 26, and all case study sections in the remaining chapters

F.   *Theory and principles emphasis*, concentrating on what one can learn about software engineering and its underpinnings
Principles and introduction chapters: Chapters 1, 2, 3, 7, 15, 22, and 25, followed, as time allows, by Chapters 14 and 21 (emerging topics)

G.   *Quality assurance and testing emphasis*
Principles and introduction: Chapters 1, 3, 7, and 10; Chapters 2, 5, 9, 13, 20, 23 (quality); and Chapters 25, 26, 27, and 28 (testing).

The web site for this book, including review questions and the Encounter game case study, is www.wiley.com/college/braude.

Eric Braude
Michael Bernstein
Boston, MA
January 2010

Acknowledgments

We owe a debt of gratitude to our students at Boston University's Metropolitan College. Working in myriad industries and businesses, they have given us invaluable feedback. The College itself has provided a model place for the teaching and learning software engineering. Our thanks go to Dick Bostwick and Tom VanCourt, much of whose work in the first edition carries over to this one. We are grateful to the people of Wiley for working with us through the painstaking process of writing and publishing this book. We are particularly appreciative of the help from our editors, Dan Sayre and Jonathan Shipley; from Georgia King, Yee Lyn Song, and the indefatigable staff. We thank the reviewers of our manuscript, whose feedback has been invaluable:

Arvin Agah, University of Kansas
Steven C. Shaffer, Pennsylvania State University
Stephen M. Thebaut, University of Florida
Aravinda P. Sistla, University of Illinois, Chicago
James P. Purtilo, University of Maryland
Linda M. Ott, Michigan Technological University
Jianwei Niu, University of Texas, San Antonio
William Lively, Texas A&M University
Chung Lee, California State University, Pomona
Sudipto Ghosh, Colorado State University
Max I. Fomitchev, Pennsylvania State University
Lawrence Bernstein, Stevens Institute of Technology
John Dalbey, California Polytechnic University
Len Fisk, California State University, Chico
Ahmed M. Salem, California State University, Sacramento
Fred Strauss, New York University
Kai H. Chang, Auburn University
Andre van der Hoek, University of California, Irvine
Saeed Monemi, California Polytechnic University
Robert M. Cubert, University of Florida
Chris Tseng, San Jose State University
Michael James Payne, Purdue University
Carol A. Wellington, Shippensburg University
Yifei Dong, University of Oklahoma
Peter Blanchfield, Nottingham University
Desmond Greer, Queen's University Belfast
WeiQi Yan, Queen's University Belfast
Zaigham Mahmood, Derby University
Karel Pieterson, Hogeschool Van Amsterdam

This book would not have been possible without the constant love, patience, and encouragement of our families.

1

The Goals and Terminology of Software Engineering

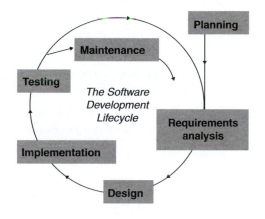

- Why is software engineering important?

- Who and what does is consist of?

- What are its main activities?

- What are the principles of software engineering?

- What ethics are involved?

- What sorts of case studies will be used to illustrate the subject?

Figure 1.1 The context and learning goals for this chapter

The goal of software engineering, and the theme of this book, is the creation of software systems that meet the needs of customers and are reliable, efficient, and maintainable. In addition, the system should be produced in an economical fashion, meeting project schedules and budgets. This is no easy task, especially for large, complex applications. This chapter introduces the field of software engineering and explains how it addresses these goals. We first explain the term "software engineering," showing that it consists of many parts.

1.1 WHAT IS SOFTWARE ENGINEERING?

Software engineering is an engineering discipline that involves all aspects of developing and maintaining a software product. Engineering disciplines such as civil, mechanical, and electrical involve the design, analysis, and construction of an artifact for some practical purpose. Software engineering is no exception to this—software products certainly have practical purposes.

The IEEE defines Software Engineering [1] as follows:

1. The application of a systematic, disciplined, quantifiable approach to the development, operation and maintenance of software; that is, the application of engineering to software.

2. The study of approaches as in (1).

As this definition suggests, it's not only what is produced that's important but also *how* it is produced. Engineering disciplines employ an established set of *systematic, disciplined,* and *quantifiable* approaches to the development of artifacts. By thoroughly applying an analogous set of approaches to the development of software, we can expect the production of software that is highly reliable, is maintainable, and meets specified requirements. A disciplined approach is particularly important as the size of a software project grows. With increased size comes greatly increased complexity, and applying a systematic and disciplined approach is critical.

One of the first uses of the phrase "software engineering" was in 1968, by a NATO Study Group on Computer Science [2]. A conference was organized at that time, motivated by the "rapidly increasing importance of computer systems in many activities of society." The Study Group focused their attention on the problems with software, and held a working conference on Software Engineering that turned out to see far into the future. The following are some quotes from the conference that summarize the cause for their concern:

> The basic problem is that certain classes of systems are placing demands on us which are beyond our capabilities and our theories and methods of design and production at this time . . . It is large systems that are encountering great difficulties. We should not expect the production of such systems to be easy.

> Particularly alarming is the seemingly unavoidable fallibility of large software, since a malfunction in an advanced hardware-software system can be a matter of life and death.

> Programming management will continue to deserve its current poor reputation for cost and schedule effectiveness until such time as a more complete understanding of the program design process is achieved.

> One of the problems that is central to the software production process is to identify the nature of progress and to find some way of measuring it.

> Today we tend to go on for years, with tremendous investments to find that the system, which was not well understood to start with, does not work as anticipated. We build systems like the Wright brothers built airplanes—build the whole thing, push it off the cliff, let it crash, and start over again.

The Study Group discussed possible techniques and methods that might lead to solving these problems. They deliberately and provocatively used the term "software engineering," with an emphasis on engineering, as they wanted to "imply the need for software manufacture to be based on the types of theoretical foundations and practical disciplines that are traditional in the established branches of engineering." They believed that if these foundations and discipline were applied to building software systems, the quality of the resulting systems would be vastly improved.

Today, many of the issues they identified are addressed by evolving software engineering techniques and practices even as the scope of applications has increased dramatically. Throughout this book we examine these practices and explain how they contribute to producing high-quality software. Before doing that, however, it is instructive to begin examining why software fails in the first place, and how some failures can even lead to catastrophic results.

1.2 WHY SOFTWARE ENGINEERING IS CRITICAL: SOFTWARE DISASTERS

Even with the best of intentions, a large number of software projects today are unsuccessful, with a large percentage never completed. Worse, quite a few software projects still end in disaster, causing a loss of money, time, and tragically, even lives. We review some representative samples here as cautionary tales. In all cases, the methods employed were inadequate for the complexity of the required application. Failures such as these motivate us to continually ask: How can we apply software engineering methodologies to ensure the appropriate level of quality in software applications?

1.2.1 The Virtual Case File Project

The FBI's Virtual Case File system was intended to automate the FBI's cumbersome paper-based case system, allow agents to share investigative information, and replace obsolete systems. Instead, after an expenditure of $170 million, the result did not accomplish these objectives at all. The effect has been to inhibit the FBI from growing its crime-fighting mission despite the growth in terrorism and the increased sophistication of many criminal organizations. All of 700,000 lines of code, costing $100 million, had to be abandoned. Poorly defined requirements, networking plans, and software development plans were cited by investigators as causes for this disaster.

1.2.2 The *Ariane* Project

"On 4 June 1996, the maiden flight of the *Ariane 5* launcher ended in failure. Only about 40 seconds after initiation of the flight sequence, at an altitude of about 3700 m, the launcher veered off its flight path, broke up and exploded." [3] The cost of developing *Ariane* during the preceding decade has been estimated at $7 billion. A significant fraction of this was wasted on June 4, 1996. *Ariane 5* itself, including its specific development, has been valued at $500 million.

The source of the problem was described in the official report [3] as follows (italics added):

> The internal Inertial Reference System software exception was caused during execution of a data conversion from 64-bit floating point to 16-bit signed integer value. The floating-point number which was converted had a value greater than what could be represented by a 16-bit signed integer. This resulted in an Operand Error. The data conversion instructions (in Ada code) were not protected from causing an Operand Error. . . . *The error occurred in a part of the software* that only performs alignment of the strap-down inertial platform. This software module computes meaningful results only before lift-off. As soon as the launcher lifts off, this function serves no purpose.

In other words, the data conversion code itself was "correct" but was called upon to execute when it should not have been. The defect lay within controlling code. This kind of problem is easy to describe but not easy to avoid because many people are involved in large projects. Large projects become extraordinarily complex. Development efforts like *Ariane* call for extensive education and coordination within project management, quality assurance, configuration management, architecture, detailed design, programming, and testing organizations. Depending on how the project was organized and designed, any one of these organizations could have been partly responsible for seeing to it that the code in question was not called after liftoff.

1.2.3 Radiation Overdose

As software controls an ever-increasing number of devices, its reliability is coming under increasingly intense scrutiny. In the project management magazine *Baseline*, Debbie Gage, John McCormick, and Berta Ramona wrote of a lawsuit alleging "massive overdoses of gamma rays partly due to limitations of the computer program that guided use of" a particular radiation-therapy machine. They reported the following: "The International Atomic Energy Agency said in May 2001 that at least five of the deaths were probably from radiation poisoning (from the machine) and at least 15 more patients risked developing 'serious complications' from radiation." [4] The defect did not show up until a significant time after release, and only after certain sequences of operator actions.

The following describes the software defect, and is quoted from [5].

> Setting the bending magnets takes about 8 seconds. *Magnet* calls a subroutine called *Ptime* to introduce a time delay. Since several magnets need to be set, *Ptime* is entered and exited several times. A flag to indicate that bending magnets are being set is initialized upon entry to the *Magnet* subroutine and cleared at the end of *Ptime*. Furthermore, *Ptime* checks a shared variable, set by the keyboard handler, that indicates the presence of any editing requests. If there are edits, then *Ptime* clears the bending magnet variable and exits to *Magnet*, which then exits to *Datent*. But the edit change variable is checked by *Ptime* only if the bending magnet flag is set. Since *Ptime* clears it during its first execution, any edits performed during each succeeding pass through *Ptime* will not be recognized. Thus, an edit change of the mode or energy, although reflected on the operator's screen and the mode/energy offset variable, will not be sensed by *Datent* so it can index the appropriate calibration tables for the machine parameters.[1]

This is a fairly involved explanation but not at all beyond the complexity of many software systems in existence today. When should this type of error have been found? If sound software engineering discipline had been employed during all phases of the project, there would have been several opportunities in the development process to detect it.

1.2.4 More Software Disasters

Readers who wish to know about more software disasters, big and small, are referred to Neumann [6], who discusses risks, problems, defects, and disasters relating to reliability, safety, security vulnerabilities, integrity, and threats to privacy and well-being. Another source is the ACM publication *Software Engineering Notes* and its Risks Forum [7].

1.3 WHY SOFTWARE FAILS OR SUCCEEDS

Thankfully, not all software projects end in the types of disasters described above, but far too many end in failure. What does it mean for a software project to be unsuccessful? Simply put, an unsuccessful project is one that fails to meet expectations. More specifically, the undesirable outcomes may include the following:

- Over budget

- Exceeds schedule and/or misses market window

- Doesn't meet stated customer requirements

- Lower quality than expected

- Performance doesn't meet expectations

- Too difficult to use

---

[1] Levenson, Nancy, and Turner C.S., "An Investigation of the Therac-25 Accidents," IEEE Computer, Vol. 26, No. 7, July 1993, pp. 18–41, copyright © 1993 IEEE.

Failing to meet just one of these objectives can cause a project to be deemed unsuccessful. For example, if a project is completed under budget, meets all requirements and functionality, has high quality, good performance and is easy to use, it still may not be successful if the schedule was missed and no customers are willing to purchase it as a result.

Charette [8] notes that there are many underlying reasons software projects are unsuccessful, including:

- Unrealistic or unarticulated project goals
- Poor project management
- Inaccurate estimates of needed resources
- Badly defined system requirements
- Poor reporting of the project's status
- Unmanaged risks
- Poor communication among customers, developers, and users
- Inability to handle the project's complexity

Other contributing factors are:

- Poor software design methodology
- Wrong or inefficient set of development tools
- Poor testing methodology
- Inadequate test coverage
- Inappropriate (or lack of) software process[2]

Unsuccessful software projects usually fall victim to several of these. To reiterate, the goal of software engineering, and the theme of this book, is the creation of software systems that are reliable, efficient, maintainable, and meet the needs of customers. Software engineering provides the tools and methodologies necessary to accomplish these goals, resulting in the development of successful software systems.

We'll end this section on a positive note. The authors feel that software engineering has improved greatly, when measured fairly. Projects of equal ambition can typically get done far more successfully now than 10 years ago. The issue really is that the ambition and scope of applications have grown enormously. The Eclipse software development platform, which this book uses as a case study, is an excellent example of a successful application. This is largely due to its flexible design, inclusive requirements process, and thorough testing.

1.4 SOFTWARE ENGINEERING ACTIVITIES

The production of software systems can be extremely complex and present many challenges. Systems, especially large ones, require the coordination of many *people*, called stakeholders, who must be organized into teams and whose primary objective is to build a *product* that meets defined requirements. The entire effort must be organized

---

[2] Charett, Robert, "Why Software Fails," IEEE Spectrum, Vol. 42, No. 9, September 2005, pp. 42–49, copyright © 2005 IEEE.

- **People**
  - Project stakeholders.
- **Product**
  - The software product plus associated documents.
- **Project**
  - The activities carried out to produce the product.
- **Process**
  - Framework within which the team carries out the activities necessary to build the product.

Figure 1.2 The four ''P's'' that constitute software engineering

into a cohesive *project*, with a solid plan for success. Finally, to successfully develop the product, the activities of the people must be organized through use of an orderly and well-defined *process*. Collectively, these activities are known as the 4 P's of software engineering: people, product, project, and process. Successful software projects must adequately plan for and address all of them. Sometimes, the needs of each of the P's conflict with each other, and a proper balance must be achieved for a project to be successful. Concentrating on one P without the others can lead to a project's failure. For example, if people are organized into efficient teams and given the resources they need to perform their roles, a project can still be unsuccessful if there's no defined software process to follow, as chaos can ensue. The 4 P's are summarized in Figure 1.2 and are discussed in the sections that follow.

1.4.1 People

People are the most important resource on a software project. It is through their efforts that software is successfully constructed and delivered. Competent people must be recruited, trained, motivated, and provided with a growth path, which is no easy task. They are the lifeblood of any successful project. Software development is often dictated by tight, market-driven deadlines and demanding lists of required product features. Because of this, only well-organized groups of engineers, educated and experienced in the methods of software engineering, are capable of consistently carrying out these activities to everyone's satisfaction. The alternative is often chaos and, all too frequently, disaster.

Typically, several groups of people are involved with and have a stake in a project's outcome. These are called its *stakeholders*. They include business management, project management, the development team, customers, and end users. Although each group is motivated to see the project succeed, given their diverse roles each has a different perspective on the process. This is discussed next, for each of the groups cited.

Business Management

These are people responsible for the business side of the company developing the software. They include senior management (e.g., V.P. Finance), marketing (e.g., Product Manager), and development managers. Their primary focus is on business issues including profit, cost effectiveness, market competitiveness, and customer satisfaction. They are typically not particularly knowledgeable about or involved in the technical aspects of the project.

Project Management

Project managers are responsible for planning and tracking a project. They are involved throughout, managing the people, process, and activities. They continuously monitor progress and proactively implement necessary changes and improvements to keep the project on schedule and within budget.

Development Team

Software engineers are responsible for developing and maintaining the software. Software development includes many tasks such as requirements gathering, software architecture and design, implementation, testing, configuration management, and documentation. This book will have much to say about each of these topics. Software engineers are motivated by many factors including technical innovation, low overhead (e.g., a minimum of business-type meetings), and having the time and support to stay involved in technology.

Customers

Customers are responsible for purchasing the software. They may or may not actually use the software. Customers may be purchasing it for use by others in their organization. They are primarily interested in software that is cost-effective, meets specific business needs, and is of high quality. They are typically involved in some aspect of specifying requirements, and since they are paying for the project, they have the ultimate say in defining the requirements.

End Users

End users are people who interact with and use software after it is finished being developed. End users are motivated by software that's easy to use and helps them perform their jobs as efficiently as possible. For example, once they become accustomed to and are effective using a particular user interface, they are typically reluctant to accept major changes to it.

1.4.2 Product

The products of a software development effort consist of much more than the source and object code. They also include project documentation (e.g., requirements document, design specification), test plans and results, customer documentation (e.g., installation guide, command reference), and productivity measurements. These products are often called *artifacts*, and are summarized in Figure 1.3. This book describes the complete set of artifacts.

Part III, on software management, describes project metrics and how they are collected and used to measure productivity.

- **Project documentation**
  Documents produced during software definition and development.

- **Code**
  Source and object.

- **Test documents**
  Plans, cases, and results.

- **Customer documents**
  Documents explaining how to use and operate product.

- **Productivity measurements**
  Analyze project productivity.

Figure 1.3 The main product artifacts of a software project

Part IV, on requirements analysis, explains how to produce requirements that specify what the product is intended to be.

Part V explains how to specify software designs. Chapter 20 describes software architectures. Chapter 21 describes how to specify the detailed designs. Design patterns, a standard means of communicating intelligently with each other about design, are described in Chapter 19.

Part VI discusses implementation (programming), emphasizing standards and precision. A major goal is to help developers to write programs that are much easier to verify for correctness.

Part VII describes how to test the parts of an application, as well as the whole. It includes test procedures that specify how tests are conducted and the test cases that specify the input data for tests. Part VII also describes the types of customer documentation artifacts that are produced and their purpose.

1.4.3 Project

A software project defines the activities and associated results needed to produce a software product. Every project involves a similar set of activities: planning, determining what's required, determining how the software should be built to meet the requirements, implementing the software, testing the software, and maintaining it once delivered to customers. These major project activities are summarized in Figure 1.4.

In addition to these activities, various development paradigms, techniques, and tools exist and are employed on different projects. A development paradigm is a way of thinking about the process of producing software.

An example of a development paradigm, and one that is in wide use today, is the *object-oriented paradigm*. It was invented to make designs and code match the real world. That is, an object as represented in a software design is patterned after a real-world object. For example, suppose that a banking application is to be built that includes support for customers, bank accounts, and transactions on the accounts. In an object-oriented paradigm, these real-word concepts are represented in the design and implementation by corresponding

---

- **Planning**

  - Plan, monitor, and control the software project.

- **Requirements analysis**

  - Define what to build.

- **Design**

  - Describe how to build the software.

- **Implementation**

  - Program the software.

- **Testing**

  - Validate that software meets the requirements.

- **Maintenance**

  - Resolve problems; adapt software to meet new requirements.

Figure 1.4 Major activities of a software project

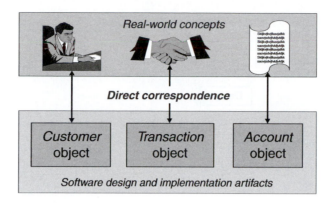

Figure 1.5 A key role of the object-oriented paradigm

Source: Graphics reproduced with permission from Corel.

classes. This greatly facilitates identifying and applying modifications to a design necessitated by changes to real-world requirements. For example, if the steps executed during a particular *transaction* need to change, the design can more easily accommodate this since there's a corresponding *transaction* object in the design. The design representation for transactions is encapsulated within the transaction object, and modifications can be applied more easily. This is illustrated in Figure 1.5. In non-object-oriented languages, the representation of a real-world concept such as a customer may be spread across many disconnected pieces of source code.

1.4.4 Process

A *software process* is a framework for carrying out the activities of a project in an organized and disciplined manner. It imposes structure and helps guide the many people and activities in a coherent manner. A software project progresses through different *phases*, each interrelated and bounded by time. A software process expresses the interrelationship among the phases by defining their order and frequency, as well as defining the deliverables of the project. Figure 1 names the major phases and indicates the order in which they are usually performed.

Specific software process implementations are called *software process models*. There are several such models, but most are based on either the *waterfall* or *iterative development* models. Each of these is briefly described below. Part II covers the evolution of software processes and details these plus several other of the most important process models.

The *waterfall process* is the simplest software process model, and forms the basis for most others. A pure waterfall process dictates that phases are implemented in sequence, with no phase starting before the previous one has almost completed. That is, phases are executed in a strictly sequential order, usually with small overlaps. Once a waterfall phase is finished it's deemed complete for the project and there is no need to return to it. Variations of waterfall exist where already completed phases may be revisited and minor updates applied, as a result of work done on subsequent phases. Waterfall begins with an inception phase, where the product is conceived and business objectives defined. Next is the specification of the requirements, followed by the design phase, the implementation phase, the testing phase, and finally the maintenance phase. Figure 1.6 illustrates the main phases and their sequence. This means that the process goes around the circle of Figure 1.1 just once.

Software development rarely occurs in the strict waterfall sequence. Instead, it skips back and forth somewhat among requirements, design, implementation, and testing. In practice, then, we often use *iterative*

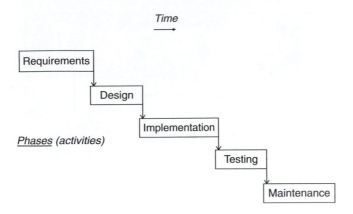

Figure 1.6 The waterfall software development process

processes for software development, in which all or some of the waterfall process is repeated several times. Some processes dictate that activities may be carried out in parallel. In the *agile* process, programmers typically view implementation as part of design rather than an entirely separate phase. Here, most phases in the circle of Figure 1.1 are repeated frequently—as often as every two weeks. This book makes frequent reference to agile methods.

When performed in a disciplined manner, iterative styles can be highly beneficial. They are especially useful when the requirements are only sketchily known at the start of a project. A subset of the system is constructed from a partial list of requirements, customer feedback is obtained, and additional requirements are generated. This cycle repeats until the complete system is built.

Since policy decisions about software process take place at an organizational level (company, department, group, etc.), there is a need to assess the software development capabilities of organizations. The Capability Maturity Model^{SM} (CMM) is such a measure. The CMM and its successor, the CMMI, were developed by the Software Engineering Institute. The software engineering capability of individual engineers can be developed and measured by the Personal Software Process^{SM} (PSP) created by Humphrey [9]. The highlights of CMMI and PSP are woven through some chapters of this book. A third level of software organization is Humphrey's Team Software Process^{SM} (TSP) [10], which describes the process by which teams of software engineers get their work done. The International Standards Organization (ISO) defines quality standards against which many organizations assess their software development processes.

Well thought-out documentation standards make it much easier to produce useful, reliable artifacts. Several standards are available. Many companies provide in-house standards. For the most part, this book applies the IEEE (Institute of Electrical and Electronics Engineers) software engineering standards, many of which are also sanctioned by ANSI (American National Standards Institute). Standards focus the process by providing a baseline for engineer, instructor, and students. In practice, they are modified and tailored to specific projects.

Software process is the subject of Part II of this book.

1.5 SOFTWARE ENGINEERING PRINCIPLES

The field of software engineering has matured greatly since it began over 40 years ago. Throughout this time practitioners have learned valuable lessons that contribute to the best practices of today. Some have become outdated, but many are still very relevant and widely implemented today. In his book [11], Alan Davis

1. *Make Quality Number 1*

2. *High-Quality Software Is Possible*

3. *Give Products to Customers Early*

4. *Use an Appropriate Software Process*

5. *Minimize Intellectual Distance*

6. *Inspect Code*

7. *People Are the Key to Success*

Figure 1.7 Major principles of software engineering

gathered 201 principles that form the foundation of software engineering. Figure 1.7 highlights some of the most important, and we explore each of them.

Make Quality Number 1

There is nothing more important than delivering a quality product to customers—they simply will not tolerate anything less. However, different people have different ideas of what quality means, and it therefore must be specified and measured. Prime examples of quality are how closely software meets the customer's requirements, how many (or few) defects it has, and how much it costs to produce. Quality measures need to be specified in advance to ensure the correct targets are being pursued and met. This book contains several chapters devoted to quality but, more important, the notion of quality is behind most of its content.

High-Quality Software Is Possible

Although it may be difficult to produce high-quality software, following modern software engineering methods and techniques has proven to meet reasonable quality goals. Examples include involving the customer, prototyping, conducting inspections, and employing incremental software processes.

Give Products to Customers Early

Many software projects fail because customers are given their first look at software too late in the development cycle. This was a major motivation for the introduction of agile methods. It's virtually impossible to know all the requirements in advance, and involving customers as early as possible is critical to getting the requirements right. Their early involvement in helping to specify requirements is very important, but giving them working software and having them use it is critical to understanding what they really need. Customers may think they want a particular feature, or think they want a user interface to look a certain way, but until they get a version of software to work with you can never be sure. Employing techniques such as agile processes, prototyping, or incremental processes allow customers to get software into their hands early in the development cycle.

Use an Appropriate Software Process

There are many software process models, and no single one is appropriate for every type of project. For example, the waterfall process works well for projects where all of the requirements are well known up front. Conversely, agile and other iterative processes are called for when few requirements are known in advance. Good software engineers and project leaders take the time to understand the type of project being undertaken and use an appropriate model.

Minimize Intellectual Distance

This principle says that for any software solution to a real-world problem, the structures of both the software solution and real-world problem should be as similar as possible. This was illustrated in Figure 5, showing how object-orientation can achieve this objective. The closer the structures are to each other, the easier it is to develop and maintain the software.

Inspect Code

This should be extended to read "Inspect All Artifacts," where artifacts are defined as any product of the software development process including technical specifications, test plans, documentation, and code. Inspections have been proven to find errors as early as possible, increase quality, and decrease overall project cost.

People Are the Key to Success

Highly skilled, motivated people are probably the most important factor contributing to the success of a software project. Good people can make up for a variety of obstacles including poor tools, insufficient processes, and unforeseen problems. Good people will figure out a way to overcome these obstacles and make the project a success. Poor performers without any of these obstacles will probably still fail. Hiring and retaining the best people is critical to producing high-quality and successful software.

So far, we have discussed the parts, principles, and activities of software engineering. Assuming that these are understood and assembled, we need to understand the societal responsibilities of software engineers.

1.6 ETHICS IN SOFTWARE ENGINEERING

Reliance on the ethics of software engineers has become an essential part of contemporary culture. To take an example, it is simply not possible for a car driver to verify and validate the code for his car's cruise control or for a patient or radiologist to verify the correctness of the code controlling the X-ray machine pointing at his head. At some point, there is no choice but to assume that the software created and installed in these and other systems has been implemented correctly, and in a manner consistent with the public interest. This is a matter of *ethics*.

The *Merriam-Webster* [12] online dictionary defines ethics as:

1. the discipline dealing with what is good and bad and with moral duty and obligation

2. a set of moral principles

Most disciplines operate under a strict set of ethical standards, as published in a corresponding code of ethics, and software engineering is no exception. The ACM and IEEE have jointly developed a *Software Engineering Code of Ethics and Professional Practice* [13]. The ACM/IEEE-CS Joint Task Force on Software Engineering Ethics and Professional Practices has recommended the document, and the ACM and the IEEE-CS have jointly approved the standard for teaching and practicing software engineering. The code includes a short and long version, with the short version listed in Figure 1.8. The short version describes the code at a high level of abstraction. The long version contains a number of clauses corresponding to each of the eight principles in the short version, with each clause providing more details and examples. Both versions are contained in [13].

PREAMBLE

The short version of the code summarizes aspirations at a high level of the abstraction; the clauses that are included in the full version give examples and details of how these aspirations change the way we act as software engineering professionals. Without the aspirations, the details can become legalistic and tedious; without the details, the aspirations can become high sounding but empty; together, the aspirations and the details form a cohesive code.

Software engineers shall commit themselves to making the analysis, specification, design, development, testing and maintenance of software a beneficial and respected profession. In accordance with their commitment to the health, safety and welfare of the public, software engineers shall adhere to the following Eight Principles:

1. PUBLIC - Software engineers shall act consistently with the public interest.

2. CLIENT AND EMPLOYER - Software engineers shall act in a manner that is in the best interests of their client and employer consistent with the public interest.

3. PRODUCT - Software engineers shall ensure that their products and related modifications meet the highest professional standards possible.

4. JUDGMENT - Software engineers shall maintain integrity and independence in their professional judgment.

5. MANAGEMENT - Software engineering managers and leaders shall subscribe to and promote an ethical approach to the management of software development and maintenance.

6. PROFESSION - Software engineers shall advance the integrity and reputation of the profession consistent with the public interest.

7. COLLEAGUES - Software engineers shall be fair to and supportive of their colleagues.

8. SELF - Software engineers shall participate in lifelong learning regarding the practice of their profession and shall promote an ethical approach to the practice of the profession.

Figure 1.8 Software Engineering Code of Ethics and Professional Practice

Source: ACM/IEEE-CS, Software Engineering Code of Ethics and Professional Practice, copyright © IEEE.

These precepts have practical consequences and can help guide a software engineer toward a course of action when confronted with a difficult situation. A few examples follow:

Example 1. Suppose that your manager asks you to join a team at work and assumes you are sufficiently skilled in Java. However, you don't know Java, but really want to work on the project and think you'll be able to learn it quickly and learn a valuable skill. Do you mention your lack of Java knowledge to your manager and risk being pulled from the project, or do you say nothing, even though your inexperience could jeopardize the success of the project? Clause 6.05 provides guidance: "Not promote their own interest at the expense of the profession, client or employer." Knowing this, you could inform your manager that you do not currently have the necessary Java knowledge, but present a case at the same time for how you will learn enough in time.

Example 2. A software engineer working on several government contracts is "encouraged" by management to charge time against the contract with the highest number of available hours. What do you do? Guidance for this is provided by clause 4.04: "Not engage in deceptive financial practices such as bribery, double billing, or other improper financial practices."

Example 3. You are asked to develop a complex, critical piece of software for a commercial product you're working on. You discover a public domain version of the source code. You're tempted to use the source code as it will save much time and effort and allow you to move onto the development of another important part of the system sooner than expected. However, it's not licensed to be used for commercial purposes. What do you do? Clause 2.02 provides guidance: "Not knowingly use software that is obtained or retained either illegally or unethically."

These are just a few examples of how software engineers can be confronted with ethical dilemmas. Having a set of guidelines greatly assists the engineer in making the right decisions.

1.7 CASE STUDIES

Reading about software engineering concepts alone is insufficient for gaining a thorough understanding of the subject. The best way to unify and reinforce the many topics presented in this book is to (1) learn how they are applied to the development of real software applications and (2) gain hands-on experience developing a software application as part of a team. To meet the first objective, case studies have been developed or described and are presented throughout the book. They serve as concrete examples of software applications, and include appropriate artifacts as they are discussed and presented in the text. The case studies are introduced in the next few sections. To meet the second objective, students working in teams are provided guidance as they apply software engineering concepts to the

development of a group project. As they progress, students will generate project artifacts and working code. Artifacts generated as part of the case studies can also be used as guidance in developing artifacts for the group project.

There are three cases studies used in the text, as illustrated in Figure 1.9. The *Encounter video game* is a single-player, stand-alone video game application that is completely implemented through the course of this book in conjunction with online components. In addition, two open source projects are used to illustrate how open source projects are developed: the *Eclipse* integrated development environment and the *OpenOffice* office productivity suite. Open source projects are developed differently from traditional software in that many

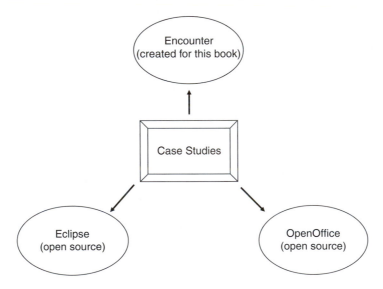

Figure 1.9 The main case studies used in this book

different people, from various organizations, develop features and functions and then contribute them back to the base software application. In this way an open source application grows in functionality and all new features are freely available for others to use and build on.

Various other examples are used in this book, including a video store application.

1.7.1 Encounter Video Game

The Encounter video game is a single-player, standalone video game application. A player is assigned a main character, and Encounter simulates all or part of the lifetime of that character. Success in playing the game is measured by attaining a *life points* goal for the player or by the ability of the player to survive for a given time limit. Figure 1.10 shows a typical screen shot: the courtyard area containing a player-controlled character, Elena.

Game characters begin with a fixed number of points allocated equally among qualities including *concentration, stamina, intelligence, patience,* and *strength.* The game consists of movement among a set of areas. The main character moves between them, encountering a game-generated character called

the *foreign* character. Characters engage each other when they are in the same area at the same time. The result of an engagement depends on the values of the characters' qualities and on the location where it occurs. Once an engagement is complete, the player's character is moved to a random area. Players can set the values of their qualities except while engaging a foreign character. The new quality values take effect only after a delay.

1.7.2 Eclipse Open Source Project

The second case study is Eclipse. Eclipse [14] is an extensible, highly configurable open source IDE (integrated development environment). An IDE provides an environment and set of tools for the development of software applications. It provides tools to build, run, and debug applications, the ability to share artifacts such as code and object with a team, and support for and integration with version control. Because Eclipse is open source, its source code and design are freely available and readily extensible by third parties through the use of plug-ins. In fact, Eclipse is considered a *platform.* It isn't a "finished" product, and is intended for continuous and indefinite extension [15]. Numerous open

Figure 1.10 Snapshot from the Encounter case study video game: Elena in the courtyard

source extensions can be found at the home of the Eclipse project, www.eclipse.org.

Eclipse has been successfully used as a tool for wide-ranging application types such as Java development, Web services, embedded device programming, and game programming contests. The Eclipse platform itself provides a programming language-agnostic infrastructure. Support for specific languages is provided by plug-ins, and each plug-in must adhere to the same rules as all the other plug-ins that use the platform [15]. Support for the Java programming language is provided by the Java Development Tools (JDT), which is built on the Eclipse platform and provides a full-featured Java IDE.

A typical Eclipse screenshot is shown in Figure 1.11.

1.7.3 OpenOffice Project

The third case study that we will use in this book is OpenOffice (openoffice.org), "a multi-platform office productivity suite. It includes the key desktop applications, such as a word processor, spreadsheet, presentation manager, and drawing program, with a user interface and feature set similar to other office suites such as Microsoft Office. OpenOffice.org also works transparently with a variety of file formats, including those of Microsoft Office" [16]. A typical OpenOffice screenshot is shown in Figure 1.12.

The OpenOffice project encourages participation by developers, as the typical developer-oriented Web page shows in Figure 1.13.

We will discuss the management of the OpenOffice project in Part III. Here is a summary, quoted from an OpenOffice Web site:

> There are three categories of active projects in OpenOffice.org: *Accepted*, which is where most technical projects are located, *Incubator*, which houses experimental projects and endeavors, and *Native-Lang*, which includes projects providing information, resources, builds, and forums in a user's native language.

The Accepted Projects at a point in time are shown in Figures 1.14 and 1.15.

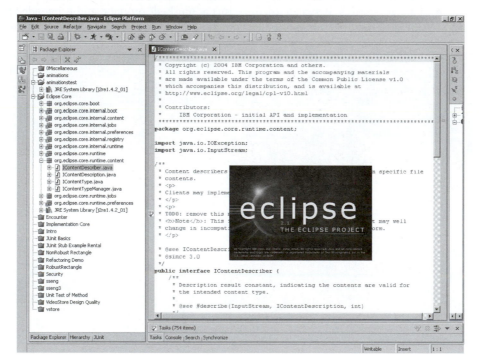

Figure 1.11 A typical screenshot of the Eclipse interactive development environment

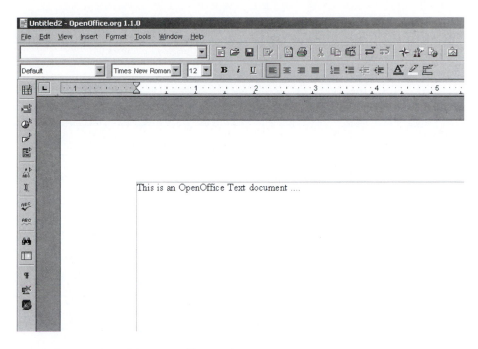

Figure 1.12 A typical screenshot of the OpenOffice word processor

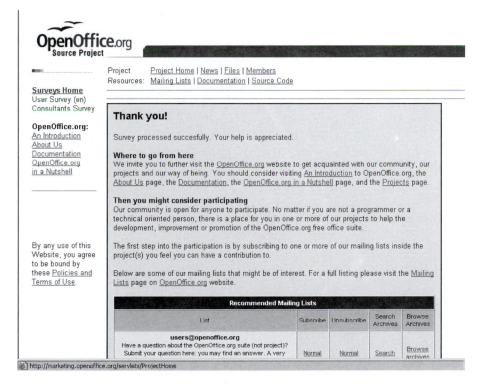

Figure 1.13 Typical OpenOffice communication with development

Project	Lead/Co-Lead	Short Name	Description
API	Michael Hoennig, Juergen Schmidt	api	The application programming interface.
Application Framework	Mathias Bauer, Carsten Driesner	framework	The framework for applications.
Build Tools and Environment	Martin Hollmichel	tools	The tools used in build process and the build environment.
Database Access	Frank Schoenheit, Dirk Grobler	dba	The database access for the applications.
Documentation	Scott Carr	documentation	End-user documentation for the various components making up OpenOffice.org.
External	Martin Hollmichel (acting)	external	This project will host all the external code allowed.
Graphic Applications	Kai Ahrens, Christian Lippka	graphics	The graphic applications such as Draw and Impress.
Graphic System Layer	Christof Pintaske, Hennes Rohling	gsl	The Visual Class Library and other modules.
Installation	Dirk Voelzke	installation	Creating the installation set.
Lingucomponent	Kevin Hendricks	lingucomponent	Creating dictionaries, thesaurii, and other related tools.

Figure 1.14 Accepted OpenOffice projects at a point in time, 1 of 2

Source: OpenOffice, http://projects.openoffice.org/accepted.html.

Localization	Dieter Loeschky, Nils Fuhrmann Pavel Janik	l10n	Localization. This project includes Internationalization (i18n).
Marketing	Jacqueline McNally	marketing	The project furthering the growth and use of OpenOffice.org technology. Efforts include: developing collateral, logos, public outreach.
Porting	Martin Hollmichel, Kevin Hendricks	porting	Porting to new platforms.
Quality Assurance	Michael Bemmer, Scott Carr, Gordon Shum	qa	Quality Assurance: testing and qualifying all builds of OpenOffice.org.
Spreadsheet	Niklas Nebel, Eike Rathke	sc	The spreadsheet application.
Universal Content Broker	Matthias Huetsch, Andreas Bille	ucb	Allows the applications to transparently access content with different structures.
UNO Development Kit / Component Technology	Kay Ramme, Kai Sommerfeld	udk	Object model development and component technology. Includes the old OI and Scripting projects.
User Interface	Oliver Specht	ui	Common user interface for OpenOffice.org applications.
Utilities	Hennes Rohling	util	Utilities used in development.
Website	Louis Suárez-Potts, Kay Schenk,	www	The OpenOffice.org website; the project for establishing the appearance of the Project.
Word Processing	Andreas Martens, Caolan McNamara	sw	The Word Processing Application

Figure 1.15 Accepted OpenOffice projects at a point in time, 2 of 2

Source: OpenOffice, http://projects.openoffice.org/accepted.html.

1.8 SUMMARY

Developing complex software systems in a successful manner has historically been very difficult. The goal of software engineering is to define a framework for creating software systems that are reliable, efficient, and maintainable, and meet the needs of customers. As illustrated in Section 1.2 on software disasters, producing software that is unreliable can have catastrophic consequences. Although most software does not end in disaster, care must be taken to avoid the many common pitfalls and mistakes that can plague a software project.

The 4 P's of software engineering—people, product, project, and process—encompass the different aspects of defining, building, and managing software. The people are the most important part, as they not only create the software but also are the customers for who the work is being done. The work products include not only source and object code, but also a complete set of artifacts describing the system. A software process model defines a framework for carrying out the different phases of a software project. It imposes order and structure to a project.

Underlying software engineering is a set of time-tested principles. Knowing these principles helps to understand the motivation for the software engineering methodology presented in this book.

Software engineering is a profession that carries with it certain ethical responsibilities. The ACM and IEEE have jointly published a code of ethics to help guide software professionals in their work.

This book uses three main case studies throughout as realistic examples of software projects.

1.9 EXERCISES

1. Besides those listed in this chapter, what additional expectations do you think software products may fail to meet?

2. Research a recent real-world "software disaster." In your own words, describe the underlying cause of the problem. What could have been done to avoid it?

3. What are the four P's of software engineering? (Recall them without consulting the book.) Briefly describe each.

4. In a paragraph, name at least two of the most important deficiencies you can think of in the *reporting* of project progress that contribute to an unsuccessful project outcome.

5. Explain in your own words why people are invariably the most important resource on a project.

6. For the stakeholder groups listed in the text, give an example of a project motivation for each.

7. You are developing a second-generation custom order entry application for a particular customer. Explain and give examples of at least two types of problems that can arise if the customer is not involved in defining the new application, and their first use of the application is after it is completed.

8. Why does the use of standards make it easier to generate useful, reliable documents? Why isn't their use a *guarantee* that high-quality documents will be produced?

9. Explain the difference between a software process and a software process model.

10. Figure 8 lists the *ACM/IEEE Software Engineering Code of Ethics and Professional Practice*. Drawing either from your own experience or from a hypothetical situation, describe a scenario that adheres to one of the eight principles. Now describe a scenario that violates one of the principles.

BIBLIOGRAPHY

1. "IEEE Standard Glossary of Software Engineering Terminology," IEEE Std 610.12-1990, December 1990, p. 67.
2. Naur, Peter, and Randell, Brian, (Editors), "Software Engineering, Report on a conference sponsored by the NATO Science Committee," Garmisch, Germany, 7th to 11th October 1968, Brussels, Scientific Affairs Division, NATO, January 1969, pp. 8–10.
3. Lions J. L., (Chairman of the Inquiry Board), "Ariane 5 Flight 501 Failure, Report by the Inquiry Board," Paris, July 1996, http://www.ima.umn.edu/~arnold/disasters/ariane5rep.html [accessed November 1, 2009].
4. McCormick, John, and Thayer, Berta Ramona, "We Did Nothing Wrong," Baseline, March 2004, p. 1, http://www.baselinemag.com/c/a/Projects-Processes/We-Did-Nothing-Wrong/ [accessed November 1, 2009].
5. Levenson, Nancy, and Turner C.S., "An Investigation of the Therac-25 Accidents," *IEEE Computer*, Vol. 26, No.7, July 1993, pp. 18–41.
6. Neumann, P. G., "Computer Related Risks", *Addison-Wesley/ACM Press*, 1995, p. 384.
7. Neumann, Peter G. (moderator), "The Risk Digest, ACM Committee on Computers and Public Policy." http://catless.ncl.ac.uk/Risks/ [accessed November 1, 2009].
8. Charette, Robert, "Why Software Fails," *IEEE Spectrum*, vol. 42, no.9, September 2005, pp. 42–49.
9. Humphrey, W. S., "PSP: A Self-Improvement Process for Software Engineers," 2005, Addison-Wesley, p. 368.
10. Humphrey, W. S., "Introduction to the Team Software Process," 2000, Addison-Wesley, p. 368.
11. Davis, Alan, *"201 Principles of Software Engineering,"* 1995, McGraw Hill.
12. Merriam-Webster Online Dictionary. http://www.merriam-webster.com/home.htm [accessed November 1, 2009].
13. "Software Engineering Code of Ethics and Professional Practice (Version 5.2) as recommended by the ACM/IEEE-CS Joint Task Force on Software Engineering Ethics and Professional Practices, 1999. http://www.acm.org/about/se-code [accessed November 1, 2009].
14. E.O.S. Project. Eclipse Open Source Project. http://www.eclipse.org/.
15. The Eclipse Project Wiki. http://wiki.eclipse.org/Main_Page.
16. OpenOffice Project. http://www.openoffice.org/.

2

Introduction to Quality and Metrics in Software Engineering

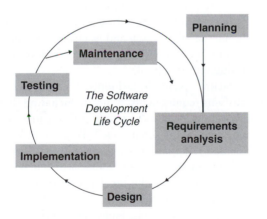

- What does "software quality" mean?

- What are "defects" in applications?

- What is the difference between *verification* and *validation* in software development?

- How do you measure software quality?

Figure 2.1 The context and learning goals for this chapter

Building software that exhibits a high level of quality is one of the major themes of this book and is a critical factor in the production of successful software systems. However, achieving a high quality level is no easy task. Quality must be integrated into projects from the beginning and during every phase of product development. This is why quality is discussed throughout the book and is being introduced at this early stage.

Throughout the life of a software project, data—or measurements—are collected to ascertain the effectiveness of the processes employed and the software being constructed. Such data are called *metrics*.

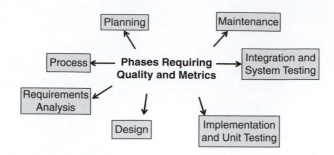

Figure 2.2 Software development phases requiring the application of metrics

These measure various aspects of a project such as the quality level of the software itself, and also the degree of the project's adherence to its schedule and other measurables such as the productivity of engineers. This chapter provides an overview of software metrics and an explanation of how they relate to software quality.

Each of the major parts of this book contains a chapter relating how quality is practiced and metrics collected and applied to the development phase covered in that part. Figure 2.2 depicts the different phases requiring quality practices and metrics collection.

So far, we have used the term "software quality" quite freely. Now we'll provide a concrete definition.

2.1 THE MEANING OF SOFTWARE QUALITY

Everyone wants "quality," but what exactly does software quality mean? There are varying views on this. Some measure quality in terms of categories such as reliability, portability, and so on. However, if one of these—portability, for example—is not a requirement of the product in any form, then it is not relevant. Some feel that the more an application changes the world for the better, the more quality it possesses. Others define software quality in terms of how well a development process is followed, or how extensively the emerging product is tested. Ultimately, it is best for an organization to define for itself and its customers what it means by "quality." Above all, it is important that "software quality" has a consistent meaning within the project's stakeholders. A definition follows that will be used throughout this book.

To give some background, let us first consider a "quality" plain old-fashioned lead pencil (frequently yellow). All would agree that such a pencil must first satisfy its requirements, typically including that it "shall be solid wood; shall have a lead core with designated hardness; shall have an eraser that can erase most of what the lead has deposited on plain paper; shall have the required length; etc." To be a *quality* old-style pencil, however, we expect additional attributes such as that it is "harder than usual to break, lasts twice as long as average pencils, has a very effective eraser, etc." To summarize, a quality *conventional* item has attributes beyond its requirements. In software engineering, however, this is *not* the typical definition of quality.

What is different about software applications is that they inevitably contain defects. Every defect is a deviation from requirements, regardless of whether the requirements are carefully written down. Hence we cannot think about the quality of software the same way we think about the quality of a lead pencil. Instead, a good definition of software quality is the following:

The more closely a software product meets its requirements, the higher its quality.

Figure 2.3 illustrates this view of quality.

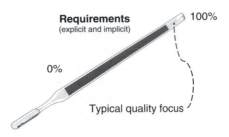

Requirements
(explicit and implicit)

100%

0%

Typical quality focus

Figure 2.3 The meaning of software quality: the degree to which the actual requirements are met

Source: Graphics reproduced with permission from Corel.

We have not yet discussed how requirements are gathered and generated. For now, let us assume that requirements are generated with the best knowledge available during requirements analysis. Even in this case, after the software has been developed and the product has been shipped to customers, it may be discovered that some requirements are in fact incorrect or missing. In these cases the software is constructed using the requirements as documented, and we would say the software meets all its *explicitly specified* requirements but it may not fully satisfy its customers. There are a number of different ways this can happen.

As an example, if customers are not consulted during requirements definition the system is constructed without their input. When they eventually use the software they may find it does not function as they wish and are dissatisfied. Even if customers are consulted and provide input, it is possible they will still be dissatisfied on using the software. For example, suppose that a software system implements a user interface, with screen layouts and menus specified in a requirements document. If customers are not given an opportunity to use the interface before the product is released, they may find that what appears to work well on paper is actually cumbersome to use. In these scenarios and others, we would say the product does not exhibit high quality because it does not satisfy the customer. Therefore a more complete definition of quality would be:

> The more closely a software product meets its specified requirements, and those requirements meet the wants and needs of its customers, the higher its quality.

Techniques for gathering requirements and ensuring customer satisfaction are covered in Part IV on requirements analysis.

Besides the benefit of customer satisfaction, producing high-quality software provides other advantages. It has often been shown that a correlation exists between products with the least number of defects and the shortest schedules. There is also a correlation between poor quality and schedule overruns, and between poor quality and increased project costs. The more defects there are in software, the more time engineers spend fixing them, taking time from other important project tasks. Also, the more defects that exist, the more likely that software changes necessitated by fixing these defects will themselves result in more defects. For all these reasons and more, quality is one of the most important attributes in software and a key contributor to its success.

2.2 DEFECTS IN SOFTWARE

A *defect* in a phase of software application is defined as a deviation from what's required for that phase. In practice, most software systems contain defects and therefore do not entirely meet their requirements. The software disasters described in Chapter 1 illustrate the cost of defects in the tens—and even hundreds—of millions of dollars. Defects can be introduced at any stage in the development process. A major goal of software engineering is identifying and removing as many defects as possible, as early as possible, throughout product development, either by inspection of artifacts or testing of the system. For example, if software is in the implementation phase, the code may deviate from the software design produced in the previous design phase, or it may be coded in such a way as to produce an incorrect output. The result of either case is considered a defect. In this particular case, an inspection of the code prior to testing is conducted, with a goal of identifying as many defects as possible. Once the software is fully integrated into a system, testing is conducted to ensure that it conforms to the specified requirements.

Defects are the clearest manifestation of a quality shortfall. The later in the development cycle they are discovered the more they cost to repair. Therefore two quality goals of software development processes are as follows [1]:

1. To remove as many defects as is reasonably possible before the product is delivered to the customer.

2. To remove as many of these defects as early in the development process as possible.

To the first point, defects discovered and repaired during software development will not be found by customers, of course. The more defects that can be removed, the higher the quality of software is likely to be, and the more the customer will be satisfied.

To the second point, as software is developed and defects are introduced (which is, in practice, inevitable), the earlier they are discovered the less they cost to repair.

According to Boehm [2] and others, the cost of defect repair after software is released to customers can be 100 times greater as compared to fixing the same defect early in the development cycle. Various studies show various cost escalation factors, but they all report a dramatic rise in the cost of detection and repair. Figure 2.4 shows one estimate of the relative cost of defect repair during each stage of development. For example, if a defect is introduced during the requirements phase, assume that it costs $1 to detect and repair if done during that same phase. If it slips through to the implementation phase, the same defect will cost $20 to repair. If it falls all the way through to maintenance, which is when customers are using the software, the cost can be $100 to repair.

The reason for this increase in repair cost in subsequent phases can be illustrated with an example [1]. Suppose you have an application that performs a large number of file reads and writes. As part of your development process, at the end of the design phase you conduct an inspection of the design and discover two defects: one in the algorithm that performs file reads and writes; the other in the allocation of memory to hold the file records. Assume that the work required to fix these defects after the inspection takes two days to complete, and the steps taken are as follows:

1. Modify the algorithm to fix the defect.

2. Conduct an inspection of the reworked design to verify its correctness.

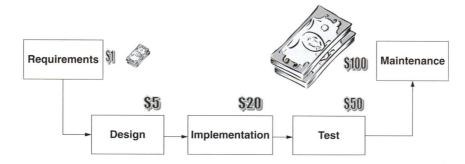

Figure 2.4 Cost of detecting and repairing a defect during maintenance, depending on the phase in which it was injected

Suppose, instead, that the defects went undetected and passed through to the implementation phase. The defects would be harder to detect and could now affect several hundred lines of code. If the defects are detected during a code inspection, the work required to fix them could take a week to complete. The step required would be as follows:

1. Modify the algorithm to fix the defect.

2. Conduct an inspection of the reworked design to verify its correctness.

3. Recode the affected portion of the code.

4. Conduct an inspection of the reworked code to verify it is correct and conforms to the reworked design.

Suppose now that the defects went undetected and passed through to the testing phase. The defects would be even harder to detect and now take more time to fix. In addition to the one week required if found during code inspection, the following additional work would be required:

5. Assistance from the tester to recreate the defects.

6. Discovery of the exact cause of the defect within the software.

7. Dedicated machine time to support debugging.

8. Retesting the fix to ensure it works correctly.

These activities can take an additional week to a month, depending on how difficult it is to isolate and repair the defect. This example illustrates the cost of not detecting and repairing defects as close to their injection as possible and why every effort must be made to detect and repair defects as early as possible.

2.3 VERIFICATION AND VALIDATION

Software verification and validation (V&V) is a process implemented throughout the software life cycle to ensure the following.

1. Each step in the development process is carried out correctly. This is called *verification*.

2. Each artifact produced meets its requirements as specified in prior phases. This is called *validation*.

The IEEE Glossary [3] defines these terms as follows:

Verification: "The process of evaluating a system or component to determine whether the products of a given development phase satisfy the conditions imposed at the start of that phase." For example, is the software design sufficient to implement the previously specified requirements? Does the code fully and correctly implement the design?

Validation: "The process of evaluating a system or component during or at the end of the development process to determine whether it satisfies specified requirements." In other words, does the implemented system meet the specified user requirements?

Verification is comparable to keeping your balance current in your checkbook based on your daily activity. As you write checks and make deposits, you enter the amount in the checkbook register and update the balance.

Each time you make an entry you check that your arithmetic is correct and your new balance is right. This is analogous to ensuring that each phase in the software development process is carried out correctly.

Validation is comparable to balancing your checkbook when the bank's statement arrives. You match all the transactions in the monthly statement with those in your register, ensuring that none have been omitted or entered incorrectly and that the transaction amounts in your register match those in the statement. In addition, you validate that the ending balance in your register matches that in the statement. Even though you kept your balance up-to-date, mistakes may have been made. Validation catches those mistakes and ensures the correctness of your balance. This is analogous to testing of a software system.

The two main activities involved during V & V are inspections and software testing. Inspections, and also reviews, are verification activities and involve peer examination of project artifacts (requirements, design, code, etc.) to discover defects. The idea is to find as many defects as possible as early as possible. Inspections are covered in greater detail in Chapter 5. Testing is the principal part of validation.

Software testing is primarily a validation activity, occurring at the end of a development cycle to ensure that software satisfies its user requirements. Testing involves providing the system with a set of inputs, and validating that the system behavior and output match what is expected. Any deviation from an expected outcome is considered a defect. Testing is covered in detail in Part VII.

Note that it is a combination of verification—primarily in the form of inspections—and validation—primarily in the form of testing—that consistently produces high-quality software. Testing alone is not sufficient. No matter how talented software engineers are at fixing defects, if the quality level is low entering validation, as measured by latent defects (those present but not necessarily known), there is a high probability that validation will take significantly longer than expected and the quality level will remain lower than desired. As many defects as possible must be removed from the artifacts before validation begins.

V&V and quality practices, as they relate to each major software phase and activity, is included in the quality chapter near the end of each part of this book. Figure 2.5 summarizes these V&V concepts.

To reinforce the verification/validation distinction, let us perform V&V on a simple example. Suppose that the customer wants an application that "solves linear equations of the form $ax + b = c$." We translate this into user requirements such as:

1. The user shall be able to input numbers a, b, and c up to 10 digits each, with up to four places following the decimal point.

2. The application shall produce a solution to the equation $ax + b = c$ that is within $1/1000$ of the mathematically exact answer.

Then we implement a program to satisfy these requirements.

- Verification: Ensuring that each artifact is built in accordance with its specifications

    - "Are we building the product right?"
    - Mostly inspections and reviews.

- Validation: Checking that each completed artifact satisfies its specifications.

    - "Are we building the right product?"
    - Mostly testing.

Figure 2.5 Verification vs. validation

It is our responsibility to ensure that we have built the application correctly by checking that we proceeded appropriately from the beginning of the process to the end. This is the *verification* process. For convenience, we will number the development phases as follows.

1. Get the customer's requirements.

2. Write down the requirements in detail.

3. Obtain the customer's approval of the requirements statement.

4. Code the application. (For simplicity, we have omitted a design phase.)

5. Test the application.

Verification checks the following questions:

1. Do the requirements express what the customer really wants and needs? Some verification issues here are as follows: Is $ax + b = c$ the correct form? What are the precision requirements? What if 0 is entered for a?

2. Are we carrying out the process of obtaining the customer's approval in an appropriate manner? Some verification issues here are as follows: Are we allowing the customer adequate time? Are we explaining all needed terms to the customer?

3. Does the code implement the written requirements in every respect? This requires an inspection of the code itself, in which the requirements are considered one at a time and the matching code is perused. This could include a mathematical proof. (Strictly speaking, verification does not call for executing the code.)

4. Do the proposed tests adequately cover the application? For an application of realistic size, this would include an inspection of the test plans, test cases, and test procedures. This is separate from testing itself, a validation step discussed below.

Validation of this product consists of obtaining the customer's approval of the written, completed requirements and executing a set of tests on the completed code. For example, we enter a = 1, b = 1, and c = 1, and validate that the program produces x = 0.

To summarize our discussion of the V&V process, at any given moment a software engineer is either creating an artifact, verifying it as he does so, or validating a completed artifact. This is illustrated in Figure 2.6.

2.4 PLANNING FOR QUALITY

Since quality practices are implemented throughout the software life cycle, it is important to express quality approaches and goals in writing early in a project—in other words, well before the goals are used in tracking the project's quality.

Agile projects emphasize the attainment of quality through continual interaction with the customer in person, early implementation, and continual, cumulative testing. The IEEE has published several standards to help meet this objective. These, and standards like them, tend to be employed in larger projects that are not agile or that employ agile methods only partially.

The Software Quality Assurance Plan (SQAP) (IEEE Std 730-2002) is a document for expressing an overall approach to quality that is conducted throughout the entire software life cycle. Major topics

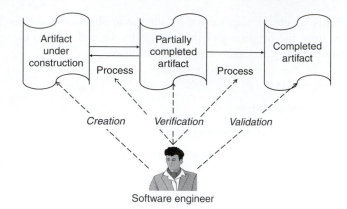

Figure 2.6 Verification and validation of an artifact: before completion vs. after

Source: Graphics reproduced with permission from Corel.

included in the plan are listed below. Details of the SQAP are covered in Chapter 5. The plan includes the following:

- The organizational structure of the quality team
- A list of documentation to be created governing the development, verification and validation, use and maintenance of the software (e.g., software requirements specification, verification and validation plan, software design specification, etc.)
- The definition and schedule of inspections to be conducted and how they are to be conducted
- The metrics to be collected, monitored, and analyzed
- References to software test plans
- How problem reporting is to be managed and conducted

The V&V Plan is the manner in which the Software Quality Assurance Plan is supported by verification and validation. The IEEE has published a Software Verification and Validation Plan (SVVP) framework (IEEE Std 1012–2004) to assist in documenting the specific V&V practices to be implemented. The contents and application of the SVVP are covered in Chapter 9.

2.5 METRICS

Metrics are numerical measures that quantify the degree to which software or a process possesses a given attribute. Examples of metrics are "defects per thousand lines of code" and "average software module size." Metrics are collected and analyzed throughout the software life cycle, and help with the following:

- Determining software quality level
- Estimating project schedules
- Tracking schedule progress
- Determining software size and complexity

- Determining project cost

- Process improvement

When goals such as software quality level and project cost are not expressed specifically enough, they may be subject to differing interpretations. These differences can cause confusion and conflict. For example, a goal stated as "The application should crash *very seldom*" is not specific. How do you measure "very seldom"? Is it once per day? Per week? Per year? A more precise goal would be "The application should crash no more than 3 times per year." Stated this way, the goal is not open to interpretation and is measurable.

Without quantifiable, objective measures to provide visibility into a project it is difficult to measure a project's progress in terms of whether it is on schedule, whether it is meeting its quality goals, and whether it is ready to ship to customers. In addition, "you can't improve what you don't measure." Continuous improvement of an organization's processes and software is predicated on collecting metrics and setting quantitative improvement goals for future projects.

To be successfully utilized, metric collection commences at the onset of a project and continues throughout the entire life cycle, through maintenance. Metric collection and analysis can take a significant amount of managerial and engineering effort, but the payoff is well worth it.

Software metrics can be classified into two broad categories: *product* metrics and *process* metrics. Product metrics measure characteristics of the software product, or system, including its size, complexity, performance, and quality level. For example, *size* can be expressed in the number of lines of code, *performance* as the number of transactions per second, and *quality level* as number of defects per thousand lines of code, which is commonly referred to as defect density.

Process metrics measure attributes of the software processes, methods, and tools employed during software development and maintenance of a software system. Process metrics include project effort, schedule adherence, defect repair rate, and productivity. For example, *project effort* can be expressed as the number of person months of development, and *defect repair rate* as the number of defects repaired per week. Many other metrics can be collected, and they are discussed in greater detail in the quality and metrics chapters later in the book. Chapter 9 describes metrics collection and utilization in more detail. The next section discusses metrics and their use in measuring quality.

2.5.1 Quality Metrics

Since quality is the degree to which software satisfies its requirements, we must be able to measure this degree of compliance. It is useful to identify a set of software quality metrics, which are a subset of the total metrics collected for a project. These metrics are specifically focused on the quality characteristics of software and of the processes employed during the software life cycle.

As described by Kan [4], important quality metrics include the following:

- Defect density

- Mean time to failure

- Customer problems

- Customer satisfaction

Defect density is the number of defects relative to the software size. Size is typically expressed in thousands of lines of code (KLOC), so defect density is expressed as defects/KLOC. Remember that a defect is defined as a deviation from user requirements, so defect density is one of the most basic metrics used to measure quality. In general, the higher the defect density, the lower the quality. Organizations typically characterize defects by type or by severity, to distinguish their relative importance. The following is an example of how a high-severity defect would be defined and of a quality goal based on the definition:

> A class 1 defect is defined as a requirement listed in section 3 of the Software Requirements Specification that the application fails to satisfy. The application shall have no more than 5 class 1 defects reported per 1,000 users during the first month of operation.

Note that this definition and goal are very specific and measurable. Again, when goals are not expressed in a quantifiable form, they may be subject to differing interpretations. For example, consider an alternative definition to the one above: "there should be very few class 1 defects reported in the first few months of operation." There is no way to measure "very few" and therefore to validate compliance.

A common indicator of software quality is the reliability of a system, as measured by its availability or the frequency of system crashes over a period of time. The typical metric used is *mean time to failure* (MTTF) and is the amount of elapsed time between system crashes. The MTTF metric is often used with safety-related systems such as the airline traffic control systems, avionics, and weapons. For instance, the U.S. government mandates that its air traffic control system cannot be unavailable for more than three seconds per year [4]. Another example can be seen in many telecommunications switches, such as those used in cellular networks. Large network providers mandate that this equipment must have "five 9's" availability, which is an uptime of 99.999% per year. This translates to a total yearly downtime of 5 minutes, 15 seconds. The reader may well ask, "Why not make the required MTTF 100%?" The answer is that this is generally not attainable, and so no development organization would sign up to do the job.

Customer problems are classified as the total number of problems encountered by customers while using the product. Some of the problems may be caused by valid defects in the software. Others may be caused by non-defects, such as a confusing user interface, poorly written documentation, or duplicate defects (i.e., defects that were already reported and/fixed but not known by the reporting party). Duplicates can be an important indicator as to how widespread a defect is, based on the number of times the same defect is reported by different users. In all these cases, whether a problem is caused by a defect or not, customers are encountering perceived usability problems and as a result may not be satisfied with the software. This makes the *customer problems* metric an important indicator of quality. This metric is typically expressed as problems/user/month. It and other metrics collected after a software product is released are discussed in Part VII on testing, release, and maintenance.

Customer satisfaction metrics are commonly collected through the administration of customer satisfaction surveys. Companies such as Cisco Systems [5] collect feedback from their customers, with satisfaction measured on a 5-point scale (5 = Very Satisfied; 1 = Very Dissatisfied). IBM includes the CUPRIMDSO categories (Capability/functionality, Usability, Performance, Reliability, Installability, Maintainability, Documentation/information, Service, and Overall). Hewlett-Packard uses the FURPS categories (Function-ality, Usability, Reliability, Performance, and Service) [4]. Results of these surveys are used to drive improvement initiatives in their respective organizations.

2.6 SUMMARY

Quality software is a major theme of this book. Quality can be defined as "the more closely a software product meets the wants and needs of its customers." There are many advantages to producing quality software including increased customer satisfaction, reduced development schedules, and reduced project cost. Quality practices are implemented at the beginning of the software life cycle and last through product release into maintenance.

Defects in software are deviations from requirements. As many defects as possible should be removed during product development, so these defects will not be delivered to customers. The earlier in the life cycle defects are detected, the easier they are to repair and the less they cost to fix. Studies have shown that defects detected and repaired after software is released to customers can cost up to 100 times as much as if the same defects were repaired shortly after they were introduced.

Verification and validation (V&V) is a process for verifying that artifacts produced during the life cycle contain as few defects as possible and validating that software satisfies its requirements. Verification answers the question, "Are we building the product right?" Validation answers the question, "Are we building the right product?"

Metrics are numerical measures collected throughout the software life cycle, and quantify the degree to which software and processes possess certain attributes. They help with determining quality level, estimating schedules, tracking schedule progress, determining software size and complexity, determining project cost, and improving processes. Metrics related to quality include defect density, mean time to failure, customer problems, and customer satisfaction.

2.7 EXERCISES

1. In addition to the reasons stated in this chapter, name at least two other advantages to producing quality software.

2. It has been noted that the later in the life cycle defects go undetected, the harder they are to discover and repair. In your own words, describe two reasons why this is true.

3. (a) Describe in your own words the difference between *verification* and *validation*.
   (b) What are the advantages and disadvantages of specifying a V&V plan before a plan for conducting your specific project?

4. (a) What are metrics?
   (b) Give a reason why you understand metrics to be important.

5. (a) In your own words, describe the difference between *product* and *process* metrics.
   (b) For each of the following objectives, state a metric you would use to help in achieving the objective, state whether it is a product or process metric, and explain how it would be applied.

      i. Avoid project schedule delays.
      ii. Measure continuous quality improvement from one project to the next.
      iii. Identify software parts that are exhibiting quality problems.
      iv. Establish a baseline for improving schedule accuracy.

BIBLIOGRAPHY

1. Whitten, Neal, *"Managing Software Development Projects,"* John Wiley & Sons, p. 195, 1995.
2. Boehm, Barry, *"Software Engineering Economics,"* Prentice-Hall, 1981.
3. "IEEE Standard Glossary of Software Engineering Terminology," IEEE Std 610.12-1990, December 1990, pp. 80-81.
4. Kan, Stephen N., 2003, *"Metrics and Models in Software Quality Engineering,"* Second Edition, Addison-Wesley, Pearson Education Inc., pp. 86–100.
5. Cisco Systems, Customer Satisfaction Metrics. http://www.cisco.com/web/about/ac50/ac208/about_cisco_approach_to_quality_customer_sat_survey.html [accessed Nov 4, 2009].

3

Software Process

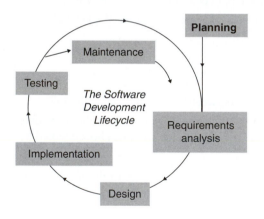

- What are the main activities of software processes?

- What are the main software process types?

- How would a team such as a student team go about selecting a process?

Figure 3.1 The context and learning goals for this chapter

A software project progresses through a series of activities, starting at its conception and continuing even beyond its release to customers. There are numerous ways for individuals and teams to organize these activities. Typically, a project is organized into *phases*, each with a prescribed set of activities conducted during that phase. A *software process* prescribes the interrelationship among the phases by expressing their order and frequency, as well as defining the deliverables of the project. It also specifies criteria for moving from one phase to the next. Specific software processes, called software process *models*—or *life cycle* models—are described. This chapter is organized to first describe the individual activities of software processes, and then to describe process models—the various ways in which these activities can be pursued.

In addition to the activities prescribed by process models, there is a set of generic activities, called *umbrella activities*, that are implemented throughout the life of a project. For instance, projects contain certain risks that if they come to pass can affect the successful outcome of the software. Risks need to be identified, monitored, and managed throughout the life of a project. This is an umbrella activity known as risk management. Other umbrella activities include project management, configuration management, and quality management. Project management is covered in Part III, configuration management in Chapter 6, and quality management throughout, but especially in Part VII.

People sometimes associate process with overhead, unnecessary paperwork, longer schedules, and so on. In other words, they feel that process doesn't add value, or worse, that it adversely affects the success of a project. When implemented incorrectly, software processes can indeed lead to undesirable results. However, as we explain in this chapter, if processes are applied with a degree of flexibility and adaptability, they are of great benefit and invaluable to the successful outcome of projects.

In certain situations, a version of working software containing a subset of the overall product functionality is required early in the overall schedule. This version of the emerging product, called a *prototype*, typically implements functionality that is deemed a risk to the project. Typical reasons to build prototypes include proving technical feasibility and validating the usability of a user interface. Prototypes are covered in detail in Section 3.2.3.1.

To reinforce the contents of this chapter and to provide guidance to students at the same time, this chapter ends with a section devoted to getting student teams started with a term project.

3.1 THE ACTIVITIES OF SOFTWARE PROCESS

Most software process models prescribe a similar set of phases and activities. The difference between models is the order and frequency of the phases. Some process models, such as the waterfall, execute each phase only once. Others, such as iterative models, cycle through multiple times. This section describes the phases that are prevalent in most software process models, and is summarized in Figure 3.2. The phases in Figure 3.1 and Figure 3.2 are identical, except that Figure 3.1 combines inception and planning. The parts are explained below. Specific process models and how they implement the phases are covered in Section 3.2.

---

1. **Inception**
   Software product is conceived and defined.

2. **Planning**
   Initial schedule, resources and cost are determined.

3. **Requirements Analysis**
   Specify what the application must do; answers *"what?"*

4. **Design**
   Specify the parts and how they fit; answers *"how?"*

5. **Implementation**
   Write the **code**.

6. **Testing**
   Execute the application with input test data.

7. **Maintenance**
   Repair defects and add capability.

Figure 3.2 The main phases of a software project, showing Inception as a separate phase

Inception

This is the phase where initial product ideas are formulated and a vision of the software is conceived. Whether it is a brand new product or an improvement to existing software, every project starts with an idea of what is to be built. Major functionality and project scope is defined. Target customers and market segments are identified. Customers and stakeholders may be consulted for high-level input into software functionality. However, stakeholder involvement at this stage is different from that during the subsequent requirements analysis phase. During inception, the goal is to gather very high level feedback. As an example, suppose a company is considering building a video store application. A market analysis may be conducted to determine the existence of competing video store applications. A summary of their features and an analysis of their strengths and weaknesses is compiled. The commercial success of the proposed application is determined by identifying potential new customers and contacting them for information concerning:

- Their satisfaction with their current application

- Ideas for needed functionality and features

- Their likelihood of adopting a new product

As an example, suppose that a currently deployed system requires custom hardware, but potential customers would prefer using standard Windows PCs. Based on this analysis and feedback, the need for and viability of the proposed application is determined. If it is deemed promising, high-level functionality for the application is defined based on the feedback received, and the project proceeds to the planning phase.

Planning

Once a high-level idea for the application is developed, a plan is formulated to produce it. Since this is still very early in the overall life cycle and detailed information is not yet available, the plan will be a rough estimate. However, some plan must be in place to understand the scope and cost of the project. A project plan that identifies the high-level activities, work items, schedule, and resources is developed. From this information a cost estimate can be developed. This step is very important to determine the feasibility of a project. For example, if the cost is deemed to be too high, a reduction in features may necessary. If the product release date is too late, more resources may be added. It is critical that these types of problems be identified as early as possible so corrective action can be taken.

The results of this phase are typically captured in a Software Project Management Plan (SPMP). The SPMP and project management are covered in Part IV. Because the plan is only a rough one at this stage, it is necessary to modify and adapt it throughout the life of the project. For example, suppose that during subsequent requirements analysis potential new customers are identified and additional functionality is requested. Using the video store application as an example, suppose a request is received to add additional workstations to stores so customers can retrieve detailed movie information, such as release date, movie studio, cast, director, producer, genre, and so on. This new functionality may require additional project resources and changes to the schedule. The SPMP would be updated as a result. Some life cycle models, such as the spiral model described below, prescribe specific points in the process where planning information is revisited and updated when required. Agile projects, as will be seen, keep planning to a minimum.

In addition to the activities described above, a plan is developed for managing project artifacts such as technical specifications and source code. This is known as *configuration management*, and includes tasks such as tracking changes to artifacts and handling multiple versions. Configuration management is planned at this early project stage, before the first project artifacts are generated. Configuration management is covered in detail in Chapter 6.

Requirements Analysis

During this phase, detailed information regarding customer wants and needs, and problems the software is intended to solve are gathered. Information gathered and documented is in much greater detail than it was in the inception phase. During inception, only enough information is required to start planning the project. During requirements analysis, specific product functions and features are defined along with requirements such as performance, reliability, and usability. Requirements are generated in a form that is completely readable and understandable by customers. High-level requirements in particular are typically expressed in ordinary English (or the local language). Various techniques are used to obtain this information, including customer interviews and brainstorming sessions. Requirements describe *what* the application is intended to accomplish. They are specified in sufficient detail so they can be used as input for the subsequent design phase, which defines *how* the software will be built. The results of the analysis are typically captured in a formal Software Requirements Specification (SRS), which serves as input to the next phase.

Software Design

The purpose of software design is to define how the software will be constructed to satisfy the requirements. That is, the internal structure of the software is defined. The two main levels of software design are software architecture and detailed design. Software architecture is analogous to the overall blueprints of a house as a whole. Blueprints specify the number of rooms and their layout, door and window locations, number of floors, and so on. Software architecture specifies how the software is broken into subsystems or modules and the software interfaces between them. For example, the architecture for a video store application may consist of components such as a user interface module, a problem domain module, and a database module. Agile projects generally perform design, implementation, and much testing in an interweaved fashion rather than calling out design as a separate phase.

The detailed design is analogous to the details contained in a house blueprint. In house plans, details such electrical wiring and plumbing are specified. In software, details such as algorithms and data structures are specified. Other aspects of software design include user interface design and database design. The output of software design is specified in a Software Design Document (SDD) and is used as input to the implementation phase. Software design is covered in detail in Part V.

Implementation

This phase consists of programming, which is the translation of the software design developed in the previous phase to a programming language. It also involves integration, the assembly of the software parts. The output consists of program code that is ready to be tested for correctness. For agile techniques, design implementation and much testing are performed in tandem.

Testing

In this phase, the code produced during the implementation phase is tested for correctness. Testing is performed at three levels. First, individual modules are tested by developers. Second, modules are integrated and tested to ensure that they interface properly. Third, once all the modules have been integrated, the entire system is tested to ensure that it meets the user requirements. System testing is typically conducted by an independent quality assurance (QA) team. Recall from Chapter 2 that this testing process is called *validation*. Once system testing has been completed, several levels of customer testing are conducted. During *beta testing* the software is as close to the final release as possible, and is given to part of the customer community with the understanding that they report any defects they find. The goal is to uncover a set of problems that could only be discovered with this type of "real-world" testing. Once beta testing is complete, *acceptance testing* is conducted on the "final" release of software. Acceptance tests are comprised of a subset of system tests, and are conducted by either the customer or a representative of the customer to ensure that it meets the customer's criteria for release. Sometimes a round of acceptance testing is conducted prior to beta testing, to make sure that the system meets certain criteria before it is given to customers for beta testing.

Maintenance

After the software is officially released to customers, the maintenance phase commences. During maintenance, modifications are made to the software that arise through one of the following:

- The repair of software defects that are discovered during normal customer use of the system

- Customer requests for enhancements

- A desire to improve attributes of the system such as performance or reliability

Modifications to the software are bundled together, and new versions of the software with these modifications are released. Maintenance is discussed in detail in Chapter 29.

Figure 3.3 shows examples of artifacts produced during each phase for our example video store application.

- **Inception**

    " . . . An application is needed to keep track of video rentals . . . "

- **Planning** (Software Project Management Plan)

    " . . . The project will take 12 months, require 10 people and cost $2M . . . "

- **Requirements Analysis** (Product: Software Requirements Spec.)

    " . . . The clerk shall enter video title, renter name and date rented. The system shall . . . "

- **Design** (Software Design Document: Diagrams and text)

    " . . . classes *DVD, VideoStore,* . . . , related by . . . "

- **Implementation** (Source and object code)

    . . . class DVD{ String title; . . . } . . .

- **Testing** (Software Test Documentation: test cases and test results)

    " . . . <u>Ran test case:</u> *Rent "The Matrix" on Oct 3; rent "SeaBiscuit" on Oct 4; return "The Matrix" on Oct 10 . . .* <u>Result:</u> *"SeaBiscuit" due Oct 4, 2004 balance of $8. (correct) . . .* "

- **Maintenance** (Modified requirements, design, code, and text)

    Defect repair: "Application crashes when balance is $10 and attempt is made to rent *"Gone With the Wind"* . . . "
    Enhancement: "Allow searching by director."

Figure 3.3 The main phases applied to a video store application

3.2 SOFTWARE PROCESS MODELS

Software process models define the order and frequency of phases in a project. The following sections describe the most important process models, starting with the classical waterfall process.

3.2.1 The Waterfall Process Model

One of the oldest software process models was defined by Royce [1] and is called the *waterfall process.* Despite its many weaknesses (described later in the section), the waterfall process is still in widespread use today and is the basis for many other more effective processes.

Figure 1.6 in Chapter 1 illustrates the phases of the waterfall process. Note that Royce's model begins with the requirements phase—he did not include inception and planning phases. In practice, organizations implementing a waterfall process would typically start with these phases. The waterfall executes in a sequential manner through each phase, concluding with maintenance. The output from one phase is used as input for the next, implying that a phase is not started until the previous one has completed. It is accepted in waterfall processes that there is a small overlap between adjacent phases. As an example, some personnel will be performing the last part of requirements analysis while others will have already started the design phase.

The waterfall process is characterized by documents generated by the time each phase is completed. These include requirements specification and design specification, for example. Also, there are usually entrance and exit criteria between phases to ensure that a phase is completed successfully before moving on.

In practice, an iterative relationship between successive phases is usually inevitable. For example, after the requirements are completed, unforeseen design difficulties may arise. Some of these issues may result in the modification or removal of conflicting or non-implementable requirements. This may happen several times, resulting in looping between requirements and design. Another example of feedback is between maintenance and testing. Defects are discovered by customers after the software is released. Based on the nature of the problems, it may be determined there is inadequate test coverage in a particular area of the software. Additional tests may be added to catch these types of defects in future software releases. A general guideline, often accepted to still be within the waterfall framework, is that feedback loops should be restricted to adjacent phases. This minimize potentially expensive rework if the feedback were to span multiple phases. An modified model illustrating this iterative relationship is shown in Figure 3.4.

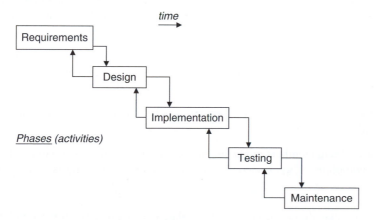

Figure 3.4 The waterfall software development process in practice: feedback is inevitable

A major limitation of the waterfall process is that the testing phase occurs at the end of the development cycle—the first time the system is tested as a whole. Major issues such as timing, performance, storage, and so on can be discovered only then. Even with thorough up-front analysis, these kinds of factors are difficult to predict until encountered during testing. Solutions may require either complex design changes or modifications to the requirements that the design is based on, necessitating iteration beyond adjacent phases. Discovering and repairing these types of defects so late in the development cycle can jeopardize the project schedule.

Major advantages and disadvantages of the waterfall process are summarized below.

Advantages

- *Simple and easy to use*: Phases are executed and completed serially, with specific entrance and exit criteria for moving between phases. Orderly execution of phases is easy to comprehend.

- *Practiced for many years and people have much experience with it*: The process is well understood, and many people are comfortable with its execution.

- *Easy to manage due to the rigidity of the model*: Each phase has specific deliverables and a review process.

- *Facilitates allocation of resources* (due to sequential nature of phases): Distinct phases facilitate allocation of personnel with distinct skills.

- *Works well for smaller projects where requirements are very well understood*: It isn't necessary to add complexity of iteration if requirements are well known up front.

Disadvantages

- *Requirements must be known up front*: It's difficult to imagine every detail in advance. Most projects start out with some uncertainty, and more details are learned as the project progresses.

- *Hard to estimate reliably*: To gain confidence in an estimate, there may be the need to design and implement parts, especially riskier ones. Estimates become more precise as the project progresses.

- *No feedback of system by stakeholders until after testing phase*: The process does not facilitate intermediate versions. Stakeholders often need reassurance of progress and confirmation that what is being developed meets requirements.

- *Major problems with system aren't discovered until late in process*: The testing phase is where these problems are found, but it leaves very little time for correction, resulting in potentially disastrous effects on project schedule and cost.

- *Lack of parallelism*: Each phase is executed to completion. Disjointed parts of the system could otherwise be completed in parallel.

- *Inefficient use of resources*: Team members can be idle while waiting for others to complete their dependent tasks or for phases to complete. Also, someone good at requirements analysis is not necessarily good at programming.

Because of factors like these, alternative (but related) processes are often employed, and these are covered in subsequent sections.

3.2.2 Iterative and Incremental Development

The waterfall process is characterized by a sequential execution through the phases. It is generally agreed that the order of the phases dictated by the waterfall is fundamental: gather requirements, create a software design to realize the requirements, implement the design, and test the implementation. The problem arises, however, when this is scaled up to gather *all* the requirements, do *all* of the design, implement *all* of the code, and test *all* of the system in a linear fashion [2]. Except for the smallest of projects this is impractical. As the system is developed and refined, more is learned and a need arises to revisit each of the phases. That is, software is more naturally developed in a cyclical manner, where a part of the system is developed and tested, feedback is gathered, and based on the feedback more of the system is developed. This reflects the fact that not everything is understood at the start of a project. *Iterative* processes accept this cyclical nature and are discussed in the rest of this section. Figure 3.1 is drawn in a way that reflects this.

An *iterative* process is typified by repeated execution of the waterfall phases, in whole or in part, resulting in a refinement of the requirements, design, and implementation. An iterative process is *incremental* if each iteration is relatively small. At the conclusion of such an iteration, a piece of operational code is produced that supports a subset of the final product functionality and features. Project artifacts such as plans, specifications, and code evolve during each phase and over the life of the project. Artifacts are considered complete only when the software is released.

As defined by Cockburn [3], incremental development is "a scheduling and staging strategy that allows pieces of the system to be developed at different times or rates and integrated as they are completed." This implies that iterations need not be executed serially, but can be developed in parallel by separate teams of people. Successive increments implement an increasing set of functionality and features until the final iteration, which produces the final product. Figure 3.5 illustrates this concept for a project with three iterations. Note that the output of each testing phase is a working subset of the final product that incrementally contains more functionality.

An iteration other than an incremental one is sometimes defined as "a self-contained mini-project, with a well-defined outcome: a stable, integrated and tested release" [2]. That is, each iteration is a self-contained

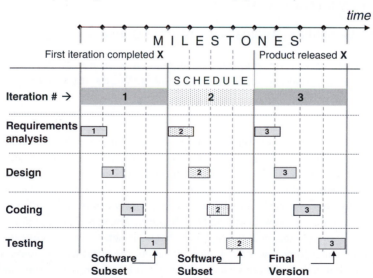

Figure 3.5 The iterative software development process: an example with three iterations

Source: Cockburn, Alistair. "Unraveling Incremental Development," January 1993, http://alistair.cockburn.us/Unraveling+incremental+development.

project with its own set of activities, plan, objectives, and measurable evaluation criteria. The "release" is a working version of software that is either used internally by the project team or externally by stakeholders and customers. Types of releases can be [2]:

- A *proof of concept*, or *feasibility study*, that is used to demonstrate or investigate feasibility of a particular aspect of the software. This includes producing software or simulations. These are covered in Section 3.2.3.2.

- A *prototype* that is a working version of software demonstrating a particular capability that is deemed high risk. Prototypes are covered in Section 3.2.3.1.

- An "internal" release that is only used by the development team and is used to ensure that development is on track, elicit feedback, and provide a basis for further development and additional capabilities.

- An "external" release that is shipped to customers for evaluation.

Treating each iteration as a self-contained project allows clear and manageable objectives to be set, and reduces overall project complexity by breaking it down into smaller pieces. By producing working software at the end of each iteration, project progress can more easily be monitored and planned, and feedback can be elicited to ensure that its capabilities are meeting stakeholder requirements. Typically, early iterations generate software releases that address aspects of the project with the highest risk. In this way, as the project progresses the overall project risk level is reduced.

An example of an iterative and incremental process that is used within parts of Microsoft is reported by Cusumano and Selby [4], to which they give the name "synch-and-stabilize." Product features are defined at a high level during the initial phase of a project, with the idea that many will evolve as product development proceeds. The product is divided into parts, each consisting of a set of features, with small teams assigned to each part. The project is also divided into parts, or iterations, each with its own completion milestone. Each iteration includes several features. Feature teams employ incremental synchronization by combining their work and stabilizing the resulting system on a daily or weekly basis. In this way the evolving software application is continually kept in a "working" state.

3.2.3 Prototyping, Feasibility Studies, and Proofs of Concept

Prototypes and feasibility studies are important techniques in software development, and are explicitly included as formal steps, or phases, in several process models. We discuss them now in more detail.

3.2.3.1 Prototyping

On beginning a software project, we are usually faced with factors that we do not yet fully understand. The look and feel of graphical user interfaces (GUIs) that will satisfy the customer is one common example. Timing is another. For example, suppose that we plan to build a Java application to control an airplane. A critical issue to pin down very early would be: Will the Java Virtual Machine be fast enough? Each unknown factor or *risk* is best confronted as soon as possible so that its severity can be assessed and a plan developed to deal with it. Risk management is dealt with in detail in Chapter 8. *Prototyping* is an important risk management technique. It is a partial implementation of the target application useful in identifying and retiring risky parts of a project. Prototyping can also be a way to obtain ideas about the customer's requirements. An increase in one's understanding of what is to come can save expensive rework and remove future roadblocks before they occur. Agile processes contain some of the benefits of prototyping because they deal at all times with working code. However, they do not have all of the benefits, since prototypes proceed in parallel with the main thread of the project, whether agile or not.

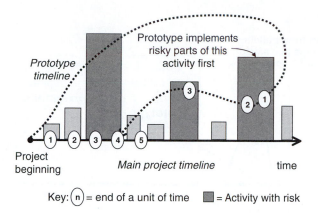

Figure 3.6 An illustration of prototyping in the context of a development project

As Figure 3.6 shows, work on a prototype typically progresses in parallel with regular work on the project. The risks are prioritized and the prototype is geared toward as many of the most important ones as time allows. In the example shown in Figure 3.6, the prototype ignores the large risk near the beginning of the project because it will be dealt with early in the ordinary course of the project in any case.

Large programs, such as billion dollar defense projects, utilize extensive prototyping to retire risks and to guide the requirements and design of the real thing. For example, before the U.S. Navy built the Aegis generation of shipboard systems, it built an entire scaled-back version, complete with software and hardware, installed on a ship for the purpose. This prototype served to indicate to the Navy what the main problems might be with the eventual systems. It also helped the Navy to develop the requirements and design of the eventual system.

Simple graphics showing GUIs using paint-type tools may be sufficient if the prototype's goal is to envision the interfaces. The more extensive the prototype, the more risks can be retired with it and the more easily a customer's requirements can be understood. On the other hand, prototypes are themselves software applications, so extensive prototypes are expensive. A rough assessment as to whether or not to build a prototype is shown in Figure 3.7. The table in the figure illustrates, for example, that a relatively inexpensive prototype with high value should probably be built. "High value" means that building the prototype helps the

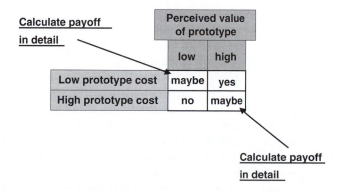

Figure 3.7 A rough calculation of whether developing a prototype would be worth it

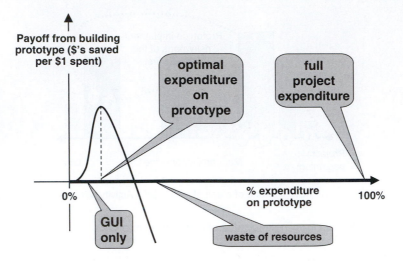

Figure 3.8 Concept of when it is worthwhile to build a prototype (near the beginning)

customer understand better what kind of product is likely to emerge, helps the engineers understand better what kind of product should emerge, and/or retires a development risk.

Many cases fall into the "maybe" category of the table in Figure 3.7, and more detailed analysis is required to assess the value of prototyping. We are seeking an optimal level of effort to be spent on a prototype, as suggested by Figure 3.8. As the expenditure on a prototype increases, its usefulness increases, but so does its drain on the project's budget. As a result, there is a point at which the payoff is optimal (the maximum point for the curve), and some point beyond which funds are actually being squandered (where the curve drops below the horizontal axis).

As an example, consider an e-commerce application in which a clothing company wants to sell goods online, retain customer profiles, and allow customers to obtain pictures of themselves wearing clothing from the catalog. A typical calculation about prototypes factors the cost of prototyping features and the potential for using prototype code in the final product. Figure 3.9 gives financial estimates for prototyping four parts of the clothing vendor application:

1. GUI screenshots

2. Transaction security

3. Complete transaction

4. Customer tries on clothing

For each of the four application features considered for the prototype, several estimates can made: the cost of building the feature, the percentage of the feature's implementation that will be reused in the application itself (i.e., not discarded), and the "gross benefit" from the effort. The gross benefit here estimates the gain from prototyping the feature, excluding reuse of the code and excluding all expenses. For example, as shown in Figure 3.9, we have estimated that if the "Customer tries on clothing" feature were to be prototyped, it would save a minimum $20,000 in development costs. This estimate is based on factors such as the following:

	Estimated cost	Gross Benefit excluding code reuse		Percentage of prototype code reused in application	Net Payoff		
		min	max		min	max	average
Prototype feature	B	D	E	C	D-(1-C)B	E-(1-C)B	
1. GUI screenshots	$10,000	$10,000	$80,000	50%	$5,000	$75,000	$40,000
2. Transaction security	$50,000	$10,000	$300,000	80%	$0	$290,000	$145,000
3. Complete transaction	$80,000	$10,000	$400,000	50%	−$30,000	$200,000	$85,000
4. Customer tries on clothing	$120,000	$20,000	$140,000	30%	−$64,000	$56,000	−$4,000

Figure 3.9 Payoff calculation example for building a prototype for a clothing application

- Preventing time wasted on proposed requirements that the prototype shows are not really needed (e.g., minimum of three unneeded requirements out of 100; $300,000 budgeted for the requirements phase = $9000 saved)

- Implementing a software design for the "trying on clothes" feature, thereby retiring some development risks (e.g., estimate that this will save a minimum of one person-week of design time = $2000)

- Rework that would have resulted from the customer changing requirements only after seeing the developed product (e.g., rework minimum of three requirements at $3000 each = $9000)

The minimum savings therefore is $9000 + $2000 + $9000 = $20,000$. Estimating the cost of building the prototype can use approximation techniques like those described in Chapter 8. An estimation of code reuse can be performed by identifying the classes of the prototype and determining which are likely to be usable in the actual application.

This type of estimation often consists of adding up the estimation of smaller parts, which is often more feasible. Bracketing each estimate between a minimum and a maximum can help to make this process a little easier for the estimator.

Once these estimates are made, the best- and worst-case scenarios for each feature can be computed. This is shown in Figure 3.9. The minimum payoff value is obtained by taking the most pessimistic combination: the highest costs, the lowest gross benefits, and the lowest reuse percentages. The maximum payoff is calculated correspondingly. For example, the maximum payoff (the most optimistic alternative) for the "GUI screenshot" prototype feature is as follows:

[maximum estimated benefit] − [minimum estimated costs]
= $80,000 − [(minimum estimated cost) × (percent not reusable)]
= $80,000 − [$10,000 × 50%] = $75,000

Averaging is one way to deal with the spread between best and worst cases. The result suggests a positive payoff for all proposed prototype features except for the "trying on clothes" feature, which projects −$4000: an overall waste of $4000. The latter negative result is due to relatively low payoff, high development cost, and low reuse.

It may be advisable for the prototype to evolve into the application itself, but this should be planned for, not accidental. By their nature, prototypes are rapidly constructed and rarely documented. They can be implemented using languages that get results quickly but may be unsuitable for the application itself.

3.2.3.2 Feasibility Studies

It is sometimes uncertain whether proposed requirements can actually be implemented in practice. In other words, an entire project is at risk rather than a few specific requirements. In addition, the project would not be feasible if the risk were to be realized. In such cases, *feasibility studies* may be advisable. These are partial implementations or simulations of the application. For example, consider the feasibility of a Java Internet-based Encounter video game, and let's say we suspect performance will be so slow that the game would be of negligible interest to anyone. A feasibility study could consist of setting up a message-passing simulation at the anticipated rate from a number of players, but with dummy content. Delays could then be estimated by clocking the simulation.

Simulations can be expensive to create since they are applications in themselves, sometimes requiring software engineering artifacts of their own such as a requirements specification! The author was once involved with a simulation of a large system under development. The simulation grew into a large program, which was needed while engineers developed the real system. No one took the requirements for the simulation seriously because it was not "the real thing." As a result, even though the development community relied on the simulation, the cost of maintaining and using it became astronomical. Making changes required tracking down an employee who "knew the system." Feasibility simulations are common in large defense programs that involve extensive software and hardware.

3.2.4 Spiral Model

One of the earliest and best known iterative processes is Barry Boehm's Spiral Model [5]. It is called a spiral because Boehm conceptualized development iterating as an outward spiral, as shown in Figure 3.10.

Boehm's spiral model is a risk-driven process in which iterations have the specified goals shown in Figure 3.10. (Recall that risks are potential events or situations that can adversely affect the success of a project.) A project starts at the center, as it were, and each cycle of the spiral represents one iteration. The goal of each cycle is to increase the degree of system definition and implementation, while decreasing the degree of risk. Risk management is built into the process in that very early in each iteration, project risks are identified and analyzed and a plan for the iteration is created that includes mitigating some or all of the risks. As an example, suppose that at the beginning of a cycle a risk is identified with the screen layout of a portion of the user interface. Software could be developed to implement part of the user interface so feedback can be elicited from stakeholders. Doing this mitigates risk early in a project and leaves ample time to implement necessary changes. Thus the overall project risk reduces the further along you are in the process. After the major risks are addressed and mitigated, the project transitions to a waterfall model, as shown in the outer spiral of Figure 3.10.

Each iteration in Boehm's spiral model consists of the following steps:

1. Identification of critical objectives and constraints of the product.

2. Evaluation of project and process alternatives for achieving the objectives.

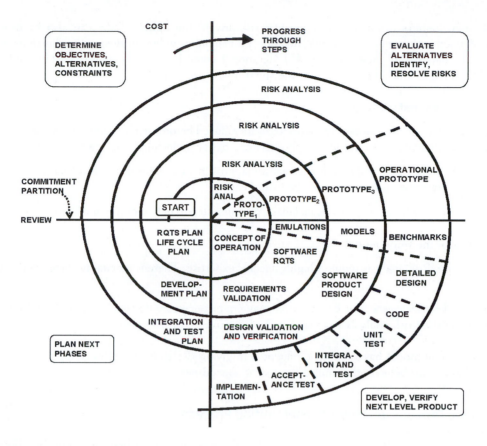

Figure 3.10 Boehm's spiral model for software development

Source: Boehm, B. W., ''A Spiral Model of Software Development and Enhancement.'' IEEE Computer, Vol. 21, No. 5, May 1988, pp. 61–72.

3. Identification of risks.

4. Cost-effective resolution of a subset of risks using analysis, emulation, benchmarks, models, and prototypes.

5. Development of project deliverables including requirements, design, implementation, and testing.

6. Planning for next and future cycles—the overall project plan is updated, including schedule, cost, and number of remaining iterations.

7. Stakeholder review of iteration deliverables and their commitment to proceed based on their objectives being met.

Each traversal of the spiral results in incremental deliverables. Early iterations produce either models, emulations, benchmarks, or prototypes, and later iterations follow a more waterfall-like process and incrementally produce more complete versions of the software. This implies that early iterations may exclude step 5, and later iterations may exclude step 4. Although Figure 3.10 shows four iterations, the process does not prescribe a set number of cycles. The number is dictated by the size of a project, the number of risks identified, and their rate of retirement.

Although Boehm's original conception was risk-driven, the Spiral Model can also be driven by a sequence of functionality sets. For example, iteration 1 for an online video-on-demand application could be to implement the database of videos and its API; iteration 2 could be to implement the GUIs, and so on.

Key advantages and disadvantages of the spiral model are listed next.

Advantages of the spiral model

- *Risks are managed early and throughout the process*: Risks are reduced before they become problematic, as they are considered at all stages. As a result, stakeholders can better understand and react to risks.

- *Software evolves as the project progresses*: It is a realistic approach to the development of large-scale software. Errors and unattractive alternatives are eliminated early.

- *Planning is built into the process*: Each cycle includes a planning step to help monitor and keep a project on track.

Disadvantages of the spiral model

- *Complicated to use*: Risk analysis requires highly specific expertise. There is inevitably some overlap between iterations.

- *May be overkill for small projects*: The complication may not be necessary for smaller projects. It does not make sense if the cost of risk analysis is a major part of the overall project cost.

Boehm's spiral model has been very influential in giving rise to many styles of iterative development models, including, we believe, the unified process, discussed next.

3.2.5 Unified Process and the Rational Unified Process

The Unified Software Development Process (USDP) was first described by Jacobson, Booch, and Rumbaugh in 1999 [6] and is an outgrowth of earlier methodologies developed by these three authors—namely, Jacobson's "Objectory methodology," the "Booch methodology" [7], and Rumbaugh et al.'s Object Modeling Technique [8]. The USDP is generically referred to as the *Unified Process* (UP). IBM's Rational Software division has developed a detailed refinement to the UP called the *Rational Unified Process* (RUP), which is a commercial product providing a set of process guidelines and tools to help automate the process.

The UP is a "use-case driven, architecture-centric, iterative and incremental" software process [6]. Iterations are grouped into four "phases," shown on the horizontal axis of Figure 3.11: *Inception, Elaboration, Construction*, and *Transition*. The UP's use of the term "phase" is different from the common use of the term. In fact, referring to the figure, the term "discipline" is the same as the common use of "phase" that we use in this book.

Each UP "phase" consists of one or more iterations, shown across the bottom of Figure 3.11. Iterations are relatively short (e.g., three weeks), the outcome of which is a tested, integrated, and executable partial system. Iterations are built on the work of previous iterations, and thus the final product is constructed incrementally. Each iteration cycles through a set of nine disciplines, which are shown on the vertical axis of Figure 3.11: business modeling, requirements, design, implementation and test activities, plus supporting activities such as configuration management, project management, and environ-ment [9]. For example, during an iteration some requirements may be chosen, the design enhanced to support those requirements, and the requirements implemented and tested. The horizontal "humps" next to each discipline show the relative effort expended on each discipline during iterations. For example, the

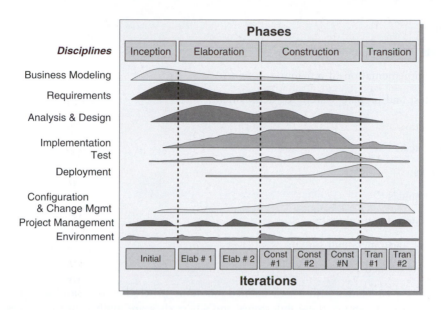

Figure 3.11 The unified software development process: its "phases" vs. traditional phases

Source: Adapted from Ambler, S. W., "A Manager's Introduction to the Rational Unified Process (RUP)." Ambysoft (December 4, 2005)., http://www.ambysoft.com/downloads/managersIntroToRUP.pdf.

largest requirements effort is expended during Inception and Elaboration, and the largest implementation effort during Construction.

The following are descriptions of the work conducted during each of the UP "phases":

Inception

- Establish feasibility

- Make business case

- Establish product vision and scope

- Estimate cost and schedule, including major milestones

- Assess critical risks

- Build one or more prototypes

Elaboration

- Specify requirements in greater detail

- Create architectural baseline

- Perform iterative implementation of core architecture

- Refine risk assessment and resolve highest risk items

- Define metrics

- Refine project plan, including detailed plan for beginning Construction iterations

Construction

- Complete remaining requirements

- Do iterative implementation of remaining design

- Thoroughly test and prepare system for deployment

Transition

- Conduct beta tests

- Correct defects

- Create user manuals

- Deliver the system for production

- Train end users, customers and support

- Conduct lessons learned

Each UP phase concludes with a well-defined milestone, where key decisions are made and specific goals defined. Figure 3.12 shows these milestones and where they are fulfilled in the process.

The typical amount of time spent in each UP phase is shown in Figure 3.13 [10]. However, this varies depending on the type of project. For example, projects that contain only minor enhancements with known requirements may spend more time in the Construction phase, while projects for which very little is known about requirements may spend more time in the Inception and Elaboration UP phases.

The advantages and disadvantages of the unified rocess are summarized below.

Advantages of the unified process

- *Most aspects of a project are accounted for*: The UP is very inclusive, covering most work related to a software development project such as establishing a business case.

- *The UP is mature*: The process has existed for several years and has been quite widely used.

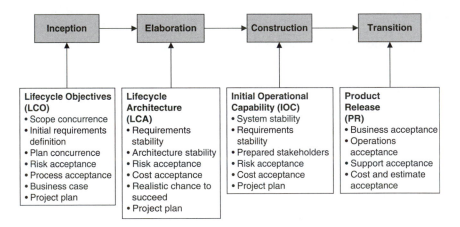

Figure 3.12 Objectives for the Unified process

Source: Adapted from Ambler, S. W., ''A Manager's Introduction to the Rational Unified Process (RUP).'' Ambysoft (December 4, 2005)., http://www.ambysoft.com/downloads/managersIntroToRUP.pdf.

UP Phases - Typical Time Distribution

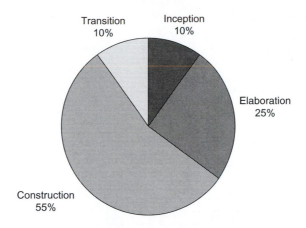

Figure 3.13 Typical time distribution of the rational unified process's "phases"

Source: Adapted from Ambler, S. W., "A Manager's Introduction to the Rational Unified Process (RUP)." Ambysoft (December 4, 2005)., http://www.ambysoft.com/downloads/managersIntroToRUP.pdf.

Disadvantages of the unified process

• *The UP was originally conceived of for large projects*: This is fine, except that many modern approaches perform work in small self-contained phases.

• *The process may be overkill for small projects*: The level of complication may not be necessary for smaller projects.

Practitioners and vendors of the unified process have modified it to be more like an agile process, discussed next.

3.2.6 Agile Processes

This section introduces agile processes. Chapter 4 is devoted entirely to agile methods, and agility is referenced and compared throughout this book.

In 2001, a group of industry experts, disillusioned with some commonly held software engineering beliefs and practices, met to discuss ways to improve software development. Their goal was to produce a set of values and principles to help speed up development and effectively respond to change. The group called themselves the Agile Alliance, in essence to capture their goal or producing a methodology that was efficient and adaptable. The result of their work was the *Manifesto for Agile Software Development* [11], also known as the *Agile Manifesto*, which contains the values and principles they defined. An *agile* software process is one that embraces and conforms to the Agile Manifesto, which is summarized in Figure 3.14.

Agile processes are highly iterative and incremental. They commonly employ the following:

• Small, close-knit teams

• Regular, frequent, disciplined customer requirements meetings

• A code-centric approach, documentation on an as-needed basis (e.g., high-level requirements statements only)

Agile processes value . . .

- . . . **individuals and interactions**

   over processes and tools

- . . . **working software**

   over comprehensive documentation

- . . . **customer collaboration**

   over contract negotiation

- . . . **responding to change**

   over following a plan

Figure 3.14 Main points of the Agile Manifesto

- Customer representatives working within the team
- The use of user stories as the basis for requirements—end-to-end accounts of how users need to accomplish individual tasks
- Refactoring, a kind of disciplined code improvement explained full in Chapter 24
- Pair programming, in which two programmers work at a single workstation
- Continual unit-testing, and acceptance tests as means of setting customer expectations

Figure 3.15 shows how the repeated iterations of an agile process are executed over time. "Story" is a task required of the application as the customer conceives it.

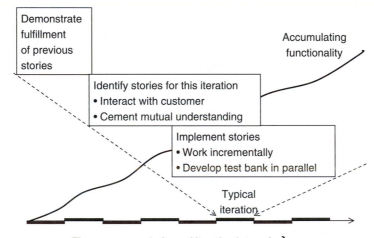

Figure 3.15 The agile process

Key advantages and disadvantages of agile processes are summarized below.

Advantages of an agile process

- *The project always has demonstrable results*: The end product of each iteration is working software.

- *Developers tend to be more motivated*: Developers prefer to produce working artifacts and tend not to like creating documentation.

- *Customers are able to provide better requirements because they can see the evolving product.*

Disadvantages of an agile process

- *Problematical for large application*: Agile methods are more readily used for smaller projects. There is debate about their utility for large projects.

- *Documentation output is questionable*: Since documentation takes second place, there is a question as to whether necessary documentation will ever be produced.

3.2.7 Open-Source Processes

Open-source software is developed and maintained by people on a volunteer basis. All project artifacts, from requirements documents through source code, are available to anyone. There are several open-source software development Web sites on the Internet that aggregate and reference open source projects, including SourceForge.net and Freshmeat.net. As of 2009, SourceForge.net hosted more than 100,000 projects and had over 1,000,000 registered users. Hosting sites provide source code repositories and utilities for project management, issues discussion, and source control. The case studies in this book illustrate two well known open source projects: Eclipse and OpenOffice.

Open-source projects typically get started when someone develops an application and posts it to a host Web site. Virtually anyone can propose new requirements, and since the source code is freely available, anyone can implement requirements that are not part of the official baseline. There is a process by which proposals and implementations are elevated in priority and a process for accepting new code and capability into the baseline. If defects are found, they are reported and others may work on fixing them. This process is repeated, and the application grows in capability and stability. In this way, open-source projects are developed in an iterative manner. In addition, by exercising an application many times, the open-source community affects a huge testing process.

Some reasons why an individual or company makes a project open source are listed in Figures 3.16 and 3.17, and reasons why they may not are listed in Figure 3.18. A primary reason to make a project open source is to leverage a large number of resources that might not otherwise be available. A principal reason to not make software open source is to keep artifacts hidden from current and prospective competitors. Some (e.g., Ferguson [12] and Kapor) believe that open source may become the dominant process for producing software.

An interesting article written by Alan Joch illustrates how the bank Dresdner Kleinwort Wasserstein (DrKW) turned its internally developed back-end Java integration tool, OpenAdapter, into open source and how it benefited from the decision. The following is an excerpt from that article.

Samolades et al. [13] studied open-source development and compared it with closed-source software. Using common metrics, OSS code quality was found roughly equal to that of CSS, and found to be superior for maintainability, or at worst equal. Some of their results are shown in Figures 3.19 and 3.20.

Open-source users find rewards in collaborative development

By Alan Joch
2/1/2005 http://www.adtmag.com/article.aspx?id=10544

Banks pride themselves on playing things close to the vest. So, when Dresdner Kleinwort Wasserstein's IT group shared the code of OpenAdapter, an internally developed tool, with the development community, it caused a sensation. "It was astonishing," recalls Steve Howe, DrKW's global head of open-source initiatives. "They found it difficult to believe a bank was open sourcing something."

OpenAdapter, a back-end Java integration tool that helps integrate bank apps with little or no custom programming, had become "a famous piece of software within DrKW," Howe says. "Half of the decision to open source it into the wider financial community was to try to replicate that enthusiasm."

DrKW's motive for releasing the tool was hardly altruistic. By releasing the tool to the wider financial community, the investment bank hoped to benefit from the bug fixes and refinements other programmers in Europe and North America might make.

However, Howe and other open-source experts warn that corporations' code-sharing projects require a number of safeguards to protect intellectual property and keep companies from becoming unwitting victims or distributors of destructive code. Some companies believe such risks outweigh the potential benefits and resist open-source business applications. DrKW and other firms believe careful open-source collaboration gives them a competitive advantage.

. . .

Banking on open source

Dresdner Kleinwort Wasserstein (DrKW) believes it found development success with OpenAdapter by creating a variation on the collaborative model the open-source community pioneered. . . . . "We open sourced the tool within DrKW and told people that if they needed to change OpenAdapter slightly, they were free to do that," Howe says. "A lot of developers decided they could make a name for themselves by contributing to the software." Today, more than 100 applications in the bank use the integration tool.

To tap similar expertise outside DrKW, the bank turned to CollabNet, a commercial project-development platform from CollabNet in Brisbane, California. CollabNet provides a number of services, including version control tools and discussion forums common in free open-source clearing-houses such as SourceForge. . . . CollabNet helped the bank establish a separate legal entity called the Software Conservancy, which owns the intellectual rights to OpenAdapter.

The site publishes the latest stable build of the software, which anyone can download. Users can also send in complaints and error reports and suggest bug fixes. So far, DrKW has received input from developers at competing banks and from companies outside the financial industry. Collaboration consists of technical subjects, not information that involves trade secrets or confidential customer data.

Developers interested in becoming more involved in OpenAdapter's evolution can gain access to the source code by signing a legal agreement that assigns the intellectual property rights of their code to the Software Conservancy. About 20 developers now hold such status.

Companies mix and match open-source and proprietary processes according to business needs. Figure 3.21 suggests that the proportion of open-source or proprietary software used is a business decision, taken in the context of expenses and revenues over time. An important factor is the expense of tailoring and maintaining open source.

☺ Leveraging large number of resources

☺ Professional satisfaction

☺ To enable tailoring and integration

☺ Academic and research

☺ To gain extensive testing

☺ To maintain more stably

Figure 3.16 Some reasons *for* making a project open source, 1 of 2

☺ To damage the prospects of a competitor's product

☺ To gain market knowledge

☺ To support a core business

☺ To support services

Figure 3.17 Some reasons *for* making a project open source, 2 of 2

☹ Documentation inconsistent or poor

☹ No guarantee that developers will appear

☹ No management control

☹ No control over requirements

☹ Visibility to competitors

Figure 3.18 Some reasons *against* making a project open source

Project Mnemonic Code	Application Type	Total Code Size (KLOCs)	No, of releases measured	Project Evolution Path
OSSPrA	Operating system application	343	13	OSS project that gave birth to a CSS project while still evolving as OSS
CSSPrA	Operating system application	994	13	CSS project initiated from an OSS project and evolved as a commercial counterpart of OSSPrA

Figure 3.19 Maintainability index comparing OSS and CSS for the same application, 1 of 2

Source: Samoladas, Ioannis, I. Stamelos, L. Angelis, and A. Oikonomou. "Open source software development should strive for even greater code maintainability." Communications of the ACM, Vol. 47, No. 10, October 2004, copyright © 2004. Association for Computing Machinery, Inc. Reprinted by permission.

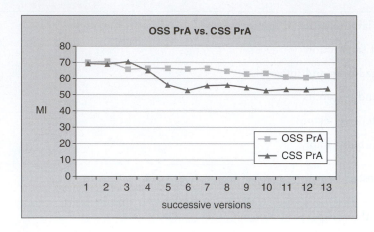

Figure 3.20 Maintainability index comparing OSS and CSS for the same application, 2 of 2

Source: Samoladas, Ioannis, I. Stamelos, L. Angelis, and A. Oikonomou. "Open source software development should strive for even greater code maintainability." Communications of the ACM, Vol. 47, No. 10, October 2004; copyright © 2004. Association for Computing Machinery, Inc. Reprinted by permission.

Various tools and environments are available to facilitate open-source development. Figure 3.22 shows a schematic diagram of one such tool, Collabnet. "Subversion" is an open-source version control system used for many open-source projects.

Key advantages and disadvantages of open-source processes are summarized below.

Advantages of open source

- *The work of many may be obtained free*: For projects that motivate others, work can be obtained from motivated outsiders.

- *Developers tend to be more motivated*, because they choose to work on it.

- *Open-source applications are very well tested*, because they are continually exercised by many and usually have efficient testing processes.

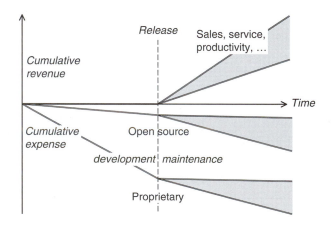

Figure 3.21 Hybrid open-source/proprietary processes

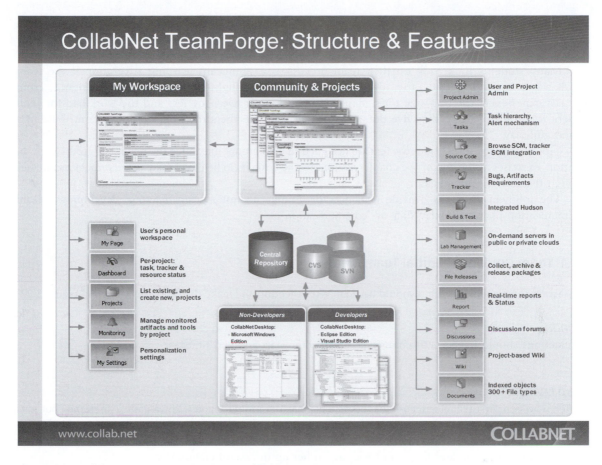

Figure 3.22 CollabNet TeamForge: Structure and Features

Source: CollabNet, http://www.open.collab.net/products/sfee/capabilities.html.

Disadvantages of open source

- *They are available to one and all*: This is part of the bargain.

- *Documentation is questionable*: Developers are not consistent in what they produce

- *Design documentation tends to be poor*: It seems that the open-source process has especially great trouble keeping designs and code synchronized, and so design documents are often poor or even nonexistent.

    To reinforce the concepts on processes described in this chapter, we continue with case studies.

3.3 CASE STUDY: STUDENT TEAM GUIDANCE

To reinforce the many software engineering concepts and practices introduced in this book, it's best if you are developing a software project in parallel. You will gain the most if the project is a team effort, as this is how most real-world software projects are executed. At the end of most major parts of the book, a section (such as this one) entitled *Team Guidance* can be found, guiding you through the different phases of your group project.

You will be asked to generate specific artifacts, and examples will be provided showing how real and hypothetical teams go about developing applications. We will often use the Encounter video game case study as an example to illustrate team guidance.

Many students look back on their team process as a significant learning adventure. If the team avoids a few common pitfalls, the adventure can be a most enlightening and useful experience. From our past experience, the best size for student groups is four or five. Any less and the workload for each student is too great. More than five doesn't afford all team members the opportunity to contribute in a meaningful way.

Tips distributed throughout the text are designed to help groups maximize the benefit of group work. In addition, exercises at the end of the chapter assign specific artifacts to be developed as the project progresses through the software life cycle.

The following sections provide guidance for holding an initial team meeting, developing a team communication plan, and exercising the communication plan.

3.3.1 Team Guidance—Initial Team Meeting

To start off the project, the team should have an initial meeting and make the decisions shown in Figure 3.23.

Agenda
All meetings should have a written agenda and specific start and end times.

Team Leader
Decide who your first team leader will be (being a team leader provides you with valuable experience but puts additional demands on your time and communication skills). To distribute the benefit of team leadership practice, it can be beneficial to swap team leadership about halfway through the project. Both team leaders can be chosen up front, and they can back each other up in case of emergency.

---

1. Set **agenda** and time limits.

2. Choose the team **leader**.

3. Get everyone's **commitment** to required time.
   - Define an expected average number of hours per week.
   - Gather dates of planned absences.

4. Take a realistic census of **team skills**.
   - Common problem: inflated programming skill claims.

5. Begin forming a **vision** of the application.

6. Decide how team will **communicate**.

7. Take **meeting minutes** with concrete action items.

Figure 3.23 Initial student team meeting—general issues

Time Commitment

A big source of frustration in student teams is a lack of commitment of some team members. It is far better to discuss commitments at the beginning than to try to fix a problem after the project is under way. To reduce the resentment that follows when some team members feel they are contributing much more than others, set in advance an expected number of hours of commitment per week. This also helps to make members work more efficiently.

Team Skills

For student projects there is often a trade-off between producing an impressive-looking product and learning new skills. To produce the most impressive product, team members would specialize along the lines of their greatest strengths. This is a typical industrial mode. They may also be tempted to skimp on documentation in order to demonstrate more features. To learn the most, however, team members need to try activities with which they are inexperienced (e.g., team leadership). They also need to do things right. Teams decide how and when to trade off between goals by specifying when they will specialize and when they will try new roles. Instructors try to establish evaluation criteria that encourage learning.

Vision

All projects start out with a vision for the software to be developed. In industry this is typically initiated by the marketing department, which develops business requirements for the product. For student projects, the product vision includes the purpose of the application, major functionality and operations, and major inputs and outputs.

Communication Plan

Decisions need to be made as early as possible as to how the team will handle communication. The next section covers this in detail.

Meeting Minutes

During team meetings, a member is designated to write the meeting minutes. The purpose of meeting minutes is twofold. First, all important decisions or agreements that are reached are recorded, so they are not forgotten and can be referred back to if necessary. As an example, during the meeting it may be decided that Google Docs will be used for storing all project specifications. This decision is recorded in the meeting minutes. The second purpose of meeting minutes is to record unresolved issues that require follow up action. These are referred to as *action items*. Each action item is assigned to one or more team members with a target date for completion. An example action item might be that Joe is to investigate and recommend a source control tool for managing the project's source code, and is to complete his action in one week. It is a good idea to review open action items at the start of each team meeting.

3.3.2 Team Guidance—Communication Plan

When a software project is initiated in industry, a set of project guidelines, tools, and communication procedures is typically established to ensure that the project is executed as efficiently as possible. This should also be done for your group project.

Many team problems arise from a failure to communicate fully. This problem is not limited to student projects. Real-world teams suffer from it as well. Effective verbal communication means making sure your thoughts are fully understood and listening to what others are saying. This is critical for teams to be

1. Listen to all with concentration

   • Don't pre-judge.

2. Give all team members a turn

   • See the value in every idea.

3. Don't make assumptions.

   • Ask questions to clarify.

4. When in doubt, communicate

Figure 3.24 Key precepts of communication

successful. The precepts shown in Figure 3.24 will help you avoid many communication problems. They sound simple but can be hard to follow, especially during times of stress.

Create *policies* for communicating and sharing information with each other, including guidelines for group editing and merging of documents, setting up and agreeing to meeting times, sharing project artifacts, and so on.

Decide on procedures for how you will generate documents for the project. You probably have to deal with discussing the scope and contents of a document, writing initial drafts, editing the drafts, getting group agreement on edits, merging drafts and producing the final document.

Many teams—including some student teams—are widely distributed geographically, and the means of communication becomes especially important. Large projects are often developed by multiple groups at multiple sites, sometimes in multiple countries. Mergers, acquisitions, "offshoring," dispersed specialists, and joint ventures often result in people at multiple sites working together on projects.

An increasing number of products are available to facilitate group work, including groupware, video conferencing, and instant messaging. Each communication medium has specific strengths. In any case, well-run face-to-face meetings are very hard to beat. If possible, schedule regular face-to-face meetings at least once a week for an hour. It is hard to convene an unscheduled meeting but easy to cancel a scheduled meeting. You can make it a goal to limit actual meetings to less time. However, if the committed time is short—say a half hour —you will find it very difficult to make longer meetings because people will build the short time limit into their schedules. If you think that your team may need to meet additionally, it is advisable to agree on when that would be each week. Set aside the time and aim to avoid a meeting. This provides a positive goal and it avoids the problem of repeatedly trying to find a common time when meetings are needed. When you set meeting times, specify an end time. Meetings typically expand to fill the allotted time. You should always have an agenda for your meetings, otherwise your meetings will be less organized and not as productive as they could be.

E-mail is an essential tool, but can be problematic due to unpredictable delays. Messages can become unsynchronized, damaging the threads of dialogs. This is especially serious near the end of a project when communication is frequent and of immediate importance.

Use a shared Web site, wiki, or chat-type facility. For example, at the time of this writing, a number of free collaboration tools are available from Google.

Do not merely state that you will use a particular tool such as Microsoft Word for word processing. Specify a version number, and exchange a few documents to be sure everyone can read and edit them. Don't change versions during the project without ensuring compatibility first.

Document your decisions in a team *Communication Plan*, as outlined in Figure 3.25.

1. **Meetings**: Team will meet each Monday from . . . to . . . in . . .
   Caveat: do not replace face-to-face meeting with remote meetings unless remote meetings are clearly effective.

2. **Meeting alternative**: Team members should keep Fridays open from . . . to . . . in case an additional meeting is required.

3. **Standards**: Word processor, spreadsheet, compiler, ...

4. **E-mail**: Post e-mails?; require acknowledgement?
   Caveat: e-mail is poor for intensive collaboration

5. **Collaboration**: Tools for group collaboration and discussion —
   e.g. Yahoo Groups, Wiki tool, Google tools, . . .

6. **Other tools: Microsoft Project (scheduling), Group calendar, . . .**

Figure 3.25 Communication planning—forms of communication

3.3.3 Team Guidance—Test Communication Plan

It is important to test the methods specified in your Communication Plan so you can make necessary adjustments as early as possible in the project. This will avoid scrambling for alternatives as the project workload increases.

Search the Web for the latest information on a topic determined by the instructor. Note at least four of its basic goals and at least five of the techniques it uses. Have everyone in the group contribute some information. Create a document containing your group's results, and practice how you will utilize your procedures for group editing and reviews. How will you organize this random activity? How can you obtain a useful result instead of a conglomeration of unconnected text?

3.4 SUMMARY

A software project progresses through a series of activities, starting at its conception and continuing all the way through its release. Projects are organized into phases, each with a set of activities conducted during that phase. A *software process* prescribes the interrelationship among the phases by expressing their order and frequency, as well as defining the deliverables of the project. Specific software processes are called *software process models* or *life cycle models*.

Most software process models prescribe a similar set of phases and activities. The difference between models is the order and frequency of the phases. The phases include planning, requirements analysis, design, implementation, testing, and maintenance.

The *waterfall* process is one of the oldest and best known software process models. Projects following the waterfall process progress sequentially through a series of phases. Work transitions to a phase when work on the previous phase is completed.

Iterative and *incremental* processes are characterized by repeated execution of the waterfall phases, in whole or in part, resulting in a refinement of the requirements, design, and implementation. At the conclusion of an iteration, operational code is produced that supports a subset of the final product's functionality. Project artifacts such as plans, specifications, and code evolve during each phase and over the life of the project. Examples of iterative processes include the spiral model, the unified process, and agile processes.

Agile processes are highly iterative, and emphasize working code throughout, as well as frequent interactions with the customer.

A *prototype* is a partial implementation of the target application useful in identifying and retiring risky parts of a project. It can sometimes be a way to obtain ideas about the customer's requirements. An increase in understanding what is to come can save expensive rework and remove future roadblocks before they occur. Many iterative process models incorporate prototypes in one or more of their iterations.

Sometimes, it is unclear whether certain requirements can be implemented in practice, placing the entire project at risk. In such cases, *feasibility studies* may be advisable, which are partial implementations or simulations of the application.

In open-source processes, software is developed and maintained by people on a volunteer basis. Source code is open to all, and there is a process for virtually anyone to suggest and implement enhancements and submit and repair defects. This process is repeated and the application grows in capability and stability. In this way, open-source projects are developed in an iterative manner. In addition, by exercising an application many times, the open-course community functions as a huge testing process.

3.5 EXERCISES

1. During which process phase(s) would each of the following activities occur?
   a. Creating a project schedule
   b. Determining the need for a bar code reader
   c. Requesting the addition of a file backup capability
   d. Performing a feasibility analysis
   e. Documenting the software interface to an SQL database
   f. Acceptance of the software application by the customer

2. Give an example of a software project that would benefit much more from using the waterfall process than from using most of the alternative processes. Explain your reasoning.

3. Describe the difference between *iterative* and *incremental* development. Describe the ways in which they are related.

4. Give an example of a software project that would benefit more from using an iterative and incremental process than from using most of the alternative processes. Explain your reasoning.

5. a. In your own words, explain how the spiral model utilizes risk analysis and risk mitigation.
   b. Explain why the outer spiral of the spiral model utilizes the waterfall process, and how the spiral model mitigates the inherent disadvantages of the waterfall process.

6. Give an example of a software project that would benefit much more from using the spiral process than from using most of the alternative processes. Write a paragraph explaining your answer.

7. How do the phases of the unified process (UP) differ from the phases usually defined for software processes?

8. Describe the pros and cons of each value listed in the Agile Manifesto (see Figure 3.14).

TEAM EXERCISES

Communication

For the following exercises, consider as a group how you will perform them, check the hints below, then carry out the assignments.

T1. Decide who your team leader(s) will be. Note that being team leader provides you with practice that may be hard to get otherwise.

T2. Decide how your team will communicate, specify your communication tools and methods, and test your communication methods. Be specific: you may change the specifics later.

T3. Search the Web for the latest information on a topic determined by the instructor (e.g., the TSP). Note at least four of its basic goals and at least five of the techniques it uses. Post the references to the course forum or Web site if there is one, and annotate your posting with the name of your group. State individual or group opinions of the topic or issue.

Your team response should be 4–7 pages long.

Hints for Team Exercises

T1 hints: To distribute the benefits of team leadership practice, it can be beneficial to swap team leadership about halfway through the semester. Both team leaders can be chosen up front, and they can back each other up in case of emergency. Such backing up is a good practice in any case, because the probability of a team leader having to quit a project or a class can be high. Note that the second half of a project typically requires the team leader to make decisions more quickly than the first half.

T2 hints: Examples are telephone, meetings, e-mail, forums, chat facilities, and Web sites.

1. Schedule regular face-to-face meetings at least once a week, if possible. It is hard to convene an unscheduled meeting but easy to cancel a scheduled one.
2. E-mail is an essential tool, but can be problematic due to unpredictable delays. Messages can become unsynchronized, damaging the threads (subjects) of dialogs. This is especially serious near the end of a project when communication is frequent and of immediate importance.
3. Use a shared Web site or chat-type facility. Free services are available at http://groups.yahoo. com/, for example.
4. Do not merely state, "We will use Superword for word processing." Specify a version number, and exchange a few messages to be sure. Don't change versions during the project without ensuring compatibility first.
5. Try out all the standards and methods you have chosen.

Throughout this program of study, validate your plans and intentions with practical tests whenever possible. Try to use at least two independent tests. In general, assume that your project will be much more demanding in the future than it is at the beginning.

T3 hints: Use this activity to stress your communication system. For example, you may want to set up a Web site to which team members are to add new TSP information. How will you organize this random activity? How can you obtain a useful result instead of a conglomeration of unconnected text?

BIBLIOGRAPHY

1. Royce, W. W., "Managing the Development of Large Software Systems: Concepts and Techniques," *IEEE WESCON 1970*, August 1970, pp.1–9.
2. Bittner, Kurt, and Spence, I., 2007, *"Managing Iterative Software Development Projects,"* Addison-Wesley, Pearson Education, Inc.
3. Cockburn, Alistair. "Unraveling Incremental Development," January 1993. http://alistair.cockburn.us/Unraveling+incremental +development [accessed November 5, 2009].
4. Cusumano, Michael, and R. W. Selby. "How Microsoft Builds Software." *Communications of the ACM*, Vol. 40, No. 6(1997), pp.53–61.
5. Boehm, B. W. "A Spiral Model of Software Development and Enhancement." *IEEE Computer*, Vol. 21, No. 5 (May1988), pp.61–72.
6. Jacobson, Ivar, J. Rumbaugh, and G. Booch. *The Unified Software Development Process*, Addison-Wesley, 1999.
7. Booch, Grady. *Object-Oriented Analysis and Design with Applications*, Addison-Wesley,1994.
8. Rumbaugh, James, M. Blaha, W. Premerlani, F. Eddy, and W. Lorenson, *"Object-Oriented Modeling and Design,"* Prentice Hall, 1990.
9. Larman, Craig, *"Applying UML and Patterns: An Introduction to Object-Oriented Analysis and Design and Iterative Development,"* Prentice Hall, 2005.
10. Ambler, S. W., *"A Manager's Introduction to the Rational Unified Process (RUP)."* Ambysoft (December 4,2005). http://www.ambysoft.com/unifiedprocess/rupIntroduction.html [accessed November 5, 2009].
11. Beck, Kent, Mike Beedle, Arie van Bennekum, and Alistair Cockburn, "Manifesto for Agile Software Development," Feb 2001. http://agilemanifesto.org/ [accessed November 5, 2009].
12. Ferguson, Charles, "How Linux Could Overthrow Microsoft," *Technology Review* (June2005). http://www.technologyreview.com/computing/14504/ [accessed November 5, 2009].
13. Samoladas, Ioannis, I. Stamelos, L. Angelis, and A. Oikonomou, "Open source software development should strive for even greater code maintainability." *Communications of the ACM*, Vol. 47, No. 10, October 2004.

4

Agile Software Processes

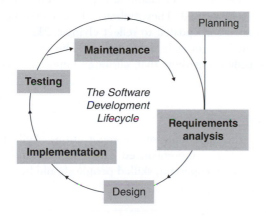

Planning

Requirements analysis

Design

Implementation

Testing

Maintenance

The Software Development Lifecycle

- How did agile methods come about?

- What are the principles of agility?

- How are agile processes carried out?

- Can agile processes be combined with non-agile ones?

Figure 4.1 The context and learning goals for this chapter

In the 1990s, agile software development came into being as an alternative to the existing classical approaches to software engineering that were perceived to be too "process-heavy." These classical approaches emphasize the need to plan projects in advance, express requirements in writing, provide written designs satisfying the requirements, write code based on these designs satisfying the written requirements, and finally to test the results. As we discussed in Chapters 1 and 3, however, many projects following these steps exhibit major problems. A primary reason is that stakeholders do not usually know at the inception of a project entirely what they require. Agile processes address this shortcoming. This chapter defines what is meant by agile development, describes several specific software processes that adhere to agile principles and are thus considered agile processes, and discusses how agile and non-agile processes can be combined.

4.1 AGILE HISTORY AND THE AGILE MANIFESTO

A group of industry experts met in 2001 to discuss ways of improving on the then current software development processes that they complained were documentation driven and process heavy. Their goal was to produce a set of values and principles to help speed up development and effectively respond to change. Calling themselves the Agile Alliance, the group's goal was, in essence, to produce a development framework that was efficient and adaptable. During the 1990s, various iterative software methodologies were beginning to gain popularity. Some were used as the basis for the agile framework. These methodologies had different combinations of old and new ideas, but all shared the following characteristics [1].

- Close collaboration between programmers and business experts

- Face-to-face communication (as opposed to documentation)

- Frequent delivery of working software

- Self-organizing teams

- Methods to craft the code and the team so that the inevitable requirements churn was not a crisis

As a result of their meeting, the Agile Alliance produced the Agile Manifesto [1] to capture their thoughts and ideas, and it is summarized in Figure 4.2.

Note that the Agile Manifesto is not anti-methodology. Instead, its authors intended to restore balance. For example, they embrace design modeling as a means to better understand how the software will be built, but not producing diagrams that are filed away and seldom used. They embrace documentation, but not hundreds of pages that cannot practically be maintained and updated to reflect change [2].

The four points of the Agile Manifesto form the basis of agile development. The first part of each statement specifies a preference. The second part specifies something that, although important, is of lower priority. Each of the four points is described next.

Individuals and Interactions (over processes and tools)

For decades, management practice has emphasized the high value of communications. Agile practices emphasize the significance of highly skilled individuals and the enhanced expertise that emerges from interactions among them. Although processes and tools are important, skilled people should be allowed to

---

We are uncovering better ways of developing software by doing it and helping others do it. Through this work we have come to value:

1. **Individuals and interactions** over processes and tools

2. **Working software** over comprehensive documentation

3. **Customer collaboration** over contract negotiation

4. **Responding to change** over following a plan

That is, while there is value in the items on the right, we value the items on the left more.

Figure 4.2 The Agile Manifesto

adapt the process and modify the tools as appropriate to get their job done as efficiently as possible. As suggested in [3], agile methods offer generative values rather than prescriptive rules: a minimum set of values, observed in all situations, that generate appropriate practices for special situations. Individuals and teams use these rules when problems arise as a basis for generating solutions that are appropriate for the project. Creativity is emphasized as a major means for problem solving. This is in contrast to more rigid software processes, which prescribe a set of predetermined rules and force teams to adapt themselves to these rules. Agile practices suggest that the latter approach is not effective and actually adds to the risk of project failure.

Working Software (over comprehensive documentation)

Working software is considered the best indicator of project progress and whether goals are being met. Teams can produce pages of documentation and supposedly be on schedule, but these are really promises of what they expect to produce. Agile practices emphasize producing working code as early as possible. As a project progresses, software functionality is added in small increments such that the software base continues to function as an operational system. In this way team members and stakeholders always know how the real system is functioning.

Although significant, working software is of greatly diminished value without reasonable documentation. Agile practices emphasize that project teams determine for themselves the level of documentation that is absolutely essential.

Customer Collaboration (over contract negotiation)

This statement emphasizes the fact that development teams are in business to provide value to customers. Keeping as close as possible to your customer is a long-established maxim of good business practice. Many programmers are disconnected from the customer by organizational layers and intermediaries; it is highly desirable to remove this barrier. All stakeholders, including customers, should work together and be on the same team. Their different experiences and expertise should be merged with goodwill that allows the team to change direction quickly as needed to keep projects on track and produce what is needed. Contracts and project charters with customers are necessary, but in order to adapt to inevitable change, collaboration is also necessary [3].

Responding to Change (over following a plan)

Producing a project plan forces team members to think through a project and develop contingencies. However, change is inevitable, and agile practitioners believe that change should not only be planned for but also embraced. Very good project managers plan to respond to change, and this is a requirement for teams operating at the most effective levels, as you will see when we discuss the highest capability levels of the CMMI in Section III of this book. As changes to the plan occur, the team should not stay focused on the outdated plan but deal instead with the changes by adapting the plan as necessary [3]. Agile practices rely on short iterations of one to six weeks to provide timely project feedback and information necessary to assess project progress and respond as necessary.

4.2 AGILE PRINCIPLES

In addition to the values described in Figure 4.2, the authors of the Agile Manifesto outlined a set of guiding principles that support the manifesto. These are quoted from [1] (bold added).

- "Our highest priority is to **satisfy the customer** through early and continuous delivery of valuable software.

- **Welcome changing requirements**, even late in development. Agile processes harness change for the customer's competitive advantage.

- **Deliver working software frequently**, from a couple of weeks to a couple of months, with a preference to the shorter timescale.

- Business people and developers must **work together daily** throughout the project.

- Build projects around **motivated individuals**. Give them the environment and support they need, and trust them to get the job done.

- The most efficient and effective method of conveying information to and within a development team is **face-to-face** conversation.

- **Working software** is the primary measure of progress.

- Agile processes promote **sustainable development**. The sponsors, developers, and users should be able to maintain a constant pace indefinitely.

- Continuous attention to **technical excellence and good design** enhances agility.

- **Simplicity**—the art of maximizing the amount of work not done—is essential.

- The best architectures, requirements, and designs emerge from **self-organizing teams**.

- At regular intervals, **the team reflects** on how to become more effective, then tunes and adjusts its behavior accordingly."

Many of these principles are implemented in practice by the agile methods described in the next section.

4.3 AGILE METHODS

This section describes some of the methods by which many agile processes practice the principles in the Agile Manifesto.

Figure 4.3 shows the manner in which agile methods implement the Agile Manifesto, as follows. Agile processes commonly employ small, close-knit teams; periodic customer requirements meetings; a code-centric approach; documentation on an as-needed basis (e.g., high-level requirements statements only); customer representatives working within the team; refactoring; pair programming; continual unit-testing; and acceptance tests as a means of setting customer expectations.

We next elaborate on the topics not already explained above.

Pair programming is a form of continual inspection by one team member of the work of a teammate. Typically, while one programs, the other inspects and devises tests. These roles are reversed for periods of time that the pair determines.

Documenting on an as-needed basis usually involves writing some high-level requirements but not detailed requirements. These are frequently collected in the form of *user stories*. A user story is a significant task that the user wants to accomplish with the application. According to Cohn [4], every user story consists of the following:

- A written description

- Conversations with the customer that establish a mutual understanding of its purpose and content

- Tests intended to validate that the user story has been implemented

MANIFESTO → RESPONSES:	1. Individuals and interactions over processes and tools	2. Working software over comprehensive documentation	3. Customer collaboration over contract negotiation	4. Responding to change over following a plan
a. Small, close-knit **team** of **peers**	y			y
b. Periodic **customer** requirements **meetings**	y		y	y
c. **Code-centric**		y		y
d. **High-level** requirements statements only			y	y
e. **Document as** needed			y	y
f. **Customer reps** work within team	y			y
g. **Refactor**				y
h. **Pair** programming and no-owner code	y			
i. Unit-test-intensive; Acceptance-**test-driven**		y	y	
j. **Automate** testing		y	y	

Figure 4.3 Ways to address the principles of the Agile Manifesto

Examples of user stories for a video store application are as follows:

- "The user can search for all DVDs by a given director."

- "The user can establish an account that remembers all transactions with the customer."

- "The user can view all available information on any DVD."

Continual interaction and contact with the customer is achieved in two ways. First, the work periods (1–6 weeks, usually) in which the each batch of requirements are to be fulfilled are specified with a team that involves the customer. Second, a customer representative is encouraged to be part of the team.

The emphasis on *working software* is realized by means of coding versions of the application and showing them to the customer. These are usually closely tied to corresponding tests. Indeed, *test-driven development*, an agile approach, actually has developers write tests even before developing the code.

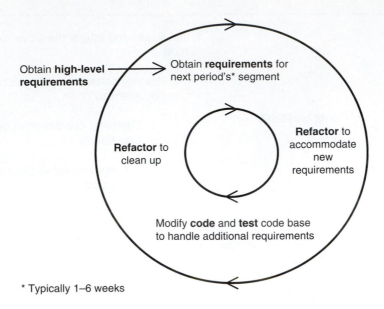

Figure 4.4 A typical agile development iteration

Refactoring is a process of altering the form of a code base while retaining the same functionality. The usual goal of a refactoring is to make the design amenable to the addition of functionality, thereby satisfying the agile desire to respond well to change. The very fact that the discipline of refactoring has been developed is a major factor making agile methods possible. This book covers refactoring in Chapter 24. Although refactoring is discussed later in the book, much of it will be useful before then and can be referred to throughout the book.

Agile methods employ the development cycle shown in Figure 4.4. Typically, the requirements are expressed in terms of user stories. Past experience in the project allows the team to assess its *velocity*: an assessment of the relative difficulty of stories and the rate at which it is able to implement them.

The schedule effects of agile methods can be seen in Figure 4.5. Planning is attenuated because there is less to plan. Requirements analysis, design, and testing are often confined to high levels. The emphasis is mostly code centered.

4.4 AGILE PROCESSES

"Agile development" isn't itself a specific process or methodology. Instead, it refers to any software process that captures and embraces the fundamental values and principles espoused in the Agile Manifesto. The following sections illustrate and describe three agile processes as representative examples.

- Extreme programming (XP)
- Crystal
- Scrum

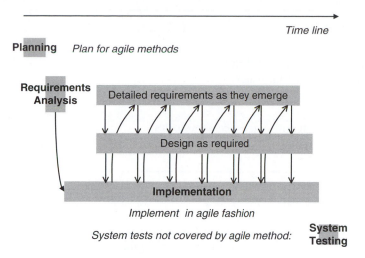

Figure 4.5 The agile schedule

4.4.1 Extreme Programming

In 1996, Kent Beck and colleagues began a project at DaimlerChrysler [5] using an approach to software development that appeared to make matters much simpler and more efficient. The methodology he developed and used became known as *Extreme Programming (XP)* [6].

Beck [6] cites four "values" guiding extreme programming: communication, simplicity, feedback, and courage. These are summarized in Figures 4.6 and 4.7. XP programmers communicate continually with their customers and fellow programmers. They keep their design simple and clean. They obtain feedback by testing their software, starting on day one. They deliver parts of the system to the customers as early as possible and implement changes as suggested. With this foundation, XP programmers are able to "courageously" respond to changing requirements and technology [5].

XP was created to deal effectively with projects in which requirements change. In fact, XP expects requirements to be modified and added. On many projects, customers start with only a vague idea of what they want. As a project progresses and a customer sees working software, specifics of what they want become progressively firm.

---

1. **Communication**

   - Customer on site
   - Pair programming
   - Coding standards

2. **Simplicity**

   - Metaphor: entity names drawn from common metaphor
   - Simplest design for current requirements
   - Refactoring

Figure 4.6 The "values" of extreme programming, 1 of 2

Source: Beck, Kent, "Extreme Programming Explained: Embrace Change," Addison-Wesley, 2000.

1. **Feedback** always sought

   - Continual testing
   - Continuous integration (at least daily)
   - Small releases (smallest useful feature set)

2. **Courage**

   - Planning and estimation with customer user stories
   - Collective code ownership
   - Sustainable pace

Figure 4.7 The "values" of extreme programming, 2 of 2

Source: Beck, Kent, "Extreme Programming Explained: Embrace Change," Addison-Wesley, 2000.

XP projects are divided into iterations lasting from one to three weeks. Each iteration produces software that is fully tested. At the beginning of each, a planning meeting is held to determine the contents of the iteration. This is "just-in-time" planning, and it facilitates the incorporation of changing requirements.

As code is developed, XP relies on continual integration rather that assembling large, separately developed modules. In the same spirit, releases are modest in added capability. The idea is to bite off a small amount of new capability, integrate and test it thoroughly, and then repeat the process.

Extreme programming recognizes the all-too-frequent breakdown in customer developer relationships, where each party develops a separate concept of what's needed and also how much the features will cost to develop. The result of this mismatch is, all too often, a mad dash for deadlines, including long working hours and an unsustainable pace. In response, extreme programming promotes a modus vivendi that's sustainable in the long term. In addition, it requires every developer to acknowledge up front that all code is everyone's common property, to be worked on as the project's needs require. In other words, no code "belongs" to a programmer. This is in keeping with engineering practice, where a bridge blueprint, for example, is the product of an organization and not the personal property of one designer.

XP is unique in using twelve practices that dictate how programmers should carry out their daily jobs. These twelve practices are summarized next [7].

1. **Planning Process.** Requirements, usually in the form of user stories, are defined by customers and given a relative priority based on cost estimates provided by the XP team. Stories are assigned to releases, and the team breaks each story into a set of tasks to implement. We described user stories in Section 4.3.

2. **Small Releases.** A simple system is built and put into production early that includes a minimal set of useful features. The system is updated frequently and incrementally throughout the development process.

3. **Test-Driven Development.** Unit tests are written to test functionality, before the code to implement that functionality is actually written.

4. **Refactoring.** Code is regularly modified or rewritten to keep it simple and maintainable. Changes are incorporated as soon as deficiencies are identified. We introduced refactoring in Section 4.3 and cover it in detail in Chapter 24.

5. **Design Simplicity.** Designs are created to solve the known requirements, not to solve future requirements. If necessary, code will be refactored to implement future design needs.

6. **Pair Programming.** This was described in Section 4.3.

7. **Collective Code Ownership.** All the code for the system is owned by the entire team. Programmers can modify any part of the system necessary to complete a feature they're working on. They can also improve any part of the system.

8. **Coding Standard.** For a team to effectively share ownership of all the code, a common coding standard must be followed. This ensures that no matter who writes a piece of code, it will be easily understood by the entire team.

9. **Continuous Integration.** Code is checked into the system as soon as it's completed and tested. This can be as frequent as several times per day. In this way the system is as close to production quality as possible.

10. **On-Site Customer.** A customer representative is available full-time to determine requirements, set priorities, and answer questions as the programmers have them. The effect of being there is that communication improves, with less hard-copy documentation—often one of the most expensive parts of a software project.

11. **Sustainable Pace.** XP teams are more productive and make fewer mistakes if they're not burned out and tired. Their aim is not to work excessive overtime, and to keep themselves fresh, healthy, and effective.

12. **Metaphor.** XP teams share a common vision of the system by defining and using a common system of describing the artifacts in the project.

4.4.2 Scrum

Scrum is an agile methodology developed in the early 1990s. It is named after the part of a rugby game that, in U.S. football terms, is a cross between the kickoff and a quarterback snap. As defined by the Merriam Webster dictionary, a scrum is "a rugby play in which the forwards of each side come together in a tight formation and struggle to gain possession of the ball using their feet when it is tossed in among them." In other words, scrum is a process that follows "organized chaos." It is based on the notion that the development process is unpredictable and complicated, and can only be defined by a loose set of activities. Within this framework, the development team is empowered to define and execute the necessary tasks to successfully develop software.

The flow of a typical scrum project is shown in Figure 4.8.

A project is broken into teams, or scrums, of no more than 6–9 members. Each team focuses on a self-contained area of work. A scrum master is appointed and is responsible for conducting the daily scrum meetings, measuring progress, making decisions, and clearing obstacles that get in the way of team progress. The daily scrum meetings should last no more than 15 minutes. During the meeting the scrum master is allowed to ask team members only three questions [8]:

1. What items have been completed since the last scrum meeting?

2. What issues have been discovered that need to be resolved?

3. What new assignments make sense for the team to complete until the next scrum meeting?

At the beginning of a project, a list of customer wants and needs is created, which is referred to as the "backlog." The scrum methodology proceeds by means of agile 30-day cycles called "sprints." Each sprint takes on a set of features from the backlog for development. While in a sprint, the team is given complete

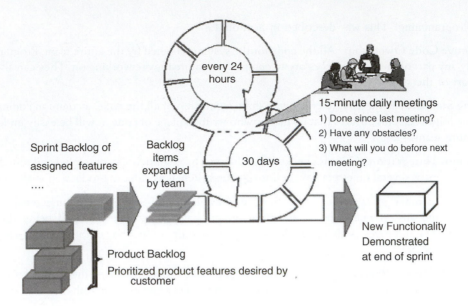

Figure 4.8 The scrum work flow

Source: Quoted and edited from http://www.controlchaos.com/about.

control of how they are to successfully complete the sprint. At the end of a sprint a customer demonstration is conducted for the customer. It serves several purposes, including [8]:

1. Demonstrating to the customer what has been accomplished.

2. Giving the developers a sense of accomplishment.

3. Ensuring that the software is properly integrated and tested.

4. Ensuring that real progress is made on the project.

At the conclusion of the demonstration, the leftover and new tasks are gathered, a new backlog is created, and a new sprint commences.

4.4.3 Crystal

Crystal is a family of agile methods developed by Alistair Cockburn. Each Crystal method shares common characteristics of "frequent delivery, close communication, and reflective improvement" [9]. Not all projects are the same, so different Crystal methodologies were created to address differences in project size and criticality. Figure 4.9 shows the different methodologies and the size project they are best suited to. Crystal methods are characterized by a color, starting at *clear* for small teams and progressing through to *orange, red,* and so on as the number of people increases. For example, Crystal Clear is geared for small teams of approximately 6 people; Yellow for teams of 10–20 people; Orange for teams of 20–40 people, and so on. The other axis defines the criticality of a project, where L is loss of life, E is loss of essential monies, D is loss of discretionary monies, and C is loss of comfort. Note that the row for loss of life is not shaded in Figure 4.9. This is because Cockburn had no experience applying Crystal to these types of projects when he created the

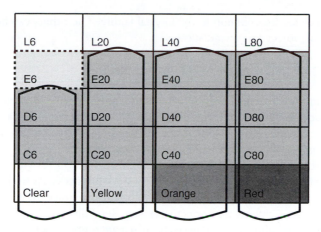

L = loss of life
E = loss of essential monies
D = loss of discretionary monies
C = loss of comfort

Figure 4.9 Coverage of various Crystal methodologies

Source: Adapted from Cockburn, Alistair, "Crystal Clear: A Human-Powered Methodology for Small Teams," Addison-Wesley, 2005.

chart. Crystal Clear doesn't explicitly support the E6 box, although Cockburn notes that teams may be able to adapt the process to accommodate such projects. Another restriction of Crystal is that it is applicable only to colocated teams.

Cockburn believes that developers do not readily accept the demands of *any* process (documentation, standards, etc). He strongly recommends accepting this by introducing the most limited amount of process needed to get the job done successfully, maximizing the likelihood that team members will actually follow the process.

All Crystal methodologies are built around three common priorities [9]:

1. Safety in the project outcome.

2. Efficiency in development.

3. Habitability of the conventions (i.e., the ability of developers to abide by the process itself).

Crystal projects exhibit seven properties to varying degrees [9]:

1. Frequent delivery.

2. Reflective improvement.

3. Close communication.

4. Personal safety.

5. Focus.

6. Easy access to expert users.

7. Technical environment with automated testing, configuration management, and frequent integration.

The first three properties are common to the Crystal family. The others can be added in any order to increase the likelihood of project safety and success.

4.5 INTEGRATING AGILE WITH NON-AGILE PROCESSES

The advantages of agile methods include the ability to adjust easily to emerging and changing requirements. The disadvantages include awkward roles for design and documentation. Cockburn's Crystal family of methodologies already acknowledges that different kinds of applications must be treated differently, even when the methods are agile.

Software process, after all, concerns the order in which we perform activities: For example, designing first and then coding from the design. One extreme is the waterfall process. As we have seen, there are many limitations in our ability to thoroughly perform the waterfall sequence once, or even a few times, iteratively. Changeable and unknown requirements are a principal reason. Regardless of the development process we use, we must make trade-offs in deciding how extensively to pursue a phase before moving to another phase. Consider, for example, the issue of how much effort to spend on planning a software enterprise.

One extreme project situation is when we are certain of obtaining all of the requirements of the end date, of the high-level design, and of who will be working on the job. In that case, we can and probably should develop a detailed plan.

The other extreme project situation is when we have little idea of any of these factors, believing that they will become clear only after the project is under way. In that case, planning at a detailed level would be a waste of time at best because it could not be even nearly accurate, and would probably even be misleading. We have no choice in this case but to begin the process, and revisit the plans as required. The extremes are illustrated in Figure 4.10.

Agile methods provide benefits but also costs, and these depend on several factors. Some are shown in Figure 4.11.

In order to gain the advantages of both agile and non-agile[1] processes, we try to integrate them. The means by which this can be performed depend on several factors, but particularly on the size of the job. As of

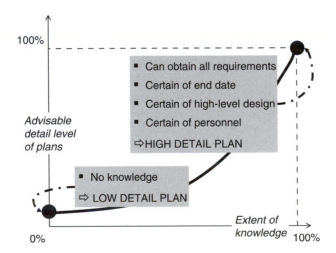

Figure 4.10 How detailed should plans be?

---

[1] Some authors characterize non-agile processes. For example, one practice is to call them "plan-based." The authors do not believe in a single characterization like this of non-agile processes; hence the blanket term "non-agile."

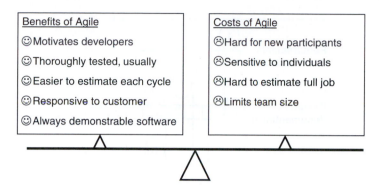

Figure 4.11 Trade-offs between agile and non-agile processes

2009, the conventional wisdom concerning the agile/non-agile split is shown roughly in Figure 4.12: The larger the job, the more non-agile process is required.

Agile processes emphasize code first, whereas non-agile ones advocate coding only from well-documented designs and designing only from well-documented requirements. These approaches appear to be almost contradictory, so combining them requires substantial skill and care. We will concentrate on methods for doing this in large jobs, where the challenges are greatest. We will call the two options *non-agile-driven* and *agile-driven* and will compare them.

4.5.1 A Non-Agile-Driven Approach

A common non-agile-driven approach is to initially approach the job without agility, then fit agile methods into the process after sufficient work has been done to define the agile roles and portions. We develop a plan, create a careful high-level design, and decompose the work into portions that can be implemented by teams in the agile manner. One can superimpose upon each agile team a process by which the accumulating

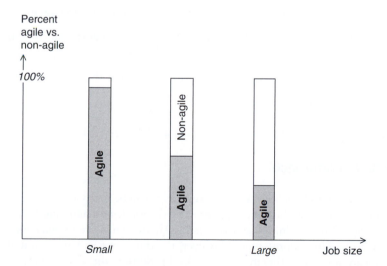

Figure 4.12 Conceptual agile/non-agile combination options: some conventional wisdom, circa 2009

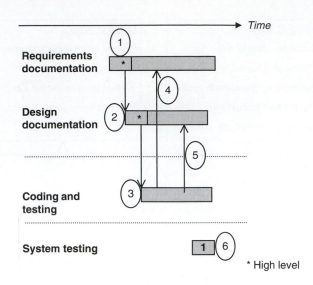

Figure 4.13 Integrating agile with non-agile methods 1: time line for a single iteration

requirements are gathered, and placed within a master requirements document. The same can be done with the accumulating design. Doing this with design is more difficult because design parts may actually be replaced and modified as refactoring takes place. Requirements tend to accumulate as much as they change.

The sequence of events is as follows:

1. High-level requirements are developed for the first iteration.

2. A high-level design is developed based on the high-level requirements.

3. Agile development by teams begins, based on these high-level documents.

4. Full requirements documentation is gathered from the work done by the agile teams as it progresses.

5. The design documentation is gathered from the agile teams at regular intervals to update the design document.

6. System testing not covered by the agile process is performed at the end, if necessary.

7. The process is repeated for each iteration.

This is illustrated for one waterfall iteration in Figure 4.13. Figure 4.14 shows this for multiple iterations.

4.5.2 An Agile-Driven Approach

For an agile-driven approach to large jobs, a (small) agile team can be set to work on significant aspects of the project until the outlines of an architecture appear. At that point, non-agile methods are used. This may involve reintegrating agile programming again as described in the non-agile-driven approach above. This has much in common with building a prototype. However, the difference is that the initial work is performed largely to develop an architecture rather than retire risks. In addition, the work is not planned as throw-away code. One agile-driven approach is shown in Figure 4.15.

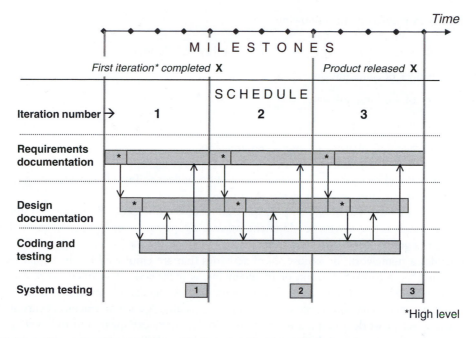

Figure 4.14 Integrating agile with non-agile methods 2: time line for multiple iterations

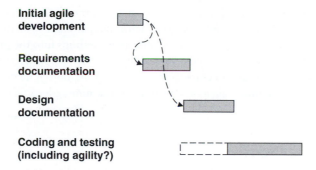

Figure 4.15 An agile-driven approach to large jobs

The case study sections for this part of the book (which appear in Chapters 5 and 6) contain two case studies that combine agile and non-agile methods.

4.6 SUMMARY

Agile software development was created as an alternative to existing plan-based approaches that were perceived to be too process heavy and rigid. A group of industry experts met in 2001 to share their vision for an alternative to these types of processes. They created the Agile Manifesto to capture their thoughts for a process that was adaptable, lean, and agile.

Agile processes emphasize the following:

- The need to collaborate closely with customers and other stakeholders
- Communication over documentation
- Frequent delivery of working software
- Self-organizing teams
- The need to embrace and plan for changing requirements

Any process that embraces the fundamental values of the agile manifesto is considered an agile process. Examples include extreme programming, scrum, and Crystal.

Extreme programming is based on four principles: communication, feedback, simplicity, and courage. It promotes practices such as test-driven development, refactoring, pair-programming, collective code ownership, continuous integration, and on-site customer.

Scrum defines a framework, or a loose set of activities that are employed by the scrum team. At the beginning of a project, a *backlog* of work, or requirements, is identified. Developers work on a subset of requirements in the backlog in 30-day *sprints*. Once a sprint begins, the team is given the freedom to employ any methods deemed necessary to complete their work successfully. A customer demo occurs at the end of each sprint. A new set of work is defined from the backlog for the next sprint and the cycle continues.

Crystal is a family of methodologies that address projects of different size and criticality. Crystal methods share the following characteristics: frequent delivery, reflective improvement, close communication, personal safety, focus, and easy access to expert users, and a technical environment with automated testing, configuration management, and frequent integration.

Agile and non-agile process can be integrated on projects in order to gain the advantages of both. The means by which this can be performed depend on several factors but particularly on the size of the project. One approach is to initiate a job without agility, then incorporate agile methods into the process after enough work has been accomplished in defining agile roles and responsibilities. Another approach is to initiate a job with an agile approach until the outlines of an architecture appear. At that point, non-agile methods are used. This may involve reintegrating agile programming again as described in the non-agile-driven approach above.

4.7 EXERCISES

1. The Agile Manifesto favors working software over extensive documentation. Under what circumstances can this cause problems if taken to an extreme?

2. a. In your own words, explain how agile processes adapt to and embrace changing requirements.
   b. Describe a scenario in which this might be counterproductive.

3. Name three benefits of the XP practice of testing software from "day one," always having working software available.

4. During the daily 15-minute scrum meeting, the leader is only allowed to ask the same three questions. What two additional questions might you want to ask? For each, explain its benefit toward achieving the goals of the meeting.

5. In your own words, explain how Crystal adapts to various types of projects.

BIBLIOGRAPHY

1. Beck, Kent, Mike Beedle, Arie van Bennekum, and Alistair Cockburn, *"Manifesto for Agile Software Development,"* Feb 2001. http://agilemanifesto.org/ [accessed November 5, 2009].
2. Highsmith, Jim, *"History: Agile Manifesto,"* 2001. http://www.agilemanifesto.org/history.html [accessed November 5, 2009].
3. Highsmith, Jim, and A. Cockburn, "Agile Software Development: The Business of Innovation," *IEEE Computer*, Vol. 34, No. 9, September 2001, pp. 120–122.
4. Cohn, Mark, *"User Stories Applied: For Agile Software Development,"* Addison-Wesley, 2004.
5. Wells, Don, *"Extreme Programming: A Gentle Introduction."* http://www.extremeprogramming.org/ [accessed November 15, 2009].
6. Beck, Kent, *"Extreme Programming Explained: Embrace Change,"* Addison-Wesley, 2000.
7. Jeffries, Ron, *"XProgramming.com: An Agile Software Development Resource."* http://xprogramming.com [accessed November 15, 2009].
8. Beedle, Mike, Martine Devos, Yonat Sharon, and Ken Schwaber, *"SCRUM: An extension pattern language for hyperproductive software development."* http://jeffsutherland.com/scrum/scrum_plop.pdf [accessed November 15, 2009].
9. Cockburn, Alistair, *"Crystal Clear: A Human-Powered Methodology for Small Teams,"* Addison-Wesley, 2005.

5

Quality in the Software Process

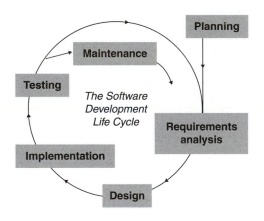

- • What are the principles of managing quality?

- • How do you plan for "quality?"

- • What are inspections and how do you carry them out?

- • How do you carry out reviews and audits?

- • How do you measure and improve software processes?

- • In what way does CMMI assess organizational quality?

- • What does a software quality plan look like?

Figure 5.1 The context and learning goals for this chapter

This chapter discusses the manner in which we integrate and manage quality throughout the software development process. This is an integral part of project planning, and it affects every phase of development. As part of planning, documents are produced detailing the quality approach to be taken, including specific quality goals, techniques to be employed, metrics to be collected, tests to be run, and the manner in which

- Quality principles
  —overarching quality guidelines

- Quality planning
  —quality plan defines overall approach to quality

- Inspections
  —peer processes focused on quality

- Reviews and audits
  —external quality assessment

- Defect management
  —identification, tracking, and resolution of defects

- Process improvement
  —continuous upgrading of process effectiveness

- Organizational quality
  —engineering competence levels (e.g., CMMI)

Figure 5.2 Quality in the software process

defects are to be handled. All of these contribute to an effective development process with a focus on quality, resulting in the development of a high-quality software product. The integration of quality in the software process is summarized in Figure 5.2. Each topic mentioned in the figure is described in this chapter.

5.1 PRINCIPLES OF MANAGING QUALITY

An overall approach to quality is guided by several principles. The planning and practices described in this chapter are implemented with these principles in mind, as follows.

First and foremost, quality is something the entire development team is responsible for, not just the quality assurance team. This is the meaning of the first point in Figure 5.3: focusing "continuously on quality." It is thus an integral part of the development process, and each phase must incorporate quality practices. For example, peer inspections are carried out for each artifact when it is generated. Depending on the artifact under review, stakeholders from different functions such as marketing, customer service, software development, customers, and so on participate in the inspection. Inspections are discussed in detail in Section 5.4. Another example is test-driven development (TDD), which is prevalent in various agile processes. It dictates

1. Focus continuously on quality.

2. A quality assurance process must be defined.

3. The organization must follow its quality assurance process.

4. Find and repair defects as early in the development process as possible.

Figure 5.3 Key principles of managing quality

Reason (by one estimate):	If defect found . . .	
	. . . soon after creation	. . . at integration time
Hours to ..		
.. detect	0.7 to 2	0.2 to 10
.. repair	0.3 to 1.2	9+
Total	**1.0 to 3.2**	**9.2 to 19+**

Figure 5.4 Cost to repair a defect, depending on time elapsed since injection

that developers write tests before coding, and then write code to pass their tests. TDD is discussed in more detail in Chapter 27.

Quality assurance (QA) refers to actions taken to assure that a product under construction attains required levels of quality. The second and third principles listed in Figure 5.3 state that a QA process must be defined and followed. This is how so much quality has been encouraged by the International Standards Organization (ISO) standard 9001 "Quality Systems—Model for quality assurance in design, development, production, installation, and servicing." Many companies have created documents describing their official QA process. ISO insists on the existence of such documents for companies seeking its certification. However, ISO recognized that a documented procedure is only a part of quality assurance. In practice, documented quality procedures are often ignored with impunity; hence ISO's second principle, which ensures that employees actually following quality procedures. Quality planning is discussed in more detail in Section 5.3.

The fourth software quality principle listed in Figure 5.4 is to find and fix defects as early as possible: i.e., to prevent them from persisting for more than a single phase. Figure 5.4 provides data from one of the author's clients on the relative cost of allowing a defect to persist. Many organizations have tried to measure the difference in cost, and it is always found to be very large. A rule of thumb sometimes used is that a defect costing a dollar to find and repair soon after its creation costs a hundred dollars to find and repair if delivered to the customer. The main consequence of this principle is that it most often pays to spend significant resources finding and fixing defects as early as possible rather than allowing them to remain undetected and active.

5.2 MANAGING QUALITY IN AGILE PROCESSES

Agile and non-agile projects are equally concerned with producing quality products, but agile methods go about this in different ways. In particular, agile responses to the principles of Section 5.1 are as follows:

1. Focusing continuously on quality
   Agile processes fulfill this principle by creating increments from close customer contact, by testing them during development, and via prearranged customer acceptance tests.

2. Defining a quality assurance process

Agile processes rely on the activities just listed for a QA process, rather than on documentation such as the IEEE standards discussed in this chapter. Whether this is sufficient, especially for large projects, remains a subject of debate.

3. Following the organization's quality assurance process

Whether or not one doubts the adequacy of agility for quality in large projects, team members are generally well motivated, and they usually follow agreed-upon methods very faithfully.

4. Finding and repairing defects as early in the development process as possible

Here, agile methods show their greatest strength, since they are code centric and thus try out implementation and testing of the pieces as soon as it is possible.

5.3 QUALITY PLANNING

We begin planning for quality early in the development life cycle. Documents are written that define an overall approach, including quality goals and techniques for every development phase (the Software Quality Assurance Plan), how the product will be verified and validated (the Software Verification and Validation Plan), and how testing is planned, specified, and reported (the Software Test Documents). The Software Quality Assurance Plan (SQAP) is described below, the Software Verification and Validation Plan (SVVP) is described in Chapter 9, and the Software Test Documents (STD) are described in the testing chapters of Part VII.

5.3.1 Software Quality Assurance Plan

The Software Quality Assurance Plan (SQAP) specifies the overall quality plan, policies, and procedures that will be followed by the team. It provides guidelines so that quality actions are not an afterthought but something consciously and deliberately striven for and practiced throughout the development process. It orients the project toward prevention—defining procedures for proactively monitoring and improving processes and quality, ensuring that quality practices are defined and implemented, and ensuring that problems are identified and resolved as early as possible. To do this, the SQAP answers the questions posed in Figure 5.5.

The rest of this section addresses these questions in turn.

1. Who will be Responsible for Quality?

An individual or group is identified as being responsible for assuring quality on a project. The individual or group is tasked with ensuring that quality is integrated into all activities: their existence does not alter the principle that quality is everyone's responsibility. For very small projects, there may be no explicit QA organization, making QA the responsibility of the project management plan. Large projects require several QA people, led by a QA manager. Sometimes an organization's QA manager is the QA lead on several projects. For truly large projects, the QA function has its own management hierarchy. In the author's experience, a project requires roughly one QA person-month for every 3 to 7 developer person-months. This excludes developer testing, which is usually considered internal because it requires intimate knowledge of the design and implementation. An example of estimated QA requirements is summarized in Figure 5.6.

2. What Quality Documentation is Generated?

The SQAP specifies the documents to be generated for a project and how they are to be checked for accuracy. Examples of documents are the Software Requirements Specification (SRS), Software Design Document

1. **Who** will be responsible for quality?

   A person, a manager, a group, an organization, etc.

2. What **documentation** will be generated to guide development, verification and validation, use and maintenance of the software?

3. What **standards** will be used to ensure quality?

   Documentation standards, coding standards, etc.

4. What **metrics** will be used to monitor quality?

   Product and process metrics

5. What **procedures** will be used to **manage** the quality process?

   Meetings, audits, reviews, etc.

6. What kind of **testing** will be performed?

7. What quality assurance **techniques** will be used?

   Inspections, proofs of correctness, tests, etc.

8. How will **defects** be handled?

Figure 5.5 What's needed from a quality plan

(SDD), Software Verification and Validation Plan (SVVP), User Documentation, and the Software Configuration Management Plan (SCMP). The SRS defines the requirements for the software, and the SDD describes how the software is designed to meet the requirements. The SRS and requirements are covered in Part IV. The SDD and software design are covered in Part V.

The SVVP describes methods used to verify that the requirements specified in the SRS are the right set of requirements, that the requirements are correctly implemented by the SDD, and that the design in the SDD is correctly implemented by the code. Verification methods include inspection, analysis, and testing. Inspection is described in detail in Section 5.4. User documentation describes how the software shall be successfully and correctly used. It also describes error messages and corrective actions to take as a result. The SCMP details how changes to software and documents are managed, and is described in greater detail in Chapter 7.

- 1 QA person per 3–7 developers

- Excludes developer testing counted as developer time

- Includes post-developer testing

- Ideally performed by external QA personnel

Figure 5.6 Typical estimate of QA requirements per developer

3. What Standards will be Used to Ensure Quality?

Adopting consistent document templates contributes to the production of quality documentation. The use of IEEE standard documents—as outlined in this text, for example—ensures that documents contain all the necessary content and can be easily read and understood by team members.

Coding standards dictate such things as variable and module naming, commenting, and logic structure. Consistently developed code aids in different team members being able to better understand it and make updates.

4. What Metrics will be Used to Monitor Quality?

The SQAP defines the quality metrics to be collected and analyzed. Examples of quality metrics include defect density, mean time to failure, customer problems, and customer satisfaction. Metrics are discussed in detail in Chapters 3 and 9, among others.

5. What Procedures will be Used to Manage the Quality Process?

Meetings, audits, and reviews are some of the techniques employed to manage the quality process. They are described in more detail in Section 5.5.

6. What Kind of Testing will be Performed?

Both the Software Verification and Validation Plan and the Software Test Documents specify the tests to be executed.

7. What Quality Assurance Techniques will be Used?

Inspections, proofs of correctness, tests, and so on are all techniques used to assure product quality. Section 5.4 in particular describes the inspection process in greater detail. Proofs of correctness and testing are described in this book as well.

8. How will Defects be Handled?

As defined in Chapter 2, defects are deviations from requirements. Procedures for identifying and managing them are defined in the SQAP. Defect management is covered in detail in Section 5.6.

5.3.2 IEEE Quality Documents

The IEEE has published several standards related to software quality, as follows:

- IEEE 730-2002: Standard for Software Quality Assurance Plans

- IEEE 1012-2004: Standard for Software Verification and Validation

- IEEE 829-1998: Standard for Software Test Documentation

These documents relate to the software development phases as shown in Figure 5.7.

Figures 5.8 and 5.9 summarize the contents of IEEE Standard 730-2002 Standard for Software Quality Assurance Plans. The case study section near the end of this chapter contains a sample SQAP for the Encounter video game.

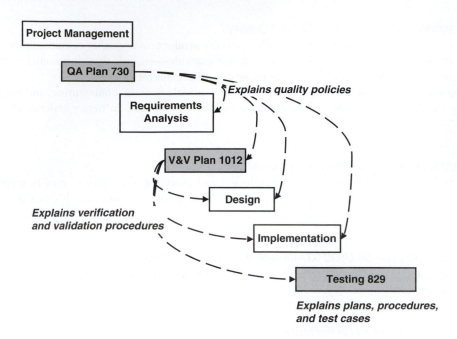

Figure 5.7 The main IEEE software quality documents

1. **Purpose**

2. **Referenced documents**

3. **Management**

   3.1   Organization

   3.2   Tasks

   3.3   Responsibilities

   3.4   QA estimated resources

4. **Documentation**

   4.1   Purpose

   4.2   Minimum documentation requirements

   4.3   Other

5. **Standards, practices, conventions, and metrics**

   5.1   Purpose

   5.2   Content

6. **Reviews**

   6.1   Purpose

   6.2   Minimum requirements

       6.2.1   Software specifications review

       6.2.2   Architecture design review

       6.2.3   Detailed design review

       6.2.4   V&V plan review

       6.2.5   Functional audit

       6.2.6   Physical audit

       6.2.7   In-process audits

       6.2.8   Managerial review

       6.2.9   SCMP review

       6.2.10   Post-implementation review

   6.3   Other reviews and audits

7.–15. See next figure

Figure 5.8 IEEE Software Quality Assurance Plan table of contents 1 of 2

Source: IEEE Std 730–2002.

7. Test

— may reference Software Test Documentation.

8. **Problem reporting and corrective action**

9. **Tools, techniques, and methodologies**

— may reference SPMP.

10. **Media control**

11. **Supplier control**

12. **Records collection, maintenance, and retention**

13. **Training**

14. **Risk management**

— may reference SPMP.

15. **Glossary**

16. **SQAP change procedure and history**

Figure 5.9 IEEE Software Quality Assurance Plan table of contents 2 of 2
Source: IEEE Std 730–2002.

5.4 INSPECTIONS

An *inspection* is a quality technique that focuses on reviewing the details of a project artifact (requirements, designs, code, etc.) in an organized and thorough manner. Inspections are performed periodically during all software engineering phases by the artifact's author and by other engineers. The purpose is to assure the artifact's correctness by seeking defects. A meeting of inspectors is held at which defects are identified. The repair of defects is the author's responsibility.

The inspection concept was developed by Michael Fagan [1] while he was at IBM. He observed that the author of a work is usually able to repair a defect once he recognizes its presence. Thus, a process is needed whereby the defects in a work are called to the author's attention as early as possible. This implies that inspections should be a peer process because inspections are performed on work in process rather than on finished product.

Since inspections were originally introduced to improve code, they are often referred to as "code inspections," but their value has been shown to be greatest when used early in the process, long before code is produced. They are used profitably as soon as the first project documents are produced. For example, requirements specifications, project management, and configuration plans should all be inspected.

5.4.1 Inspection Principles

Guiding principles for conducting inspections are listed below. The sections that follow describe each of these:

1. Peer process

2. Specified roles

3. Defect detection instead of defect repair

4. Use of checklists

5. Artifact readiness

6. Adequate preparation

7. Metrics collection

8. Time limit

1. Peer Process

Inspections are conducted by a group of individuals who are familiar with the artifact under review. They may be software engineers, members of other departments such as software quality assurance, marketing, sales, or customers. The inspection is a peer process with an overriding goal of discovering defects. The work in progress is under inspection, not the performance of the author, and therefore it is not a supervisor-subordinate process. An author is responsible mainly for the product he or she submits *after* inspection, not before. The work brought to the inspection should be the author's best effort, not a draft.

2. Specified Roles

Inspections work best when specific roles are assigned to each participant.

The *moderator* is responsible for leading the inspection and seeing that it is conducted in a productive and efficient manner. The moderator schedules the meeting and ensure that it starts and ends on time, with the latter being accomplished by maintaining an appropriate pace throughout. It is very easy for participants to get bogged down in details and to try to solve problems during the meeting. It is the job of the moderator to prevent this from happening and to keep the meeting moving along. However, the moderator must also ensure that the pace is not too fast as to miss defects. When defects are identified, the moderator is responsible for ensuring that there is consensus from the team. Thus, to be effective a moderator should be technically competent. The moderator is also an inspector. The job can sometimes involve sensitive issues, such as having to moderate among hostile participants with differing opinions. As described by Wiegers, "Moderators should be trained in how to conduct inspections, including how to keep participants with strong technical skills but low social skills from killing each other." [2]

The *author* is the person responsible for the work product itself, and repairs all defects found (offline). The author is also an inspector, looking for defects along with other inspectors. In order to avoid bias, the author should not serve in any other role. Authors must remain objective throughout the inspection and not become defensive. This can be hard as others are finding "faults" with their work.

The *recorder* is responsible for writing down descriptions and classifications of the defects found, and for recording the action items. If the inspection team is very small, the moderator could also take on this role, but it usually is best to have someone else assume this responsibility. The recorder is also an inspector.

A *reader* is responsible for leading the team through the work in an appropriate and thorough manner. This person selects the most effective sequence for presenting the work product and answer questions posed by the inspection team. The reader is also an inspector. In many cases, the role of the reader is handled by the moderator or author.

An *inspector* is a participant who attempts to identify defects in the artifact under review.

All participants in an inspection act as inspectors, in addition to any other responsibilities they may have. It is important to invite people who can make a significant contribution and have the expertise to identify defects to the inspection. Examples of people who should attend are other project members, those responsible for testing or maintaining the product, and depending on what artifact is being developed, customer and business representatives. Depending on the artifact being inspected, there may be a requirement for specialized inspectors. For example, a *focused inspector* inspects for a specific criterion (e.g., reliability). A *specialized inspector* is a specialist in the area covered by the artifact under inspection (e.g., a radar expert for a radar control application).

3. Defect Detection, not Defect Repair

Inspections should focus on identifying defects, and specifically exclude any discussion of their repair. The repair process is left to the author, and no time should be spent during inspections even suggesting repairs. All repair suggestions should be made offline. This is typically one of the hardest things to control—many participants love to discuss potential solutions and it is quite easy to fall into interminable technical discussions regarding the best approach. This is where a strong moderator is essential. It is key to not let this type of discussion continue and instead to remind people that the goal of the meeting is to identify defects, not repair them.

4. Checklists

A checklist can be very useful in providing guidance to inspectors, describing specific areas to pay attention to. Each type of artifact such as project plan, requirements specification, design specification, configuration management plan, source code, and so on should have its own checklist, as each requires different areas of focus. Example questions to ask when examining a requirements specification might be as follows: Is each requirement verifiable by testing? Is each requirement uniquely identified? For code inspections, questions to ask might be: Are there any variables that are unused or redundant? Is the code adequately commented? Good examples of checklists can be found in [3].

5. Artifact Readiness

The artifact under review should be in the best state of readiness that the author is capable of. For documents there should not be many, if any, sections with "to be determined." Code should compile cleanly. When a group of people takes time to identify a defect that the author would have found with reasonable effort, a significant amount of time is wasted.

6. Adequate Preparation

Inspections are not the same as reviews, management overviews, or education sessions. Inspectors have to work at the same level of detail as the author. (This is what makes inspections time-consuming and thus expensive.) The artifact under review is distributed several days before the meeting, allowing inspectors adequate time to study the material, identify defects, and prepare questions to ask at the inspection. Inspection-aiding software can save time by allowing inspectors to enter descriptions of defects they discover while preparing. The recorder accesses and edits these at inspection meetings.

7. Metrics Collection

During inspections, metrics are collected and analyzed. Examples of metrics to collect are as follows:

- Number of defects discovered, by severity and type

- Number of defects discovered by each category of stakeholder inspecting the artifact

- Number of defects per page reviewed

- Review rate (number of pages/hour)

For severity, a simple classification such as *trivial*, *minor*, and *severe* can be used. For type, categories such as missing function, incorrect function, performance, and usability can be used. This classification topic is discussed in Section 5.6.1.

The metrics collected from inspections are analyzed and the results used for several purposes. First, they are used to predict the efficiency of future reviews. If a company has information on the rate of review for a particular artifact, it can use that to predict how long to schedule for a future review of a similar artifact. Second, counting the number of defects discovered during each stage of development is useful in predicting the number of defects in future projects. Even more specific, counting the number of defects discovered by a *particular stakeholder* (e.g., marketing, customer, QA) is also useful. For example, if during a requirements review fewer than expected defects are discovered by the customer representative, it could indicate either a lack of preparation or misunderstanding of requirements by that person. In either case, this would raise a red flag and a follow-up meeting with the customer would ensue to understand the cause for the discrepancy.

8. Time Limit

Inspections should not be marathon sessions, which can occur if the moderator does not keep the meeting moving along. After a certain amount of time, participants will not be as focused as needed. Each session should be kept to a maximum of two hours, and if it is not completed by then a follow-up session should be rescheduled.

5.4.2 Inspection Process

The inspection process follows an orderly flow of steps, each adhering to the principles described above. The steps are summarized in Figure 5.10.

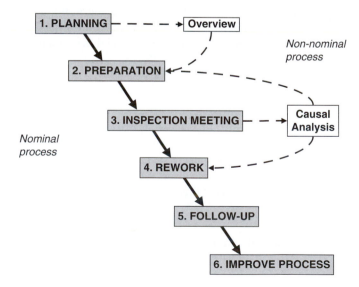

Figure 5.10 The parts of the inspection process, emphasizing the main sequence of activities

1. **Planning.** The process begins with planning. This includes deciding which inspection metrics to collect, identifying tools to be used in recording and analyzing these data, deciding who will participate in inspections and when they will take place, and distributing the materials several days prior to the meeting. Typically, the moderator is responsible for these tasks.

   1A. **Overview meeting.** If necessary, an overview meeting can be organized to explain the artifact under inspection. Since meetings are expensive, this should be avoided unless obviously necessary.

2. **Preparation.** The next step for each inspection consists of preparation. Here, inspectors review the work in complete detail at their own workstations (e.g., checking that the code under inspection correctly implements the detailed design), possibly using checklists provided for guidance. What makes the inspection process valuable, but also expensive, is the fact that this time-consuming process is performed by several people in complete detail. The process is not a "review," because inspectors work at the same level of detail as the author. Inspectors frequently enter the defects they find into a database (e.g., Web-accessible) together with descriptions and classifications. This helps to prevent duplication, and it minimizes unnecessary meeting time. Some prefer to use paper to record their defects, and some consider the number of inspectors who recognize a given defect to be a useful metric.

3. **Inspection meeting.** When every participant is prepared, the inspection meeting takes place. During this meeting, the participants honor their designated roles. Of particular importance is to not try and *solve* problems that are raised, but instead to ensure that they are recognized as defects, to record them as action items only, and to move on.

4. **Rework.** Normally, the author is able to repair all defects, working alone. This is the rework phase. If the inspection meeting decides, however, that the defects are so pervasive that a reinspection is required, then the item is recycled through the process.

   4A. **Causal analysis.** If the defects are due to a misunderstanding or widespread misconception, it may be necessary to call a separate meeting at which these causes are analyzed and discussed. Again, since meetings are expensive, these should not be scheduled casually.

5. **Follow-up.** After the author repairs the defects identified during the inspection meeting, a brief follow-up meeting is conducted at which the moderator and the author confirm that the defects have indeed been repaired. This is not intended to be a detailed review by the moderator. The onus for repair is on the author, who is responsible for the work. If the number of defects repaired is high, a follow-up inspection may be required.

6. **Improve process.** Organizations should always analyze the efficacy of their processes and strive to improve them. For inspections, the group meets from time to time to review the inspection process itself, and decides how it can be improved. They examine the metrics collected, including the list of defects, and decide how the development process can be improved to reduce and/or prevent the same types of defects in the future.

Figure 5.11 shows the average relative times for each inspection process step, used as reference data by one of the author's clients.

The inspection meeting time in Figure 5.11 is shown as one hour for the sake of reference. Individual companies or development groups record inspection times and quantities inspected, and they estimate future inspections based on these historical data. The times shown in Figure 5.11 may disturb the uninitiated, who may wonder whether it really does take that long to check code. Producing professional-quality products does indeed take a substantial amount of time, and any failure to recognize the true costs ends up consuming far more time in the end. Inspections have been estimated by Gehani and McGettrick [4] to consume as much as 10-15 percent of the development budget.

	One company's estimates
Planning	**1 hr ×(1 person)**
Overview	*1 hr × (3–5 people)*
Preparation	**1 hr × (2–4 people)**
Inspection meeting	**1 hr × (3–5 people)**
Rework	**1 hr × (1 person)**
Analysis	*1 hr × (3–5 people)*
Total:	**7–21 person-hours**

Figure 5.11 Inspection time/costs per 100 non-commented lines of code

Inspections are expensive because they consume the time of several engineers. Nevertheless, various studies (for example, [1]) have shown that they pay off handsomely. This is due to the astronomical cost of detecting and repairing defects undiscovered until close to delivery time. Quantified benefits of inspections from sources such as IBM, ICL, and Standard Bank, for example, are summarized in [5].

Appendix D of the case study shows an example of a form for reporting the results of an inspection.

5.5 QA REVIEWS AND AUDITS

The QA organization works with the project leadership to define the manner in which external quality assessment will be performed, specifies this in the SQAP, and executes it during the course of the project. External QA activities are either *reviews* (sometimes called *walk-throughs*), which are scheduled in advance, or *audits*, which are not so scheduled. A project can expect both types of activities. Figures 5.12 and 5.13 show the range of options for QA involvement in reviews and audits, starting from the most invasive to the least.

- Participate in all meetings
  Including formative sessions and inspections.

- Review all documents
  Participate in all inspections
  (but do not attend all meetings).

- Attend final reviews and review all completed documents

- Review select completed documents
  But do not participate otherwise.

Figure 5.12 Options for QA reviews

- Audit at unrestricted random times
  Includes visiting with engineers.
  Includes inspecting any document at any time.

- Audit random meetings

- Audit randomly from a specified list of meetings

- Audit with notice

- No auditing

Figure 5.13 Options for QA audits

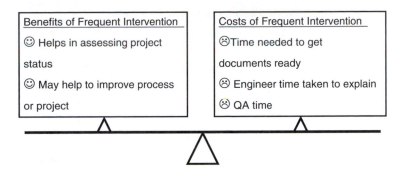

Figure 5.14 Comparing frequent vs. occasional QA intervention

Frequent intervention by QA has the advantage of providing QA personnel with greatly improved understanding of the health of the project, but it may disrupt the project by frequently calling for documents or for engineers' time. This trade-off is summarized in Figure 5.14.

5.6 DEFECT MANAGEMENT

Projects encourage the submission of defect reports by all team members. Usually, a screening process that ensures defect reports are valid and accurate is put in place. To manage defects, QA standardizes on the manner in which defects are defined and tracked. These data can then be compared between different projects so that estimates can be made regarding new projects. We explain this standardization next.

5.6.1 Classifying Defects

Teams classify each defect by its *severity* (how serious it is), *priority* (indicating when it will be handled), its *type* (the kind of problem) and its *source* (the phase during which it was injected). These classifications are illustrated in Figure 5.15.

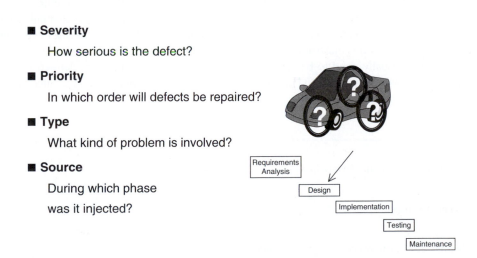

Figure 5.15 Defect classification

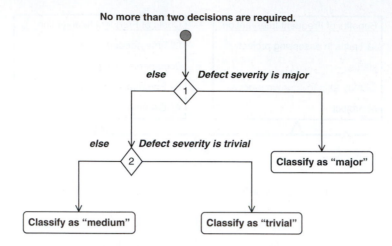

Figure 5.16 The triage decision method applied to defect severity classification

A single severity classification scheme can be used for all artifacts. It is possible to be very discriminating among levels of severity, but this consumes time. The results should be worth the time. One of the authors has frequently encountered teams using discriminating classification schemes that consume significant decision-making time and yet the data that they produce are not utilized by the organization.

Deciding the severity level of a defect falls into can sometimes be difficult. Triage is a useful and simple decision-making technique when confronted with a large number of possibilities, a situation occurring often in software engineering. Utilizing triage for defect classification has the advantage of being fast to perform because each classification requires answering just one or two questions as shown in Figure 5.16. Once a list of defects develops, the team approaches the major ones first (they can be placed in order with the "major" category if necessary). Once they have been attended to, the medium severity defects can be handled. The team gets to the trivial ones only after this, if time allows.

A simple way to classify the severity of defects when using triage is shown in Figure 5.17.

Although triage is fast, the three-category classification lumps together all defects that fail requirements, whether serious or not. Thus, "name field is not purple, as required" and "system crashes every minute" (a "showstopper" since its effects are catastrophic for the application) are given the same severity, which is rather extreme. Showstoppers usually need to be separated. To address this, the IEEE has defined a more refined classification of defect severity as shown in Figure 5.18. The "None" category is added to collect unprioritized defects.

- **Major**
  Causes a requirement to be unsatisfied.

- **Medium**
  Neither *major* nor *trivial*.

- **Trivial**
  Defect doesn't affect operation or maintenance.

Figure 5.17 Classifying defect severity by triage

- **Urgent**
  Failure causes system crash, unrecoverable data loss, or jeopardizes personnel.

- **High**
  Causes impairment of critical system functions, and no workaround solution exists.

- **Medium**
  Causes impairment of critical system functions, though a workaround solution does exist.

- **Low**
  Causes inconvenience or annoyance.

- **None**
  None of the above.

Figure 5.18 IEEE 1044.1 Severity classification

A defect's *priority* is the order in which the team plans to address it. This is somewhat aligned with the defect's severity but is not identical. For example, a defect can be classified as "urgent" but it may not be necessary to repair it immediately. For the sake of project efficiency, for example, its repair may be batched with a set of repairs to the same part of the product.

Different phases use different defect *type classifications*. For example, a defect in the requirements may concern ambiguity but "ambiguity" does not apply very well to code. On the other hand, code may have a logic defect but "logic" does not apply to requirements in the same way. Some types of defects *are* common to all artifacts, as listed in Figure 5.19.

The *source* of a defect is the phase in which it was introduced (or *injected*). For example, you may discover while testing a video store application that it does not—but should—accept the video *It's A Mad, Mad, Mad, Mad World* because the requirements document stated that no word in a title should be repeated more than once (supposedly to prevent bad data entry). Even though the defect may have been discovered during the testing phase, its *source* phase was requirements analysis.

5.6.2 Tracking Defects

Table 5.1 shows a typical way to track known defects. The information is used to manage ongoing work and to record defect history for postmortem and estimation purposes.

- **Omission**
  Something is missing.

- **Unnecessary**
  The part in question can be omitted.

- **Nonconformance with standards**

- **Inconsistency**
  The part in question contradicts other part(s).

- **Unclassified**
  None of the above.

Figure 5.19 Common defect types across all artifacts

Many bug-tracking programs are indispensable in tracking and managing defects. *Bugzilla* is an example of an open source defect-tracking system. It was originally written by Terry Weissman. Bugzilla features include the following:

> inter-bug dependencies, dependency graphing, advanced reporting capabilities extensive con-figurability, a very well-understood and well-thought-out natural bug resolution protocol, email, XML, console, and HTTP APIs. (It is) available integrated with automated software configuration management systems, including CVS [6].

Appendix B of the case study contains an example of the way in which defects can be reported, and Appendix A contains an example of the way in which they can be tracked.

5.7 PROCESS IMPROVEMENT AND PROCESS METRICS

Even a very good process has to adapt to changes such as new technology and new kinds of requirements. For these reasons, very effective software development organizations include a *meta-process* with every software process: a process for improving the process itself. This usually takes the form of meetings at the end of phases to review the effectiveness of the process used with a view to improving it for future projects. A meta-process is outlined in Figure 5.20.

To measure the effectiveness of a process, an organization has to use it for several projects and then compare the project metrics. Table 5.2 gives an example.

These results suggest that process U is the most effective, since it produces the best results in every category. Process V is the worst for the opposite reasons. Matters are not often so simple, however. For example, suppose that we had to choose between Waterfall and "Waterfall + Incremental." The latter process is superior in defect count, developer cost, and customer satisfaction, but it scores worse in the other categories. Making the call depends on the relative importance of the factors to the organization.

Figure 5.21 lists a sequence of actions that can be taken throughout the life of a project in order to continually improve the process.

Figure 5.22 is an example of the kind of data that can be collected about the process. It is applied to the process of collecting detailed requirements, which is covered in Part IV, but the table is applicable to most phases. The numbers are illustrative only, and should not be regarded as industry standards. A comparison with the organization's normative (typical) data reveals deficiencies in the team's meeting process and in their individual execution (i.e., the actual writing process). This exposes problems in meetings, for example, which were subjectively evaluated 2 out of 10 by the team. It was determined (though not visible in the data) that the meeting process would improve if the straw man proposal brought to the meeting was more complete i.e. an explicit proposal that can be used as a basis for discussion.

The other problem observed in the example shown in Figure 5.22 seems to occur during the execution step, where the actual work of writing the requirements is performed. The defect rate is higher than normal (5 versus 3) and the self-assessed quality is a little below average (4). Compared with company norms, there appears to be room to spend more time executing the work (i.e., as individuals), thereby reducing the defect count and improving the subjective self-assessment. You can observe from this process that a standard for counting the parts of the phase is fundamental to our ability to measure it. In this case, we are counting "detailed requirements," a concept that will be explained in Chapter 4.

Even in the absence of historical data, the team predicts what the values of the metrics should and will be. With these advance predictions, teams tend to work better, and they tend to remember results. The data collected become the basis for future historical data. Managing all of this is not technically difficult, but it has

Table 5.1 A typical way to track known defects

Defect Tracking

No.	Name	Description	Discovering engineer	Responsible engineer	Date opened	Source	Severity	Type	Status
1	Checkout flicker	Checkout screen 4 flickers when old DVDs are checked out by hitting the Checkout button.	Kent Bain	Fannie Croft	1/4/04	Integration	Med	GUI	Being worked; begun 2/10/04
2	Bad fine	Fine not correct for first-run DVDs checked out for 2 weeks, as displayed on screen 7.	Fannie Croft	April Breen	1/4/06	Requirements	High	Math	Not worked yet
…	…	…	…	…	…	…	…	…	Tested with suite 9023
…	…	…	…	…	…	…	…	…	Resolved
…	…	…	…	…	…	…	…	…	…

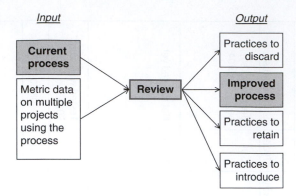

Figure 5.20 The process improvement meta-process

to be done at the same time as many other urgent activities. For this reason, the assignment of clear responsibilities and the regular review of the metric data are worked out at this early stage in the process. As you will see in the next section, process improvement feedback separates great development organizations from merely good ones.

Table 5.2 Data from multiple projects used to compare processes

Process →	Waterfall	Waterfall + Incremental	Process U	Process V
Average over 10 projects:				
Major defects identified within first 3 months per 1000SLOC in delivered product	1.3	0.9	0.7	2.1
Development cost per detailed requirement	$120	$100	$85	$135
Developer satisfaction index (1 to 10 = best)	4	3	4	3
Customer satisfaction index (1 to 10 = best)	4	6	6	2
Cost per maintenance request	$130	$140	$95	$165
Variance in schedule on each phase : $100 \times \dfrac{\text{actual duration} - \text{projected duration}}{\text{projected duration}}$	+20%	+70%	−10%	+80%
Variance in cost : $100 \times \dfrac{\text{actual cost} - \text{projected cost}}{\text{projected cost}}$	+20%	+65%	−5%	+66%
Design fraction : $\dfrac{total\ design\ time}{total\ programming\ time}$ Humphrey: Should be at least 50%.	23%	51%	66%	20%

1. **Identify and define** metrics team will use by phase.

   Include . . . **time spent on research, execution, and review**
   . . . **size (e.g., lines of code)**
   . . . **number of defects detected per unit (e.g., lines of code)**
   include source
   . . . **quality self-assessment of each on scale of 1–10**
   maintain bell-shaped distribution

2. **Document** these in the SQAP.

3. **Accumulate** historical **data** by phase.

4. Decide **where** the metric data will be **placed.**
   As the project progresses SQAP? SPMP? Appendix?

5. **Designate engineers** to manage collection by phase.
   QA leader or phase leaders (e.g., design leader)

6. **Schedule reviews** of data for lessons learned.
   Specify when and how to feed back improvement.

Figure 5.21 A process for gathering process metrics

Requirements Document: 200 detailed requirements	Meeting	Research	Execution	Personal Review	Inspection
Hours spent	0.5 × 4	4	5	3	6
% of total time	10%	20%	25%	15%	30%
% of total time: norm for the organization	*15%*	*15%*	*30%*	*15%*	*25%*
Self-assessed quality 1–10	<u>2</u>	8	<u>5</u>	<u>4</u>	6
Defects per 100	N/A	N/A	N/A	5	<u>6</u>
Defects per 100: organization norm	*N/A*	*N/A*	*N/A*	*3*	*4*
Hours spent per detailed requirement	0.01	0.02	0.025	0.015	0.03
Hours spent per detailed requirement: organization norm	0.02	0.02	0.04	0.01	0.03
Process improvement	**Improve strawman brought to meeting**		**Spend 10% more time executing**		
Summary	**Productivity: 200/22 = 9.9 detailed requirements per hour**				

Figure 5.22 Collecting project metrics for phases

5.8 ORGANIZATION-LEVEL QUALITY AND THE CMMI

Software development organizations periodically assess and upgrade their overall capability. In the 1980s the nonprofit Software Engineering Institute (SEI) established a classification of capabilities for contractors on behalf of the U.S. Department of Defense (DoD). The DoD's plan was to restrict bidding on government software development contracts to contractors with specified capability levels. The SEI's system, now expanded into the *Capability Maturity Model Integration* (CMMI), succeeded in providing concrete software engineering competence goals for organizations. Actually, the scope of CMMI is larger than software engineering, but we will restrict our attention to the latter, termed *CMMI-SW*. Many organizations, defense and commercial alike, have used the CMMI and its predecessor, the CMM, to assess the quality of their development process.

Software development organizations are assessed at a CMMI level between 1 (worst) and 5 (best). The CMMI distinguishes two kinds of assessments: *staged* and *continuous*. The staged assessment consists of identifiable steps. We will not discuss the continuous kind here. The CMMI classifies staged organizational capability with the steps shown in Figure 5.23 (from [7]). These are elaborated on in Table 5.3.

5.8.1 Level 1: Initial

The "Initial" CMMI level is the most primitive status that a software organization can have. Organizations at level 1 can be said only to be capable of producing software (i.e., "something"). The organization has no recognized process for software production, and the quality of products and projects depends entirely on the individuals performing the design and implementation. Teams depend on methods provided by members of the group who take initiative on the process to be followed. From project to project, these could be very good or very poor. The success of one project has little relation to the success of another unless they are similar and employ the same software engineers. When a project is completed, nothing is known or recorded about its cost, schedule, or quality. New projects are as uncertain of success as past ones.

For most organizations, this is unacceptable.

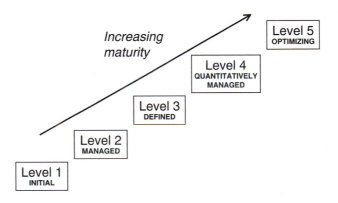

Figure 5.23 CMMI model for organization with staged processes

Table 5.3 SEI specifications of capabilities required for each level (see [7] for a full description)

Level, Title, and Summary	Expected Outcome	Characteristics
1. INITIAL		
Undefined; ad hoc	Unpredictable; depends entirely on team individuals	Organizations often produce products, but they are frequently over budget and miss their schedules.
2. MANAGED	Preceding level plus:	
Measurement and control	Project outcomes are qualitatively predictable	Respect organizational policies Follow established plans Provide adequate resources Establish responsibility and authority Provide training Establish configuration management Monitor and control: Take corrective action Evaluate process and product relative to plans: address deviations
3. DEFINED	Preceding level plus:	
Processes standardized	Projects consistent across the organization; qualitatively predictable	Establish process objectives Ensure process objectives met Establish orderly tailoring Describe processes rigorously Be proactive
4.QUANTITATIVELY MANAGED	Preceding level plus:	
Processes measured	Metrics available on process; quantitatively predictable	Set quantitative goals for key subprocesses Control key subprocesses with statistical techniques Identify and remedy variants
5. OPTIMIZING	Preceding level plus:	
Improvement meta-process	Processes improved and adapted using process metrics	Establish quantitative process improvement objectives Identify and implement innovative process improvements Identify and implement incremental process improvements Evaluate process improvements against quantitative objectives

5.8.2 Level 2: Managed

The "Managed" CMMI level applies to organizations capable of tracking projects as they unfold. Such organizations make plans, manage configurations, and maintain records of project costs and schedules. They also describe the functionality of each product in writing. It is therefore possible to predict the cost and schedule of very similar projects performed by a very similar team.

Although level 2 organizations track projects, no standard development process for the organization is guaranteed.

5.8.3 Level 3: Defined

The "Defined" CMMI level applies to organizations that document and enforce a standard process. Such a process is typically one of those described in the previous chapters (waterfall, spiral, etc.). Some organizations adopt existing standards such as IEEE's, while others define their own. Roughly speaking, as long as management enforces coordinated, professional standards, and engineers implement them uniformly, the organization is at level 3. Training is typically required for an organization to reach level 3. Teams are allowed flexibility to tailor the organization's standards for special circumstances. Level 3 includes organization-wide standards for project management, complete configuration management, inspections, design notation, and testing.

Level 3 organizations lack general predictive capability. They are able to make predictions only for projects that are very similar to ones performed in the past.

5.8.4 Level 4: Quantitatively Managed

The "Quantitatively Managed" CMMI level applies to organizations that can predict the cost and schedule of jobs. A common way to do this is to use statistical techniques and historical data. Such an organization classifies jobs and their components; it measures and records the cost and time to design and implement these; then it uses these metric data to predict the cost and schedule of subsequent jobs. As Humphrey has pointed out, this is not "rocket science," but it does require a significant amount of organization, as well as an ability to analyze the data. Level 4 requires a complete, metric-oriented quality plan.

Even though level 4 is a high level of capability, it is not the highest. Software engineering changes rapidly. For example, the object-oriented paradigm made rapid inroads in the 1990s: reuse and new component concepts are having a growing impact. Future improvements and paradigms are unpredictable. Thus, the capabilities of a level 4 organization that does not adapt and improve may actually decline over time.

5.8.5 Level 5: Optimizing

Rather than trying to predict future changes, it is preferable to institute permanent *procedures* for seeking and exploiting new and improved methods and tools. Level 5 organizations, at the "Optimizing" CMMI level, build in process improvement. In other words, their process (actually a meta-process) includes a systematic way of evaluating the organization's process itself, investigating new methods and technologies, and then improving the organization's process. Many organizations aspire to this impressive capability.

5.8.6 Relationship of the CMMI to the PSP, TSP

As we have seen, the CMMI is a measure of capability at the organizational/corporate level. Watts Humphrey and the Software Engineering Institute have also defined coordinated process models at the team level and at the individual engineer level. These are called the *Team Software Process* (TSP) and the *Personal Software Process* (PSP), respectively. The PSP, TSP, and CMMI frameworks form a relatively coordinated set of capabilities and procedures at the individual, team, and organizational levels, respectively. We will describe the TSP in the project management chapters and the PSP in the implementation chapters.

5.8.7 Relationship of the CMMI to Agile Methods

CMMI appears to be almost contradictory to agility because it is process heavy. However, CMMI and agility are at different levels. CMMI is used to assess the capability of organizations as a whole to produce good applications. Those that use agile methods are just as interested in such an assessment as those that are not, and it is reasonable to assume that CMMI will evolve to assess development organizations of all kinds.

5.9 CASE STUDY: SOFTWARE QUALITY ASSURANCE PLAN FOR ENCOUNTER

The Software Quality Assurance Plan (SQAP) for Encounter is based on *IEEE Std 730-2002 Standard for Software QualityAssurance Plans*. The table of contents was outlined in Figures 5.8 and 5.9.

ENCOUNTER SOFTWARE QUALITY ASSURANCE PLAN

The author is indebted to his students for inspections of this document and for their improvements to the original.

> Note to the Student:
> Organizations usually have a standard quality assurance procedure. The SQAP for each project relies on this and provides project-specific QA plans. We will effectively combine two such documents here.

Approvals:

Title	Signature	Date
Engineering Manager	*P. Jones*	6/15/04
QA Manager	*L Wilenz*	6/11/04
Project Manager	*A. Pruitt*	6/7/04
Author	*E. Braude*	6/1/04

The table of contents of this SQAP follows that of IEEE standard 730-2002 in most essentials.

Revision History

> This assumes the existence of a method whereby revision numbers of documents are assigned.

Version 1

1.0.0 E. Braude: created 1/17/99

1.1.0 R. Bostwick: reviewed 5/30/99, added substance to Sections 7 through end

1.1.1 E. Braude: integrated and revised contents 5/31/99

Version 2

2.0.0 E. Braude: significant edits of Section 5.2 1/18/04

2.0.1 E. Braude: edits 1/23/04

2.1.0 E. Braude: edits in many sections responding to reviews by students 6/17/04

Table of Contents
1. Purpose
2. Referenced Documents

3. Management

   3.1 Organization

   3.2 Tasks

   3.3 Responsibilities

   3.4 QA Estimated Resources

4. Documentation

   4.1 Purpose

   4.2 Minimum documentation requirements

   4.3 Other

5. Standards

   5.1 Purpose

   5.2 Content

6. Reviews

   6.1 Purpose

   6.2 Minimum requirements

   6.3 Other reviews and audits

7. Test

   7.1 Unit Test

   7.2 Integration Test

   7.3 System Test

   7.4 User Acceptance Test

8. Problem Reporting and Corrective Action

9. Tools, Techniques, and Methodology

10. Media Control

11. Supplier Control

12. Records Collection, Maintenance, and Retention

13. Training

14. Risk Management

15. Glossary

16. Sqap Change Procedure and History

Appendix A – Metric History for this Project

Appendix B – Problem Reporting Form

Appendix C – Change Reporting Form

Appendix D – Inspection Meeting Report Form

Appendix E – Document Baselining Checklist

> Typically, most of the content of a SQAP are common to all of the organization's projects. Engineers would need simply to tailor parts to the project in question.

1. Purpose

This document describes the means by which the Encounter project will produce and maintain a high-quality product. It is also intended to describe mechanisms for improving the quality assurance process itself. "Quality" is defined as the degree to which the application satisfies its requirements.

> There is no separate "scope" section in the IEEE standard, so we have inserted it here. "Scope" contains vital information such as whether this document applies to the first release only or to maintenance as well.

The scope of this document comprises the artifacts of all releases.

2. Referenced Documents

See Section 4.2.

3. Management

3.1 Organization

> State the roles that are involved in ensuring quality. Actual names are provided in Section 3.3. The process described in this case is a mix of internal and external quality assurance.

This section assumes the description of the organizational structure of the Encounter project in 4.2 of the SPMP.

This document will refer to the quality work of developers as "internal." In addition, for the first three iterations of Encounter, a quality assurance engineer will be designated who will be responsible to the manager of QA. The QA leader will take the lead for project-wide quality issues. QA tasks will be referred to as "external."

3.2 Tasks

> Summarize what needs to be done.

External QA tasks shall include, for all iterations:

- Maintaining this document

- Documenting the quality of the evolving product and associated artifacts

- Managing external review meetings

- Ensuring that verification takes place and logging verification

- Preparing for and attending all inspections

- Post-unit testing as per the Software Test Documentation

- Engaging in activities designed to improve the quality assurance process itself

- Keeping the project leader apprised of QA progress through weekly written reports

- Carrying out the audits specified in Section 6 of this document

- Providing the development team with feedback from QA's activities

- Assign defect repair to software engineers

- Identifying methods and tools for collecting and maintaining metrics

Internal QA tasks shall include, for all iterations:

- Each team member responsible for the quality of his or her work, as defined in this document

- Maintaining an issue database

- Collecting the metrics designate by this and other project documents

- Carrying out the reviews and inspections specified in Section 6 of this document

- Unit testing as per GCI manual 023.2

3.3 Responsibilities

> State what roles will fulfill what job functions.

It is the quality assurance leader's responsibility to see to it that the tasks in Section 3.2 are performed and to ensure that the prescriptions in this document are followed, including scheduling the reviews specified. For the first three iterations, the QA leader will perform all of the quality control (QC) functions.

For subsequent iterations, the QC team, appointed by the QA department manager, will take over this function. The quality leader and the QC team are responsible for all non-unit testing. (See Part VII of the book for background information on these types of tests). A description of the QC team will be supplied.

The project leader will be responsible for ensuring that inspections and unit tests are performed. The schedules are to be placed in the SPMP.

> No names are assigned to these roles here because they are in the Software Project Management Plan, which is their proper place. Duplicating a name here would require us to update more than one document when there are changes.

The leaders designated in the SPMP are responsible for the quality of their respective areas (requirements, design, etc.). They shall ensure that the designated metrics are collected and that the quality self-assessments as outlined in Section 5.2 of this document are conducted.

Each member of the Encounter development team is responsible for quality as specified in Section 4.5 of the company document "Quality responsibilities of engineers at GCI." This includes testing individual methods and combinations of methods in a class ("unit testing").

3.4 QA Estimated Resources

The estimated resources required for QA on Encounter are as follows:

- One engineer working half time for the first third of the project
- One engineer working full time for the second third of the project
- One engineer working full time for the last third of the project
- An additional engineer working half time for the last third of the project

4. Documentation

4.1 Purpose

The purpose of this section is to identify the documentation that will be used to ensure quality.

4.2 Minimum Documentation Requirements

> This section lists all of the project documentation, since the documentation is a major factor ensuring the quality of the product. Note that the User's Manual is excluded: it is a deliverable rather than a project document.

The following documents will be produced:

- Software Quality Assurance Plan (SQAP; this document)
- Software Configuration Management Plan (SCMP)
- Software Project Management Plan (SPMP)
- Software Requirements Specifications (SRS)
- Software Design Document (SDD)
- Software Test Documentation and the test document that it refers to (STD)

- Software Verification and Validation Plan (SVVP)
- Software Verification and Validation Report (SVVR) (*Note:* This book does not cover the SVVR.)
- Maintenance Plan

In addition to these documents, the Java source code will utilize *Javadoc* to generate package-, class-, and function-level documentation. (See http://java.sun.com/j2se/javadoc/ for Javadoc specifications.)

4.3 Other

—intentionally left blank

> It is customary to make a comment like this so that no one wastes time looking for what may be missing.

5. Standards, Practices, Conventions, and Metrics

5.1 Purpose

This section describes the standards, practices, conventions, and metrics to be used for the Encounter project. These are intended not only to ensure quality of the Encounter product but also to obtain quantitative metric data on the SQA process itself. These data are to be used to help elevate the CMMI level of Gaming Consolidated Industries (GCI) from level 2 to level 3.

5.2 Content

> Describe the standards, practices, conventions, and metrics to be used. Organization-wide quality goals can be supplied here or in a separate appendix. The contents of this section should be as specific as possible. For example, statements such as "quality should be as high as possible" should be avoided.

Standards:

The IEEE documentation standards as of July 1, 2004, with appropriate modifications, are to be used for all documentation. The standards for Javadoc commenting will be followed as found at http://java.sun.com/j2se/javadoc/writingdoccomments/index.html and http://java.sun.com/j2se/javadoc/writingapispecs/index.html. Documentation standards or templates developed by the company may supersede these at the discretion of management.

Unified Modeling Language standards, as specified in . . . shall be used in this project.

Refer to the Conventions section below for additional standards.

Practices:

1. Because delaying quality is expensive, GCI Inc. strongly encourages engineers to apply quality precepts while working, rather than as an afterthought. This is referred to in the company as "internal quality." It includes all unit testing.

2. GCI Inc.'s policy is that the QA department provides independent, external testing. The QA department at GCI also has a role in educating engineers in the practice of internal quality and working with project mangers to ensure that it takes place.

3. All project artifacts are inspected and are made easily available to the team once released by the developer.

4. All project artifacts are placed under configuration management, where the contents can be seen by anyone in the team at any time (see the Software Configuration Management Plan for details).

5. The development process is to be reviewed at least once for improvement, and the written results forwarded to the software engineering laboratory (see Section 6.2.10).

Conventions:

Where feasible, writing conventions should conform to the suggestions in *Writing for Computer Science: The Art of Effective Communication* by Justin Zobel (Springer Verlag.

The coding conventions as found at http://java.sun.com/docs/codeconv/html/CodeConventions.doc.html will be followed.

Metrics:

> This section is liable to be extensive. The numbers used here would be based on historical data obtained from the group that is developing Encounter.

GCI's list of standard metrics, found at http://xxx, should be gathered as specified there. The following includes some of them.

For every process and document, metrics shall include the following:

1. Time spent by individuals on preparation and review.

2. Number of defects per unit (e.g., lines of code), classified per Section 8 of this document.

3. Quality self-assessment of the QA process and performance on a scale of 1 through 10, approximately in a bell-shaped distribution; self-assessment scores will not be used for the evaluation of personnel by management; failure to produce them, however, may negatively affect the evaluation of an engineer by management, however.

> We would specify all metrics to be collected on this project. Possible metrics are described in Chapter 6.

The standard for defect classification is given in Section 8 of this document.

Quality Goals:

GCI quality goals for delivered products are as follows, measured in terms of defects detected within two months of delivery.

- No known "critical" or "serious" defects remain in any delivered artifact.

  In addition:

- Requirements: No more than one "medium," and no more than three "trivial" defective detailed requirements per 100

- Design: No more than one "medium" defect per five diagrams. A "diagram" is any figure that uses about a page of easily legible parts.

- Pseudocode: No more than two "medium" defects per 1000 lines pseudocode is described in Chapter 19.

- Code: No more than two "medium" defects per KLoC (1000 lines of non-commented code)

The data from this project are to be reported as Appendix 1 to this document.

6. Reviews and Audits

6.1 Purpose

The purpose of reviews and audits is to continually focus engineers' attention on the quality of the application as it develops. *Reviews* effect this in a scheduled and thorough manner. *Audits* do so on the basis of random sampling with short notice.

6.2 Minimum Requirements

> Large projects require the full set of reviews and audit listed here. Student teams should try to conduct reviews and inspections of requirements and design, as well as postmortem reviews. "Reviews" are discussions of proposed artifacts. "Inspections" are conducted on completed artifacts presented to the team. The SQAP does not call out inspections as a heading, so the author has inserted section "A"'s for this purpose.

6.2.1 Software Requirements Reviews

These are walk-throughs of all proposed requirements in the presence of the entire team and at least one responsible customer representative. They will be led by the requirements leader, who will determine their frequency and scope.

6.2.1A Software Requirements Inspections

After they have been reviewed, all requirements will be inspected in accordance with GCI, Inc.'s document GCI 345678 "Inspections and Review procedures at GCI." Requirements sections must be completed and signed within a week of beginning the design.

6.2.2 Architecture Design Reviews

This is a review of alternative architectures with the entire team. The review will be led by the design leader in accordance with GCI 345678 on a frequency to be determined. The team will provide feedback, which will be reflected in the final design.

6.2.2A Architecture Design Inspections

After they have been reviewed, architectures will be inspected in accordance with GCI, Inc.'s inspection process manual, document GCI 345678. Architecture sections must be completed and signed off within a week of beginning detailed design.

6.2.3 Detailed Design Reviews

These are reviews of all proposed detailed designs in the presence of the entire development team. They will be led by the design leader, who will determine their frequency and scope, but at least one design review will be conducted per iteration. If possible, the architecture will be decomposed into detailed designs of its parts, and these will undergo separate detailed design reviews.

6.2.3A Detailed Design Inspections

After they have been reviewed, detailed designs will be inspected in accordance with GCI, Inc.'s inspection process manual, document GCI 345678. Detailed design sections must be completed and signed off within a week of beginning implementation.

6.2.3 Test Plan Reviews

These are reviews of all proposed test plans in the presence of the entire team. They will be led by the

QA leader, who will determine their frequency and scope. The test plan will be decomposed into parts, and these will undergo separate reviews.

6.2.3A Test Plan Inspections

After they have been reviewed, test plans will be inspected in accordance with GCI, Inc.'s inspection process manual, document GCI 345678. Test plan sections must be completed and signed off within a week of beginning testing.

6.2.4 Verification and Validation Plan Review

V&V is to be conducted by an independent team (i.e., not associated with QA), following the process detailed in GCI 345678. The QA engineer will review the SVV plan prior to its execution.

6.2.5 Functional Audits

The QA leader shall be responsible for auditing the product relative to the SRS. The audit will follow company guidelines in "GCI 8902: Release Procedures."

6.2.6 Physical Audits

Prior to each delivery, the QA leader is responsible for checking that the physical software and its documentation designated for delivery are complete and the correct version.

6.2.7 In-Process Audits

Project personnel should expect random audits of their work. These will consist of visits to the work site by individuals or teams designated by division management. A day's notice shall usually be given for all visits, but audits without notice shall take place as well. The subject of these audits will be the current work of teams and individuals that has been allocated to the project. All project artifacts will be made freely available to all team members and auditors at all times. It will be organized in a clear, standard fashion, so that audits will be possible without any notice.

6.2.8 Managerial Review

The Encounter project shall be reviewed by the VP for Engineering during the first week of every month:

exceptions are at the discretion of the VP for Engineering. It is the project leader's responsibility to schedule this review and provide the appropriate documentation and software demonstrations.

6.2.9 SCMP Review

The QA leader shall review the status of configuration management on a monthly basis in a manner independent of the procedures specified in the SCMP.

6.2.10 Post-Implementation Review

As with all GCI projects, the Encounter team shall conduct post-implementation reviews to provide data for future projects. These will include reviews of the project phase just completed and reviews of the QA process itself. The QA team or QA leader shall file a process improvement report for every phase, and for the QA process itself, with the manager of the software engineering laboratory.

6.3 Other Reviews and Audits

—intentionally left blank

7. Test

This section describes how testing is to be managed. The text here should refer to, but not duplicate, the software test documentation.

The responsibilities for testing were described in Section 3.3. Refer to the Software Test Documentation for details on testing Encounter.

8. Problem Reporting and Corrective Action

This section explains how defects come to be recognized, described, and repaired. They do not follow the details of IEEE standards. The reader is referred to the IEEE standards, as well as to Humphrey [8] for additional defect severity and type classifications.

The team will use the Bugzilla defect management system.

> Instead of describing Bugzilla, we will describe a hypothetical manual defect system for the sake of clarity, even though a software-based system is common practice and far preferable. Such systems also allow for a dialog thread involving, typically, testers and developers.

The Problem Reporting Form to be used by the Encounter development team in response to a software problem report generated by QA is shown in Appendix B.

To use this form, engineers should retrieve the form from www.a.b.c.d. The defect number will appear automatically, and the site will ensure that the appropriate fields are filled in.

The values for *severity* are as follows:

• *Critical*: Causes the application to crash with significant frequency

• *Serious*: Causes at least one documented requirement to be unmet

• *Trivial*: Could be allowed to stand ad infinitum without impeding the user from exercising a required feature

• *Medium* : Is neither serious nor trivial

The documentation defect types are as follows:

• Incorrect

• Missing material

• Unclear

• Ambiguous

• Incomplete

• Redundant (within or between documents)

• Contradictory

• Obsolete

The code *and pseudocode* defects types are as follows:

• Syntax

• Logic

• Data (i.e., allows a wrong variable value)

• Insecure (allows unacceptable security breach)

The workflow of a defect status is:

1. Open: defect found by tester

2. Assigned: defect assigned to an engineer

3. Corrected: defect fixed by engineer

4. Closed: defect closed by tester

If the defect is reopened, the defect will move from the Corrected state to an Open state.

The QA leader will create and the QA team will maintain a database of problem reports that describe the deficiencies, discrepancies, and anomalies for Encounter. They will ensure that defects are consistently recorded on this form and that they are routed and repaired in a consistent manner. Problem reports shall be routed in accordance with the SCMP. Full traceability as to their effects and status shall be maintained, including after they are repaired.

After iteration three, when a problem is encountered, the QA manager will distribute the problem report to the members of the Change Control Board (CCB). For the first three releases, the configuration specialist will carry out the functions of the QA team, and the project leader will perform all of the CCB functions in accordance with the SPMP. The CCB evaluates the problem report and then assigns a priority to the report of either *immediate, to be done,* or *optional.* The problem report is then assigned by the CCB to the Encounter development team, QA, or CM for resolution. The CCB determines the schedule for problem report resolution based on problem report priority and analysis report results. After the problem in the report is corrected, the QA team reviews the results and the QA manager reports on the review to the CCB. If necessary, the process is repeated.

9. Tools, Techniques, and Methodologies

SQA techniques include the auditing of standards, requirements tracing, design verification, software inspections, and the verification of formal methods. The SQA tools consist of software verification programs, checklists, media labels, and acceptance stamps. Checklists will be obtained from the company's software engineering laboratory, and tailored for Encounter. These are augmented by NASA checklists at [9]. Checklists include the following:

- Review checklists are used at formal meetings, for document reviews, and for inspections.

- Checklists will be used for verifying the quality of the following activities and documents: Preliminary Design Review, Critical Design Review, Test Readiness Review, Functional Configuration Audit, Physical Configuration Audit, SRS, SDD, SPMP, and Software Development Folders.

- Separate checklists and forms are used for software audit purposes.

> This book contains checklists throughout. These checklists involve meeting and inspection procedures, for example. Teams often begin with published checklists, and augment them according to additional specific needs of their projects.

Additional SQA tools, techniques, and methodologies for configuration management are described in the SPMP.

10. Media Control

> Describe the means by which disks, tapes, and so on will be managed.

The SQA team verifies that the software media are built and configured per the SCMP and that authorized changes have been installed and tested. In addition, the SQA team verifies that the software media are duplicated using only the procedures identified in the SCMP. SQA acceptance is indicated by an SQA stamp on the media label. The SQA audit reports for media control are intended as further evidence that QA procedures have been followed. All backup media will be stored offsite as described in the SCMP.

11. Supplier Control

> This section concerns relationships with suppliers of software and hardware. It describes how and by whom these relationships are to be handled.

The SQA team verifies all commercial third-party products provided by the suppliers during incoming inspection by reviewing the packing slips that identify the products and their version numbers. The QA manager is responsible for ensuring that all third-party software and hardware meets the expected requirements. The products will be validated by the QA manager through installation and acceptance tests. A QA representative will be responsible for testing all new versions. He will also be responsible for the relationship with the external vendor.

12. Records Collection, Maintenance, and Retention

> This section describes how physical records will be handled and who will be responsible for them. Include disk files that are not under configuration control.

The SQA records collected and archived shall include the following:

- Task reports

- Anomaly reports not handled by the regular problem-reporting mechanism

- Memos, including recommendations to responsible parties

- Logbooks of SQA activities

- Audit reports

- Signed-off checklists from reviews and audits

- Minutes of inspections

- Metrics for the QA process itself

Besides verifying the archive procedures specified in the SCMP, SQA shall separately archive its own records at least once a week. These records are retained throughout the operation and maintenance phase.

13. Training

Includes SQA training specific to this project.

The SQA organization will conduct an initial four-hour orientation on quality for the development team. This will include a presentation on the metrics to be used and a workshop on how to use tools for recording metrics. SQA will also conduct monthly three-hour classes for development team members to keep them informed of quality goals, tools, and techniques. Team members can waive attendance at these meetings by scoring perfectly on a multiple-choice quiz available at GCI/monthly/SQA/quiz.

Each team member is required to attend a three-hour course on writing styles and conventions conducted by QA.

14. Risk Management

SQA team members are encouraged to identify risks as early as possible and direct them to the project leader. The procedures for risk management are specified in Section 5.4 of the SPMP.

15. Glossary

. . . .

16. SQAP Change Procedure and History

. . .

(The material in the following appendices was supplied by Jane Dyson.)

Appendix A: Metric History for This Project

Product	Defect Unit	Expected Rate	Actual Rate	Preparation Time		Review Time	
				Expected Time	Actual Time	Expected Time	Actual Time
SCMP	Section	1 minor defect per section					
SPMP	Section	1 minor defect per section					
SQAP	Section	1 minor defect per section					
SRS	Section	1 minor defect per section					
SDD	Section	1 minor defect per section					
STP	Section	1 minor defect per section					
SVVP	Section	1 minor defect per section					
SVVR	Section	1 minor defect per section					
Requirements	D-Requirement	1 medium and 3 trivial defects per 100					
Design	Diagram	1 minor defect per 5					
Pseudocode	KLOC	2 medium defects					
Code	KLOC	2 medium defects					

Code Defects

A free online tool called "RefactorIt" from http://www.refactorit.com shall used by the Project Manager to estimate LOC, NCLOC, and CLOC.

Appendix B: Problem Reporting Form

1. Defect number:_____

2. Proposed by: _____

3. Documents / sections affected: _____

4. Document defect type:

   a. _____ Missing material

   b. _____ Unclear

   c. _____ Ambiguous

   d. _____ Incomplete

   e. _____ Redundant (within or between documents)

   f. _____ Contradictory

   g. _____ Obsolete

      Source code affected (for source code defects):

5. Package(s) _____

6. Class(es)_____

7. Method(s)_____

8. Severity:

   a. _____ High

   b. _____ Medium

   c. _____ Low

9. Code defect type:

   a. _____ Syntax

   b. _____ Logic

   c. _____ Data (i.e., allows a wrong variable value)

   d. _____ Insecure (allows unacceptable security breach)

10. Phase injected (earliest phase with the defect):

   a. _____ Requirements

   b. _____ Architecture

   c. _____ Detailed design

   d. _____ Code

   e. _____ Implementation

11. Detailed description: _____

12. Priority: a. _____ Immediate   b. _____ Intermediate   c. _____ Deferred

13. Resolution: _____

14. Status: a. _____ Closed   b. _____ Open

      Sign-off:

15. Description and plan inspected: _____

16. Resolution code and test plan inspected: _____

17. Change approved for incorporation: _____

Appendix C: Change Reporting Form

1. Change number: _____

2. Proposed by: _____

3. Documents/sections affected: _____

4. Reason for change or addition: _____
   . . .

5. Enhancement:_____
   _____
   . . .

6. Details: _____
   . . .

   Signatures:

   Description and plan inspected (QA team leader) _____

   Resolution code and test plan inspected (QA team leader) _____

   Change approved for incorporation (Team leader) _____

Appendix D: Inspection Meeting Report Form

A completed Inspection Meeting Report must be included at the end of each document. Only the latest report is required.

Inspection Meeting Report

PROJECT:		
DATE:	STARTING TIME:	ENDING TIME:
PRODUCED BY:		
TYPE OF INSPECTION:	☐ INITIAL INSPECTION	☐ REWORK INSPECTION
DOCUMENT NUMBER AND REVISION:		
BRIEF DESCRIPTION:		

APPRAISAL OF THE WORK UNIT:

☐   Inspection not completed (continuation scheduled for _____)

☐   No further inspection required

☐   Minor revisions required

☐   Major revisions required

MATERIALS PRODUCED

☐   Issues List (Not Author's Responsibility)

☐   Issues List for Author

☐   Traceability Issues?

Participant	Role(s)	Org./Dept.
	Author	
	Moderator	
	Recorder	
	Inspector	
	Inspector	
	Inspector	
	Inspector	
	Inspector	

Inspection Meeting Report Issues List

ISSUES, NOT FOR AUTHOR			
Issue	Issue must be resolved prior to Document Baseline? Y/N	Assigned To	Response
1.			
2. etc.			

ISSUES FOR AUTHOR	
Issue	Response
1.	
2. etc.	

Appendix E: Document Baselining Checklist

Document Baselining Checklist

	Item	Comment / Initials
☐	Inspection Meeting Report completed and all issues resolved.	
☐	Revised document sent out for consensus after Inspection.	
☐	All comments accepted via Word's Track Changes. Track changes feature then turned off.	
☐	Check for clean requirements traceability completed. (*SRS only*)	
☐	All high-level requirements have been allocated to detailed requirements. (*SRS only*)	
☐	Final traceability report generated and stored. (*SRS only*)	

5.10 SUMMARY

Quality practices are integrated throughout the development process. They start with planning, when specific documents such as the Software Quality Assurance Plan (SQAP) and the Software Verification and Validation Plan (SVVP) are produced, describing the quality policies, procedures, and practices to be implemented.

The SQAP is the master quality plan and specifies the people and organizations responsible for quality, the project documentation to be produced, the metrics to be collected, the procedures to be practiced, and the techniques to be implemented. It is an important document as it sets the expectations regarding quality early in a project and helps guide its implementation.

Inspections are an important quality technique that involve peer review of all project artifacts including documents, test plans, and code. Their goal is to identify defects as close to their introduction as possible so that they can be repaired quickly. Considerable research has shown that the cost to repair a defect increases dramatically the longer it is allowed to persist in the software.

Quality reviews and audits by a quality assurance (QA) organization are beneficial. An external QA group is independent of the people developing the software and other artifacts and can objectively assess quality. Again, assessing quality and addressing it throughout the development process helps identify problems as early as possible.

Problems are identified by team members throughout the development process and are submitted as *defects*. A screening process is implemented to ensure that the defects are accurate and valid. A classification system is employed to understand the severity of each defect and priority for its repair. In addition, maintaining metrics such as number of defects, time to repair, and so on is useful for comparison with other projects and in making estimates for future projects.

Improving the effectiveness of the overall software process is accomplished through implementation of a meta-process. This includes the collection of process metrics, and meetings at the end of projects phases to analyze the metrics. In addition, lessons-learned meetings are conducted at the end of a project to analyze project successes and identify areas of improvement.

The Software Engineering Institute has developed a comprehensive meta-process for assessing an organization's overall capability. The process is called the Capability Maturity Model Integration (CMMI), and it defines several levels of capability and maturity an organization can measure itself against. The levels range from the lowest, Level 1 Initial, to the highest, Level 1 Optimizing. At the Initial level an organization can produce software but has no recognized process. At the Optimizing level, an organization implements a meta-process for process improvement.

5.11 EXERCISES

1. In a paragraph, explain why it is important to document quality procedures at the beginning of a project rather than later on.

2. The number of people attending an inspection can have a direct impact on the effectiveness of the review. List the disadvantages of having either too few or too many people attend an inspection.

3. Give two advantages and two disadvantages to using standards for documentation of the various software phases.

4. Why is it generally a good idea to have a cross-functional group be part of an inspection team? What type of review (that is, during what development phase) might it not be a good idea?

5. Your instructor will pair up student project teams. Conduct an inspection of an artifact produced by the other team, such as a SCMP or SPMP. Use an inspection checklist, such as one found in [3], to guide your inspection.

6. Give an example of a defect that might be classified with a high severity but a low priority. Be specific with your answer.

7. (a) In your own words, describe each of the CMMI levels.

   (b) How does applying the CMMI levels promote organizational quality? Explain this in a paragraph or two, using your own words.

BIBLIOGRAPHY

1. Fagan, M. "Design and Code Inspections to Reduce Errors in Program Development." *IBM Systems Journal*, Vol. 15, No. 3, 1976, pp. 182–211.
2. Wiegers, Karl, "Improving Quality Through Software Inspections," *Process Impact*, 1995. http://www.processimpact.com/articles/inspects.html [accessed November 15, 2009].
3. Wiegers, Karl, "Goodies for Peer Reviews," *Process Impact*, "http://www.processimpact.com/pr_goodies [accessed November 15, 2009].
4. Gehani, Narain, and A. McGettrick, *"Software Specification Techniques,"* International Computer Science Series, Addison-Wesley, 1985.
5. Gilb, T., and D. Graham, *"Software Inspection,"* Addison-Wesley, 1993.
6. Bugzilla. http://bugzilla.org/about.html [accessed December 10, 2009].
7. Capability Maturity Model® Integration (CMMI[SM]), Version 1.1, http://www.sei.cmu.edu/pub/documents/oz-reports/pdf/02trf012.pdf [accessed December 8, 2009].
8. Humphrey, Watts S., *"A Discipline for Software Engineering,"* SEI Series in Software Engineering, Addison-Wesley, 1995.
9. NASA Goddard Space Flight Center Software Assurance Web site. http://sw-assurance.gsfc.nasa.gov/disciplines/quality/index.php (2006) [accessed November 15, 2009].

6

Software Configuration Management

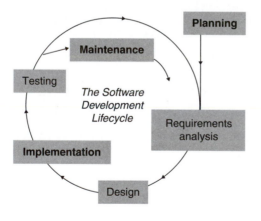

- **Planning**
- **Maintenance**
- Testing
- *The Software Development Lifecycle*
- Requirements analysis
- **Implementation**
- Design

- What is the purpose of software configuration management?

- What activities does it consist of?

- How do you plan for configuration management?

- What tools are available to support it?

- How is configuration management handled in large projects, in practice?

Figure 6.1 The context and learning goals for this chapter

Many artifacts are produced in the course of developing a software product, such as specifications (e.g., requirements, design), source and executable code, test plans and test data, user documentation, and supporting software (e.g., compilers, editors). Each undergoes numerous revisions, and keeping track of the various versions needs to be managed in a reliable and consistent manner. *Software Configuration Management* (SCM) is the process of identifying, tracking, and storing all the artifacts on a project. In the context of SCM, each of these artifacts is referred to as a Configuration Item (CI).

SCM contributes to overall software quality in that it supports a reliable way to control a project's artifacts. For example, the SCM process ensures that the proper source files are included when building the software system and that the correct project documentation is retrieved when required.

Many activities contribute to configuration management, including identification of artifacts as configuration items, storage of artifacts in a repository, managing changes to artifacts, tracking and reporting these changes, auditing the SCM process to ensure it's being implemented correctly, and managing software builds and releases. Many of these activities are labor intensive, and SCM systems help automate the process.

6.1 SOFTWARE CONFIGURATION MANAGEMENT GOALS

We first define the overall goals of software configuration management: *baseline safety, overwrite safety, reversion, and disaster recovery*.

Baseline safety is a process of accepting new or changed CIs for the current version of the developing product (the baseline), and safely storing them in a common repository so that they can be retrieved when needed later in a project.

Overwrite safety means that team members can safely work on CIs simultaneously, and changes can be applied so they do not overwrite each other. Overwrite safety is needed when the following kind of sequence occurs.

1. A. Engineer Alan works on a copy of CI X from the common repository.

    B. Brenda simultaneously works on an identical copy of X.

2. Alan makes changes to X and puts the modified X back in the repository.

3. Brenda also makes changes to X and wants to replace the version of X in the common repository with the new version.

Overwrite safety assures that Brenda's changes don't simply replace Alan's, but instead are added correctly to Alan's.

Reversion occurs when a team needs to revert to an earlier version of a CI. This is typically required when mistakes transition a project to a bad state—for example, when it is found that a new version of a CI turns out to cause so many problems that it is preferable to revert to a previous version. Reversion requires knowing which version of each CI makes up a previous version of the project.

Disaster recovery is a stronger form of reversion—it is the process of retaining older versions of an application for future use in case a disaster wipes out a newer version.

These four goals, fundamental for configuration management, are summarized in Figure 6.2.

6.2 SCM ACTIVITIES

There are several SCM activities and best practices that are implemented to successfully meet the goals just described. They are mainly the following:

1. Configuration identification.

2. Baseline control.

3. Change control.

4. Version control.

- **Baseline Safety**

  Ensure that new or changed CIs are safely stored in a repository and can be retrieved when necessary.

- **Overwrite Safety**

  Ensure that engineer's changes to the same CI are applied correctly.

- **Reversion**

  Ensure ability to revert to earlier version.

- **Disaster Recovery**

  Retain backup copy in case of disaster.

Figure 6.2 Major goals of configuration management

5. Configuration auditing.

6. Configuration status reporting.

7. Release management and delivery.

Each of these is described in the following sections.

6.2.1 Configuration Identification

The first step in configuration management is to identify a project's artifacts, or configuration items (CI), that are to be controlled for the project. As described in the introduction, candidate CIs include source and object code, project specifications, user documentation, test plans and data, and supporting software such as compilers, editors, and so on. Any artifact that will undergo modification or need to be retrieved at some time after its creation is a candidate for becoming a CI. Individual files and documents are usually CIs and so are classes. Individual methods may also be CIs, but this not usually the case. A CI may consist of other CIs.

CIs are too large when we can't keep track of individual items that we need to and we are forced to continually lump them with other items. CIs are too small when the size forces us to keep track of items whose history is not relevant enough to record separately.

Once selected, a CI is attached with identifying information that stays with it for its lifetime. A unique identifier, name, date, author, revision history, and status are typical pieces of information associated with a CI.

6.2.2 Baselines

While an artifact such as source code or a document is under development, it undergoes frequent and informal changes. Once it has been formally reviewed and approved, it forms the basis for further development, and subsequent changes come under control of configuration management policies. Such an approved artifact is called a *baseline*. IEEE Std 1042 defines a baseline as a "specification or product that has been formally reviewed and agreed to by responsible management, that thereafter serves as the basis for further development, and can be changed only through formal change control procedures."

Baselines not only refer to individual CIs but also to collections of CIs at key project milestones. They are created by recording the version number of all the CIs at that time and applying a version label to uniquely identify it. Milestones can occur when software is internally released to a testing organization, or when a

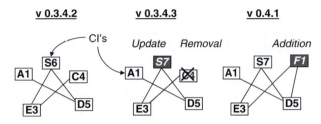

A baseline is an individual or group of CIs
labeled at a key project milestone.

Each version below is a baseline.

Figure 6.3 Transitioning from one baseline to the next

version of software is packaged for release to a customer. For example, a new software version is created and a set of source files and documentation that constitute software release 1.0 are grouped together, given a unique label such as "version 1.0," and are recorded as belonging to the same baseline. This allows all the files constituting software release 1.0, and their correct versions, to always be correctly identified and grouped together. If files belonging to a baseline are added, deleted, or modified, an updated baseline is created with a new version number. Figure 6.3 illustrates this concept.

Once baselines are created and labeled, they are utilized in a project for three primary reasons [1]:

1. Reproducibility
2. Traceability
3. Reporting

These are explained next.

1. **Reproducibility** means that you can reproduce a particular software version or set of documentation when necessary. This is required during product development as well as during maintenance. For example, software is shipped to customers, and different customers may use different versions. In the meantime, the project team is developing a new software release, and as a result is updating many of the CIs used in previous software releases. If a problem is reported by a customer running an older software version, because it was saved as a baseline the older version can by resurrected by the project team and used to identify and repair the source of the problem.

2. **Traceability** means that relationships between various project artifacts can be established and recognized. For example, test cases can be tied to requirements, and requirements to design.

3. **Reporting** means that all the elements of a baseline can be determined and the contents of various baselines can be compared. This capability can be utilized when trying to identify problems in a new release of software. Instead of performing a lengthy debugging effort, differences in source files between the previous and current software versions can be analyzed. This may be enough to identify the source of the problem. If not, knowing exactly what changes occurred can point to potential root causes, speeding up the debugging effort and leading to faster and easier problem resolution. Baselines are also useful to ensure that the correct files are contained in the executable file of a software version. This is used during configuration audits, and is covered in Section 6.2.5.

6.2.3 Change Control

Configuration items undergo change throughout the course of development and maintenance, as a result of error correction and enhancement. Defects discovered by testing organizations and customers necessitate repair. Releases of software include enhancements to existing functionality or the addition of new functionality. *Change control*, also known as configuration control, includes activities to request, evaluate, approve or disapprove, and implement these changes to baselined CIs [2].

The formality of these activities varies greatly from project to project. For example, requesting a change can range from the most informal—no direct oversight for changing a CI—to a formal process—filling out a form or request indicating the CI and reason for change, and having the request approved by an independent group of people before it can be released. Regardless of the formality of the process, change control involves identification, documentation, analysis, evaluation, approval, verification, implementation, and release as described next [2].

Identification and documentation

The CI in need of change is identified, and documentation is produced that includes information such as the following:

• Name of requester

• Description and extent of the change

• Reason for the change (e.g., defects fixed)

• Urgency

• Amount of time required to complete change

• Impact on other CIs or impact on the system

Analysis and evaluation

Once a CI is baselined, proposed changes are analyzed and evaluated for correctness, as well as the potential impact on the rest of the system. The level of analysis depends of the stage of a project. During earlier stages of development, it is customary for a small group of peer developers and/or the project manager to review changes. The closer a project gets to a release milestone, the more closely proposed changes are scrutinized, as there is less time to recover if it is incorrect or causes unintended side effects. At this latter stage, the evaluation is often conducted by a change control board (CCB), which consists of experts who are qualified to make these types of decisions. The CCB is typically comprised of a cross-functional group that can assess the impact of the proposed change. Groups represented include project management, marketing, QA, and development. Issues to consider during the evaluation are as follows:

• Reason for the change (e.g., bug fix, performance improvement, cosmetic)

• Number of lines of code changed

• Complexity

• Other source files affected

• Amount of independent testing required to validate the change

Changes are either accepted into the current release, rejected outright, or deferred to a subsequent release.

Approval or disapproval

Once a change request is evaluated, a decision is made to either approve or disapprove the request. Changes that are technically sound may still be disapproved or deferred. For example, if software is very close to being released to a customer, and a proposed change to a source file requires many complex modifications, a decision to defer repair may be in order so as to not destabilize the software base. The change may be scheduled for a future release.

Verification, implementation, and release

Once a change is approved and implemented, it must be verified for correctness and released.

6.2.4 Version Control

Version control supports the management and storage of CIs as they are created and modified throughout the software development life cycle. It supports the ability to reproduce the precise state of a CI at any point in time. A configuration management system (also known as a version control system) automates much of this process and provides a repository for storing versioned CIs. It also allows team members to work on artifacts concurrently, flagging potential conflicts and applying updates correctly.

A good version control system supports the following capabilities:

1. Repository

2. Checkout/Checkin

3. Branching and merging

4. Builds

5. Version labeling

These are explained in the following sections.

6.2.4.1 Repository

At the heart of a version control system is the repository, which is a centralized database that stores all the artifacts of a project and keeps track of their various versions. Repositories must support the ability to locate any version of any artifact quickly and reliably.

6.2.4.2 Checkout and Checkin

Whenever a user needs to work on an artifact, they request access (also known as *checkout*) from the repository, perform their work, and store the new version (also known as *checkin*) back in the repository. The repository is responsible for automatically assigning a new version number to the artifact.

Files can usually be checked out either *locked* or *unlocked*. When checking out locked, the file is held exclusively by the requester and only that person can make modifications to the file and check in those changes. Others may check out the file unlocked, which means it is read-only and they only receive a copy. Concurrent write privileges can be achieved by branching, which is explained in the next section.

When checking in a file, version control systems record the user making the change and ask the person to include an explanation of why the file was changed and the nature of the changes. This makes it easier to see how a file has evolved over time, who has made the changes, and why they were made.

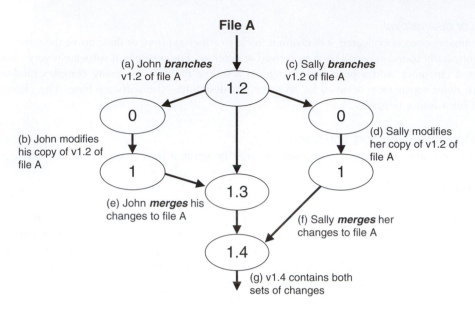

Figure 6.4 Branching and merging changes

6.2.4.3 Branching and Merging

Projects are most often developed by teams of people. Version control systems provide mechanisms to allow team members to work on the same set of files concurrently (*branching*) and correctly apply changes to common files so that none are lost or overwritten (*merging*). This is also known as overwrite safety.

Figure 6.4 depicts an example, in which John creates a *branch* by checking out version 1.2 of file A. A branch is a private work area in a version control system that allows you to make changes to baselined files without conflicting with other team members. John maintains a private copy of the file on his branch and makes his changes. Concurrently, Sally also needs to work on file *A,* so she creates her own branch and checks out version 1.2. Her copy starts out the same as John's since he has not yet checked in his updates. Once John finishes his changes, he checks in his files to the repository, and the file is given a new version number 1.3. Later, Sally finishes her modifications to *A* and wants to check in the file. If the version control system allowed her to just replace the current copy of file *A* (version 1.3, which now includes John's changes) with her copy, John's changes would be lost. Instead, the version control system supports *merging*, which intelligently applies Sally's changes to version 1.3 and creates a new version 1.4 with both of their changes applied correctly. If the set of changes are made to various parts of the same file, the system can usually perform the merge operation automatically. If the changes conflict with each other, as when the same lines of code are changed, the system will ask the user to merge the changes manually. In this case the system will show the user which lines overlap so that person can apply the changes correctly.

6.2.4.4 Builds

Version control systems provide support so as to reliably and reproducibly compile and build the latest version of software files into an executable, usable file. A user can specify which branch of code to build from, allowing concurrent development. In addition to the executable file, builds produce logs containing the file versions comprising the build.

6.2.4.5 Version Labeling

Versions are created by applying a label to all files comprising a software build. The label is usually a version number, such as "version 1.0". This allows software versions to easily be referenced and reconstructed if necessary, and supports the construction of baselines.

6.2.5 Configuration Audits

As defined by IEEE 1028-2008 [3], a software audit is "an independent examination of a software product, software process, or set of software processes performed by a third party to assess compliance with specifications, standards, contractual agreements, or other criteria." In the context of configuration management, the goals of a configuration audit are to accomplish the following:

- Verify that proper procedures are being followed, such as formal technical reviews.

- Verify that SCM policies, such as those defined by change control, are followed.

- Determine whether a software baseline is comprised of the correct configuration item. For example, are there extra items included? Are there items missing? Are the versions of individual items correct?

   Configuration audits are typically conducted by the quality assurance group.

6.2.6 Configuration Status Reporting

Configuration status reporting supports the development process by providing the necessary information concerning the software configuration. Other parts of the configuration process, such as change and version control, provide the raw data. Configuration status reporting includes the extraction, arrangement, and formation of reports according to the requests of users [4]. Configuration reports include such information as the following:

- Name and version of CIs

- Approval history of changed CIs

- Software release contents and comparison between releases

- Number of changes per CI

- Average time taken to change a CI

6.2.7 Release Management and Delivery

Release management and delivery define how software products and documentation are formally controlled. As defined in IEEE 12207-1998 [5], "master copies of code and documentation shall be maintained for the life of the software product. The code and documentation that contain safety or security critical functions shall be handled, stored, packaged and delivered in accordance with the policies of the organizations involved." In other words, policies must be implemented to ensure that once software and documentation is released it must be archived safely and reliably, and can always be retrieved for future use.

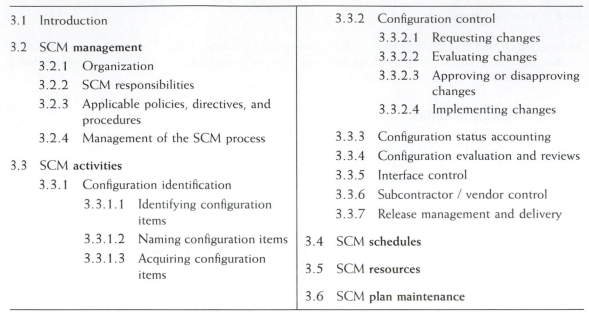

Figure 6.5 IEEE 828-2005 Software Configuration Management Plan table of contents

Source: IEEE Std 828–2005.

6.3 CONFIGURATION MANAGEMENT PLANS

To specify how the software configuration is to be managed on a project, it is not sufficient merely to point to the configuration management tool that will be used. There is more to the process, such as what activities are to be done, how they are to be implemented, who is responsible for implementing them, when they will be completed, and what resources are required—both human and machine [2]. The IEEE has developed a standard for software configuration management plans, IEEE 828-2005. This can be very useful in making sure that all bases have been covered in the process of CM. Figure 6.5 shows the relevant contents of this standard, which are included in Chapter 3 of the plan.

    The topics to be specified in Section 3.3 of the SCMP are largely covered in Section 6.2 of this chapter. Section 3.3.3 of the SCMP documents the means by which the status of SCM is to be communicated (e.g., in writing, once a week). Section 3.3.6 applies if a CM tool is used or if configuration management is handled by a subcontractor. The IEEE standard describes the purpose of each section of the above outline in detail. IEEE 828-2005 is used in the Encounter case study later in this chapter.

6.4 CONFIGURATION MANAGEMENT SYSTEMS

For all but the most trivial application, a configuration management system (also known as a version control system) is indispensable for managing all the artifacts on a project. Microsoft's SourceSafe™ is in common use. CVS is a common environment, as well as Subversion and others.

6.4.1 Concurrent Version System (CVS)

The Concurrent Version System (CVS) is a commonly used, free, open source configuration management system. CVS implements a client-server architecture, with users running client CVS software on their

- **Up-to-date**

  Is identical to the latest revision in the repository.

- **Locally Modified**

  File has been edited but has not replaced latest revision.

- **Needs a Patch**

  Someone else has committed a newer revision to the repository.

- **Needs Merge**

  You have modified the file but someone else has committed a newer revision to the repository.

- **Unknown**

  Is a temporary file or never added.

Figure 6.6 File status possibilities in CVS

machines, and a CVS server storing a repository of project files. Users check out projects (using the *checkout* command); make changes; check in (using the *commit* command); and merge with the changes of others who checked out at the same time (using the *update* command). CVS automatically increments the version number of files or directories (e.g., from 2.3.6 to 2.3.7). The status possibilities for a file are shown in Figure 6.6.

6.5 CASE STUDY: ENCOUNTER VIDEO GAME

What follows is a configuration management plan for Encounter. The Software Configuration Management Plan (SCMP) for Encounter is based on IEEE Std 828-2005 Standard for Software Configuration Management Plans. The table of contents of the relevant sections is outlined in Figure 6.8, which is Chapter 3 of the IEEE specification.

Title	Signature	Date
Engineering Manager	*P. Jones*	6/15/04
QA Manager	*L Wilenz*	6/11/04
Project Manager	*A. Pruitt*	6/7/04
Author	*E. Braude*	6/1/04

ENCOUNTER SOFTWARE CONFIGURATION MANAGEMENT PLAN

APPROVALS

Note to the Student:
It is a good idea to have each team member sign off on the physical document. This process focuses their attention on the fact that they are accountable for its contents, and they will be more likely to ensure that it is the document they intend.

Revision History

This assumes the existence of a method whereby revision numbers of documents are assigned.

Version 1

1.0.0 E. Braude: Created first draft 5/1/98

1.1.0 R. Bostwick: Reviewed 1/10/99

1.1.1 E. Braude: Expanded 3.2 1/18/99

1.2.0 E. Braude: Reviewed for release5/18/99

1.2.1 E. Braude: Final editing4/30/99

Version 2

2.0.0 E. Braude: significant edits of section xx 5/2/99

2.0.1 E. Braude: edits 5/13/04

The table of contents of this SCMP follows that of IEEE standard 828-2005.

3.1. Introduction

This Software Configuration Management Plan (SCMP) describes how the artifacts for the Encounter video game project are to be managed.

3.1.1 Definitions
Approved CIs: CIs signed off by project management
Artifact: A final or interim product of the project (e.g., a document, source code, object code, test result)
Master file: A particular designated file for this project, defined in Section 3.3.1.2

3.1.2 Acronyms
CI: configuration item—an item tracked by the configuration system
CM: configuration management—the process of maintaining the relevant versions of the project
SCMP: the Software Configuration Management Plan (this document)

3.2. SCM Management

3.2.1 Organization

State how this is to be managed. Supply role (s), but no names or responsibilities. Names are supplied in a later section.

A specific engineer, provided by the QA organization, will be designated as the "configuration leader" for the duration of the project.

3.2.2 SCM Responsibilities

State the tasks that each role must carry out. If this is not stated, essential activities will not be done, and some activities will be done by more than one team member. Include backup responsibilities in case the main individual is incapacitated.

3.2.2.1 Configuration Leader

"Responsible" does not necessarily imply that the individual does all of the work—merely that he or she organizes the work and sees to it that the work is done.

The configuration leader shall be responsible for organizing and managing configuration management (CM). Whenever possible, the configuration leader shall discuss CM plans with the development team prior to implementation. He or she will maintain this document (the SCMP). The configuration leader is responsible for the installation and maintenance of the configuration management tool(s) specified in Section 3.2.3. Archiving is to be performed in accordance with department policies 12345.

The SCM leader shall be responsible for acquiring, maintaining, and backing up the configuration tools used. He or she shall also develop a plan of action if tools become unsupported (e.g., by discontinuance of the vendor). Additional responsibilities of the configuration leader are stated in Sections 3.1-3.6.

3.2.2.2 Project Leader
The project leader and his or her manager will take over the configuration leader's function only under exceptional circumstances. They are responsible for knowing all the

relevant means of access to documents throughout the life of the project. The project leader shall ensure that archiving is performed in accordance with the policies in Section 3.2.3 below.

Additional responsibilities of the managers are stated in Sections 3.3.3 and 3.3.4.

3.2.2.3 Engineers

It is the responsibility of each engineer to abide by the CM rules that the configuration leader publishes. Engineers are also referred to "Standard Engineering Responsibilities," document 56789.

Additional responsibilities of the engineers are stated in Section 3.3 below.

3.2.3 Applicable Policies, Directives, and Procedures

> Activities such as CM are generally conducted in accordance with group or corporate guidelines. Student teams should identify and list their policies in this section. Policy 3 should be included.

1. Configuration management for this project shall be carried out in accordance with the corporate guidelines for configuration management, corporate document 7890 version 6 (8/15/98).

2. In accordance with division software improvement policies, midstream and post-project review sessions are required, where improvements to these guidelines are to be documented for the benefit of the organization. These sessions are required to help prepare the division for level 5 CMM certification. The self-assessment results are to be sent to the manager of Software Self-Assessment within three weeks of the assessment session. All "room for improvement" sections are to contain substantive material, with specific examples.

3. All current and previously released versions of CIs will be retained.

4. The master file (defined in Section 3.3.1.2) can be accessed only by the configuration leader and, in his or her absence, the department manager.

5. CM passwords should be changed in accordance with corporate security practices, with the following addition: No password shall be changed until the project leader, his manager, and the manager of QA have all been notified and have acknowledged the notification.

6. The project leader and department manager are to have complete access to all documents under configuration at all times. Access verification form www.ultracorp.division3.accessVerification is to be submitted every two weeks by the project leader to his or her manager.

7. The Encounter project will use SuperCMTool release 3.4, a configuration management product by SuperCMTool.

> These are fictitious names.

8. Archiving is to be performed in accordance with department policies 123456.

3.3. SCM Activities

3.3.1 Configuration Identification

> This section states how configuration items (CIs) come into being and how they get their names. Without such procedures being stated and followed, chaos results.

3.3.1.1 Identifying Configuration Items

The project leader shall be responsible for identifying all CIs. Engineers wishing to propose CIs shall secure his or her agreement, via e-mail or otherwise. If the project leader is unavailable for one business day following the engineer's e-mailed proposal for inclusion, the configuration leader shall have the authority to accept the proposed item.

3.3.1.2 Naming Configuration Items

The configuration leader shall have the responsibility for

labeling all CIs. The file conventions shall be as follows:

Root directory: Encounter

Subdirectory: SRS or SDD or . . .

File N-N-N.xxx corresponding to version N.N.N

For example, version 2.4.8 of the SRS will be on file Encounter/SRS/2_4_8.txt.

The text file Master in the root directory states the versions of the CIs that comprise the current and prior states of the project. For example, Master could include information such as:

The current version of Encounter is 3.7.1. It comprises version 2.4.8 of the SRS, version 1.4 of the SDD.

The previous version of Encounter was 3.6.11. It comprised version 2.4.8 of the SRS, version 1.3 of the SDD.

This information shall be maintained in a table of the following form.

Encounter SRS version SDD version. . . .

Release

3.3.1.3 Acquiring Configuration Items

In specifying this section, imagine the most stressful part of the project, which is the implementation phase, involving several people in parallel. The process has to be very orderly, but it also has to allow engineers reasonable access to the parts of the project so that they can start work quickly.

Engineers requiring CIs for modification shall check them out using SuperCMTool's checkout procedure. Note that SuperCMTool prompts the user with a form requesting an estimate of how long the checkout is anticipated, and stores this information for all requesters of the CI. Anyone requiring a CI that is currently checked out should negotiate with the current owner of the CI to transfer

control through SuperCMTool. A read-only version of the CI is available to all engineers. Under no circumstances may an engineer transfer a CI directly to anyone.

3.3.2 Configuration Control

This section spells out the process whereby configuration items are changed. This process should be flexible enough to allow quick changes, but controlled enough to keep changes very orderly so that they improve the application, not damage it.

3.3.2.1 Requesting Changes As specified in the Software Project Management Plan (see Part III), the team will designate an "inspector" engineer who is allocated to each team member. Before requesting a change, engineers must obtain an inspection of the proposed change from an inspection team or, if this is not possible, from their inspector engineer. To request the incorporation of a changed CI into the baseline, form www.ultracorp.division3.Encounter .submitCI must be submitted to the configuration leader and the project leader, along with the changed CI and the original CI.

3.3.2.2 Evaluating Changes

For larger projects, a group of people, often called the Change Control Board, evaluates and approves changes. Student teams must make this process reasonably simple.

The project leader or designee will evaluate all proposed changes. The project leader must also specify the required quality standards for incorporation.

3.3.2.3 Approving or Disapproving Changes

The project leader must approve proposed changes. If the project leader is unavailable for three business days following the submission of a proposed change, the configuration leader shall have the authority to approve changes.

3.3.2.4 Implementing Changes

> To avoid chaos, it is natural to give to the CM leader the responsibility for incorporating changes; this can create a bottleneck at implementation time, however. Before this "crunch" occurs, the CM leader should find ways to remove this bottleneck by distributing as much work as feasible to the engineers making the changes.

Once a CI is approved for incorporation into the baseline, the configuration leader shall be responsible for coordinating the testing and integration of the changed CI. This should be performed in accordance with the regression test documentation described in the Software Test Documentation. In particular, the configuration leader shall coordinate the building of a version for testing. Version releases must be cleared with the project leader, or with the manager if the project leader is absent.

3.3.3 Configuration Status Accounting

The configuration leader shall update the configuration summary at least once a week on the project configuration Web site www.ultracorp.division3/Encounter/Configuration. SuperCMTool's status report will be a sufficient format for the summary.

3.3.4 Configuration Audits and Reviews

> In industry, random audits are often employed. They are not commonly conducted by student teams due to a lack of resources, although some teams have carried them out successfully. Periodic reviews, as part of the regular team meetings, do not take much time, and they are recommended.

The project manager shall schedule a review by the CM leader of the configuration at least once every two weeks, preferably as an agenda item for a regularly scheduled weekly project meeting. The CM leader shall review CM status, and report on the proposed detailed procedures to be followed at code and integration time.

Configuration efforts will be subject to random audits throughout the project's life cycle by the IV&V team.

3.3.5 Interface Control

The CM system interfaces with the project Web site. This interface shall be managed by the configuration leader.

3.3.6 Subcontractor/Vendor Control

The configuration leader shall track upgrades and bug reports of SuperCMTool. He or she should be prepared with a backup plan in case the maintenance of SuperCMTool is discontinued. This plan is to be sent to the project leader within a month of the project's inception.

3.4 SCM Schedules

> The SCM schedule can be provided here, or combined with the project schedule in the SPMP. In the latter case, this section would not repeat the schedule, but would merely point to the SPMP.

The schedule for configuration management reporting, archiving, and upgrading is shown in Figure 6.7.

3.5 SCM Resources

The configuration leader will require an estimated average of six hours a week to maintain the system configuration for the first half of the project, and twelve hours a week for the second half. We have chosen not to call out separately the time spent by the other team members on configuration management.

3.6 SCM Plan Maintenance

> All project documents undergo change throughout the duration of the project. The SCMP is especially sensitive to change, however, because it controls change itself.

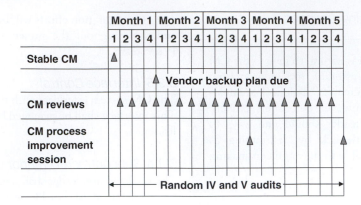

Figure 6.7 Configuration management schedule

Due to the importance of a stable SCM plan, all changes to this document must be approved by the entire CM team.

In view of the software development organization's goal to attain CMM level 5, the configuration leader will do the following for the CM process improvement sessions:

- Review the effectiveness of this plan

- Quantify losses due to defects in this plan

- Review the effectiveness of Super CMTool

- Investigate the literature for new CM methods; quantify the costs and benefits of improvements

- Investigate new CM tools

- Suggest specific improvements to this CM process

- List the benefits of improvements

- Provide cost estimates on effecting the improvements

- Prioritize the cost/benefit ratios of all the suggested changes

6.6 CASE STUDY: ECLIPSE

CONFIGURATION MANAGEMENT IN ECLIPSE[1]

Open source projects such as Eclipse are developed by geographically dispersed engineers who have different source code access requirements. Most are developing their own plug-ins, which are extensions to existing Eclipse code and functionality, and only require access to Eclipse source code for debugging their work. Others may want to change existing Eclipse source code if they are fixing a bug, or add code if they are developing a feature. These developers require write-access to Eclipse code.

Source code is managed in Eclipse using CVS (Concurrent Versioning System), which is the de facto version control system for open source projects. Eclipse integrates a built-in CVS GUI, making version control very easy to use. CVS implements a client-server architecture, with the Eclipse repository housed on a central server at dev.eclipse.org that stores all the Eclipse source code.

In general there are two classes of Eclipse users as follows:

1. Those that want to read and/or modify Eclipse code but don't have write access to the CVS repository.

2. Those that do have write permission for the Eclipse source code and can modify and update the CVS repository. These people are call *committers*.

The following is quoted from [7] and describes these two classes of users.

---

[1] This section is based on information from [6].

Anonymous CVS

For people who actually want to change Eclipse code but who do not have the required commit rights in that area, all elements of the Eclipse project are available via anonymous access to the development CVS repository. Using anonymous access you can checkout code, modify it locally, but cannot write it back to the repository. This is handy if you would like to fix a bug or add a feature. Get the code via anonymous access, do your work, and then pass the work on to a committer for inclusion in the repository. . . .

All committers must use SSH (Secure SHell) to access the CVS repository if they wish to use their user id and password (i.e., if they want to write to the repository).

Full CVS

Developers with commit rights have individual user ids and passwords in the Eclipse project development repository. As a committer you can use SSH (Secure SHell) to connect to the CVS repository as follows. . . . . Once your information is authenticated, you can browse the repository and add projects to your workspace. If you do some changes that you'd like to contribute, after testing and ensuring that you have followed the contribution guidelines, you are free to release your changes to the repository. Of course, you can only release changes to projects for which you have commit rights.

Note that you can use the SSH protocol and your Eclipse user id to access projects for which you are not a committer, but you will not be able to release changes.

These points are summarized in Figure 6.8.

VERSION NUMBERING

Eclipse plug-ins use a version-numbering scheme that captures the nature of the changes implemented by the plug-in. Version numbers are composed of four parts as follows:

Major, minor, service, and qualifer. *Major, minor,* and *service* are integers, and *qualifier* is a string.

- Major—this number is incremented each time there is a breakage in the API

- Minor—this number is incremented for "externally visible" changes

- Service—this indicates a bug fix or other change not visible through the API

- Qualifier—this indicates a particular build

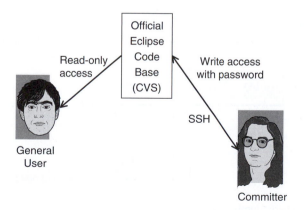

Figure 6.8 Eclipse configuration management

First development stream

> 1.0.0

Second development stream

> 1.0.100 (indicates a bug fix)
> 1.1.0 (a new API has been introduced)
> The plug-in ships as 1.1.0

Third development stream

> 1.1.100 (indicates a bug fix)
> 2.0.0 (indicates a breaking change)

The plug-in ships as 2.0.0

Maintenance stream after 1.1.0

> 1.1.1

The plug-in ships as 1.1.1

Figure 6.9 Eclipse plug-in version numbering 1 of 2

Source: Eclipse Wiki, http://wiki.eclipse.org/Version_Numbering.

The example shown in Figure 6.9 and 6.10, taken from http://wiki.eclipse.org, shows how the version number changes as a result of plug-in development. The description shows that bug fixes, new application programming interfaces, and shipping to the community are reflected in the numbering in particular ways.

6.7 STUDENT TEAM GUIDANCE: CONFIGURATION MANAGEMENT

Student teams should create a Software Configuration Management Plan (SCMP) for their project using IEEE Std 828-2005 as a template and the Encounter SCMP in Section 6.5 guidance. The rest of this section describes how to organize for this task.

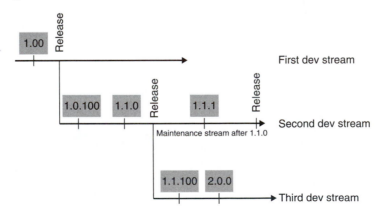

Figure 6.10 Eclipse plug-in version numbering 2 of 2

Source: Eclipse Wiki, http://wiki.eclipse.org/Version_Numbering.

1. Roughly sketch out your SCMP
   - Determine procedures for making changes.
   - Omit tool references unless already identified one.
   - See the case study for an example.

2. Specify what you need from a CM tool
   - For class use, maybe only locking and backup.

3. Evaluate affordable tools against needs and budget
   - Commercial tools are in wide use.
   - For class use, try free document storage Web sites; simple method of checking out, e.g., renaming, can be too simple.

4. Finalize your SCMP

Figure 6.11 Planning configuration management

Figure 6.11 shows how teams can go about deciding their configuration management methods.

When there is insufficient time to learn a CM environment, teams have succeeded reasonably well with simple Web sites, such as www.yahoogroups.com, that allow document storage. A simple checkout system is needed, one of which is to change the document type. For example, when the SQAP is checked out to Joe, the file is changed from *sqap.txt* to *sqap.joe*. Although configuration management applies to both documents and source code, the file-naming convention usually has to be planned separately. For example, we cannot change *myClass.java* to *myClass.joe* without disrupting compilation. Some groups maintain two directories. One contains the current baseline, which cannot be changed without a formal process. The other directory contains versions that are currently being worked on.

Trial CM tools or free ones such as CVS and Subversion are available. Google supports free document hosting with Google Docs and has support for version control. Be sure that your process does not rely on excessive manual intervention, and that it does not result in a bottleneck where one person is overloaded. If you are considering using a tool, be sure that the length of the learning curve justifies its use. There are many other software engineering aspects to learn besides using a particular CM tool. Whatever system you select, try it out first on an imagined implementation. Make sure that the process is smooth. You do not want to worry about your CM process during the implementation phase, when time is limited. In the work world, however, professional CM tools are a necessity.

6.8 SUMMARY

Software configuration management (SCM) is a process for managing all the artifacts produced on a software project, including source code, specifications, and supporting software. Planning for SCM starts early in a project, starting with the Software Configuration Management Plan. It specifies the SCM activities to be implemented throughout development and software maintenance, such as identification, change control, version control, audits, status reporting, and release management.

Early in a project, artifacts are identified as configuration items (CI) to be stored in a repository and managed. After a CI is reviewed and approved it becomes part of a baseline and is officially managed by SCM policies. Artifacts go through inevitable change, being newly created or modified due to either error correction or enhancement. SCM defines activities to request, evaluate, approve or disapprove, and implement changes to baselined CIs.

A key requirement of SCM is the ability to reproduce the precise state of all CIs at any point in time. A version control system (also known as a configuration management system) automates much of this process and provides a repository for storing versioned CIs. It also allows team members to work on artifacts concurrently, flagging potential conflicts and applying updates correctly. Version control systems include functionality for checking in and checking out files, branching and merging, building the software, and creating software versions.

Configuration audits, which are typically conducted by the quality assurance group, are used to ensure that agreed upon SCM procedures and policies are being followed, and that software being produced is comprised of the correct components.

Configuration status reports support the audit process by providing a detailed history for each CI including when it was created and modified, how it was modified, and by whom.

6.9 EXERCISES

1. In your own words, define the term *configuration item* and describe its purpose.

2. Why is it necessary for compilers to be identified as configuration items? Describe a scenario that illustrates when this is necessary.

3. Describe the four goals of configuration management in your own words, and explain why each is important.

4. If you are developing a software application using an incremental process, at what points would you minimally create baselines?

5. Explain the difference between change control and version control.

6. Agile processes promote continuous integration, which results in branching and merging at very frequent intervals (as often as every few hours). Describe one advantage and disadvantage of branching and merging so frequently. Describe one advantage and disadvantage of branching and merging less frequently.

7. As mentioned in the Team Guidance section (Section 6.6), for small teams it may not be necessary to utilize an automated configuration management system. Describe the process you would follow to perform branching and merging without such a system.

8. Research a configuration management system such as Subversion or CVS. Describe how it implements the seven SCM activities listed in Section 6.2.

TEAM EXERCISE

For the team exercise, consider as a group how you will perform it, check the hints below, and then carry out the assignment.

CM Plan

Produce a software configuration management plan for your team project using IEEE standard 828-1990. The case study should guide your team, but your document will be more specific, reflecting the particular resources available to you. Do not include material unless it contributes to the document's goals. Avoid bottlenecks and unnecessary procedures. Include procedures for what to do if people cannot be reached and deadlines loom.

Before you begin, estimate the number of defects per page the team thinks it will discover during the final review. Keep track of and report the time spent on this effort by individual members and by total team effort. State the actual defect density (average number of defects per page). Assess your team's effectiveness in each stage on a scale of 0 to 10. Summarize the results using the numerical results, and state how the team's process could have been improved.

Criteria:

1. Practicality: How well does the plan ensure that documents and their versions will be secure, coordinated, and available? (A = plan very likely to ensure coordination and availability)

2. Specifics: How specific is the plan in terms of suitably naming places and participants? (A = no doubt as to what engineers must do)

3. Process assessment and improvement: To what degree did the team understand the strengths and weaknesses of its process, and how specific are its plans for improvement? (A = full, quantitative understanding, with plans for improvement very specific and realistic)

Hints for Team Exercise

Do not fill in sections that are as yet unknown; add only parts that you are confident of being able to implement within the semester. Make your plan realistic. For example, don't state that "all other team members will review each contributor's work" unless you are reasonably sure that this can be done within the probable constraints of your project. It is too early to make any assumptions about the architecture and design of the application.

BIBLIOGRAPHY

1. Bellagio, David, and T. Milligan, "Software Configuration Management Strategies and IBM Rational Clearcase: A Practical Introduction," IBM Press/Pearson plc, 2005, p. 7.
2. "IEEE Standard for Software Configuration Management Plans," *IEEE Std 828-2005*, August 2005.
3. "IEEE Standard for Software Reviews and Audits," *IEEE Std 1028-2008*, August 2008.
4. Hass, Anne M. J., *"Configuration Management Principles and Practice,"* Addison-Wesley, 2003, p. 25.
5. "Systems and software engineering—Software life cycle processes," *IEEE Std 12207-2008* Second edition, January 2008, p. 69.
6. Eclipse, http://www.eclipse.org [accessed August 13, 2009].
7. Eclipse, http://www.eclipse.org/eclipse/ [accessed August 13, 2009].

7

Principles of Software Project Management I: Organization, Tools, and Risk Management

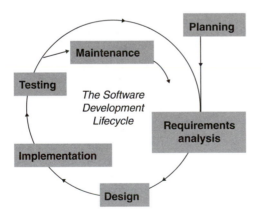

- How are software development projects organized?

- What is an appropriate team size?

- What happens when teams are geographically distributed?

- What tools and techniques are available to support projects?

- How do you handle risks?

- How are projects managed in practice? In student teams?

Figure 7.1 The context and learning goals for this chapter

Software project management is the process of planning, organizing, and monitoring the development of a software project from its inception to its completion. It incorporates a set of tools and techniques practiced by the person or people responsible for a project during every phase of development. The person responsible is the *project manager* (a term usually used for larger projects) or *team leader* (a term typically used for smaller

- **Customers** are **seldom sure** of what they want.

- Customers **change** their requirements and plans may not be updated.

- It is **hard to estimate** up front the magnitude of the effort required.

- It is **hard to coordinate** the many **requirements**, the **design** elements corresponding to each requirement, and the corresponding **code**.

- There may be unforeseen **technical difficulties** to overcome.

- It is not easy to maintain constructive **interpersonal** team **dynamics**. Time pressures cause stress, and team members have differing opinions.

But these obstacles can all be overcome!

Figure 7.2 Some challenges of software project management

projects or teams). Sometimes the person responsible is called the project manager and has one or more subordinate team leaders. In all cases, these people practice project management. Critical to the success of a project is the organization of the project team. Many different organizational structures are possible, each with a set of strengths and weaknesses.

It is very difficult to deliver a quality, fully accepted software application on time and within budget. Figure 7.2 gives some of the main reasons. Software project management addresses these issues by incorporating a range of activities and structure into a project, including project organization, tools, and support, management of project risks, project estimation and scheduling, project documentation and tracking. These are summarized in Figure 7.3 and explained in this chapter.

- **Organization**
  - How is the project team structured?

- **Project Management Tools**
  - What tools are available to support project management?

- **Risk Management**
  - How are risks to the project's success identified and mitigated?

- **Estimation**
  - How long will the project take to complete and how many resources are required?

- **Scheduling**
  - What are the different parts of the project, in what order will they be completed, and who will work on each part?

- **Documentation and Monitoring**
  - How is a project plan created, and how is the plan monitored to ensure that the project is progressing on time and within budget?

Figure 7.3 What does software project management address?

The rest of this chapter focuses on the organizational structures, tools, and risk management that support project management. The next chapter, which completes our discussion of project management principles, covers methods that can be employed, including estimation, scheduling, and planning.

7.1 SOFTWARE PROJECT ORGANIZATION

The way in which a company is organized has a direct bearing on how projects are executed. Some companies organize around their projects. In these companies project managers have great autonomy, with team member directly reporting to them. Other companies organize around functional areas such as development, marketing, finance, and so on, giving project managers responsibility for monitoring and reporting on project progress. Other companies employ an organization that mixes both of these. In general, there are three types of organizational structure: *project-oriented*, *function-oriented*, and *matrix*. We examine each of these in the sections that follow.

7.1.1 Project-Oriented Organization

In *project-oriented organizations*, personnel are organized around the projects of the company. When a new project is initiated, a project manager is assigned to head up the project. One of their first tasks is forming the team, which is made up of new hires or people who are finishing other projects. The project team comprises people from multiple functional areas such as marketing, finance, development, and so on. Team members report to the project manager, who is their ultimate boss. They are attached in all ways to a particular project, and have no organizational affiliation with people on other projects. This type of organization is illustrated in Figure 7.4.

The principal reason to organize around projects is to develop loyalty to the project rather than to the functional manager [1]. Since employees are dedicated to a single project, they can focus their time and energy on that project. This increases the predictability of schedules as there is less chance of team members spending unscheduled time on other projects. However, this type of organization has the potential disadvantage of isolating engineers professionally and reducing the amount of reuse and professional stimulation between projects as a result of this isolation.

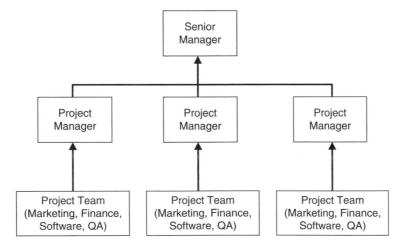

Figure 7.4 Project-oriented organization

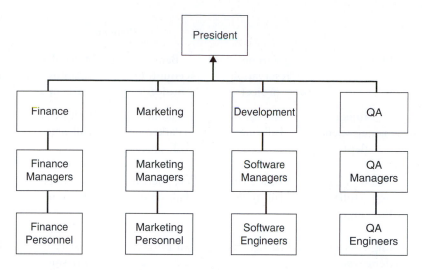

Figure 7.5 Function-oriented organization

7.1.2 Function-Oriented Organization

Function-oriented organizations are a very common type of structure. A company is organized into groups based on their functions, such as marketing, finance, development, QA, and so on. This type of structure is illustrated in Figure 7.5.

In this form, functional organizations have projects, but the scope of their projects is limited to the boundaries of their group responsibilities. As an example, if a software functional group is working on the user interface (UI) software of a larger software product, only the UI software being developed is considered the current project for that group.

Functional managers in this kind of organization act as project managers, responsible for their projects as well as the hiring, firing, and salary of their team members. Managers may be responsible for multiple projects. This structure has the advantage of clear and responsible decision-making channels. However, because managers are responsible for multiple projects, their knowledge of projects is necessarily limited by their available time. In addition, they must weigh carefully the needs of each and ensure that they don't favor one over the other. If one of their projects is falling behind schedule, for example, they may shift personnel from another project to the lagging project. This may cause a delay in the other project.

7.1.3 Matrix Organization

Matrix organizations are a cross between project- and function-oriented organizations. They try to gain the advantages of both project-oriented and function-oriented organizations. In a matrix organization, employees belong to a functional group (e.g., marketing, engineering) but are loaned to projects based on their expertise. Thus, a software engineer's supervisor—who is responsible for evaluating that person—would be a member of the software engineering functional unit. Within each project on which the person is working, however, he or she would be supervised by a project leader. Engineers are usually involved on a regular basis with one project, sometimes two, but seldom more.

Figure 7.6 illustrates the reporting structure of a matrix organization. In this structure, a project manager is assigned to each project. For example, Oscar Mart is a member of the marketing department and assigned to the airline reservation project, headed by Al Pruitt. For all project-related activities, Oscar reports directly to Al.

Matrix Organization		Project			
		Airline reservation project	**Bank accounting project**	**Molecular analysis project**	**Fluid mechanics project**
Functional Unit	**Project management dept**	Al Pruitt Full time	Quinn Parker Full time	Ruth Pella Full time	Fred Parsons Full time
	Marketing dept (Julia Pitt, mgr)	Oscar Mart Full time	Pete Merrill Full time	Sue More Half time	Elton Marston Full time
	Engineering dept (Joe Roth, mgr)	Hal Egberts	Ben Ehrlich	Mary Ericson	Len Engels . . . . . .

Figure 7.6 Matrix organization

However, Oscar's boss is Julia Pitt, a manager in the marketing department. Julia would consult with Al when doing performance appraisals.

An advantage to this approach is that project managers maintain focus and have responsibility for the success of their projects. Functional managers are focused on the content of their functional area and can more easily coordinate the efforts of their group members, some of whom may work on multiple projects. For example, the software manager of a database group might recognize that multiple projects have similar requirements for accessing a database. The manager can coordinate a software design that is general enough to be used by multiple projects. We will consider team size next.

7.1.4 Agile Organization

Agile teams consist of technical people. Their principal nontechnical contact is with the customer. Still, functions of the kind mentioned above continue to be required. An example is finance. Every organization needs to understand the costs and benefits of projects. Agile teams become adept at estimation, and so finance people—who are not part of the agile team itself—have good short-term data and forecasts but are required to be agile as well. This is because agile teams are not plan-driven. The upshot is that the nontechnical people must base their work on good but relatively short-term data. They perform their work by interacting with the customer and with the development team.

7.2 TEAM SIZE

To be precise, a "team" is a group of people who work closely together on a daily basis. One might imagine that the appropriate size of a team depends strongly on the size of the application (large teams for large applications, etc.) but this is not so. Large teams (not necessarily *groups*—keep the definition of "team" in mind) have the advantage of dividing the work into many parts but the disadvantage of communication that is

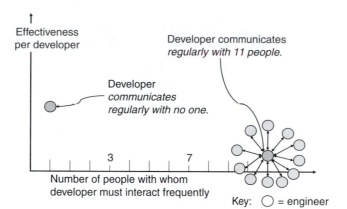

Figure 7.7 Options for team size showing extremes

time-consuming and error-prone. A significant aspect of such communication is the need for team members to explain what they are doing. Having to keep forty people up-to-date on a daily basis, for example, requires a lot of meeting time. In his classic work, *The Mythical Man-Month* [2], Fred Brooks pointed out that adding people to a failing project invariably makes matters *worse*. In other words, for many projects the disadvantage of increased communication channels, which are particularly heavy during the learning process of new team members, may often outweigh the advantage of division-of-labor.

What is the optimal size of a team? This is a matter of trading off the benefit of having many helping hands against the cost of communication among them. The optimal size depends on the nature of the project: Routine projects can usually benefit from larger team sizes because a lot is understood about what each person should do. Let's consider extremes for a typical project, shown in Figure 7.7. The vertical axis reflects the effectiveness per developer.

Experience of the authors and others shows that the number of developers with whom each developer needs to interact on a regular basis should normally be between three and seven. (Humphrey [3] suggests four to eight.). Formal studies on the effect of team size on performance are rare. At one extreme shown in Figure 7.7, the developer works without interacting regularly with anyone on an individual basis. Although no time is spent on communication, such isolation typically results in misunderstandings of what is required of that developer, leading to a relatively low level of effectiveness. At the other extreme, the developer has to interact regularly with so many individuals that there is not enough time left to perform development itself, again resulting in relative ineffectiveness. In particular, true "regular communication" could entail speaking with someone for an average of approximately two hours a week. If an engineer were in regular communication with ten others, then fully one half of his time would be spent communicating, leaving only half of the week for his individual contribution. Project organizers, whether planning twenty-person or hundred-person projects, have to account for this. Figure 7.8 illustrates these points as follows. If you pick a team size—such as three—and draw a vertical line, it intersects the blue area between two values of "effectiveness per developer." The inexactness of this measure leads us to talk in terms of ranges rather than absolutes. We are interested in picking a team size that yields the most efficient work on a per-developer basis. Figure 7.8 shows this occurring between team sizes of about three and seven.

As the number of participants in a project grows, an organization where everyone is a peer becomes impossible to use because the number of communication links (between all of the pairs) grows with the square of the number of participants. Three people entail three lines of communication, four people entail six, five people ten, six people fifteen: n people require $(n - 1) + (n - 2) + \cdots + 1 = n(n - 1)/2$ lines of communication. This grows with the square of n. One hundred people would have to participate regularly in 4,950 lines of communication! One alternative for large projects is the organization shown in Figure 7.9, in which peer

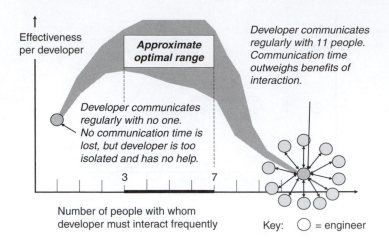

Figure 7.8 Range of optimal size for beneficial interaction

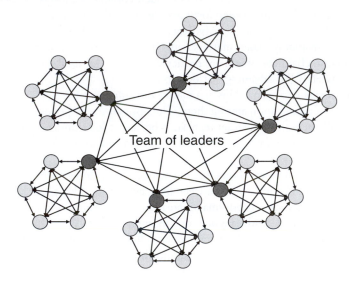

Figure 7.9 A peer organization arrangement for larger projects

groups remain small, and one member of each group is designated the communicator with the other peer groups. This type of organization tries to preserve the benefits of small teams, but it harnesses the large number of people to build a large application. Note that team leaders have double the amount of communication time than non-team leaders.

7.3 GEOGRAPHICALLY DISTRIBUTED DEVELOPMENT

Independent of whether a team is project-oriented, function-oriented, or matrixed, team members may be either collocated or geographically distributed. The latter presents a unique set of challenges.

Managers naturally try to make use of worldwide programming talent to optimize costs and improve quality, a process sometimes called *offshoring*. The Internet and collaboration tools have made offshoring increasingly practical. The per-hour costs of remote programmers are traded off against the communication

- Same office area
  - + ideal for group communication
  - − labor rates suboptimal

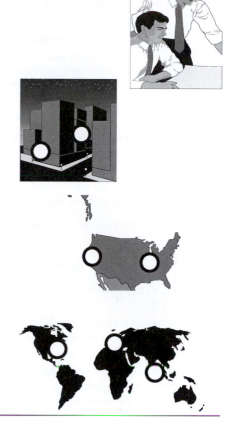

- Same city, different offices communication fair
  - + reasonably good communication
  - + common culture
  - − labor rates suboptimal

- Same country, different cities
  - + common culture
  - − communication difficult

- Multi-country
  - + labor rates optimal
  - − communication most difficult
  - − culture issues problematical

Figure 7.10 Possible locations of distributed team

Source: Graphics reproduced with permission from Corel.

problems incurred by physical remoteness. This trade-off depends largely on the degree of need for continual interaction with the customer. Options for remote teams are illustrated in Figure 7.10.

Bob Schudy, a colleague of the authors who has extensive experience with offshoring, lists its advantages:

- Work can be done around the clock
- Good-quality work is available
- There is potential for cost saving

He lists the following as disadvantages:

- Increased difficulty for the offshore personnel to understand requirements
- The lack of informal "chatter" that can smooth progress
- Time differences for (virtual) meetings

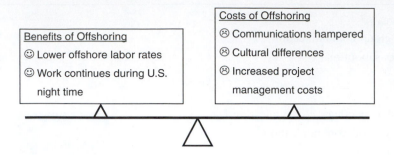

Figure 7.11 To offshore or not to offshore

- Surprises in skill sets
- Traveling ills, especially for westerners in the East

Schudy includes the following in his remedies for these disadvantages.

- Meet face-to-face initially and periodically.
- Use various media (chat, VOIP, conference calls, etc.).
- Make sure there is strong onsite management.

Some of the trade-offs that are accounted for in deciding whether and how much to offshore are shown in Figure 7.11.

Figure 7.12 is an example of how a project can be distributed among "near-shore" (same country; remote location) and offshore. Figure 7.13 shows how tasks could be allocated in a distributed development project. The particular allocations are shown as examples only, and were quoted by a group at IBM.

IBM lists the methods in Figures 7.14, 7.15, and 7.16 for dealing with distributed development. The word "requirements" in the figures refers to what is needed about the process, not the requirements of any one application. GDD stands for geographically distributed development. UML is a design notation covered in this book.

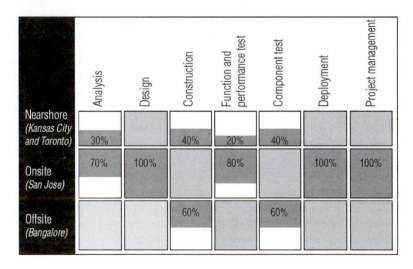

Figure 7.12 Example of how tasks can be allocated in a distributed development project.

Source: IBM, copyright © International Business Machines Corporation, reprinted with permission, http://www3.software.ibm.com/ibmdl/pub/software/rational/web/guides/GC34-2500-00.pdf.

In-house team	Remote subcontractor
• **Business analysis** • **New feature** development and related testing • **Requirements**: capturing, documenting, and managing • System **architecture**, modeling • **Project management**	• **Testing** on pre-release builds • **Testing** maintenance releases of current version • Build and deployment • Selected project management • **Maintaining** current version • **Unit testing** components modified during maintenance • Creating and modifying requirements for maintenance

Figure 7.13 An allocation of tasks

Source: IBM, copyright © International Business Machines Corporation, reprinted with permission, http://www-128.ibm.com/developerworks/rational/library/apr05/cammarano/index.html.

REQUIREMENTS	IBM RESPONSE
United teams despite diverse languages and cultures	• Enable browser-based access to the same knowledge base for all teams • Provide easy access to guidelines, template and tool mentors based on underlying best practices • Visually communicate discipline workflow and interactions with the Unified Modeling Language (UML)
Reduction in work transfer issues	• Implement a framework based on core process workflows from business modeling through deployment • Use a phased approach to software development that details execution for each discipline
Easy-to-navigate process that is not overwhelming for users	• Jump-start planning and get new team members up to speed fast with knowledge assets and guidance • Allow users to create personal process views that are central to individual needs • Provide intuitive navigation with a browser-based interface
Demonstrated progress toward expected return on investment for GDD projects	• Track metrics throughout the project life cycle • Report on variance measurements and adjust process to achieve desired results • Track project progress and quality through quantitative analysis
Ability to assess and manage distributed resources efficiently	• Maintain a broad and deep understanding of an organization's capacity, skills inventory, total workload and resource demand • Optimize skill usage with resource planning to align mission-critical resources with high-priority projects

Figure 7.14 Tools and methods for distributed development, IBM, 1 of 3

Source: IBM, copyright © International Business Machines Corporation, reprinted with permission, http://www3.software.ibm.com/ibmdl/pub/software/rational/web/guides/GC34-2500-00.pdf.

Demonstrated progress toward expected return on investment for GDD projects	• Track metrics throughout the project life cycle • Report on variance measurements and adjust process to achieve desired results • Track project progress and quality through quantitative analysis
Ability to assess and manage distributed resources efficiently	• Maintain a broad and deep understanding of an organization's capacity, skills inventory, total workload and resource demand • Optimize skill usage with resource planning to align mission-critical resources with high-priority projects
Scalable project management solution	• Centralize sensitive schedule, budget and resource data while allowing secure, high-performance access anywhere in the world • Implement native scheduling, resource loading and "what-if" scenarios that avoid performance issues by integrating with third-party scheduling products
Consistently executed processes	• Capture and reuse successful GDD engagement models, work breakdown structures and workflows to ensure execution against IT governance requirements and best practices • Enable reusable project templates and task guidance based on a proven process, so teams never have to start planning from scratch
Accurately tracked labor costs for in-house or external resources	• Accurately track labor expenses and budget for time and materials or fixed-bid resources

Figure 7.15 Tools and methods for distributed development, IBM, 2 of 3

Source: IBM, copyright © International Business Machines Corporation, reprinted with permission, http://www3.software.ibm.com/ibmdl/pub/software/rational/web/guides/GC34-2500-00.pdf.

REQUIREMENTS	IBM RESPONSE
Quick and easy Implementation to start collaborating in days, not months	• Facilitate discussions, set up chat rooms and combine team calendars with ready-to-use templates • Leverage out-of-the box functionality that users can customize themselves • Centralize installation on one server
Consolidated work area where teams can more effectively communicate and collaborate on project issues	• Create a centralized location to post and share project documents that can be viewed and modified by other team members • Share team member project calendars • Track feedback from other team members • Enable the creation of forums and participation in threaded discussions • Allow team members to share files in real time via Web conferencing

Figure 7.16 Tools and methods for distributed development, IBM, 3 of 3

Source: IBM, copyright © International Business Machines Corporation, reprinted with permission, http://www3.software.ibm.com/ibmdl/pub/software/rational/web/guides/GC34-2500-00.pdf.

REQUIREMENTS	IBM RESPONSE
On demand communication options for distributed team members	• Let users know which team members are available for collaboration through integrated presence awareness • Provide instant messaging for real-time, person-to-person communication • Leverage browser-based conferencing to share presentations and meeting materials
Ability for all disparate project members to securely connect to the team workplace through the intranet, Internet or mobile devices	• Enable full-featured browser-based and mobile access to presence, instant messaging and team spaces

Figure 7.16 (*Continued*)

7.4 THE TEAM SOFTWARE PROCESS

Teams avoid reinventing procedures that are common to several software development projects: Organizations create procedures or guidelines in advance for teams to apply. Watts Humphrey's *Team Software Process*[SM] (TSP) [3] does this in a detailed manner. The TSP provides guidance to groups on each of the project development phases after requirements analysis. Humphrey has reported encouraging results in establishing maturity goals and procedures for software teamwork. The objectives of the TSP are shown in Figures 7.17 and 7.18. Whether or not a team uses the TSP, much can be learned from it. TSP shares several characteristics with agile teams, such as the autonomy of teams. TSP is heavily metric-oriented, and although agile methods are not, they do take seriously the velocity measure.

The TSP's emphasis on team initiative and bottom-up interaction encourages an increased degree of professionalism among software engineers. For example, Humphrey states that it is unprofessional for engineers to provide management with schedules that cannot be accomplished, even when requested to do so. He counsels negotiation in such a situation. The philosophy here is similar to that for agile projects.

• Build self-directed teams
  • 3–20 engineers
  • establish *own* goals
  • establish *own* process and plans
  • track work
• Show managers how to manage teams
  • coach
  • motivate
  • sustain peak performance

Figure 7.17 Objectives of the Team Software Process, 1 of 2

Source: Graphics reproduced with permission from Corel.

- Accelerate CMM improvement

  - make CMM 5 "normal"

- "Provide improvement guidelines to high-maturity organizations"

- "Facilitate university teaching of industrial-grade teams"

Figure 7.18 Objectives of the Team Software Process, 2 of 2

Professionalism, Humphrey reminds us, involves an obligation to serve society responsibly, in addition to serving employers. Also noteworthy is the TSP's emphasis on "coaching" by management external to the team. Management is expected not simply to give orders and specify deadlines, but to provide guidance, tools, and other required resources. In this respect, TSP is better able to handle teams with varying degrees of experience and skills. TSP is organized around iterations of the waterfall sequence; it requires that the team "launch" each iteration at a meeting where a number of predefined issues are addressed. Humphrey provides numerous detailed scripts and checklists to support the TSP. Figure 7.19 summarizes these points regarding TSP.

The phases can be iterated several times, requiring several launches. Launch issues to be settled are shown in Figure 7.20.

Humphrey recommends that the items listed in Figure 7.21 be produced by each phase launch. Much of this is covered by procedures and IEEE documents discussed in this book.

7.4.1 Introductory Team Software Process (TSPi)

Formal training for TSP is beyond the scope of a student team working together during a software engineering course. For example, it requires the already extensive Personal Software Process. The *TSPi* is a scaled-down version of the TSP designed to fit in an academic semester. The TSPi roles are *team leader*, *development manager, planning manager, quality/process manager,* and *support manager*. In the TSPi the "support manager" is responsible for obtaining and supplying all the tools and environments, such as compilers, for example.

Humphrey describes a specific semester-long schedule for the TSPi, consisting of three iterations (he calls them "cycles") as shown in Figure 7.22.

The idea of this schedule template is that data obtained from each cycle is used to estimate the metrics for the next cycle. Cycle 1 is comparatively long because it includes the team's first progression through the stages. It is intended to be a "minimal function working subset of the final product." Cycle 3 is long enough to

- Team initiative

- Bottom-up interaction

- Professionalism among software engineers

- Negotiate schedules

- Emphasis on "coaching" by management Provide guidance, tools, and other required resources

- Participants required to be PSP trained

- Organized around iterations Each requires a "launch"

- Numerous detailed scripts

Figure 7.19 TSP practices

☐ Process to be used

☐ Quality goals

☐ Manner of tracking quality goals

☐ How team will make decisions

☐ What to do if quality goals not attained
  ○ **fallback positions**

☐ What to do if plan not approved
  ○ **fallback positions**

☐ Define team roles

☐ Assign team roles

Figure 7.20 Issues to settle at TSP launch

Source: Humphrey, Watts S., ''Introduction to the Team Software Process (The SEI Series in Software Engineering),'' Addison-Wesley, 2000, p. 496. Graphics reproduced with permission from Corel.

wrap up the job completely. This leaves a relatively short middle cycle. "Strategy" (phase 1 of an Iteration in Figure 7.22) refers to the overall way in which the team will go about building the cycle in question. This requires a high-level discussion of the requirements, a conceptual design, and an overall assembly plan for the components. The results are then made into the concrete plan (phase 2), the written requirements (phase 3), and so on.

7.5 SOFTWARE PROJECT TOOLS AND TECHNIQUES

Project managers and teams use a variety of tools and techniques to manage a software project, such as CASE tools, build vs. buy decisions, language selection, decision making with triage, and the use of project variables. Each is described in the sections that follow.

1. Written team goals

2. Defined team roles

3. Process development plan

4. Quality plan

5. Project's support plan computers, software, personnel, etc.

6. Overall development plan and schedule

7. Detailed plans for each engineer

8. Project risk assessment

9. Project status report

Figure 7.21 Artifacts to be produced at launch

Source: Humphrey, Watts S., ''Introduction to the Team Software Process (The SEI Series in Software Engineering),'' Addison-Wesley, 2000, p. 496.

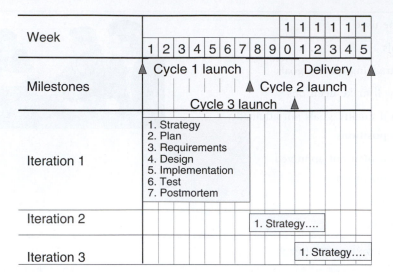

Figure 7.22 TSPi cycle structure (Humphrey)

Source: Humphrey, Watts S., "Introduction to the Team Software Process (The SEI Series in Software Engineering)," Addison-Wesley, 2000, p. 496.

7.5.1 Tool Selection

A number of vendors sell tools and environments for helping engineers to develop software applications. These are sometimes referred to as computer-aided software engineering (CASE) tools, and sometimes as "integrated tools." Many are packaged with or connected with development environments such as Microsoft's Visual Studio. They may also be a collection of tools obtained from unrelated sources. Figure 7.23 lists some possible tools. They include scheduling tools such as Microsoft Project, configuration management tools such as SourceForge or CVS, requirements management tools such as Rational's RequisitePro, design representation, typically with UML tools such as Borland's Together, code-building tools like Ant, and testing support tools such as Rational's TestManager. Large projects simply cannot be managed without at least some of these components; in particular, configuration management tools are indispensable.

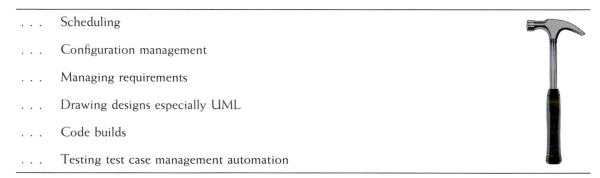

. . .   Scheduling

. . .   Configuration management

. . .   Managing requirements

. . .   Drawing designs especially UML

. . .   Code builds

. . .   Testing test case management automation

Figure 7.23 Potential CASE tool components

Source: Graphics reproduced with permission from Corel.

	Build cost	Buy cost	Comments
	(in thousands)		multi-year costs not accounted for
Supplies	$ 0	$40	Purchase Ajax engine
First-person perspective	$ 5	$ 0	Ajax has this feature
3-D	$10	$ 1	Customize Ajax application
Light reflection	$15	$10	Customize Ajax application
TOTALS	$30	$51	

Build, do not buy

Figure 7.24 Example of build vs. buy decision making for a video game graphics engine

7.5.2 Build or Buy Decisions

Tools and applications that promise to help or form the basis for new applications are often available. For example, in planning for a Web-based auction application, we would compare the purchase of ready-made auction software with developing our own application from scratch. Typically, we delay these decisions until the requirements are known, but they are discussed here since they are a part of project management.

A rational manner for approaching this kind of decision is to make a list of expenses and to estimate the magnitude of each alternative. An example is shown in Figure 7.24, which illustrates the decision-making process concerning the purchase of the (hypothetical) Ajax graphics software that would help us enhance the graphics of our video game.

Figure 7.24 reduces the decision to a comparison of numbers, which is a common way of deciding among alternatives. In other words, it computes the bottom line with and without purchasing Ajax's software. It breaks out the relevant desired graphics features and estimates the cost of each. Ajax implements Feature 1, first-person perspective, completely (i.e., continually displays the view of the scene from the player's perspective). On the other hand, Ajax does not do a complete job of handling 3-D (Feature 2), so we will have to program to compensate for this. Finally, we need light reflection (Feature 3), where the scene gives the impression of a light source shining onto it from a single direction. Ajax helps here, but we will have to perform considerable programming to make it work. The table in Figure 7.24 could be an appendix to the project plan or the Software Design Document. A more realistic version of the table would compare the costs on a multiyear basis, and would include maintenance expenses. The more features we are required to implement ourselves, the less attractive the purchase.

Many decisions can be framed in a cost comparison form like this. Maintaining a written record of decisions such as quantitative build-or-buy trade-offs helps in communicating these decisions to the team and others. The form can be refined and updated as more information becomes known, and it aids postmortems and process improvement.

7.5.3 Language Selection

Although the identification of an implementation language or languages is frequently a design decision, languages are often identified near the beginning of the project. Sometimes this decision is straightforward, as when the organization mandates a language, or when a language is the only one capable of implementing the

Factor	Weight (1-10)	Benefit of Language 1 1 to 10 = best	Benefit of Language 2 1 to 10 = best
Internet-friendly	3	8	2
Familiarity to development team	8	3	9
Compilation speed	5	2	8
Runtime speed on processor p	1	7	3
	Score	$3*8+8*3+5*2+ 1*7 = 65$	$3*2+8*9+5*8+ 1*3 = 121$

Figure 7.25 Example of method for deciding language choice

requirements. Sometimes, however, the implementation must be chosen from several alternatives. A common way to decide among alternatives is to first list the factors involved, and then to give factor each a weight (measure of importance). After that, each alternative is scored relative to each factor. Calculations are then made that produce a total score for each alternative. Figure 7.25 shows examples of factors and weights that could enter into such a determination. The weights are factors in arriving at the bottom line. For example, the score for language 1 is $3*8+8*3+5*2+1*7$ (weights underlined).

Decision-making tables such as this are not substitutes for making judgments: they merely decompose large decisions (e.g., what language to choose) into smaller ones (e.g., Java is more Web-friendly than C++). Such decompositions provide more stability, but the conclusions that they provide are sensitive to the weighting chosen, the factors selected, and the judgments made. Their results should be compared with common sense conclusions.

7.5.4 Decision Making with Triage

Executing projects is frequently an overwhelming experience. For example, a "to do" list of wants and needs accumulates quickly, grows during the project more than it shrinks, and can easily induce a feeling of futility. The natural way to deal with this is to prioritize. A complete prioritization is frequently overwhelmed by events, however. For example, if we have a list of 100 things to do, and time for probably only 20 of them, then it is a waste of time to meticulously order all 100. *Triage* can be useful for situations like this.

Instead of a lengthy decision process, triage requires one to make no more than two decisions about each item, as shown in Figure 7.26. Once this has been performed, items from the "do at once" category are

---

• *Among top items in importance?*

   If so, place it in ⟦do at once⟧ category

• Otherwise, *could we ignore without substantially affecting project?*

   If so, place it in ⟦last to do⟧ category

• Otherwise (*do not spend decision time on this*)

   Place in ⟦middle⟧ category

Figure 7.26 Using triage in project management

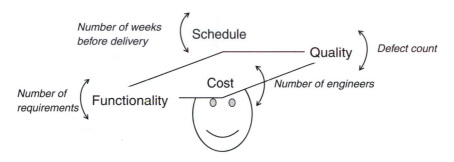

Figure 7.27 Variables available to the project manager

carried out until they are exhausted (if ever), and then we move on to the middle list, and so on. When necessary, items can be prioritized within their category. The benefit of this is that little time is wasted in splitting hairs or wondering about the exact order of actions that will never be performed. As reported in *Business Week* [4], for example, triage teams were used by Microsoft in combing through bug reports during the debugging of Windows^{TM} 2000.

Next, we consider what tools the project manager has at hand to steer his or her project to success.

7.5.5 Project Variables

To achieve project objectives, the project leader has four variables that conceivably can be manipulated: *cost*, *schedule*, *quality*, and *functionality*. As Figure 7.27 suggests, this is something of a balancing act, because there are many trade-offs among these four attributes.

For example, if the project leader is asked to spend less time producing the application (affecting *schedule*), he or she has to negotiate for reduced requirements (affecting *functionality*), increased defect expectations (affecting *quality*), or increased labor (affecting *cost;* assuming that more people can be used effectively) in order to offset the reduced time.

Project management deals constantly with trade-offs among these variables. To make the best decisions, we quantify these trade-offs whenever we can. One way to visualize them is by means of a "bulls-eye" diagram, suggested for this purpose by Humphrey. In a bulls-eye diagram, each of the variables is plotted by means of an axis originating at the center. This is shown for the *cost* parameter in Figure 7.28.

The axes are drawn symmetrically relative to each other. In the bulls-eye diagram shown in Figure 7.29, there are four variables, so that they form 90-degree angles.

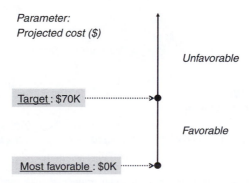

Figure 7.28 Introduction to bull-eye figure for project variables

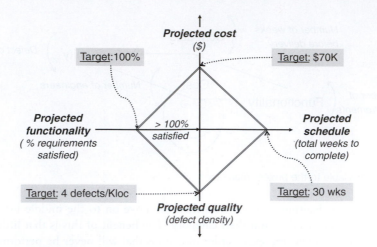

Figure 7.29 Bulls-eye framework example for project variables

The variables have to be arranged so that on each of these axes, the *origin* is the *most favorable* value, and the target value is marked on each axis the same distance from the origin, forming a quadrilateral. (If there were five variables, they would form a regular pentagon, etc.) For example, on the "projected functionality" axis, the origin denotes "many more than the designated requirements satisfied," while the unit mark represents "100% of the requirements satisfied." The actual values could lie outside the polygon if they exceed goals, as shown in Figure 7.30.

The status of a project can be visualized using the solid polygon obtained by joining the values on the axes and filling in the resulting polygon. The more the resulting polygon lies within the original regular polygon, the healthier the project. The example project shown in Figure 7.30 falls short on two of the variables but performs well for the other two. This visualization helps a project manager to alter priorities and achieve goals in an even manner. For example, the leader of the project represented in the figure should cut costs and push for an increase in functionality, even if this results in higher defect rates and longer project duration.

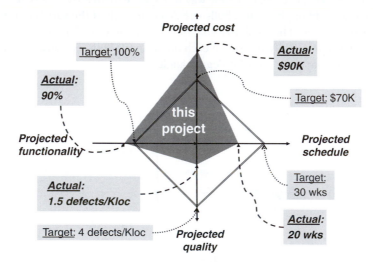

Figure 7.30 Bulls-eye figure for project variables on a particular project

Organizational

1. The team may not have the required **Java skills** to execute the job on time because several of them have not used Java in a business environment.

2. We may **lose** a team **member**.

Technical

3. An off-the-shelf **database management system** may not be versatile enough to cover the types of operations required of a video store.

4. We intend to use **Web services**, but no one in the team has used these before.

Figure 7.31 Example risks in video store application

7.6 RISK MANAGEMENT

All projects involve a degree of *risk*. These are issues that can potentially cause problems such as a delay of the schedule or increased project costs. Figure 7.31 shows some risks from the video store example.

We try to confront risks as soon as possible rather than waiting for them to confront us in the process of building the application. This is called *risk management*, and it consists of the activities in Figure 7.32.

Perhaps the hardest part of risk management is identification, because it requires imagining parts of the process that may not seem at first to harbor any risks. Once a risk is identified, it is important and very useful to express the risk with as much precision as possible. For example, "a team member may get sick" is too vague a description. Much better would be "sick time will exceed the company norm by 50% due to an unusual number of young parents in the team."

Figure 7.33 illustrates a way to thinking about risks. It shows two obstacles to a project.

We generally deal with risks with one of two different strategies. They are *conquest* (such as building a traffic light at the road) or *avoidance* (e.g., routing the path around the house). These two strategies are illustrated in Figure 7.34.

Teams develop a plan to address each risk and assign an individual who sees to it that the plan is carried out. The challenge here is to develop a concrete plan and avoid general statements such as "we will all learn Java." For example, we can address the "inadequate Java skills" risk mentioned in Figure 7.31 by conquest: "Tom, Sue, and Jack will pass level 2 Java certification by December 4 by attending a Super Education Services

1. **Identify** risks by imagining all worst-case scenarios: lasts for approximately first third of project.

2. **Analyze** each risk to understand its potential impact on the project.

3. Typically too many risks given time. Hence, **prioritize** identified risks to enable focus on most serious.

4. In dealing with each risk, choose to **conquer** or **avoid** it. Conquering a risk means investigating it and taking action so that the event does not materialize. Avoiding means changing plans so that the issue never occurs.

5. Finally, develop a **plan** to retire each risk.

Figure 7.32 The main risk management activities

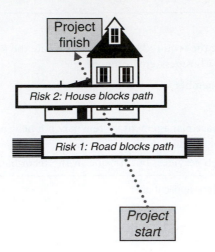

Figure 7.33 Retirement by conquest or avoidance—risk examples

Source: Graphics reproduced with permission from Corel.

Intermediate Java course." Alternatively, the risk can be retired by avoidance: "Use C++ instead of Java" (assuming that the team is skilled in C++). A retirement strategy for the "Web services knowledge immature" risk is to set up a couple of sample Web services and write access code for key video store functions that use them. If the results are satisfactory, we will have employed risk retirement by conquest.

Table 7.1 illustrates one way to perform risk prioritization. First, the risks themselves should be described fully. The priority depends on factors such as the likelihood of the risk and the seriousness of its impact on the project. A high-priority task has a low-priority *number* because people usually refer to their "highest priority" as priority number 1. The more expensive it is to deal with a risk, the lower its priority. In particular, when managing a risk becomes a very large amount of work, we may be better off not working on it

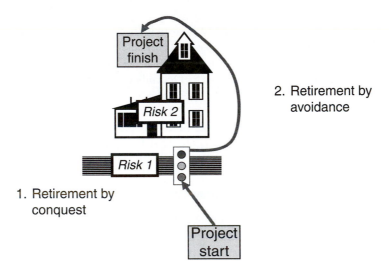

Figure 7.34 Retirement by conquest or avoidance

Source: Graphics reproduced with permission from Corel.

Table 7.1 A way to perform risk prioritization

No.	Title	Estimated likelihood of occurring (L: 1-10 with 1 lowest like-lihood)	Estimated impact (I: 1-10 with 1 lowest impact)	Estimated cost of managing (M: 1-10 with 1 lowest cost)	Priority number (lowest number handled first) $(11-L)*(11-I)*M$	Retirement plan	Responsible person	Target completion date
1	Insufficient Java skills: See note 1	8	9	9	$3 * 2 * 9 = 54$	See note 3	Jared	10/15
2	Web services immature: See note 2	3	7	2	$8 * 4 * 2 = 64$	See note 4	Jen	8/3
...								

in advance at all, but simply dealing with the issue involved when it actually arises. For example, if the only way to anticipate a risk is to construct an expensive simulation, then we may simply have to accept the risk.

Note 1. The risk is that the team does not have enough skill in Java to handle the programming required by this project within the time required.

Note 2. The risk is that although Web Service technology is a good choice, technically speaking, it is new to the industry at the time of this project, and its immaturity may create difficulties.

Note 3. Jen, Oscar, and Alf should pass level two Java certification by October 15 by attending an Ajax Education Services Intermediate Java course.

Note 4. Jen will install three Web services typical of DVD inventory management, and run 1,000 typical transactions against these, gathering timing data.

Not every risk can be dealt with earlier than its natural occurrence. To take an extreme example, suppose that the team has a week to add significant functionality to an application. The goal would be: Add the capability to show future investment growth graphically for a financial application. There is probably little to be gained from performing risk analysis and retirement in this case. Since the time frame is so short, the team's time may be better spent simply starting the design at once. Doing so takes a chance, but the time required for risk analysis may not leave enough time to do the job.

7.7 STUDENT TEAM GUIDANCE: ORGANIZING THE SOFTWARE PROJECT'S MANAGEMENT

This section describes how the student team organizes for the development task, provides a hypothetical account of interactions among students, and guides students in producing a Software Project Management Plan.

7.7.1 Team Guidance—Student Team Organization

Student teams are usually organized as peers. To make peer teams effective, the team leader encourages consensus but keeps the schedule firmly in mind, making clear and timely decisions when required. In student teams, team leaders tend to intervene too little. Meetings drag on unreasonably in the quest for consensus or agreement, and the team leader is not experienced enough to make a resolution. Being firm without alienating team members is a valuable skill. A key to this is ensuring that team members' opinions are respected— whether adopted or not.

Figure 7.35 lists the steps for organizing a team, particularly a student team.

One effective management arrangement for a team is to pair up developers by having them work together some—or even all—of the time. The latter is called *pair programming*. Another way is to designate team members as leads for the project phases with a backup for each. Typically, the lead and the backup work together, or the backup serves as a continual inspector, ready to take over the lead role if necessary. The project arrangement shown in Figure 7.36 is designed to make each person the backup for the activity on which his or her primary activity is dependent.

Once a project leader has settled the procedural aspects of team organization, it is time to consider what really counts with team members: how they feel about what they are doing. If a person belongs to a motivated and well-organized team, he will probably enjoy his work and the team will probably produce a good product. People are motivated when they are respected and are engaged in an activity that they feel enriches them. Part of each member's job is to create those conditions for himself and others. The project leader creates a well-organized project by setting schedules and limits, with the team's agreement. In particular, when it comes to meetings the issues in Figure 7.37 can be useful.

In the case of student teams, *uneven contribution* is often a major problem: some team members may feel that a member is not contributing enough. A team member who feels this way should discuss the issue with the project leader. If there is general agreement about this, the project leader should speak privately to the

1. **Select** team **leader.**
   Responsibilities:
   - ensure that all project aspects are active
   - fill all gaps

2. **Designate** leader **roles** and document responsibilities.
   team leader: *proposes and maintains*   ... SPMP
   configuration management leader: ... SCMP
   quality assurance leader: ... SQAP, STP
   requirements management leader: ... SRS
   design leader: ... SDD
   implementation leader: ... *code base*

3. **Specify leaders' responsibilities.**
   - propose a straw-man artifact (e.g., SRS, design)
   - seek team enhancement and acceptance
   - ensure that designated artifact is maintained and observed
   - maintain corresponding metrics if applicable

4. Designate a **backup** for each leader

Figure 7.35 One way to organize a team

individual. If no significant change is observed in that person's behavior after about a week, the project leader should confirm the team's concern and then discuss the issue with the instructor. Instructors will either remove the individual from the team or discuss ways to apportion credit accordingly.

7.7.2 Team Guidance—Team Meetings

One activity regularly required of project managers is to hold meetings. Figure 7.38 lists some good meeting practices from which all team members can benefit.

The items marked with a single asterisk should be performed before the meeting. Since groups are not particularly good at creating artifacts from scratch (especially designs), it is far better for someone to bring to the meeting a tentative ("straw-man") version of the artifact to form the basis for discussion. For example, the design leader brings a tentative design, or the team leader brings a tentative work breakdown. The version should not be overly specific, because there must be plenty of room for input by the members.

Figure 7.36 A way to back up leaders within a team

- Develop an **agenda** in advance of meeting, with everyone's agreement.

- Set **time limits** for meeting as a whole and for each agenda item. Allow extra ten or fifteen minutes for unanticipated items.

- Designate someone to take **minutes**, at least for action items.

- At meeting, **begin by** briefly **reviewing** the agenda and time limits.

- Designate someone to **watch time** and warn of time limits.

- Insist on one person speaking at a time. **Listen** to people, even if their ideas seem outrageous. (Probably aren't.)

- Move unproductive discussions **offline**.

Figure 7.37 Planning and conducting meetings

Many meeting participants, but especially students, complain that meetings last too long without accomplishing enough. When the approximate time for discussions is agreed to in advance, however, members tend to focus on the issues to be resolved, and meetings can be quite effective. Deciding when to allow further discussion and when to break it off is a duty of the team leader. The keys to doing this are whether the discussion is productive, and whether the discussion of the present topic is preventing the discussion of more important ones, given the time remaining. It is also the leader's task to ensure that the discussion remains focused and that a conclusion is reached. At times, the leader must step in and make a decision, because consensus is not always possible. The member recording action items also records decisions taken. This should generally be done in a crisp form—minutes are meant primarily to remind everyone of the decisions made.

1. *Distribute start time, end time, and agenda with approximate times.
   o List important items first.

2. *Ensure that "straw-man" items are prepared.

3. Start on time.

4. Have someone record action items.‡

5. Have someone track time and prompt members.

6. Get agreement on the agenda and timing.

7. Watch timing throughout, and end on time.
   o Allow exceptions for important discussion.
   o Stop excessive discussion; take offline.

8. Keep discussion on the subject.

9. **E-mail action items and decision summary.

*in advance of meeting   ‡actions members must perform   **after meeting

Figure 7.38 Team guidance—team meetings

1. Get agreement on agenda and time allocation

2. Get volunteers to:

    . . . record decisions taken and action items
    . . . watch time and prompt members

3. Report progress on project schedule — *10 min*

4. Discuss strawman artifact(s) — *x min*

5. Discuss risk retirement — *10 min*

6. , 7., . . . <more agenda items> (Include metrics and process improvement?)

n. Review action items — *5 min*

Figure 7.39 Specifying agendas

One good management practice is to create and follow agendas for meetings. Some items, such as concise status reviews, are almost always appropriate. Risk retirement (covered in Section 10.4) should be a mandatory agenda item at most meetings during the first third of the project. Metrics and process improvement are sometimes appropriate topics. These are discussed after a phase has been completed, not necessarily at every meeting. An example of a generic agenda is shown in Figure 7.39.

7.8 SUMMARY

Software project management is the process of planning, organizing, and monitoring the development of a software project from inception to completion. A project is typically headed by a project manager, who is responsible for the daily project activities.

Companies can be organized in several different ways, each having an effect on how a project team is organized and run. In a *project-oriented* organization, people are organized around the projects of the company. Every employee is assigned to a project, which is their primary focus. In a *function-oriented* organization, people belong to a functional group such as marketing or software development. Each functional group has its own projects centered around their area of responsibility. Managers assume the role of project managers. A *matrix* organization is a cross between project- and function-oriented organizations. Employees belong to a functional group (e.g., marketing, engineering) and are loaned to projects based on their expertise. They directly report to their functional manager, who is responsible for directly supervising them. They also indirectly report to the project manager, who is responsible for the daily activities of the project.

The size of a project team has a direct effect on the success of a project. Teams that are large can divide the work into manageable parts. However, large teams have the disadvantage of requiring communication that is time-consuming and error-prone. Experience shows that the optimal number of people with whom a person needs to interact with on a regular basis should normally be between three and eight.

Not all project teams are collocated. With the advent of using remote developers, project teams may be split across continents. This is known as offshoring. There are many advantages to using remote teams, such as cost savings and the benefit of quality work. However, there are disadvantages to be overcome, such as time zone differences, cultural differences, and potential communication difficulties. Setting up regular face-to-face meetings and having strong on-site management are key elements to making offshoring work.

Watts Humphrey's *Team Software Process*[SM] (TSP) defines a set of detailed procedures for building project teams, establishing team goals, and distributing team roles. It emphasizes team initiative and encourages an increased degree of professionalism among software engineers. As an example, Humphrey states that it is unprofessional for engineers to provide management with schedules that cannot be accomplished, even when requested to do so.

Project managers and teams carry out many tasks as part of their job, including project scheduling, configuration management, requirements management, drawing designs, building code, and testing. As much as possible, they utilize automated tools to support their work. These tools are sometimes called computer-aided software engineering (CASE) tools.

When planning and developing an application, existing software may be available that can form the basis for the new application. In order to determine whether it makes sense to build from scratch or leverage existing software, project teams make a rational decision by comparing the costs of each option.

Another decision to make is the use of programming language. A decision-making table helps to determine the pros and cons of different language choices.

Project managers have several variables at their disposal that are manipulated as they manage a project: *cost, schedule, quality,* and *functionality.* Changing one variable has a direct effect on the others. For example, a project manager may want to speed up a project by pulling in the completion date (schedule). In that case, one or more of the other variables must be adjusted—you cannot pull in a schedule unless you change something else. The manager must reduce *functionality,* add resources (*cost*), or reduce *quality.* Bulls-eye figures can be useful in visualizing these variables in a project and as an aid in seeing how each variable affects the others.

All projects contain some amount of *risk,* which are issues that can potentially cause problems such as a delay of the schedule or increased project costs. Risks are of two basic types. *Organizational* risks are primarily caused by people's behavior, such as resigning from the company. *Technical* ones are caused primarily by errors in hardware or software, such as a defect in a third-party application. Early in a project risks are identified and mitigation strategies created. Each risk is actively managed throughout the project.

7.9 EXERCISES

1. a. Describe in your own words the structure of a project-based organization, and explain how it promotes the successful delivery of software.
   b. Name two long-term disadvantages of a project-based organization.

2. a. Describe in your own words the structure of a function-based organization, and explain how it promotes the successful delivery of software.
   b. Name two long-term disadvantages of a function-based organization.

3. a. Describe in your own words the structure of a matrix organization, and explain how it promotes the successful delivery of software.
   b. Name two long-term disadvantages of a matrix organization.

4. Write a paragraph explaining why adding people to a project does not necessarily improve its schedule—and may worsen it.

5. Consider a project team you have been a member of, either as part of a student team or in industry. Describe the organization of the team, and describe in sufficient detail two aspects that worked well and two that did not work well.

6. Consider a software project under development, with half of the engineers in one time zone and the other half in another time zone twelve hours away. How would you recommend the project

team be organized? Describe two challenges that need to be overcome due to the time-zone difference.

7. a. Explain how a bulls-eye diagram can help visualize the progress of a software project.

 b. Suppose you are managing a project that has the following goals:

 -Cost: 100K
 -Schedule: 12 months
 -Quality: 12 defects/Kloc
 -Functionality: 90% requirements implemented

 Draw a bulls-eye diagram that shows only one of these goals being met or exceeded.

8. Why plan for risk identification and retirement when developing a project plan? In a paragraph or two, answer this in your own words.

9. Describe a kind of project under which risk identification and retirement would probably *not* pay off. Explain.

10. Suppose that your team is tasked to implement a system that provides Web-based books. The application is intended to execute on desktops, be downloadable, and be automatically upgraded over time via the Internet. You are to assume the following:

 i. The team includes employees who are based at a new offshore site.

 ii. The application is to be ready in a month.

 iii. Preliminary plans call for a Java implementation on a PC model that is due to arrive in two weeks. No one in the team is well versed in Java. They all know C++ well.

 You are concerned about the risks associated with items (i) and (iii) above. Explain the kinds of risks these are, your specific responses, and the kind of solutions you are proposing.

11. You have been tasked to build a system for managing online DVD rentals. Describe four plausible risks and indicate how you would retire them. Be as concrete as possible in describing the risks.

BIBLIOGRAPHY

1. Heldman, Kim, *"PMP Project Management Professional Exam: Study Guide,"* Sybex/Wiley Publishing Inc., 2007, p. 17.
2. Brooks, Frederick P., *"The Mythical Man-Month: Essays on Software Engineering, Anniversary Edition,* Addison-Wesley, 1995.
3. Humphrey, Watts. S., *"Introduction to the Team Software Process (The SEI Series in Software Engineering),"* Addison-Wesley, 2000, p. 496.
4. *"The Mother of All Software Projects," Business Week,* February 22, 1999.

8

Principles of Software Project Management II: Estimation, Scheduling, and Planning

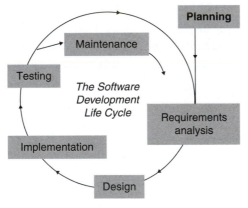

Planning

Maintenance

Testing

The Software Development Life Cycle

Requirements analysis

Implementation

Design

- How do you estimate the cost of a software job?

- What are good ways to go about creating a project schedule?

- What does a Software Project Management Plan look like?

- How are projects planned in practice?

- What are good ways for student teams to plan their projects?

Figure 8.1 The context and learning goals for this chapter

This chapter explains the methods that project managers use to estimate the costs of a project and ways to schedule it. It also explains how to write a project plan.

8.1 COST ESTIMATION

The process of estimating project costs (i.e., for fixed capabilities, quality level, and schedule) often starts at the inception of a project and continues even after coding has begun. There are several specific techniques used to estimate costs that are described in the following sections. Before doing so, however, let's examine how precise we can expect such estimates to be.

8.1.1 Estimate Precision

When a project is initiated, the team can typically have only a vague idea of its cost. The more we learn about the requirements for the product and the more design we perform, the more precise we can be about its cost. This is illustrated in Figure 8.2. Since complete precision is a practical impossibility in most cases, a range is a good way to express projected cost. There is always a need to estimate a "ballpark range" from a summary requirements statement, hence the cost estimation following conceptualization shown in Figure 8.2.

Our assumption here is that the goal consists of attaining a set of capabilities rather than starting with a fixed amount and asking what capabilities can be implemented for that amount (a related but different process).

The fourfold estimation error shown in Figure 8.2 is from a study reported by Boehm [1]. For an application that will eventually cost $100,000, for example, estimates made after the application's concept has been developed can be as low as $25,000 and as high as $400,000! We use various techniques to sharpen our estimate of a project's cost as early as possible, which amounts to reducing the height of the vertical lines in Figure 8.2. Only at the latter end of implementation can we have complete confidence in our estimates. (The estimates are far less useful at that time, however, since most of the funds will already have been spent!)

It puzzles some people that we can even begin to think about the costs of a project without detailed requirements, but this is a common practice in other fields. For example, one can gain a rough estimate of the cost of building a house without any design or detailed requirements. One can use rules of thumb such as

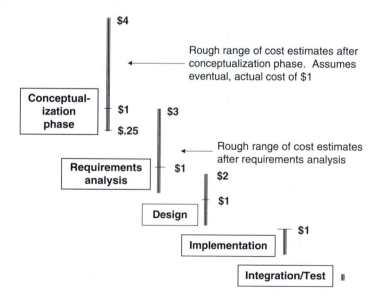

Figure 8.2 Range of error in estimating costs narrows as the project progresses

"houses in this area cost about $100 per square foot to build," and so a 1,000-square-foot house will cost about $100,000.

A good way to approach project cost estimation at the very early stages of a project is to develop estimates in several independent ways and then combine the results. One can even weigh the estimates obtained according to one's level of confidence in each of them.

It takes experience to properly use cost estimation tools, and the first time one uses them the results are often unreliable. With time, feedback, and calibration, however, one learns to use them with increasing precision. The rest of this section describes the techniques used to estimate projects in summary form. The chapter then describes them in detail.

8.1.2 Estimation Methods

Cost estimation methods for agile projects, described in Section 8.1.6, focus on estimating the upcoming iteration ("sprint" in scrum terms), based on its required user story or stories, as well as experience from past iterations. These are small-scale estimates but it is part and parcel of the agile philosophy that large projects are composed of small deliveries. Now let's turn to estimation of projects in the large that are not necessarily agile in whole or in part. Whether or not one actually uses the methods described, they do contain many hard-won ideas that can be configured for various situations, including variations in agile estimation.

Figure 8.3 shows a typical road map for the early estimation of project cost and duration. The next section shows an example of the use of lines of code and past projects. The function point methodology and COCOMO (Constructive Cost Model) are explained below.

8.1.3 Estimating Lines of Code without Function Points

This section discusses ways to estimate lines of code at a very early stage, well before any design has been performed. Once design work is performed, the methods are based on the parts of the design and become far more precise, as indicated in Figure 8.2.

Several estimation methods, notably the COCOMO and COCOMO II model, depend on the number of lines of code. "COCOMO" stands for Boehm's "Constructive Cost Model" [1]. At the very early stages of a project, COCOMO may not sound very useful because coding is a long way off when one is in the project planning stage. By comparing the product with other products, however, estimating lines of code may well be feasible. For example, we could estimate that our current satellite control job is comparable to our last satellite job, which required 3 million lines of FORTRAN. However, our current job has the additional requirement of being able to monitor hurricanes. It may be possible to roughly estimate the size of this additional piece based on other hurricane trackers (700,000 lines of FORTRAN, for example). When implementation languages change, industry-standard language conversion factors are used.

---

1. Use comparisons with past jobs to estimate cost and duration directly or to estimate lines of code. and / or
   Use function point method to estimate lines of code.
   i.   Compute unadjusted function points.
   ii. Apply adjustment process.
2. Use lines of code estimates to compute labor and duration using COCOMO (II) formulas.

Figure 8.3 A roadmap for estimating the cost of a software project

Organizations working above Capability Maturity Models level 1 must be able to record the person-hours and duration of the parts of jobs. In the absence of such data, we would have to compare our Encounter video game, for example, with other games. It is difficult, impossible even, to obtain data directly from companies other than one's own, although trade publications and general industry studies sometimes provide partial data. For example, we may know from industry announcements that "BugEye Inc." has worked on its new game for two years: The announcement may even mention a number of programmers. Such data is suspect, however, since companies regard their development knowledge as a corporate asset, and commonly exaggerate or underreport numbers as the case may be.

In the absence of historical data, it may be necessary to compare the project with related projects, (simulations, for example, in the case of our video game). Let's say that we have very little experience programming games, and some experience programming simulations and Java. Our lines-of-code estimation may have to be something like the following:

> I once wrote a nongraphical simulation of a simple queue in C++, which required about 4-8 pages of code. At about 30-50 non-comment lines per page, this totals 120–400 lines. We will assume that Java requires the same number of lines. The first commercial release of Encounter has 4–15 such queues and 30–90 additional components of comparable size to make it interesting, so that yields between $[(120 \text{ lines}) \times (34 \text{ components})]$ minimum and $[(400 \text{ lines}) \times (105 \text{ components})]$ maximum as our range, or approximately 5,000 to 42,000 lines of code. The use of graphics multiplies the effort by 1.5 to 4, depending on the degree of sophistication, so this gives us a range of $1.5 \times 5,000$ to $4 \times 42,000 = 7.5$ to 170 K-lines (thousands of lines) of code. (*Note:* The case study in this book encompasses a prototype, which is far less ambitious than the version on which this estimate is based.)

By documenting such data on a spreadsheet, we establish a baseline, and we can then sharpen our estimates as the project goes forward. Note that the range 7.5 to 170 K-lines is consistent with Figure 8.2, in which a 16-fold range in estimates is expected at the conceptualization stage. The preceding calculation is a bottom-up approximation, since it estimates the cost of the whole from the cost of the parts.

An example of a top-down approximation follows, using industry data (or, preferably, historical data from the organization performing the work). Suppose we know that a very good video game required the services of 5–20 expert programmers for 1–2 years. Since we can invest only 1/10 of the amount that was invested in that game, we will assume that ours will have about 1/10 of its capability. Assuming 5–25 lines of (fully tested!) Java code per day, this yields

$$(1/10 \text{ capability of the famous game}) \times (5 - 25 \text{ lines per day}) \times (5 - 20 \text{ programmers}) \times (1 - 2 \text{ years})$$
$$\times (48 - 50 \text{ weeks per year}) \times (35 - 60 \text{ hours per week})$$
$$\cong 4.2 - 300 \text{ K} - \text{lines of code}$$

This range is different from the bottom-up estimate obtained previously, but it helps to ground our ideas about the job's magnitude, since the method used this time is quite different.

Free estimation tools, such as those at www.construx.com, are also available on the Web.

8.1.4 Function Points

Starting in 1979 with Albrecht [2], the more fundamental notion of *function points* was developed to assess the size of a project without having to know its design and without having to make any a priori assumptions about code size. The function point technique is a means of calibrating the capabilities of an application in a uniform manner, as a single number. This number can then be used to estimate lines of code, cost, and duration by comparison with the function point values of other projects. Function points are attractive in concept, since they try to get to the heart of a future product's capability. However, it takes a great deal of practice to apply them in an accurate and consistent manner.

8.1.4.1 Calculating Function Points

Function point calculation comprises the following steps:

Function Point Step 1

Identify the functions (e.g., "retrieve," "display") that the application must have. The International Function Point Users Group (IFPUG; see [3]) has published criteria as to what constitutes a "function" of an application in this sense. They consider user-level functionality, rather than programming-level functions as in C. Typically, a function is the equivalent of processing a screen or form on the monitor. For our role-playing video game prototype, for example, we can identify the following functions.

1. Set up the character representing the player.

2. Encounter a foreign character.

Function Point Step 2

For each such function, compute its function point contribution from the sources shown in Figure 8.4.

The following summarizes the sense of each contributing factor. The guidelines have to be carefully followed, otherwise it is hard to obtain consistent estimates.

- *External inputs*: Only inputs that affect the function in a different way from each other are counted as separate. Thus, a function of an application that subtracts two numbers would have EI = 1, not EI = 2. On the other hand, if the character A can be input to request an addition and S for subtraction, these would contribute 2 to EI.

- *External outputs*: Only outputs that account for true separate algorithmic or nontrivial functionalities should be counted. For example, a process that outputs a character in several fonts would be counted as 1; error

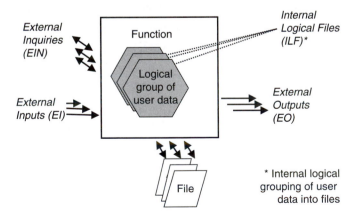

Figure 8.4 Function point computation for a single function

Source: International Function Point Users Group, http://www.ifpug.org.

PARAMETER	Simple			Complex		
Ext. inputs *EI* ✗	. . . 3	or	. . . 4 or	. . . 6 = ___		☐
Ext. outputs *EO* ✗	. . . 4	or	. . . 5 or	. . . 7 = ___		☐
Ext. inquiries *EIN* ✗	. . . 3	or	. . . 4 or	. . . 6 = ___		☐
Int. logical files *ILF* ✗	. . . 7	or	. . . 10 or	. . . 15 = ___		☐
Ext. logical files *ELF* ✗	. . . 5	or	. . . 7 or	. . . 10 = ___		☐
				Count Total		☐

Figure 8.5 Function point computations (IFPUG)

messages are not counted. Chart representations of data are counted as 2 (1 for the data and 1 for the formatting), and data sent to separate nontrivial destinations (e.g., printer) [3].

- *External inquiry*: Each independent inquiry is counted as 1.

- *Internal logical files*: This counts each unique logical group of user data created by or maintained by the application. Combinations of such logical groupings are not counted; each functional area of the application dealing with a unique logical grouping increases the count by one.

- *External logical files*: This counts each unique grouping of data on files external to the application.

Function Point Step 3

As shown in Figure 8.5, each of these parameter values is then factored by a number, depending on the degree of complexity of the parameter in the application. IFPUG [3] has published detailed descriptions of the meaning of "simple" and "complex" in this context.

Applying this process to the two selected functions of the Encounter video game mentioned above, we obtain the spreadsheet tables shown in Figures 8.6 and 8.7. These figures are highly preliminary, but they do begin to provide estimate parameters for the job. The total unadjusted function point estimate for these two Encounter functions is 25 + 16 = 41.

Function Point Step 4

Next, one computes weights for the fourteen general characteristics of the project, each between 0 and 5. This is shown for the two selected Encounter functions in Figures 8.8 and 8.9. We have actually used a range for each of these to reflect our current uncertainty about the application. Once again, it takes consistent experience to assess the appropriate values for these variables. For example, factor 6 asks for the degree of certainty that online data entry is required. We are certain that the user will need to input characteristics for the game characters, and so the value chosen is the highest: five.

The total General Characteristics value (1 through 14) is between 24 and 41.

	count	Simple Factor	count	Medium factor	count	Complex factor	Sub-totals		Total
Ext. inputs	1	3	1	4	1	6	13		
comments:	Name		Ready/move		Qualities				
Ext. outputs	0	4	0	5	0	7	0		
Ext. inquiries	0	3	0	4	0	6	0		25
Int. logical files	1	7	0	10	0	15	7		
comments:	Data about the user's character								
Ext. interface files	1	5	0	7	0	10	5		
comments:	Data about the user's character								

Figure 8.6 Unadjusted function point computation for first Encounter functions: "Set up player character."

	count	Simple factor	count	Medium factor	count	Complex factor	Sub-totals		Total
Ext. inputs	0	3	0	4	0	6	0		
Ext. outputs	1	4	0	5	0	7	4		
comments:	Report on results								
Ext. inquiries	0	3	0	4	0	6	0		16
Int. logical files	1	7	0	10	0	15	7		
comments:	Data about the user's character								
Ext. interface files	1	5	0	7	0	10	5		
— comments on about the user's character									

Figure 8.7 Unadjusted function point computation for first Encounter functions: "Encounter foreign character."

Incidental   Average   Essential

0 ——— 1 ——— 2 ——— 3 ——— 4 ——— 5

None   Moderate   Significant

	Case Study
1. Requires backup/recovery?	0–2
2. Data communications required?	0–1
3. Distributed processing functions?	0
4. Performance critical?	3–4
5. Run on existing heavily utilized environment?	0–1
6. Requires online data entry?	5
7. Multiple screens for input?	4–5

(continued)

Figure 8.8 General characteristics for function point adjustment, numbers 1–7

Function Point Step 5

Finally, the (adjusted) function point total is calculated by the formula shown in Figure 8.10. This equation states that if there are no special demands at all on the application (total general characteristics $= 0$), then the function point measure should be scaled down from the unadjusted (raw) score by 35% (which explains the "0.65"). Otherwise the measure should be scaled up from the unadjusted amount by one percentage point for each general characteristic unit.

For the case study, a reasonable allocation of general characteristics is shown in Figures 8.8 and 8.9. The total value of these is between 24 and 43, so the final (i.e., adjusted) function point computation is

$$41 \times [0.65 + 0.01 \times (24 \text{ to } 41)] = 41 \times [0.89 \text{ to } 1.06] \approx 36 \text{ to } 43$$

8.1.4.2 Converting Function Points to Lines of Code

Once accurately obtained, function points are very useful. For example, they can be used as comparison metrics, allowing organizations to estimate jobs based on function point metrics of previous jobs. They can be converted to lines of code using standard tables. Lines of code can then be used to estimate total effort in person-months as well as duration (see the next section on COCOMO). For example, [4] estimates 53 lines of Java source per function point. Using this factor for the Encounter example, we anticipate

Incidental   Average   Essential

0 ——— 1 ——— 2 ——— 3 ——— 4 ——— 5

None   Moderate   Significant

	Case Study
8. Master fields updated online?	3–4
9. Inputs, outputs, inquiries of files complex?	1–2
10. Internal processing complex?	1–3
11. Code designed for reuse?	2–4
12. Conversion and installation included?	0–2
13. Multiple installation in different organizations?	1–3
14. Must facilitate change and ease of use by user?	4–5

Figure 8.9 General characteristics for function point adjustment, numbers 8–14

$$(\text{Adjusted}) \text{ Function Points} =$$
$$[\text{Unadjusted function points}] \times$$
$$[0.65 \ + \ 0.01 \times (\text{ total general characteristics})]$$

Figure 8.10 Computation of adjusted function points

(36 to 44) $53 \approx 1.9 - 2.3$ K-lines of Java source. As expected, this is much lower than the previous estimates of 4.2-300 and 7.5-170 K-lines of Java source. This is true because it applies to only two "functions" for Encounter, whereas the larger estimates were for a full game.

8.1.4.3 A Further Function Point Example

Let's consider a system that tracks video rentals. We will confine the application to a customer-oriented application, in which customers rent videos and need information about availability.

We assume that the application requires two files only: one for customers and a second for videos. The unadjusted function point computation is as shown in Figure 8.11.

Now we estimate the adjustment factors, as shown in Figure 8.12, yielding a "General Characteristics" total of 35.

		Simple		Medium		Complex		Sub-	Total
	count	factor	count	factor	count	factor		totals	
Ext. inputs	2	3	1	4	0	6		10	
— *explanation:*	*Name, ph. #*		*Video data*						
Ext. outputs	0	4	1	5	0		7	5	
— *explanation:*			*Amount due*						
Ext. inquiries	0	3	1	4	0	6		4	33
— *explanation:*			*Availability*						
Int. logical files	2	7	0	10	0	15		14	
— *explanation:*	*Customers; Videos*								
Ext. interface files	0	5	0	7	0	10		0	

Figure 8.11 Unadjusted function point scores for vide store example

None	Incidental	Moderate	Average	Significant	Essential
0 ———	1 ———	2 ———	3 ———	4 ———	5

1. Requires backup/recovery?............................... 4
2. Data communications required? 0
3. Distributed processing functions? 0
4. Performance critical? 3
5. Run on existing heavily utilized environment? 1
6. Requires online data entry?............................ 5
7. Multiple screens for input? 3
8. Master fields updated online?........................ 5
9. Inputs, outputs, inquiries of files complex?..... 2
10. Internal processing complex?........................ 1
11. Code designed for reuse? 3
12. Conversion and installation included? 3
13. Multiple installation in different orgs.?......... 3
14. Must facilitate change case of use by user?... 2   *Total*

                                                                             35

Figure 8.12 FP adjustment factors for video store example

The Function Point formula gives

$$\text{Function points} = [\text{unadjusted function points}] \times [0.65 + 0.01 \times (\text{total general characteristics})]$$
$$= 33 \times [0.65 + 0.01 \times 35]$$
$$= 33$$

This yields $33 \times 53 = 1,749$ lines of non-commented source lines of Java code.

The function point method is summed up by Capers Jones in [5], a practiced advocate of function point application. See also [6].

8.1.5 Estimating Effort and Duration from Lines of Code

Once lines of code have been estimated, either through use of historical data, by comparison to related projects, or via function points, they can be used to estimate labor requirements and project duration using Barry Boehm's COCOMO models [1]. COCOMO is based on the idea that project outcomes, plotted as graphs, have a consistent basic shape. A parameterized formula is found for the shape, so that to obtain the graph for a particular project, he simply has to determine the parameters for it.

8.1.5.1 COCOMO I

Boehm observed that the labor required to develop applications tends to increase faster than the application's size. He found in his initial research that the exponential function, with exponent close to 1.12, expresses this relationship quite well. Boehm's model also says that the duration increases exponentially with the effort, but with an exponent less than 1 (the exponent used in this case is close to 0.35). This reflects the observation that after a certain size (the "knee" in curve (2)), additional required effort has only a gradual lengthening effect on the time it takes to complete the project. These are illustrated in Figure 8.13, where LOC is short for "lines of code."

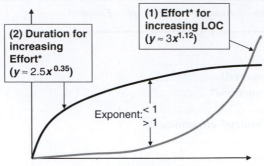

Figure 8.13 Meaning of the COCOMO formulas

Source: Boehm, Barry, "Software Engineering Economics," Prentice Hall, 1981.

Using data from numerous projects, Boehm estimated the parameters for these relationships, assuming an exponential relationship. His formulas are illustrated in Figure 8.14. In this system, *organic* applications are stand-alone applications such as classical (i.e., non-Web-enabled) word processors—or our Encounter case study. *Embedded* applications are integral to hardware-software systems (e.g., an antilock braking system). *Semi-detached* applications are in between. A Web-enabled Encounter, for example, is semi-detached: it is not organic, but neither is it as heavily embedded as the code in an antilock braking system, for example. Encounter would communicate with the Internet via signals that are only occasional when compared with the frequency of CPU instruction execution.

Boehm's model says first that the required effort and duration have separate models (formulas) for each type of application (differing in factors *a* and *b*). For example, a stand-alone job with 20,000 lines of code would take $2.4 \times 20^{1.05} \approx 51$ person-months duration if organic (stand-alone) but about $3.6 \times 20^{1.2} \approx 76$ person-months if embedded.

The duration formula can be expressed directly in terms of line of code (KLOC) as follows:

$$\text{Duration} = c \times \text{Effort}^d = c \times (a \times \text{KLOC}^b)^d = c \times a^d \times \text{KLOC}^{bd}$$

At first glance, Boehm's duration formula may appear strange because the relationship between effort and duration seems to be simpler than his formula indicates. For example, if we know that a job requires 120

$$\text{Effort in Person-months} = a \times KLOC^b$$
$$\text{Duration} = c \times Effort^d$$

Software Project	a	b	c	d
Organic	2.4	1.05	2.5	0.38
Semi-detached	3.0	1.12	2.5	0.35
Embedded	3.6	1.20	2.5	0.32

Figure 8.14 Original COCOMO I formulas

Source: Boehm, Barry, "Software Engineering Economics," Prentice Hall, 1981.

person-months, and we put ten people onto it, won't it get done in 12 months? This would indeed be the case if we could usefully and consistently employ all 10 people on the project from day 1 through day 365, but this is not usually possible. Consider, for example, day 1. Since all the engineers can't know much about the project (it has just begun), what useful activities could all ten engineers do that day? It follows that if we allocate 10 engineers from the first day, the 120 person-month job will actually take longer than 12 months.

Boehm's duration formula has the strange property of being independent of the number of people put on the job! It depends only on the size of the job. Actually, the formula assumes that the project will have roughly an appropriate number of people available to it at any given time (for example, one on day 1, thirty on day 100, assuming that is what's needed).

Boehm's model, which has been tested extensively and is widely respected, has been refined over time, and has been largely updated with the more complex COCOMO II, described next. A great deal of practice is required to use even COCOMO I effectively. It is best used along with an independent method and a healthy dose of common sense (sometimes called a "sanity check"). Using Boehm's basic formula on the prototype version of Encounter (consisting of two basic functions), with 4-300 K-lines of code, we obtain 10 to 1,000 person-months of effort, and 6 to 35 months in duration, as shown in Figure 8.15.

8.1.5.2 COCOMO II

COCOMO (I) is somewhat identified with the Waterfall process because it does not specifically account for iterative development. It must be used anew for each iteration, and does not account for factors such as whether the iteration is early or late in the process. For this reason and others, Boehm updated it to COCOMO II. (See, for example, http://sunset.usc.edu/research/COCOMOII/.) The a of COCMO I can be interpreted as a scaling factor. COCOMO II replaces it with a product of various scaling factors SF_1, SF_2, SF_3, SF_4, and SF_5. This allows for a more refined set of parameters. The b parameter in COCOMO I expressed the number of times KLOC is multiplied. COCOMO II replaces this with a product of seventeen quantities EM_i

		$\underline{a}$	$\underline{K}$	$\underline{b}$		approx.
Effort						$a\mathrm{K}^{\wedge}\mathrm{b}$
	LO	2.4	4.2	1.05		10
	HI	2.4	300	1.05		1000

		$\underline{c}$	$\underline{P}$	$\underline{d}$		approx.
Duration						$c\mathrm{P}^{\wedge}\mathrm{d}$
	LO	2.5	10	0.38		6
	HI	2.5	1000	0.38		35

Figure 8.15 Using COCOMO I to estimate the magnitude of the Encounter effort

$$\boxed{\begin{array}{l} \text{Effort in Person-months} \\ = a \times \Pi_{i=1}{}^{17}\text{EM}_i \end{array}}$$

where $a = 1.01 + \sum_{j=1}{}^{5} SF_j$
EM_i are multiplicative cost drivers
SF_j are scaling cost drivers

Figure 8.16 Basic COCOMO II Formula

Source: Boehm, Barry, "Software Engineering Economics," Prentice Hall, 1981, http://sunset.usc.edu/research/COCOMOII/.

(so each replaces *KLOC* in COCOMO I). These are called *multiplicative cost drivers*, and they allow for more refinement in describing the product and project.

The COCOMO II *Effort* formula is shown in Figure 8.16. The symbol ? (capital p) is the product symbol. For example, $\Pi_{k=1}^{4} k^2$ means $1^2 \times 2^2 \times 3^2 \times 4^2$.

Figure 8.17 lists the types of the quantities SF_i and EM_j. The SF_5 parameter, for example, allows for factoring in the maturity of the development organization. The SF_3 parameter allows for the degree of risk remaining in the project. The value of SF_3 is high for initial iterations and low for later ones. The EM_{16} parameter accounts for the modern practice of developing in several physical locations. Each of the parameters has a defined scale.

8.1.6 Assessments for Agile Projects: Story Points and Velocity

This section discusses estimation techniques for agile projects. In order to commit to delivering capability at the end of a cycle, a team must assess the effort required. As with function points, *story points* are a means by which to measure the size of a story as it relates to implementation. Unlike function points, however, which attempt absolute measurement, story points are a relative measure. In other words, they compare stories within a project only. The size range is typically between 1 and 10, and the size of a story is based on the team's history of implementing stories in past cycles of the project. One way to establish story points is to take an executed story that the team considers to be average, assign it 5 story points, and use it as a yardstick for future stories. Another is to select a very small implemented story, count it as 1 point, and then calculate all other stories as multiples of it. A more sophisticated way is to create a plot as shown in Figure 8.18.

A big advantage of agile methods is that they involve many entire creation cycles. In a pure waterfall, team members find it difficult to estimate the size and completion time of a job because they will not usually have performed one just like this in the past, with the same participants. Agile methods, on the other hand, facilitate the assessment of how much completed work a team is capable of producing by relying on observed past performance within the same project. Recall that in physics, velocity is defined as *distance covered per time unit*. Similarly, agile project velocity is defined as the *amount of functionality created per time unit*. This translates into story points per cycle. Assuming the constancy of cycles (e.g., always two weeks), the reliability of a velocity calculation depends only on the ability to accurately assess story points. With the experience of repeatedly making this estimate, teams increase their estimation accuracy as the project progresses. See Figure 8.19.

As effective as this kind of agile estimation is, it requires augmentation when larger scale estimation is required. The reader is referred to Cohn, *Agile Estimating and Planning*, Prentice Hall, for example, for further reading.

Sym.	Abr.	Name
SF_1	PREC	Precendentedness
SF_2	FLEX	Development Flexibility
SF_3	RESL	Architecture and Risk Resolution
SF_4	TEAM	Team cohesion
SF_5	PMAT	Process Maturity
EM_1	RELY	Required Software
EM_2	DATA	Data Base Size
EM_3	CPLX	Product Complexity
EM_4	RUSE	Required Reusability
EM_5	DOCU	Documentation Match to Life-cycle Needs
EM_6	TIME	Time Constraint
EM_7	STOR	Storage Constraint
EM_8	PVOL	Platform Volatility
EM_9	ACAP	Analyst Capability
EM_{10}	PCAP	Programmer Capability
EM_{11}	AEXP	Applications Experience
EM_{12}	PEXP	Platform Experience
EM_{13}	LTEX	Language and Tool Experience
EM_{14}	PCON	Personnel Continuity
EM_{15}	TOOL	Use of Software Tools
EM_{16}	SITE	Multi-Site Development
EM_{17}	SCED	Required Development Schedule

Figure 8.17 Basic COCOMO II cost drivers

Source: Boehm, Barry, ''Software Engineering Economics,'' Prentice Hall, 1981, http://sunset.usc.edu/research/COCOMOII/.

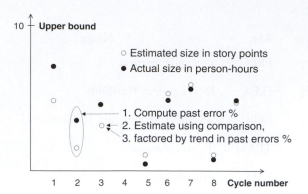

Figure 8.18 Estimating story points

- Definition: Number of **story points** the team can execute **per cycle**

- Relies on **history** of performance and consistency of story points
  - ○ Within this project and past ones

- Depends on accurate story points

Figure 8.19 Velocity in agile development

8.2 SCHEDULING

Project estimates are used as input for constructing project *schedules*. Teams develop schedules so that everyone knows what to expect, what to do, and when to do it. Figures 8.20, 8.21, and 8.22 step through a typical schedule construction using a spreadsheet. Substantial projects are best performed with specialized tools such as Microsoft Project.

Software project scheduling confronts a fundamental chicken-and-egg problem, as follows. Part of a software engineering project is to gather the requirements but until we know the requirements for the application, we can't say how long it will take to do the job and so, strictly speaking, we can't schedule it. There are several approaches to breaking out of this loop. One is to develop a schedule only after the requirements have been specified. Although this is logical, it is not often used. The main reasons for this are as follows:

1. As mentioned before, it is usually impractical to specify all requirements up front.

2. Management usually needs to know up front how much time the project will consume and how much it will cost.

A common way to approach these issues is to begin with deadlines and to accomplish as many of the important requirements as possible with the specified time and financial resources, and then to iterate this process. For the purposes of discussion, this is the approach used here.

The first step is to show the deadlines for deliverables to the customer. In our case, we will suppose that the customer wants to see a prototype after four weeks and the completed project after four months. One

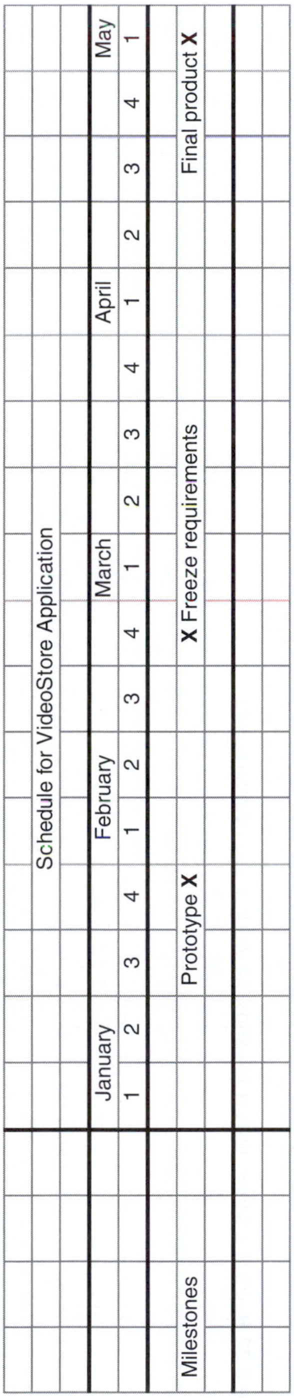

Figure 8.20 Building a schedule Part I—setting milestones

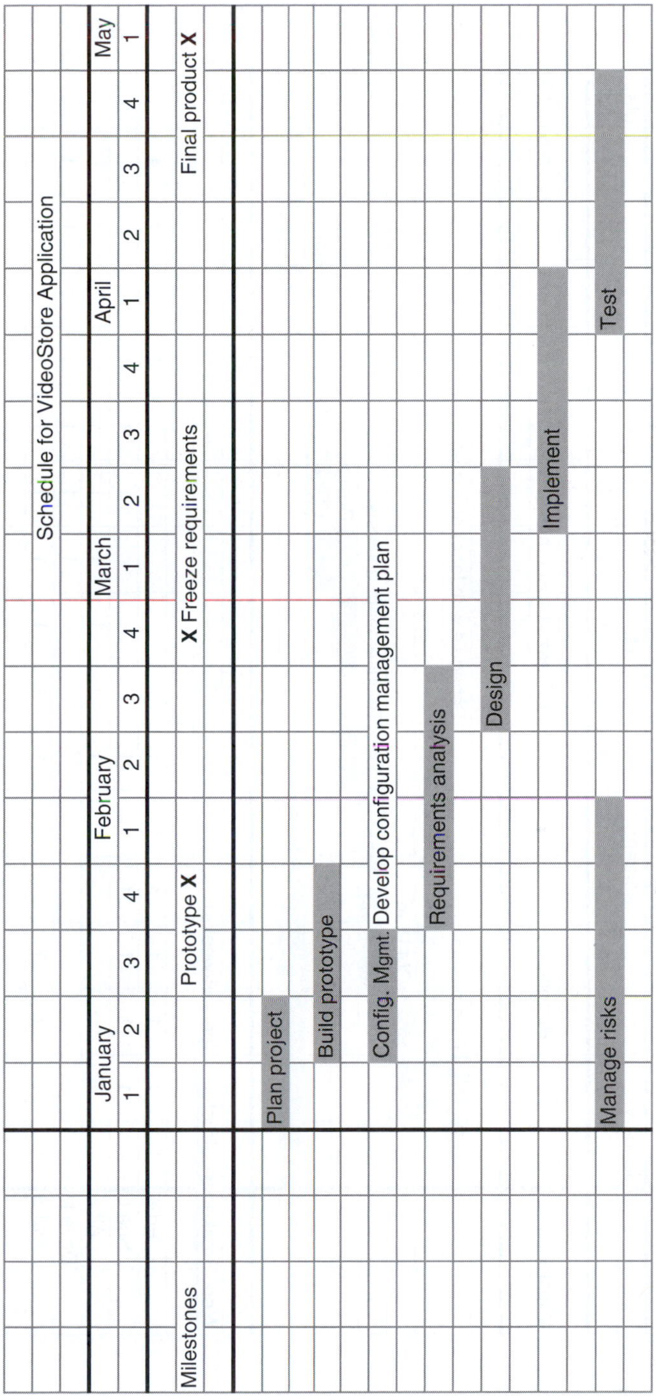

Schedule for VideoStore Application

	January				February				March				April				May
	1	2	3	4	1	2	3	4	1	2	3	4	1	2	3	4	1
Milestones			Prototype **X**						**X** Freeze requirements						Final product **X**		

Figure 8.21 Building a schedule Part II—showing phases

Schedule for VideoStore Application

	January				February				March				April				May
	1	2	3	4	1	2	3	4	1	2	3	4	1	2	3	4	1
Plan project																	
Build prototype																	
Config. Mgmt. Develop configuration management plan																	
Requirements analysis																	
Design																	
Implement																	
Test																	
Manage risks																	
Milestones			Prototype **X**						**X** Freeze requirements						Final product **X**		

Schedule for VideoStore Application

	January 1	2	3	4	February 1	2	3	4	March 1	2	3	4	April 1	2	3	4	May 1
Milestones				Prototype **X**					**X** Freeze requirements							Final product **X**	
Plan project	2	1	1	1													
CM Plan			1														
Build prototype				1	1												
Manage risks	1	1	1	1	1	1	1										
Requirements analysis					2	2	2	2	2	2							
Design											2	2	4				
Implement													3	2	3	3	
Test																2	2

Schedule with labor allocated

Work Breakdown Structure (person-weeks)

	January 1	2	3	4	February 1	2	3	4	March 1	2	3	4	April 1	2	3	4	May 1
Ed A	1	1	1	1	1	1	1		1	1	1	1	1	1	1	1	1
Sue C		1	1	1	1	1	1	1	1	1	1	1	1	1	1		
Alf K	1	1					1	1	1	1	1	1	1	1			
Dave M									1	1	1	1	1	1	1	1	1
Pat S	1	1	1	1	1		1		1	1	1	1	1		1		
Weekly totals	3	4	3	3	3	2	4	2	2	3	3	4	5	3	3	2	
Cumulative	3	7	10	13	16	18	22	24	26	29	33	37	42	45	48	50	

Figure 8.22 Building a schedule Part III—showing work breakdown structure

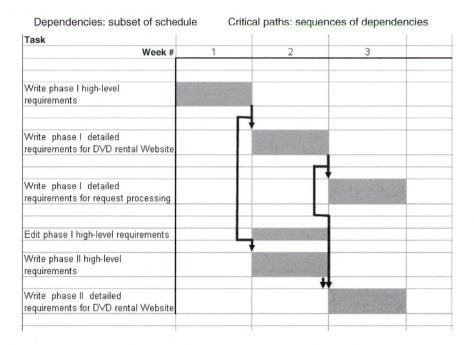

Figure 8.23 Dependencies shown in schedules

technique used in setting a schedule is to build in buffers to compensate for factors that we don't or can't know about. For example, our schedule assumes four weeks per month, which provides at least one unscheduled week. This is shown in Figure 8.20. Some project managers frown on approaches like this because they hide things.

Now we work backward from the milestones to show the times for the various phases, as shown in Figure 8.21.

Finally, the team needs to ensure that people are available to do the work. This requires a *work breakdown structure* (WBS) showing who will do what work. Figure 8.22, for example, includes a WBS.

In the example of Figure 8.22, the last week of design requires just one person and the first week of implementation requires two engineers.

Schedules show the intended order of tasks. If task *A* is scheduled to be performed prior to task *B*, this does not necessarily imply that *B* depends on *A*. For example, we may have selected the order because it is more convenient to perform task *A* before *B*. However, if task *X* depends on task *Y*, then task *Y* should be scheduled to complete before task *X* begins, and the dependency should be made clear on the schedule.

We can denote dependencies on a schedule, as shown in Figure 8.23. These become important whenever we want to alter the schedule. They are also necessary in determining the project's *critical paths*: the sequence of activities that *must* be performed, and the order in which they must be performed. To summarize: The dependencies form a subset of the schedule, and the critical paths are sequences of dependencies.

8.3 THE SOFTWARE PROJECT MANAGEMENT PLAN

The project plan is documented so that everyone knows what to do and when to do it. There are many formats for such a plan. We will use IEEE Software Project Management Plan (SPMP) standard 1058-1998 for this purpose. The table of contents for 1058-1998 is shown in Figure 8.24, and is used in the case study in

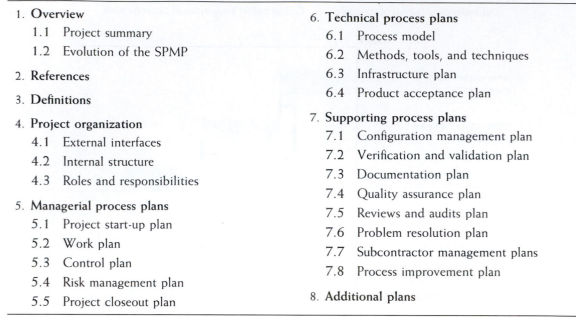

1. **Overview**
   - 1.1 Project summary
   - 1.2 Evolution of the SPMP

2. **References**

3. **Definitions**

4. **Project organization**
   - 4.1 External interfaces
   - 4.2 Internal structure
   - 4.3 Roles and responsibilities

5. **Managerial process plans**
   - 5.1 Project start-up plan
   - 5.2 Work plan
   - 5.3 Control plan
   - 5.4 Risk management plan
   - 5.5 Project closeout plan

6. **Technical process plans**
   - 6.1 Process model
   - 6.2 Methods, tools, and techniques
   - 6.3 Infrastructure plan
   - 6.4 Product acceptance plan

7. **Supporting process plans**
   - 7.1 Configuration management plan
   - 7.2 Verification and validation plan
   - 7.3 Documentation plan
   - 7.4 Quality assurance plan
   - 7.5 Reviews and audits plan
   - 7.6 Problem resolution plan
   - 7.7 Subcontractor management plans
   - 7.8 Process improvement plan

8. **Additional plans**

Figure 8.24 IEEE 1058-1998 Software Project Management Plan table of contents

Section 8.4. The IEEE standard is sometimes viewed as belonging only to "document-heavy" projects. In fact, its parts should be used when and only when they provide value. Agile project leaders can gain by perusing the topics and deciding how and when the issue mentioned is to be handled. Non-agile projects are not bound to use a section unless the effort is worth it. Problems arise when needed issues are ignored and when documentation is used for no productive purpose.

Section 1.1 in the SPMP—the overview—should identify the project but should not cover its requirements (i.e., descriptions of its behavior). These are covered in the Software Requirements Specification, described in Part II of this book. Repeating that material in the SPMP would violate the principle of single-source documentation (to say each thing in one place only). Section 1.2 describes the ways in which the SPMP itself is expected to grow and change. The Software Configuration Management Plan (SCMP) should have been developed by this time (see Chapter 6), so that versions of the SPMP can be properly controlled. A reference to the SCMP is provided here.

Section 4.1 describes the ways in which organizations will communicate with the development team. This depends on the project's stakeholders (the people who have an interest in it). For example, how will engineering interface with marketing (regular meetings, E-mail, etc.)? Section 4.3 specifies the responsibilities of project personnel.

Section 5.2, the Work Plan, can contain the project's schedule. Section 5.3, the Control Plan, specifies who will manage, control, and/or review the project, together with how and when this is to be done. For example, senior management needs to know how projects are progressing, so we would describe the process for keeping them informed here. Risk management (Section 5.4) was described in Chapter 7.

Constraints on the languages and tools used are provided in the "technical process plans," Section 6—for example, "This project shall use Java from Sun, version 1.2.1, and Rational Rose version 1." Section 6.1 refers to the software development process to be used (e.g., waterfall, spiral, incremental). Possible "organizational structures" were discussed in Chapter 7. Section 6 can include information on reuse requirements.

In Section 7, the "Supporting Process Plans" references or describes activities that support the development process, such as configuration management and quality assurance. If the support function is described in separate documents (e.g., the configuration management plan or the quality plan), we reference those documents. Otherwise, we describe the support function in full. These and other aspects of the SPMP are explained further in the case study at the end of this part of the book.

The reader will find a sample SPMP for the Encounter cases study in Section 8.4 of this chapter, which conforms to IEEE standard 1058-1998. Excerpts from management documentation for the Eclipse and OpenOffice open source projects can be found in Sections 8.5 and 8.6 respectively. In comparing them, the reader will notice the benefits of using a standard but also some of the limitations in flexibility.

8.4 CASE STUDY: ENCOUNTER PROJECT MANAGEMENT PLAN

The Software Project Management Plan for Encounter shown in this section is based on *IEEE Std 1058-1998 Standard for Software Project Management Plans*. Figure 8.24 is the table of contents for the document.

Approvals

Title	Signature	Date
Engineering Manager	*P. Jones*	7/15/04
QA Manager	*L Wilenz*	7/11/04
Project Manager	*A. Pruitt*	7/7/04
Author	*E. Braude*	7/1/04

Revision History

Version 1

　1.0.0 E. Braun: Created first draft 6/1/98

　1.1.0 R. Chadwick: Reviewed 1/11/99

　1.1.1 E. Braun: Expanded 3.2 1/19/99

　1.2.0 R. Chadwick: Reviewed for release 5/19/99

　1.2.1 V. Brahms: Final editing 4/30/99

Version 2

　2.0.0 E. Braun: Updated to 1998 standard 5/18/2004

1. Overview

1.1 Project Summary

> Note to the Student:
> This should be at a high enough level that it does not need to change much over time. Details should appear in subsequent sections, not this one. This summary should not substitute for any part of the requirements document.

This project is organized to produce a role-playing video game called Encounter. This game will be developed in several stages since the customer intends to specify the requirements in stages, with each stage following the demonstration of each version. The early versions are intended for educational purposes, as examples of software engineering practice, and as legacy systems on which students may build their own video games. The later versions are expected to be either freeware games or commercial products marketed by a game marketing organization.

1.2 Evolution of the SPMP

> Explains how and by whom this document will be maintained. It will have to be modified in several ways (e.g., with a more detailed schedule as more is known about the requirements). If a concrete plan is not put in place to maintain this document, it will be worked on sporadically or not at all.

This document will be maintained on a weekly basis by the project leader. It is subject to configuration management by means of the SCMP. It is the project leader's responsibility to submit this document as a CI, and to keep it up to date. This SPMP mainly follows the format of IEEE 1058.1-1998.

2. References

[IEEE] The applicable IEEE standards are published in "IEEE Standards Collection," 1997 edition.

[MPACL5] This document is to conform to the company's "Master Plan for the Attainment of CMM Level 5."

[Braude] The principal source of textbook reference material is *Software Engineering: An Object-Oriented Perspective* by E. Braude (Wiley, 2000).

3. Definitions

$$
\begin{aligned}
&\text{CI} = \text{Configuration Item}\\
&\text{CMM} = \text{Capability Maturity Model, the}\\
&\qquad\text{SEI's model for organizational}\\
&\qquad\text{improvement}\\
&\text{IEEE} = \text{Institute of Electrical and Electronics Engineers}\\
&\text{QA} = \text{Quality Assurance}\\
&\text{SEI} = \text{Software Engineering Institute, Pittsburgh, PA}\\
&\text{SCMP} = \text{Software Configuration Management Plan}
\end{aligned}
$$

SPMP = Software Project Management Plan (this document)
SRS = Software Requirements Specification
SDD = Software Design Document
STP = Software Test Plan
tbd = to be decided

4. Project Organization

4.1 External Interfaces

> Name the people and organizations with whom the team should communicate.

The project team will interface with the following individuals and organizations: VP, Engineering (for technical and standards direction), Marketing (for requirements), Game Laboratory (for advanced game features), and the quality assurance engineer.

4.2 Internal structure

Figure 8.25 shows the organization of the Encounter project within Gaming Industries Consolidated.

The project will be organized as a team of peers with designated roles. The roles are team leader, configuration management leader, quality assurance leader, requirements management leader, design

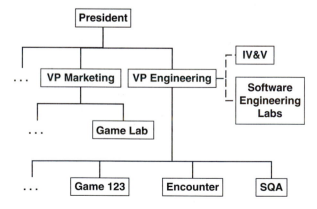

Figure 8.25 Organization of Gaming Industries Consolidated

Member	Team leader	CM Leader	QA leader	Requirements Management Leader	Design Leader	Implementation Leader
Liaison Responsibility	VP Engineering			Marketing	Software engineering lab	
Document Responsibility	SPMP	SCMP	SQAP STP	SRS	SDD	Code base

Figure 8.26 Encounter project responsibilities

leader, and implementation leader. In addition, there are liaison roles to marketing and to the software engineering laboratory.

4.3 Roles and Responsibilities

The responsibilities of the participants in the project are shown in Figure 8.26.

Being responsible for a document includes the following:

- Making sure that the document is created on time

- Having the team leader identify the writers of the document

- Keeping the document up-to-date throughout the project life cycle

5. Managerial Process Plans

5.1 Project Startup Plan

> This section specifies the planning activities that will be conducted once the project is under way. It is a plan to conduct planning—a meta-plan, if you like.

5.1.1 Estimation Plan

> As a project progresses, our ability to estimate its cost and duration improve (but also become progressively less useful). This section explains when and how we intend to perform these estimations.

Estimations of project cost and duration will be made following the specification of high-level requirements (using function points), detailed requirements (using a method to be determined), and after high-level design. The latter estimates will be made by comparison with past projects.

Before beginning requirements analysis, we have estimated the size of this effort in three different ways:

1. Using an informal top-down estimate based on the experience of team members with somewhat similar projects.

2. Using a top-down approximation with industry game development data.

3. Using function points on two known functions, extrapolating to the entire application.

The results are shown in Figure 8.27.

Method*	Mini	Max	Comment
(1)	7.5**	170	
(2)	4.2	300	
(3)	11.4	46	1.9-2.3 for two identified functions: 6-20 times as many in complete application
Most conservative	11.4	300	Maximum of minimums and maximum of maximums
Least conservative	4.2	46	Minimum of minimums and minimum of maximums
Widest range	4.2	300	Minimum of minimums and maximum of maximums
Narrowest range	11.4	46	Maximum of minimums and minimum of maximums

Figure 8.27 Very rough estimate of application size prior to requirements analysis

There are many ways of presenting this data, depending on the needs of management and the development staff. Some of these are shown in Figure 8.27. In the absence of written requirements, estimates are necessarily very rough. The estimates themselves can be an appendix to this document instead of here within the body, and updated as the project progresses.

The reason for the very wide range is that the figures have been obtained with negligible interaction with the customer.

5.1.2 Staffing Plan
The roles will be filled as follows.

5.1.3 Resource Acquisition Plan

This section indicates how resources will be obtained other than staff (computers, software, etc.)

The implementation leader will ensure that all team members are supplied with the selected development environment within two weeks of project start.

5.1.4 Project Staff Training Plan
All staff members whose Java proficiency level is less than "advanced," as defined by the Ajax certification, will be trained by Universal Training Inc. courses within the first month of the project. The objective will be to attain advanced-level proficiency.

5.2 Work Plan

5.2.1 Work Activities

This section specifies how the work will be subdivided.

The work on this project will be divided into configuration management, quality assurance (including testing), requirements analysis, design, and

Responsibilty	Leader	Facilitator	Marketing liaison	QA liaison	Game lab liaison	Risk retirement
Report at weekly meeting	X		X	X		X
Circulate weekly report				3*		
Circulate biweekly report					4*	
Circulate monthly report	1*		2*			
*Report formats						
1	see CI 34: "monthly project status form"					
2	see CI 87: "monthly marketing status form"					
3	see CI 344: "weekly QA status form"					
4	see CI 48: "biweekly game lab result form"					

Figure 8.28 Program monitoring and control

Name	Team Leader	CM Leader	QA Leader	Requ. Mngmnt Leader	Design Leader	Implementation Leader
Ed Braun	X					X
Al Pruitt		X				
Fern Tryfill			X			
Hal Furnass				X		
Karen Peters					X	
Liaison with	VP Eng.			Marketing	Soft. Eng. Lab	

Figure 8.29 Staffing plan for Encounter

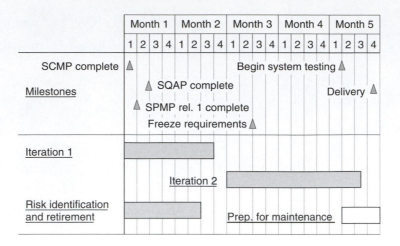

Figure 8.30 High-level chart of tasks with fixed delivery date, ordered by completion

implementation. The project roles and responsibilities are shown in Figure 8.26.

5.2.2 Schedule Allocation

> If we are given a fixed completion date and have identified the process that we will use, we may have enough information to provide a high-level schedule. We increase the amount of detail in the schedule as more becomes known about the design.

The schedule is shown in Figure 8.30. Refer to the SQAP for the schedule of quality activities.

5.2.3 Resource Allocation

The work breakdown structure is shown in Figure 8.31. The bottom line shows the person-months available for each month.

> We have not yet performed any design, so it is too early to name the engineers who will work on specific parts. These names will be added here after the designs for the various configurations have been determined.

5.2.4 Budget Allocation

The budget allocation, shown in Table 8.1, matches the work breakdown structure shown in Figure 8.32, and includes an additional 10 percent to cover unanticipated costs. Loaded[1] labor rates are $4,000 per week.

5.3 Control Plan

> The IEEE describes this section as "metrics, reporting mechanisms, and control procedures necessary to measure, report, and control the product requirements, the project schedule, budget, resources, and the quality of work processes and work products."
>
> It is usually advisable to schedule regular team meetings (typically weekly; sometimes short daily stand-up meetings). When there is no business to conduct, such meetings can easily be canceled. On the other hand, scheduling a meeting on short notice may be difficult when team members have other commitments. Even teams that work together every day need to schedule regular review meetings to avoid drifting. The meeting convener should normally cancel a meeting if there are no agenda items.

---

[1] i.e., including benefits

	Month 1				Month 2				Month 3				Month 4				Month 5			
	1	2	3	4	1	2	3	4	1	2	3	4	1	2	3	4	1	2	3	4
Milestones	△ SCMP	△ SQAP / △ SPMP rel. 1									△ Freeze requirements							Complete testing △		Delivery △
Tasks	Iteration 1								Iteration 2											
	Risk I&R																			
E. Braude	1	1	1	1	1	1	1	1	1	1	1	1	1	1	1	1	1	1	1	1
J. Pruitt	1	1	1	1	1	1	1	1	1	1	1	1	1	1	1	1	1			
F. Tryfill	1	1	1	1	1	1	1	1	1	1	1	1	1							
H. Furnass	1	1	1	1	1	1	1	1	1	1	1	1		1	1	1	1	1	1	1
K. Peters	1	1	1	1	1	1	1	1						1	1	1	1	1	1	1
F. Smith (tech support)	.5	.5	.5	.5	.5	.5	.5	.5	.5	.5	.5	.5	.5	.5	.5	.5	.5	.5	.5	.5
TOTAL	5.5	5.5	5.5	5.5	5.5	5.5	5.5	5.5	4.5	4.5	4.5	4.5	4.5	4.5	4.5	4.5	4.5	4.5	3.5	3.5

Figure 8.31 Work breakdown structure, excluding clerical work

The entire team will meet at the beginning of each phase (requirements, design, and implementation) within each iteration. There will be weekly project meetings on Tuesdays from 10:00 a.m. to noon. Team members are requested to keep Friday mornings from 9:00 a.m. to 11:00 a.m. open for an additional meeting, in case such a meeting becomes necessary. The team leader will inform the team by Thursday at 4:30 p.m. if the latter meeting is to take place.

5.3.1 Requirements Control Plan
The requirements leader will report to the project leader on the status of the SRS in writing each Tuesday.

5.3.2 Schedule Control Plan
The project leader will report to the team on the status of the schedule in writing each Monday.

5.3.3 Budget Control Plan
The project leader will report to management on the status of the budget in writing every second Monday.

5.3.4 Quality Control Plan
The QA representative will provide written reports to the manager of QA, with copies to the project

Table 8.1 Budget allocation

Month Number	Allocation
1	$96,800
2	$96,800
3	$87,120
4	$87,120
5	$77,440
Total	$445,280

#	Risk Title (details given above)	Likelihood 1-10 1 = least likely	Impact 1-10 1=least impact	Retirement Cost 1-10 1=lowest cost	Priority (lowest number handled first)	Retirement / Mitigation Plan	Responsible Engineer	Target Completion Date
1	Superimpose images	3	10	1	8	Experiment with Java images	P. R.	2/1/99
2	Deficient Java skills	9	6	8	80	H.T., K.M, V.I.,and L.D. to attend training course beginning 1/5/99 at Ultra Training Corp, obtain Java level 2 certification by 3/1/99 and level 3 certification by 4/15/99	H. L.	4/15/99
3	Alan Gray maybe pulled off this project	3	7	9	288	Susan Ferris to inspect all of Alan's work	S.F.	Continual
...	...	...	...	...	...	...	...	...

Figure 8.32 Sample risk analysis for Encounter case study

leader, on a schedule to be determined by the manager of QA.

5.3.5 Reporting Plan

The written reports referred to in this section (5.3) will be via e-mail. Issues affecting human safety will be reported to all project personnel and management, regardless of the plans in this document.

5.3.6 Metrics Collection Plan

See the Software Quality Assurance Plan.

5.4 Risk Management

Elaborate on the risks as specific "bad happenings"; do not leave as generic titles. For example, "deficient Java skills" by itself does not specify the issue. Perhaps the project can be performed adequately by a team whose Java skills have deficiencies.

Figure 8.32 shows a format for risk reporting and retirement. Each project meeting is to have an agenda item for risk identification brainstorming and reporting on risks that have been identified.

Risk #1: "Superimposing images" concerns image manipulation in Java. This is a required capability, because characters have to move about, superimposed on background images. No one in the team has experience with placing the image of a character against a background without carrying a rectangle along with the character. We do not know whether this is easy, difficult, or impossible to do.

Risk #2: "Deficient Java skills" indicates the fact that 40 percent of the team is not sufficiently skilled in Java to implement the movement and interaction of character images. We anticipate that it will also be necessary to scale the game environment, but no one on the team has any experience with this. We do not know whether the capabilities that our customer has in mind are doable with Java,

and even if they are, we do not know how long it will take to come up to speed. This could damage the project irreparably.

. . . .

5.5 Project Closeout Plan

Encounter will not be maintained and released beyond 2006. A phase-out plan for the second half of 2006 will be developed.

6. Technical Process Plans

Here is where we describe the process to be used (waterfall, iterative, etc.).

6.1 Process Model

The first two versions of this project will be executed using a spiral development process with an iteration corresponding to each version. The first iteration will be a working prototype but will be fully documented. The second iteration will result in version 1 of Encounter. The number of subsequent iterations and the nature of version 2 are to be decided after the customer has witnessed a demonstration.

6.2 Methods, Tools, and Techniques

The Encounter project will use Rational Rose™ for design and will be implemented in Java. Object-Orientation is to be used throughout. Javadoc will be used for documentation as much as possible (see the SRS for this requirement). Refer to Section 2.1 (process model) for a description of the process.

6.3 Infrastructure Plan

The Encounter team will require model 981234 PCs, Internet access, 100 GB storage on Felix, and the Ajax team collaboration application support.

The hardware resources required are . . . .

6.4 Product Acceptance Plan

Management and investor representatives will finalize acceptance criteria within three weeks of project start. Acceptance tests will take place at the MGC offices within a week of the project completion date.

7. Supporting Process Plans

> This section references plans supporting processes that span the duration of the software project such as the SCMP, SVVP, and SQAP.

8. Additional Plans

None

8.5 CASE STUDY: PROJECT MANAGEMENT IN ECLIPSE

The material in this section is quoted, edited, or adapted from the Eclipse Web sites as they existed at various points in time. It is not a formal SPMP but rather a description of how project management is implemented for Eclipse. The shaded material consists of the authors' comments.

ECLIPSE DOCUMENTATION

The home page for Eclipse documentation is at http://www.eclipse.org/eclipse/index.php — "documentation." This includes user manuals. Documentation is classified as a subproject in itself.

> Note to the Student:
> Documentation is so substantial that it is designated as a (sub)project unto itself.

ORGANIZATION OF THE ECLIPSE PROJECT

> The Eclipse project consists of several "Top-Level Projects." A management committee is responsible for each of these. Each top-level project consists of several (non-top-level) projects. Each project has a project lead, the project plans, and the development team. The development team consists of developers and "committers." Only the latter have the authority to commit artifacts to the baseline. These are explained later in this section. This is largely special to open source projects.

See Figure 8.33 for the project structure.

Proposed Eclipse Project Structure and Roles

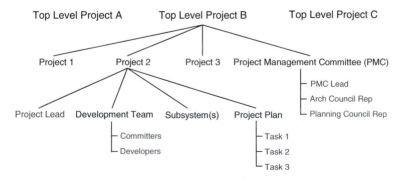

Figure 8.33 Eclipse project—proposed structure and roles

Source: Eclipse Project, http://www.eclipse.org/org/documents/Eclipse%20Development%20Process%202003_11_09%20FINAL.pdf.

CHARTER FOR THE ECLIPSE TECHNOLOGY (TOP-LEVEL) PROJECT

> The "Eclipse Technology Project" differs from the "Eclipse Project." The following document includes a description of project management in Eclipse. It is found at http://eclipse.org/technology/technology-charter.html and has been reformatted and annotated by the author. As described below, a project can migrate from being an "Eclipse Technology Project" to being an "Eclipse Project." This "charter" document mainly describes organization and management. Without committing this kind of thing to paper, there would be little chance of a successful outcome.

Overview

> This is a good overview. It includes the overall motivation for the project and, as with all good overviews, does not attempt to provide complete descriptions. It starts by providing the motivation for Eclipse.

The Eclipse Technology Top-Level Project (the "Eclipse Technology Project") is an open source software research and development project, which encapsulates three related activity streams, each of which is based on or uses the Eclipse Platform and/or Eclipse Tools:

1. Academic research projects and other exploratory investigations ("Research Stream");

2. Development of educational materials, teaching aids, and courseware ("Education Stream");

3. Incubation of small-scale, innovative platform and tools projects ("Incubators Stream").

Mission

The mission of the Eclipse Technology Project is to provide a home within the Eclipse Foundation for small, informally structured projects that add new capabilities to the Eclipse software base (Incubators Stream), foster greater community awareness and understanding of Eclipse (Education Stream), or explore research issues in Eclipse-relevant domains such as programming languages, tools, and development environments (Research Stream). The Eclipse Technology Project is intended to:

1. Provide the open source community with a lighter-weight alternative to the larger scale, more structured development activities carried out by other PMCs, and

2. Create opportunities for researchers, academics, and educators to play a significant role within the Eclipse community.

Scope

> A "Scope" section in a document often refers to the scope of the document itself; that is, the extent that the document is intended to cover. That is not the case here. This section describes the scope of the actual Eclipse Technology Project.

The scope of the Eclipse Technology Project will encompass a wide variety of small projects rather than a few large ones. Although anticipating enormous diversity in the content of these activities, from a process-oriented viewpoint they will all share important common characteristics, which argues for a common management envelope:

• Focus on precompetitive development and research

• Use of informal development processes

• Fluid project tracking due to frequent plan changes

• Flexible milestones that adapt based on partial results

• Small teams

• Resource commitments tentative, due to volunteer labor or lack of sponsor funding

- Development often cross-cuts the scope of several other Eclipse Foundation Projects

The Eclipse Technology Project serves as a single point of focus for such teams, and provides them with a home within the Eclipse community . . . In many cases successful Research Projects will evolve into incubators, and incubators in turn may migrate to other Project Management Committees (PMCs), either by merging into an existing project, or by forming the basis for a new one. . . .

Project Management Committee

> This section specifies the Eclipse project management by specifying the responsibilities of the project management committees.

The projects under this charter are managed by a group known as the Project Management Committee. PMCs are expected to ensure that:

- Each project operates effectively by providing leadership to guide the project's overall direction and by removing obstacles, solving problems, and resolving conflicts.

- All project plans, technical documents, and reports are publicly available.

- All projects operate using open source rules of engagement: meritocracy, transparency, and open participation. These principles work together. Anyone can participate in a project. This open interaction, from answering questions to reporting bugs to making code contributions to creating designs, enables everyone to recognize and utilize the contributions.

The PMC has the following responsibilities:

- Providing the leadership and vision to guide the project's overall direction in a manner consistent with the Eclipse Foundation Architectural Roadmap.

- Providing assistance and support to the developers and researchers working on the project by removing obstacles, solving problems, and resolving conflicts.

- Ensuring that project plans are produced.

- Working with the Eclipse Management Organization (the EMO) to establish the development processes and infrastructure needed for the development team to be effective.

> Documents should explain abbreviations the first time they are introduced, like this, but also include them in a glossary so that the reader knows where to look for an explanation. The reader is expected to know the meaning of "the Eclipse Management Organization." This is normal: the project management for a software development effort typically reports to a higher-level person or body within the company.

- Recommending new projects to the EMO.

- Recommending the initial set of project committers for each new project overseen by the PMC, and establishing the procedures consistent with this charter for voting in new committers.

- Helping to ensure that the projects overseen by the PMC have enough contributors, and working to fill vacancies in roles.

- Producing "how to get involved" guidelines to help new potential contributors get started.

- Coordinating relationships with other Eclipse Foundation Projects.

- Facilitating code or other donations by individuals or companies.

- Making recommendations to the Eclipse Foundation Board

> (This is the overall controlling body for Eclipse.)

regarding contributions proposed under licenses other than the standard one used by Eclipse.

- Working with the EMO and committers to ensure that in-bound contributions are made in accordance with the Eclipse Foundation IP.

(Intellectual Property)

Policy.

- Acting as a focal point for the community in representing the projects it oversees.

Since Eclipse is open source, this documentation has to include procedures that ensure the continued existence and health of the Project Management Committees (PMCs) themselves.

The PMC lead is appointed by the Board. The initial PMC is selected by the PMC lead. Thereafter, to become a member of the PMC, an individual must be nominated by another member of the PMC and unanimously approved by all PMC members.

In the unlikely event that a member of the PMC becomes disruptive to the process or ceases to contribute for an extended period, the member may be removed by unanimous vote of remaining PMC members. PMC members may resign at any time by delivering notice of their resignation to the PMC lead.

The PMC is responsible for producing and maintaining the project charter. Development must conform to any rules or processes outlined in the charter, so a change to the development process may necessitate a change to the charter. Changes to the charter are approved by the board.

The work of the PMC is shared by the PMC members. All PMC members are expected to contribute actively. In particular, PMC members are expected to take responsibility for overseeing certain areas of work in the project, and reporting to the PMC on these areas.

Active participation in the user newsgroups and the appropriate developer mailing lists is a responsibility of all PMC members, and is critical to the success of the project. PMC members are required to monitor the main roject mailing list and the developer mailing lists for all projects and components they are overseeing.

Roles

Many roles in an open source development are typically different from commercial development roles. They depend on volunteers and not paychecks. For that reason, there is increased potential for participants to come and go. This document describes policies to deal with this.

The projects under this charter are operated as meritocracies: the more you contribute, and the higher the quality of your contribution, the more you are allowed to do. However, with this comes increased responsibility.

Users

Users are the people who use the output from the project. Output will typically consist of software and research. Software in this context means intellectual property in electronic form, including source and binary code, documentation, courseware, reports, and papers.

Developers

Users who contribute software or research become developers. Developers are encouraged to participate in the user newsgroup(s), and should monitor the developer mailing list associated with their area of contribution. When appropriate, developers may also contribute to development design discussions related to their area of contribution. Developers are expected to be proactive in reporting problems in the bug tracking system.

Committers

Developers who give frequent and valuable contributions to a project, or component of a project (in the case of large projects), can have their status promoted to that of a "committer" for that project or component respectively. A committer has write access to the source code repository for the associated project (or component), and gains voting rights allowing them to affect the future of the project (or component).

> The following paragraph describes a formal process, which is essential to the smooth running of the Eclipse project.

In order for a developer to become a committer on a particular project overseen by the PMC, another committer for the same project (or component as appropriate) can nominate that developer, or the developer can ask to be nominated. Once a developer is nominated, the committers for the project (or component) will vote. If there are at least three positive votes and no negative votes, the developer is recommended to the PMC for commit privileges. If the PMC also approves, the developer is converted into a committer and given write access to the source code repository for that project (or component). Becoming a committer is a privilege that is earned by contributing and showing discipline and good judgment. It is a responsibility that should be neither given nor taken lightly.

> A good management document anticipates negative circumstances like the following.

At times, committers may go inactive for a variety of reasons. The decision-making process of the project relies on active committers who respond to discussions and votes in a constructive and timely manner. The PMC is responsible for ensuring the smooth operation of the project. A committer that is disruptive, does not participate actively, or has been inactive for an extended period may have his or her commit status removed by the PMC.

Active participation in the user newsgroup and the appropriate developer mailing lists is a responsibility of all committers, and is critical to the success of the project. Committers are required to monitor and contribute to the user newsgroup.

Committers are required to monitor the developer mailing list associated with all projects and components for which they have commit privileges. This is a condition of being granted commit rights to the project or component. It is mandatory because committers must participate in voting (which in some cases requires a certain minimum number of votes) and must respond to the mailing list in a timely fashion in order to facilitate the smooth operation of the project. When a committer is granted commit rights he or she will be added to the appropriate mailing lists. A committer must not be unsubscribed from a developer mailing list unless their associated commit privileges are also removed.

Committers are required to track, participate in, and vote on relevant discussions in their associated projects and components. There are three voting responses: +1 (yes), −1 (no, or veto), and 0 (abstain).

Committers are responsible for proactively reporting problems in the bug tracking system, and annotating problem reports with status information, explanations, clarifications, or requests for more information from the submitter. Committers are responsible for updating problem reports when they have done work related to the problem.

Projects

The work under this Top-Level Project is further organized into projects. New projects must be consistent with the mission of the Top-Level Project, be recommended by the PMC, and confirmed by the EMO. Projects can be discontinued by decision of the board.

When a new project is created, the PMC nominates a project lead to act as the technical leader and nominates the initial set of committers for the project, and these nominations are approved by the EMO. Project leads are accountable to the PMC for the success of their project.

Project Organization

> This section describes the organization of projects within Eclipse.

Given the fluid nature of Eclipse Technology Projects, organizational changes are possible, in particular: dividing a Project into components; dividing a Project into two or more independent Projects; and merging two or more Projects into a single Project. In each case the initiative for the change may come either from within the Project or from the PMC, but the PMC must approve any change, and approval must be confirmed by the EMO.

If a project wishes to divide into components, commit privileges are normally granted at the component level, and the committers for a given component vote on issues specific to that component. Components are established and discontinued by the PMC. When the PMC creates a component it appoints a component lead to act as the technical leader and names the initial set of committers for the component. The component lead is designated as a committer for the project and represents the component in discussions and votes pertaining to the project as a whole. Component committers do not participate in votes at the level of the project as a whole, unless they are also the component lead.

In cases where new projects are being created, either by splitting or by merging, the usual procedures as set forth in this charter are followed. In particular, developers will not necessarily have the same rights after an organizational change that they enjoyed in the previous structure.

Infrastructure

> This section is a useful checklist for most software projects.

The PMC works with the EMO to ensure the required infrastructure for the project. The project infrastructure will include, at minimum:

- Bug Database—Bugzilla database for tracking bugs and feature requests.

- Source Repository —One or more CVS repositories containing all the software for the projects.

- Web Site—A Web site will contain information about the project, including documentation, reports and papers, courseware, downloads of releases, and this charter.

- General Mailing List—Mailing list for development discussions pertaining to the project as a whole or that cross projects. This mailing list is open to the public.

- Project Mailing List—Development mailing list for technical discussions related to the project. This mailing list is open to the public.

- Component Mailing List—Development mailing list for technical discussions related to the component. This mailing list is open to the public.

The Development Process

In this section, the phrase "release cycle" will refer to a significant block of project activity, which corresponds to an actual release cycle in the case of incubators or Education Projects, or to a major stage of a phased Research Project.

> This assumes an interactive development process. However, each iteration is actually released, and so must be a usable version of the product.

Each project lead must produce a development plan for the release cycle, and the development plan must be approved by a majority of committers of the project. The plan must be submitted to the PMC for review. The PMC may provide feedback and advice on the plan, but approval rests with the project committers.

> The document mandates here that each project provide a requirements document. It would have been better to be more specific about where such documents are deployed: it is not easy to find Eclipse requirements documents in practice, and it is questionable that they exist in many cases. Even for non-open source projects, it can be difficult to understand the extent of documentation. This is greatly clarified when an organization standardizes on documentation types (e.g., selected IEEE standards).

Each project must identify, and make available on its Web site, the requirements and prioritizations it is working against in the current release cycle. In addition, each project must post a release plan showing the date and content of the next major release, including any major milestones, and must keep this plan up to date.

The committers of a project or component decide which changes may be committed to the master code base of a project or component, respectively. Three +1 ("yes" votes) with no −1 ("no" votes or vetoes) are needed to approve a code change. Vetoes must be followed by an explanation for the veto within 24 hours or the veto becomes invalid. All votes are conducted via the developer mailing list associated with the project or component.

Special rules may be established by the PMC for projects or components with fewer than three committers. For efficiency, some code changes from some contributors (e.g., feature additions, bug fixes) may be approved in advance, or approved in principle based on an outline of the work, in which case they may be committed first and changed as needed, with conflicts resolved by majority vote of the committers of the project or component, as applicable.

The master copy of the code base must reside on the project Web site, where it is accessible to all users, developers, and committers. Committers must check their changes and new work into the master code base as promptly as possible (subject to any check-in voting rules that may be in effect) in order to foster collaboration among widely distributed groups and so that the latest work is always available to everyone. The PMC is responsible for working with the Eclipse Foundation to establish a release engineering and build process to ensure that builds can be reliably produced on a regular and frequent basis from the master code base and made available for download from the project Web site. Builds in this context are intended to include not only code but also reports, documentation, and courseware.

Each project is responsible for establishing test plans and the level of testing appropriate for the project.

> This document does not establish quality goals. As a result, there is significant variation in the quality of Eclipse projects. A commercial effort would be much more specific in this respect.

All development technical discussions are conducted using the development mailing lists. If discussions are held offline, then a summary must be posted to the mailing list to keep the other committers informed.

Licensing

All contributions to projects under this charter must adhere to the Eclipse Foundation Intellectual Property Policy."

Eclipse is organized into the Platform, JDT, and PDE subprojects as follows [7].

> In describing the management of a project, it may be necessary, as here, to refer to particular requirements or design issues. Otherwise, we try to separate project processes from requirements. Requirements are not known during the first iteration of project management documents but they do become known more during subsequent iterations.

Platform

"The platform project provides the core frameworks and services upon which all plug-in extensions are created. It also provides the runtime in which plug-ins are loaded, integrated, and executed. The primary purpose of the platform subproject is to enable other tool developers to easily build and deliver integrated tools."

JDT

"The JDT (*Java Development Tools*) project provides the tool plug-ins that implement a Java IDE supporting the development of any Java application, including Eclipse plug-ins. It adds a Java project nature and Java perspective to the Eclipse Workbench as well as a number of views, editors, wizards, builders, and code merging and refactoring tools. The JDT project allows Eclipse to be a development environment for itself."

PDE

"The PDE (*Plug-In Development Environment*) project provides a number of views and editors that make is easier to build plug-ins for Eclipse. Using the PDE, you can create your plug-in manifest file (plugin. xml), specify your plug-in runtime and other required plug-ins, define extension points, including their specific markup, associate XML Schema files with the extension point markup so extensions can be validated, create extensions on other plug-in extension points, etc. The PDE makes integrating plug-ins easy and fun."

These subprojects are further decomposed. For example, the Platform subproject is broken down into components. Each component operates like a project unto its own, with its own set of committers, bug categories, and mailing lists. These are as follows [8]:

Project Name	Description
Ant	Eclipse/Ant integration
Compare	Universal compare facility

. . . .

DRAFT PROJECT PLAN FOR ECLIPSE RELEASE 3.0

The following is excerpted and quoted from the project plan for release 3 of Eclipse [9]. It provides an example of a specific project plan when compared with the charter.

Last revised Friday, January 30, 2004 (' marks interesting changes since the previous draft of October 27, 2003).

A method of providing some short-term document history.

Please send comments about this draft plan to the eclipse-dev@eclipse.org *developer mailing list.*

As an application, Eclipse has *features*. As a platform, Eclipse has to have *an API set*: a means for interfacing with it for programmers extending it.

This document lays out the feature and API set for the next feature release of Eclipse after 2.1, designated release 3.0 (Why Eclipse "3.0"?).

A hyperlinked table of contents like the following is useful. Notice the emphasis here on deliverables and schedule, expressed in the first item.

Release deliverables

Release milestones

Target operating environments

Compatibility with previous releases

Eclipse Platform subproject

Java development tools (JDT) subproject

Plug-in development environment (PDE) subproject

This part is a scope statement. It also specifies the management of this document and provides an overview.

Plans do not materialize out of nowhere, nor are they entirely static. To ensure that the planning process is transparent and open to the entire Eclipse community, we (the Eclipse PMC) post plans in an embryonic form and revise them throughout the release cycle.

> PMC = Project Management Committee.

The first part of the plan deals with the important matters of release deliverables, release milestones, target operating environments, and release-to-release compatibility. These are all things that need to be clear for any release, even if no features were to change.

The remainder of the plan consists of plan items for the various Eclipse subprojects. Each plan item covers a feature or API that is to be added to Eclipse, or some aspect of Eclipse that is to be improved. Each plan item has its own entry in the Eclipse bugzilla database, with a title and a concise summary (usually a single paragraph) that explains the work item at a suitably high enough level so that everyone can readily understand what the work item is without having to understand the nitty-gritty detail.

> Note that, in place of a detailed requirements document, the detailed requirements are effectively provided via the Bugzilla database, where there is no real distinction between required features and a bug in what's been implemented. Bugzilla is an open source defect tracking application. See http://www.bugzilla.org/. A reference on Eclipse's specific use of Bugzilla is at https://bugs.eclipse.org/bugs/docs/html

. . . .

> A series of dots, as here (an "ellipsis"), indicates that the author omitted material from the original in the interest of brevity. The activities listed in the next paragraph are considered "maintenance," the topic covered in the last part of this book.

With the previous release as the starting point, this is the plan for how we will enhance and improve it. Fixing bugs, improving test coverage, documentation, examples, performance, usability, and so on, are considered routine ongoing maintenance activities and are not included in this plan unless they would also involve a significant change to the API or feature set, or involve a significant amount of work. All interesting feature work is accounted for in this plan.

> This provides more on the scope of this document. The activities listed are considered "maintenance," covered in the last part of this book. A three-part scheme for requirements priority is used, with the added "rejected" category. This merely keeps track of requirements that were proposed at some point and rejected.

The current status of each plan item is noted:

Committed plan item—A committed plan item is one that we have decided to address for the release.

Proposed plan item—A proposed plan item is one that we are considering addressing for the release. Although we are actively investigating it, we are not yet in a position to commit to it or to say that we won't be able to address it. After due consideration, a proposal will either be committed, deferred, or rejected.

Deferred plan item—A reasonable proposal that will not make it in to this release for some reason is marked as deferred with a brief note as to why it was deferred. Deferred plan items may resurface as committed plan items at a later point.

Rejected plan item—Plan items that were proposed but judged unworkable are marked as rejected plan items, with an accompanying summary of why they were dismissed. Keeping track of rejected items avoids repeating the discussion.

> This is more or less a triage classification, except that items considered and rejected are maintained for reference.

Release Deliverables

The release deliverables have the same form as previous releases, namely:

- Source code release for Eclipse Project, available as versions tagged "R3___0" in the Eclipse Project CVS repository.

- . . . .

Release Milestones

Release milestones occurring at roughly six-week intervals exist to facilitate coarse-grained planning and staging. The milestones are as follows.

> There is an attempt here to pace milestones at regular intervals to facilitate regular communication. Otherwise, long gaps would occur in which no communication is guaranteed, which is undesirable.

- Friday June 6, 2003—Milestone 1 (3. 0 M1), stable build reflecting progress

- Friday July 18, 2003—Has been tested and validated in the target operating configurations listed below.

- . . . .

> The remainder of the material at http://www.eclipse.org/eclipse/development/eclipse_project_plan_3_0.html consists of requirements, and are excerpted in Chapter 18, the Requirements Analysis part of this book.

8.6 CASE STUDY: PROJECT MANAGEMENT FOR OPENOFFICE

The case study in this section provides excerpts from the OpenOffice project management plan. For the most part, we will use the same headings as found in the official OpenOffice documentation.

OPENOFFICE PROJECT GUIDELINES

> Note to the Student:
> The following is taken from http://www.open-office.org/dev___docs/guidelines.html, with minor editing. It is titled "Guidelines for Participating in OpenOffice.org" and constitutes a project management subject.

OpenOffice.org is an open source project through which Sun Microsystems has released the technology for the StarOffice$^{(TM)}$ productivity suite. Sun sponsors and participates in OpenOffice.org; CollabNet hosts and helps manage the project. The overall name of the Project is OpenOffice.org, as is the name of the software product.

OpenOffice.org's main features include the following:

- Downloadable sources and information

- Community and communication mechanisms, such as mailing lists and forums

OpenOffice.org has established the necessary facilities to make this open-source technology available to all interested participants. Principal project objectives are as follows:

- Establishment of open, XML-based standards for office productivity file formats and language-independent bindings to component APIs

- Open access to the source code via CVS versioning to enable innovation for building the next generation of open-network productivity services

GOVERNANCE

> For a proprietary project, this would corre-
> spond to a management section.

OpenOffice.org is governed by the Community Council, which is constituted by members from the OpenOffice.org community. They created the charter establishing the Council. The Council holds periodic meetings by IRC as well as conducting business via discuss@council.openoffice.org mail list. Both IRC records and mail-list archives are public. Agenda items may be proposed by any member and should be sent to agenda@council.openoffice.org. For more information, go to the Council Web site.

The following sections describe guidelines regarding technical roles and responsibilities at OpenOffice.org and handling of source code. Substantial enhancements or modifications of these guidelines need approval of the Community Council.

For guidelines on the protocols for proposing projects to OpenOffice.org, please see Protocols for Project Proposal.

ROLES AND RESPONSIBILITIES

Everybody can help no matter what their role. The more a person gets involved in the project, the more he or she develops a trusting relationship with others. Those who have been long-term and valuable contributors to the project earn the right to commit directly to the source repository.

OpenOffice.org respects the rights of its community to post messages and use the mailing lists to further the aims of the project. In fact, we encourage people to use the mailing lists. To this end, we will do our best to limit "spam" and to ensure that communication among community members is carried out politely and efficiently. We have posted some "Mail-List Guidelines" that detail our commitment.

> We would state here something like the fol-
> lowing: "There are several categories of

> OpenOffice participant: members, developers,
> and project leads. These are explained next."

MEMBERS

"Members" refers to those persons who have joined the project by registering with OpenOffice.org and have a username. A member may not have subscribed to a mailing list, and a subscriber to a mailing list who is using the project may not have registered; only those who have registered are members. It is strongly encouraged that all members join the general and relevant specific project lists as well as joining a particular project. Initially, one can only join as an observer, a role that allows one to contribute to the project and otherwise participate in it.

DEVELOPERS

> Written rules like these are essential for get-
> ting the job done. Without them, there would
> be chaos and no OpenOffice.

Project members who give frequent and valuable contributions to a project can have their status promoted to that of a "developer" for that project. A developer has write access to the source code repository. A "content developer" has write access to a project's documentation but not to the source code.

In order for a contributor to become a developer, another developer has to nominate that contributor. The project lead may convert the contributor into a developer and give write access to the source code repository for the project.

At times, developers may go inactive for a variety of reasons. A developer who has been inactive for six months or more may lose his or her status as a developer. In this case or if the value of a developer's contributions diminishes, write access may be revoked by the responsible project lead.

A committed change must be reversed if this is requested by the responsible project lead or by the Community Council or its delegates and the conditions cannot be immediately satisfied by the equivalent of a "bug fix" commit. The situation must be rescinded before the change can be included in any public release.

> This paragraph belongs in a location where specific rules are given for committing code to OpenOffice.

PROJECT LEADS

There are three main categories of public projects in OpenOffice.org:

- Accepted projects ("projects")
- Incubator
- Native-lang

All accepted projects must have two leads. It is up to each project to determine the actual content of the roles each lead will take on. Native-lang and incubator projects may have one lead. Size and complexity are the determining factors: a large project requires two leads.

> Presumably, the requirement for two committed project leads minimizes the risk that a lead becomes unavailable, thereby threatening the health of the project. This is a facet of risk management.

A project lead is responsible for giving guidance and directions for his or her project and its part in the OpenOffice.org effort. The lead especially should make sure that questions about his or her project are answered and that a friendly and supportive environment is created. Contributions, maillist discussions, and forum interchanges, as well as issues and other administrative duties should be handled in an encouraging and productive fashion.

Loss of project lead status may occur not only due to contribution inactivity (as described for developers) but also because of missing fulfillment of responsibilities for the project the project lead is in charge of. Any member of the affected project may ask for the Community Council to reconsider a project lead, or to intervene in disputes or questions concerning project leadership. A decision by the Community Council is required to revoke project lead status.

Any member of a project is eligible for election to project lead of that project. Elections are arranged by the project concerned. A list of our current project leads can be found in the list of projects.

SCHEDULE

See http://development.openoffice.org/releases/OOo_2_0_timetable.html.

SOURCES

> This section is effectively a Software Configuration Management Plan.

The codebase is maintained in shared information repositories using CVS. Only developers and project leads have write access to these repositories. Everyone has read access via anonymous CVS or the Web front end.

All source code committed to the project's repositories must be covered by LGPL and SISSL. Files in the repository must contain a header according to the OpenOffice.org templates (available for code and makefiles). Contributors of source code larger than small changes must have signed the joint copyright assignment form before their contribution can be committed to the repository.

Straightforward patches and feature implementations can be committed without prior notice or discussion. Doubtful changes and large-scale overhauls need to be discussed before committing them into the repository. Any change that affects the semantics of an existing API function, configuration data, or file formats or other major areas must receive approval. A project lead may informally approve changes within his or her project. There are three different types of changes:

Info	Informational notice about an API change; no developer action necessary.
Recommended	Use the new API as soon as possible. The old API is obsolete and might go away in the near future. New code should always use the new API.
Required	Not complying with the new API will break the build or cause runtime failure. Developer action is mandatory.

> This gives a great deal of discretion to project leads. A more formal process, involving more people, may be impractical for an open source project like this.

Proposals for interproject changes of type "recommended" or "required" must be published with the suggested change date to the interface discussion mailing list. After one week of review, a change announcement must be published to the interface announce mailing list. During this announcement period, depending projects have to prepare their projects for the changes so that the following build will not break. They are responsible for reflecting the change in their project, not the requester. Within the two weeks of discussion/announcement, project leads may raise a flag, and project leads majority has to decide about cancellation of the change request.

> These documents provide a flavor for the management of the OpenOffice project. They are not intended to be complete.

8.7 CASE STUDY: STUDENT TEAM GUIDANCE

This section describes a hypothetical account of interactions among students as they prepare and conduct a project planning meeting, and guides students in producing a Software Project Management Plan.

8.7.1 Team Guidance: Steps to a Project Management Plan for Encounter

> Note to the Student:
> This section explains how the principles explained in this part of the book are translated into practice by a hypothetical student project team, using the Encounter case study as an example.

Before beginning the Software Project Management Plan (SPMP), the team met at least once to discuss the project in general terms, and Ed Braun was selected as team leader. The configuration management plan (SCMP) and quality plan (SQAP) were written.

PREPARING FOR THE PROJECT PLANNING MEETING

Well before the meeting, Ed looked through the IEEE SPMP headings (refer to Figure 8.24) for the major issues, and drafted material for each of them. In the case of the Encounter video game, he considered these to be the project organization (primary and backup roles, and their responsibilities) (Section 4.3 in Figure 8.1), risk management (5.4), and the schedule (5.2). Ed also drafted a brief paragraph for Section 1.1 (project summary). He left the staffing plan blank (i.e., who fills what role) because he felt it best to have members volunteer for roles at the meeting. He planned for the remaining issues to be filled in after the meeting. Via e-mail, Ed asked for a volunteer to perform cost estimation, since this is a technical task that requires significant lead time, and is best done by one or at most two people.

Ed wrote up options for objectives and priorities rather than selecting the top priority, since he did not want the group to feel railroaded into a decision. He included "attaining quality goals," "developing something that the members can use" (a favorite of his), and "complete project on schedule" as options for the top priority. He was pretty sure that the group would agree to a flat role-based organization as described in Section 9.4, so he wrote this into the straw man document.

Via e-mail, Ed asked team members to think about the risks that they consider threatening to the project, and to send write-ups to him 48 hours before the meeting, in the form of Table 8.1 in Section 10.4. Karen was concerned about the group's Java capabilities. She communicated with the rest of the team about their knowledge of Java, and described this risk as specifically as she could. She also researched companies that provide on-site training at short notice. Her step-by-step risk retirement plan was included in the material she sent to Ed. Hal Furnass had a concern about superimposing images in Java, and he sent his risk identification and retirement write-up to Ed. The latter collected these in the straw man SPMP, and listed them in priority.

Ed then drafted the following agenda for the meeting.

Meeting to be held in Engineering 397 at 10:00 a.m. to 11:30 a.m. Friday, September 1

1. Appoint record keeper and time keeper (5 minutes, 10:05)

2. Approve agenda and times for this meeting (5 minutes, 10:10)

3. Review SPMP sections supplied by Ed (25 minutes, 10:35)

4. Allocate remaining SPMP section to writers (20 minutes, 10:55)

5. Arrange review process (via e-mail and/or meeting) (5 minutes, 11:00)

6. Brainstorm for additional risks (10 minutes, 11:10)

7. Review action items (5 minutes, 11:15)

8. Miscellaneous business (10 minutes, 11:25)

Ed e-mailed the agenda and his straw man SPMP to the team members two days before the meeting, and asked them to read it over before the meeting. His version of the SPMP contained all of the IEEE headings.

THE INITIAL PROJECT PLANNING MEETING

At the meeting, Ed asked Fern to record action items and major decisions, and asked Al to watch the time and remind the team if it exceeded planned limits. It was understood that these two roles would rotate among the members in future meetings. Most of Ed's ideas were accepted. Several changes to Ed's proposed schedule were suggested. Hal pushed very hard for a buffer week in which no tasks are assigned. Karen pointed out that no work should be assigned during the week before the midterm. There was also a discussion of using a simple waterfall to avoid the complications of revisiting document, but this was dismissed as not reflecting the real world. Fern pushed for incremental development because she wanted to begin coding as soon as possible, but there was little support for this because the team did not even have architecture yet. Members felt that "quality" was an area they needed the most practice with.

After considerable debate about building an exciting computer game, the team decided that "the attainment of the specified quality parameters" would be its top priority. It was recognized that a quality game worth playing was out of the question in the time available, and that the actual capabilities would be have to be minimal. When the team arrived at role allocation, Karen volunteered immediately for the "design leader" role. There were three volunteers for "implementation leader" and none for QA leader. Ed compromised by suggesting that two of the three people split roles as QA and implementation leaders, switching halfway through the semester. The other roles were filled, and Ed reminded them of their responsibilities, and of their additional backup roles, as stated in the SPMP.

The discussion of how to allocate the writing of the SPMP went over its planned limit, but the discussion was productive and to the point, so Ed did not try to curtail it. It was decided that only two team members besides Ed would write the SPMP, and the rest would review their writing, since it would be too difficult in a short time to manage more people writing. After 10 minutes, the team found itself discussing very small sections, and Ed cut off discussion, promising to resolve the small differences offline, and e-mail the two members concerned a detailed allocation of the sections. The team decided that the writers would complete their sections by Friday at 6:00 p.m., and Ed would create the document from these and circulate the results to the team by Saturday at 3:00 p.m. Everyone would provide comments to Ed by Sunday at 3:00 p.m., and Ed would take all of these comments into account to finalize the document. A tentative meeting was set for Monday at 11:00 a.m. in Arts 283 in case it was necessary, and Ed was tasked with informing the team by Sunday night at 8:00 p.m. whether the meeting would be required or not.

Fern reviewed the decisions made, who was to write what sections, and when the due dates were. The meeting adjourned.

COMPLETING THE PROJECT MANAGEMENT PLAN

In writing the document details, the team realized that various issues had not been discussed at the meeting, including the details of "monitoring and controlling" (Section 5.3 in Figure 8.24). Hal's initial write-up of this section spoke of many meetings at which the project was to be reviewed, but most of the other members felt that many of the meetings were unnecessary. After reading several proposals, Ed tried to resolve the e-mail discussion by proposing that project monitoring be accomplished at weekly meetings, supplemented by meeting at the inception of each phase (which he would try to fold into weekly meetings as well). The team agreed. To allow for the possibility that more project meetings would be needed, a second weekly time was selected which members would keep available, but would be used only if required.

> The case study contains material concerning liaison activities. These are shown for illustration purposes, and would not normally be the responsibility of student teams. Some teams might want to designate a member as liaison to the instructor. This is usually best performed by the team leader. If the project has a true customer (i.e., the project is not just an invention of the team itself), then a liaison to the customer would be required: the requirements leader would normally have this task. If the project were an agile one, a customer representative would be part of the team.

8.7.2 Team Guidance—Software Project Management Plan

Student teams should create a Software Project Management Plan (SPMP) for their project using IEEE Std 1058-1998 as a template, the Team Guidance in the previous section, and the Encounter SPMP in Section 8.4 as guidance.

8.8 SUMMARY

Project costs are estimated as early as project initiation, well before the requirements are defined. The earlier the estimate is made the greater the margin of error, and we therefore use ranges as a way to calculate estimates. For example, during conceptualization, cost estimates can have a fourfold estimation error; after design, a twofold error.

Project estimates are done by first finding something objective to measure, such as lines of code (LOC). Since this is done before any code is written, the application is compared to the LOC of similar or related software produced in the same company, and the LOC of the new application is extrapolated from that. Another way to produce LOC is to compute *function points*, which objectively measure the intended functionality of the new software. The function point calculation produces a single number that is then converted to lines of code using a standard conversion. Once LOC are calculated, the COCOMO model can be used to compute an effort estimate.

Agile projects can be estimated by the use of story points, which are assigned based on a comparison of new stories to existing stories. For example, an average story is given a score of 5, and all new stories are compared to that story.

Once an estimate is made, a detailed schedule is constructed that lists all the tasks, their duration, their dependence on each other, and the resources assigned.

A project plan is created that includes all project information including project organization, roles and responsibilities, project estimate, schedule, and risks. It also includes references to such documents as configuration management, and verification and validation plans.

8.9 EXERCISES

1. Describe in at least one paragraph at least two consequences of failing to develop a written project plan.

2. Suppose you are tasked with computing the number of function points for a small application. Assume the application implements the following functionality measures, all of which can be characterized as having medium complexity:

   - number of external inputs: 4
   - number of external outputs: 5
   - number of external queries: 2
   - number of internal logical files: 2
   - number of external files: 3
   - Suppose also that the application has the following general characteristics:
   - requirements backup: 0
   - data communications: 0
   - distributed processing: 1
   - performance critical: 2
   - heavily utilized: 1
   - online entry: 4
   - multiple screens: 3
   - master fields: 3
   - file inquiries: 2
   - internal processing: 3
   - reuse: 2
   - conversion and installation: 1
   - multiple installations: 0
   - change and ease of use: 5

Compute the number of function points for this application.

3. Cost estimation is important, but can you cite a circumstance under which it is probably not worthwhile performing at all? Explain your answer.

4. Give one major advantage and one major disadvantage to the use of function points in estimation.

5. List a part of the SPMP that your student team is probably unable to supply at this stage of the project. This refers to a part you will have to return to after more work has been performed on the project.

6. Explain why project planning is considered one of the phases in the software life cycle and also an umbrella activity that stretches across several phases.

TEAM EXERCISE

SPMP

Develop a Software Project Management Plan for your project. Use (or tailor, or improve upon) the IEEE standard, as shown in the case study below. Include at least two iterations in the schedule. Obtain a rough estimate of the size of the product.

Before you begin, estimate the number of defects per page the team thinks it will discover during its final review. Keep track of, and report the time spent by individual members and by total team effort in the following stages: research, document preparation, review (including inspections). Show the actual defect density (average number of defects per page). Assess your team's effectiveness in each stage in a scale of 0 to 10. Summarize in a narrative, using the numerical results, and state how the team's progress could have been improved. The team is encouraged to use additional metrics if they contribute to effectiveness in this and future efforts.

Criteria:

1. Degree of clarity of the plan and addendum. (A = very clear writing; all specifics included, especially of risk retirement)

2. Degree of realism of the plan and addendum. (A = sets realistic goals and procedures (neither too ambitious nor too modest))

3. Extent to which the plan and addendum include all relevant specifics. (A = > 95% of knowable, relevant specifics included)

4. Extent to which the plan and addendum exclude irrelevant material. (A = < 5% if details supplied irrelevant)

5. Usefulness of your self-assessment.

BIBLIOGRAPHY

1. Boehm, Barry, *"Software Engineering Economics,"* Prentice Hall, 1981.
2. Albrecht, A. J., "Measuring Application Development Productivity," *Proceedings of the Joint SHARE/GUIDE/IBM Application Development Symposium,* October 1979, pp. 83–92.
3. International Function Point Users Group (December 1999). http://www.ifpug.org [accessed November 15, 2009]
4. "Function Point Languages Table Version 3.0," Quantitative Software Management, April 2005. http://www.qsm.com/?q=resources/function-point-languages-table/index.html [accessed November 15, 2009]
5. Jones, Capers, *"Applied Software Measurement: Global Analysis of Productivity and Quality,"* 3rd edition, McGraw-Hill Osborne Media, 2008.
6. Dorfman, M., and R. A. Thayer (eds and contributors), "Software Engineering," *IEEE Computer Society,* November 1999.
7. Eclipse. http://www.eclipse.org/eclipse/index.php [accessed December 10, 2009].
8. Eclipse. http://www.eclipse.org/platform/index.php.
9. Eclipse. http://www.eclipse.org/eclipse/development/eclipse_project_plan_3_0.html.

9

Quality and Metrics in Project Management

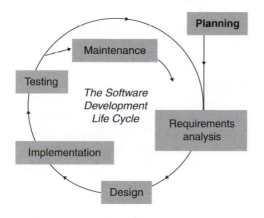

- How do you cultivate a quality mind-set in a project?

- What are examples of project metrics?

- How do you use metrics to improve projects?

- What is a software verification and validation plan?

- What is a good example of a planned verification and validation?

Figure 9.1 The context and learning goals for this chapter

Software quality does not come about by accident. Achieving it starts by cultivating a quality culture within the project team. It also requires careful planning and monitoring, with project managers continuously asking questions such as the following throughout the life of a project.

- Is the project on schedule? Is it late?

- Are too many defects being discovered? Too few?

- Are defects being fixed too slowly?

- Is testing progressing at the desired pace?

Agile teams become adept at answering these questions for team-level work. Continual interaction with the customer, short, mutually defined sprints, and continual testing mean that questions like these are being continually asked and answered in the context of the team and customer representative. On the other hand, the scope of the project can exceed a single group, in which case various non-agile techniques are applied as well.

As introduced in Chapter 2, the answers to these and similar questions are provided by metrics, which are data collected and analyzed throughout a project.

Examples of project metrics are *defects per KLOC* (thousand lines of code), *lines coded per man-month* (MM), and *test case execution rate*. Each provides an objective measure of a project and its processes. Metrics are an important tactical tool of the project manager. They allow the manager to continuously assess project quality and schedule, identify problem areas, and gain insights into the project that allow him or her to make proactive decisions to head off problems. As an example, if during the testing of the software an unusually high number of defects are discovered in a particular software module, action can be taken to proactively remedy the root cause, such as conducting a code inspection, redesigning the module, or executing unit tests. Without metrics, it is difficult to know how a project is executing and the quality level of the software. Metrics help not only current projects but also future ones. This is because future projects base metric targets on past ones.

Targets must be established to effectively utilize the metrics collected. For example, if 50 test cases are executed during the first week of system testing, is the testing team making good progress or poor progress? The answer depends on the test case execution goal defined during project planning. If the plan called for executing 100 test cases, then the answer is poor progress; if the plan was 20 test cases, then the answer is good progress. This also assumes a standard for "test case." The goals are established by analyzing metrics collected during prior projects and using them as baselines.

9.1 CULTIVATING AND PLANNING INTERNAL QUALITY

Internal quality refers to the quality activities undertaken by the development team itself. This calls for cultivating a quality culture among the development team, an attribute of good leadership. The essential goal here is a sense of shared responsibility and pride among the team members. Fundamental gains in a quality attitude accrue when the project leader continuously ensures that the work is very orderly, and that the team's efforts are focused on appropriate priorities.

We plan for the management of a project and its internal quality assurance procedures at the same time. Internal quality procedures, standards, and habits are active throughout the project management plan, the requirements, the design, and the code.

External provision for quality is specified in a separate set of documents: the quality assurance plan, the verification and validation plan, and the test documentation. The relationship of internal and external quality activities is illustrated in Figure 9.2.

The internal management of quality is as much a mind-set as a document set. It begins with a configuration management plan that ensures consistent and safe documentation. (For example, if we were to implement the wrong version of the design document, the code would not match the requirements for the implementation, and thus would hardly be a high-quality product!)

Most project management plans designate team members with specific responsibilities. Table 9.1 shows an example of responsibility designation in which each member also has a backup responsibility. Each activity

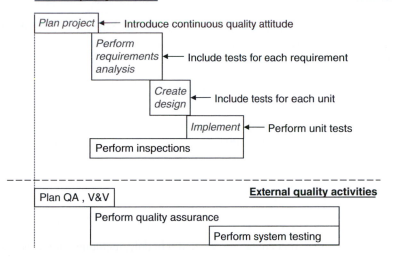

Internal quality activities

Plan project ◄── Introduce continuous quality attitude

Perform requirements analysis ◄── Include tests for each requirement

Create design ◄── Include tests for each unit

Implement ◄── Perform unit tests

Perform inspections

External quality activities

Plan QA , V&V

Perform quality assurance

Perform system testing

Figure 9.2 Managing quality—internal and external activities to promote quality in projects

leader promotes an attitude of quality for his activity. The backup members can act as pair inspectors for each leader.

9.2 PROJECT METRICS

Project metrics are those that apply across the board or have broad implications during a project rather than being very focused. The metrics process starts by identifying which metrics to collect, setting target goals for each, and regularly monitoring and reviewing them throughout the project. This is described in detail in the sections that follow.

Table 9.1 Example of responsibilities for documentation, with backup

Name	Primary Responsibility	Backup Responsibility
Alice Jarman	Team leader	Configuration management
Bruce Stern	Configuration management	Security
Bob Crowder	Internal quality	Team leader
Sarah Fournier	Security	Internal quality
Hans Lightman	Requirements	Release
Vladimir Norsk	Design	Requirements
John Green	Implementation	Design
Susan Klein	Release	Implementation

9.2.1 Identification

During project planning, the metrics to be collected are identified. Some are applicable to all phases (e.g., defects) while others only apply to a specific phase (e.g., test case execution). While there are many metrics to chose from, some of the most useful are as follows [1]:

- Project milestones

- Testing progress

- Defect detection and defect injection per phase

- Defect resolution

We discuss each of these next.

Project Milestones
A plan is created early in a project that contains a detailed schedule, including milestones, which are concrete objectives that must be achieved at specific times. A project manager monitors the progress of a project against these milestones to determine whether it is on schedule. Project scheduling and the establishment of milestones were covered in Chapter 10. The obvious metric here is the number of days between a milestone's schedule and the day on which it was actually reached.

Testing Progress
A test plan is usually constructed before any formal testing commences. It includes information regarding the types of test cases to run and detailed information regarding each test case. The most common metrics to collect during formal testing are the *rate of test case execution* and the *number of passed test cases*. With these two metrics, project managers can determine whether testing is proceeding on schedule.

Defect Injection and Detection
Defect metrics are probably the most common type of metric collected. Defects occur during each development phase, but such defects may have been incurred (or "injected") during a previous phase. The *defect detection rate* is measured for a given detection phase and a given injection phase. For example, a "defect detection rate of 0.2 per 100 requirements defects at the implementation phase" means that one defect in the requirements is detected, on average, when implementing a set of 500 requirements. Figure 9.3 shows an example project in which these data have been collected. It also shows the longevity of defects: phase of injection vs. phase of detection. For the sake of simplicity, we have omitted the test and post-delivery phases, which would complete the picture.

Let's focus on the detailed requirements part of Figure 9.3. It shows that two defects per 100 were detected during the requirements phase (assessed by means of inspections). This compares favorably with the organization's norm of 5 per 100. Looking across the "detailed requirements" row, we observe that our process detected fewer than the normal rate of requirements defects during subsequent phases. This seems to tell us that our project, and possibly the process we are using, is comparatively effective when it comes to producing quality requirements. However, it is also possible that our detection process is worse than usual! This bears investigation. To complete the table, we would include similar defect data collected during testing, and during a specific time (e.g., three months) after product delivery.

The results for *design* defects in Figure 9.3 are as follows. We detected more than the usual number of design defects during inspections at the time they were injected, but recognized fewer design defects at later

Defects detected: Per 100 requirements/per . . . in the design/per KLoC, etc. **This project**/*norm*		Phase in which defect was **detected**			
		Detailed requirements	Design	Implementation	Deployment
Phase in which defect was **injected**	Detailed requirements	2/5	0.5/1.5	0.1/0.3	3/1
	Design		3/1	1/3	3/2
	Implementation			2/2	5/3
	Deployment				3/12

Figure 9.3 Examples of defect count—injection phase vs. detection phase

stages. Since it is more expensive to detect and repair a defect later in the process, this indicates that our project seems to be superior to the organization norms. Figure 9.3 also contains information about defects detected after deployment to customers, which is surely the most important metric in the end.

Defect Resolution

Tracking defect detection tells us the rate at which we are finding defects, giving an indication of the quality of the evolving product. Equally important is the metric *defect resolution*, which measures the rate at which defects are being resolved. Defect detection and defect closure are complimentary. For example, even if defect detection is meeting or beating the plan, if the defect resolution rate is below plan, the backlog of open defects increases and the quality and schedule of the project suffer.

9.2.2 Planning

Once the set of metrics to be collected is identified, a plan is established with targets for each metric. The best way to derive targets is to use the metrics collected during previous projects as a baseline, adjusted as necessary. Without projections based on previous projects, it is very difficult for project managers to know whether a project is meeting expectations. An example of a plan used to track *defect detection* and *defect resolution* is shown in Figure 9.4.

Figure 9.4 tracks the number of defects submitted and resolved weekly versus the plan. Each week the actual number of defects discovered is filled in and compared with the plan. In this example, note that the number of open defects for the first three weeks is greater than what had been anticipated. At the end of week 3/10–3/16, 103 defects are open vs. a plan of 66. Armed with this knowledge, the project manager can take appropriate corrective action. Similar plans are created for each of the other metrics collected.

9.2.3 Monitor and Review

During the life of a project it is a good idea for key members of the project team to review the metrics on a regular basis, usually weekly. One good way to do this is for the project manager to create a packet of information containing metrics charts as shown in Figure 9.4. This helps present the information in a concise format for easier review. However, just presenting these overview charts may not be enough. For example, in addition to the defect plan shown in Figure 9.4, additional information such as detailed

Week of	Build	Plan			Actual		
		Submitted	Resolved	Open	Submitted	Resolved	Open
2/17 - 2/23	44			66			66
2/24 - 3/02	45	40	40	66	52	42	76
3/03 - 3/09	46	40	40	66	48	42	82
3/10 - 3/16	47	40	40	66	56	35	103
3/17 - 3/23	48	40	40	66			
3/24 - 3/30	49	30	54	42			
3/31 - 4/07	50	20	44	18		TROUBLE!	
4/08 - 4/14	51	10	28	0			
4/15 - 4/21	52	10	10	0			
4/22 - 4/28	53	5	5	0			
4/29 - 5/05	54	3	3	0			
5/06 - 5/12	55	3	3	0			

Figure 9.4 Example of tracking defect resolution—recognizing problems with defects remaining open

defect reports may be included to better understand the source of the problems being discovered. If this is done for each of the metrics included in the report, the amount of information can become overwhelming. Although it is still a good idea to include it all, it is common to create a summary, sometimes in the form of a *project dashboard*. A dashboard presents a concise, graphical summary of essential information regarding the general health of a project. This is analogous to an automobile dashboard, which contains gauges such as fuel level, odometer, and engine temperature, to quickly ascertain the general status and health of a car. Figure 9.5 shows an example dashboard from the

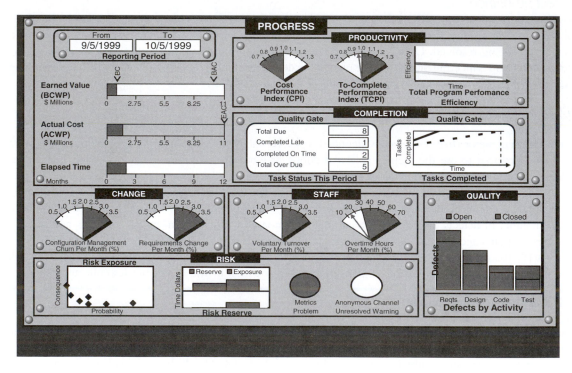

Figure 9.5 Example of a project management dashboard

Source: Software Program Managers Network (SPMN), http://www.spmn.com. Provided by AMERICAN SYSTEMS with permission.

Software Program Manager's Network [2]. The type of information contained in a dashboard includes the following:

- Milestone completion

- Requirements changes

- Configuration changes

- Staff turnover

- Staff overtime hours

- Quality metrics such as defects per phase

- Risk analysis

With this concise project information, stakeholders can focus their attention only on those metrics not conforming to plan. For example, it can be noted from Figure 9.5 that the plan calls for two requirements changes per month, but in the period covered by the dashboard three requirements changed. Stakeholders can now look at more detailed information regarding the requirements that changed to determine whether they pose a risk to the project. Other metrics that are meeting or beating the plan need not be examined in great detail.

9.3 USING METRICS FOR IMPROVEMENT

Companies strive to improve their project execution in two ways:

- By improvement within a project, from one phase to the next

- By improvement across projects, from one project to the next

But how do you identify what needs improvement? There is a wise saying that "you can't improve what you don't measure." Metrics provide the measures that allow project managers to identify how a project is performing, the areas requiring the most improvement, and the objective data needed to measure the rate of improvement. The next two sections describe how this is accomplished within and across projects.

9.3.1 Improvement within a Project

The first step to improve quality from one development phase to the next is to collect metrics during each phase. Table 9.2 shows a summary chart that can be used, which includes provisions for comparison with past projects. The data can be used in two ways:

1. To assess the health of each phase's artifacts.

    For example, if the defect rate for our requirements is 0.7 per page and the company's average is 0.3 per page, then we have identified an issue with our requirements. (The concept of a defect in a page of documentation has to be carefully defined to ensure consistency.)

2. To assess our management of this project.

    For example, if our defect rates are lower than the company's norms for most phases so far, then we are probably managing our project well. A final judgment on this would depend on the defect rate of the delivered project compared with the norm.

Table 9.2 Data on activities relating to document creation and error rates

	Research	Meeting	Drafting[T0]	Reviewing[T1]	Finalizing[T2]	Post-mortem	TOTAL
Time[L1]	120	30	210	130	140	30	660
% Time	18%	5%	32%	15%	21%	10%	N/A
(Average % time)[L2]	−14%	−7%	−15%	−30%	−16%	−18%	N/A
Quantity[L3]	N/A	N/A	22	N/A	N/A	N/A	28
Productivity	TBD[I1]	TBD[I1]	6.3	TBD[I1]	TBD[I1]	N/A	2.5[I2]
(Average productivity)	TBD[I1]	TBD[I1]	TBD[I1]	TBD[I1]	TBD[I1]	TBD[I1]	18.3[I2]
Self-assessed quality[L4]	3	5	2	1	5	9	N/A
Defect rate[L5]	N/A	N/A	1.5[I3]	N/A	TBD[I4]	N/A	N/A
(Average defect rate)	N/A	N/A	(1.1)	N/A	TBD	N/A	N/A
Process improvement note #	(1)		(2)	(3)		(4)	

The information in Table 9.2 is examined, column by column, identifying data that are different from par. For each datum below par, we devise concrete actions that the team will perform differently for the next phase. For each datum above par, we look for beneficial techniques that may be applied in future phases. "Self-assessments" are comparative, subjective scores that the team assigns various activities. One way to collect them for four activities, let us say, is to ask each team member to allocate $5 \times 4 = 20$ points among the four activities, each score being between 0 and 10. The averages indicate how well the team as a whole thinks it performed on each activity. This is a subjective measure that can be profitably compared with other metrics.

Here is an explanation of the superscripts in Table 9.2.

Left-Hand Column

[L1] Spent by entire team, in person-hours

[L2] The average amount of time spent on these activities in one of the following (select one): entire organization on all projects, entire organization on similar projects (the ideal), this department on all projects, this department on similar projects, this team on prior phases.

[L3] For documents: total number of pages produced in the case of documents. For code: ×1000 lines of non-commented code. A line of non-commented code is defined as <A precise definition is provided here, perhaps showing examples of how to count lines for common constructs such as *for* loops.>

[L4] This is a judgment that the team makes about the quality of the activity's product. It is subjective but can be very useful. A good way to obtain self-criticism is to force the average of these numbers to be five on a scale of 0 to10.

[L5] This is a key metric. It is necessary to define the following:

- What severity of defects will be counted (usually any besides trivial)

- When in the process these are counted (so as to be consistent for the sake of comparison)

Top Row

[T0] Spent by team members preparing the artifact to the best of their ability; before submitting artifact to the rest of the team for review

[T1] Includes inspections

[T2] After review; responding to comments from the rest of the team

Interior of Table

[I1] Measuring productivity for these activities is a more advanced concept and is covered later.

[I2] Pages per hour = (total pages)*60/(total time in minutes)

[I3] Found during the "finalizing" stage

[I4] This metric is determined by the end of the project—or even during maintenance—when defects are detected that were injected during this phase.

The following notes correspond to the last row in Table 9.2 and are examples of specific process improvement actions.

1. Our self-assessed quality measure on *research* was 3. The team spent a percentage of time on this activity that is close to the norm, so the remedy is not to spend more time on research. If there were known reasons why research was on the poor side (e.g., a new procedure or very unfamiliar type of application) then the data here may not be a cause for alarm. Otherwise, the team would discuss how to improve the research process in the future.

2. The *drafting* of the artifact was poor in several respects. It took more than twice as long to draft a page than is usual; the product of drafting was significantly poorer than the self-assessed average of five; and the defect rate was significantly higher than the norm. The table by itself provides no explanations or trade-offs to deal with this, it merely indicates the problem. The team considers the particular circumstances of the activity and decides what went wrong and how to fix it. For example, perhaps the main reviewer was Ed and his mother became ill during the activity. The team may conclude that there was not enough backup for lead writers, for example.

3. The next problematical activity was *reviewing*, where the score was lowest: 1. Since the team spent 20 percent of its time reviewing compared with the norm of 30 percent, the team's first conclusion is probably to spend more time reviewing. This has to come at the expense of another activity. The team would probably take the time from the *postmortem* activity, where its score was very high, and *finalizing*, where it spent more than the usual amount of time.

4. To capture beneficial practices for the future, the team notes areas where it performed well. This applies to the *postmortem* activity, where it performed highly to its satisfaction and used less time than is usual. The team must identify the reasons. An example is any unusual activity, such as team members bringing to the postmortem prepared statements of process improvement.

Our self-evaluation gives scores of **3 to review and 8 to research** out of a forced average of 5. We spent 15% of our time on review and 25% on research. **We will spend 20% on each** of these activities for the next phase.

Our **defect rate** declined steadily except for this phase, when it **rose**. This seemed to be due to a lack of common vision prior to dividing the writing. In past phases, we succeeded in establishing a common vision of what we wanted to do before beginning to write our parts. Before beginning to write the next document we will confirm a **shared vision**.

The **ratio of requirements time to design** time was 1.2, which is lower than this ratio from past successful projects in the company. Our design self-evaluation was 6, more than average. On our next project, we plan to **spend 10% more time on requirements analysis** at the expense of design time.

Figure 9.6 Using project metrics to improve software development processes

Teams set aside time at the end of each phase to assess the conclusions drawn from metrics, and to write down how it will improve its process during the next phase. Figure 9.6 shows examples of improvement conclusions.

9.3.2 Improvement across Projects

Companies strive to improve their performance from project to project. No matter how efficient they are, the best organizations know they can always improve. They identify areas for improvement and specify actions that will lead to the desired improvements in those areas on subsequent projects.

Steps that can be taken to achieve these improvements are as follows:

1. Identify several areas for improvement that are important to the company. Examples include *quality*, *schedule predictability*, and *efficiency*.

2. Identify and collect metrics that measure performance in each of these areas. These metrics are used as baselines for setting goals in future projects.

3. As part of project planning for a future project, establish goals for improvement in each of the identified areas, using metrics from prior projects as a baseline.

4. Identify specific actions to implement that will support achievement of the goals.

As an example, Figure 9.7 lists four areas that have been identified for improvement: *schedule, predictability, efficiency*, and *time-to-market*. A metric is identified to accurately measure project performance in each area. Note that there may be several appropriate metrics to use in each area, but for simplicity we are only identifying one. An improvement goal is identified for each category, and specific actions are defined to be implemented in the next project in order to reach the targeted improvement goal.

Figure 9.8 contains a generic set of actions to be implemented in order to reach the first quality improvement goal listed in Figure 9.7: reducing *defects/KLOC* by 10 percent. Note that in this example we are only focusing on the *defects/KLOC* as a measure of quality; in practice there are others we would focus on as well.

The first of the improvement steps is to identify those parts of the software that contained the most defects during the prior release. The areas are then targeted for additional design and code reviews to understand why they contained a high number of defects, and a plan is devised to refactor those areas during the subsequent project to improve their quality. Provisions are made in the planning of the subsequent project to incorporate these actions.

Category	Metric	Description	Improvement Goal
Quality	Defects/KLOC	New defects found during formal QA testing, per churned KLOC	10%
Predictability	% schedule accuracy improvement	% improvement across releases	5%
Efficiency	MM/KLOC	Pre-QA development effort per churned KLOC	10%
Time to Market	Calendar time/KLOC	Pre-QA calendar time per churned KLOC	15%

Figure 9.7 Improving projects across the organization—examples of improvement goals

9.4 SOFTWARE VERIFICATION AND VALIDATION PLAN

Recall that *verification* responds mainly to the question "Are we correctly building those artifacts in the present phase that were specified in the previous phases?" *Validation* responds to the question "Do the artifacts just completed in the present phase satisfy their specifications from previous phases?"

IEEE 1012-2004 Software Verification and Validation Plan, whose headings are reproduced in Figure 9.9, provides a framework for expressing the manner in which V&V is to be carried out. This specification is written during initial project planning, and compliments the Software Quality Assurance Plan covered in Chapter 6 and the case study in Chapter 8.

The annexes to IEEE V&V Standard 1012-1998 are as follows:

Annex

A. Mapping of ISO/IEC 12207 V&V requirements to IEEE Std 1012 V&V activities and tasks

B. A software integrity level scheme

C. Definition of independent verification and validation (IV&V)

Improvement Category: Quality

Actions:

1. Identify components of software that contained most defects.

2. Plan to conduct design and code reviews in these areas.

3. Plan to refactor several of these areas during subsequent project.

Figure 9.8 Example improvement plan

1. **Purpose**

2. **Referenced documents**

3. **Definitions**

4. **V&V overview**
   4.1 Organization*
   4.2 Master schedule
   4.3 Software integrity level scheme
   4.4 Resource summary
   4.5 Responsibilities
   4.6 Tools, techniques, and methodologies

5. **V&V processes**
   5.1 Management of V&V
   5.2 Acquisition V&V
   5.3 Development V&V

5.4 Operation V&V
5.5 Maintenance V&V

6. **V&V reporting requirements**
   6.1 Reporting
   6.2 Administrative
   6.3 Documentation

7. **V&V administrative requirements**
   7.1 Anomaly reporting and resolution
   7.2 Task iteration policy
   7.3 Deviation policy
   7.4 Standards, practices, and conventions

8. **V&V documentation requirements**

*Subheadings are typical examples (IEEE)

Figure 9.9 IEEE 1012-2004 Software Verification and Validation Plan—table of contents
Source: IEEE Std 1012-2004.

C.1 Technical independence

C.2 Managerial independence

C.3 Financial independence

C.4 Forms of independence

   C.4.1 Classical IV&V

   C.4.2 Modified IV&V

   C.4.3 Internal IV&V

   C.4.4 Embedded V&V

D. V&V of reusable software

E. V&V metrics

   E.1 Metrics for evaluating software development processes and products

   E.2 Metrics for evaluating V&V tasks and for improving the quality and coverage of V&V tasks

F. Example of V&V organizational relationship to other project responsibilities

G. Optional V&V task descriptions

H. Other references

I. Definitions from existing standards (normative)

Copyright © IEEE 2003

An ideal procedure is for an outside group to perform V&V. This is called *Independent Verification and Validation* (IV&V).

The next section in the chapter gives an example of a SVVP case study.

9.5 CASE STUDY: SOFTWARE VERIFICATION AND VALIDATION PLAN FOR ENCOUNTER

> Note to the Student:
> This section shows an example of Software Verification and Validation Plan for the Encounter video game project, organized in accordance with IEEE 1012-2004. In the interests of space, various sections have been omitted.

1. Purpose

This document provides the verification and validation procedures that will be followed for the development of the Encounter video game.

2. Referenced Documents

Software Project Management Plan
Software Configuration Management Plan

3. Definitions

None

4. V&V Overview

4.1 Organization

> This section describes how the V&V effort will be organized (in terms of roles) and how it relates to the development phases.

The verification and validation of Encounter is coordinated with each phase of every iteration.

4.2 Master Schedule

Because of the organization of V&V as described in Section 4.1, the V&V schedule follows directly to the project schedule as defined in the SPMP.

4.3 Resource Summary

> This section describes the person-hours required for V&V or the amount required to fund an external organization for IV&V.

Verification will be performed internally. Validation will be performed partly by project engineers. The costs of this internal work are built into the SPMP. Validation will also be performed by one external QA engineer. This person will consume four person-months.

4.4 Software Integrity Level Scheme

> The integrity level of software expresses how critical it is. Software components that potentially threaten safety have the highest integrity level. The IEEE standard describes four levels: high, major, moderate, and low. A tool supporting informal research, for example, would probably be required to have only a low integrity level.

The Encounter application is required to have moderate integrity.

4.5 Responsibilities

The development team members will

- Perform verification activities throughout the project, including inspections within all phases

- Perform and document all unit testing using JUnit

- Validate requirements documents with the marketing manager

The QA engineer will

- Verify that the team has followed its documented procedures, including those described in this document

- Perform all post-unit testing
- Report the results to the team and management
- Maintain this document

4.5 Tools, techniques, and methodologies

To be supplied

5. Life Cycle V&V

5.1 Management of V&V

The V&V effort on Encounter (internal and external) will be supervised by the manager of Quality Assurance.

> Each of the following sections describes how V&V of every process will be conducted. When this is to be performed internally, it can be included in the corresponding document (SPMP, SRS, etc.), and this V&V document can refer to those.

5.2 Acquisition V&V

> "Acquisition" is the process by which an organization obtains software. Using third-party software relieves the development organization of having to reinvent the wheel. However, it places a burden on the organization to certify the quality of such software. Many disasters have been experienced because this step was avoided.

Each vendor-supplied tool used for the development of Encounter will be validated by the QA engineer.

5.3 Development V&V

5.3.1 Concept V&V
Conceptual work on the Encounter game concept will be verified by answering the following questions:

- Are all critical marketing factors identified?
- Does any concept imply a significant risk to project completion? If so, should that concept be mitigated?

5.3.2 Requirements V&V
The Encounter SRS will be verified by answering the following questions:

- Are all critical requirements that were identified during the concept phase specified?
- Is the SRS organized in a way that facilitates traceability?
- Does the SRS account for all required interfaces with other systems?
- Does any requirement imply a significant risk to project completion? If so, should that requirement be mitigated?

The Encounter SRS will be validated by exposing it to the marketing department and to a sample of 30 game players.

5.3.3 Design V&V
The Encounter SDD will be verified by answering the following question:

- Are all requirements accommodated by the design?

5.3.4 Implementation V&V
The implementation of Encounter will be verified by answering the following questions:

- Are all requirements fully verified?
- Is the code organized in a way that facilitates traceability back to design and requirements?
- Is all code documented according to standards?
- Is all code thoroughly documented?

5.3.2 Test V&V
The test documentation of Encounter will be verified by answering the following verification questions, and the validation questions that follow.

- Are all critical requirements intended to be fully tested at every level of detail (e.g., human safety)?

- Is the test philosophy adequate for the requirements?

- Are the test plans complete as specified in the test philosophy?

- Are the test cases complete as specified in the test philosophy?

For the test plans and procedures, the reader is referred to the Software Test Documentation. These plans and procedures are designed to accommodate the following validation questions.

- Do the defect count, defect rate, outstanding defects, and defect severity attest to an acceptable product?

- If not, what success rate will be required to attain acceptability?

- Do they account for all of the metrics specified in the SQAP?

5.8 Operation V&V

> This part verifies that the application is appropriately supported after deployment to users.

To be supplied

5.9 Maintenance V&V

The maintenance plan shall be verified against company maintenance criteria, specified in the company's maintenance requirements and procedures, document 890.23.

6. Reporting Requirements

> This includes who reports the results of the V&V effort and to whom do they provide these reports.

6.1 Reporting

The QA person attached to the project reports the status of V&V weekly to the manager of QA and copies the team leader.

6.2 Administrative

> This describes who is responsible for the V&V reporting effort.

The project leader is responsible for ensuring that all V&V reporting is performed.

6.3 Documentation

A single report that includes all versions of the results of the tasks described in this document is maintained.

7. V&V Administrative Requirements

> This describes who is responsible for the V&V effort.

7.1 Anomaly Reporting and Resolution

The QA engineer attached to the Encounter project will maintain the current state and the history of each defect found. The QA engineer will maintain all metrics identified in the SQAP on a Web site and will e-mail a list of all anomalies (including defects) that he or she deems to have excessive repair timelines. This includes defects with no repair duration estimates and those that have exceeded their planned completion date. The Bugzilla facility will be used.

7.2 Task Iteration Policy

> This section explains the circumstances under which V&V tasks are repeated because of results obtained or because of changes in the project.

V&V tasks will be repeated at the discretion of the QA representative, but these will include the following criteria.

- An inspection whose defects count is more than 20 percent greater than the norm.

- A test whose defects count is more than 20 percent greater than the norm.

- An entire phase if the previous phase changes by more than 20 percent.

7.3 Deviation Policy

> Describes the procedures required to deviate from this plan.

Any proposal to deviate from this plan requires the approval of the QA manager and the project manager.

7.4 Standards, Practices, and Conventions

These are set down for all company projects at http:// . . . .

8. V&V Documentation Requirements

> Section 6 described what should be reported. Section 8 covers the means for noting in writing the results of V&V. It specifies the form that all V&V documentation must take. For example, it could be organized as an appendix to this document.

9.6 SUMMARY

Quality in project management begins by cultivating a quality culture within the project team. Members develop a shared responsibility and pride. Many projects designate team members with specific responsibilities, and each activity leader promotes an attitude of quality for his activity.

Ensuring quality requires careful planning and monitoring throughout. Metrics are collected and analyzed, providing means of concretely assessing how well a project is executing. There are many useful metrics; some of the most basic are *project milestone planned vs. fulfilled*, *defect counts*, and *test execution*.

After identifying the metrics to be collected, a plan is created with goals for each. Targets are created by analyzing previous projects and using metrics from those as a baseline. If targets aren't established, project managers will not know whether a project is on track.

During the course of a project, the team meets regularly to review the metrics. In addition to the detailed data, a graphical summary often known as a *project dashboard* is created. The dashboard presents the key metrics in a clear, concise manner, allowing the team to quickly ascertain how each is aspect of the project is performing against the plan.

Successful companies strive to improve the overall quality of their performance, both during the course of a project and between successive projects. Metrics are analyzed in each case to identify areas requiring the most improvement. Specific actions are then enacted, and metrics objectively measure whether the improvements are providing the anticipated results.

The Software Verification and Validation Plan is an important part of project quality. It specifies a plan for generating artifacts based on specifications of previous phases (*verification*), and for building software that meets customer's wants and needs (*validation*). IEEE 1012-2004 provides a framework for this document.

9.7 EXERCISES

1. In your own words, define "project metrics" and explain how they are used in managing a project.

2. The defect plan in Figure 9.3 shows the number of open defects falling behind plan starting in week 1. Assuming you are the project manager, at what point would you start taking corrective action?

Would it be after the first week, or would you wait a number of weeks to see whether the situation improves? Are there any other metrics you might collect to help you decide? Write a paragraph to explain your answer.

3. Describe in your own words how a project manager could utilize a project dashboard in managing a project.

4. What metrics related to software testing might you include in a weekly project metrics report to provide insight into the status of the testing process? Explain your choices.

5. For each of the remaining categories in Figure 9.7 (predictability, efficiency, time to market), create an action plan to reach the stated improvement goals. Use Figure 9.8 as a template for your plans. Include a minimum of three actions to take for each category.

TEAM EXERCISE

V&V Plan

T1. Produce the relevant parts of a V&V plan using IEEE standard 1012-1986. Measure and report on the metrics described in Team Exercise T1 in Chapter 6.

Criteria:

1 Practicality: How well does the plan ensure that the work will be adequately verified and validated? (A = completely practicable in the environment of the project)

2 Specifics: How specific is the plan in terms of suitably naming places and participants? (A = spells out exactly how V&V will be performed in the environment of the development)

3 Team participant perception: To what degree are participants likely to perceive your plan as a help to them? (A = written in a way that respects the time and efforts of engineers)

SQAP

T2. Produce a realistic software quality assurance plan for your project. Measure the time spent on this effort by individual members and by the complete team. Provide the corresponding metric data and self-assessment for this assignment, as described in Team Exercise in Chapter 8.

Criteria: as for Team Exercise in Chapter 8.

BIBLIOGRAPHY

1. Laird, Linda M., and M. Carol Brennan, "Software Measurement and Estimation: A Practical Approach," *Wiley-Interscience*, 2006, pp. 181–192.
2. Software Program Managers Network (SPMN). http://www.spmn.com.

10

Principles of Requirements Analysis

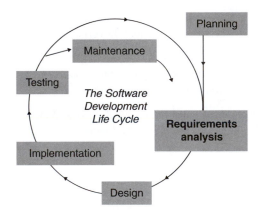

- Planning
- Maintenance
- Testing
- *The Software Development Life Cycle*
- **Requirements analysis**
- Implementation
- Design

- Why the term requirements "analysis?"

- What is the value of written requirements?

- Where do requirements come from?

- What is the difference between high-level and detailed requirements?

- What is the difference between functional and nonfunctional requirements?

- How do you document requirements?

- What does traceability mean?

- How do agile teams handle requirements?

- How can student teams gather requirements?

Figure 10.1 The context and learning goals for this chapter

Before a software system is designed and implemented, one needs to understand what that system is intended to do. This intended functionality is referred to as the *requirements*, and the process of gaining the necessary understanding of this is called *requirements analysis*. An application for video store management, for example, could mean different things to different people, each a somewhat differing set of requirements. One interpretation could be an application that tracks employee time and outputs paychecks; another, an e-mail

- The process of **understanding what's wanted** and **needed** in an application. For example, you may know that you *want* a colonial house in New England, but you may not know that you will probably *need* a basement for it.

- We express requirements **in writing** to complete our understanding and to create a contract between developer and customer.

Figure 10.2 The meaning of requirements analysis

application that processes customer rental requests; a third, an application that records rented videos and computes charges; and so on. As in most business endeavors, the reliable and professional way to specify what is agreed upon is to express it in writing. Therefore the output of requirements analysis is a software requirements specification (SRS). These points are summarized in Figure 10.2.

A requirement specifies *what* the customer wants. This normally does not include anything about *how* the application is designed or programmed. Specifying a requirement is like telling a contractor that you want a 12 foot by 15 foot room added to your house. You generally do not specify how you want the contractor to build the addition—that is a design and construction issue.

10.1 THE VALUE OF REQUIREMENTS ANALYSIS

A defective requirement (i.e., one not repaired before the requirements document is finalized) turns out to be very expensive. It is an estimated 20 to 100 times more expensive to repair if allowed to slip through the development process compared with repairing it soon after it is incurred. In financial terms, if the cost of finding and repairing a defect at requirements time is $1, then the cost of finding and fixing that same defect at the end of the development process is $20 to $100. The damage that results from the customer's poor experience with the application is a factor additional to the expense involved.

Given the tremendous benefit of detecting and repairing defects at requirements time, why are so many projects damaged by poor or nonexistent requirements analysis? A principal reason is that customers usually do not know at the beginning of a project all that they want or need. Instead, they learn to understand what they themselves want only while the project progresses. The Encounter case study is an example of this uncertainty; it has a purpose, but one whose details are still in formation. This book emphasizes iterative development and the close alignment between the requirements, design, and implementation. Agile methods are a prime example. Engineers using a well-organized iterative process gather requirements, design for those requirements, and implement for them in coordinated iterations.

10.2 SOURCES OF REQUIREMENTS

We usually think of *customers* as the source of requirements since applications are built for them. In practice, matters are rarely simple here because the people paying for an application, the people who will be using the application, and the people designated to work out the requirements may be different. It is wisest to consider the wishes and needs of a spectrum of people. All of the people with an interest in an application's outcome are known as its *stakeholders*. To simplify matters in this chapter, however, we will usually use the term "customer."

There are two main requirements analysis challenges. First, as already mentioned, customers rarely know exactly what they want when a project begins. The complexity of modern applications makes such completeness all but impossible. Second, customers rarely know all that they *need*, either. Sometimes, they are not equipped to know it. To return to the house addition analogy, it may take time for a homeowner to realize that for the addition he wants, he will desire windows on all walls. He may have to be educated to understand that he needs to support the addition with piers rather than with a regular foundation.

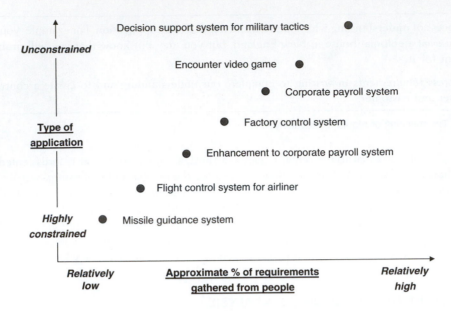

Figure 10.3 Source of requirements—people and other sources

Source: Adapted from "Software Requirements–SEI Curriculum Module SEI-CM-19-1.2." by John W. Brackett, copyright © 2009 Carnegie Mellon University with special permission from its Software Engineering Institute.

Requirements arise from multiple sources: mostly from stakeholders, but also from documents and even from books. As shown in Figure 10.3, Brackett [1] has plotted several types of applications to illustrate the degree to which requirements are gathered from people, as opposed to other sources such as written material.

Figure 10.3 classifies applications by the degree to which they are constrained by nature—restrictions on the application that cannot be altered. For example, an application that describes the trajectory of a ball is constrained by gravity; chemical reactions are constrained by physical laws. Generally speaking, the less constrained a problem, the more its requirements must be obtained from people. At one constraint extreme, for example, is our video game case study. Being the product of pure imagination, it relies on people for most of its requirements.

10.3 *HIGH-LEVEL* VS. *DETAILED* REQUIREMENTS

A typical requirements document is large. A detailed description of every requirement, although necessary in some form or other, can be mind-numbing to read. Imagine, for example, a document that spells out every detail of every property of Microsoft Word™. It would certainly not read like a novel! For this reason, we often divide requirements documents into two parts: *high-level* and *detailed*.

The first part of a requirements document is an overview, which is relatively readable and is well suited to customers. Its contents are referred to as the *high-level* or *business* requirements. Anyone wanting to get an idea of what the application is all about reads the high-level requirements. In many organizations, the marketing department prepares this material based on market research and conversations with customers. Although not formally necessary, the high-level requirements often include a description of *why* the application is being built, and they state the benefits to both the developing organization and the customer [2]. In some organizations the high-level requirements form a separate document such as a "market requirements" document. In this book we will include the high-level requirements in the SRS. As an example, the video store application high-level requirements might contain sentences like the following:

The Video Store application shall enable clerks to check DVDs in and out.

The following shows a sketch of the main user interface: . . .

The second part of a complete requirements document consists of the complete particulars. They are especially useful for developers, who need to know precisely what they have to build. These are the *detailed requirements*. Although detailed requirements are used frequently by developers, they should be understandable to the customer, and should not contain developer jargon where possible. Here are some examples from the video store application.

The daily late charge on a DVD shall be computed at half the regular two-day rental rate, up to the value of the DVD listed in the "Intergalactic Video Catalog." When the amount owed reaches this value, the total late charge is computed as this amount plus $5.

When the "commit" button is pressed on GUI 37, the GUI shall disappear and GUI 15 shall appear with a superimposed green border (RGB = 6, 32, 8) and the name and address fields filled with the data for the customer.

One challenge of writing the high-level and detailed requirements is to ensure that they remain consistent over time. This is facilitated by keeping the high-level requirements at a high enough level—for example, "Clerks can enter customer particulars." This kind of statement tends not to change very much. On the other hand, the details are provided in full in the detailed requirements and are much more liable to evolve. A corresponding example is, "Clerks can enter the customer's first name of 1 to 10 alphabetical characters in the text field shown in figure 34, a second name of 1 to 15 alphabetical characters . . . ."

10.4 TYPES OF REQUIREMENTS

Requirements are commonly classified as either *functional* or *nonfunctional*. This classification applies to both high-level and detailed requirements. Each type is described in the sections that follow.

10.4.1 Functional Requirements

Functional requirements, also known as *behavioral* requirements, specify services that the application must provide (e.g., "The application shall compute the value of the user's stock portfolio."). An application allows entities interacting with it (typically users) to accomplish tasks. Such an entity is frequently a person, but it can also be a machine or even another program. A *functional requirement* specifies something specific that the application allows such an entity to accomplish. In our video store application, for example, the following are functional requirements.

The application allows clerks to check out DVDs.

The application allows clerks to display the customer's account status.

10.5 NONFUNCTIONAL REQUIREMENTS

Any requirement that does not specify functionality provided by the application is *nonfunctional*. For example, a requirement such as "the application shall display a customer's account status in less than two seconds" is not functional, because it does not specify a specific service. Instead, it *qualifies* a service or services (specifies something about them). Nonfunctional requirements need to be specific, quantifiable, and testable. Consider a nonfunctional requirement that reads:

> The system shall retrieve user information quickly.

This requirement is vague (e.g., what does *retrieve* mean?), not quantifiable (e.g., how fast is *quickly?*), and therefore not able to be tested. An improved version of the requirement would be as follows.

> Once the OK button is pressed on the "Retrieve Account Information" screen, the user's account information shall be displayed in less than 3 seconds.

This requirement is specific (because it identifies a specific button on a specific screen), quantifiable (because of the specific response time), and testable. The documentation should make it clear exactly what "the OK button" refers to.

Major nonfunctional categories are: *qualities* (e.g., reliability, availability, maintainability, etc.), *constraints* (on the application or its development), *external interfaces* (hardware, software, communication) and *error conditions*. These are summarized in Figure 10.4 and elaborated upon in succeeding sections.

10.5.1 Quality Attributes

Reliability requirements specify "the ability of the software to behave consistently in a user-acceptable manner when subjected to an environment in which it was intended to be used." [3]. In other words, it is the extent to which defects will be detected by users during normal operation. This kind of requirement recognizes that applications are unlikely to be perfect, but limits the extent of imperfection in quantified terms. The following is an example, and assumes that a definition of "level one faults" has been provided.

> The Airport Radar Application (ARA) shall experience no more than two level-one faults per month.

- **Quality attributes**

  - **Reliability and availability** (observed faults, average uptime)
  - **Performance** (speed, throughput, storage)
  - **Security** (malicious and nonmalicious compromise of data or functionality)
  - **Maintainability** (cost to maintain)
  - **Portability** (move to a different operating environment)

- **Constraints** on the application or its development

- **External interfaces** that the application "talks to"

  - Hardware
  - Other software
  - Communication with external agents

- User interfaces

- Error handling

Figure 10.4 Nonfunctional requirement categories

Availability, closely related to reliability, quantifies the degree to which the application is to be available to its users. The following is an example.

ARA shall be available at level one on either the primary or the backup computer 100% of the time.

ARA shall be unavailable on one of these computers at level one or two for no more than 2% of the time in any 30-day period.

Often, high-availability requirements are specified in terms of "the nines." For example, five-nines, or 99.999% availability, means that a system can only have a yearly downtime of 5.256 minutes. This type of requirement might be documented as follows.

The system shall support "five-nines" availability.

Performance requirements specify timing constraints that the application must observe. These include elapsed time for computations (speed), throughput, and storage (e.g., RAM usage, secondary storage usage, etc). The following is an example.

The Stress Analyzer shall produce a stress report of type five in less than a minute of elapsed time.

Performance requirements are a critical part of *real-time* applications, where actions must complete within specified time limits. Examples include collision avoidance software, flight control applications, and antilock brake controls. The following is an example.

The computation of brake fluid pressure shall complete within one millisecond.

Security requirements concern malicious intent toward a system. This makes security different from other requirements, which specify application behavior when used by well-intentioned people. One can specify requirements that contribute towards security. These call for concrete measures, such as login procedures, password lengths, and so on, that contribute to making the product more secure. On the other hand, implicit security requirements are far more difficult to deal with. Implicitly, no one wants an application that is vulnerable to attack, so the requirement exists in the abstract. However, the nature of many future attacks is not predictable, and so there is no way to specify a requirement for their defense except in general terms that are of little value.

Maintainability requirements specify how easy or difficult it is to modify the software, as a result of fixing a defect or implementing an enhancement. For example, the easier it is to understand the software, the easier it is to maintain. Maintainability can be measured by the time it takes to repair defects. The following is an example of a maintainability requirement.

The average time for a maintenance engineer to repair a severity-2 defect shall be no greater than 8 person-hours.

Portability requirements identify those parts of the software that may need to run in different operating environments, as well as how easy or difficult it is for those parts to be ported. The following is an example.

The graphics subsystem shall be designed so it can run in both the Windows and Linux operating systems.

- **Platform**

  - Example: The application must execute on any 1GH Linux computer.

- **Development Media**

  - Example: The application must be implemented in Java.
  - Example: Rational Rose must be used for the design.

Figure 10.5 Examples of constraints

The maximum amount of effort to port the graphics subsystem from Windows to Linux shall not exceed 2 person-months.

10.5.2 Constraints

A *constraint* on an application is a requirement that limits the available options for developing it. Recall that requirements are generally "what" statements. "How" is usually left to the design. Constraints can be thought of as exceptions to this. Figure 10.5 shows some examples.

Design or implementation constraints describe limits or conditions on how the application is to be designed or implemented. These (nonfunctional) requirements are not intended to replace the design process—they merely specify conditions imposed upon the project by the customer, the environment, or other circumstances. They include *accuracy*, as in the following example.

The damage computations of the Automobile Impact Facility (AEF) shall be accurate to within one centimeter.

Tool and language constraints are often imposed. These include historical practices within the organization, compatibility, and programmer experience. Here is an example.

The AEF is to be implemented in Java and developed on the Eclipse platform.

Design constraints are imposed on the project because stakeholders require them. They can be specified in the requirements document or the design document. Such constraints restrict the design freedom of developers. The following requirement is an example.

The AEF shall utilize the Universal Crunch Form to display impact results.

The constraint of having to follow certain *standards* is often determined by company or customer policies. Here are examples.

Documentation for AEF shall conform to Federal Guideline 1234.56.

The AEF code is to be documented using company code documentation guidelines version 5.2.

Projects are frequently constrained by the hardware platforms they must use. The following is an example.

AEF shall run on Ajax 999 model 12345 computers with at least 128 megabytes of RAM and 12 Gigabytes of disk space.

- Hardware

  - Example: "The application must interface with a model 1234 bar code reader."

- Software

  - Example: "The application shall use the company's payroll system to retrieve salary information."
  - Example: "The application shall use version 1.1 of the Apache server."

- Communications

  - Example: "The application shall communicate with human resources applications via the company intranet."
  - Example: "The format used to transmit "article expected" messages to cooperating shipping companies shall use XML standard 183.34 published at http://. . . . "

Figure 10.6 Types of external interface requirement for an application, with examples

10.5.3 External Interface Requirements

Applications are frequently required to interface with other systems. The Internet is a common example of such an external system. Interface requirements describe the format with which the application communicates with its environment. Figure 10.6 shows the common types, with examples of each.

10.5.4 User Interface Requirements: Principles

User interface design is sometimes included with the "design" phase of software development, but it can more properly be considered part of the requirements phase. This book takes the latter perspective, including only *software* design in the "design" phase, and not graphic design.

Customers commonly conceive of an application by visualizing its graphical user interface (GUI), so a good way to help them describe the application is to develop draft GUIs. Our goal here is to provide some of the essentials of user interface design. This is quite different from the *technical* design of the application, which is covered in Part IV. The latter includes considerations of what GUI classes to select and how to relate them to other classes.

In developing user interfaces for applications, it is ideal to work with a professional designer, who is trained in user behavior, color usage, and techniques of layout design. For many projects, however, especially smaller ones, software engineers must design user interfaces with no such assistance. Thus, we list some guidelines for user interface design.

Galitz [4] provides eleven steps for developing user interfaces. We have adapted these, as shown in Figure 10.7. Each of these steps is applicable to the high-level requirements process and/or the detailed requirements processes. Steps 1 and 2 are described in Chapter 11. Steps 3–11 are explored in Chapter 12.

10.5.5 Error-Handling Requirements

Requirements analysis deals with two kinds of errors. The first are those that actors make (entities interacting with the application such as a user or other system); the second consists of errors that developers make. Error-handling requirements specify how the application responds to different types of errors. Figure 10.8 lists some of the ways of dealing with errors.

Regarding the first kind of error, error-handling requirements explain how the application must respond to anomalies in its environment. For example, what should the application do if it receives a message from

Step 1: Know your user	(H[2])
Step 2: Understand the business function in question	(H)
Step 3: Apply principles of good screen design	(H, D[3])
Step 4: Select the appropriate kind of windows	(H, D)
Step 5: Develop system menus	(H, D)
Step 6: Select the appropriate device-based controls	(H)
Step 7: Choose the appropriate screen-based controls	(H)
Step 8: Organize and lay out windows	(H, D)
Step 9: Choose appropriate colors	(D)
Step 10: Create meaningful icons	(H, D)
Step 11: Provide effective message, feedback, and guidance	(D)

Figure 10.7 Steps for constructing user interfaces

Source: Adapted from Galitz, W., ''The Essential Guide to User Interface Design: An Introduction to GUI Principles and Techniques,'' John Wiley & Sons, 1996.

- Ignore

- Warn user

- Allow unlimited retries

- Log and proceed anyway

- Substitute default values

- Shut down

Figure 10.8 Options for error-handling requirements

another application that is not in an agreed-upon format? It is preferable to specify this in the requirements document rather than leave the course of action to programmers alone.

The second kind of error refers to actions that the application should take if it finds *itself* having committed an error—that is, because of a defect in its construction. This kind of error requirement is applied very selectively, because our aim is to produce defect-free applications in the first place rather than cover our mistakes with a large set of error-handling requirements. In particular, when a function is called with improper parameters, we program a continuation of the application only if such an erroneous continuation is preferable to the actual cessation of the application. As an example, suppose that we have to specify the requirements for a device that automatically applies doses of intravenous drugs. Users are entitled to assume that the application is thoroughly specified, designed, implemented, and inspected, so that the drug composition and dosage computations are correct. Nevertheless, it would be wise in a case like this to specify an independent check of the composition and dosage of the drugs before administering them, and to specify error handling accordingly. Error-processing requirements in this case may consist of a complete stop of the application, or a temporary halt and a notification to the operator of the device indicating the problem.

10.6 DOCUMENTING REQUIREMENTS

The output of requirements analysis is what the IEEE calls the software requirements specification (SRS). There are several ways in which an SRS can be organized. As we will see in Chapter 11 and beyond, the Eclipse open source project is organized around three "subprojects." Within each, requirements are organized

1. **Introduction**
   1.1. Purpose
      1.2. Scope
      1.3. Definitions, acronyms, and abbreviations
      1.4. References
      1.5. Overview
2. **Overall description**
   2.1. Product perspective
      2.1.1. System interfaces
      2.1.2. User interfaces
      2.1.3. Hardware interfaces
      2.1.4. Software interfaces
      2.1.5. Communications interfaces
      2.1.6. Memory constraints
      2.1.7. Operations
      2.1.8. Site adaptation requirements
   2.2. Product functions
   2.3. User characteristics
   2.4. Constraints
   2.5. Assumptions and dependencies
   2.6. Apportioning of requirements
3. **Specific requirements**

   (see Figure 9)

Appendixes

Figure 10.9 IEEE 830-1998 Software Requirement Specifications table of contents, 1 of 2

Source: IEEE Std 830-1998.

around several "themes." The OpenOffice open source project organizes its requirements in four main parts: a word processor, a spreadsheet, a presentation facility, and an illustration tool.

In this book we will often use—and modify—IEEE standard 830-1998 [6], shown in Figures 10.9 and 10.10. The IEEE standard was developed and maintained by a committee of very experienced software engineers. It is very helpful, but it requires modification and tailoring to respond to changes in tools, languages, and practices. The first two sections of the standard, "Introduction" and "Overall description," correspond to the high-level requirements and are covered in Chapter 11. Section 3 of the standard, the "Specific requirements," corresponds to the detailed requirements. It is expanded and applied in Chapter 12.

Next we turn our attention to the essential links of the SRS to the rest of the project.

10.7 TRACEABILITY

Traceability is the ability to readily understand how the parts of separate project artifacts relate to each other. In particular, it links individual requirements with other project artifacts. (See, for example, [7]). A detailed requirement is traceable if there are clear links between it, the design element that accommodates it, the code that implements it, the inspection that verifies it, and the test that validates it. Figure 10.11 shows relationships between the artifacts, based on a single requirement.

Table 10.1 is an example of how a change in a requirement for DVDs in the video store application causes changes in the remaining artifacts.

Hyperlinking is a convenient way to transition easily between artifacts. In particular, the requirements document can be placed on the Internet or an intranet, and dependent artifacts can be connected via hyperlinks.

10.8 AGILE METHODS AND REQUIREMENTS

Agile processes specify requirements analysis by first establishing a shared vision of the application. This is done via discussions among the team members and the customer. After that the requirements are gathered in relatively small stages. The vision stage is intended to form a concept of the ultimate product that is simple

3.1 **External interfaces**

3.2 **Functional requirements**

   —organized by feature, object, user class, etc.

3.3 **Performance requirements**

3.4 **Logical database requirements**

3.5 **Design constraints**
   3.5.1 Standards compliance

3.6 **Software system attributes**
   3.6.1 Reliability
   3.6.2 Availability
   3.6.3 Security
   3.6.4 Maintainability
   3.6.5 Portability

3.7 **Organizing the specific requirements**
   3.7.1 System mode – or
   3.7.2 User class – or
   3.7.3 Objects (see right) – or
   3.7.4 Feature – or
   3.7.5 Stimulus – or
   3.7.6 Response – or
   3.7.7 Functional hierarchy – or

3.8 **Additional comments**

Figure 10.10 IEEE 830-1998 Software Requirement Specifications table of contents, 2 of 2—detailed requirements
Source: IEEE Std 830-1998.

and clear enough for all stakeholders to understand and relate to. This vision is kept as concise as possible without compromising the shared vision itself. Examples are as follows:

   An application that allows video store personnel to manage DVD rentals

   A Web-based calendar program for individuals and departments

   A system that analyzes individuals' susceptibility to disease based on their genetic information

   The vision stage is followed by multiple iterations that are typically 2–4 weeks in duration. Such an iterative style has the advantage of keeping misunderstandings to a minimum and allowing all concerned to grapple with the requirements being considered. The requirements for each cycle are gathered by means of *user stories*—narratives, always told from the user's perspective, of how the application is to be used. This process is summarized in Figure 10.12 and described in more detail in the sections that follow.

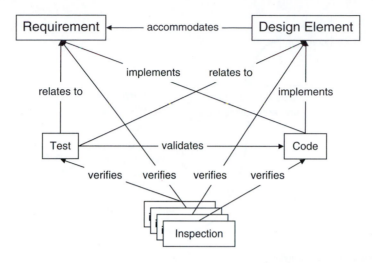

Figure 10.11 Traceability among project artifacts

Table 10.1 How a change in a requirement for DVDs in a video store application causes changes in other artifacts

Artifact	Original version	Revised version
Requirement	The title of a DVD shall consist of between 1 and 15 English characters.	The title of a DVD shall consist of between 1 and 15 characters, available in English, French, and Russian.
Design element	DVD title: String	DVD ◆ Title title: String

Code	class DVD
	{
	   String title . . . .
	}
		class DVD
		{
		   Title title . . . .
		}

		class Title . . .
Inspection report	Inspection # 672:	Inspection # 935:
	4 defects; follow-up inspection #684.	1 defect; no follow-up inspection required.
Test report	Test # 8920 . . .	Test # 15084 . . .

10.9 UPDATING THE PROJECT TO REFLECT REQUIREMENTS ANALYSIS

A project's document set is a living entity—it has to be "fed and cared for" at regular intervals throughout the life of the project. Typically, when a phase is executed, several documents must be updated.

For very large projects, the process of analyzing the customer's requirements is formal and organized. For example, the U.S. Department of Defense (DoD) often publishes a request for proposals (RFP) to develop

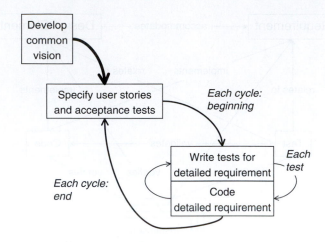

Figure 10.12 Agile requirements analysis

an SRS alone. Such an RFP contains a very high level description of the project. The RFP can be thought of as specifying the high-level requirements. Contractors respond to the RFP, and a winner is chosen who creates detailed requirements. To ensure that the requirements are satisfactory, numerous meetings are held. These involve contractor personnel, civil servant specialists and managers, uniformed officers of the Navy or Air Force, and others. The resulting SRS can be thousands of pages long. The winning contractor may or may not be chosen to perform the actual design and development of the application.

Once high-level requirements have been gathered, the SPMP can be updated as shown in Figure 10.13. Such updating occurs throughout the life cycle of an application.

The resulting schedule would typically be like that shown in Figure 10.14, containing more detail than the schedule shown when the SPMP was originally drafted (Chapter 8) but still not very detailed. In

	Status after Initial Draft	Status after Obtaining High-Level Requirements
Milestones	Initial	More milestones; more specific
Risks	Identify initial risks	Retire risks identified previously; identify more risks now that more is known about the project
Schedule	Very rough	Preliminary project schedule
Personnel	Designate high-level requirements engineers	Designated engineers for detailed requirements analysis
Cost Estimation	Very rough	First estimates based on job content

Figure 10.13 Updating project plans after obtaining high-level requirements

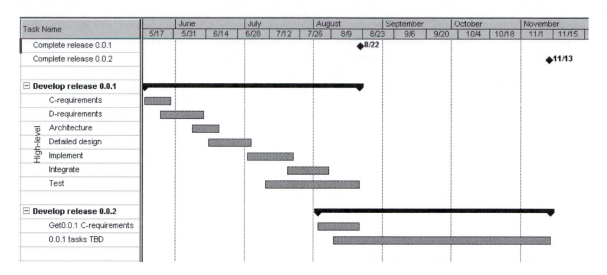

Figure 10.14 Typical schedule after obtaining high-level requirements

particular, we may know that release 0.0.2 should be made on November 13, but it may be too early to decide other parts of the schedule.

Cost estimation can be improved once high-level requirements have been analyzed. The main improvement stems from the increased understanding that developers gain concerning the scope and nature of the application. Function point estimates (described in Chapter 8) can be made more complete, and so can the estimates derived from them for schedule and labor. Direct bottom-up estimates can be improved as well.

Another factor limiting the number of iterations of the requirements is the high degree of coordination required to keep the project documents and the source code coordinated. This is one reason that highly iterative development techniques such as agile methods do not really attempt to write detailed requirements documents.

10.10 SUMMARY

Requirements analysis is the process of understanding what's wanted and needed in an application. The output of requirements analysis is a software requirements specification (SRS), which serves as input into the design process. The SRS document used in this book is IEEE standard 830-1998.

Requirements are divided into high-level and detailed requirements. High-level requirements are also called business requirements. These describe why the application is being built and state the benefits to both the developing organization and the customer. Detailed requirements provide complete specifics about the requirements that developers must know in order to implement the application.

Project requirements often change and evolve throughout the life of a project. When they do, other project artifacts such as the design and implementation must change accordingly. *Traceability* allows for maintaining associations between individual requirements and other project artifacts to facilitate updating them.

Both high-level and detailed requirements are classified as either functional or nonfunctional. Functional requirements specify services that the application must provide to the user. Nonfunctional requirements specify qualities, constraints, interfaces, and error handling of the application.

Agile requirements analysis starts by defining a concise vision statement about the intended application. Next, 2–4 week development cycles are executed, with the first step of each defining the requirements for that iteration. Each requirement is usually based on a *user story* along with an explicit acceptance test. A user story is a high-level piece of required functionality as seen by the anticipated user. Detailed requirements are usually expressed in terms of unit tests rather than being written explicitly.

After requirements analysis is completed (or after each iteration in an iterative process), the project plan is updated to reflect the new details known about the application. The more requirements that are known, the closer the schedule comes to being finalized.

10.11 EXERCISES

1. Explain why a defective requirement could be 100 times more expensive to fix after software is deployed versus being fixed during requirements analysis.

2. Give an example of a software application in which the customer is the same as the end user. Give an example in which they are different. In each case, identify the customer and end user.

3. In your own words, explain the difference between high-level and detailed requirements. Give an example of a high-level and detailed requirement for a typical word processing application.

4. In your own words, describe the difference between functional and nonfunctional requirements.

5. Explain why the following requirement is not sufficient. How would you amend it?
   " The order entry system shall not crash more than 5 times per year. The system shall recover from each crash as quickly as possible to avoid down time."

6. Brackett makes the point that the more constrained an application, the less reliance we have on people as the source of requirements. (Refer to his graph in Figure 10.3 comparing "approximate percent of requirements gathered from people" with "type of application.") Can you think of any applications that do not fall on the graph's diagonal?

7. Agile requirements gathering calls for a customer representative to work continually with the development team generating requirements. Describe a scenario in which this type of arrangement may produce poor requirements.

8. What are three major advantages and disadvantages of describing detailed requirements with unit tests?

BIBLIOGRAPHY

1. Brackett, J. "Software Requirements: SEI Curriculum Module SEI-CM-19-1.2," January 1990. http://www.sei.cmu.edu/library/abstracts/reports/90cm019.cfm [accessed November 15, 2009].
2. Wiegers, Karl E., *"More About Software Requirements,* Microsoft Press, 2006, p 5.
3. Davis, Alan M., *"Software Requirements: Objects, Functions, and States,* Prentice Hall, 1993, p. 310.
4. Galitz, W., *"The Essential Guide to User Interface Design: An Introduction to GUI Principles and Techniques,"* John Wiley & Sons, 1996.
5. Alexander, Ian, and Neil Maiden (Editors), *"Scenarios, Stories, Use Cases: Through the Systems Development Life-Cycle"* (paperback), John Wiley & Sons, 2004.
6. "IEEE Recommended Practice for Software Requirements Specifications," *IEEE Std 830-1998*, June 1998.
7. Wiegers, Karl E., *"Software Requirements,"* Microsoft Press, 2003.

11

Analyzing High-Level Requirements

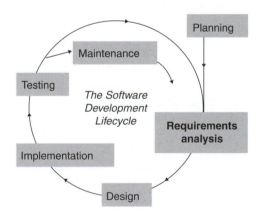

- What are examples of customer wants?

- What does stakeholder vision mean?

- How do you interview for and document requirements?

- How does one write an "overview" requirements section?

- How do you write "main functions" and use cases?

- What agile methods are there for dealing with high-level requirements?

- How do you specify user interfaces at a high level?

- How does one frame security requirements?

- How do you use diagrams for high-level requirements?

- What are examples of high-level requirements in practice?

Figure 11.1 The context and learning goals for this chapter

High-level requirements describe the purpose of an application and its intended functionality. They can also describe the application's benefits to both the customer and the developing organization. This chapter describes the process whereby we collect, analyze, and specify the requirements at a high level. It is helpful to express high-level requirements using both text and diagrams, in order to convey a complete understanding of the intended application. High-level requirements are of great interest to all stakeholders, particularly customers, who purchase and ultimately use the application based on its requirements.

11.1 EXAMPLES OF CUSTOMER WANTS

Typically, at the time that requirements analysis commences, the customer is still forming concepts of what he or she wants and needs. This is analogous to the requirements-gathering phase between an architect and a client. For example, a client may want a house with four bedrooms and a large living room, but nevertheless relies on the architect to help clarify what he wants and needs (e.g., a ranch house with a living room with seating for ten).

As an example, consider the Encounter case study. The following is a fragment of customer thinking obtained by a mythical marketing department.

Encounter is to be a role-playing game that simulates all or part of the player's lifetime. It should be of interest to both male and female game players.

Figures 11.2 and 11.3 summarize the high-level requirements for the Encounter case study. The complete description of Encounter high-level requirements is contained in Section 2 of the SRS: Overall Description. The requirements statements in Figures 11.2 and 11.3 are at a very high level with detail purposely omitted. For example, the requirement "Each quality has a value" does not specify what those values are. Specific values are documented in the detailed requirements of Section 3 of the SRS.

- Role-playing game that simulates all or part of the lifetime of the player's character.
- Game characters not under the player's control called "foreign" characters.
- Game characters have a number of *qualities* such as *strength, speed, patience,* etc.
- Each quality has a value.
- Characters "encounter" each other when in the same area, and may then "engage" each other.

Figure 11.2 High-level requirements for Encounter, 1 of 2

- The result of the engagement depends on the values of their qualities and on the area in which the engagement takes place.
- Player characters may reallocate their qualities, except while a foreign character is present.
- Reallocation takes effect after a delay, during which the player may be forced to engage.
- Success is measured . . .
  - by the "life points" maximum attained by the player – or –
  - by living as long as possible.

Figure 11.3 High-level requirements for Encounter, 2 of 2

At this stage in requirements analysis, there are usually unresolved issues such as whether there is to be one or several characters under the control of the player, what should occur when two characters interact, and whether the game can be played over the Internet. It is the task of the development team to work with customers to clarify their wants and needs. A common process is to interview the customer, which is described in Section 11.3.

Customer *needs* can be subtler to classify than their *wants*, since customers are typically less conscious of them. For example, a customer may *want* a music application that allows computer novices to write music but may *need* a periodic auto-save function to avoid losing work. Whether such a feature is a requirement or part of the design depends on what is agreed between the developer and the customer. If the customer, having understood auto-saving, wants this feature, then it becomes a requirement. The customer may be content, however, to leave it to the designer as to how to accommodate the computing needs of novice users. In that case, auto-saving would not be a requirement, but a design element.

11.2 STAKEHOLDER VISION

The people who have some interest in the outcome of the product are called its *stakeholders*. As an example, consider the creation of an e-commerce Web site. One set of stakeholders consists of the site's visitors. Typically, their primary requirement is the ease with which they can find and purchase needed items. The company's owners are stakeholders, too. Their primary requirement may be profit, short- or long-term. For this reason, they may want the site to emphasize high-margin items. Marketing, another group of stakeholders, may require the Web site to track visitors. The application's developers are stakeholders, too. For example they may want to use new development technology to keep up to date.

In the case of packaged (shrink-wrapped) applications such as word processors, spreadsheets, and development environments, as well as their equivalents (such as downloaded applications), the development team pays a great deal of attention to the acceptability of the application by as many users as possible. Although this can be a difficult marketing problem, it is clear that the users are the most significant stakeholders. For many large projects, identifying the most important stakeholders is complex. The "customer" is often the party paying to have the application developed, but even this is not clear-cut. For example, the Navy may be paying for an application, but the developers' day-to-day customer may be a civil servant rather than a naval officer. Then again, are not the taxpayers the "customers," since they are actually paying for the application? The customer of a subcontractor is the prime contractor. The customer for shrink-wrapped applications is a composite of potential customers established by the marketing department. When an application is intended for internal company use, such as claims processing within an insurance company, the customer is an internal organization.

Conflicting stakeholder interests can easily result in inconsistent requirements. An example of this occurs when two different groups within a company, with different motivations, apparently want the "same" application built. When requirements cannot be reconciled, projects tend to flounder and are frequently canceled. Even when stakeholders' requirements are consistent, they may be too expensive to satisfy entirely.

Developers—yet another stakeholder community—are subject to professional responsibilities, which can profoundly affect requirements. Suppose, for example, that developers are asked to build software for a medical device with a fixed budget, but they come to understand that the required features cannot all be adequately tested within that budget. Unless the budget is changed, they would need to eliminate features for professional reasons.

A good deal of stakeholder identification and management involves managing the scope of the requirements to make them buildable within given budgetary and schedule constraints. The good project leader surmounts these difficulties—a process that requires managerial, personal, business, and political skills.

Customers develop a vision—sometimes unconscious or incomplete—of how their application will operate. This vision is sometimes referred to as the application's *model* or *concept of operations*. Different people may hold differing concepts of what a software application entails. For example, the possible concept of operations for "a weather system" could be

- a facility for turning raw weather service information into graphical form
      or
- a real-time system for forecasting the weather
      or
- an application for alerting users to weather anomalies

These differing concepts of operations lead to very different applications!

The project manager or requirements engineer helps the stakeholders to clarify their concept of operations. Since customers usually lack the means with which to express such concepts, engineers can propose appropriate techniques such as use cases, data flow diagrams, or state transitions, which are described below. These techniques are also used for design, as shown in Part IV.

11.3 THE INTERVIEW AND DOCUMENTATION PROCESS

Much of the analysis of requirements is a person-to-person activity, organized to produce an application satisfying the customer. Figure 11.4 summarizes the process of preparing for and interviewing the customer to elicit their requirements.

Since there are typically several stakeholders who want to provide their input, the first issue is deciding whom to interview. Recall that requirements coming from different stakeholders may be contradictory. It is often effective to interview a small number of primary stakeholders, and then solicit comments from other key stakeholders. Two interviewers at each session are preferable to one, since a typical interviewer tends to miss points. Bringing a recorder can help, with permission requested in advance. The most significant person to interview is often the most difficult to schedule time with, so perseverance is called for. Interviewing the wrong

---

Before interview:
1. List and **prioritize** "customer" interviewees.
   - most likely to determine project's success.
2. **Schedule** interview with fixed start and end times.
   - at least two from development team should attend.
   - prepare to record?

At interview:
3. Concentrate on **listening**.
   Don't be passive: probe and encourage.
   - persist in understanding *wants* and exploring *needs*.
   - walk through use cases, also data flow? state diagrams?
   Take thorough notes.
4. Schedule **follow-up** meeting for validation.

After interview:
5. **Draft SRS** high-level requirements using a standard.
6. **Contact customer** for comments.

Figure 11.4 One way to handle interviews with the customer

people can result in wasted time and effort. The *scrum* agile process in particular insists that the customer community supply just one representative for requirements. This puts the onus on the stakeholders to provide consistent requirements rather than having developers adjudicate among differing customer communities.

Although it is important to listen carefully to the customer at the interview, one usually cannot obtain requirements by one-way listening alone. Typically, the customer formulates some of the requirements as he goes along, and needs help. Although the vision created is primarily the customer's, the interviewer and the customer develop a vision jointly to an extent. Customers usually require some prompting to fill out their vision, a little (but not too much!) like a witness on the stand. Dennis [1] suggests asking three types of questions: close-ended, open-ended, and probing. Close-ended questions, such as, "How many videos do you expect to keep in stock?" provide important detailed information about the system. Open-ended questions, such as, "What are the shortcomings of your current video store system?" allow the interviewee to elaborate on his requirements. Probing questions, such as "Can you give me an example of why the user interface is difficult to use?" are follow-up questions designed to gather more detailed information.

Use cases, described in Section 11.5 are an effective way to obtain and express requirements for a wide variety of applications. Some requirements need to be diagrammed, and ways to do this are described in Section 11.9. To validate the requirements as written out, the interviewers follow up via e-mail, holding a subsequent meeting if necessary. Recall that the *detailed* requirements have yet to be gathered and require additional meeting time.

After the meeting, the high-level requirements are drafted in a format such as the IEEE standard. The draft should be provided to the customer community for comments, and successive interviews are conducted until there is satisfaction with the high-level requirements.

The great challenge we face is expressing clearly what customers want and need. Words alone can be appropriate, but for many applications, narrative text needs to be supplemented by figures of various kinds. The following sections describe how to express high-level requirements.

11.4 WRITING AN OVERVIEW

An overview is intended to allow readers to quickly understand the main purpose of the intended application. Otherwise, it should be as short as possible and should seldom need alteration when project details change. The challenge of writing a good overview is usually underestimated, probably because it is often thought that if one knows what a subject is about then summarizing it should not be difficult.

The following is an example for the video store application; in this case, a single sentence suffices.

VStore is intended to help video stores manage DVD inventory and rentals.

It is tempting to add more details to this, but good requirements documents are organized to provide details in orderly stages, so adding more details here would result in duplication and could reduce readability. "Manage DVD inventory and rentals" provides substantive information but is general enough so that changes in requirements details are unlikely to force it to change.

11.5 DESCRIBING MAIN FUNCTIONS AND USE CASES

Following an overview section, high-level requirements usually list the major functions such as "enter new video" and "rent video." Since users typically utilize applications through a relatively small number of common back-and-forth interactions, this can be a good way to summarize functionality. An effective way to document these interactions is through writing *use cases*, originally coined by Jacobson [2]. Use cases describe the typical sequence of interactions between users of an application and the application itself, and provide a narrative of how the application is used [3]. They have become a very effective way to express many functional high-level requirements. As an example, when using a word processor, we usually (1) retrieve a file, (2) change and add text, and then (3) store the result. Functional high-level requirements are often naturally expressed as an interaction between the application and agencies external to it, such as the user.

Agile projects tend to employ the idea of *user stories*. These are similar to use cases but are broader in scope and have distinct criteria. User stories are described in Section 11.6.

A use case is identified by its name and by the type of user of the application, called the *actor*. The main part of a use case documents a typical interaction between an actor and the application, often called a *scenario*. A scenario consists of a numbered list of steps. Each step should be simply described and include who is carrying out the step. A good way to start writing a use case is to list the *main success scenario*, which is the sequence of steps that lead to a successful outcome. A single use case should not attempt to account for a significant number of branches. Other scenarios of the use case, such as error conditions, are typically documented as *extensions*. For example, *Retrieve a File* would be a typical use case for a word processor, with the user as actor. The main success scenario contains the following sequence of seven steps. Note that each step starts with the entity that executes the step. In the case of an error in opening the selected file, an alternative is documented in the Extensions section.

Retrieve a File

Main Success Scenario

1. User clicks File menu

2. System displays options new and open

3. User clicks open

4. System displays file window

5. User enters directory and file name

6. User hits open button

7. System retrieves referenced file into word processor window Extensions

7a. System displays error indicating file could not be opened

It is possible for a single person to use a system in several different ways, adopting the roles of different actors. In UML, a use case diagram shows the actors, the use cases, and the relationship between them. A use case diagram is a useful tool for diagrammatically summarizing the set of actors and use cases without having to show all the details of the use cases. Figure 11.5 is an example of a use case diagram, with the names of the use cases shown in the ovals, and the actors drawn outside the rectangle with lines connecting them to the use cases they interact with.

As further examples of use cases, Figures 11.6 and 11.7 contain examples of use case scenarios for the *Initialize* and *Engage Foreign Character* use cases for the Encounter case study.

The actor in each of these use cases is the player of Encounter. Each use case is a sequence of actions taken by the player and the Encounter game, as shown for the *Initialize* use case. The *Engage Foreign Character* use case is a typical sequence of actions by Encounter and the player, whenever the player's main character and a foreign character are in the same area at the same time. The actor in the *Set Rules* use case is a game designer. The actor describes the ability of Encounter to support the editing of rules for character interaction. The *Travel to Adjacent Area* use case is explained in the case study accompanying this book. The *Set Rules* use case is not included in the case study requirements.

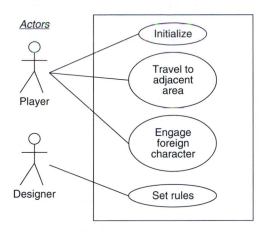

Figure 11.5 Use cases for Encounter—a UML use case diagram

Initialize

1. *System* displays player's main character in the dressing room.
2. *System* displays a window for setting his character's qualities.
3. *Player* allocates the qualities of his main character.
4. *Player* chooses an exit from the dressing room.
5. *System* moves player's main character into the area on the other side of the exit.

Figure 11.6 *Initialize* use case

Engage Foreign Character

1. *System* displays the foreign character in the same area as the player's.
2. *System* exchanges quality values between the two characters.
3. *System* displays the results of the engagement.
4. *System* displays player's character in a random area.

Figure 11.7 *Engage Foreign Character* use case

The actor need not be a human role—it can be another system that uses the application. For example, if the application under development is a robot control system, then the actor could be a factory automation system that uses the robot control system.

Use cases can handle limited branching, but if there is more than one level of branching, the extension idea, described above, can be tried. Otherwise the use case should probably be decomposed into other use cases. Even a single branch in a use case leads to an awkward description. For example, the following could be a use case for a personal budgeting application.

1. User selects "add checks" or "reconcile account"

2. If "add checks" selected:

3. One action happens

4. Another action happens

5. . . . . (one or more steps)

6. If "reconcile account" selected:

7. One action happens

8. Another action happens

9. . . . .

This would be better decomposed into "select options," "add checks," and "reconcile account" use cases.

Use cases are like stories and so they provide excellent insight into applications. They can be expressed at differing levels of generality. The Unified Software Development Process [4] recommends using detailed use cases to specify a large fraction of the requirements.

A use case that is similar to an existing one yields little additional value. Use cases should be *sequential*, or else *orthogonal* to each other. Two use cases are sequential if one can follow the other. *Orthogonal* is not a precisely defined term, but orthogonal use cases take completely different views or options. For example, in a warehouse application, use cases based on a foreman actor and a financial analyst actor would typically be orthogonal. In the Encounter case study, *Set Rules* is orthogonal to *Engage Foreign Character*. Chapter 14 shows how use cases are combined to produce new use cases; it also introduces inheritance among use cases.

Jacobson's [2] inspiration for the idea of use cases was that, despite the huge number of potential executions, most applications are conceived of in terms of a relatively small number of typical interactions. He suggests starting application design by writing use cases, then using them to drive class selection. This technique is demonstrated in Chapter 12. Use cases are also the basis for system-level test plans.

Many established documentation standards, including the IEEE's, predate use cases and they must be augmented to accommodate them. The Encounter case study describes them in Section 2.2 "Product Functions" of the SRS, as this is the section that describes the functional high-level requirements. Although use cases are often identified with object-oriented methods, they can be used with any development methodology.

11.6 AGILE METHODS FOR HIGH-LEVEL REQUIREMENTS

High-level requirements for agile projects are collected and understood in a manner similar to that for non-agile methods except that the requirements process operates in pieces and continues continuously through most of the life of the project. Non-agile processes require a time when requirements are frozen (i.e., beyond which the customer has no right to change them). Agile processes, on the other hand, accept frequent changes in requirements as a necessity. How can one of these be a valid approach without the other being invalid? The difference lies in the level of trust engendered by very close customer contact. If the customer's trusted representative works continually as part of the development team, it is unlikely that he will suddenly ask for unreasonable requirements. In agile processes, selected high-level requirements are elaborated upon within each iteration. Each is usually based on a *user story* or *stories*, each accompanied by an explicit acceptance test. A user story is a high-level piece of required functionality as seen by the anticipated user. According to Beck and West [5] a user story must be discrete, estimable, testable, and prioritized, as described in Figure 11.8. Compared with use cases, user stories are described less by their form than by these qualities. Having to be estimable is one difference, and this is illustrated in the example below. User stories can also be more extensive than use cases.

1. From **user's perspective**
2. **Discrete**
   - Single functionality, feature, or expectation.
   - Not necessarily precise.
3. **Estimable**
   - Developers can estimate required effort.
4. **Testable**
5. **Prioritized**
   - By customer, in consultation.
6. Can be fit in a **single cycle**.

Figure 11.8 Required qualities of a user story

Beck and West [5] give an example of how to gather user stories. The customer starts with the following story.

0.0 *Will outperform all other vending machines*

This is fine except that it's not estimable—there is no way to estimate the effort required to carry out this job. Consequently, the developer probes for more specific stories to obtain estimable ones, a process known as *splitting*.

1.0 Payment. *Will accept all kinds of payments*

2.0 Freshness. *Will sell no stale or outdated merchandise*

3.0 Restocking. *Will automatically request restocking of items selling best in the area*

4.0 Communication. *Will communicate with the customer to prevent transaction errors*

This is an improvement, but these are still not estimable, so further splitting is required. Recall that prioritization is also called for. The agile programmer then requests more specifics concerning the highest priority story. If this were *1.0 Payment*, the user might provide the following:

1.1 *Accept coins*

1.2 *Accept currency*

1.3 *Accept debit card*

1.4 *Accept credit card*

1.5 *Accept debit or credit card via Web transaction*

1.6 *Accept foreign coins and currency; at least euros for sales in Europe*

1.7 *Convert currencies*

1.8 *Ensure that payment meets or exceeds the cost of the selected product*

1.9 *Make change*

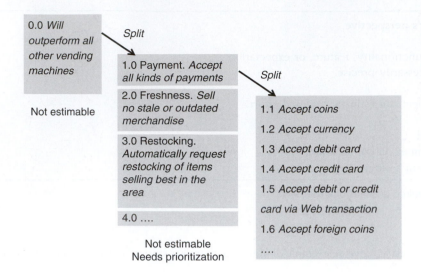

Figure 11.9 Splitting user stories

The splitting process is illustrated in Figure 11.9.

11.7 SPECIFYING USER INTERFACES: HIGH LEVEL

The specification of a user interface at a high level is often included in the high-level requirements. Recall from Section 10.6.4 the following steps in specifying user interfaces.

Step 1. Know your user

Step 2. Understand the business function in question

Step 3. Apply principles of good screen design

Step 4. . . . .

We will discuss Steps 1 and 2 in this chapter as they apply only to high-level requirements. The remaining steps are described the next chapter, on detailed requirements.

11.7.1 Step 1: Know Your User

This step involves understanding the nature of the application's eventual users. Figure 11.10 outlines some of the factors involved. The checklist is a way of ensuring that we know the basic characteristics of the anticipated users, and that we document our assumptions. These characteristics determine the nature of the user interface. In general, users with less education, training, skill, and motivation require greater simplicity, more explanation, and more help. This may have to be traded off against efficiency and speed. It is often desirable to provide several levels of user interface, depending on the level of the user.

11.7.2 Step 2: Understand the Business Function

This step requires the designer to understand the purpose of the particular proposed user interface in terms of the application's overall purpose. For example, if the business purpose is the stocking of a warehouse, we may

- **Level of knowledge and experience**
  - Computer literacy (high; moderate; low)
  - System experience (high; moderate; low)
  - Experience with similar applications (high; moderate; low)
  - Education (high school; college; advanced degree)
  - Reading level (>12 years schooling; 5–12; < 5)
  - Typing skill (135 wpm; 55 wpm; 10 wpm)
- **Characteristics of the user's tasks and jobs**
  - Type of use of this application (mandatory; discretionary)
  - Frequency of use (continual; frequent; occasional; once-in-a-lifetime)
  - Turnover rate for employees (high; moderate; low)
  - Importance of task (high; moderate; low)
  - Repetitiveness of task (high; moderate; low)
  - Training anticipated (extensive; self-training through manuals; none)
  - Job category (executive; manager; professional; secretary; clerk, etc.)
- **Psychological characteristics of the user**
  - Probable attitude toward job (positive; neutral; negative)
  - Probable motivation (high; moderate; low)
  - Cognitive style (verbal vs. spatial; analytic vs. intuitive; concrete vs. abstract)
- **Physical characteristics of the user**
  - Age (young; middle aged; elderly)
  - Gender (male; female)
  - Handedness (left; right; ambidextrous)
  - Physical handicaps (blind; defective vision; deaf; motor handicap)

Figure 11.10 Know your user when developing requirements

Source: Adapted from Galitz, W., "The Essential Guide to User Interface Design: An Introduction to GUI principles and techniques," John Wiley & Sons, 1996.

want the user interface to reflect the layout of the warehouse floor. The sequence of screens that appear typically reflects the manner in which users normally carry out their tasks for the business at hand.

Sometimes the execution of a program can be envisaged by displaying a series of GUI images. For example, one could provide a fair conception of Encounter by displaying a sequence of screen shots. Figures 11.11 and 11.12 are examples of preliminary GUI sketches for setting the qualities of an Encounter character.

Upon being shown GUIs, the customer typically realizes that he needs more or wants something different. In the example shown in Figure 11.11, it could well occur to the customer that the GUI for changing

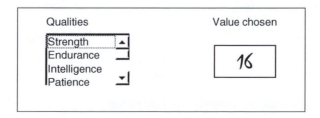

Figure 11.11 Preliminary sketch of user interface for setting game character qualities

Figure 11.12 Preliminary Encounter screen shot

Source: Graphics reproduced with permission from Corel.

the value of qualities is awkward because the total number of points may not change. The customer would also probably observe that the GUI is not visually appealing. The process of finalizing the GUI is very interactive. The detailed requirements provide precise GUI specification, as explained in Chapter 12.

11.7.3 GUI Transitions

Applications typically involve multiple GUIs. The high-level requirements describe the required mouse actions that take the user from one GUI to another. Figure 11.13 shows a useful way to represent the transitions between GUIs. When a particular GUI is present on the monitor, the application can be considered to be in a particular *state*. Changing from one GUI state to another is called a *transition*. States and transitions are actually more general concepts, and are described further in Section 11.9.2.

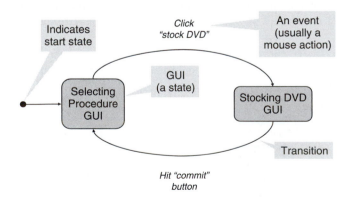

Figure 11.13 GUI transitions for video store application—Introduction

Source: Copyright © E. J. Braude, John Wiley & Sons, 2003.

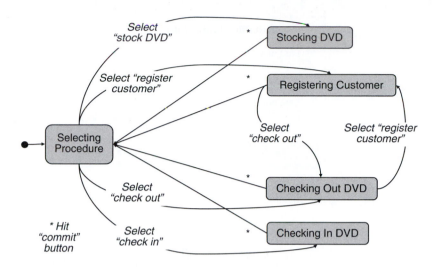

Figure 11.14 GUI transitions for video store application

A typical GUI/transition diagram for the video store example is shown in Figure 11.14.

While a particular GUI is being displayed, an application is said to be in a particular *state*. We explore states further in Section 11.9.2.

Figures 11.15–11.19 show rough sketches of the GUIs referenced in Figure 11.14. The detailed requirements provide compete detail.

Figure 11.15 Rough sketch of "Select Procedure GUI" referenced in Figure 11.14

Figure 11.16 Rough sketch of "Sketch of Stock DVD GUI" referenced in Figure 11.14

Figure 11.17 Rough sketch of "Register Customer GUI" referenced in Figure 11.14

Figure 11.18 Rough sketch of "Check out DVD GUI" referenced in Figure 11.14

Figure 11.19 Rough sketch of "Check in DVD GUI" referenced in Figure 11.14

11.8 SECURITY REQUIREMENTS

Many security requirements can be effectively expressed at a high level because we can express security goals without having to anticipate all of the specific breaches that can occur. Here is an example from the Eclipse project.

> The Eclipse Platform should provide the basic framework for a security mechanism that can be used by all plug-ins, including a simple credentials store and user authentication. Additionally,

- **Confidentiality "C"**
  - Data passed not visible to the unauthorized.
- **Nonrepudiation**
  - Parties can prove the existence of agreements.
- **Integrity "I"**
  - Ability to validate not/altered in transit.
- **Authentication "A"**
  - Ability to validate user's identity.
- **Authorization**
  - Permission to deal with the subject.
- **Availability**
  - For example, as compromised by denial-of-service attacks.

Figure 11.20 Common security requirements

key parts of the Platform itself should be secured, such as the ability to install plug-ins, which might need to be restricted in certain products or for certain users.[1]

Standard classifications for high-level security requirements are shown in Figure 11.20. They are sometimes collected into the acronym "CIA," which stands for "Confidentiality, Integrity, and Authentication." Figure 11.20 adds *nonrepudiation*, which is the ability for parties to a contract to prove reliably that the contract was indeed made. It also adds *authorization*, which specifies who may access what particular information, and availability, which specifies reaction to denial-of-service attacks. Denial-of-service attacks are activities, such as flooding a Web site automatically with requests, that make is difficult for anyone else to access it.

We ensure that these properties are satisfied by suitable corresponding requirements at the detailed level. However, ill-meaning perpetrators devise ways to compromise systems by exploiting combinations of properties that the system does *not* possess. To explain this, consider a (non-software) set of requirements that were already devised to ensure that the funds in a prominent Irish bank were secure. These required that two bank managers, each possessing a different key, were required to unlock a major safe. They also required constant guards for the managers. Both procedures were faithfully observed. It is important to understand that for perpetrators, existing security measures simply constitute a set of constraints within which they work, setting them to seek opportunities that the constraints do not cover. In the case of the bank example, there was no requirement for guards on the families of these two officials. Observing this combination of properties that the system did *not* possess, criminals took hostage the families of both managers and by this means coerced the officers into obtaining the bank's cash on their behalf.

Privacy is often linked with or considered part of security. This is because the purpose of many exploits is to gain access to data to which the perpetrator is not entitled, thereby compromising its privacy.

One example of privacy regulations is the Health Insurance Portability and Accountability Act of 1996 (HIPAA), which regulates health information created or maintained by health care providers who engage in designated electronic health care transactions. The Department of Health and Human Services is responsible for implementing and enforcing HIPAA. The act took effect in April 2003.

The main thrust of HIPAA is to ensure that an individual's health information is used for health purposes alone. "The final rules for security protect the confidentiality, integrity, and availability of individual health information and will provide a standard level of protection in an environment where health information

---

[1] https://bugs.eclipse.org/bugs/show_bug.cgi?id=37692.

- The Health Insurance Portability and Accountability Act passed in 2000 and 2002; **2003** compliance
- Regulates health **information** created or maintained by **health care providers**
- U.S. Department of Health and Human Services responsible for implementing and enforcing
- Main thrust: Ensure that an individual's health information is **used only for health** purposes

  - Ensures **confidentiality**, **integrity**, and **availability**
  - Mandates **safeguards** for physical storage, maintenance, transmission, and access

Figure 11.21 Main points of HIPAA

Source: HIPAA Act of 1996.

pertaining to an individual is housed electronically and/or is transmitted over telecommunications systems/ networks. The standard mandates safeguards for physical storage and maintenance, transmission, and access to individual health information. Entities required to comply with the standard include any health care provider, health care clearinghouse, or health plan that electronically maintains or transmits health information pertaining to an individual." Figure 11.21 summarizes these points.

11.9 USING DIAGRAMS FOR HIGH-LEVEL REQUIREMENTS

According to Davis [6] and Wiegers [7], no single view of requirements gives a complete understanding, and it is often helpful to represent high-level requirements using diagrams. What is often needed is a combination of text and diagrams to convey a complete picture of the intended application. We introduce two types of diagrams used to describe high-level requirements: *data flow* and *state transition* diagrams. We are using them here to express requirements. They are often used to express designs as well, and this can be confusing. The difference to watch for is not so much the form of expression as whether the attempt is to express "what" (requirements) or "how" (design).

11.9.1 Data Flow Diagrams

Some requirements are naturally described as the flow of data among processing elements. For example, imagine that our customer is trying to explain what he wants from an ATM banking application, starting with deposits and affecting accounts at several locations. In a *data flow diagram*, the *nodes*, shown as circles or rectangles, represent processing units. The *arrows* between nodes denote the flow of data. The arrows are annotated with the data's type. *Data stores*—places where data reside, such as databases—are denoted by a pair of horizontal lines enclosing the name of the data store. *External agencies* such as the user and printers are represented by rectangles.

For the ATM application, the *deposit* functionality might get the deposit from the user and check the deposit transaction to ensure that it is legitimate. These functions are represented by circles in Figure 11.22. Next, the type of data flowing between the functions is noted on the figure—the account number and the deposit amount. The user is involved, too, and so is represented. A function to create a summary of accounts, to give another example, requires input from a store, as shown.

A more complete data flow diagram for the ATM requirements would be as shown in Figure 11.23.

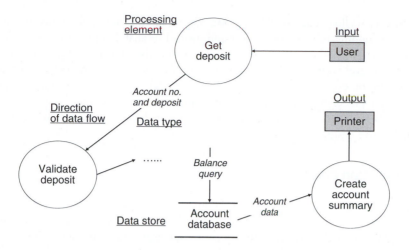

Figure 11.22 Data flow diagram—explanation of symbols

The complete diagram of Figure 11.23 includes the "member banks" data store, which is a list of banks allowing a deposit at this ATM. It also shows the data flow for the response to a query, in which details about an account are displayed. Expressing these requirements in text form only would be more difficult than using a data flow diagram to help describe them. Notice that data flow diagrams do not show control. For example, the ATM application does not indicate what function occurs first. Standards used for the symbols differ among organizations (e.g., rectangles can be used for the processing elements rather than circles).

Whether or not data flow diagrams are helpful for expressing requirements depends upon the application. For example, the ATM data flow diagram in Figure 11.23 clarifies for many readers what behavior the application is meant to exhibit, whereas video game requirements would probably not be

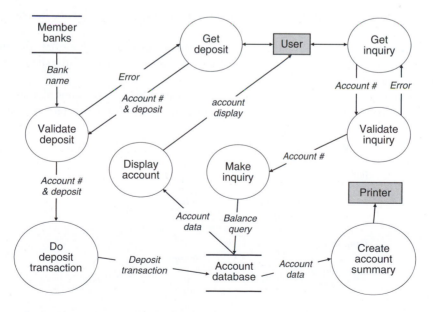

Figure 11.23 Partial data flow diagram for ATM application

described well using a data flow diagram. When using these diagrams for requirements specification, there is a significant danger of slipping into performing design instead of analyzing requirements. For example, if an application is required to track the flow of orders within a company, then a data flow diagram (DFD) showing this process at a high level would be an appropriate form for high-level requirements because the DFD is needed to express the outcomes. On the other hand, consider an application that is required to apply a complex formula. A DFD explaining the calculation process would be part of the design, but not the requirements—the formula would be sufficient for expressing the requirements. We will revisit data flow diagrams in Part IV, the design section of the book.

11.9.2 State Transition Diagrams

Sometimes, an application, or part thereof, is best thought of as being in one of several *states*. The state of an application is its situation or status. States are sometimes called "phases" or "stages." Although a state often corresponds to a GUI and vice versa, the state concept is more general than GUIs. The idea is to divide the application into states so that the application is always in one of these states. Note that the states we are defining are based on the requirements of the application—not its software design. For example, it might be useful to think of an online shopper at a bookselling site as being either in "browsing" state (looking at book information) or in "purchasing" state (providing credit card information, etc.). A diagram that depicts the different states and the transitions between states is called a *state transition diagram*.

There are several possible Encounter states:

- *Setting up:* the state during which the game is being set up

- *Preparing:* equipping the player's character with qualities such as "strength" and "intelligence" can be performed as long as no foreign character is present

- *Waiting:* nothing is happening in the game that is experienced by the user

- *Engaging:* the state in which the player's character and the foreign character are exchanging quality values

These states are shown in a UML state transition diagram in Figure 11.24. For event-driven applications, diagrams like this can be an effective way for the customer and developer to obtain a shared concept of how the application is meant to work.

After identifying the states, the *transitions* between states are added. Transitions, denoted by arrows, are each labeled with the name of the *event* that causes the object to change from one state to another. Events are

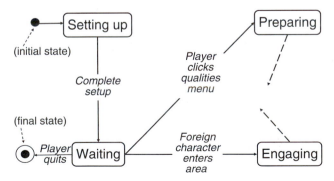

Figure 11.24 Partial Encounter state transition diagram

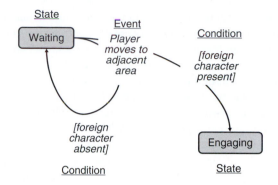

Figure 11.25 Using conditions in state transition diagrams

occurrences that can cause a change in the object's state. A typical event on a GUI is a mouse click. The solid circle denotes the starting state. The final state is depicted by the solid circle inside another circle.

States and transitions can apply to entities at many levels. For example, a ship can be in one of several states, such as *Sailing*, *Docking*, or *Docked*. Parts of the ship can be in several states: For example, a cabin can be in *Occupied* or *Unoccupied* state.

Sometimes, when an object is in a given state and an event occurs, the object can transition to one of several states, depending on a condition. For example, when the player decides to move her character to an adjacent area, the game transitions from the *Waiting* state into one of two states. One possibility is to transition back to *Waiting* state (if the foreign character is absent from the entered area); the other is to transition to the *Engaging* state (if the foreign character is present in the entered area). In UML, conditions are denoted by square brackets, as shown in Figure 11.25.

The complete state transition diagram for Encounter is shown in Figure 11.26. Once the player has finished setting up the Encounter game, the latter transitions from *Setting Up* state into *Waiting* state. If Encounter is in

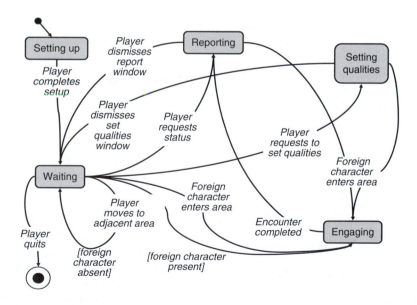

Figure 11.26 Encounter state transition diagram

Waiting state and a foreign character enters, then *Encounter* transitions into *Engaging* state. Figure 11.26 indicates that the process of setting quality values and the process of reporting the results of an encounter can be interrupted by the arrival of the foreign character. The latter causes a new encounter to commence immediately.

A state transition model is a good way to explain the concept of operations of Encounter. State transition models are commonly used as design tools as well (see Chapter 16). Whether or not they should be used to express high-level requirements, as we are doing here, depends on the application in question and how helpful doing so is for the customer. This may require some education of the customer.

For many applications, each state corresponds to a GUI. However, there is a wide variety in what we may define as a state. The state diagram in Figure 11.26 corresponds roughly to the presence of visual artifacts on the monitor, but these are not GUIs. For example, when the foreign character Freddie appears on the monitor, the application transitions to *Engaging* state, but Freddie is just an additional graphical element, not a separate GUI.

11.10 CASE STUDY: HIGH-LEVEL SOFTWARE REQUIREMENTS SPECIFICATION (SRS) FOR THE ENCOUNTER VIDEO GAME

Note to the Student:
Using a standard to write the SRS helps one to cover all of the aspects of requirements that readers need to know about, and provides a recognized structure. Several standards are available, but we will concentrate on the IEEE standard. The complete IEEE 830-1998 standard can be found in [8]. Most organizations allow modification of the standard to tailor it for their own use. In fact, the template used below modifies the standard by omitting some less important sections and by adding sections on concept of operations and use cases. The reader can compare the case study headings with the standards shown in Figures 8 and 9 of Chapter 10.

In the case study portion of this chapter, Sections 1 and 2 cover the high-level requirements. The remainder of the document, Sections 3 and 4, containing the detailed requirements, is provided in the case study at the end of Chapter 12. Recall that customer requirements are not intended to be detailed enough to develop the design and implementation—this is the purpose of the detailed requirements.

History of versions of this document:

1/19/98 Hal Furness: Initial draft

1/29/98 Karen Peters: Reviewed for technical accuracy; changes made throughout

2/1/98 Hal Furness: Entire document reviewed for small improvements

2/19/98 Karen Peters: Document reviewed and suggestions made

2/29/98 Karen Peters: Moved use cases to Section 2.2

3/1/98 Hal Furness: Improved wording throughout; sense not changed

5/20/04 Eric Braun: Updated to 830-1998 standard

14/20/08 Eric Brannen: Edited to improve assorted clarifications

1. Introduction

1.1 Purpose

The purpose of this entire document (not the purpose of the application).

This document provides all of the requirements for the Encounter video game. Parts 1 and 2 are intended primarily for customers of the application, but will also be of interest to software engineers building or maintaining the software. Part 3 is intended primarily for software engineers, but will also be of interest to customers.

1.2 Scope

> (The aspects of the application this document is intended to cover.)

This document covers the requirements for release 0.0.1 of Encounter. Mention will be made throughout this document of selected probable features of future releases. The purpose of this is to guide developers in selecting a design that will be able to accommodate the full-scale application.

1.3 Definitions, Acronyms, and Abbreviations

See Table 3.3.

1.4 References

Software Configuration Management Plan (SCMP) for Encounter version 1.0

Software Design Description (SDD) for Encounter version 1.2

Software Project Management Plan (SPMP) for Encounter version 1.2

Software Quality Assurance Plan (SQAP) for Encounter version 1.0

Software User Documentation Plan (SUDP) for Encounter version 1.0

Software Test Documentation (STD) for Encounter version 1.0

1.5 Overview

Intentionally omitted.

> The author of this document felt no need for this section, and intends to cover the overview in Section 2.

2. Overall Description

> Make this general enough so that it is unlikely to change much in future versions. Avoid statements that are repeated in later sections.

Encounter is to be a role-playing game that simulates the lifetime of the player's main character. It should be of interest to both men and women. The measure of "success" in playing Encounter is up to the player. Typically, success will be measured by the "life points" maximum attained by the player or by the ability of the player to live as long a life as possible.

Some game characters are to be under the control of the player. The rest, called "foreign" characters, are to be under the application's control. Game characters will have a fixed total number of points allocated among qualities such as strength, stamina, patience, and so on. Characters encounter each other when they are in the same area at the same time, and may then engage each other. The result of the engagement depends on the values of their qualities and on the environment in which the engagement takes place. Engagements are not necessarily violent or adversarial. Players have restricted opportunities to reallocate their qualities. One of the player-controlled characters will be referred to as the "main" player character.

In early versions of this game, there will be only one player-controlled character and one foreign character.

The eventual nature of the characters is to be determined from insights gained from surveys and focus groups. It is expected that initial releases will not have animation. Encounter should eventually be highly customizable, so that users can either start with predefined games, substitute predesigned characters and rules of engagement, or devise their own characters and rules of engagement.

The design should support expansion into a family of games, including Internet-based multiple-player versions.

2.1 Product Perspective

> In this section, Encounter is compared with other related or competing products. This is a useful way to provide perspective on the application. Subheading 2.1.1 of this section has been changed from the IEEE standard to accommodate "concept of operations."

Encounter is intended to fulfill the need for programmers to have a greater influence over the contents of video games with additional programming. It is also intended for a somewhat mature clientele. Encounter is intended to appeal to both genders. The design and documentation for Encounter will make it convenient to expand and modify the game. It is anticipated that Encounter will be used as a legacy application for expansion into applications such as office interaction simulations.

2.1.1 Concept of Operations

> This section conveys the overall concept of the application by whatever means are most natural for doing so. In the case of Encounter, the requirements developers decided that state/transitions best convey the concept.

Encounter can be in one of the following states (also shown in Figure 11.26):

- **Setting up.** The state in which the game is being set up by the player

- **Reporting.** The system is displaying a window showing the status of the player's character(s).

- **Setting qualities.** Equipping the player's character with qualities. This process consumes arbitrary amounts of time, and can be performed as long as no foreign character is present.

- **Engaging.** The state that applies whenever a foreign character and the player's main character are present in an area at the same time.

- **Waiting.** The player and the foreign character(s) are not active.

This state/transition is tested by integration test <to be supplied>.

2.1.2 User Interface Concepts

> The following figures are preliminary sketches of key user interfaces only, used to provide perspective on the product. All the user interfaces are specified in detail in Section 3. We have modified

the standard IEEE heading "user interfaces" to emphasize that these are not the detailed GUIs.

2.1.2.1 Area User Interface Concept The areas in which encounters take place shall have an appearance very roughly like that shown in Figure 11.12.

2.1.2.2 User Interface Concept for Setting Quality Values When setting the values of game characters under his control, the player uses an interface of the form sketched approximately in Figure 11.11. The scroll box is used to identify the quality to be set, and the text box is used for setting the value.

2.1.3 Hardware Interfaces
None. Future releases will utilize a joystick.

2.1.4 Software Interfaces
None.

2.1.5 Communications Interfaces
None. Future releases will interface with the Internet via a modem.

2.1.6 Memory Constraints
Encounter shall require no more than 16 MB of RAM and 20 MB of secondary storage (see test plan <test reference to be supplied>).

2.1.7 Operations

> Normal and special operations required by the user, such as modes of operation, data processing support functions, and backup and recovery operations.

It shall be possible to save and retrieve a game.

2.1.8 Site Adaptation Requirements

> Requirements for execution on a particular installation; versions in various languages (e.g., French, Japanese, Spanish).

None.

2.2 Product Functions

> Summary of the major functions of the application. This section is more detailed than Section 1.5, but does not attempt to supply all details, as done in Section 3. The writers of this SRS decided that use cases are an appropriate manner in which to specify the overall functionality of Encounter.

This section specifies the required overall functionality of the application, but is not intended to provide the complete specifications. Section 3 provides the requirements in complete detail.

2.2.1 *Initialize* Use Case

Actor: Player of Encounter

Use case: Figure 11.27 gives the text of the *Initialize* use case. The use case is shown in context with the *Encounter foreign character* use case and the *Set rules* use case. Initialize is the typical sequence users execute at the beginning of a session.

This use case corresponds to test <test reference to be supplied> in the Software Test Documentation.

2.2.2 *Travel to Adjacent Area* Use Case

Actor: Player of Encounter

Use case:

1. Player hits hyperlink connecting displayed area to adjacent area

2. System displays the indicated adjacent area including player's character

2.2.3 *Encounter Foreign Character* Use Case

Actor: Player of Encounter

Use case:

1. System moves a foreign game character into the area occupied by the player, or Player moves into an area containing a foreign character

2. System causes the two characters to engage

3. System displays the result of the engagement

4. If either the player's character or the foreign character has no points, the game terminates

5. Otherwise, System moves the player's character to a random area different from that in which the encounter took place, and displays it there

2.3 User Characteristics

> Indicate what kind of people the typical users are likely to be. Examples: novice, software professional, accountant with five years of computer usage, etc.

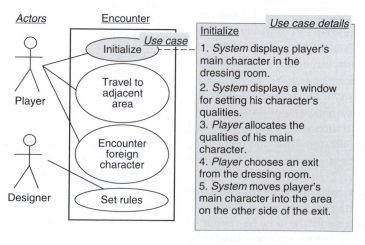

Figure 11.27 *Initialize* use case for Encounter

The user is expected to be approximately 20–35 years of age.

2.4 Constraints

> These are all conditions that may limit the developer's options. They can originate from many sources.

Encounter shall operate on PCs running Windows XP or later at a minimum speed of 500 MHz. Java shall be the implementation language.

2.5 Assumptions and Dependencies

> (Any assumptions being made—for example, future hardware.)

None.

2.6 Apportioning of Requirements

> (Order in which requirements are to be implemented.)

The requirements described in Sections 1 and 2 of this document are referred to as "customer requirements"; those in Section 3 are referred to as "detailed requirements." The primary audience for customer requirements is the customer community, and the secondary audience is the developer community. The reverse is true for the detailed requirements. These two levels of requirements are intended to be consistent. Inconsistencies are to be logged as defects. In the event that a requirement is stated within both the customer requirements and the detailed requirements, the application shall be built from the detailed requirement version since it is more detailed.

"Essential" requirements (referred to in Section 3) are to be implemented for this version of Encounter. "Desirable" requirements are to be implemented in this release if possible, but are not committed to by the developers. It is anticipated that they will be part of a future release. "Optional" requirements will be implemented at the discretion of the developers.

11.11 CASE STUDY: HIGH-LEVEL REQUIREMENTS FOR ECLIPSE

> Note to the Student:
> This section discusses published requirements for Eclipse. There is no single requirements document for Eclipse—the requirements are spread over multiple documents. The authors have reconstructed a partial requirements document from these sources at a single point in time, placing them roughly in IEEE format for the sake of comparison. The result is necessarily incomplete, and illustrates a shortcoming of many open source projects. Most of the material below is quoted directly (but selectively, of course) from the Eclipse documentation online at the time.

"The Eclipse Project is an open source software development project dedicated to providing a robust, full-featured, commercial-quality, industry platform for the development of highly integrated tools. The mission of the Eclipse Project is to adapt and evolve the eclipse technology to meet the needs of the eclipse tool building community and its users, so that the vision of eclipse as an industry platform is realized."[2]

"The Eclipse workbench consists of *windows*. Each window contains *parts*. Each part can be a *view* or an *editor*. A *perspective* is a physical configuration of parts. Figure 11.28 shows a typical Eclipse screenshot."[3] This example is a Java perspective (as indicated in the shortcut bar). This perspective consists of a Windows Explorer–type of view, an editor, and other parts, including the console view.

> This particular window is used merely as an example, to make the specification more understandable—not as a detailed specification.

---

[2] From http://www.eclipse.org/projects/index.html.

[3] Ibid.

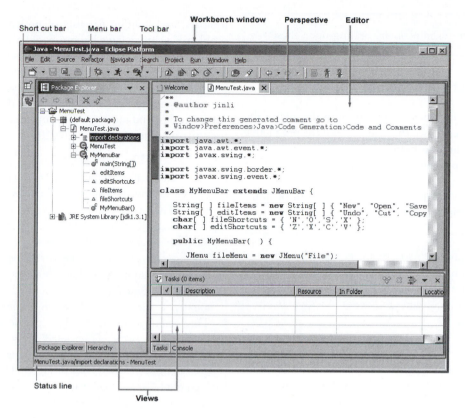

Figure 11.28 Eclipse GUI

Source: Eclipse, http://www.eclipse.org/articles/Article-UI-Guidelines/Index.html.

The following three sections are quoted from Eclipse documentation with some adaptation.

11.12 ECLIPSE PLATFORM SUBPROJECT (FIRST OF THREE)

Note to the Student:
Since Eclipse is organized around three sub-projects, it is natural to organize the summary requirements in the same way. Within each project, summary requirements are organized around several "themes." This is a way to organize the (high-level) requirements and allow latitude at the same time. The themes do provide content, but they avoid specifying details.

The Eclipse Platform provides the fundamental building blocks of the Eclipse projects. Plan tasks are new features of the Eclipse Platform or significant reworking of existing features. Many of the changes under consideration for the next release of the Eclipse Platform address three major themes, as follows:

- **User experience theme.** Improving Eclipse from the point of view of the end user.

- **Responsive UI theme.** Making it easier to write Eclipse plug-ins that keep the UI responsive.

- **Rich client platform theme.** Generalizing Eclipse into a platform for building non-IDE applications.

In addition, there are important Eclipse Platform improvements that do not naturally fit into any of the above themes. These are categorized as follows:

- Other Eclipse Platform items

> Below are examples elaborating upon these.

User Experience Theme

This theme includes improving both the "out of the box" experience so that new users are productive faster, and finding better ways to scale up to large numbers of plug-ins without overwhelming the user.

Committed Items (Eclipse Platform subproject, User Experience theme)

> The requirements here are grouped by priority. "Committed" is the highest priority. The others are "proposed" and "deferred." Completion of a requirement is denoted with a green check mark.

Improve UI scalability

"Despite efforts to ensure UI scalability with a large base of available tools, the Eclipse workbench still intimidates many users with long menus, wide toolbars, and lengthy flat lists of preferences. This problem is acute in large Eclipse-based products. The Platform should provide additional ways for controlling workbench clutter, such as further menu and toolbar customizability, distinguishing between novice and advanced functions, supporting different developer roles, and more specific object contributions for particular file types . . . (37929)"

> The number given above in parentheses is a link to the following bug entered in Eclipse's Bugzilla bug database: https://bugs.eclipse.org/bugs/ show_bug.cgi?id=37929. This and other requirements are managed in the same way as defects. The reason is that both define work to be done on an existing application. Each Bugzilla location contains extensive discussion about the requirement and the progress made implementing it. This amounts to the detailed specification—a common way of specifying detailed requirements in open source projects. The beginning of Bugzilla item 37929 is shown in Figure 11.29 and Figure 11.30. We will return to the subject of requirements tools in Chapter 12.

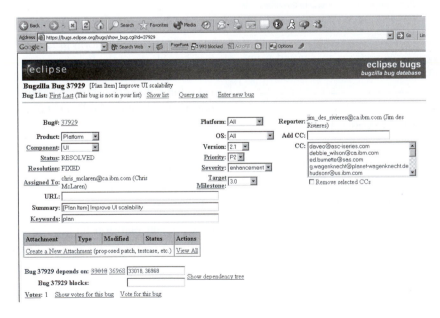

Figure 11.29 Using Bugzilla in Eclipse to track bugs and detailed requirements, 1 of 2

⊙ Leave as **RESOLVED FIXED**
○ Reopen bug
○ Mark bug as **VERIFIED**
○ Mark bug as **CLOSED**

`Commit`

View Bug Activity | **Format For Printing**

Description:

```
Improve UI scalability. Despite efforts to ensure UI scalability with a large
base of available tools, the Eclipse workbench still intimidates many users
with long menus, wide toolbars, and lengthy flat lists of preferences. This
problem is acute in large Eclipse-based products. The Platform should provide
additional ways for controlling workbench clutter, such as further menu and
toolbar customizability, distinguishing between novice and advanced functions,
supporting different developer roles, and more specific object contributions
for particular file types. [Platform UI, Platform Debug, JDT UI] [Theme: User
experience]
```

------- *Additional Comment #1 From Jim des Rivieres 2003-05-21 11:18* -------

```
*** Bug 36954 has been marked as a duplicate of this bug. ***
```

------- *Additional Comment #2 From MorPheus 2003-06-08 14:40* -------

```
Hi,

    I am glad after reading the Eclipse Project Draft 3.0 plan that in eclipse
3.0 that this bug going to be addressed, but I also want the people who is
going to address this bug to provide api's to do the menu and toolbar
customization(i.e, allow us to remove unwanted menu items programmatically).If
you are just providing the option to customise the menubar toolbar manually
```

Figure 11.30 Using Bugzilla in Eclipse to track bugs and detailed requirements, 2 of 2

Improve initial user experience

Users who are new to an Eclipse-based product can find their first experiences with it overwhelming, even daunting. The initial experience would be improved if a product could preconfigure the workbench to show only the subset of function that a new user really needs; welcome pages could be personalized for particular users roles or levels of experience. . . . (37664)

Improve UI affordances

. . . (37671) ✔ *Work completed*

> This is a way of tracking the status of requirements.

Proposed Items (Eclipse Platform subproject, User Experience theme)

> The "proposed" category is the second most important priority. Note that these requirements are expressed in an exploratory, less specific, manner. Requirements analysis still has to be performed to transform these into committed items.

The following work items are being actively investigated, but we are not yet able to promise any solution for this release.

Allow editors to open files outside workspace

A common request is to be able to use Eclipse to open a file that is not part of the workspace, or perhaps even one on a remote system. In addition, applications would like to provide file extension associations so that double-clicking on a file in the OS desktop would open the associated Eclipse editor. The operations and capabilities available on these "outside of the workspace" files would need to be defined. (37935)

Improve workspace synchronization with file system. . . .

> Details omitted

Content-type-based editor lookup. . . .

> Details omitted

Deferred Items (Eclipse Platform subproject, User Experience theme)

> The Eclipse project tracks requirements that may never be implemented. This enables them to be revived, provides history, and discourages them from being proposed again. It helps to clarify the project's direction.

These items are next in line for this release. As committers complete their assigned tasks or additional help becomes available, some of these items may be committed for this release:

Add table of contents support to wizards (36947) . . .

> Details omitted

Add project templates (36960) . . .]
. . . .

(■ recently de-committed item) Aid ongoing learning (37666)

> More tracking the status of requirements. "De-committed" means, effectively, "dropped."

(■ recently deferred item) Provide a general purpose navigator (36961) . . .

> These are just a few examples that illustrate the organization of these documents.

Other Eclipse Platform Items

> The following are examples from the Eclipse Platform subproject within this "theme."

Design Constraints: Compatibility of Release 3. 0 with 2.0 and 2.1

> This section is quoted from note[4]. It consists of nonfunctional requirements, and one example is expanded here. A "breaking" change is one that prevents some applications from executing on the new version that did execute on the old one. Note also that this paragraph contains policy elements for requirements rather than requirements themselves.

"Eclipse 3.0 will be compatible with Eclipse 2.0 and 2.1 to the greatest extent possible. The nature and scope of some of the key plan items are such that the only feasible solutions would break compatibility. Since breaking changes are a disruption to the Eclipse community, they cannot be taken lightly. We (the Eclipse PMC) will have an open discussion with the community before approving a proposed breaking change for inclusion in 3.0. In other regards, Eclipse 3.0 will be compatible with 2.0 and 2.1. We also aim to minimize the effort required to port an existing plug-in to the 3.0 APIs. We will provide a comprehensive *Eclipse 3.0 Porting Guide* that covers all areas of breaking API changes and describes how to port existing 2.1 plug-ins to 3.0. Up-to-date drafts of the *Eclipse 3.0 Porting Guide* will be included with milestone builds so that it's possible to climb aboard the 3.0 release wagon at the early stages, or to estimate the amount of effort that will be involved in eventually porting existing plug-ins to 3.0."

---

[4] http://www.eclipse.org/eclipse/development/eclipse_project_plan_3_0_20040130.html.

11.13 CASE STUDY: HIGH-LEVEL REQUIREMENTS FOR OPENOFFICE

This section is intended to give the reader an idea of the OpenOffice requirements.

> Note to the Student:
> The prose below has been adapted by the authors from http://www.openoffice.org/product/ which was written with a partially marketing flavor. For example, we have replaced "WRITER is a powerful tool . . . " with "WRITER is a tool . . . " "You can easily integrate images" has been replaced by "It facilitates integrating images." OpenOffice requirements are decomposed at this top level as shown next.

OpenOffice consists of the following:

- WRITER is a tool for creating professional documents, reports, newsletters, and brochures. It facilitates integrating images and charts in documents, creating everything from business letters to complete books with professional layouts, as well as creating and publish Web content.

- CALC is a spreadsheet that facilitates the absorption of numerical information. It enables users to calculate, analyze, and visually communicate data. Advanced spreadsheet functions and decision making facilitate sophisticated data analysis. Charting tools generate 2D and 3D charts.

- IMPRESS is used for the creation of multimedia presentations. It allows special effects, animation, and drawing tools.

- DRAW facilitates the production of everything from simple diagrams to dynamic 3D illustrations and special effects.

- The Database User Tools facilitates day to day database work in a simple spreadsheet-like form. They support dBASE databases and ODBC or JDBC.

High-Level Requirements for WRITER

> It appears that the only high-level description of WRITER is written in a style to attract users

> rather than to specify its requirements. The following is found at http://www.openoffice.org/product/writer.html.

"WRITER has everything you would expect from a modern, fully equipped word processor. It's simple enough for a quick memo, powerful enough to create complete books with contents, diagrams, indexes, etc. You're free to concentrate on your message, while WRITER makes it look great.

The *Auto-Pilot* takes all the hassle out of producing standard documents such as letters, faxes, agendas, minutes. You are of course free to create your own templates.

The *Stylist* puts the power of style sheets into the hands of every user.

You're free to add words and phrases to the *AutoCorrect dictionary*, which can check your spelling as you type.

AutoComplete suggests common words and phrases to complete what you are typing.

AutoFormat takes care of the formatting as you write, leaving you free to concentrate on your message.

Text frames and *linking* mean you are free to lay out newsletters, flyers, etc. exactly the way you want them to be.

Increase the usefulness of your long, complex documents by generating a table of contents or indexing terms, bibliographical references, illustrations, tables, and other objects. You are free to choose your own email software—WRITER offers direct connection to email software. Make your documents freely available with WRITER's HTML export to the Web, or publish in Portable Document Format (.pdf) to guarantee that what you write is what your reader sees. Of course, you are free to use old Microsoft Word documents, or save your work in Word format for sending to people who are still locked into Microsoft products."

> We would express these more like the following.

WRITER shall be a full-featured word processor. It shall allow the creation of simple documents and complete books with contents, diagrams, indexes, etc. An example is shown in Figure 11.31.

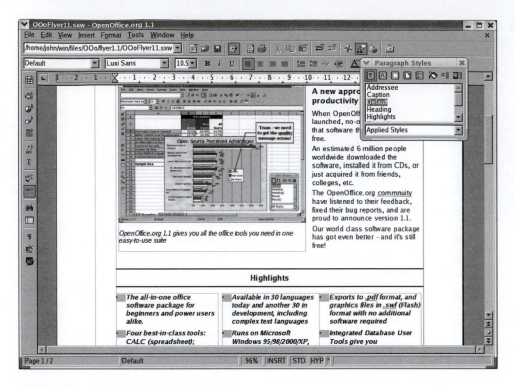

Figure 11.31 Example of document open in WRITER

Source: OpenOffice, http://www.openoffice.org/product/pix/writer-big.png.

WRITER's *Auto-Pilot* feature shall facilitate the creation of standard documents such as letters, faxes, agendas, minutes. The *Stylist* feature shall allow the user to easily vary the style of a document. The *AutoCorrect dictionary* feature shall check spelling during or after test entry. The *AutoComplete* feature shall suggests common words and phrases to complete a partially typed sentence. The *AutoFormat* feature shall handle formatting while the user enters text. *The text frames* and *linking* features shall allow the user to flexibly format newsletters, flyers, etc.

WRITER shall generate a table of contents, indexes, bibliographical references, illustrations, and tables. It shall provide direct connection to e-mail software, export HTML to the Web, publish in Portable Document Format, and save work in Microsoft Word format.

> We will skip additional requirements for OpenOffice. It carries many of its detailed

requirements in an application called (rather unpoetically) *Issuezilla*. Issuezilla consists of "issues." An issue could be a bug but it could also be a task. This is similar to Eclipse's use of Bugzilla. Some OpenOffice projects have created more careful requirements documents. For example, the OpenOffice PROJECT Management Toolset (draft at [5]) and the OpenOffice Bibliographic module (draft at [6]).

---

[5] http://oopm.openoffice.org/files/documents/177/1843/OOPM_Requirements_Discussion_Draft_A1a.pdf as of 2005.

[6] http://www.geocities.com/manish_k_agrawal/Biblio_req.html as of 2005.

11.14 SUMMARY

This chapter has described the process whereby the high-level requirements for a product are obtained and recorded in a manner clear to the customer and developing organization. High-level requirements describe the purpose of an application, its intended functionality, and its benefits. The high-level requirements are documented in a form such as Sections 1 and 2 of IEEE 830-1993 Software Requirements Specifications. Various techniques for eliciting and recording high-level requirements are used. One way to gather requirements is to interview stakeholders and potential customers.

A combination of text and diagrams is used to document the requirements. The following guidelines can be used to choose the appropriate form.

- If a requirement is simple and stands alone, express it in clear sentences within an appropriate section of the SRS.

- If a requirement is an interaction between the user and the application, express it via a use case.

- If the requirement involves process elements, each taking inputs and producing outputs, use a data flow diagram.

- If a requirement involves states that the application can be in (or parts can be in), use a state transition diagram. States often correspond to GUIs.

Use cases are widely applicable for describing customer requirements because they capture user application interactions. If a state transition diagram expresses what the customer wants and needs and the customer understands the diagram, then its use is appropriate. The same holds for data flow diagrams.

User interfaces are specified as part of the high-level requirements. Two important principles for defining high-level user interfaces are to (1) know your user and (2) understand the business function in question.

High-level requirements for agile projects are collected continuously through most of the life of the project. Each requirement is expressed with a *user story*. A user story is a high-level piece of required functionality as seen by the anticipated user.

11.15 EXERCISES

1. Describe in your own words the difference between customer *wants* and customer *needs*. Provide an example that illustrates the difference.

2. List four of what you consider to be the most important high-level requirements for an application that tracks bar-coded invoices within a company.

3. Interview two separate people about their high-level requirements for the bar-code application specified in Exercise 2. Compare the requirements gathered from each interviewee. How similar or different an application did each of them envision? How did it compare with the high-level requirements you generated? Write a paragraph summarizing the similarities and differences, the importance of interviewing different stakeholders for their vision of a software application, and how you might reconcile the differences.

4. What is a use case? Is the following a use case? Why or why not?
   "The system shall provide advice for the beginning Windows user on how to execute Windows operations."

5. Write a use case for one of the high-level requirements listed in Exercise 2.

6. Why is it important to show customers preliminary sketches of GUIs as early in the development cycle as possible? Give what you consider to be one or two of the most important reasons.

7. Your customer needs to specify user interfaces. Discuss two or three of each of the pros and cons of the following means for doing this in the context of the application (large or small) and the nature of the GUI (complex or simple).
   a. Sketching using hand drawings, your own or drawn by a graphic artist
   b. Sketching using graphics tools, such as Paint or PowerPoint
   c. Using the GUI-building features of the target language of the application

8. Draw a data flow diagram to express the high-level requirements of an application that tracks the flow of orders within a company.

9. Consider an application that manages patients in a doctor's office. Patients call for an appointment and their information is entered into the application. Patients can call to reschedule or cancel appointments. After a patient is seen by a doctor, the patient may be referred to another doctor for treatment if necessary. Draw a state-transition diagram to express the high-level requirements for this application.

TEAM EXERCISES

T11.1 Write the high-level requirements for an application decided upon by the team. Follow the form of IEEE830-1993. Track the amount of time spent doing this exercise. Decide what fraction of the requirements are understood by the team. Estimate how long it would take to obtain 95 percent of the requirements. State how the process you used could have been improved. Be specific, and provide examples.

T11.2
a. Identify an individual outside the team who needs a modest application. You will be gathering high-level requirements from this individual, then showing them to him or her.
b. With your "customer," identify metrics for how he or she will evaluate your high-level requirements. Also determine the time limit for an interview (e.g., a half hour).
c. Interview the customer, and write the high-level requirements.
d. Have the customer evaluate and comment on your high-level requirements in accordance with the chosen metrics.

BIBLIOGRAPHY

1. Dennis, Alan, Barbara Wixom, and David Tegarden, *"Systems Analysis and Design with UML Version 2.0: An Object-Oriented Approach,"* John Wiley & Sons, p. 139, 2005.

2. Jacobson, Ivar, *"Object Oriented Software Engineering: A Use Case Driven Approach,"* (Addison-Wesley Object Technology Series), Addison-Wesley, 1994.

3. Fowler, Martin, *"UML Distilled Third Edition: A Brief Guide to the Standard Object Modeling Language,"* Addison-Wesley, p. 99, 2004.

4. Jacobson, Ivar, Grady Booch and James Rumbaugh, *"The Unified Software Development Process,"* (Addison-Wesley Object Technology Series), Addison-Wesley, 1999.

5. Alexander, Ian, and Neil Maiden (Editors), *"Scenarios, Stories, Use Cases: Through the Systems Development Life-Cycle"*, John Wiley & Sons, 2004.

6. Davis, Alan, *"201 Principles of Software Engineering,"* McGraw Hill, 1995.

7. Wiegers, Karl, *"Software Requirements,"* Microsoft Press, pp. 193–4, 2003.

8. "IEEE Recommended Practice for Software Requirements Specifications," IEEE Std 830-1998, June 1998.

12

Analyzing Detailed Requirements

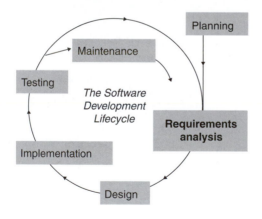

- What ways are there to organize detailed requirements?

- How do you express user interfaces in detail?

- How do you express security requirements in detail?

- What kinds of error conditions can be specified?

- What is traceability and why is it important?

- What ways are there to prioritize requirements?

- Why associate requirements with tests?

- How do agile methods relate to detailed requirements?

- How do you use tools for requirements analysis?

Figure 12.1 The context and learning goals for this chapter

After high-level requirements are specified, typically for an iteration, the next step in requirements analysis is to define the detailed requirements. The purpose of detailed requirements is to provide the reader with absolutely all that's required of the application. With one exception, there is nowhere else for the team to state *exactly* what this consists of. For example, if we do not state here that the title of a video must appear in a 16-point font on the monitor, then we assume that this will not appear in the product.

The "exception" mentioned above refers to the possibility of either stating each detailed requirement as a comment in the source code or of expecting source code and its unit tests to effectively specify the requirement. This tends to be the approach of agile projects, which we discussed previously. Agile projects do not rule out the kind of documentation that we discuss in this chapter, but they value working code ahead of such separate documentation.

This chapter concentrates on written detailed requirements. However, whether one writes down detailed requirements in these ways or not, there is no choice but to eventually think them through. In fact, they form a common currency of applications, as it were. Detailed requirements are usually divided into sections, including functional requirements, nonfunctional requirements, and GUI details.

12.1 THE MEANING OF DETAILED REQUIREMENTS

Detailed requirements provide software engineers with a basis for design and implementation. They are sometimes called "specific requirements," "functional specifications," or "developer requirements." Detailed requirements consist of a complete list of specific properties and functionality that the application must possess, expressed in complete detail. Each of these requirements is labeled, and tracked through implementation. Detailed requirements are consistent with, and elaborate upon, the high-level requirements. They are intended to be read primarily by developers—however, customers are interested in them as well, and should be able to understand and comment on them with few exceptions. Recall that the primary audience for the high-level requirements consists of customers.

As the case studies in this book demonstrate, when it comes to software engineering, "the devil is in the details." For example, in 1999 NASA lost a weather satellite worth a reported[1] $125 million, reportedly because control data they had assumed to be in metric form was not [1].

> . . . the root cause for the loss of the MCO spacecraft was the failure to use metric units in the coding of a ground software file, "Small Forces," used in trajectory models. Specifically, thruster performance data in English units instead of metric units was used in the software application code titled SM_FORCES (small forces). A file called Angular Momentum Desaturation (AMD) contained the output data from the SM_FORCES software. The data in the AMD file was required to be in metric units per existing software interface documentation, and the trajectory modelers assumed the data was provided in metric units per the requirements.[2]

This description implies that the requirements stated the need for metric units but the software did not implement the requirements correctly. A fascinating fact is that this defect was identified within mere days *after* the disaster. This means that it may not be hard to locate a defect once we know it is present. The problem is often our ignorance of its presence. The detailed requirements form the first line of defense against the corruption or omission of details. Far from being the mindless activity that it might first appear, getting all the requirements down in complete detail involves the difficult tasks of organizing people and their thought process. To understand this challenge, imagine the task of organizing a 20-volume requirements document set so effective

---

[1] http://news.bbc.co.uk/1/hi/sci/tech/514763.stm.

[2] ftp://ftp.hq.nasa.gov/pub/pao/reports/1999/MCO_report.pdf.

that a NASA engineer, for example, would know exactly where to add or look for a specific requirement. Storing and maintaining these requirements in a searchable database helps a great deal, but the task remains difficult indeed.

12.2 ORGANIZING DETAILED REQUIREMENTS

Requirements change constantly, and so written requirements should be well-organized and easy to update. To appreciate the value of carefully organizing detailed requirements, consider the following rather random attempt at writing detailed requirements for the Encounter game. Note that these requirements are still raw and are not inspected.

Every character in the Encounter video game shall have a name.

Every game character has the same set of qualities, each with a floating point value.

Encounter shall take less than a second to compute the results of an engagement.

Each area has a specific set of "qualities needed." For example, combat areas require strength and stamina; living rooms require sensitivity and intellect.

When two Encounter game characters are in the same area at the same time they may either choose or be obliged by the game to engage each other.

Every game character shall have an amount of life points.

The sum of the values of qualities of a game character relevant to the area in question shall be referred to as the character's area value. In an engagement, the system compares the area values of the characters and computes the result of the engagement.

The name of any character in Encounter shall have no more than 15 letters.

As it grows, an unorganized list like the one above quickly becomes unmanageable.

- Its very size makes it hard to understand as a unit even before it grows into the hundreds, if not thousands.

- The requirements are of mixed types: performance requirements must be dealt with differently from functional requirements, for example.

- Some requirements naturally belong with related ones.

- It is difficult to locate a specific requirement.

Functional detailed requirements can be organized according to several classifications, including by feature, use case, GUI, state, and class. We describe each method in more detail in subsequent sections. Tools for managing requirements can help a great deal. Nevertheless, the decision as to how to organize detailed requirements in the first place is important because teams refer to them continually if the document is well done.

The IEEE standard 830-1998 provides document templates for several ways to classify the detailed requirements. Figure 12.2 shows the conventional and the object-oriented classification templates of the IEEE 830-1998 standard. The object-oriented classification uses classes/objects as a method of organizing the functional requirements. The SRS is often tailored to corporate or team needs by adding or modifying sections as appropriate. For example, the OO organization lacks a section equivalent to 3.4 in the non-OO organization "logical database requirements." The Encounter case study uses a modified form of the IEEE OO

3. **Specific requirements (<u>non-OO</u>)**

3.1 **External interfaces**

3.2 **Functional requirements**

3.3 **Performance requirements**

3.4 **Logical database requirements**

3.5 **Design constraints**

   3.5.1 Standards compliance

3.6 **Software system attributes**

   3.6.1 Reliability

   3.6.2 Availability

   3.6.3 Security

   3.6.4 Maintainability

   3.6.5 Portability

3.7 **Organizing specific requirements**

   3.7.1 System mode – or

   3.7.2 User class – or

   3.7.3 Objects (see right) – or

   3.7.4 Feature – or

   3.7.5 Stimulus – or

   3.7.6 Response – or

   3.7.7 Functional hierarchy – or

3.8 **Additional comments**

---

3. **Specific requirements (<u>OO</u>)**

3.1 **External interface requirements**

   3.1.1 User interfaces

   3.1.2 Hardware interfaces

   3.1.3 Software interfaces

   3.1.4 Communications interfaces

3.2 **Classes/Objects**

   3.2.1 Class/Object 1

      3.2.1.1 Attributes

      3.2.1.2 Functional requirements

      3.2.1.3 Events . . .

. . . . . .

3.3 **Performance requirements**

3.4 **Design constraints**

3.5 **Software system attributes**

3.6 **Other requirements**

Figure 12.2 IEEE 830-1998—specific requirements, OO and non-OO organizations

Source: IEEE Std 830-1998.

style and includes a section for use cases. Figure 12.3 maps the detailed requirements sections of Section 3 to the requirements category it describes.

It may be advisable to organize detailed requirements into a *combination* of classifications. For example, a feature-based organization could be used within the *configuring*, *executing*, and *backing up* states of an accounting application. The requirements for a factory automation system could be organized at the highest level by function (intake, part manufacturing, and assembly); they could then be organized by class within each.

This means the method of organizing detailed requirements is sometimes related to the probable architecture or implementation of the application. For example, if the design is to be object-oriented, detailed requirements organized by use case or class should be considered because they facilitate traceability. If the application lends itself to an obvious functional breakdown, then organizing the requirements by feature hierarchy may be appropriate.

12.2.1 Organizing Detailed Requirements by Feature

The oldest manner of organizing detailed requirements is by feature. This amounts to providing a simple list of functionality such as the following, for the Encounter video game. Many features are defined by a stimulus-and-response pair, as for requirement 127.

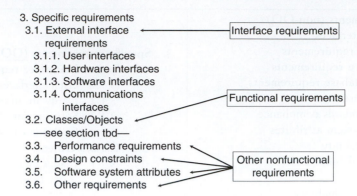

Figure 12.3 IEEE 830-1998—specific requirements, OO style interpreted as functional and nonfunctional detailed requirements

Source: IEEE Std 830-1998.

125. There shall be a set of hyperlinked locations at every exit to every area.

126. The foreign character shall move from area to adjacent area at random times, with an average of three seconds.

127. When the user clicks on the "Set qualities" button, the window in figure xx appears on the monitor.

Arranging requirements by feature has the advantage of simplicity but the disadvantage of inaccessibility; this is because it allows jumping from a feature in one part of the application to a feature in a completely different part. For example, if we wanted to change the manner in which the foreign character moves about, we would have to determine that the relevant requirement is number 126. How would we know what other requirements are affected? Search tools can help a great deal. Another disadvantage is the lack of traceability. For example, what part(s) of the code does requirement 125 map to?

One way to impose order on functional feature lists is to arrange them in a function *hierarchy* (i.e., by decomposing the application into a set of high-level functions, and then these into subfunctions, etc.). For example, the requirements for a home budget program could be decomposed into (1) *checking* functions, (2) *savings* functions, and (3) *investment* functions. The required *checking* functionality could be further decomposed into *checkbook* functions, *reconciliation*, and *reporting*, and so on.

12.2.2 Organizing Detailed Requirements by Use Case

Use cases (introduced in Chapter 11) exploit the observation that many requirements occur naturally in operational sequences. For example, an individual requirement such as "a video store application shall allow entering the title of a new video" typically takes place as part of a *sequence* of transactions. A use case diagram showing a collection of use cases for a video store application is illustrated in Figure 12.4.

The authors advocate providing use cases for high-level requirements. One may have the option of using this same organizing principle for detailed requirements. In this case we would group the detailed requirements according to each use case, fleshing out the steps of each use case in complete detail. The following is an example of how one such grouping of requirements would appear in the SRS.

3.7.1 Checking in DVDs

This is a detailed version of section xx. (Note 1; see the "Note" explanations on the next page)

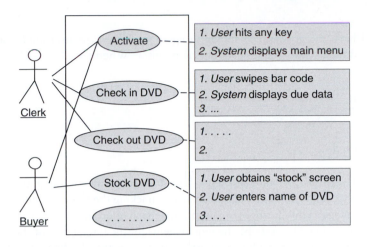

Figure 12.4 Organizing requirements by use case for the video store example

The application shall provide the following capability to interact with store clerks. These requirements assume that the main screen is on the monitor. (Note 2)

3.7.1.1 Step 1: *Check In* button (Note 3)

The clerk shall be able to hit the *Check In* button, whereupon the *Check In* screen will appear (described in section xx above).

3.7.1.2 Step 2: Filling in fields (Note 4)

The clerk shall be able to fill in the following text fields in the *Check In* screen . . . .

3.7.1.2.1 Video name field

This field shall allow for 30 alphanumeric characters, including blanks.

. . .

Note 1: This paragraph corresponds to the *Checking in DVD* use case described in the high-level requirements.

Note 2: This section introduces the use case and states *preconditions*, if any. A precondition is a fact assumed true at the inception of the use case.

Note 3: This corresponds to the first step of the use case.

Note 4: Since these are the detailed requirements, they must specify the requirements completely. The details will not be specified elsewhere.

The Unified Software Development Process favors organizing all requirements by use cases. Agile methods de-emphasize detailed requirements in favor of working code, but they emphasize organization of requirements by user story.

12.2.3 Organizing Detailed Requirement by GUI

Applications display GUIs, and these are the means by which users think of them, so it can be natural to provide requirements organized in this way. Using this style, the requirements for the Encounter video game would be something like the following:

1. <u>Area GUIs</u>
   Area GUIs shall have the appearance shown in figure xx. When the user clicks on the "Set qualities" button, the window in figure xx appears on the monitor. When the user clicks on . . . .

2. <u>Dungeon GUI</u> . . .

3. <u>Living Room GUI</u> . . .

4. <u>Set Quality GUI</u> . . . .

5. <u>View Qualities Window</u> . . .

The advantage of organizing requirements by GUI is its direct connection with the use of the application. Another advantage is traceability: we have a good chance of tracking the requirements associated with a given GUI class. One disadvantage of this means of organization is that it often fails to cover all of the requirements. In the Encounter example, we need to describe the requirements for the interaction of the player's character and the foreign character. No GUI paragraph is a natural container for this. Perhaps the closest is "Area GUIs." However, this is not a suitable place for specifying the manner in which characters exchange points. Another disadvantage is that given functionality is often associated with several GUIs.

As an example, Figure 12.5 illustrates an organization of the video store requirements by GUI. Specification of individual GUIs is discussed further in Section 12.3.

3.1 <u>Selecting Procedures</u>

The GUI for selecting procedures shall be as shown in Figure 1. It shall be possible to select from the following procedures by clicking on a radio button, followed by the "go" button. …

Figure 1

3.2 <u>Stocking DVDs</u>

The GUI for stocking DVDs shall be as shown in Figure 2. It shall be possible to enter a DVD into the system using the GUI in figure … The application shall save the title—expressed in up to 30 alphanumeric characters—and the number of copies. The latter shall range between 1 and 100, inclusive. …

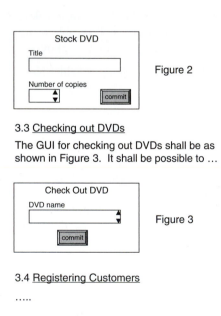

Figure 2

3.3 <u>Checking out DVDs</u>

The GUI for checking out DVDs shall be as shown in Figure 3. It shall be possible to …

Figure 3

3.4 <u>Registering Customers</u>

…..

Figure 4

Figure 12.5 Organizing requirements by GUI, for the video store example

12.2.4 Organizing Detailed Requirements by State

This style consists of collecting in one place the detailed requirements that apply to each state. For example, the requirements for an application that controls a chemical process might be best classified by the states in which the process can find itself (*starting up*, *reacting*, *cooling*, etc.). Within each state classification, the *events* that affect the application while in that state are listed. Classification by state can be appropriate when the requirements for each state are quite distinct. For example, an accounting system may be required to behave entirely differently depending on whether it is in the *configuring*, *executing*, or *backing up* state. Although the Encounter case study requirements could be organized by state, we decided that there are more advantages to organizing them by class, which we describe next.

12.2.5 Organizing Requirements by Class

In the object-oriented (or "class") style for organizing requirements, a categorization is first performed equivalent to selecting classes; then the individual requirements are placed into the resulting classes. Classes used to categorize the requirements are known as *domain* classes. Domain classes represent real-world objects or concepts in the application. For example, a banking application would have domain classes such as *bank customer*, *checking account*, and *savings balance*. A common first step in identifying domain classes is to gather the nouns or their equivalent used in the high-level requirements. We then make each functional detailed requirement correspond to a function in the target language. This promotes one-to-one traceability from detailed requirements to methods. Agile methods use a similar approach in that detailed requirements are organized by tests of classes.

One disadvantage of organizing requirements by classes is the risk that we later change the classes, thereby breaking the correspondence between requirements and design. This is discussed by Jordan, Smilan, and Wilkinson in [2]. In fact, some developers use classes for organizing the requirements but do not seriously aim to use these classes for the design. In this case, traceability is compromised, but there is less pressure to identify lasting classes very early in the process. Another disadvantage of this classification is that it requires us to select classes very early in the development cycle, and many argue that we are effectively performing design in doing so. Let's look at the *Encounter* game case study as an example. Picking classes such as *PlayerCharacter* and *Area* at requirements time is harmless since the implementation is very likely to use these classes. On the other hand, it can be reasonably argued that having the *AreaConnection* objects reference the *Area* objects that they connect is a design decision.

The great advantage to organizing requirements by classes that will be used in the design is that it promotes tight correspondence between requirements, design, and implementation. This is a key benefit for using the OO paradigm in any case. In addition, classes that correspond to real-world concepts are much more likely to be reused than those that do not. For many applications, the benefits of using a class-oriented classification method outweigh its drawbacks in the authors' opinions.

A typical sequence for obtaining functional detailed requirements using the OO style is as follows:

1. List the concepts mentioned in the use cases and other high-level requirements (usually, many of the nouns).

2. The resulting collection of classes is typically incomplete. Try to uncover remaining "domain" classes. This process is explained below. Inspect this collection of classes.

3. For each of the classes obtained, write down all of the required functionality of the application primarily pertaining to that class, as shown in the Encounter case study. This is done in the form of attributes and functions. For example, "every customer shall have a name" (an attribute listed under paragraph *Customers*)

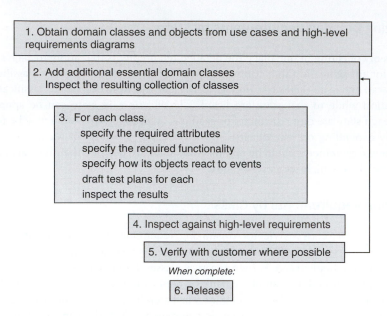

Figure 12.6 Road map for detailed requirements using the OO style

and "the application shall be able to compute the total assets of each customer" (a function listed under *Customers*). In the (requirements) document that you are writing, avoid using the term "class." Use ordinary, nontechnical English. Specify the events that the objects of the class are required to handle.

4. Inspect the detailed requirements as the process progresses.

5. Ideally, test plans for each detailed requirement should be devised at the same time, as explained below.

6. Inspected the detailed requirements against the high-level requirements.

7. Verify the detailed requirements with the customer.

8. Release the requirements, or return to Step 1 for more requirements.

Recall that the primary audience for detailed requirements consists of developers. However, customers are vitally interested in the details, too. Figure 12.6 summarizes these steps.

It is a common error when classifying requirements by class to use the language of design instead of plain English. For example, the following language is acceptable.

It shall be possible to obtain the number of days delinquent on any account.

The following is *not* acceptable in a requirements document.

getDelinquentDays() returns the number of days delinquent on the account.

In other words, object-orientation is used here only as an organizing principle for the requirements. The use of OO for design and implementation is performed later.

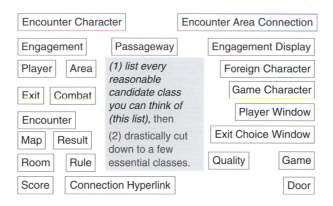

Figure 12.7 Candidate domain classes for the Encounter video game

We identify the classifying classes carefully and conservatively, identifying the domain classes of the application. As an additional example, the domain of an application simulating a bank might contain classes *Bank Customer* (the corresponding class name in Java or C++ can have no blanks, of course) and *Teller* but not *File* or *Database*—not even *Customer* or *Transaction*. The latter are not special to the application in question. Our goal is to identify a minimum but sufficient set of domain classes that include all of the specific requirements. Each GUI usually results in a domain class.

As another example of domain class selection, consider an application that manages visits to a Web site. Some candidate domain classes are *Site Visitor*, *Site Visit*, and *Site Mission*. Requirements pertaining to the visitor (e.g., data about visitors, and functionality such as displaying visitor profiles) would be collected with the *Site Visitor* classification. If the application requires us to track the reasons for each visit, then a domain class *Site Mission* would be appropriate. The corresponding requirements would be collected within *Site Mission*. For example, the requirement on the application could be that visitors submit a form stating their goals in visiting the site.

After identifying classes from the use cases and other high-level requirements, an effective way to complete the identification of key domain classes is to use a "list and cut" process. This consists of (Step 1) listing every reasonable candidate class you can think of, and then (Step 2) aggressively paring down the list to a few essential classes. We elaborate on these steps next.

(Step 1) Figure 12.7 shows candidate classes for the Encounter game selected from the text of the high-level requirements. The Unified Modeling Language (UML) notation for a class is a rectangle containing the class name.

(Step 2) We now filter the classes identified. Note first that it is far easier to add a class later than to remove one that has become embedded in the design and implementation, so that if there is doubt about the usefulness of a candidate class we eliminate it. The rationale used for the final selection of domain classes for the case study is given next.

Encounter: Change to *EncounterGame* to make its purpose clearer (we may also need the plain "encounter" concept as well).

Game: Not a domain class—too general (we may reintroduce this later when seeking useful generalizations).

Game Character: Too general to be in the domain (we may reintroduce this later when seeking useful generalizations).

Player: *Player Character* is a preferable name (more specific to the domain).

Foreign Character: OK (foreign characters act in ways that are different from player characters).

Encounter Character: OK (generalization of *PlayerCharacter*, *ForeignCharacter*, etc., is still within the domain of the application).

Quality: Omit—try to handle as simple attribute of *EncounterCharacter*.

Room: Omit—not sure if we need this; already have *Area*.

Door: Omit—not sure we'll need it.

Exit: Not sure if we need this; leads to neighboring area. Try as simple attribute of *Area*—omit for now

Rule: Omit—not sure we'll need it.

Area: OK (The astute reader will note that this decision is defective.)

Engagement: OK

Passageway. We do need to connect areas, but we do not yet know what form these connections will take. Use *EncounterAreaConnection* instead.

Result: Omit—it's vague.

Combat: Omit—not sure we'll need it—already have *Engagement*.

Score: Omit—try as attribute of other classes.

Player Quality Window: This is needed to express the Initialize use case.

Exit Choice Window: Omit—not needed—click on exit hyperlinks.

Map: Omit—not required at this stage (maybe in a future version).

Engagement Display: OK—needed by use case though will try to postpone by substituting a command line interface.

The resulting classes are shown in Figure 12.8. The figure includes the inheritance relationships present among these classes denoted with a triangle. UML notation is covered in detail in Chapter 16.

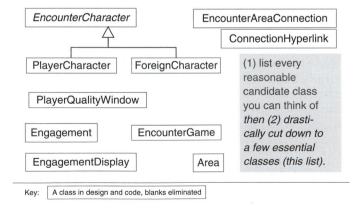

Figure 12.8 Classes for the Encounter video game, showing only inheritance relationships

The classes in Figure 12.8 may relate in ways besides inheritance. For example, *Encounter Area Connection* will probably aggregate two *Area* objects. However, our concern here is only with the core application classes, using them to organize the requirements. Relationships among classes are shown where necessary. Using inheritance enables some degree of leverage. For example, after stating the requirements for *Encounter Character* we do not need to repeat these requirements in describing *Player Character* and *Foreign Character*. The *Encounter Character* class is shown in italics in Figure 12.8 because it is abstract—this declares that there will be no actual characters besides player-controlled and foreign characters.

The IEEE 830-1998 SRS standard designates a place where the purpose of each class is stated, together with its key attributes and functions. The standard calls for using the decimal numbering system from each class (e.g., 3.2.5) to each of its attribute requirements (e.g., 3.2.5.1) and each of its function requirements (e.g., 3.2.5.2). Instead, we will arrange classes alphabetically to make it easier to add and remove classes. Such insertions are necessary as the application grows. It is important to number requirements, however, in order to be able to manage them, so we do this within each class as shown in the case study.

Sometimes, only "essential" requirements are numbered since only they must be traced for now. A good reference for this style of organizing specific requirements is Jordan, Smilan, and Wilkinson [2]. To assist in tracing detailed requirements it can help to give a name to each one, as in the case study. For example:

3.2.A.7 <u>Preferred qualities</u>

[essential] Each area shall favor a set of qualities.

Including "desirable" and "optional" detailed requirements is beneficial for several reasons. First, the scope of the application can be controlled by implementing the requirements in a planned order. Second, stating future requirements provides direction to designers, helping them to create designs that can accommodate future features. One technique for indicating which requirements have actually been designed for and implemented is to start by including a disclaimer with each, as in the following example.

When organizing detailed requirements by class, it's sometimes a challenging issue to decide under what class to state the requirement. Consider the following requirement example.

Every Encounter character shall have a name . . .

This requirement should be classified with "Encounter Characters." We will explain below the relation of this with a GUI requirement. The following requirement requires more consideration.

Whenever the player's main character enters an area, that area and all the characters in it shall be displayed on the monitor.

Class candidates to classify this function are *Player Character* and *Area*. The requirement effectively calls for an event handler. A natural triggering class for handling the entry event would be the area entered because it is aware of which characters inhabit it. The area entered could display itself and the characters it contains, so the requirement stated above could reasonably be classified under *Area*.

We often find it necessary to deal with *individuals*, *aggregations*, and *GUIs* centered on a single theme. For example, for a video store management application, we need to deal with the following.

• What are the required properties of individual DVDs? For example, what are the length limitations of their titles?

- What are the required properties of the collection of DVDs? For example, what is the requirement for stocking new GUIs?

- What are the specifications of a GUI that displays information about DVDs? For example, what are the limitations on the text shown? (GUI specifications often change frequently.)

Thinking ahead, we recognize that these will be separate classes when we come to design time, so we organize the requirements document paragraphs to anticipate this. It is usually best to begin with the paragraph that describes the requirements on the *individuals*: in this case, DVD. This specifies the required degree of detail that the application is required to store. It is referenced by other paragraphs.

3.2.DV DVDs

. . .

3.2.DV.1 Attributes of DVDs

3.2.DV.1.X Director's Name The application shall retain the name of the director of each DVD. This shall consist of the director's last name, in a form of between 1 and 30 characters, which can consist of a-z, A-Z, and a hyphen. In the case of multiple directors, only the first—alphabetically—shall be retained.

. . .

3.2.DG DVD GUI

The GUI displaying a DVD shall have the appearance of figure xx.

. . .

3.2.DG.1 Attributes of DVDs

. . .

3.2.DG.1.X Director's Name Appearance The director's name shall be displayed in the location shown in figure xx, in accordance with requirement 3.2.DV.1.X, but limited to the first 20 characters. . . .

. . .

3.2.DG.3 Events Pertaining to the DVD GUI

. . .

3.2.DG.3.X OK Button When the "OK" button is pressed . . .

. . .

3.2.DI DVD Inventory

. . .

3.2.DI.2 Functionality of DVD Inventory

. . .

3.2.DI.2.X Stocking a DVD The application shall allow new DVDs to be added to the inventory, up to a maximum of one million. . . .

. . .

Organizing principle	Advantages	Disadvantages
By Feature	☺ Maps well to why we are building the application ☺ Easy to understand	☹ Does not map well to OO code ☹ Hard to locate random requirement
By Use Case	☺ Easy to understand	☹ Use cases may overlap ☹ Hard to trace to design and code ☹ Coverage is limited
By GUI	☺ Easy to understand	☹ Not every function appears in a GUI ☹ Functionality of GUIs overlap ☹ Hard to trace to design and code
By State	☺ Easy to understand ☺ Design thinking begins early	☹ Classification can be unclear to the customer ☹ Hard to allocate requirements to state
By Class	☺ Easy to trace to code ☺ Easy to locate random requirement ☺ Design thinking begins early	☹ Classification can be unclear to the customer

Figure 12.9 Ways to organize detailed requirements—advantages and disadvantages

12.2.6 Classification Methods: Advantages and Disadvantages

Figure 12.9 summarizes the different ways to organize functional detailed requirements that we discussed in the previous sections, along with their relative advantages and disadvantages.

12.3 USER INTERFACES: DETAILED REQUIREMENTS

Recall the following steps in specifying user interfaces.

Step 1: Know your user

Step 2: Understand the business function in question

Step 3: Apply principles of good screen design

Step 4: Select the appropriate kind of windows

Step 5: Develop system menus

Step 6: Select the appropriate device-based controls

Step 7: Choose the appropriate screen-based controls

Step 8: Organize and lay out windows

Step 9: Choose appropriate colors

Step 10: Create meaningful icons

Step 11: Provide effective message, feedback, and guidance

- Ensure **consistency** among the screens of designated applications, and among screens within each
  - conventions; procedures; look-and-feel; locations
- **Anticipate** where the user will usually **start**
  - frequently upper left—place "first" element there
- Make **navigation** as **simple** as possible
  - align like elements
  - group like elements
  - consider borders around like elements
- Apply a **hierarchy** to emphasize order of importance
- Apply **principles of pleasing visuals**—usually:
  - balance; symmetry; regularity; predictability
  - simplicity; unity; proportion; economy
- Provide **captions**

Figure 12.10 Principles of good screen design

Source: Galitz, W., "The Essential Guide to User Interface Design: An Introduction to GUI Principles and Techniques," John Wiley & Sons, 1996.

Steps 1 and 2 were described in the previous Chapter 11 since they apply primarily to high-level requirements. We now describe the remaining steps for specifying detailed user interface requirements, which are essentially a detailed description of each GUI screen.

Step 3: Apply the principles of good screen design

Figure 12.10 lists some major elements of good screen design. The figure includes several factors that often apply to making an interface pleasing. Although these serve only to introduce the subject of visual effects, they are nevertheless usable by the average software engineer.

As an example, we apply some of these principles to an example of a screen used to input information about customers and their accounts. An initial attempt at a GUI is shown in Figure 12.11. To improve the interface, we start at the top left, placing the most important elements first, and grouping like elements. Figure 12.12 illustrates

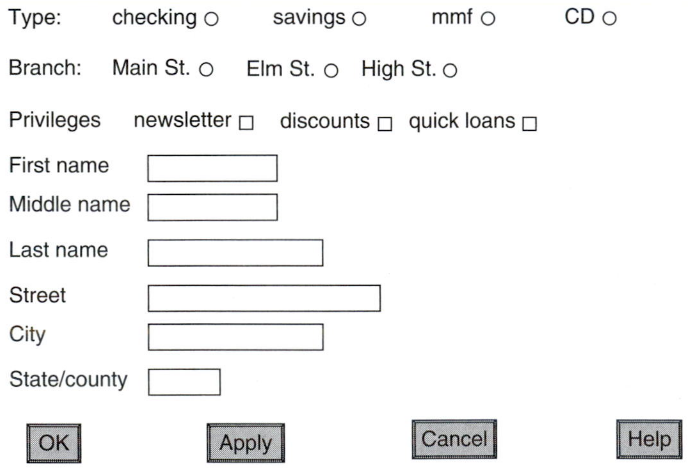

Figure 12.11 Applying principles of good screen design—"Before"

Source: Galitz, W., "The Essential Guide to User Interface Design: An Introduction to GUI Principles and Techniques," John Wiley & Sons, 1996.

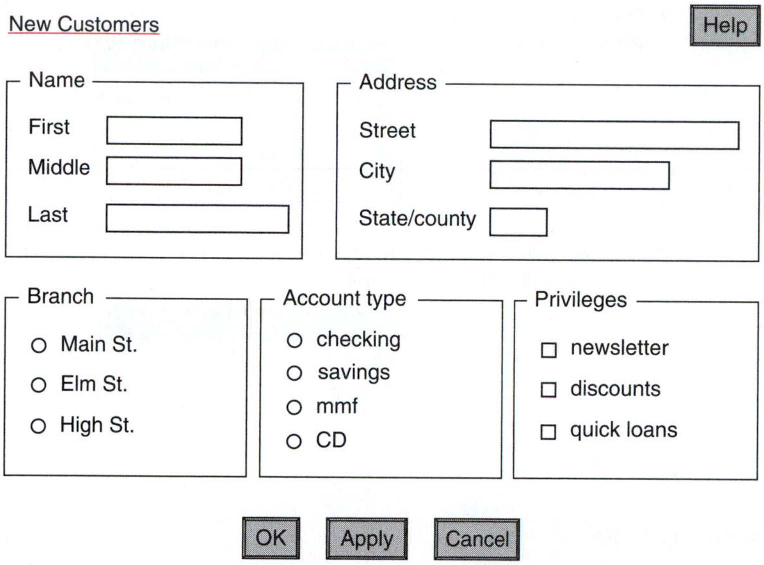

New Customers
Help
Name
First
Middle
Last
Address
Street
City
State/county
Branch
Main St.
Elm St.
High St.
Account type
checking
savings
mmf
CD
Privileges
newsletter
discounts
quick loans
OK
Apply
Cancel

Figure 12.12 Applying principles of good screen design—"After"

the improvement that the application of these principles can bring. Figure 12.13 shows where some of the principles of good screen design were applied.

Step 4: Select the appropriate kind of windows

Each user interface purpose can be served most effectively by one or two particular types of windows. Figures 12.14 and 12.15 list five common GUI purposes and a window type that satisfies each of them. The window types employ Windows™ terminology, but are typical.

New Customers
Anticipate start
Expected position
Help
Name
Address
First
Street
Ensure consitency
Align like elements
City
Last
State/co
Border around like elements
Branch
Use Captions
Account type
Privileges
Main St.
checking
newsletter
Elm St.
Symmetry
Balance
High St.
CD
quick loans
Group
like elements
Proportion
OK
Apply
Cancel

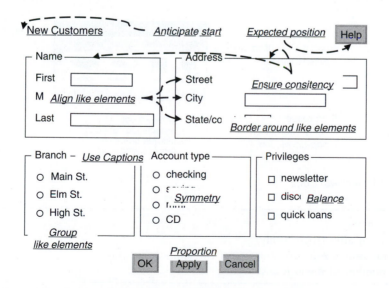

Figure 12.13 How principles of good screen design were applied

1. *Purpose*: display properties of an entity
-- *property window*

Properties of automobile 189	
Property	Value
Brand	Toyota
Model	Camry
ID	893-8913-789014

2. *Purpose*: obtain additional information so as to carry
   out a particular task or command
-- *dialog window*

Help	
Word	_____
This screen ○	All screens ○

Figure 12.14 Types of windows, 1 of 2

Step 5: Develop system menus

Some rules for the creation of main menus, provided by Galitz [3], are shown in Figure 12.16.

Users require a stable, comprehensible anchor for applications, hence the need for a constant main menu. The number of items on this menu should usually be between five and nine, because most of us feel comfortable with choices of this size. For example, the word processor with which this book is being typed has nine main menu items: *File, Edit, View, Insert, Format, Tools, Table, Window,* and *Help*. The number of items could have been far higher, since there is plenty of space for more. However, we would probably have to

3. *Purpose:*
provide information
– *message window*

ABC alert message
Caution: "age" must be < 120
OK

4. *Purpose:*
present a set of controls
– *palette window*

5. *Purpose:*
amplify information
– *pop-up window*

Figure 12.15 Types of windows, 2 of 2

- Provide a main menu
- Display all relevant alternatives (only)
- Match the menu structure to the structure of the application's task
- Minimize the number of menu levels

Figure 12.16 Developing system windows

continually search the list for the option we require, and this outweighs the benefit of increasing the choices. The main menu items are determined by the business at hand—in this case the processing of text. Thus, for example, graphics commands are placed on a secondary menu.

Step 6: Select the appropriate device-based controls

"Device-based controls" are the physical means by which users communicate their desires to the application. They include joysticks, trackballs, graphics tablets, touch screens, mice, microphones, and keyboards.

Step 7: Select the appropriate screen-based controls

"Screen-based controls" are symbols that appear on the monitor, by means of which the user notifies the application of his or her input and intentions. These include icons, buttons, text boxes, selections, and radio buttons. The rules for arranging screen-based controls in a window are virtually the same as those for screen design in general (see Figure 12.10. Their number is, again, typically between five and nine. This number can be increased, however, when a hierarchy is used. For example, in Figure 12.13 there are twenty options to select from, but the interface is manageable because these twenty items are organized into six groups.

Step 8: Organize and lay out windows

The rules for laying out multiple windows are similar to those for individual screen design (involving symmetry, proportion, etc.) as in Figure 12.10, but they involve arrangements such as tiling and cascading. The latter terms are illustrated in Figure 12.17.

Step 9: Choose appropriate colors

When used with skill and taste, color can enhance displays. Colors do not automatically make a user interface more useful or more attractive, however, and they can easily worsen it. According to renowned designer Paul

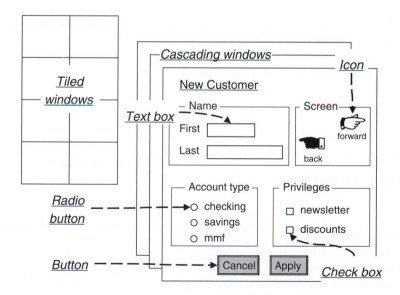

Figure 12.17 Common GUI terms

Source: Graphics reproduced with permission from Corel.

Rand, "color is complexity personified" [4]. Software engineers who do not have a professional designer with whom to work should be very sparing and conservative about the use of color. Try black and white first. If there is a clear purpose to it, introduce one color. Make sure that this helps the user. Think seriously before adding more colors.

Taking note of well-established applications, such as widely used word processors, can suggest how to use colors well. You can be assured that experienced professionals designed these interfaces, and the untrained software engineer can benefit from imitating them. The color blue is common in real-world screens of all kinds. Symmetry of colors is often recommended, and this symmetry can be of several varieties. For example, the author's word processor uses mainly three different shades of blue, which occur in a symmetrical pattern on the standard color palette. The other two colors used are yellow and, to a lesser extent, green. These are used in small quantities, accenting additional functionality only, and they do not compete with the major items, which are in black and gray.

12.4 DETAILED SECURITY REQUIREMENTS

Writing the detailed requirements for security measures is a matter of being entirely specific about the needed security measures. Some of these are shown in Figures 12.18 and 12.19. When it comes to security logoffs, for example, we may want to require that if there is no keystroke on the application for ten minutes, it logs off automatically. Audit trails for security breaches are important. Some of these requirements are easy enough to specify but difficult to implement. For example, how would an application know that it has experienced a security breach?

12.5 ERROR CONDITIONS

For each requirement, we ask what would happen if it were to take place under erroneous circumstances. As an example, let's take a requirement example put forward by Myers [5], as shown in Figure 12.20.

---

1. **User identification** capabilities
   • Rules on IDs, name clashes, restrictions, etc.
2. Person or entity **authentication** capabilities
   • Exact requirements permitting access to resources
3. Security **logoff**
   • Measures to prevent unattended or unusual usage
4. **Audit trails** of security-related events
   • Type, outcome, state at the time, date and time, source

Figure 12.18 Detailed security requirements, 1 of 2

---

5. **Password** specifications
   • Length, composition, allows characters, etc.
6. Controls to ensure data **integrity**
7. Retrievable record of encryption methods
8. Information on security attributes of the system

Figure 12.19 Detailed security requirements, 2 of 2

A function that tells whether three numbers produce an equilateral triangle (all sides equal), *an isosceles triangle* (exactly two sides equal), *or a scalene triangle* (all sides different).

Figure 12.20 Requirement example, without necessary errors

A function that tells whether a triplet of numbers produces:

1. *an equilateral triangle (whose sides are all greater than zero and equal), in which case it outputs 'E' at the prompt, or*

2. *an isosceles triangle (whose sides are greater than zero, exactly two of which are equal, and that form a triangle), in which case it outputs 'I' at the system, or*

3. *a scalene triangle (whose sides are all greater than zero, which form a triangle, and that is neither equilateral nor isosceles), in which case it outputs 'S' at the prompt, or*

4. *no triangle, in which case it outputs 'N' at the prompt.*

Figure 12.21 A more complete version, accounting for errors

This requirements specification is not complete because it does not account for error conditions. The version in Figure 12.21 is more complete. A lack of error conditions in requirements specifications becomes especially glaring when the function is tested, since the tester forces error conditions and needs to know what the required output is.

Sound requirements analysis does not turn a blind eye to "illegal" input: it deals with them directly. For example, it is tempting to assume that a GUI for the triangle requirement does not permit the input of negative numbers, and so the function does not have to deal with erroneous data. Such an assumption is unwise because it transfers the "legality" part of the triangle requirement to requirements on code clients of our triangle function. This increases the dependence among parts of the application, whereas we always try to obtain independent parts. Although it *is* good practice to trap invalid user input at the GUI level and to oblige the user to enter only legal values, this does not substitute for good requirements and error recognition elsewhere. The authors recommend requiring the trapping of incorrect data at many, if not all, possible points. This is equivalent to a long-established engineering practice of practicing redundancy to promote safety.

12.6 TRACEABILITY OF DETAILED REQUIREMENTS

Chapter 13 discusses the qualities that we want requirements to possess, and metrics for measuring them. We will call out one property here because it is fundamental to how we think about requirements: *traceability*.

Imagine an application with 1,000 specific requirements. Without a clean trace from each requirement through the design of the application to the actual code that implements it, it is very difficult to ensure that such an application remains in compliance with the requirements. When the requirements change, which is safe to assume, this becomes even more difficult. The capacity to map each detailed requirement to its relevant part(s) of the design and implementation is called traceability. We first discuss the traceability of functional requirements, then nonfunctional requirements.

One way to help accomplish traceability is to map each functional detailed requirement to a specific function of the target language. This technique is used in the Encounter case study. Figure 12.22 shows parts

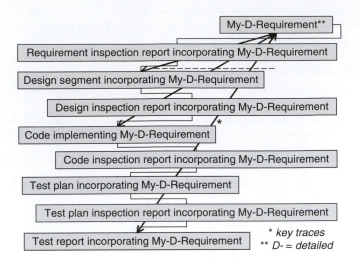

Figure 12.22 A thorough trace of an invidivual detailed requirement

of the project that we would like to keep linked to have complete traceability. Achieving and maintaining this degree of traceability during development is a major challenge.

As an example, consider the following functional requirement for the Encounter video game case study.

> When a foreign game character enters an area containing the player's main character, or vice versa, they engage each other.

The meaning of this statement is clear. What remains to be seen, however, is what part or parts of the design and code will be responsible for implementing this requirement. When using the OO paradigm we can link this requirement to a specific function of a specific class. The issue of what class is responsible for a function is not trivial, and it arises repeatedly when using the OO style. For the above example, *Area* objects would be able to recognize that an engagement is to take place since they would presumably be aware of their inhabitants. In particular, this requirement will be traceable to specific event-handling code for the *Area* class.

As the project proceeds, the requirements document should be kept consistent with the design and the implementation. When requirements are hard to trace through design and code, however, developers tend to avoid updating the requirements document when making changes to the source code because of the extensive effort required. Ultimately, such a deterioration of documents results in escalating development and maintenance expenses. This phenomenon is illustrated by the following example.

> *Developer Bill is asked to make changes to the implementation. Bill finds it difficult to connect the code he is modifying to the corresponding parts of the requirements document; consequently, he fails to update the documentation.*
>
> *Developer Carmen is tasked to make new modifications. She implements new code, tests it, and begins updating the requirements document. However, everyone tells her not to bother, pointing out that the requirements document is out of date in several places and no one trusts it very much. They tell her it makes no sense to take the time to perfect her part when no one will read the document anyway. So Carmen moves on to do other programming. The discrepancies between the requirements document and the code continue to widen.*

	Module 1	Module 2	Module 3
Requirement			
1783	getInterest()	computeBal()	showName()
1784	showAccount()	showAddress()	showName()

Figure 12.23 Example of a requirements traceability matrix

When a requirements document as a whole is untrustworthy, even the most conscientious developer balks at properly updating his or her particular part. On the other hand, when the documents are clearly cross-referenced, and management makes documentation a job performance requirement, engineers do keep them in very good professional shape. In other words, the system used to match detailed requirements with the designs, and code that implement them, must be very clear and concrete.

When the code implementing a requirement needs to exist in several parts of the implementation, tracing is achieved by means of a requirements *traceability matrix* of which Figure 12.23 is an example. Here, requirement 1783 is implemented by the action of functions *getInterest()* in module 1, *computeBal()* in module 2, and *showName()* in module 3. A change in this requirement necessitates a change in one or more of these functions. This must be carefully managed because these functions may participate in satisfying other requirements (e.g., *showName()* is used to implement requirement 1784 as well). As a result, changes made to satisfy one requirement may compromise another. Since many-to-many relationships are difficult to manage, we try to make the mapping between requirement and function one-to-one.

We want each detailed requirement to be traceable forward and backward. The preceding discussion concerns *forward* traceability of functional requirements from detailed requirement to implementation. *Backward* traceability of a detailed requirement means that the requirement is a clear consequence of one or more high-level requirements. For example, the detailed requirement

Foreign characters should move from area to area at intervals averaging 5 seconds

can be traced back to the following high-level requirement, which was part of Section 2.0 in the SRS.

The rest [of the characters], called "foreign" characters, are to be under the application's control.

This backward traceability is a basis for the inspection of detailed requirements. Complete traceability is obtained when each detailed requirement is linked to a specific element of design, and to a unit test, as suggested by Figure 12.22. It indicates the advantage of a tight trace (correspondence) between each individual functional requirement, the part of the design intended to handle the requirement, and the part of the code that implements it. These are coupled with the focused test for the requirement, called a *unit test*. Unit tests are the subject of Chapter 26.

The preceding discussion concerned functional requirements, but how do we trace nonfunctional requirements? This can be difficult because more than one part of the design and implementation may contribute to satisfying a nonfunctional requirement. For example, a requirement that every Encounter engagement complete in less than one second could involve code in an *Engagement* class, and/or a *GameCharacter* class, and/or an *Area* class. Our objective at requirements time is to specify nonfunctional requirements as clearly as possible. In order to clarify nonfunctional requirements, we will also touch on design and implementation issues.

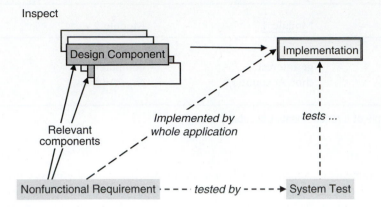

Figure 12.24 Tracing and testing functional vs. nonfunctional requirements

One goal of the design phase is to isolate each nonfunctional requirement in a separate design element. In the case of performance requirements, an attempt is made to isolate time-critical processing units. Appropriate, inspectable, nonfunctional comments accompany each function that is affected by performance requirements. Preferably, these are quantitative, as in "must complete in less than one millisecond in the worst case." Similarly, in cases where storage constraints are specified, we identify functions that generate the most storage.

Experience shows that a relatively small percentage of functions in an application account for most of the processing, so searching for a few principal time-consuming ones can be fruitful. Let's return to the "one-second" performance requirement example for Encounter engagements mentioned above. At design and implementation time, we seek typical time-consuming components in the computation of engagements. These components include loops, graphics displays, and network communication. Loops and communication are not involved in computing engagements, and a test is implemented to ensure that the graphics and GUIs required for an engagement execute fast enough. Probably, the function that consumes most of the time is either the function to "engage a foreign character" of the *Engagement* class, or the function to display engagement results.

To validate nonfunctional requirements we therefore tie each of them to a test plan, preferably at the time of writing the requirement. Figure 12.24 illustrates the typical relationship of functional and nonfunctional requirements to implementation and testing, discussed above. It illustrates the fact that several elements may contribute to nonfunctional requirements, and that system or integration testing is typically required to validate nonfunctional requirements because verifying them (i.e., prior to execution) can be difficult.

12.7 USING DETAILED REQUIREMENTS TO MANAGE PROJECTS

Detailed requirements can be considered the "currency" of a project because they track the amount that's been accomplished. For example, a project manager can track the project as in Table 12.1. Recall that it's important for developers to quickly find relevant requirements sections to enable them to easily keep a requirements document up-to-date. In the IEEE requirements format, functional requirements are in Section 3.2. If we were to number the paragraphs 3.2.1, 3.2.2, . . . , it would be time-consuming to locate the paragraph pertaining to a *Customer* class, for example. For this reason, the authors use an alphanumeric labeling such as 3.2.CU for Customers, 3.2.DV for DVDs, etc.

Table 12.1 Example of a table that facilitates the tracing of a requirement

3.2.CU This section concerns the requirements for dealing with video store customers.			
Priority (1, 2, or 3)			
Implemented yet? (Y or N)			
Attributes			
Functions			
Events			
3.2.CU.1.1	1	N	A required attribute
3.2.CU.1.2	2	Y	A required attribute
3.2.CU.2.1	1	N	A required function
3.2.CU.2.2	1	Y	A required function
3.2.CU.3.1	1	Y	A required event
3.2.CU.3.2	2	N	A required event

12.8 PRIORITIZING REQUIREMENTS

It is usually difficult—if not impossible—to implement *all* desired functionality of an application on schedule and within budget. As discussed in Chapter 8, one may trade off *capability, schedule, quality level,* and *cost.* Thus, if the schedule, budget, and quality level cannot be changed, the only alternative is to vary capability—that is, to reduce the requirements that are implemented. This reduction process is performed in a planned manner. One technique is to prioritize the specific requirements. Ranking all requirements is usually a waste of time. Instead, many organizations classify requirements into three (sometimes four) categories. We will call them "essential," "desirable," and "optional." The use of three categories is an application of triage described in Chapter 5. We first implement all of the essential requirements. The desirable and optional requirements indicate the direction in which the application is headed and thus influence the design. Figure 12.25 gives an example of requirements prioritization.

Some speculate that as much as 80 percent of the real benefits of many applications accrue from as few as 20 percent of the requirements. Thus, if prioritization is performed well (e.g., calling roughly 20 percent—no more—"essential"), one can possibly achieve most of an application's benefit with only a fraction of the work. This is a useful point to keep in mind if the project begins to run out of time.

The preliminary draft of an SRS shown in Figure 12.26 contains some prioritized detailed requirements for the first release of Encounter. They are provided here, "warts" and all, to give the reader a feel for issues that must be dealt with. Some of the "desirables" will become "essentials" in future releases. The requirements are in draft form and are clearly in need of reorganization. They are improved upon later in this chapter and in the case study.

The prioritization of requirements usually relates to the iteration that will implement them. For example, if we are not able to implement the "optional" requirement "Encounter shall take less than a second

---

[essential] *Every game character has the same set of qualities.*

[desirable] *Each area has a set of* **preferred** *qualities.*

[optional] *The player's character shall age with every encounter. The age rate can be set at setup time. Its default is one year per encounter.*

Figure 12.25 Example of prioritization of detailed requirements

PRELIMINARY DRAFT of Encounter detailed requirements
(These are not yet organized: see the case study for an improved form.)

[not inspected][essential] Every game character in the Encounter video game shall have a name.

[not inspected][essential] Every game character has the same set of qualities, each having a floating point value.

[not inspected][essential] Encounter takes place in areas, each of which is connected to other areas by exits.

[not inspected][essential] Whenever an Encounter game character enters an area containing another game character and one of them is player-controlled, the characters may either choose, or be obliged by the game, to engage each other.

[not inspected][essential] Whenever a player-controlled game character is alone, the player can change the values of its qualities.

[not inspected][desirable] The name of every character in Encounter shall have no more than 15 characters.

[not inspected][desirable] At any given time, every game character shall possess a number of living points. These are the sum of the values of its qualities.

[not inspected][desirable] Each area has a set of preferred qualities.

[not inspected][desirable] Combat areas require strength and stamina; living room areas require listening ability and intellect.

[not inspected][desirable] The sum of the values of qualities of a game character relevant to the area in question shall be referred to as the character's area value. In an engagement, the system compares the area values of the characters and transfers to the stronger half the points of the weaker. For example, suppose the player engages a foreign character in an area requiring stamina and attention to detail, and ps is the value of the player's stamina. Assuming $p_s + p_a > f_s + f_a$, we would have $p_s' = p_s + f_s/2$, $p_a' = p_a + f_a/2$, $f_s' = f_s/2$, $f_a' = f_s/2$ where x' denotes the value of x after the transaction.

[not inspected][optional] Encounter shall take less than a second to compute the results of an engagement.

[not inspected][optional] The player's character shall age with every engagement. The age rate can be set at setup time. Its default is one year per engagement.

[not inspected][optional] Player-controlled characters lose or gain the values of their characters at the end of every engagement at the rate of +2% when under 30 and −2% when over 30.

Figure 12.26 Preliminary SRS fragment showing prioritization and status of detailed requirements

to compute the results of an engagement" in the second iteration, it could appear with higher priority in a subsequent iteration. The requirements for an iteration are maintained in an identifiable manner. This helps in understanding subsequent requirements.

12.9 ASSOCIATING REQUIREMENTS WITH TESTS

As each detailed requirement is written, tests for the requirement should be developed. There are several advantages to writing tests simultaneously with the requirement. First, doing so helps to clarify the specific requirement. Second, it shifts some work from the testing phase of the project to the requirements phase. This relieves some of the pressure on the latter half of the project when there is less flexibility in the use of time. Agile processes go one step further, and *specify* each detailed requirement by means of a test.

Test input for Requirement NNN	Expected output
Harry	Harry
X	X
" " (blank)	"" (blank)
123456789012345	123456789012345
1234567890123456	123456789012345
. . . . . .	. . . . . .

Figure 12.27 Example of association between detailed requirements and their tests

To take an example, one of our requirements is as follows:

Requirement NNN. Every game character in the Encounter video game shall have a unique name containing between 1 and 15 characters.

Requirements of the attribute type like this really specify get- and set- functions, so that Figure 12.27 constitutes the beginnings of a test plan for this requirement. Part VII covers these tests in detail.

12.10 AGILE METHODS FOR DETAILED REQUIREMENTS

In an agile project, the detailed requirements are usually expressed in terms of in-code comments and unit tests rather than being written explicitly in a separate document. For example, consider a traditional requirement such as the following.

Customers shall be able to enter the name of a DVD in the text box, up to 20 alphanumeric characters. The application shall check this, with punctuation marks replaced by blanks, with the DVD inventory, and display accordingly "Sorry, we don't stock this DVD" or "Added to your list."

This is replaced with one or more tests as shown in Listing 1, augmented by code comments and equivalent data entry in the corresponding GUI. Assume that the setup code in the unit test contains the following:

Listing 1: Example of JUnit testing, typically used in agile methods

```
DVDSearch dVDSearch = new DVDSearch();

public void testLookup()
{
    // "Gone With The Wind'' should be present
    dVDSearch.doSearch( "Gone With The Wind'' );
    assertEquals( dVDSearch.searchResult, true );
    assertEquals( dVDSearch.outputMessage, "Added to your list'');
    // "War and Peace'' should be absent
    dVDSearch.doSearch( "War and Peace'' );
    assertEquals( dVDSearch.searchResult, false );
```

```
    assertEquals( dVDSearch.outputMessage, "Sorry, we don't stock
this DVD'');

    . . . . . .

}
```

Figure 12.28 summarizes this discussion.

The advantage of using tests as a requirement is that this is concrete; the disadvantage is that it is not complete. There is nothing to stop us from including thorough detailed requirements with the unit test, however, thereby gaining agile and, to some extent, non-agile advantages. This is shown in Figure 12.29.

Non-Agile

Customers shall be able to enter the name of a DVD in the text box, up to 20 alphanumeric characters. The application shall check this, with punctuation marks replaced by blanks, with the DVD inventory, and display accordingly "Sorry, we don't stock this DVD" or "Added to your list." (Excerpt from requirements document.)

Agile

```
public void testLookup() {
    //''Gone With The Wind'' should be present
    dVDSearch.doSearch( ''Gone With The Wind'' );
    . . .
    //''War and Peace'' should be absent
    dVDSearch.doSearch( ''War and Peace'' );
    . . .
```

Figure 12.28 Unit tests and code comments as detailed requirements in agile processes

```
/* Requirement 3.4.2: Customers shall be able to enter the name of a DVD in
the text box, up to 20 alphanumeric characters. The application shall
check this, with punctuation marks replaced by blanks, with the DVD in-
ventory, and display accordingly ''Sorry, we don't stock this DVD'' or
''Added to your list.'' */

public void testLookup() {
    //''Gone With The Wind'' should be present
    dVDSearch.doSearch( ''Gone With The Wind'' );
    . . .
    //''War and Peace'' should be absent
    dVDSearch.doSearch( ''War and Peace'' );
    . . .
```

Figure 12.29 Combining agile and non-agile methods in handling detailed requirements

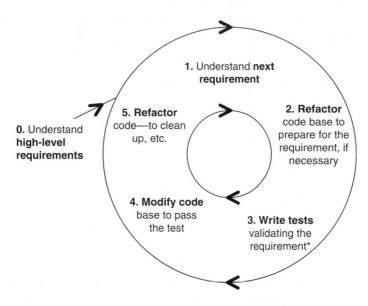

Figure 12.30 The agile programming cycle

When unit tests are used as detailed requirements, they are sometimes written *before* the code is written. This style is known as *test-driven development*. It builds upon the existing code base, and is carried out in the following sequence.

1. Understand the required new or modified functionality.

2. If needed, refactor the code to prepare it for the new functionality. Refactoring preserves the code's functionality, neither increasing nor decreasing its actual functionality. It is discussed in detail in Chapter 24.

3. Write test code that would test this functionality if it existed. This is usually done with a tool such as JUnit. This test will fail initially because the functionality it tests does not yet exist.

4. Add to the code base until the test passes.

5. If necessary, refactor the code base to make it clear and coherent.

Test-driven development is described further in Chapter 27.

Recall that agile development consists of the cycle shown in Figure 12.30. Refactoring, described in Chapter 24, is essential to the process in two ways. It is used to change the form (not the functionality) of the code base to prepare for the addition of new functionality. It is also used to make the resulting addition fit smoothly within the application as a whole.

12.11 USING TOOLS AND THE WEB FOR REQUIREMENTS ANALYSIS

Tools can help the process of capturing and managing requirements—for example, by sorting, categorizing, prioritizing, assigning, and tracking them. One benefit of such tools is to know who is working on what requirement at what time. Tools can also help to control "feature creep"—the process by which features that are not really necessary are added to the application. With the appropriate tools, a project leader can more easily assess the status of requirements analysis. For example, the leader can easily determine the percentage

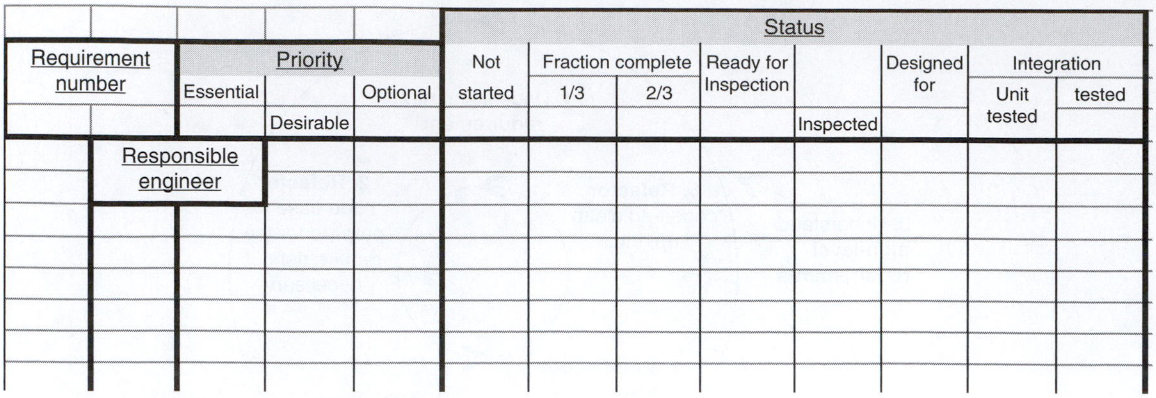

Requirement number	Priority			Status								
	Essential		Optional	Not started	Fraction complete		Ready for Inspection		Designed for	Integration		
					1/3	2/3				Unit tested	tested	
	Desirable							Inspected				
Responsible engineer												

Figure 12.31 Example spreadsheet for tracking requirements

of essential detailed requirements implemented and fully tested by QA. Bugzilla (sometimes in a version with the unappealing name "Issuezilla"), an open source tool for managing requirements, was described in the Eclipse high-level requirements case study. This section also discusses the management of requirements for simple projects, as well as IBM's commercial RequisitePro tool.

12.11.1 Simple Projects

For simple projects, much of this can be performed using a simple Web-based spreadsheet, as illustrated in Figure 12.31. However, for most reasonably sized projects a requirements tool is essential. The "designed for" designation in Figure 12.31 indicates that the requirement is accounted for in the design. "Unit tested" means that the code implementing the requirement has undergone testing in stand-alone fashion. "Integration testing" means that the application has been tested to verify that it implements the requirement. A table such as that in Figure 12.31 is maintained as part of a project status document that can be attached to the SPMP.

The cells in this matrix could be hyperlinked to relevant parts of the project's documents, thereby preserving single-source documentation for detailed requirements (i.e., eliminating duplication). For example,

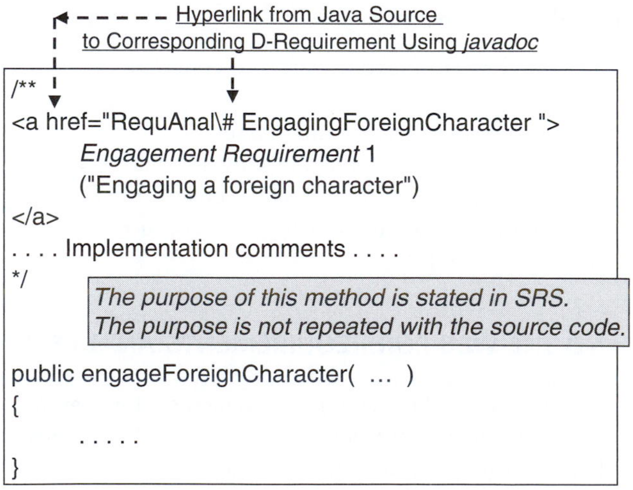

Figure 12.32 Hyperlink from Java source to corresponding detailed requirement using Javadoc

hyperlinks from the source code to the corresponding detailed requirement can be accomplished with tools such as Javadoc. Javadoc converts certain Java source code comments into an HTML document describing the classes and their methods (see, for example, [6]). By inserting hyperlinks to the SRS within these comments, the HTML document produced by Javadoc hyperlinks to the SRS. This is illustrated in Figure 12.32, where the detailed requirement corresponding to the method *engageForeignCharacter()* is hyperlinked from the document that Javadoc produces from the source code. The use of *doclets* make this process increasingly convenient.

The trend is for continual improvements in the process by which programmers will be able to more easily go back and forth between the SRS, the design, the graphical user interfaces, and the source code.

12.11.2 IBM's RequisitePro™

For substantial projects, professional tools are needed to track requirements. The sheer number of detailed requirements usually make this necessary. One example is IBM's RequisitePro™ product. The following figures, describing it, are taken from http://www.ibm.com/developerworks/rational/library/5347.html. Figure 12.33 shows a window for setting the properties of an individual detailed requirement.

RequisitePro allows various views of the requirements as a whole. This helps project managers and software engineers to manage and track their progress. Figure 12.34 is one example.

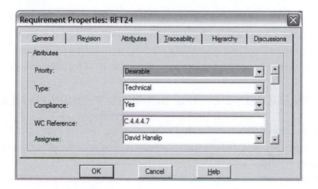

Figure 12.33 Setting properties of a requirement in IBM's RequisitePro™

Source: IBM, http://www.ibm.com/developerworks/rational/library/5247.html.

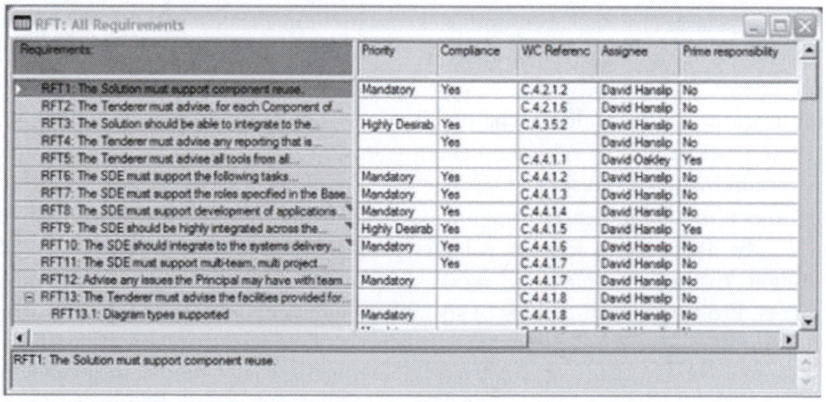

Figure 12.34 A view of a collection of requirements in RequisitePro™

Source: IBM, http://www.ibm.com/developerworks/rational/library/5247.html.

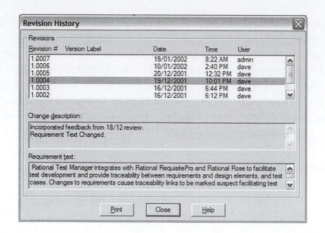

Figure 12.35 History of a requirement in RequisitePro™

Source: IBM, http://www.ibm.com/developerworks/rational/library/5247.html.

It is possible to query this requirements database—in other words, to obtain all requirements satisfying a desired criterion, such as those pertaining to security. As individual requirements are worked on by software engineers, tools like RequisitePro™ allow the "history" to be tracked, as shown in Figure 12.35. History refers to an account of the work performed to satisfy the requirement at various points in time.

12.12 THE EFFECTS ON PROJECTS OF THE DETAILED REQUIREMENTS PROCESS

Once detailed requirements have been collected, the project documents can be updated to reflect the improved project knowledge. We will take as an example the required updates to the SPMP, which can be updated as shown in Figure 12.36.

Detailed requirements are placed under configuration control. One issue to be addressed is what level of detail should be counted as a software configuration item (CI). Certainly, Section 3 as a whole ("Specific requirements") of the SRS (using the IEEE standard) could be a CI. Each class could be a CI. Individual requirements are typically too fine-grained to be CIs.

When the list of requirements grows into the hundreds, *inconsistencies* can easily arise. Classifying requirements by classes, classes by packages, and packages by subpackages, and the like becomes a necessity. The packages typically correspond to subsystems in the overall organization of the application.

Although *completeness* is a goal for which we strive in collecting requirements, it is usually an elusive goal. For substantial applications, there is seldom a natural "last" requirement—just the last one before requirements freeze. For this reason, we strive for self-completeness: ensuring that all of the requirements necessary to accompany each requirement are present.

Large-scale projects require increasing organizational formality (not to be confused with formal methods). The SRS may have to be divided into separate volumes. A single section in our (tiny!) case study could expand into a 700-page volume. Extensive management work is required to schedule the development and inspection of detailed requirements. Projects with hundreds of specific requirements need requirements management tools. The successful widespread usage of the Java packages has shown, however, that large collections of requirements are manageable when the functionality is organized by well-defined packages, subpackages, and classes.

The rewards of good requirements analysis are substantial. Conversely, the penalties for poor requirements are substantial too. For example, Faulk [7], reports on a Government Accounting Office study of the Cheyenne Mountain Upgrade project on which "requirements-related problems" resulted in a $600

	Status after initial draft	*Result of updating after high-level requirements*	Result of updating after detailed requirements
Milestones	Initial	*More detailed*	More detailed
Risks	Identify	*Retire risks identified previously; seek more risks*	Retire risks identified; identify more risks
Schedule	Very high level	*Preliminary project schedule*	More detailed: shows class and method development tasking
Personnel	Designate C-requirements engineers	*Engineers designated for D-requirements analysis*	Designate software architects
Cost Estimation	Crude estimates	*First estimates based on job content*	Improved estimate using more specific function points and/or past experience with similar requirements

Figure 12.36 Updating a project upon completion of detailed requirements analysis

million cost overrun, an eight-year delay, and diminished capability. Debates continue about the percentage of large projects that turn out badly versus the percentage that turn out well. Many large projects do a fine job of requirements analysis. The author can attest to this from personal experience.

12.13 STUDENT PROJECT GUIDE: REQUIREMENTS FOR THE ENCOUNTER CASE STUDY

This section illustrates how the requirements principles covered in this book are translated into practice, by using the video game case study as an example. It uses the object-oriented style of expressing requirements. Recall that this organizing style has the advantage of improved traceability and the disadvantage of diminished readability compared with other organizations such as by use case. The case study is continued in subsequent chapters.

1. Preparing

Hal Furness, having been elected the requirements leader, was responsible for organizing the analysis of the requirements. As per the project organization, Hal was backed up by Karen Peters. They decided to gather requirements in two stages. The first would be primarily from the customer's perspective (high-level requirements), and the second primarily for developers (detailed requirements).

Hal and Karen prepared to gather metrics on the requirements process. They classified the stages of the process by preparation, interview, write-up, and review. The metrics they chose were dictated mostly by company policy, and were as follows:

• Time taken

• Pages of high-level requirements written

- Self-assessment of the artifacts on a scale of 1–10 (not mandated by company policy)

- Defects found during inspections, as applicable

The reader is referred to Section 4 of this guide to see these metrics arranged in tabular form.

Karen made sure that the system for logging and tracking defects was in place, and that Hal was equipped with the documentation of how to use it.

The company's investors considered video games a promising area, and were willing to provide seed money for requirements analysis and a prototype. It was now Hal and Karen's task to determine with whom to speak to get high-level requirements. Hal understood that none of the team knew much about video games. He decided to interview people who frequently play games and are interested in giving their time for a modest fee. He made contact with Betty Sims, President of Amateur Gamers International, an enthusiastic game player who saw a bright future for video games as vehicles for fun, community involvement, and education. Betty also knew many gamers. Hal and Karen decided to write up requirements specifications based on Betty's input and then show the specifications to others. The rest of the team was to investigate other avenues for input at the same time.

At a weekly meeting, Hal presented a plan for requirements analysis, as follows:

Week 1:

Hal and Karen: Interview Betty; begin drafting high-level requirements.

Fern and Al: Seek other candidates for requirements input.

Week 2:

Fern and Al: Report candidates to weekly meeting.

Team: Select one or two additional people to supply requirements.

Hal and Karen: Complete draft of high-level requirements, e-mail to Betty for comments; arrange to interview the designated additional people; e-mail existing specification to them; create a complete requirements document for iteration 1; place under configuration control.

Week 3:

Team: Approve the SRS for iteration 1.

Hal and Karen: Interview designated people; edit and expand the specification; e-mail to all interviewees; collate responses; edit document, leaving selected issues for team resolution; plan detailed requirements analysis (see the Part V of this book).

Week 4:

Team: Provide input on the draft SRS; approve plan for detailed requirements analysis (see Part V of this book).

Hal and Karen: Write up SRS and e-mail to all interviewees.

Week 5:

Hal and Karen: Resolve issues raised by interviewees; write up results; e-mail to team; begin implementing detailed requirements process (see Chapter 13).

Team: Inspect high-level requirements.

Despite the expense, Hal felt it important to have the entire team inspect the high-level requirements because of the document's importance. In general, the team planned to use three-person inspection teams.

Hal scheduled the first interview with Betty in Room 1428 of the Stewart Building from 10:00 a.m. to 11:30 a.m. He e-mailed her a brief write-up of the project's history, and created the following very simple agenda.

10:00 a.m.–10:15 a.m. Hal: motives for the project

10:15 a.m.–11:30 a.m. Interview of Betty: customer requirements

Hal decided not to introduce more details because he wanted Betty's requirements to influence the rest of the meeting.

2. Interviewing the Customer

Hal and Karen arrived at the interview with Betty, equipped with good sound recording equipment. Betty could not understand why anyone would want to build a video game unless it competed with the best available. Hal explained that this was just a first step, to provide the team with experience in this kind of programming, to get an idea of the scope of work required, and to show the investors what could be accomplished with a given amount of funding. Other motives were to determine whether there was any merit to the ideas that video games have potentially wide appeal, and are applicable to education. After this, the meeting became more focused. The tape recorder was turned on and Hal and Karen began to take detailed notes.

Betty's contention was that role-playing games (not action games) held the most promise for broadening the player community. She discussed the minimum capability that a prototype would need. This included areas where the game characters would engage, ways to get from one area to the other, ways to cause interactions among characters, and what would happen when the characters engaged. Hal and Karen tried to separate the issues and features as they arose, into "crucial for the first iteration," "can be postponed," and "other" (i.e., they used a triage method). The importance of the requirements listed in "other" would be determined later.

Given the script-like nature of the requirements Betty described, Hal focused on obtaining use cases from her. He asked her to describe typical scenarios for the game. Betty described what happens when two characters interact. Karen took notes and expressed this as a use case—a sequence of actions taken by the player and/or the game—and then read it back to Betty.

Betty couldn't think of any other scenarios. Hal felt that there must be more, and asked how the game gets started. This resulted in a second use case. The third use case that they recognized explained how the player moves his character from one area to another. These three use cases seemed to be a satisfactory beginning. Hal and Karen felt that there might be additional essential use cases, but they would have to gather them later.

Betty, Karen, and Hal sketched a few screens together. One showed a typical encounter, and another showed a screen for entering the qualities of game characters. There was considerable discussion of the perspective that the player would have. Betty wanted a player perspective where the view shown on the monitor is the view seen by the player. Karen felt that the required complexity for that view would take the project well beyond their modest initial budget. It was agreed that a modified from-above view would be adequate for the prototype. The screen sketches reflected this. They agreed that considerable refinement of the user interface would be required.

Because of the interfaces that they sketched, Karen felt that the game could really be understood only by means of states. Betty was not familiar with this term, but she was comfortable describing what she called the "modes" of a typical role-playing game, which turned out to be the same concept. Karen and Hal then sketched out the required states of the game, and reviewed with Karen how the game gets from one state to another.

Hal briefly considered clarifying the game further by analyzing the flow of data, but soon realized that the data flow perspective added little value.

Karen reviewed her notes with the others. A few points needed correcting, but there was general agreement on the description.

3. Writing Up the Software Requirements Specification

Hal and Karen divided the task of writing up the SRS by sections. They used the IEEE SRS standard, Sections 1 and 2 (Section 3 consists of the detailed requirements, the process for which is discussed in the Student Project Guide for Chapter 4). To avoid conflicting write-ups, they made sure that their sections were as independent as possible. Hal remembered his previous project, where the team spent so much time reconciling pieces written by different people that it would have been quicker for one person to perform the entire task alone.

They discussed how to prioritize the requirements, because it was becoming clear that otherwise the list of requirements would become far larger than the team could handle. Hal wanted to rank them all, but Karen pointed out that the effort involved would be largely wasted—most of the top-ranking requirements would get done anyway, so their exact order would not be important. Almost none of the bottom ones would get done, so the time spent ranking them also would be wasted. They decided to use a triage method to rank requirements into essential at one extreme, optional at the other, and desirable for the middle category (which simply means neither essential nor optional). They felt that it might be necessary to rank the desirable requirements later. This saved a great deal of useless debating time. They described their classification scheme in Section 2.6 of the SRS ("Apportioning of requirements").

Section 2.1.1 (concept of operations, containing the state diagram for the game) took Hal the longest time to write because he had to translate Betty's informal comments into a concrete form. They tried to cross-reference appropriate sections of the SRS with corresponding tests even though the tests were still sketchy. This helped to clarify the requirements themselves, however. When Betty looked at the test for Section 2.1.1, she recognized that Hal and Karen did not understand some of the issues. In particular, when the game is in Reporting state and the foreign character enters the area containing the player's character, the test did not expect anything to happen. Betty saw this as detrimental and as a way for the player to effectively halt the game. The defect was added to the list of defects with a "major" categorization.

Karen sketched the user interfaces using PowerPoint™ as a drawing tool, rather than building them with Java, the target language. She considered PowerPoint adequate because the UIs in this part of the SRS are meant to be sketches—the detailed UIs are specified in Section 3—and, in any case, they were liable to be changed a great deal. This helped Hal and Karen to show the sketches to Betty and the others, obtain feedback, and then specify the UIs exactly for the detailed requirements.

4. Following Up

The SRS Sections 1 and 2 were e-mailed to Betty. She realized that Hal and Karen had included only two of the three use cases, and the third use case describing movement of the player's character was absent. This defect was logged with a high priority.

Betty was surprised to see that the SRS did not reflect several issues that she thought she had made clear were important, and was humbled to see that the SRS reflected "requirements" that she had offhandedly mentioned but now realized would be a waste of time. The latter included the ability of the player to change outfits while an engagement is progressing. She had numerous comments, most of which Hal and Karen responded to, and some of which were added to the list of defects. Hal e-mailed the SRS Sections 1 and 2 to the team to enable them to prepare for an inspection.

Team leader Ed had learned about Arlan Howard, a marketing executive who was very familiar with the video game industry. The financial backers were willing to fund further requirements analysis at the customer level, and Hal and Karen prepared to meet with Howard. The latter was not able to grant them more than half

This project // **organization norm**	Preparation	Interview	Write-up (results of inspection)	Review	Total
Time spent (minutes)	200 minutes	170 minutes	270 minutes	250 minutes	14.8 hours
% Time spent	250/890 = 28%//**20%**	170/890 = 19%//**23%**	270/890 = 30%//**27%**	200/890 = 22%//**29%**	
Quantity produced			15 pages		
Productivity (= Time/ quantity)			15/14.8 = 1.01 pgs/hr// **0.95**		
Self-assessed quality (1–10)	9	5	9	2	
Defect rate			1.3 per page// **1.01** per page		
Process improvement	Spend ~20% less time preparing	Spread interview time more evenly among people	Check material more thoroughly prior to inspection	Spend ±30% more time reviewing	

Figure 12.37 Example of postmortem data and analysis

an hour since he was very busy. Karen developed a prioritized list of questions and topics and mailed them and the existing draft of SRS Chapters 1 and 2 to Howard. They planned to wrap up the high-level requirements with Howard. The team also planned the process of developing the detailed requirements.

5. Metrics and Postmortem for High-Level Requirements
The high-level requirements were subjected to an inspection by the entire team and the defects were recorded. For the next weekly meeting, Hal and Karen summarized the metrics as shown in Figure 12.37. The team agreed on the postmortem observations shown.

6. Preparing for Detailed Requirements
Hal and Karen had completed their write-up of the high-level requirements, based on discussions and interviews with Betty Sims and Arlan Howard. They used the IEEE standard, whose headings prompted them for the nonfunctional requirements such as GUIs, performance, and hardware platforms. Now they had to identify the manner in which they would organize the functional Detailed Requirements. They anticipated having to revisit and update the SRS many times, coordinating the design and code with it: they wanted this process to be as simple as possible. As a result, their major criterion was the ability to easily maintain consistency between the SRS, the design, and the code.

They first discussed organizing the detailed requirements by states and actions, based on the state-transition diagram described in the high-level requirements. This organization method would consist of a list of the actions that a player would take, such as clicking an exit hyperlink on an area, followed by the effects of this action. They both agreed that this would be an understandable organization, but decided that it would not trace to the implementation as well as they wanted. They began searching for other ways in which to organize the detailed requirements.

Hal was in favor of organizing the functional detailed requirements by use case, especially since he wanted to follow the Unified Software Development Process. He said that, at this stage, the video game could most easily be thought of in terms of the *setting up* use case, the *moving among the game areas* use case, and the *engaging the foreign character* use case. He pointed out how convenient it would be to use just these three use cases as the total extent of the functional requirements. He was also excited about the prospect of perhaps being able to reuse these use cases for specifying future games.

Karen agreed that the requirements would be quite easy to understand if organized by use case, but she had several objections. The first was that some requirements would be part of more than one use case. An example is what happens when an exit from a room is clicked. This could be part of all of the three use cases they had identified, and so it would not be clear where to look for it. Karen's other objection was the fact that mapping from the use cases to the code would not be as clean as the organization she had in mind. Finally, she pointed out that the organization was not yet equipped to properly archive use cases for future reuse.

Karen wanted to organize functional use cases by class, which, she said, facilitated traceability from requirements to implementation. She wanted to pick them carefully enough to ensure that they would be used as part of the design (and implementation). Hal pointed out a disadvantage of this approach: the fact that it forced them to decide very early on some of the classes that they would use in implementing the application. He was worried about the possibility that they may later change their minds about the selection. After further discussion, they decided that organizing the detailed requirements by class had more benefits than drawbacks, and they committed to this method. They decided to be very conservative about class selection, however.

7. Classifying the Detailed Requirements

Hal and Karen first took each use case, and identified what object of what class initiated the action and what object has the responsibility for carrying out the action. This process prompted them to create and/or identify classes. They found it necessary to call Betty and Arlan several times to clarify use case steps they thought they had understood but really didn't.

Hal listed the classes and objects mentioned in the use cases. They then brainstormed, scouring every aspect of Encounter they could reasonable imagine for additional possible classes. As a final step in the class selection process, they drastically cut the list down to an essential few, but taking care to preserve all of the classes referred to in the use cases. The final list consisted of *Area*, *EncounterCharacter*, *EncounterGame*, *Engagement*, *EngagementDisplay*, *ConnectionHyperlink*, *ForeignCharacter*, *PlayerCharacter*, and *PlayerQualityWindow*.

They now finalized the headings of the SRS in Section 3.2 ("Specific requirements"). They collected the detailed requirements related to areas in Subsection 3.2.A, corresponding to the *Area* class. They ordered these subsections alphabetically because they anticipated adding classes later. They surmised that if they were to have ordered topics by number (e.g., *PlayerCharacter* being 3.2.14), then locating an individual requirement would have been more difficult, because the user of the SRS would have to search many of the 3.2.N subsections before finding the one applicable. The next class being *EncounterAreaConnection*, they numbered the next subsection 3.2. EAC, and so on. Within each classification, they created subsections for *attributes*, *entities*, *functionality*, and *events*.

8. Writing the Detailed Requirements

Karen and Hal wrote Section 3.1 on user interfaces by filling in details on the sketches they had made for the high-level requirements, then asking Betty, as well as the human factors department, to review them. Knowing that this would be the final document from which these were to be built, they had the customer agree on every detail.

They checked their interview notes with Betty and Arlan as to the properties ("attributes") of each classification (class). For example, they asked what properties were required for the connections between two Encounter areas. (One property of such connections was "the first area" connected, and another was "the second area.") For each class, they asked themselves what entities (instances of the class) were required for the game. For example, there would have to be a dressing room area and a courtyard area. They then asked what functionality the class had to possess. For example, a functionality of each Encounter character is the ability to configure the values of its qualities (requirement 3.2.EC.3.2). Finally, they listed all of the events that instances of the class were required to respond to (for example, clicking on an exit from an area).

One aspect that disturbed them was the time required for new values to take effect. They realized that this was a key aspect to the game: if no time were to elapse, the player would simply set the qualities pertaining to the current area to a maximum, and little skill would be required to play the game. The delay made the game interesting, but the problem was, how much delay should there be? They considered stating "to be decided" for the duration, but finally concluded that this would not help. They decided to specify four seconds, feeling that changing this amount should be straightforward.

Karen was concerned about the imprecision of some of the requirements, especially those concerning the manner in which quality points should be exchanged when two characters engage each other. She felt that programmers could easily misunderstand the requirements. This would waste time on defects and produce a defective game. She suggested using Z-specifications. Hal made the point that no one except Karen would understand them well enough, since the rest of the team did not have the required education. They compromised by agreeing to use appropriate mathematics in specifying this requirement, but not the Z-specification format. Karen made a mental note that if she ever taught software engineering, she would insist that all students to be completely comfortable with Z-specifications.

Prompted by the section headings in the IEEE SRS standard, Karen and Hal made sure to cover all of the performance requirements and checked them with Betty and Arlan, mostly pertaining to the speed that the game would have to possess to be interesting. They also thought through the memory requirements (RAM and disk). They then completed the document.

9. Following Up: Metrics and Postmortem on Detailed Requirements

The requirements analysis team asked Betty, Arlan, and the rest of the team to inspect the detailed requirements. They performed this inspection primarily against the high-level requirements by ensuring that every part of the high-level requirements were elaborated upon by detailed requirements. They also employed a checklist like the one described in Table 13.3 of Chapter 13. Several defects were found, which Hal and Karen recorded and repaired. The results of this process were similar to those described in Figure 12.37.

12.14 CASE STUDY: DETAILED REQUIREMENTS FOR THE ENCOUNTER VIDEO GAME

This section completes the requirements specification of the Encounter video game in IEEE format.

3. Detailed Requirements

> Note to the Student:
> The IEEE term used in this heading is "specific" requirements. We have substituted the term "detailed" to be consistent with the text.

3.1 External Interface Requirements

3.1.1 User Interfaces

> Section 2.1.2 in the SRS for the Encounter video game showed only sketches of user interfaces in order to provide product perspective. It lacked details and should not be regarded as the last word.
>
> If user interfaces are not completely specified later in this document, then all details should

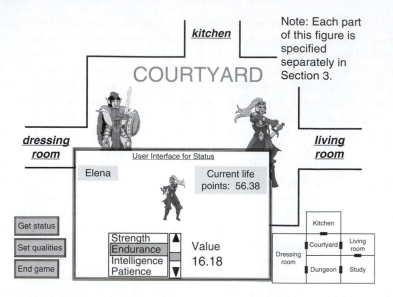

Figure 12.38 Detailed requirement for Encounter courtyard GUI

Source: Graphics reproduced with permission from Corel.

---

be given in this section. Since we are using the object style of specification in this case study, the details of each window are packaged with their classes in Section 3.2.2 in the SRS. In any case, this section should explain the physical relationships among graphical elements (e.g., cascading, tiled, superimposed).

Encounter takes place in areas. Figure 12.38 shows a typical screen shot of the courtyard area, with a player-controlled character, a foreign character, and the results of an engagement. This interface takes up the entire monitor screen. Areas have connections to adjacent areas, labeled by hyperlinks. Clicking on one of these hyperlinks moves the player's character into the corresponding area.

The entire set of interfaces is as follows:

a. One user interface for each area, specified in Section 3.2AR below.

b. A user interface for setting the quality values of the player's character, specified in Section 3.2.PQ.

c. A user interface for displaying the results of an engagement, specified in Section 3.2.ED. The

same user interface is used to show the status of the player's character.

An interface of type a above will always be present on the monitor. When called for by these requirements, interfaces of type b or c will be superimposed. This requirement is tested in Software Test Documentation (STD). <test reference goes here>.

3.1.2 Hardware Interfaces

The hardware that Encounter (which is a software application) deals with

---

None
(In a future release, Encounter will be controllable by a joystick.)

3.1.3 Software Interfaces

Other software with which Encounter must interface: an example would be a printer driver

---

None

(In a future release, Encounter will be playable from Intergalactic Internet Gaming Site.)

3.1.4 Communication Interfaces

None

(In a future release, Encounter shall interface with the Internet via a modem with at least 56 Kb/s.)

3.2 Detailed Requirements by Category

> The IEEE uses the heading "Classes/objects" for Section 3.2. This assumes an audience that knows object orientation. It is necessary to understand OO to create this section but it is not necessary in order to read and understand it.

> Since we are classifying the detailed requirements by class, we first list the classes that we have (very carefully!) chosen. These are not all of the classes that will be used by the application—merely the core classes pertaining to the domain of the application, which are adequate for organizing all of the requirements. In this case, for example, all of them are aspects of the Encounter video game.

Categories for the Encounter video game sufficient for expressing the requirements are Area, EncounterCharacter, EncounterGame, Engagement, EngagementDisplay, ForeignCharacter, PlayerCharacter, and PlayerQualityWindow.

> The numbering "3.2.Area.N.N . . . ," etc. used in Section 3.2 makes it easier for us to insert, remove, and locate requirements by organizing alphabetically the classes that contain them. Think in terms of hundreds of requirements. If we were to number the classes using "3.2.1 . . . ", "3.2.2 . . . ," etc., then inserting new classes would have to be done at the end of the list, since existing numbering, already referred to elsewhere in the project, could not be disturbed. The requirements would not be alphabetically ordered. As a result, one would have to go through the requirements one by one to locate a particular one.

3.2.AR Areas

> First, we describe what the class (i.e., this classification of requirements) refers to.

An area is a place viewable on the monitor. All activities of Encounter (including engagements) take place in areas. Rooms, gardens, and courtyards are examples of areas.

3.2.AR.1 Attributes of Areas

> Here we tell what properties each object (specific entity) of the class must possess.

3.2.AR.1.1 Area Name (essential; not yet implemented)

> The statement above in parentheses indicates the priority and the status of the requirement. Once the requirement is coded and tested, the statement "not yet implemented" is either deleted or changed to "implemented." "Essential" requirements are implemented first. Once a requirement has been designed for and implemented, "essential" can be removed. This is one technique for tracking the state of the application and its relationship with this SRS. Another technique is to specify the iteration to which the requirement applies.

Every Encounter area will have a unique name consisting of 1 to 15 characters. Acceptable characters shall consist of blanks, 0 through 9, a through z, and A through Z only.

Test plan < reference to test goes here>.

Each attribute-type requirement maps to a pair of get- and set- functions. This document suggests how each requirement can be hyperlinked to a unit test in the Software Test Documentation.

3.2.AR.1.2 Area Image (essential; not yet implemented)
There shall be an image to display each Area object on the entire monitor. The image shall fill the entire monitor.

3.2.AR.1.3 Area-Specific Qualities (essential; not yet implemented)
Only some game character qualities shall be applicable in each area. The specific qualities required for each area are specified in Section 3.2.AR.2.

3.2.AR.2 Area Entities

We designate specific area objects that must exist within the application. This section has been added to the IEEE standard. The

alternative would have been to express these requirements as functions: for example, "Encounter shall be capable of displaying XYZ area with the following characteristics."

3.2.AR.2.1 Courtyard Area (essential; not yet implemented)
There shall be an Area object with the name "courtyard" requiring the qualities stamina and strength. The preliminary courtyard image shown in Figure 12.39 includes a map of nearby areas.

3.2.AR.2.2 Dressing Room Area (essential; not yet implemented)
There shall be an area with name "dressing room" requiring no qualities. Its preliminary image, shown in Figure 12.40, includes a map of nearby areas.

3.2.AR.2.3 Dungeon Area (essential; not yet implemented)
There shall be an area with name "dungeon" requiring the qualities stamina and patience. Its preliminary image shown in Figure 12.41 includes a map of nearby areas.

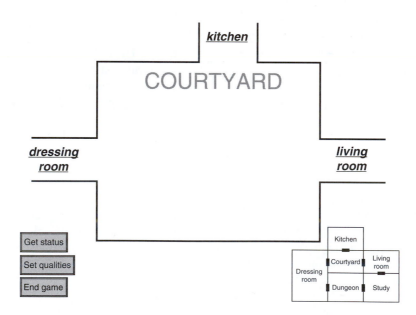

Figure 12.39 Encounter courtyard image

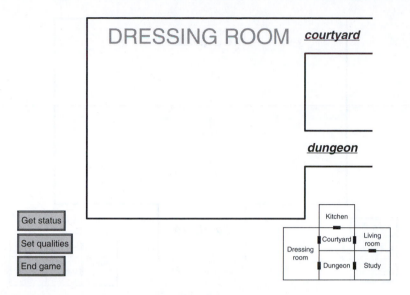

Figure 12.40 Encounter dressing room image

Source: Copyright © E. J. Braude, John Wiley & Sons, 2001.

3.2.AR.2.4 Kitchen Area (essential; not yet implemented) There shall be an area with name "kitchen" requiring the quality concentration. The preliminary kitchen image shown in Figure 12.42 includes a map of nearby areas.

3.2.AR.2.5 Living Room Area (essential; not yet implemented) There shall be an area with name "living room" requiring the qualities concentration and stamina. Its preliminary image shown in Figure 12.43 includes a map of nearby areas.

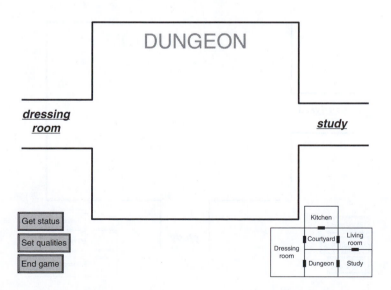

Figure 12.41 Encounter dungeon image

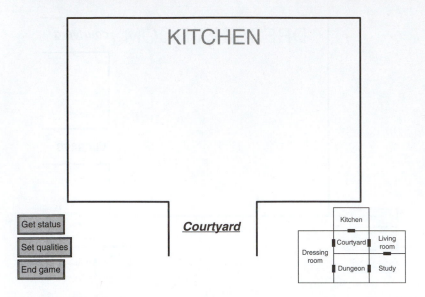

Figure 12.42 Encounter kitchen image

Source: Copyright © E. J. Braude, John Wiley & Sons, 2001.

3.2.AR.2.6 Study Area (essential; not yet implemented)
There shall be an area with the name "study" requiring the quality concentration. Its preliminary image shown in Figure 12.44 includes a map of nearby areas.

3.2.AR.3 Area Functionality

This is the required functionality that pertains specifically to areas. Every functional

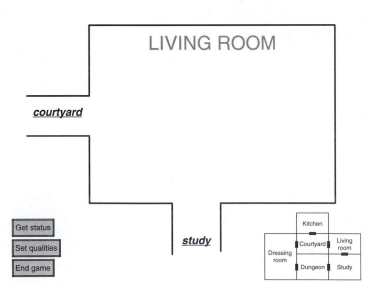

Figure 12.43 Encounter living room image

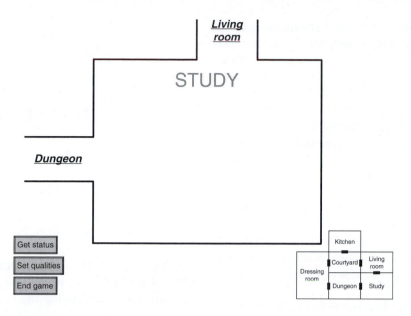

Figure 12.44 Encounter study image

capability of the application should belong to one of these sections.

None

3.2.AR.4 Events Pertaining to Areas

We separate the events that pertain to areas from the attributes, objects, and methods. An event is an action that occurs to the application and is instigated from outside of the application.

3.2.AR.4.1 Display on Entry of Player Character (essential; not yet implemented) Whenever the player's main character enters an area, that area and the characters in it shall be displayed on the monitor, filling the monitor.

3.2.AR.4.2 Handling Engagements (essential; not yet implemented) When a foreign game character enters an area containing the player's main character, or vice versa, they engage each other.

3.2.AR.4.3 Interrupting Engagements (optional; not yet implemented) Players are able to interrupt engagements on a random basis. On average, the player can stop one of every ten engagements by executing the procedure to set qualities. The user tries to interrupt an engagement by attempting to set the player's qualities. If the game does not allow this, no indication is given: the game proceeds as if the attempt had not been made.

3.2.AR.4.4 Pressing the *Set qualities* Button (essential; not yet implemented) When the user presses the *Set qualities* button, a window for setting the values of qualities appears superimposed on the area, provided that there is no foreign character in the area. See 3.2.PQ for the specifications of this window.

3.2.AR.4.5 Pressing the *End game* Button (optional; not yet implemented) When the user presses the *End game* button, the game terminates. No additional screens appear.

The previous sentence, an inverse requirement, was felt to be necessary because games often do display a summary of a session.

3.2.AR.4.6 Pressing the *Get status* Button (optional; not yet implemented)   When the user presses the *Get status* button, an engagement display window appears showing the status of the player's character before and after the last engagement.

3.2.CH Connection Hyperlinks

Between Areas Connection hyperlinks are hyperlinks placed at each area exit, showing the area to which it is connected.

3.2.CH.1 Attributes of Connections Hyperlinks

3.2.CH.1.1 Connection (essential; not yet implemented)   Each connection hyperlink corresponds to an area connection.

3.2.CH.2 Connection Hyperlink Entities (essential; not yet implemented)   There are two connection hyperlinks corresponding to each area connection, one in each area of the connection.

3.2.CH.3 Functionality of Connection Hyperlinks   None

3.2.CH.4 Events Pertaining to Connection Hyperlinks

3.2.CH.4.1 User Clicks on a Connection Hyperlink   The effect of clicking a connection hyperlink is that the player's character is displayed in the area on the other side of the area connection.

3.2.CO Connections between Areas

Characters travel from area to adjacent area by means of connections. Each of these connects two areas. Figure 12.45 shows the required connections among the areas.

3.2.CO.1 Attributes of Connections between Areas

3.2.CO.1.1 First and Second Areas (essential; not yet implemented)   Each connection shall connect a pair of areas, which we will call the "first" and "second" areas.

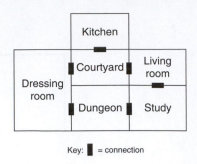

Figure 12.45 Encounter area configuration requirement

3.2.CO.2 Connections Entities

3.2.CO.2.1 Dressing Room–Courtyard (essential; not yet implemented)   There shall be a connection between the dressing room and the courtyard.

3.2.CO.2.2 Dungeon–Study (essential; not yet implemented)   There shall be a connection between the dungeon and the study.

3.2.CO.2.3 Study–Living Room (essential; not yet implemented)   There shall be a connection between the study and the living room.

3.2.CO.2.4 Courtyard–Living Room (essential; not yet implemented)   There shall be a connection between the courtyard and the living room.

3.2.CO.2.5 Dressing Room–Dungeon (essential; not yet implemented)   There shall be a connection between the dressing room and the dungeon.

3.2.CO.2.6 Courtyard–Kitchen (essential; not yet implemented)   There shall be a connection between the courtyard and the kitchen.

3.2.CO.3 Functionality of Area Connections   None

3.2.CO.4 Events Pertaining to Area Connections

3.2.CO.4.1 Moving a Character through a Connection (essential; not yet implemented)   Connections are displayed as hyperlinks at the borders of areas whenever the player's character is in the area. When the user clicks such a hyperlink, the linked area is displayed with the character in this area.

3.2.EC Encounter Characters

3.2.EC.1 Attributes of Encounter Characters

3.2.EC.1.1 Names of Encounter Characters (essential; not yet implemented) Every game character in the Encounter video game shall have a unique name. The specifications for names shall be the same as those for Area names, specified in 3.2.AR.1.

3.2.EC.1.2 Qualities of Encounter Characters (essential; not yet implemented) Every game character has the same set of qualities. Each quality shall be a nonnegative floating point number with at least one decimal of precision. These are all initialized equally so that the sum of their values is 100. The value of a quality cannot be both greater than 0 and less than 0.5.

For the first release the qualities shall be concentration, intelligence, patience, stamina, and strength.

3.2.EC.1.2 Image of Encounter Characters (essential; not yet implemented) Every game character shall have an image.

3.2.EC.2 Encounter Character Entities The characters of the game are described among the types of Encounter characters.

3.2.EC.3 Functionality of Encounter Characters

3.2.EC.3.1 Living Points (essential; not yet implemented) The Encounter game shall be able to produce the sum of the values of any character's qualities, called its living points.

3.2.EC.3.2 Configurability of Encounter Character Quality Values (essential; not yet implemented) Whenever an Encounter character is alone in an area, the value of any of its qualities may be set. The value chosen must be less than or

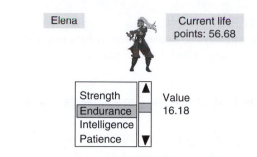

Figure 12.46 Required user interface for status
Source: Graphics reproduced with permission from Corel.

equal to the sum of the quality values. The values of the remaining qualities are automatically adjusted so as to maintain their mutual proportions, except for resulting quantities less than one, which are replaced by quality values of zero.

3.2.ED Engagement Displays (essential; not yet implemented)
There shall be a window displaying the result of engagements. The format is shown in Figure 12.46.

3.2.ED.4 Engagement Display Events

3.2.ED.4.1 Dismissing the Display (essential; not yet implemented) When the user hits OK, the display disappears.

3.2.EG The Encounter Game
The requirements in this section pertain to the game as a whole.

3.2.EG.1 Attributes of the Encounter Game

3.2.EG.1.1 Duration (optional; not yet implemented) A record shall be kept of the duration of each game, timed from when the player begins the game.

3.2.EG.2 Entities of the Encounter Game

3.2.EG.2.1 Single Game (essential; not yet implemented) There shall be a single game.

> Future releases will allow several versions of the game to run at the same time.

3.2.EN Engagements

An engagement is the interaction between a game character controlled by the player and a foreign character.

3.2.EN.1 Attributes of Engagements None

3.2.EN.2 Engagement Entities There are no permanent engagement entities.

3.2.EN.3 Functionality of Engagements

3.2.EN.3.1 Engaging a Foreign Character (essential; not yet implemented)

> This particular requirement is mathematical in nature and so there is no attempt to replace the mathematics with natural language, which would risk compromising its precision. The use of natural language to explain the mathematics is a good practice, however.

When an engagement takes place, the "stronger" of the two characters is the one whose values of area-specific qualities sum to the greater amount. The system transfers half the values of each area-specific quality of the weaker to the stronger. No transfer of points takes place if neither character is stronger.

If either character has no points after the value reallocations are made, the game ends. If the game does not end, the player's character is moved to a random area and the results of the engagement are displayed.

As an example of the value reallocations, suppose that the player engages a foreign character in an area preferring stamina and concentration. If p_s is the value of the player's stamina, and assuming $p_s + p_c > f_s + f_c$, we would have $p_s' = p_s + f_s/2$, $p_c' = p_c + f_c/2$, $f_s' = f_s/2$, and $f_c' = f_a/2$.

> The reader will recognize the defect in the last equation, which should be $f_c' = f_c/2$. We will leave the defect intact as an example.

To take a numerical example of an engagement in this area: If the player's stamina value is 7 and concentration value is 19, and Freddie the foreigner's stamina is 11 and concentration 0.6, then the player is stronger. The result of the engagement would be:

> Player: stamina $7 + 11/2 = 12.5$; concentration $19 + (0.6)/2 = 19.3[0]$
>
> Freddie: stamina
>
> $11/2 = 5.5$; concentration 0 because $(0.6)/2$ is less than 0.5

3.2.FC Foreign Characters

A foreign character is an Encounter character not under the player's control.

3.2.FC.1 Attributes of Foreign Characters See Encounter character requirements. These are initialized to be equal.

> In future releases, foreign characters may mutate into new forms.

3.2.FC.2 Foreign Character Entities

> This section tells that there is only one foreign character.

3.2.FC.2.1 Freddie Foreign Character (essential; not yet implemented) There shall be a foreign character named "Freddie," whose image is shown in Figure 12.47. This character shall initially have a total of 100 points that are distributed equally among its qualities.

3.2.FC.3 Functionality of Foreign Characters

3.2.FC.3.1 Foreign Character Movement (essential; not yet implemented) As long as it is alive, a foreign character should move from area to adjacent area at random intervals averaging two seconds. After being present in an area for a random

Figure 12.47 Foreign character Freddie image requirement

Source: Graphics reproduced with permission from Corel.

amount of time averaging one second, all of the character's life points are divided among the qualities relevant to the area, such that the values of each quality are as close to equal as possible.

3.2.PC Player Characters

These are Encounter characters under the control of the player.

3.2.PC.1 Attributes of Player Characters See Encounter character attributes. Player character images can be selected from one of the images in Figure 12.48.

3.2.PC.2 Player Character Entities

3.2.PC.2.1 Player's Main Character The player shall have control over a particular game character

called the "main" character. The nature of this control is subject to the restrictions specified in the remaining requirements. This character shall initially have a total of 100 points that are distributed equally among its qualities.

3.2.PC.2.2 Additional Characters under the Control of the Player (optional; not yet implemented) The player shall be able to introduce characters other than the main character that the player controls. Details are to be decided.

3.2.PC.3 Player Character Functionality

3.2.PC.3.1 Configurability of the Player Character Quality Values (essential; not yet implemented) Whenever all foreign players are absent from the area containing the player's main character, the player may set the value of any quality of the main character using the Player Quality window shown in Figure 12.49. The value chosen must be less than or equal to the sum of the quality values. The values of the remaining qualities are automatically adjusted so as to maintain their mutual proportions, except for resulting quantities less than 0.5, which are replaced by quality values of zero.

3.2.PC.3.2 Configurability of the Player Character Images (desirable; not yet implemented) The player shall have the option to choose the image representing his or her main character from at least two images. These options are shown in Figure 12.48.

3.2.PC.3.3 Aging of the Player Character Images (optional; not yet implemented) The main player character shall automatically increase each quality by a percentage for the first half of his or her life, then decrease each quality by the same percentage for the second half. Details are to be decided.

3.2.PQ The Player Quality Window

This is a window from which the player may allocate the values of his or her characters.

3.2.PQ.1 Attributes of the Player Quality Window The window for setting the qualities of

Figure 12.48 Player character image options

Source: Graphics reproduced with permission from Corel.

a player character in Encounter is shown by means of a typical example in Figure 12.49. The game character icon appears in the center, and its name appears at the left top of the screen. The character's life points appear in the center. On the left center is a list box displaying four of the qualities at a time. Clicking on one of these qualities allows the player to select a value for it in the text box on the right. An explanation of how the arithmetic is performed is shown in a pale yellow box in the lower part of the screen.

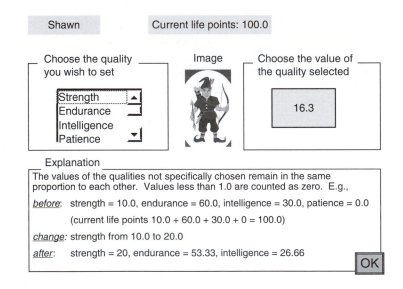

Figure 12.49 User interface required GUI for setting quality values

Source: Graphics reproduced with permission from Corel.

Color backgrounds for the name, life points, and value boxes are to be pale turquoise.

3.2.PQ.2 Player Quality Window Entity

3.2.PQ.2.1 Window for Allocating Qualities (essential; not yet implemented) A window shall be available under the conditions described above to allocate the values of the player character. The window shall have the appearance of the GUI shown in Section 3.1.1.2 of this specification.

3.2.PQ.3 Player Quality Functionality

3.2.PQ.3.1 Initiating the Display (essential; not yet implemented) The player quality menu shall be able to display itself.

3.2.PQ.4 Player Quality Window Events

3.2.PQ.4.1 Displaying the Value of a Quality (essential; not yet implemented) When the player clicks on a quality in the list box on the left, the value of that quality shall be displayed in the text box on the right.

3.2.PQ.4.2 Setting the Value of a Quality (essential; not yet implemented) When the user enters a legitimate value for a quality and hits the "enter" button, the value of that quality is set to the amount entered. If the value is invalid, an error window shall appear stating "invalid value: try again."

3.2.PQ.4.3 Dismissing the Window (essential; not yet implemented) When the user hits the OK button, a time of four seconds elapses, after which the window disappears. At the end of this time period (i.e., if there are no interruptions) the value allocations are made.

3.2.PQ.4.4 Interruption (essential; not yet implemented) Upon interruption of the display of the quality value window, the window vanishes.

Note that interruptions shall be caused by a foreign character entering the area. Note also in this case that the quality values are not changed and that an engagement takes place.

3.3 Performance Requirements

> Performance requirements include required speeds and/or time to complete. Unless documented in a different section of the SRS, they may also include memory usage (RAM and/or disk), noted either statically or dynamically (i.e., memory required at runtime).

The application shall load and display the initial image in less than a minute.

Engagements should execute in less than one second.

These requirements are tested in STD < reference to test goes here>.

3.4 Design Constraints

> This section specifies restrictions on design. If there is no material in this section, designers are free to create any (good) design that satisfies the requirements. For example, we can add the design constraint "one-story" to the following: "A house with four bedrooms, all of which are less than a thirty-second walk from the family room."

Encounter shall be designed using UML and object-oriented design. It shall be implemented in Java. The software shall run as a Java application on Windows 95. It shall be designed in a way that makes it relatively easy to change the rules under which the game operates so that others can customize the game.

3.5 Software System Attributes

3.5.1 Reliability

Encounter shall fail not more than once in every 1,000 encounters. Test documentation < reference to test goes here>.

3.5.2 Availability

Encounter shall be available for play on any PC running Windows 95 only (i.e., no other applications simultaneously). Test documentation < reference to test goes here>.

3.5.3 Security

> Future releases will allow access to saved games only with a password.

3.5.4 Maintainability

3.5.4.1 Changing Characters and Areas (essential) It shall be straightforward to change characters and areas.

3.5.4.2 Globally Altering Styles (desirable) It shall be straightforward to globally alter the style of the areas and connections. (Style changes reflect different levels of game play in the same environment.)

3.5.4.3 Altering Rules of Engagement (optional) Rules of engagement should be relatively easy to change.

3.6 Other Requirements

None

4. Supporting Information

None

4.1 Table of Contents and Index

Not included.

4.2 Appendixes

Not included.

> Appendices may include
>
> (a) Sample I/O formats, descriptions of cost analysis studies, or results of user surveys
> (b) Supporting or background information that can help the readers of the SRS
> (c) A description of the problem to be solved by the software
> (d) Special packaging instructions for the code and the media to meet security, export, initial loading, or other requirements
>
> State explicitly whether or not each appendix is to be an official part of the SRS.

12.15 SUMMARY

Detailed requirements ("developer" or "detailed" requirements) are written primarily with designers and developers in mind. They are created from high-level requirements, as well as from continued customer interaction. Detailed requirements must be testable, traceable, and consistent. Since they become numerous, they must be classified systematically. There are several ways to organize detailed requirements including by feature, use case, GUI, state, and domain class.

Agile projects tend not to create documents—separate from the code and tests—with detailed requirements.

Detailed requirements must be traceable to the design and implementation that realize them and to the tests that validate them. Without a clean trace from each requirement through the design of the application to the actual code that implements it, it is very difficult to ensure that such an application remains in compliance with the requirements. When the requirements change, which is safe to assume, this becomes even more difficult. Detailed requirements must also be traceable in the other direction, to the high-level requirements they are derived from, to ensure that all are fully specified.

Since it is difficult to implement all desired functionality, requirements are often prioritized. Categories such as *essential*, *desirable*, and *optional* are used to designate priorities. Organizations commit to delivering essential functionality, and if there is time they implement desirable and then optional features.

Once detailed requirements have been collected, the project documents are updated to reflect the improved project knowledge. For example, schedules are updated with more accurate dates and risks are retired and more information is learned.

12.16 EXERCISES

1. To what audience are detailed requirements primarily targeted?

2. Name five ways of organizing detailed requirements.

3. What is wrong with the following Detailed requirements? Explain how you would fix them.

   a. *HomeBudget* shall display a convenient interface for entering personal data.

   b. *SatControl* shall compute the predicted time it takes to circle the Earth on the current orbit, and the actual time taken to circle the Earth on the previous orbit.

   c. *InvestKing* shall determine the best investment strategy.

4. What are three advantages and three disadvantages of organizing detailed requirements by class rather than by feature?

5. Suppose that you are defining the requirements for an application that simulates the movement of customers in a bank. List five classes that can be used to organize the requirements.

6. Provide detailed requirements for each class identified in Exercise 3 by describing one attribute and one function corresponding to each class.

7. When identifying domain classes (as in Figure 12.8), why is it useful to denote the relationship between them (i.e., inheritance, aggregation)?

8. Applying the principle of good screen design outlined in Step 3 of Section 12.3 sketch good GUI screens for a home finance application that:

   a. displays a summary of a user's financial holdings, organized by type of holding, and

   b. allows a user to input the details for a new holding

9. For each detailed requirement listed in Exercise 6, assign a priority (e.g., essential, desirable, optional) and explain why you chose them.

10. Create a chart similar to Figure 12.27 that specifies test input and output for one of the attributes identified in Exercise 6.

TEAM EXERCISE

SRS

Write the SRS for your application. Use or modify the IEEE standard. If you are using an iterative approach, try to indicate what requirements are to be implemented in each iteration.

Track the time spent on this by individuals and by the group. Break this time into appropriate activities. Measure the effectiveness of your effort. (Feel free to develop your own metrics; see also team exercises in previous chapters.) Indicate how the process you used to develop the SRS could have been improved.

Evaluation criteria:

(1) Degree of clarity

(2) Extent to which the plan includes all relevant details and excludes irrelevant material

(3) Effectiveness of your self-measurement and process improvement description

BIBLIOGRAPHY

1. Booch, Grady, *"Object-Oriented Analysis and Design with Applications,"* Addison-Wesley, 1994.
2. Jordan, Richard, Ruth Smilan, and Alex Wilkinson, "Streamlining the Project Cycle with Object-Oriented Requirements," *OOPSLA Conference Proceedings* (1994), pp. 287–300.
3. Galitz, W., *"The Essential Guide to User Interface Design: An Introduction to GUI Principles and Techniques,"* John Wiley & Sons, 1996.
4. Rand, Paul, *"A Designer's Art,"* Yale University Press, 1985.
5. Myers, Glenford. J., *"The Art of Software Testing,"* John Wiley & Sons., 1979.
6. Java^{TM} SE 6 Platform Documentation, 2006.
7. Faulk, Stuart,"Software Requirements: A Tutorial," 1997, http://www.cs.umd.edu/class/spring2004/cmsc838p/Requirements/Faulk_Req_Tut.pdf [accessed November 29, 2009].
8. Mars Climate Orbiter Mishap Investigation Board Phase 1 Report, November 1999, ftp://ftp.hq.nasa.gov/pub/pao/reports/1999/MCO_report.pdf [accessed November 29, 2009].

13

Quality and Metrics in Requirements Analysis

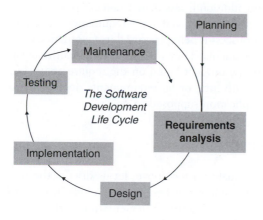

- • What is meant by the accessibility of requirements?
- • Comprehensiveness?
- • Understandability?
- • How do you assess the degree of ambiguity of requirements?
- • Consistency?
- • Prioritization?
- • What is meant by the degree of security in requirements?
- • In what sense can requirements be complete?
- • Testable?
- • Traceable?
- • What metrics are suitable for these qualities?

Figure 13.1 The context and learning goals for this chapter

This chapter describes measures of quality in requirements. The more a requirements document expresses what the customer wants and needs, the higher its quality. We usually think of details as being far less important than the "big picture," but a missing requirements detail can seriously affect projects, as numerous case studies show. Recall, for example, the overlooked detail of metric-to-nonmetric distance conversion that dispatched a $125 million spacecraft to oblivion.

How . . . **accessible** is each requirement?
. . . **comprehensive** is the SRS?
. . . **understandable** is each requirement?
. . . **unambiguous** is each requirement?
. . . **consistent** is the SRS?
. . . **effectively prioritized** are the requirements?
. . . **secure** is the requirement?
. . . **self-complete** is the SRS?
. . . **testable** is each requirement?
. . . **traceable** is each requirement?

Figure 13.2 Attributes of requirements analysis that promote quality

To help ensure that the requirements are indeed covered, we focus on qualities that requirements should possess. They should be complete and consistent; each one should be capable of being traced through to the design and implementation, tested for validity, and implemented according to a rational priority. Figure 13.2 lists these attributes and tells what we should look for in good requirements. We can systematically review and inspect requirements based on this list. For example, a set of consistent requirements is far more likely to express what stakeholders want and need than a set with contradictions.

This chapter discusses how each of these qualities can be measured. "Target values" refers to the numerical goals set in the project relative to various metrics. Metrics are most useful when their target values are specified *in advance*. For example, we could state in advance that, based on experience on past projects, requirements will be considered "complete" when the rate of modification and addition is less than 1 percent per week.

Projects are greatly improved when the QA organization is involved in the requirements analysis stage. In particular, QA verifies that the intended development process is being executed in accordance with plans. QA should participate in inspections of requirements documents. They tend to have a healthy perspective because they understand that they will have to validate the product based on the requirements. In poorly organized projects, QA may be handed an application with little or no requirements documentation and asked to test it. This begs the question, "what is the application supposed to do?"

13.1 QUALITY OF REQUIREMENTS FOR AGILE PROJECTS

Before discussing the attributes of requirements analysis quality listed above, let us discuss the quality of requirements for agile processes. The primary process for requirements here consists of eliciting user stories from the customer, along with acceptance tests, and then subjecting the implementation to those tests upon completion. In addition, the customer must feel satisfied with the result. This may or may not be supported by significant documentation. Quality has to be assessed, if not measured according to this standard. This entails computing the fraction of acceptance tests passed and making an assessment of the customer's reaction, possible via a questionnaire. Since the customer—usually in the form of a team member representative—is part of the development effort, requirements assessment includes the performance of the customer. Given the nature of requirements analysis, this is all to the good.

13.2 ACCESSIBILITY OF REQUIREMENTS

To deal with a set of requirements, we should be able to access the ones we want, when we want them. This is the quality of *accessibility*. The first property we need in this respect is a means of identifying the detailed requirements.

- **Ease of getting to statement** of detailed requirements.

- **Metric:**

  0: *extremely long average access time (compared with the organization's norm)*
  10: *average access time as fast as can be expected*

Figure 13.3 The accessibility of requirements

We do this by numbering them in some way. A good numbering system allows us to know whether the requirement has been implemented, for example, and to trace it to the code that actually carries it out.

A project's requirements change continually throughout its life cycle. For example, when a programmer tries without success to implement a requirement and explains this to the customer, the latter frequently finds missing parts in the requirement. The SRS must then be accessed to ascertain whether these missing requirements were present, and included if they were not. Taking an example from the video store case study, the customer (in this case, the video store) may question why a DVD's play time does not appear on the monitor. The developers and the customer will want to know whether this was specified in the SRS. Where in that document should they look to determine this? Rummaging through poorly organized documents is time-consuming and therefore expensive.

Here is a checklist for improving the accessibility of requirements:

- Do you know where the high-level requirements are stated?

- Do you know where the detailed requirements are listed?

- Are the detailed requirements organized in groups, preferably with each group corresponding to a high-level requirement?

- Are all of the detailed requirements organized into a list, or a clearly understood list of lists?

- Can you look up requirements by keyword? By subject matter? By use case? By GUI? By user type?

- Can you look up requirements by other criteria relevant to the particular application or project?

One accessibility metric is the *average time taken to access a detailed requirement*. To measure this, a sample would be taken of existing and missing requirements, and several people would be timed finding these or ascertaining that they are absent. Statistically speaking, 150 is a good sample size. Smaller sample sizes are unreliable but are probably better than nothing. In selecting a sample, one uses a process that is as random as time allows. For example, one could ask each of a group of people familiar with the proposed application to contribute ten potential detailed requirements, then pick at random from the combined list to obtain samples to seek. Accessibility is summarized in Figure 13.3.

13.3 COMPREHENSIVENESS OF REQUIREMENTS

A quality SRS expresses all of the requirements for a product. By *comprehensiveness*, we mean the extent to which the customer's wants and needs are included. An appropriate metric would thus be *percentage of the customer's requirements appearing in the SRS*. An obvious way to ensure this is to have the customer validate it, but this is not a simple matter, as the points in Figure 13.4 suggest.

The comprehensiveness of requirements forms an elusive and vague goal, and yet the completeness of requirements is key to the successful completion of a project and the tracking of progress. Each iteration

- Not enough **resources** to satisfy every customer wish
  - Prioritize so that comprehensive within each batch of requirements
- **Customer can't/won't read** entire SRS
  - Make SRS easy to follow
  - Use a standard
  - "Read" SRS to customer
- **Limitations of self-inspections**
  - Subject to peer inspection
- **Contradictory stakeholder requirements** need to be satisfied
  - Apply diplomatic skills and expect compromise

Figure 13.4 Issues in attaining comprehensive requirements

makes the requirements more comprehensive. One way to deal with the evolving set of requirements is to include requirements of future iterations and of all priorities in measuring completeness. An example is shown in Table 13.1. This perspective helps us to assess how close our plans are to satisfying the customer's wants and needs.

A more tractable measure is *self-completeness*, in which the requirements contain all materials that its parts reference. However, this is somewhat different, and is discussed below.

Here is a checklist for improving the comprehensiveness of requirements:

- Summarize, or give a very short preliminary description of needed requirements that have not been included yet.

- Is the customer satisfied that the requirements reflect all of his or her needs and wishes?

- What fraction of the listed requirements are slated for implementation in the current release? Future releases?

Figure 13.5 shows two useful comprehensiveness metrics.

The IEEE defines a rather complex measure of completeness in 982.2-1988 A35.1. This is a formula involving 18 observed quantities (e.g., "number of condition options without processing") and 10 weights (e.g., the relative importance of "defined functions used"). It measures the degree to which there are loose ends within a set of detailed requirements.

Table 13.1 Including future requirements

Requirement		Priority	Iteration
No.	**Description**		
780	Every DVD record shall contain the title, up to 60 alphanumeric characters	2	3
781	Every customer record shall include the customer's credit card number, consisting of 16 digits.	1	2
782	. . .		

Let T = total number of documented detailed requirements
(all priorities; all iterations)

METRIC: % Requirements implemented =

$$\frac{100 * [\text{no. of requirements implemented}]}{T}$$

METRIC: % Requirements Currently Targeted =

$$\frac{100 * [(\text{no. of requirements implemented}) + (\text{no. of top priority requirements in current iteration})]}{T}$$

Figure 13.5 Two useful comprehensiveness metrics

13.4 UNDERSTANDABILITY OF REQUIREMENTS

Understandability appears to be a highly subjective quality because it depends on peoples' opinion. However, it can be measured. For example, a random set of people from an appropriate population can be asked to express on a form their opinion of a requirements document. Table 13.2 is an example of an opinion form—in this case applied to a user interface. Here is a checklist for improving the comprehensiveness of requirements.

- Are the requirements written in language that its typical reader would understand?

- Do they use the vocabulary of the client problem domain?

- Do the requirements describe only external behavior—that is, as seen from the user's point of view? ("User" can include external systems rather than just people.)

- Do the requirements avoid stating *how* the problem is to be solved, what techniques are to be used, or how the application is to be designed? (The exceptions to this are when such specification are indeed required up front.)

13.5 UNAMBIGUITY OF REQUIREMENTS

Unless a detailed requirement is written clearly and unambiguously, we won't be able to determine whether it has been properly implemented. Figure 13.6 illustrates an example of an ambiguous requirement, followed by an improved version. The original requirement seems to allow the player to change the qualities of a game character at any time during the game. This would take the fun out of the game, because the player would simply set quality values to their largest possible relevant values and there would be little room for trying various strategies.

Here is a checklist for improving the nonambiguity of requirements:

- For each requirement, is there only one way that a typical reader would interpret it?

- For each requirement, are terms avoided that could be understood in more than one way?

Figure 13.7 shows a metric for ambiguity that depends on a triage measurement: decide whether the detailed requirement has exactly one clear meaning (score of 2); or many meanings (score 0); otherwise give it a score of 1.

The player can decide the qualities of Encounter characters.

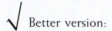At any time? Probably not. Would have to test under all circumstances, many not intended, incurring unnecessary expense and producing a wrong result.

✓ Better version:

Whenever all foreign players are absent from the area containing the player's main character, the player may change the quality values of this character, keeping the sum total of the quality values unchanged. The PlayerQualityWindow, (see Section tbd) is used for this purpose. Changes take effect four seconds after the "OK" button is pressed.

Figure 13.6 An example of ambiguity in requirements

A metric (range: 0 to 1 00)

$$\frac{100*\sum[\text{unambiguity of each detailed requirement }(0{-}2)]}{2*[\text{number of detailed requirements}]}$$

0 = could have many meanings; 2 = clearly one meaning

Figure 13.7 A metric for unambiguity

13.6 CONSISTENCY OF REQUIREMENTS

A set of detailed requirements is *consistent* if there are no contradictions among them. As the number of detailed requirements grows, inconsistency tends to become difficult to detect. Inconsistency is illustrated by the three requirements in Figure 13.8.

Requirement 14. *Only basic food staples shall be carried by game characters.*

. . . . . .

Requirement 223. *Every game character shall carry water.*

. . . . . .

Requirement 497. *Flour, butter, milk, and salt shall be considered the only basic food staples.*

Figure 13.8 Example of inconsistency in requirements

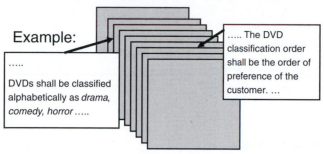

Means: **No contradiction**, in whole or in part

Example:

..... DVDs shall be classified alphabetically as *drama, comedy, horror* .....

..... The DVD classification order shall be the order of preference of the customer. ...

Metric: **Percentage of contradicted requirements**

Figure 13.9 Consistency in requirements

The object-oriented style of organization of requirements helps to avoid inconsistencies by classifying detailed requirements by class and by decomposing them into a simple form. This is not a guarantee of consistency, however, and so requirements inspections include a check for consistency. Here is a checklist for improving the consistency of requirements:

- For each requirement, are there other requirements that could lead to contradicting or annulling it?

- For each requirement, are there other requirements that are very similar and so can create inconsistencies?

- Does each requirement avoid a chain of consequences that can't be readily followed?

A consistency metric is *the percentage of detailed requirements partly or wholly contradicted elsewhere.* To obtain such a metric, one would consider a sample of detailed requirements—150 would be appropriate—and investigate each one in turn to determine whether it is contradicted elsewhere in the document. This entails comparing it to all of the remaining detailed requirements. Figure 13.9 provides another example.

This measure is imperfect because it accounts only for pairs of inconsistent requirements. As Figure 13.8 illustrates, inconsistency can result from a set of requirements.

13.7 PRIORITIZATION OF REQUIREMENTS

Since quality is ultimately defined by customer satisfaction, the requirements analysis process is continually directed toward the customer's concept of satisfaction. Teams typically show stakeholders interim accomplishments, and stakeholders then influence the course of the work accordingly. Because of this, the priority of requirements—and thus the order in which requirements are implemented, as described in Chapter 12—makes a significant difference in the customer's satisfaction. In mathematical language, this is a non-commutative operation since the SRS sequence

implement requirement A then *plan to implement requirement B*

may well produce a different product from

implement requirement B then *plan to implement requirement A*

Assume three prioritizations: *high*, *medium*, and *low*

Metric: Variation from # *high* = # *medium* = # *low*
Let T = total number of detailed requirements

$$\frac{100 * [\text{T} - |\text{T}/3 - \text{high}| - |\text{T}/3 - \text{medium}| - |\text{T}/3 - \text{low}|]}{\text{T}}$$

0 = worst; 100 = best

Figure 13.10 A metric for measuring the quality of prioritization

There are effective and ineffective prioritizations. For example, giving most requirements the highest priority indicates poor planning. Ranking low-priority requirements is usually a waste of time because they are unlikely to be all implemented. As mentioned, when stakeholders see the implementation of requirements, they tend to change subsequent requirements. An effective prioritization tries to account for these factors.

Here is a checklist for improving the prioritization of requirements:

- Is it clear what requirement should be worked on first? Second?

- Are the priorities at a high level consistent with those at the detailed level?

- Is there a prioritization process in place such that it will remain clear what is the next important requirement that should be worked on?

- Is the prioritization appropriately matched with customer expectations?

- Is the prioritization appropriately matched with project risks?

Assume that each requirement is in one of three priorities. How would we measure the quality of the prioritization? A good quality prioritization categorizes requirements into equal parts, indicating that no category has been neglected. Figure 13.10 shows a metric for this.

For example, if 900 requirements are very well prioritized, each category would contain 300 requirements, and the formula would give $100 * [900 - 0 - 0 - 0]/900 = 100\%$. On the other hand, if 700 were classified as high priority, 100 as medium and 100 as low, the metric would yield

$$100 * [900 - |300 - 700| - |300 - 100| - |300 - 100|]/900 = 100 * 100/900 = 11.1\%$$

The low percentage indicates poor prioritization.

13.8 SECURITY AND HIGH-LEVEL REQUIREMENTS

Security can be dealt with as an actual (explicit) requirement or as an attribute of requirements. For example, "All passwords shall be unavailable except to the system administrator" is an explicit requirement of an application. On the other hand, "The requirements in our SRS will cause fewer than 10 security breaches of level 1 or greater (defined elsewhere) in a century of continuous operation under the threat environment of 2009" is not a requirement in the ordinary sense. It is an attribute of the requirements.

Security in requirements is a special case in that it deals with deliberate exploits on the part of others to misuse it. Traditional requirements, after all, are intended to specify what an application *should* do, and have not addressed misuse. This is changing. To an increasing extent, requirements documents are addressing the security issue by including such content as *misuse cases*. These are similar to the idea, mentioned earlier, of inverse requirements. The following are examples of misuse cases—use cases that the system is required to *dis*allow:

> An automated user of the application enters a known user ID and more than 10 passwords per second. A user accesses more than 30 customer records in a single sitting and transmits these to another address within 10 seconds of accessing them.

Here is a checklist for improving the security aspects of requirements:

- Consider the places in the proposed application where intrusion appears to be possible. Are concrete security requirements stated for those places?

- Has the confidentiality of data, where applicable, been specifically required?

- Has the security of user identity been specified?

- Has the security of passwords been explicitly called for?

- Has the ownership of files or access been specified?

- Has encryption been called for when appropriate?

- Have specific, known security exploits ("hacks") been specified against? An example is "SQL injection shall be prevented." (SQL injection is a means of unauthorized database access.)

> Have specific and potential exploits been specified against via misuse cases?

13.9 SELF-COMPLETENESS OF REQUIREMENTS

Typically, a requirement depends on other requirements. A set of requirements is *self-complete* if it contains every part whose inclusion is necessitated by parts already present. Figure 13.11 illustrates an incomplete set of requirements. Without the specification of how a video is to be "displayed," this set of requirements is incomplete as a unit.

As another example, suppose that the SRS for a calendar application contains the following requirement.

> *The application shall retain all information entered by the user for each appointment.*

REQUIREMENTS

1. *The application shall display a DVD in stock when a title is entered at the prompt; otherwise it shall display "OUT OF STOCK."*

2. *The application shall display all of the store's DVDs by any director whose last name is entered at the prompt. These shall be displayed one by one. Advancing through the DVDs shall be controlled by the* forward *arrow key.*

Incomplete: Lacks specification on how to display a video!

Figure 13.11 An example of self-incompleteness in requirements

When a requirement is present, so must all those necessitated by its presence.

A metric (0 = best; 1 poor; no theoretical upper limit):

$$\frac{[\text{number of missing necessary associated requirements}]}{[\text{number of detailed requirements present}]}$$

Figure 13.12 A metric for self-completeness

The presence of this requirement necessitates a requirement describing means for entering appointment information. It also necessitates a requirement explaining means for displaying this information. This is the meaning of "self-completion." Here is a checklist for improving the self-completeness of requirements:

• For each requirement stated, are all the requirements present that it refers to?

• For each requirement stated, are all the requirements present that it depends on?

To measure self-completeness, we look at each detailed requirement and note any necessary associated requirement that is missing. An appropriate metric is shown in Figure 13.12.

The number of missing requirements is determined by sampling.

13.10 TESTABILITY OF REQUIREMENTS

Each detailed requirement must be *testable;* that is, it must be possible to definitely validate that the requirement is operative in the finished application by testing for it. Figure 13.13 provides an example of a nontestable requirement, and shows what it would take to make the requirement testable.

The system shall display the difference in salary
between the client and the worldwide average for the
same trade.

X—can't be tested because the average mentioned cannot be determined (even though it exists).

 Better:

The system shall display the difference in salary
between the client and the estimated worldwide average
for the same trade as published by the United Nations
on its Web site www.tbd at the time of the display . . .

Figure 13.13 An example of testability

Table 13.2 Example of a user satisfaction questionnaire

User Satisfaction	
0 = of no value; 5 = average satisfaction; 10 = a pleasure to use	
Quality	**Score**
1. Overall appearance	
2. Layout of text areas	
3. Layout of buttons	
4. Readability	
5. Ease of entering data	
6. Degree to which erroneous data entry is prevented	
. . . . . .	

Requirements that are not testable are of negligible value. It would be impossible to assess whether such a requirement has been attained. This is an all-or-nothing property. There is little value in the "degree of testability" of a requirement.

Testability can sometimes be used to specify a detailed GUI requirement. For example, instead of specifying a GUI in complete detail we may prefer to provide a test such as the following:

The GUI for entering DVDs shall have the fields and buttons listed in figure xx, and its design shall score an average of at least 8.5 out of 10 on the user satisfaction questionnaire in Table 13.2.

An effective way to ensure testability and to ensure the clarity of a requirement at the same time is to include tests with the requirement. Figures 13.14 and 13.15 illustrate an example.

Agile programming applies this test orientation but short-circuit's the prose by encoding the test up front, using it as a requirement, in effect. A reasonable testability metric is the following:

The percentage of detailed requirements that are accompanied by a test.

Even when a requirement is testable, executing a test may be difficult or time-consuming. To be complete, we sometimes need to consider the *cost of testing* as part of the consideration. A very high cost

---

The video store application shall implement a discount program as follows:

- One DVD: no discount
- Two DVDs: 20% discount for the second DVD
- Three DVDs: 40% discount for the second and third DVD
- All videos beyond the third are discounted at 40%.

Figure 13.14 Including tests with requirements, 1 of 2—the requirement

1. Customer Owen Jones rents one DVD. He is charged the regular rental of $5.00.

2. Customer Teresa Edwards rents two DVDs. She is charged the regular rental of $5.00 for the first and $4.00 (20% discount) for the second.

3. Customer Theodore List rents three DVDs. He is charged the regular rental of $5.00 for the first, $4.00 (20% discount) for the second, and $3.00 (40% discount) for the third.

4. Customer Fred Harari rents five DVDs. He is charged the regular rental of $5.00 for the first, $4.00 (20% discount) for the second, and $3.00 (40% discount) for the third. The fourth and fifth DVDs are charged at $3.00 (40% discount).

Figure 13.15 Including tests with requirements 2 of 2—the tests

influences our choice and priority of requirements. For example, suppose that we consider adding to our online video service the following requirement:

> For each movie entered by the customer, the application shall display a number from 0 to 5 that provides the system's estimate of how much he will like the movie. This estimate is based on the customer's past viewing ratings.

This can be tested, but the expense of doing so properly may dissuade us from making it a high priority. Recommendation algorithms have become a competitive activity among providers, with large rewards provided for the creators of the most (measurably) effective ones. Like this one, many requirements are strongly associated with business decisions.

Here is a checklist for improving the testability of requirements:

- Is the requirement clear enough to devise input/output data samples that exercise it? Specify the tests.

- Is there a set of tests that, if passed, provides significant confidence that the requirement will have been satisfied?

- If one reasonable person in the customer community proposed a set of tests for the requirement, would another probably agree that it tests the requirement?

13.11 TRACEABILITY OF REQUIREMENTS

Traceability was defined in Chapter 10. Our concern here is how to measure a set of requirements in this respect. A requirement is traceable if it maps in a completely clear manner to the design element that accommodates it, the code that implements it, and the tests that test it. When the OO (or "class") organization of requirement writing is used, the mapping to the class within the design and to the code can be completely clear. It requires work and clear thinking to maintain such clarity, however. For example, a *Customer* paragraph that specifies the rentals that each customer can have could compromise traceability. The design would probably have the classes *Customer*, *DVD*, *DVDRental*, and *DVDRentals*. The requirements organization should reflect this.

Organizing classes by functionality, GUIs, use cases, and so on has various advantages, as discussed in Chapter 12, but traceability is not a strength for most of them. One would have to peruse each detailed requirement and ask whether it will clearly map to a class.

(Range: 0 to 100)

$$\frac{100 * \sum [\text{traceability of each detailed requirement } (0 - 2)]}{2 * [\text{number of detailed requirements}]}$$

0 = untraceable; 2 = clearly traceable to a specific class

Figure 13.16 A traceability metric

Here is a checklist for improving the traceability of requirements:

- For each detailed requirement, is it clearly conceivable that an identifiable part of the code base will implement it? (It's ideal when a single method implements a single detailed requirement.)

- Is it clearly conceivable that a single, identifiable part of a software design and implementation could contain it? (A detailed requirement that must be spread over several probable main modules is not easily traceable.

Traceability can be measured as in Figure 13.16. Using 2 as a measure allows the application of triage for a give requirement, where 0 = *untraceable;* 2 = *fully traceable;* 1 *otherwise.*

13.12 METRICS FOR REQUIREMENTS ANALYSIS

The previous sections of this chapter described metrics for a number of requirements qualities: accessibility, comprehensiveness, understandability, unambiguousness, consistency, degree of prioritization, security, self-completeness, testability, and traceability. Additional metrics can be considered.

The following list of quality assurance metrics includes requirements analysis metrics in IEEE Standard 982.2-1988 ("IEEE Guide for the Use of IEEE Standard Dictionary of Measures to Produce Reliable Software"). Some measure the qualities we have already discussed in a different manner.

- Percentage of unambiguous specific requirements (IEEE metric 6)

- Degree of completeness (IEEE metrics 23 and 35)

- Percentage of misclassified detailed requirements (in the object-oriented style, this measures the percentage allocated to the wrong class)

- Traceability (IEEE metric 7)

- Degree of atomicity (indivisible into smaller parts)

- Consistent with the remaining requirements (IEEE metrics 12 and 23)

- Measures of the effectiveness of requirements inspection

- Percentage of missing or defective requirements found per hour of inspection

- Measures of the effectiveness of the requirements analysis process

- Cost per detailed requirement

- On a gross basis (total time spent/number of detailed requirements)

- On a marginal basis (cost to get one more)

- Rate at which specific requirements are . . .

  – modified

  – eliminated

  – added

- Measure of the degree of completeness of the requirements. This can be estimated from the rate, after the official end of detailed requirements collection, at which specific requirements are . . .

  – modified

  – added

13.13 INSPECTING DETAILED REQUIREMENTS

The reader is referred to Chapter 5 for a description of the inspection process in general.

Detailed requirements are the first software process documents that can be inspected against prior documentation (the high-level requirements). Inspectors prepare for the inspection by reading over the high-level requirements and comparing the detailed requirements with them. It can be very productive to inspect requirements against each of the qualities and metrics listed above.

The rest of this section provides an example of a detailed requirements inspection. Here is an uninspected version of detailed requirements for the Encounter video game case study on which we will perform an example inspection, entering the results in a table (see Table 13.3). We employ the technique of automatically adding the "not inspected yet" comment to each. It is removed when the inspection takes place. The final version of these requirements, resulting from the inspection, is shown in the accompanying Encounter case study.

Area Requirement 1 ("*Area* name"). (Not inspected yet) Every area shall have a name of up to 15 characters.

Area Requirement 2 ("*Area* image"). (Not inspected yet) There shall be an image in gif form to display each *Area* object.

Area Requirement 3 ("Display area method"). (Not inspected yet) Whenever a player character enters an area, that area and the characters in it shall be displayed.

Area Requirement 4 ("Courtyard object"). (Not inspected yet) There shall be an *Area* object with name "courtyard." Its image shall be that shown in Figure xx on page xx.

Area Requirement 5 ("Dressing room object"). (Not inspected yet) There shall be an Area object with name "dressing room" and blank background image. The dressing room shall be adjacent to the courtyard area.

Encounter Requirement 1 ("Engaging a foreign character"). (Not inspected yet) When an engagement takes place, the following computation is performed: The sum of the values of qualities of a game character relevant to the area in question shall be referred to as the character's area value. (In this release, all qualities will count as equal.) In an engagement, the system compares the area values of the characters and transfers to the stronger, half of the points of the weaker. For example, suppose the player engages a foreign character in an area requiring stamina and attention span, and ps is the value of the player's stamina, etc. Assuming $p_s + p_a > f_s + f_a$, we would have $p_s' = p_s + f_s/2$, $p_a' = p_a + f_a/2$, $f_s' = f_s/2$, $f_a' = f_s/2$ where x' is the value of x after the transaction.

Table 13.3 Example of a form used for the inspection of detailed requirements

No.	Requirement Description	Traceable backward	Comprehensive	Consistent	Feasible	Unambiguous	Clear	Precise	Modifiable	Testable	Traceable forward Note 14
1001	Area Requirement 1	Note 2	Note 1	Yes	Yes	No 1	Yes	No 1	No 2	No 1, 2	Yes
1002	Area Requirement 2	Yes	Yes	Yes	Yes	No 3	Yes	No 3	Note 3	Yes	Yes
1003	Area Requirement 6	Yes	Note 5	Note 5	Yes	No 3	No 3	No 5	Yes	Yes	Yes
1004	Area Requirement 3	Yes	Yes	Yes	Yes	Yes	Yes	Note 6	Note 3	Yes	Yes
1005	Area Requirement 4	Yes	Note 7	Yes	Yes	Yes	Yes	Yes	Yes	Yes	Yes
1006	Engagement Requirement 1	Note 2	Yes	Yes	Yes	Yes	Yes	Yes	Note 3	Yes	Yes
1007	EncounterCharacter Requirement 1	Yes	Note 1	Yes	Yes	No 1	Yes	No 1	No 2	No 1, 2	Yes
1008	EncounterCharacter Requirement 2	Yes	No 11	Yes	Yes	Yes	Note 8	Yes	No 6	Yes	Note 9
1009	EncounterCharacter Requirement 3	Yes	Yes	Yes	Yes	Yes	Yes	Yes	Note 3	Yes	Yes
1010	EncounterCharacter Requirement 4	Note 11	Yes	Yes	Yes	Yes	Note 12	Note 12	No 7	Yes	Yes
1011	EncounterGame Requirement 1	Yes	Yes	Yes	Yes	Yes	Yes	Yes	Note 13	Yes	Yes
1012	Foreign Character Requirement 1	Note 11	Yes	Yes	Yes	Yes	Yes	No 8, 9	Yes	Yes	Yes
1013	Player Character Requirement 1	Yes	Yes	Yes	Yes	Yes	No 10	Yes	Note 15	Yes	Yes
1014	Player Character Requirement 2	Yes	Yes	Yes	Yes	No 12	No 12	No 12	Note 3	No 12	Yes
1015	Player Character Requirement 3	Yes	Yes	Yes	Yes	Note 10	Note 10	Yes	Yes	Yes	Yes

EncounterCharacter Requirement 1 ("Name of game character"). (Not inspected yet) Every game character in the Encounter video game shall have a unique name of up to 15 characters.

EncounterCharacter Requirement 2 ("Qualities of game characters"). (Not inspected yet) Every game character has the same set of qualities, each having a floating point value. These are initialized to 100/n, where n is the number of qualities. The qualities are attention span, endurance, intelligence, patience, and strength.

EncounterCharacter Requirement 3 ("Image of game character"). (Not inspected yet) Every game character will be shown using an image that takes up no more than 1/8 of the monitor screen.

EncounterCharacter Requirement 4 ("Engagement with foreign character"). (Not inspected yet) Whenever an Encounter game character enters an area containing another game character and one of them is player-controlled, the player character may either choose or be obliged by the game to engage the other character. Whether there is a choice or not is controlled by the game in a random way on a 50% basis.

EncounterGame Requirement 1 ("Encounter game object"). (Not inspected yet) There shall be a single EncounterGame object.

ForeignCharacter Requirement 1 ("Freddie foreign character object"). (Not inspected yet) There shall be a foreign character named "Freddie," all of whose qualities have equal values and whose image is shown in Figure 4.57.

PlayerCharacter Requirement 1 ("Configurability"). (Not inspected yet) Whenever all foreign players are absent from an area, the player may set the values of his or her qualities using the PlayerQuality-Window, as long as the sum of the quality values remains the same.

PlayerCharacter Requirement 2 ("Main player character"). (Not inspected yet) The player shall have complete control over a particular game character called the main character.

PlayerCharacter Requirement 3 ("Living points") (Not inspected yet). Encounter shall produce the sum of the values of the character's qualities, called its living points.

We will show typical results of an inspection of these requirements. One inspection comment about this set as a whole is that the requirements do not support enough expansion of the game into a competitive product. A more particular defect is that the requirements do not properly specify the delay involved in setting a player's quality values; during the delay the player is subjected to an engagement in an unprepared state. (If the delay is too small, the player simply sets the qualities required for the area as high as possible and the game is not much of a challenge.) Let's inspect the list of proposed detailed requirements one at a time.

Table 13.3 is an example of a form that can be used for the inspection of detailed requirements, applied to the above list. Most of the metrics previously described in this chapter can be computed from this table.

The table contains "Notes" and "No" notes.

Here are the "No" notes:

1. Can a game character or area have a name with no characters?

2. The number 15 is rigid.

3. Only one?

4. If the player controls several characters, are all of their areas to be displayed or does this have to do only with the main player character?

5. Filling the entire monitor screen?

6. It should be easier to add new qualities or remove them.

7. When is there a Freddie? When does he appear?

8. In future releases, characters may mutate.

9. Clarify what stays the same.

10. Can the value of a quality be negative?

11. Ambiguous, because the player can't control everything that happens to the main character at all times.

12. Refine "complete control."

The "Notes" are as follows:

1. Is any keyboard character acceptable?

2. Check validity with the customer.

3. It is unclear how modifiable this should be.

4. It is hard to answer "complete" because it is unclear. See the note referenced in the "Clear" column for the issue.

5. We assume that the customer has some leeway in exactly what the "courtyard" will look like.

6. Are there dressing room exits to any other area?

7. This is somewhat clumsily written: could lead to misunderstanding.

8. It is usually preferable to have a single requirement match each attribute. This does not appear necessary, as the qualities will be treated alike.

9. Produce at any time? On request? Show at all times?

10. These details are not mentioned in the high-level requirements: check with customer.

11. Clarify "50% basis," if possible.

12. For Internet versions, it may become necessary to have more than one instance of an EncounterGame object. We will not exclude this possibility in future iterations.

13. It is not clear in what directions this could be modified.

14. Is the requirement written in such a way that it will be possible to trace it through to the code that implements it?

13.14 SUMMARY

The quality of a requirements document is reflected in how well it expresses customer wants and needs. To help ensure that requirements are of high quality, we focus on attributes they should possess. They include the following:

- Accessible

- Comprehensive

- Understandable

- Unambiguous

- Consistent

- Prioritized

- Secure

- Self-complete

- Testable

- Traceable

Requirements are inspected after they are written. They are the first software process documents that can be inspected against prior documentation (the customer requirements). It can be very productive to inspect requirements against each of the attributes listed above.

13.15 EXERCISES

1. (This is intended to be a closed book exercise.) List the qualities that requirements should possess (one example: precise). In your own words, describe the meaning of each.

2. Explain why the following requirement for a book sales site is ambiguous. Modify the requirement to make it unambiguous.

   "Orders that include special edition books and overnight delivery or exceed $100 must be processed over the phone."

3. Provide an example of three requirements for an order entry system that are inconsistent. How would you modify them to make them consistent?

4. For the order entry system in Exercise 3, provide three requirements that are not testable, and explain why each is not testable. Provide a modified version of each requirement to make it testable.

5. Your instructor will pair up student project teams. Conduct an inspection of the other team's detailed requirements. Evaluate the requirements against the list of metrics described in this chapter. Prepare a table such as Table 13.3 to summarize your results.

14

Formal and Emerging Methods in Requirements Analysis: An Introduction (Online Chapter)

To access this online chapter please visit www.wiley.com/college/braude.

15
Principles of Software Design

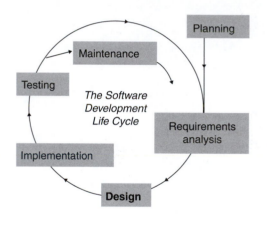

- • What are the goals of software design?

- • How do you use various design models for a single application?

- • What are use case model, class models, data flow models, and state models?

- • How are frameworks used in design?

- • What are the IEEE standards for expressing designs?

- • How does a team prepare for design in practice?

The Software Development Life Cycle

- Planning
- Maintenance
- Testing
- Implementation
- Design
- Requirements analysis

Figure 15.1 The context and learning goals for this chapter

A "software design" is a representation, or model, of the software to be built. Its purpose is to enable programmers to implement the requirements by designating the projected parts of the implementation. It is a set of documents containing text and diagrams to serve as the base on which an application can be fully programmed. A complete software design should be so explicit that a programmer could code the application from it without the need for any other documents. Software designs are like the blueprints of a building that are sufficient for a contractor to build the required building. They can be understood in two parts: high-level design, often referred to as "software architecture," which is generally indispensable, and all other design, referred to as "detailed design." It can be beneficial to make designs very detailed, short of being actual code. This is because engineers can examine a detailed design for defects and improvements prior to the creation of code rather than examining only the code. The benefits of a fully detailed design are balanced against the time required to document and maintain detailed designs. For large efforts, levels in between high level and detailed design may be identified.

This chapter introduces the concepts, needs, and terminology of software design. It sets the stage for the remaining chapters in this part of the book, which include various concrete examples.

15.1 THE GOALS OF SOFTWARE DESIGN

The first goal of a software design is to be *sufficient* for satisfying the requirements. Usually, software designs must also anticipate changes in the requirements, and so a second goal is *flexibility*. Another goal of software design is *robustness*: the ability of the product to anticipate a broad variety of input. These and other goals are summarized in Figure 15.2.

These goals sometimes oppose one another. For example, to make a design efficient it may be necessary to combine modules in ways that limit flexibility. In fact, we trade off goals against each other in ways that depend on the project's priorities.

A software design is *sufficient* if it provides the components for an implementation that satisfies the requirements. To assess such sufficiency, one needs to be able to understand it. This fact is obvious, but it has profound consequences. It can be difficult to create an understandable design for applications due to the large number of options that are typically available. OpenOffice, for example, is a very complex application when viewed in complete detail. Yet OpenOffice is simple when viewed at a high level, as consisting of a few subapplications: word processing, spreadsheet, presentations, and database.

Modularity is thus a key to understandability. Software is modular when it is divided into separately named and addressable components. Modular software is much easier to understand than monolithic software, and parts can be replaced without affecting other parts. It is easier to plan, develop, modify, document, and test. When software is modular you can more easily assign different people to work on different parts.

A design is a form of communication. In its most elementary form, it documents the result of a designer's thought process, and is used to communicate back to himself thereafter when he needs to know what he designed. This is fine if the designer is to be the only person who has this need, but a project usually involves several people throughout its lifetime. If a design is not *understandable* for them, it is of limited value, and the project's health is at risk. Design simplification, in particular, frequently results in a better design. Understandability is usually achieved by organizing the design as a progression from a high level with a manageable number of parts, then increasing the detail on the parts.

A good software architect and designer forms a clear mental model of how the application will work at an overall level, then develops a decomposition to match this mental model. She first asks the key modularity

---

- *Sufficiency:* handles the requirements
- *Understandability:* can be understood by intended audience
- *Modularity:* divided into well-defined parts
- *Cohesion:* organized so like-minded elements are grouped together
- *Coupling:* organized to minimize dependence between elements
- *Robustness:* can deal with wide variety of input
- *Flexibility:* can be readily modified to handle changes in requirements
- *Reusability:* can use parts of the design and implementation in other applications
- *Information hiding:* module internals are hidden from others
- *Efficiency:* executes within acceptable time and space limits
- *Reliability:* executes with acceptable failure rate

Figure 15.2 Principal goals of software design

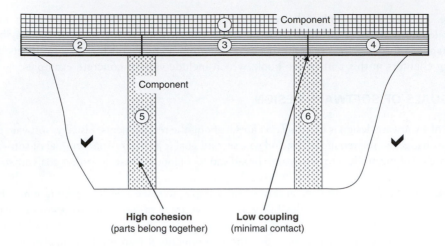

Figure 15.3 High cohesion and low coupling—bridge example

question such as: What five or six modules should we use to decompose a personal finance application? What four or five modules neatly encompass a word processing application? After deciding this, she turns to decomposing the components, and so on. This process is sometimes called "recursive design" because it repeats the design process on design components at successively fine scales. Software decomposition itself involves consideration of *cohesion* and *coupling*.

Cohesion within a module is the degree to which the module's elements belong together. In other words, it is a measure of how focused a module is. The idea is not just to divide software into arbitrary parts (i.e., modularity), but to keep related issues in the same part. Coupling describes the degree to which modules communicate with other modules. The higher the degree of coupling, the harder it is to understand and change the system. To modularize effectively, we *maximize cohesion* and *minimize coupling*. This principle helps to decompose complex tasks into simpler ones.

Software engineering uses Unified Modeling Language (UML) as a principal means of explaining design. Understanding software design concepts by means of analogous physical artifacts is helpful to some, and we will employ this means on occasion. Figure 15.3, for example, suggests coupling/cohesion goals by showing an architecture for a bridge, in which each of the six components has a great deal of cohesion and where the coupling between them is low. The parts of each bridge component belong together (e.g., the concrete and the embedded metal reinforcing it)—this is high cohesion. On the other hand, each component depends on just a few other components—two or three, in fact. This is low coupling.

The "Steel truss" in Figure 15.4, on the other hand, shows many components depending on each other at one place. We would question this high degree of coupling.

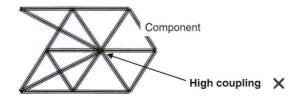

Figure 15.4 A questionable architecture—high coupling in a truss

- *Obtaining more or less of what's already present*
  Example: handle more kinds of accounts without needing to change the existing design or code
- *Adding new kinds of functionality*
  Example: add *withdraw* to existing *deposit* function
- *Changing functionality*
  Example: allow withdrawals to create an overdraft

Figure 15.5 Aspects of flexibility: ways in which an application may be required to change

Low coupling and high cohesion are particularly important for software design because we typically need to modify applications on an ongoing basis. Compare the life cycle of a typical software application with that of the bridge in Figure 15.3: the likelihood that the software will require modification is many times greater. Low coupled/high cohesion architectures are far easier to modify, since they tend to minimize the effects of changes.

The number of top-level packages in an architecture should be small so that people can comprehend the result. A range of "7 ± 2" is a useful guideline, although specific projects can vary greatly from this range for special reasons. As an example, OpenOffice would be hard to understand if we decomposed it into 100 parts instead of four as follows: "word processing, spreadsheet, presentations, and database." The mind has much trouble thinking of 100 separate things at more or less the same time. The difference between small- and large-scale projects (such as OpenOffice) is the amount of nesting of modules or packages. Projects typically decompose each top-level package into subpackages, these into subsubpackages, and so on. The "7 ± 2" guideline applies to each of these decompositions.

A design or implementation is *robust* if it is able to handle miscellaneous and unusual conditions. These include bad data, user error, programmer error, and environmental conditions. A design for the video store application is robust if it deals with attempts to enter DVDs with wrong or inconsistent information, or customers who don't exist or who have unusually long names, or if it handles late rental situations of all kinds. Robustness is an important consideration for applications that must handle communication.

The requirements of an application can change in many ways, and as a result a design must be *flexible* to accommodate these changes. Figure 15.5 illustrates ways in which an application may change.

A set of previously used *design patterns* is a useful resource for flexible designs. Design patterns are discussed in Chapter 17. We design so that parts of our own applications can be *reused* by others and ourselves. Figure 15.6 lists the types of artifacts that often can be reused.

We can reuse . . . .

- **Object code** (or equivalent)
  Example: sharing dlls between word processor and spreadsheet
- **Classes**—in source code form
  Example: Customer class used by several applications
  Thus, we write generic code whenever possible
- **Assemblies of related classes**
  Example: the java.awt package
- **Patterns** of class assemblies

Figure 15.6 Types of reuse

As an example of class reuse, consider the class *DVDRental* that associates the DVD and the customer renting it. Such a class is reusable only in another application dealing with the rental of DVDs, which is limited. If, however, we design a *Rental* class dealing with the rental of an *Item* to a *Customer*, and if *DVDRental* inherits from *Rental*, then we would be able to reuse the *Rental* portion for other applications due to its generality. Design patterns facilitate the reuse of assemblies of related classes rather than individual ones.

Information hiding is a design principle in which the internals of a module are deliberately not usable by code that does not need to know the details. This is supported in object-oriented languages by declaring a public interface through which user code accesses the objects of a class. Private methods and attributes are only accessible to the objects of the class itself. Information hiding allows the internals of a module to be modified without the users of the module having to change. It also reduces complexity because the module interface is fixed and well defined; using code need not be concerned with internal details.

Efficiency refers to the use of available machine cycles and memory. We create designs and implementations that are as fast as required, and that make use of no more than the required amount of RAM and disk. Efficient designs are often achieved in stages as follows. First, a design is conceived without regard to efficiency; efficiency bottlenecks are then identified, and finally the original design is modified. As an example, consider the use of maps on the Web. When the user browses a map and wants to move to an adjacent area, early algorithms required a separate page fetch. Algorithms were introduced, however, to automatically fetch appropriate adjacent maps after the initial fetch, improving efficiency and, with it, the user's experience. It is ideal if efficiency is considered at the time of initial design, however.

It is unrealistic to expect that a real-world application be 100 percent defect-free. An application is *reliable* if it falls within a predetermined standard of fault occurrence. Metrics make this precise, such as the average time between failures. Reliability is related to but different from robustness. Robustness is mostly a design issue because one must specifically accommodate erroneous data in advance—accommodating it does not happen by accident or experience. On the other hand, reliability is mostly a process issue, requiring thorough inspection and testing of artifacts. Design affects reliability in that clean designs make it easier for developers to produce error-free applications. However, a wide range of other factors make for reliability, because an application can fail for a wide variety of reasons.

15.2 INTEGRATING DESIGN MODELS

The architectural drawings of an office building comprise the front elevation, the side elevation, the electrical plan, the plumbing plan, and so on. In other words, several different views are required to express a building's architecture. Similarly, several different views are required to express a software design. They are called *models*.

Four important models are shown in Figure 15.7, and they are explained next. Several ideas here are taken from the Unified Software Development method of Booch, Jacobson, and Rumbaugh. Figure 15.7 includes an example from the Encounter video game case study to illustrate the four models and how they fit together.

The subsequent sections of this chapter elaborate on these models so that they can be contrasted and combined with each other. Subsequent chapters in this part of the book provide detailed examples of each.

15.2.1 Use Case Model

This section describes several levels of use cases and related concepts. The *use case model* consists of the following four parts:

1. The *business use cases*: a narrative form, suitable for developer-to-customer communication, describing the required basic sequences of actions

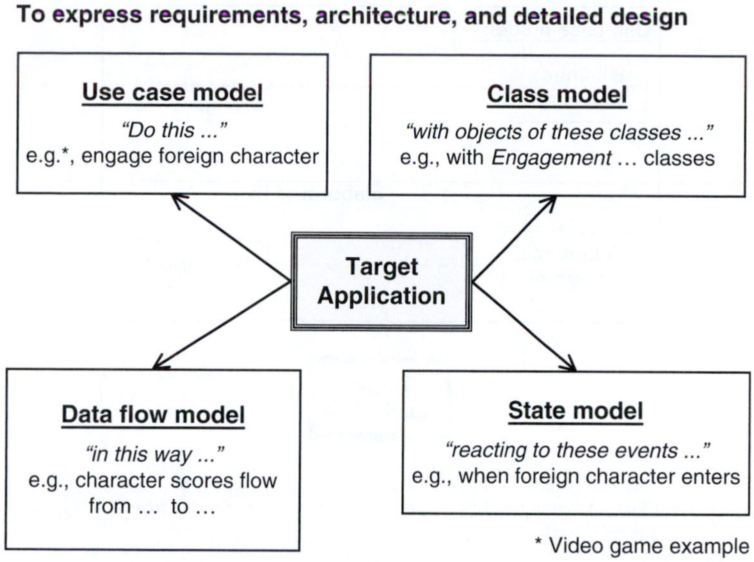

To express requirements, architecture, and detailed design

Figure 15.7 Models to express designs (and parts of requirements)

2. Their refinement into regular *use cases*, described in Chapter 11

3. Their transformation into *sequence diagrams* (covered in Chapter 16), which in turn can be in two successive stages of refinement:

   (a) With informal functionality descriptions, at first lacking all details

   (b) With specific function names and showing all details

4. *Scenarios*: instances of use cases that contain specifics, and that can be used for testing. For example, a scenario of the use case step

   Customer chooses account

   would be something like

   John Q. Smith chooses checking account 12345.

The use case model expresses what the application is supposed to do, as suggested in Figure 15.8.

15.2.2 Class Models

Classes are the building blocks—more precisely, the types of building blocks—of designs. Class models consist of *packages* (a grouping of classes) that decompose into smaller packages, and so on, which decompose into classes, and these, in turn, decompose primarily into methods. This is shown in Figure 15.9. We cover classes in more detail in Chapter 16.

15.2.3 Data Flow Models

The class model describes the *kinds* of objects involved; it does not show actual objects. The *data flow model*, on the other hand, shows specific objects and the types of data flowing between them. It is related to the class

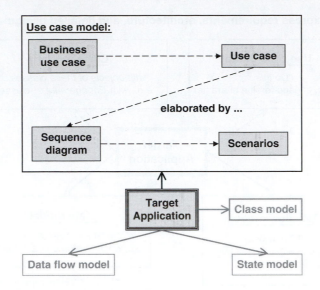

Figure 15.8 The role of use case models in design

model, because the objects involved must belong to the classes in the class model. We discuss data flow diagrams in Chapter 16. Figure 15.10 shows the parts of a data flow model.

15.2.4 State Models

State models reflect reactions to events. Events include mouse actions and changes in variable values. Events are not described in class models or component models, but they do occur in the state model. We introduced states in Chapter 11 as one way to describe the requirements of an application. The states in that context describe the external behavior of the application. The states we are referring to here reflect the state of

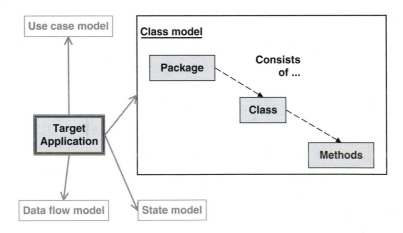

Figure 15.9 The role of class models in design

Source: Jacobson, Ivar, ''Object Oriented Software Engineering: A Use Case Driven Approach,'' Addison-Wesley, 1992.

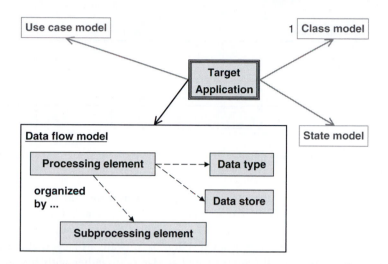

Figure 15.10 The role of component models in design

Source: Jacobson, Ivar, "Object Oriented Software Engineering: A Use Case Driven Approach," Addison-Wesley, 1992.

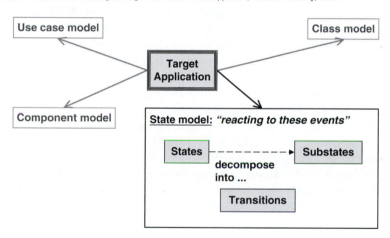

Figure 15.11 The role of state models in design

Source: Jacobson, Ivar, "Object Oriented Software Engineering: A Use Case Driven Approach," Addison-Wesley, 1992.

elements in a software design. The role of state models is shown in Figure 15.11. They are described in more detail in Chapter 16.

15.3 FRAMEWORKS

As we have seen, the *reuse* of components is a major goal in software development. If an organization can't leverage its investments in the skill of its designers and programmers by using their work several times over, competitors who do so will be faster to market with superior products. The parts of an application that are particular to it and are not reused are often called its *business logic*. Business classes are essentially the domain classes discussed in Chapter 12.

Where do we keep the classes slated for reuse? How do we organize them? Should we build in relationships among these classes? Do they control the application or does the application control them? The computing

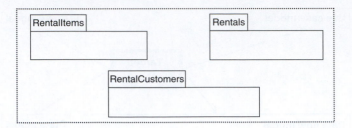

Figure 15.12 A framework for rental applications

community has learned from experience that merely making a list of available functionality does not necessarily result in reuse. We have learned, however, that arrangements like the Java API (coherent sets of classes) do indeed lend themselves to highly successful reuse. The Java APIs (*3D, 2D, Swing*, etc.) are *frameworks*.

A *framework*, sometimes called a *library*, is a collection of software artifacts usable by several different applications. These artifacts are typically implemented as classes, together with the software required to utilize them. A framework is a kind of common denominator for a family of applications. Progressive development organizations designate selected classes as belonging to their framework. Typically, a framework begins to emerge by the time a development organization develops its second to fourth application. As an example, consider the *Rental* framework shown in Figure 15.12 that our video store application could use. This architecture divides the elements into the items that can be rented (books, DVDs, etc.), the people who can rent them, and the rental records that associate members from the first two parts.

The individual classes in the framework will be supplied later. Frameworks like these are usually obtained in a combined bottom-up and top-down manner: bottom-up by examining the structure of actual application architectures such as the video store application, seeking more general forms; and top-down by conceptualizing about the needs of a particular family of applications such as rentals.

Classes within a framework may be related. They may be abstract or concrete. Applications may use them by means of inheritance, aggregation, or dependency. Alternatively, as we will see below, a framework may feel like a generic application that we customize by inserting our own parts.

Figure 15.13 shows the relationship between framework classes, domain classes, and the remaining design classes. The design for an application consists of (1) the domain classes (that are special to the

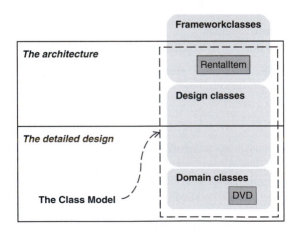

Figure 15.13 Class model vs. architecture and detailed design

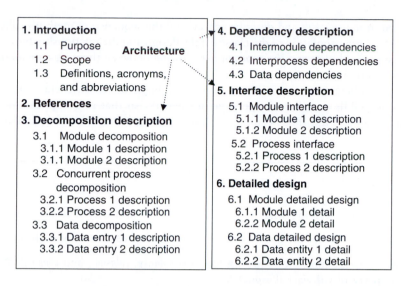

Figure 15.14 IEEE 1016-1998 SDD example table of contents

application), (2) some of the framework classes (generally speaking, not all are needed), and (3) the remaining classes needed to complete the design, which we are calling simply "design" classes. The design classes consist of those required for the architecture and those that are not. The latter are effectively the detail design classes, required to complete the design. These three constitute the class model for the application. All of the domain classes are in the detailed design because they are very specific. The framework classes used are part of the application's architecture.

The framework classes used in the design are part of an application's architecture, as shown in the figure. The domain classes are usually part of the detailed design since they are specific to the application and are not architectural in nature.

15.4 IEEE STANDARDS FOR EXPRESSING DESIGNS

The IEEE Software Design Document (SDD) standard 1016-1998 provides guidelines for the documentation of design. The table of contents is shown in Figure 15.14. IEEE guidelines explain how the SDD could be organized for various architectural styles, most of which are described above. The case study uses the IEEE standard, with a few modifications, to account for an emphasis on the object-oriented perspective. As shown in Figure 15.14, Sections 1 through 5 can be considered software architecture, and Section 6 can be considered the detailed design, to be covered in the next chapter.

15.5 SUMMARY

Software design is a model of the intended software application, as specified by its requirements. A software design is analogous to the blueprints of a house.

Good software designs should exhibit the following characteristics: sufficiency, understandability, modularity, high cohesion, low coupling, robustness, flexibility, reusability, information hiding, efficiency, and reliability.

When expressing a software design, it is helpful to use several different connected views, or models. A use case model describes what the application is intended to do from the point of view of the user. Sequence diagrams are derived from use cases and describe objects and the sequence of methods calls between them. Class models are a static representation of the classes of the design and the relationship between them. A data flow model shows specific objects and the types of data flowing between them. A state model shows design elements and their reaction to events.

Frameworks are collections of reusable software that implements a general solution to a general problem. For example, GUIs are often designed via frameworks so that new applications do not have to rewrite code to implement a GUI. They can instead leverage the existing GUI code and just add their own customization.

15.6 EXERCISES

1. Write a paragraph describing what a "software design" is, and why it is important.

2. In your own words, define the goals of software design and explain why each goal is important.

3. In your own words, define the following terms: *modularity*, *cohesion*, and *coupling*. Why is each a desirable property of software designs?

4. Can a design be cohesive and exhibit a high degree of coupling? Explain your answer and provide an example.

5. How might coupling and reusability be related? How might cohesion and reusability be related? Explain your answer and provide one example for each.

6. In your own words, explain what is meant by *robustness*. Below is code for a method *divide()*. Make the method more robust in at least two ways.

```
public double divide( Double aNumerator, Double aDenominator )
{
  return aNumerator.doubleValue() / aDenominator.doubleValue();
}
```

7. Using the Internet, research one of the many Java API frameworks (e.g., Swing, JMF, 2D, 3D). In a few paragraphs, describe the design of the framework and how it accommodates reuse.

8. Provide a modularization for an application that advises clients on stock picks, and enables them to transfer funds among various stocks and savings accounts. Explain your solution. *Hint:* One reasonable solution employs four packages.

16

The Unified Modeling Language

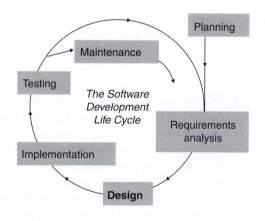

- What is the UML notation for classes and packages of classes?

- How does UML represent class relationships such as inheritance, aggregation, and dependency?

- What is a sequence diagram?

- How do UML activity diagrams relate to flow charts?

Figure 16.1 The context and learning goals for this chapter

Recall that a "software design" is a representation, or model, of the software to be built. For many years, software engineers relied on a miscellany of somewhat unrelated graphical means for getting across the point of their designs. Their principal means were data flow diagrams, flowcharts, and ways to picture the location of physical files. These were never very satisfactory. With the advent and wide acceptance of object-oriented methods, leaders in the software engineering community began to pool and relate their ideas for notation and graphical representation of software designs. Classes, for example, now needed to be represented in design figures. The Unified Modeling Language (UML) is the result.

In this chapter we introduce the UML, which is now a widely accepted, largely graphical notation for expressing object-oriented designs. The UML standard is managed by the nonprofit Object Management

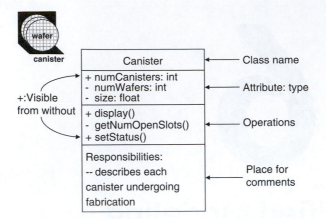

Figure 16.2 Class details in UML

Group consortium of companies (www.omg.org), and takes hundreds of pages to formally specify. As a result, UML tends to be inclusive (some say too much so), incorporating data flow and, in effect, flowcharts; but it contains much more that we do not have space in this book to include. The parts that we do cover, however, are adequate for most of our needs. UML is an excellent step in the direction of improving software engineering, but will probably be improved upon as the discipline evolves.

The chapter describes class relationships in UML, including inheritance (Class Models, Section 16.2) a way to represent control among functions (Sequence Diagrams, Section 16.5), diagrams of state, events, and transitions (Section 16.6), its modernization of flow charts (Activity Diagrams, Section 16.7), and finally data flow diagrams (Section 16.8). Section 16.9 shows an example that combines these.

16.1 CLASSES IN UML

Classes in UML are represented by rectangles containing the class name at a minimum. The detailed version includes attribute and operation names, signatures, visibility, return types, and so on. Figure 16.2 shows a class from the detailed design of an application that controls the flow in a chip manufacturing plant of canisters holding wafers.

Not all of the attributes need be specified in the class model. We show as much detail as needed, neither more nor less. Showing more detail clutters a diagram and can make it harder to understand. Some required attributes may be left to the discretion of the implementers. It is also common to omit accessor functions from class models (e.g., *getSize()* and *setSize()*) since these can be inferred from the presence of the corresponding attributes (*size*).

As an example of a class, consider an application that assists the user in drawing a simple figure of a person using geometric shapes. We'd probably want a *Rectangle* class for this with attributes such as *length* and *breadth*. Since the application is supposed to be smart, we'd want it to use the concept of a foot (e.g., to know where feet belong), so we'd probably want a *Foot* class. By introducing these classes, we are improving the cohesion of related parts, such as the attributes of a foot, the understandability of the design, and its modularity. We are also hiding information until it's needed. This example will be explored as we go through this chapter, and will be described as a whole in Section 16.9.

16.2 CLASS RELATIONSHIPS IN UML

This section discusses the way in which UML collects classes and such in packages. It also introduces relationships called associations.

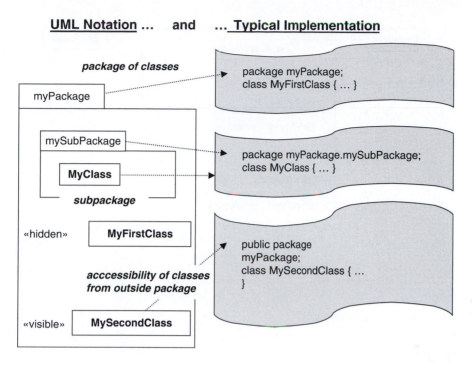

Figure 16.3 UML notation for packages and Java implementation

16.2.1 Packages

The Unified Modeling Language uses the term *package* for collecting design elements such as classes. UML packages can contain subpackages, or any materials associated with an application, including source code, designs, documentation, and so on. Figure 16.3 shows the UML notation for packages and subpackages. Classes within a package can be specified as accessible or as inaccessible from code external to the package. "Package" also happens to be the name of collections of Java classes. Java packages translate into file directories; their subpackages decompose into subdirectories, and so on. The Java implementation of this is shown in Figure 16.3.

16.2.2 Associations

Attributes are one way of showing the properties of a class, and are generally used to denote simple types such as integers or Booleans. *Association* is an additional method of indicating class properties, and is commonly used to denote that objects of two classes depend on each other in a structural way. Associations are drawn with a solid line between two classes. We can annotate the relationship, which may be one- or two-way. Two-way associations are problematical because we need to be sure that both ends of the implied information are kept consistent. This is illustrated in Figure 16.4.

Consider an application that assists the user in drawing a simple figure of a person. We may want a *FootShape* class if the shape of a foot needs to be described (promoting the "sufficiency" of the design). There would be an association between *FootShape* and *Foot*, indicating coupling between the two. This example is described as a whole in Section 16.9.

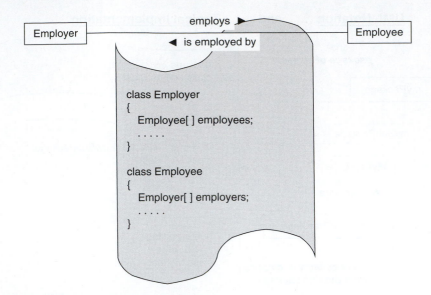

Figure 16.4 UML notation for associations

16.3 MULTIPLICITY

The ends of an association line can be annotated with *multiplicity*, which describes the numerical relationship, or the number of instances, of each class. For example, consider the *Employer/Employee* relationship as shown in Figure 16.5. The "1..3" next to *Employer* indicates that each instance (object) of an *Employee* can be associated with 1–3 instances of an *Employer*. Conversely, the "1..∗" next to *Employee* means that each instance of an *Employer* can be associated with a minimum of one *Employer* (with no maximum). In other words, the multiplicity next to a class indicates how many instances of that class are associated with one instance of the class at the other end of the association line. A single value can be used to indicate an exact number of objects. If a multiplicity is not present next to a class, the assumed value is 1. This is also illustrated in Figure 16.5, which shows that one *Employee* is associated with exactly one *PersonalInfo* instance, and vice versa.

16.4 INHERITANCE

In UML, *inheritance* describes a relationship between classes in which one class assumes the attributes and operations of another. It is often thought of as an "is-a" relationship. For example, since an *Employee* "is-a" *Person*, we can express their relationship with inheritance by saying that an Employee inherits from a *Person*. UML

Figure 16.5 Multiplicity of associations in UML

UML Inheritance   ... and   ... _Typical Implementation_

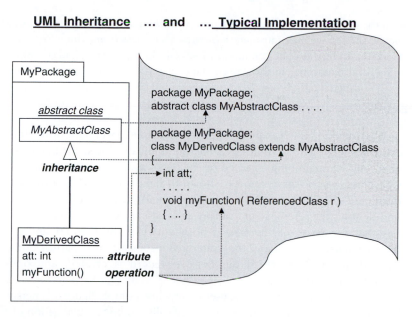

Figure 16.6 Inheritance in UML and Java implementation

indicates inheritance with an open triangle. We refer to the class being inherited from (e.g., _Person_) as a _base_ class; the class doing the inheriting (e.g., _Employee_) is a _derived_ class.

Figure 16.6 shows an example of a package consisting of two classes: _MyAbstractClass_ and _MyDerivedClass_, with _MyDerivedClass_ inheriting from _MyAbstractClass_.

Abstract classes—that is, those classes that cannot be instantiated into objects—are denoted with italics. _Interfaces_ are collections of method prototypes (name, parameter types, return types, and exceptions thrown). Classes _realize_ interfaces by implementing the methods that the interface promises. The UML notation is shown in Figure 16.7.

It is customary to arrange class models so that base classes are physically above derived classes. However, this positioning is not necessary in any technical sense.

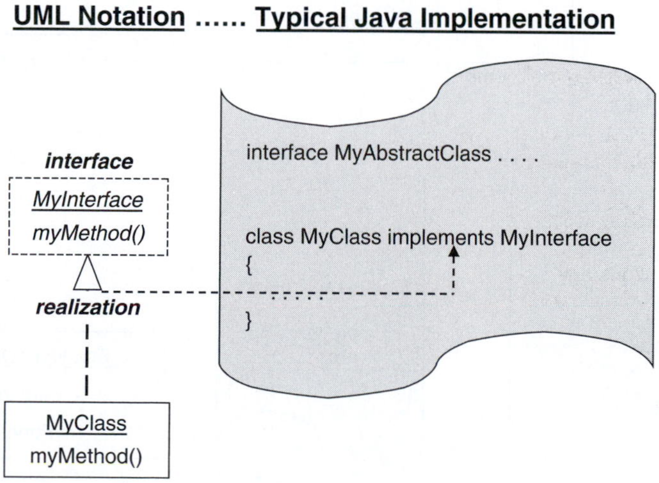

UML Notation ...... _Typical Java Implementation_

interface
MyInterface
myMethod()

realization

MyClass
myMethod()

interface MyAbstractClass . . . .

class MyClass implements MyInterface
{

}

Figure 16.7 Interfaces in UML and Java implementation

Consider again the application that assists the user in drawing a simple figure of a person. Since it deals with various geometric shapes, we may introduce a *GeometricShape* class from which *Rectangle* and such inherit. This saves us from having to repeat code common to *Rectangle*, *Circle*, *Triangle*, and so on, thereby promoting modularity, flexibility, and reusability in the design. This example is described as a whole in Section 16.9.

16.4.1 Aggregation

Aggregation is a type of association that can be thought of as a whole–part relationship. It is denoted with an open diamond next to the aggregator (whole). Aggregation indicates the structural inclusion of objects of one class by another, and is usually implemented by means of a class (whole) having an attribute whose type is the included class (part). Aggregation is shown in Figure 16.8, with both *Company* and *EmployeeDirectory* each considered a "whole," and each consisting of multiple *Employees*, the "parts." The label "emp" next to the diamond denotes the reference in *Company* and *Employer* to the aggregated *Employee*. The use of aggregation implies that if a particular *Employee* is both a part of the *Company* and part of the *EmployeeDirectory*, then the two aggregators "share" the Employee instance that is part of both. That is, if "Jane Doe" is an *Employee*, then one instance of her *Employee* record is created, and both Company and EmployeeDirectory reference that instance.

Returning to the application that assists the user in drawing a simple figure of a person, the association between *Foot* and *FootShape* probably turns out, more specifically, to be an aggregation of *FootShape* by *Foot*. This example is described as a whole in Section 16.9.

16.4.2 Composition

Composition is a stronger form of aggregation in which the aggregated object exists only during the lifetime (and for the benefit of) the composing object—no other object may reference it. The composed object is created and destroyed whenever the composing object is created and destroyed. Composition implies that the composed instance is not shared. For example, Figure 16.9 shows that *Employee* instances are structurally part of *Company* and *EmployeeDirectory*. For any given employee such as "Jane Doe," a separate instance of her Employee object is created as part of *Company* and *EmployeeDirectory*.

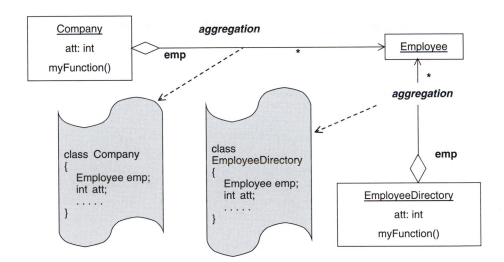

Figure 16.8 UML representation of aggregation and Java implementation

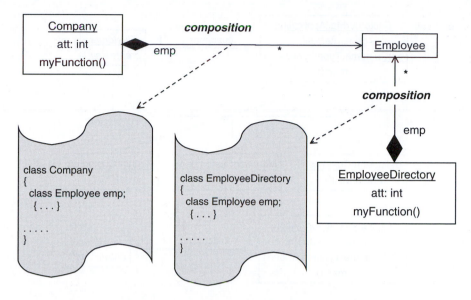

Figure 16.9 UML representation of composition and Java implementation

16.4.3 Dependency

Dependency, denoted with a dotted line arrow, means that one class depends upon another in the sense that if the class at arrow's end were to change, then this would affect the dependent class. Strictly speaking, dependency includes association, aggregation, composition, and inheritance. However, these relationships have their own notation, and we usually reserve dependency to indicate that a method of one class utilizes another class, and to relate packages. This is shown in Figure 16.10.

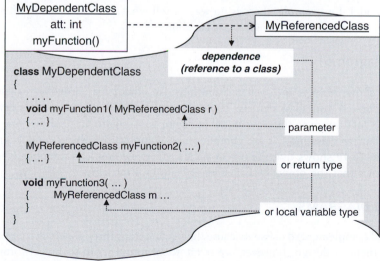

Figure 16.10 UML representation and Java implementation of dependence (excluding inheritance and aggregation)

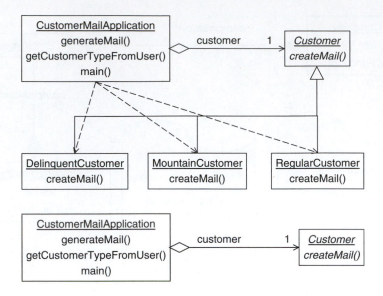

Figure 16.11 Example of a class diagram (class model) for a customer mail application

16.4.4 Class Diagrams

Class diagrams help us to visualize the design of applications. They describe the types of objects in the application, their attributes and operations, and the static relationships between them [1]. Consider an application producing e-mail text for various kinds of customers. A possible UML class diagram is shown in Figure 16.11. It says that the class *CustomerMailApplication* has a variable named *customer*, which is of type *Customer*. Since *Customer* is abstract, the *customer* variable is either a *DelinquentCustomer*, *MountainCustomer*, or *RegularCustomer*. When *customer.createMail()* is called, one of the three versions of *createMail()* is called, depending on the class that *customer* belongs to.

The strength of class diagrams is that they help us to envisage the building blocks of an application. Note, however, that they do not indicate the way in which the application executes. In the Customer Mail Application class model, for example, there is no way to tell what method executes after *main()*. Sequence diagrams, discussed in Section 16.5, provide this capability.

16.4.5 Object Diagrams

An object diagram shows objects and their relationships. An object is a particular realization of a class, so object models are derived from class models. There are many possible object models deriving from a class model. For example, let's return to the class model in Figure 16.4. Figure 16.12 shows one object model that derives from it. Whereas class models are compile-time relationships, object models are usually runtime relationships. Figure 16.12 shows that the object *ajaxCorp:Company* employs the objects *sue:Employee* and *joe: Employee*. It also shows that the object *abcCorp:Company* employs the object *joe:Employee*.

16.5 SEQUENCE DIAGRAMS

Use cases are a good complement to classes because they define steps through which a user and an application transition. To use them in design, however, we refine them into a more technical form so that class and methods that enable them can be identified. In addition, there are many sequences of actions that applications

Class Model

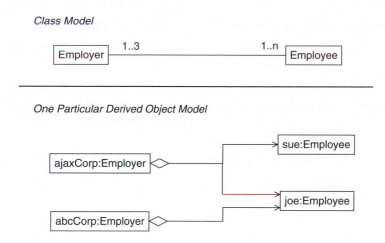

One Particular Derived Object Model

Figure 16.12 Example of a class model and a particular object model in UML derived from it

need to be designed for but are not use cases. The number of possible sequences of function calls—even common ones—is very large, whereas the number of use cases is kept relatively small (4–20 for small jobs and at most hundreds for extremely large ones). Sequence diagrams are graphical representations of control flow, and are particularly useful for describing executions that involve several *objects*, as found in the scenario of a use case. Sequence diagrams require us to think in terms of objects and functions. The lifetime of each object involved is shown as a solid vertical line, with the name of the object and its class at the top. Each interaction between objects is shown by means of a horizontal arrow from the object initiating the service to the object supplying the service. As an example we develop a sequence diagram for the *Check Out* use case for the video store application. Figure 16.13 shows a beginning sequence diagram for the use case.

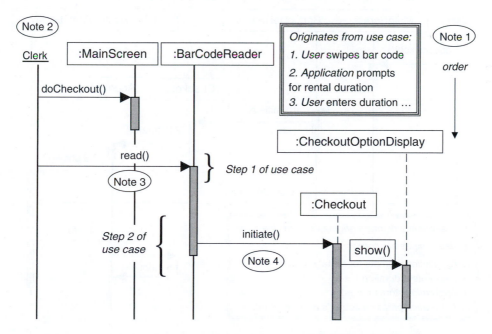

Figure 16.13 Beginning of a sequence diagram for *Check Out* use case in video store design

The following notes explain the corresponding features of the diagram:

Note 1: In a sequence diagram, time goes in a downward direction. In this example, *doCheckout()* occurs first, followed by *read()* and then *initiate()*, and so on.

Note 2: Use cases are initiated either by the user, as this one is, or by an object. Initiation begins at the top left of the diagram, and a solid vertical line beneath this symbol is drawn to indicate that the entity already exists. We can supply preconditions to specify assumptions that apply at the inception of the sequence.

Note 3: Sequence diagrams show the initiation and execution of a sequence of functions. The object at the beginning of each arrow *initiates* work; the object at the end of the arrow *carries out* the work of the method indicated. Each elongated rectangle denotes the execution of a method of the corresponding object.

In our *Check Out* sequence diagram, the clerk initiates the second function by swiping the bar code reader over the video. We then determine who or what should execute the responding function. Since a bar code reader recognizes a swipe, we may decide that a *BarCodeReader* object would be appropriate for dealing with actions relating to the physical reader, and that the required function of *BarCodeReader* will be named *read()*. There will be only one *BarCodeReader* object for the entire application, so the notation "*:BarCodeReader*" to represent this object is sufficient. There is no need to name a *BarCodeReader* object; we may decide later to make the *read()* method of *BarCodeReader* static, in which case no actual *BarCodeReader* object would be involved.

Note 4: We can capture the checkout process with a *Checkout* class. The *BarCodeReader* object then creates a *Checkout* object. We have used a factory method *initiate()* here to create and initialize the

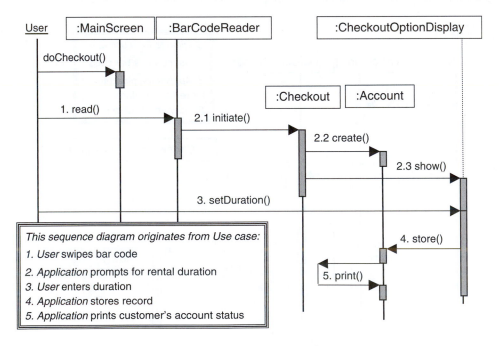

Figure 16.14 Sequence diagram for *Check Out* use case in video store design

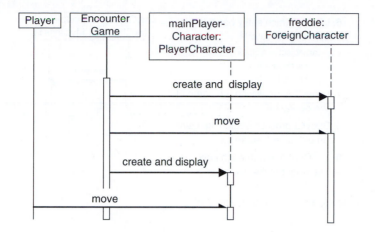

Figure 16.15 A sequence diagram showing concurrence

Checkout object. The method *initiate()* then creates a display for choosing checkout options and shows it on the console. A complete sequence diagram for the use case is given in Figure 16.14.

In the previous sequence diagrams, the solid arrow head indicates *synchronous* method calls, meaning that the caller receives control back when an operation is complete. Sequence diagrams show *asynchronous* messages using either stick arrow heads or half-arrows. An asynchronous message means that the caller does not wait for an operation to complete. Instead, control returns immediately back to the caller and the result, if any, is processed at a later time. The called method executes in a separate thread, either by spawning a new thread or executing within an existing thread. The elongated rectangle at the end of the arrow represents a thread that executes in parallel. As an example, we might want the game characters of Encounter to move independently from area to area during the action. This is shown in Figure 16.15 with both a *PlayerCharacter* and *ForeignCharacter* running in separate threads.

Figures 16.16 and 16.17 summarize the steps needed to create a sequence diagram.

When the initiator is the user, a simple label at the top suffices, rather than a rectangle. Note that the object responsible for executing the method named on the arrow is at the *end* (not the beginning) of the arrow.

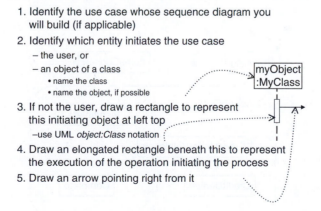

Figure 16.16 Steps for building a sequence diagram, 1 of 2

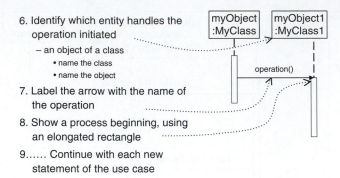

6. Identify which entity handles the operation initiated
   – an object of a class
     • name the class
     • name the object
7. Label the arrow with the name of the operation
8. Show a process beginning, using an elongated rectangle
9...... Continue with each new statement of the use case

Figure 16.17 Steps for building a sequence diagram, 2 of 2

16.6 STATE DIAGRAMS

We introduced the concept of state and transitions in Chapter 11 as a way to sometimes express requirements. A *state diagram* shows the states of the objects of a class, the events to which the object are sensitive, and the resulting transitions between them. State diagrams are also known as *state-transition diagrams* or *statecharts*.

16.6.1 States and Substates

In UML, substates of a state are simply shown as nested rounded rectangles. Figure 16.18 shows the states and substates that may be present in an *OnlineShopper* class. It shows that while a shopper is checking out, she can be having her credit validated.

   The state *Incomplete* indicates that the shopper has signaled a readiness to check out but has not yet submitted credit card information. The black dot and arrow indicate that *OnlineShopper* objects are initially in the *Browsing* state.

16.6.2 Events

In the context of state models, an *event* is something whose occurrence affects objects of the class in question. Examples of events are a button click on a *Button* object or a change in the value of an object's variable.

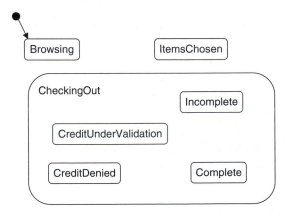

Figure 16.18 States and substates for *OnlineShopper* class

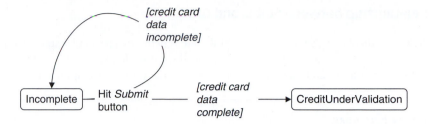

Figure 16.19 Conditions on events in UML and the resulting difference in transitions

16.6.3 Transitions

An event may cause an object to *transition* from its current state to another state. We denote a transition with an arrow, labeled with the name of the event causing the transition. For example, when a *Shopper* object in *Incomplete* state submits valid credit card information, it transitions from *Incomplete* state to *CreditUnderValidation* state.

Sometimes, when an object is in a given state and an event occurs, the object can transition to one of several states, depending on a *condition*. For example, when a shopper submits credit card information (by clicking the mouse or hitting *enter*), the resulting transition depends on whether or not the data are complete. As shown in Figure 16.19, conditions are denoted by square brackets in UML.

16.6.4 *OnlineShopper* State Diagram Example

A complete state-transition diagram for the *OnlineShopper* is shown in Figure 16.20. When the *Shopper* object enters the *CheckingOut* state, it automatically enters the substate *Incomplete* (more precisely, *CheckingOut. Incomplete*).

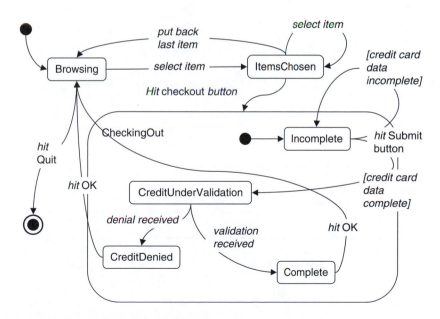

Figure 16.20 State-transition diagram for *OnlineShopper* class

16.6.5 The Relationship between States and GUIs

When an application is displaying a GUI, one can think of it as being in a particular state. Mouse or keyboard actions are *events* that affect this state. Although we may well want to define states that do not correspond to GUIs, and vice versa, a State↔GUI correspondence can be made for many applications.

16.7 ACTIVITY DIAGRAMS

Flowcharts are among the oldest graphical methods for depicting the flow of control of algorithms. The UML uses an extended form of flowcharts called *Activity Diagrams*. The notation for activity diagrams is shown in Figure 16.21. This example includes parallelism, showing the activities *Do a Task* and *Do Another Task* operating in parallel. Control is not passed to *Do Even More* until both have completed.

Figure 16.22 contains an activity diagram for a *setName()* method, showing the most commonly used flowchart constructs: decisions (diamonds) and processes (ovals).

The following example shows an activity diagram involving two classes. It describes the backward chaining algorithm for expert systems, and illustrates how flowcharting can be helpful in explaining complex algorithms. *Expert systems* are usually based on knowledge in the form of rules, which take the form

$$antecedent \text{ AND } antecedent \text{ AND } \ldots \text{ AND } antecedent \Rightarrow consequent$$

where *antecedent*s and *consequent*s are *facts*.

For example,

$$animal \text{ is } mammal \text{ AND } animal \text{ is } striped \Rightarrow animal \text{ is } zebra$$

Our facts will simply be strings such as "animal is mammal."

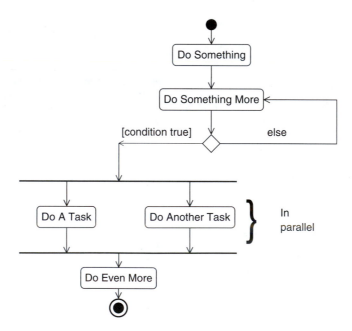

Figure 16.21 UML activity chart notation

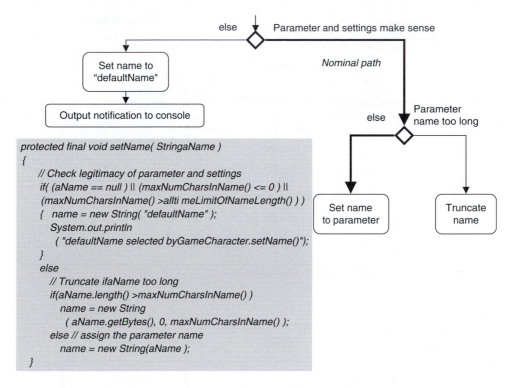

Figure 16.22 Activity diagram example

The problem is to build a program that, given the following:

- a list of facts, such as $\underline{A}$, $\underline{B}$, $\underline{Q}$, and

- a list of rules, such as $\underline{A\&R{\Rightarrow}L}$, $\underline{A\&B{\Rightarrow}C}$, and $\underline{B\&C{\Rightarrow}R}$

determines whether or not a given fact, such as L, can be deduced. The answer is "yes" for this example, because

$$A(known)\&B(known) \Rightarrow C;$$
$$B(known)\&C(just\ deduced) \Rightarrow R;$$
$$A(known)\&R(just\ deduced) \Rightarrow L.$$

We will store the current list of known facts as a static *Vector* of *Fact* called *factList*, and the list of known rules as a static *Vector* of *Rule* called *ruleBase*. We will simplify the setup of these lists by hard coding the example given above in the *Fact* and *Rule* classes. This is shown in Figure 16.23.

Our emphasis is on the harder part: the "backchaining" algorithm *proveBack()* for establishing whether or not a given fact, which we will name *soughtFact*, can be deduced from the given facts and rules. A flowchart for this algorithm is shown in Figure 16.24.

This activity diagram helps to simplify an otherwise complex algorithm. An inspection of the activity diagram might uncover the fact that it fails to terminate if there is a circular chain in the rule base such as $X \Rightarrow Y$ and $Y \Rightarrow X$.

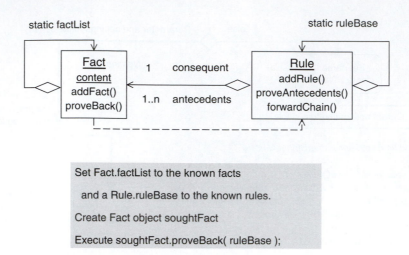

Figure 16.23 A class model for chaining rules in expert systems

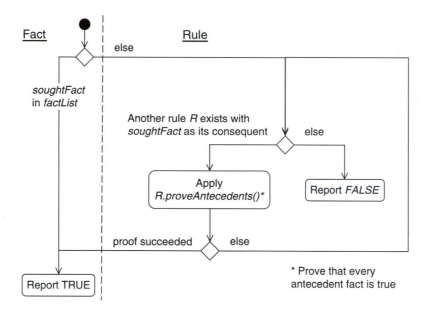

Figure 16.24 Activity for *soughtFact.proveBack()* involving two classes

16.8 DATA FLOW MODELS

Data flow models were introduced in Chapter 11 when we discussed requirements. Recall that they consist of *actions*, each of which takes place at a *node*. The UML notation for this is exemplified in Figure 16.25. Each node has input and output *pins* indicating the corresponding data type. Data stores are shown with rectangles and a *datastore* stereotype.

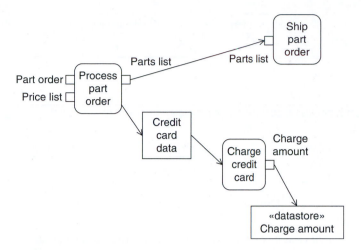

Figure 16.25 Data flow models in UML—an example

Source: Adopted from Jacobson, Ivar, Grady Booch and James Rumbaugh, ''The Unified Software Development Process,'' (Addison-Wesley Object Technology Series), Addison-Wesley, 1999.

16.9 A DESIGN EXAMPLE WITH UML

As an example that illustrates several parts of the UML notation in this chapter, consider a graphics studio specializing in drawing stick people. A GUI for this is illustrated in Figure 16.26.

We will focus only on the "foot" requirements. Certainly, there is a need for *Rectangle* and *Ellipse* classes. The first question is whether we need a *Foot* class. When we drag a rectangle near the end of a leg, the application has to know that we want it to be placed at the end of that leg in a standard position. Although it may well be possible to do this without the application "knowing" about legs and feet, it is much easier to

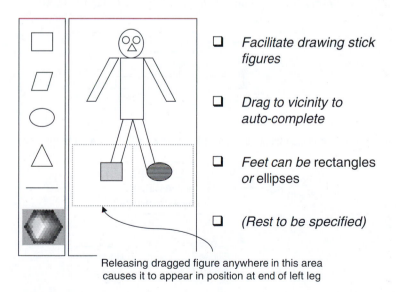

Figure 16.26 Specifications for figure-drawing example application

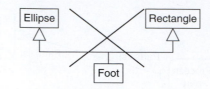

Figure 16.27 Bad attempt at class model for "A foot is either an ellipse of a rectangle"

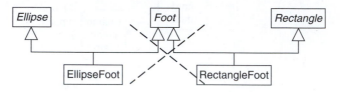

Figure 16.28 Better attempt at class model for "A foot is either an ellipse of a rectangle"

carry out if *Leg* and *Foot* classes are used. (For example, a *Leg* object would aggregate a *Foot* object). The next question is how to relate the classes *Foot*, *Rectangle*, and *Ellipse*. Consider the possibility shown in Figure 16.27.

This class model says that a *Foot* object is both an ellipse and a rectangle, which is not correct. A better option is the class model in Figure 16.28.

This model is at least not incorrect as the first attempt was. It is a little clumsy, however, in that it proliferates classes (*EllipseFoot*, *RectangleFoot*, etc.). This is not tenable (do we need *ReactangleEar*, etc.?). It also uses multiple inheritance, which is problematical in general, and not available in Java. Now consider the option shown in Figure 16.29.

This is a reasonable solution except for one very awkward issue: it makes every *Ellipse* in our application a kind of *FootShape*, and likewise for every *Rectangle*. For one thing, this certainly limits the reusability of the *Ellipse* class. For another, it is rather strange to think of ellipses as *FootShapes* in any case. Finally, if we continue with this, *Ellipse* may also have to be a *HandShape* object etc. One way to deal with these problems is for *FootShape* to depend only "lightly" on *Ellipse* and *Rectangle* as shown in Figure 16.30.

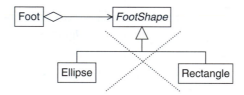

Figure 16.29 Another attempt at class model for "A foot is either an ellipse of a rectangle"

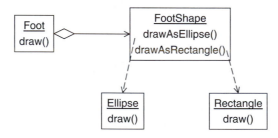

Figure 16.30 Best attempt so far at class model for "A foot is either an ellipse of a rectangle"

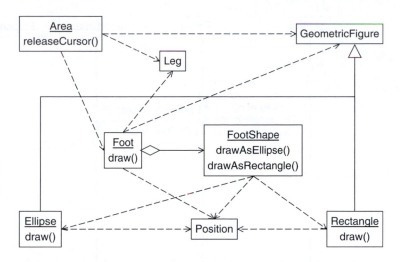

Figure 16.31 A class model showing all dependencies in drawing application class model

This class model shows that the restrictions on the shape of *Foot* objects are reflected in the methods of *FootShape*. They reference only *Ellipse* and *Rectangle* at this point, but can readily be augmented to accept other geometric shapes. We can now fill in more details, as shown in Figure 16.31.

The Area's *releaseCursor()* method handles the auto-placement (at the end of legs in the cases shown), and this information is passed along to the anatomical object (*Foot* in this case); otherwise the *draw()* of *Ellipse* and *Rectangle* are used to do actual drawing. The class *Position* could be avoided. It contains the x- and y-coordinates. For example, *drawAsEllipse(Position aPosition)* in *FootShape* could have the following form.

```
void drawAsEllipse( Position aPosition )
{
    Ellipse ellipse = new Ellipse();   // the dependency shown in the
                                       class model
    ellipse.draw( aPosition );         // the actual work drawing the
                                       ellipse
    . . . .
}
```

Showing all of the dependencies in a class model can make for a complicated diagram, and for this reason dependencies are often omitted. (This is perhaps like sweeping things under the rug!) The sequence diagram in Figure 16.32 specifies how the classes and methods work together, and shows details about parameters.

The sequence diagram specifies that when a geometric figure is dragged to an area and the cursor it released, the *releaseCursor()* method of *Area* executes with the *GeometricFigure* as parameter. The *Area* object deduces which anatomical object is involved (*Foot* in this case), so it calls upon that object to draw itself; it also knows what geometric form is required.

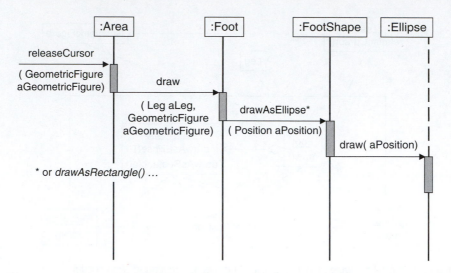

Figure 16.32 Sequence diagram for figure drawing application

16.10 SUMMARY

The Unified Modeling Language (UML) is a widely accepted graphical notation for expressing object-oriented designs. UML defines several ways classes can be related. These are summarized in Figure 16.33.

UML models are diagrams that show either the classes of a software design and how they are related, or the flow of control of a design. Figure 16.34 summarizes the UML models covered in this chapter.

- **Package**
  - Group of related classes
- **Inheritance**
  - Take on attributes and operations from other classes
    - "is-a" relationship
  - For example, an Employee "is-a" Person
- **Association**
  - Structural relationship between classes
- **Aggregation**
  - Structural inclusion of object on one class by another
    - "whole-part" relationship
- **Composition**
  - Stronger form of aggregation
  - Included object is created and destroyed when including object is created and destroyed
- **Dependency**
  - One class depends on another
  - Changes to depended-on class affect dependent class

Figure 16.33 Various relationships between classes that can be shown in UML class diagrams

- **Class Models**
  - classes of a design and their relationship
- **Object Model**
  - objects of a design and their relationship
- **Sequence Diagrams**
  - sequence of method calls among objects
  - usually corresponds to a use case
- **State Diagrams**
  - states of a design element
  - transitions among states caused by events
- **Activity Diagrams**
  - flow of control
  - similar to flow charts
- **Data Flow Model**
  - show processing elements and the data that flow between them

Figure 16.34 UML models

16.11 EXERCISES

1. Name three major relationships that could exist between classes *A* and *B*. Describe them in your own words. Express each in UML and in a typical Java implementation.

2. Explain the difference between aggregation and composition. Give an example to support your answer.

3. Which of the following classes inherit from which? Explain your reasoning.
   Worm, Ellipse, Animal, 2DFigure, Circle

4. Draw the class diagram for the following code. Explain the correspondence between the code and the diagram.

```
abstract class A ( )

class B
(
    B ( ) ( )
)

class C extends A
(
    B b = new B ( );
)
```

5. A library has a collection of items (books and magazines) available to loan patrons. For each item in the collection, the system maintains data about its title, author, and unique id. In addition, the

copyright year is maintained for books, and the edition number is maintained for magazines. Draw a UML class diagram representing the library items. Be sure to include the required attributes. *Hint:* Use inheritance in your model.

6. Show a class diagram for an application that displays automobiles. Depending on the user's request, it displays a typical Ford, Toyota, or Chevy, together with interactive pages of information about each. We want to be able to easily add new automobile brands to the application in the future and to reuse parts of the design where possible.

7. Suppose that your car has a built-in application that displays the status of the engine parts at all times. Draw a UML state diagram for the *Starter* class that describes the automobile's starter only. Explain your reasoning.

   Note that the starter is sometimes connected to and sometimes disengaged from the car's motor. The starter reacts to actions involving the car key. The key can be in one of three positions: vertical, 90°, and 180°.

8. Consider an application used at a doctor's office. The application schedules patient appointments and maintains patient medical histories. Suppose the application design contains an *Appointment* class to track appointments, and a *MedicalHistory* class for each patient. How would you draw the UML class relationship between these two classes?

9. Consider the following use case for a web e-commerce application:

   Use Case Name: "Select Item"
   Actor: Shopper
   Precondition: Actor has requested product list

   Scenario:

   1. Application displays product list
   2. User selects item on product list
   3. User clicks "add item to shopping cart" button
   4. System acknowledges item placed in shopping cart

   Draw a UML sequence diagram for this use case. Explain your reasoning.

10. Draw a UML activity diagram for the "Select Item" use case in Exercise 9. Explain your reasoning.

BIBLIOGRAPHY

1. Fowler, Martin, *"UML Distilled: A Brief Guide to the Standard Object Modeling Language,"* 3rd ed. Addison-Wesley, p. 99, 2004.
2. Jacobson, Ivar, Grady Booch and James Rumbaugh, *"The Unified Software Development Process,"* (Addison-Wesley Object Technology Series), Addison-Wesley, 1999.

17

Software Design Patterns

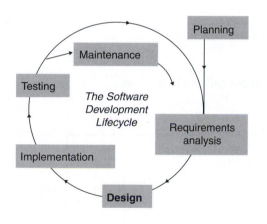

- What are examples of a recurring design purpose?

- What are "creational" design patterns?

- What are "structural" design patterns?

- What are "behavioral" design patterns?

- Can design patterns be thought of in terms of roles and basic forms?

Figure 17.1 The context and learning goals for this chapter

Design patterns concern class combinations and accompanying algorithms that fulfill common design purposes. Each design pattern expresses a design concept rather than an inflexible class combination. The accompanying algorithms express the pattern's basic operation. This chapter is intended to familiarize the reader with the purposes of design patterns, probing their overall forms and usage, summarizing the major ones, and examining several in some depth. These are taken from Gamma et al. [1], the classic reference for the subject. Chapter 15 described typical software design goals and purposes. We will start here with an example design purpose and follow it with a design pattern satisfying that purpose.

17.1 EXAMPLES OF A RECURRING DESIGN PURPOSE

17.1.1 A Simple Example

There are many applications in which we define a class but for which only one instance will be needed. As an example, householders are forever contemplating the modernization of their kitchens, often using software to visualize the possibilities. Using a *Kitchen* class would be natural. Now suppose that a requirement is that the application does not allow more than one kitchen to be under consideration. It is always a good idea for an application to enforce what it intends, so the pattern needed here is the enforcement of the one-instance-only requirement. The Singleton design pattern, described in Section 17.5.1, fits this bill.

17.1.2 A More Complex Example

Let's continue with the kitchen application, which we will call *KitchenViewer*. It enables the user to first lay out the parts of a kitchen without committing to a style. The overall interface is shown in Figure 17.2.

Here is a use case.

Lay out a Kitchen

Preconditions: None

1. *User* clicks on the "wall cabinet" icon.

2. *Application* displays a wall cabinet in the center of the work area.

3. *User* resizes the wall cabinet.

4. *User* drags the wall cabinet to a position in the upper half of the work area.

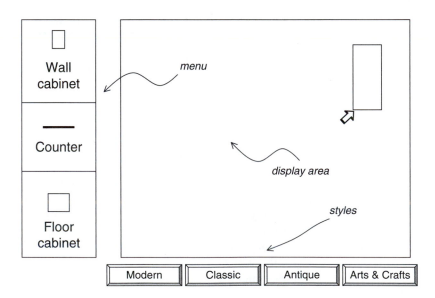

Figure 17.2 Graphical interface to the KitchenViewer example application

5. *User* releases the cursor.

6. *Application* places the wall cabinet in the nearest conforming position.

7. *User* clicks on the "floor cabinet" icon.

8. *Application* displays a floor cabinet in the center of the work area.

9. . . . . . .

Once the layout process is complete, the kitchen appears as in the example shown in Figure 17.3.

After a kitchen has been sketched in the above manner, KitchenViewer allows the user to try various styles for the wall cabinets, floor cabinets, and countertops. When the user selects "Antique," for example, the design appears as in Figure 17.4.

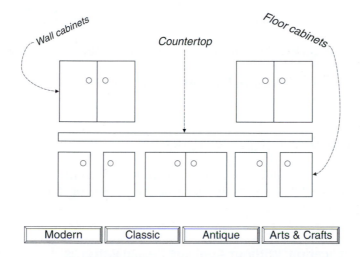

Figure 17.3 An example of a kitchen being designed with KitchenViewer

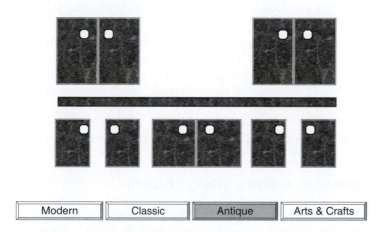

Figure 17.4 Selecting an antique style using KitchenViewer

What are our specific design purposes for KitchenViewer? The procedure of rendering the various styles is basically the same, regardless of the style, and we should *not* have more than one copy of this procedure in our application. In particular, we should avoid code such as the following.

```
Counter counter = new Counter( );
draw( counter );
```

This is because no amount of added code will enable this to draw variable types of counters at runtime. Better design thinking than this is required, and it is usually set up to allow *polymorphism*: a single block of code that executes in several possible ways, depending on the context. One approach is to design the kitchen application so as to provide a method such as *renderKitchen(myStyle)*, somehow parameterizing the rendering procedure with a required style. We would need to figure out what kind of a thing *myStyle* should be, and how *renderKitchen()* uses it. This kind of design purpose recurs, and we can describe it as follows.

An application must construct a family of objects at runtime: The design must enable choice among several families of styles.

This purpose can be approached with the Abstract Factory design pattern, which is discussed in Section 17.5.2.

17.2 AN INTRODUCTION TO DESIGN PATTERNS

To illustrate how patterns express ideas, think about how you might describe your housing preferences to a realtor. The term "ranch style," for example, denotes a useful house pattern. It conveys an idea rather than a completely specific design.

17.2.1 Example Application: Without Applying Design Patterns

As an example of a software design pattern, let's return to the KitchenViewer example. Recall that we want to be able to provide a method such as *renderKitchen(myStyle)*. Now we need to elaborate on what *myStyle* means.

The method *renderKitchen()* uses the classes *Kitchen*, *WallCabinet*, and so on, and we will make it a member of a class called *Client*. If we temporarily forget our purpose of parameterizing the style, the method *renderKitchen()* would look something like Listing 17.1.

This code would have to be repeated for every style, resulting in more error-prone and far less maintainable code. (Sooner or later, code that is supposed to be duplicated becomes different in different places.) A class diagram for this would look like Figure 17.5.

The result is repetitive and complicated. As a result, it is inflexible, hard to prove correct, and hard to reuse.

17.2.2 Example Application: Applying a Design Pattern

Now let's fulfill our KitchenViewer design purpose by applying the Abstract Factory design pattern. We'll assume that some object will have the responsibility for creating the kitchen. Here is the key: Instead of that object directly creating *AntiqueWallCabinet* objects, for example, a parameterized version of *renderKitchen()*

Listing 17.1:   The method *renderKitchen()* in KitchenViewer

```
// VERSION IGNORING OUR DESIGN PURPOSES

// Determine the style
...                                     // case statement?
// Assume that the antique style was selected.

// Create the antique wall cabinets
AntiqueWallCabinet antiqueWallCabinet1 = new AntiqueWallCabinet ();
AntiqueWallCabinet antiqueWallCabinet2 = new AntiqueWallCabinet ();
...

// Create the antique floor cabinets
AntiqueFloorCabinet antiqueFloorCabinet1 = new AntiqueFloorCabinet
  ();
AntiqueFloorCabinet antiqueFloorCabinet2 = new AntiqueFloorCabinet
  ();
...

// Create the kitchen object, assuming the existence of add() methods
Kitchen antiqueKitchen = new Kitchen();
antiqueKitchen.add( antiqueWallCabinet1, ... ); // rest of
  parameters specify location antiqueKitchen.add
  ( antiqueWallCabinet2, ... );
...
antiqueKitchen.add( antiqueFloorCabinet1, ... );
antiqueKitchen.add( antiqueFloorCabinet2, ... );
...

// Render antiqueKitchen
...
```

delegates their creation, replacing phrases such as the following:

```
new AntiqueWallCabinet();          //applies only to antique style: Replace! with the following.
myStyle.getWallCabinet();          //applies to the style chosen at runtime
```

At runtime, the class of *myStyle* determines the version of *getWallCabinet()* executed, thereby producing the appropriate kind of wall cabinet. To carry out this delegation of responsibility, we introduce a new class, which we'll call *KitchenStyle*, supporting methods *getWallCabinet()*, *getFloorCabinet()*, and so on. *KitchenStyle* will

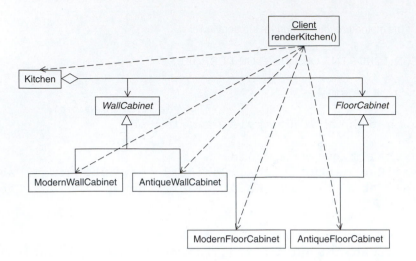

Figure 17.5 A design for KitchenViewer without design patterns

have subclasses, which we'll name *ModernKStyle*, *AntiqueKStyle*, and so on, each supporting separate implementations of *getWallCabinet()*, *getFloorCabinet()*, and so on. This is shown in Figure 17.6.

Recall that, due to polymorphism, executing *myStyle.getFloorCabinet()* has different effects when *myStyle* is an object of *ModernKStyle* versus an object of *AntiqueKStyle*. The class model in Figure 17.7 is a more complete version.

Notice that the client code references *Kitchen*, *KitchenStyle*, *WallCabinet*, and *FloorCabinet*, but does not reference specific wall cabinet styles or floor cabinet styles. For example, the class *AntiqueWallCabinet* does not appear in the client code. To see how this works, let's assume that at runtime, *myStyle* is an object of the class *ModernStyle*. In this case, when the method *renderKitchen()* executes a statement such as

```
WallCabinet wallCabinet7 = myStyle.getWallCabinet();
```

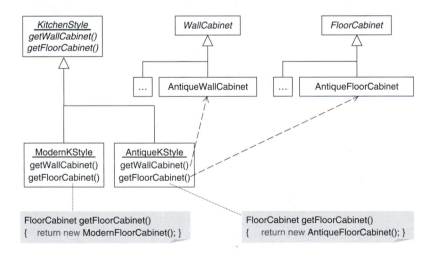

Figure 17.6 The idea behind the *Abstract Factory* design pattern

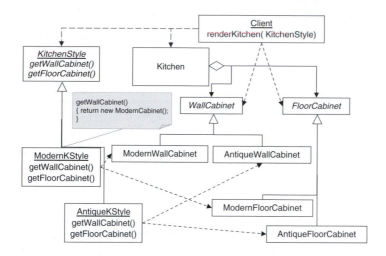

Figure 17.7 The *Abstract Factory* design pattern applied to KitchenViewer

the method *getWallCabinet()* is the version defined in the class *ModernStyle*, and so it actually returns a *ModernWall* object.

The method *renderKitchen(KitchenStyle myStyle)* looks like Listing 17.2.

This version of *renderKitchen()* is much more versatile than the previous version since it is not written for any particular style. Figure 17.8 describes the Abstract Factory design pattern in general.

Listing 17.2:   The method *renderKitchen(KitchenStyle myStyle)* in KitchenViewer

```
// Create the wall cabinets: Type determined by the class of myStyle
WallCabinet wallCabinet1 = myStyle.getWallCabinet();
WallCabinet wallCabinet2 = myStyle.getWallCabinet();
. . .

// Create the floor cabinets: Type determined by the class of myStyle
// Create the kitchen object (in the style required)
FloorCabinet floorCabinet1 = myStyle.getFloorCabinet();
FloorCabinet floorCabinet2 = myStyle.getFloorCabinet();
. . .

Kitchen kitchen = new Kitchen();
kitchen.add( wallCabinet1, . . . );
kitchen.add( wallCabinet2, . . . );
. . .

kitchen.add( floorCabinet1, . . . );
kitchen.add( floorCabinet2, . . . );
. . .
```

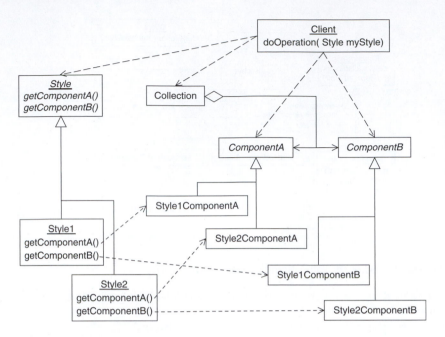

Figure 17.8 The *Abstract Factory* design pattern

The client method *doOperation(Style myStyle)* builds an instance of *Collection* in the style indicated by *myStyle* by calling *myStyle.getComponentA()* and *myStyle.getComponentB()*. If *myStyle* is a *Style1* object, for example, these two operations produce *Style1ComponentA* and *Style1ComponentB* objects, respectively. The pattern thus ensures a consistent style throughout.

We have mentioned that design patterns should not be regarded in a literal manner. For example, the design in the above figure could also appear as shown in Figure 17.9.

In this alternative, *Collection* aggregates *Style*, *Client* does not reference *Style* directly, *doOperation()* takes no parameters, and *Collection* has methods for getting the various components. *Collection*'s aggregated *Style* object is instantiated at runtime, perhaps with separate setup code. When *doOperation()* calls *getComponentA()* in *Collection*, control is delegated to *getComponentA()* in the aggregated *Style* object. This is still the Abstract Factory pattern. The Abstract Factory pattern is described in more detail in Section 17.5.2.

17.3 SUMMARY OF DESIGN PATTERNS BY TYPE: CREATIONAL, STRUCTURAL, AND BEHAVIORAL

Gamma et al. [1] classified design patterns in one of three categories, depending upon whether it has to do with one of the following:

• Creating a collection of objects in flexible ways (*creational* patterns)

• Representing a collection of related objects (*structural* patterns)

• Capturing behavior among a collection of objects (*behavioral* patterns)

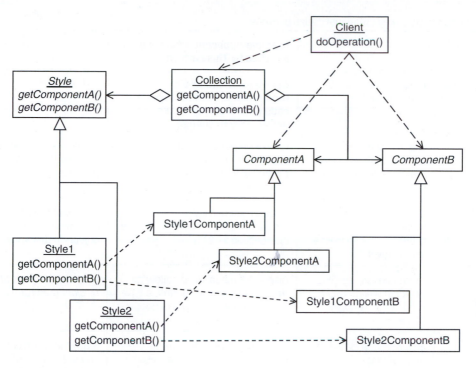

Figure 17.9 The Abstract Factory design pattern alternative

These categories are useful for recognizing when a pattern may be needed and as the beginning of a guide to selecting which one may be appropriate. Next, we will elaborate on each using example applications.

17.3.1 Creational Design Patterns

Creational design patterns help us to flexibly set up collections of objects for subsequent processing. They allow the creation of several possible collections from a single block of code, but with properties such as:

• Creating many *versions* of the collection at runtime

• *Constraining* the objects created: for example, ensuring that there is only instance of its class

Table 17.1 summarizes the use and nature of key creational design patterns. The abstract factory and singleton patterns are described in more detail in subsequent sections.

17.3.2 Structural Design Patterns

Structural design patterns help us to arrange collections of objects in forms such as linked lists or trees. They are useful when we want to manage complex data consisting of associated objects. Table 17.2 summarizes the use and nature of key structural design patterns. The Adapter and Facade patterns are described in more detail in subsequent sections as representative examples of structural design patterns.

Table 17.1 A summary of key creational design patterns

Design Pattern Name	*Approximate Design Purpose Satisfied by This Pattern*	**Example Application Purpose Satisfied by This Pattern** **Design for the following requirements without repeating code unnecessarily. Make the design easy to change.**	*Outline of the Design Pattern*
Factory	*Create objects at runtime with flexibility that constructors alone cannot provide.*	From a single version of control code, generate mail messages tailored to various customers.	*Create desired objects by using methods that return the objects.*
Abstract Factory (see Section 17.5.2)	*Create coordinated families of objects at runtime, chosen from a set of styles.*	Display a kitchen layout, allowing the user to select a style at runtime. (See Section 17.2.2.)	*Encapsulate each family in a class whose methods return objects in that style.*
Prototype	*Create an aggregate object in which selected parts are essentially copies.*	Display a kitchen layout, allowing the user to select at runtime a type of wall cabinet, or a type of floor cabinet, etc.	*Create the objects of the type by cloning a prototype.*
Singleton (see Section 17.5.1)	*Ensure that a class has at most one instantiation, accessible throughout the application.*	Build an application to evaluate the results of a lab experiment. Ensure that there is exactly one *Experiment* object at runtime, and ensure that it can be accessed by any method in the application. (See Section 17.5.1.4.)	*Make the constructor private and obtain the unique object by means of a public method that returns it.*

Table 17.2 A summary of key *structural* design patterns

Design Pattern Name	*Approximate Design Purposes Satisfied by This Pattern*	**Example of Design Purposes Satisfied by This Pattern** **Design for the following requirements without repeating code unnecessarily. Make the design easy to change.**	*Summary of the Design Pattern*
Composite	*Represent a tree of objects.* Allow client code to access uniform functionality distributed in the subtree rooted by any node.	Represent the organization chart of a company. Allow client code to call *printOrganization()* on any *Employee* object, printing the names of the employee and all subordinates, if any. Allow the addition and removal of subtrees at runtime.	*Have composite objects aggregate other composite objects.*
Decorator	*Allow objects and functionality to be added to an object at runtime.*	Allow the user of an online clothing store to see his or her image dressed in a variety of clothes.	*Link the objects using aggregation.*

(*continued*)

Table 17.2 (*continued*)

Adapter (see Section 17.6.2)	*Allow an application to make use of external (e. g., legacy) functionality.*	Design a loan application from scratch, but allow it to use any vendor's classes that compute monthly payment calculations.	*Introduce an inherited intermediary class relating the application and the class with desired functionality.*
Facade (see Section 17.6.1)	*Manage software architectures involving large numbers of classes.*	Design the architecture of a student loan software application so that one group of developers can concentrate on the loan option database, another on the user interface (simultaneously), and a third on payment calculations. Minimize coordination problems.	*For each package, introduce an object that is the sole access to objects within the package.*
Flyweight	*Obtain the benefits of having a large number of individual objects without excessive runtime space requirements.*	We want to be able to visualize a room with stenciling. There are five stencil patterns but thousands of potential stencil marks on the walls. This might be easy to do if each mark were a separate object, but we can't afford the memory required, and it's impractical to name all of these separate objects.	*Share objects by parameterizing the methods with variables expressing the context.*
Proxy	*Some methods are remote, or require lots of resources to execute (time or space). Ensure that they can be executed, but no more often than necessary.*	Assume that rendering an image consumes a significant amount of time and space because the image data has to be read from a file, fill a buffer, and then be rendered. If the buffer is already filled by a previous invocation of the method, then invoking the function should not repeat this step.	*Introduce a class standing between the requesting methods and the resource.*

17.3.3 Behavioral Design Patterns

When an application runs, much behavior generally occurs among the objects. An example is when a method in one object calls several methods in an object of a different class. Sometimes we want to control and label behavior in order to parameterize it or reuse it. Each behavioral pattern captures a kind of behavior among a collection of objects. Let's consider the following example of mutual behavior among *Ship* and *Tugboat* objects. Let's say that we want to estimate the amount of time required to bring ships into and out of a harbor and transport them to dry dock for maintenance, based on their size, and so on. Imagine that this is a complex calculation that requires a systematic simulation of the transportation process. Figure 17.10 suggests a configuration.

The classes *Ship* and *Tugboat* are natural class choices, but objects of these classes play different roles, depending on whether the ship is entering, leaving, or heading for dry dock. Since there are many potential applications in which we can use *Ship* and *Tugboat*, we do not want these classes to depend on each other, as suggested by Figure 17.11.

We have a *behavioral* design purpose here because we want to separate the interdependent behavior of these objects from the objects themselves. The Mediator design pattern does this. Figure 17.12 shows the core idea of Mediator.

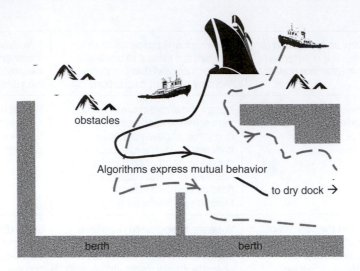

Figure 17.10 Example of behavioral design goal—tugboat and ship port entry

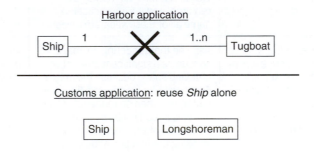

Figure 17.11 Avoiding design dependency in port entry example

In this design, *Ship* and *Tugboat* classes do not refer to each other. Instead, the *LeavingPort* class controls how objects of *Ship* and *Tugboat* behave to estimate the time for that maneuver.

The full Mediator pattern allows for the fact that the mediated classes may need to communicate (e.g., to respond to events on either of them). To accomplish this, the mediated classes can be made to subclass a base class that aggregates a generic mediator class (*PortMission*). This is shown in Figure 17.13.

Note that in Figure 17.13 the *Ship* class does depend on the class *Vessel*, which depends on *PortMission*, so we cannot use the *Ship* class without these two. These dependencies are much more acceptable, however, than

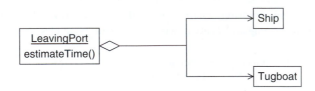

Figure 17.12 The Mediator design pattern concept applied to the port entry example

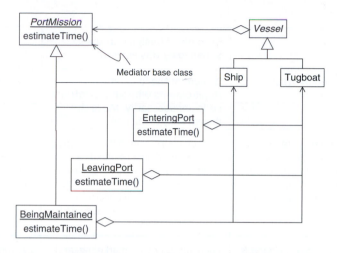

Figure 17.13 Applying the Mediator design pattern to the port entry example

having *Ship* depend for all time on *Tugboat*. Ships are always vessels, and they usually have missions, but they are only sometimes associated with tugboats. Table 17.3 summarizes the use and nature of key behavioral design patterns. The Interpreter, Observer, and State patterns are described in more detail in subsequent sections as examples of structural design patterns.

Table 17.3 A summary of key behavioral design patterns

Approximate Design Pattern Name	*Design Purposes Satisfied by This Pattern*	Example of Design Purposes Satisfied by This Pattern	*Summary of the Design Pattern*
		Design for the following requirements without repeating code unnecessarily. Make the design easy to change.	
Chain of Responsibility	*We want a collection of objects to exhibit functionality. At design time we want to be able to easily add or delete objects that handle all or part of the responsibility.*	Design a GUI for a Web application to view automobiles with requested color, etc. The display is dynamic, depending on the model, etc. chosen. Reuse the GUI parts among the displays.	*Link objects to each other via aggregation. Each performs some of the work, and then calls on the next object in the chain to continue the work.*
Command	*Make the execution of operations more flexible. For example, enable "undoing."*	Allow users of an application to retract their last four decisions at any time (the "undo" problem).	*Capture each command in a class of its own.*
Interpreter (see Section 17.7.1)	*Parse an expression.*	Design an application that takes as input an order for a network of PCs, expressed in a standard syntax. The output consists of instructions for assembling the network. (See Section 17.7.1.5.)	*Introduce a class to capture expressions, and allow expression classes to aggregate expression classes.*

(continued)

Table 17.3 (*continued*)

Approximate Design Pattern Name	*Design Purposes Satisfied by This Pattern*	**Example of Design Purposes Satisfied by This Pattern** **Design for the following requirements without repeating code unnecessarily. Make the design easy to change.**	*Summary of the Design Pattern*
Mediator (see above)	*Capture the interaction between objects without having them reference each other (thus permitting their reuse).*	Build an application that estimates the amount of time required to bring ships into and out of a harbor, and to transport them to dry dock for maintenance, but ensure that the *Ship* and *Tugboat* classes can be reused separately.	*Capture each interaction in a separate class, which aggregates the objects involved.*
Observer (see Section 17.7.2)	*A set of objects depends on the data in a single object. Design a way in which they can be updated when that single object changes attribute values.*	Keep management, marketing, and operations departments up to date on sales data. Each of these departments has different requirements for the data.	*Capture the data source as a class. Allow it to loop through the observer objects, calling an update() method.*
State (see Section 17.7.3)	*At runtime, vary the effect of invoking an object's methods depends upon the object's state.*	Customers fill out an order form on a Web site, and then hit the "enter" button. The result must depend upon the state of the form data: "Product Information Complete," "Personal Information Incomplete," "Credit Check In Progress," etc.	*Aggregate a class representing the state with operative method doAction(). Subclasses effect the required actions of substates with their own versions of doAction().*
Template	*Allow an algorithm to execute partial variants at runtime.*	Organize the huge number of traffic light algorithms in a city by arranging them into a few basic forms, with variants tailored to specific locations.	*Have a base class contain an overall method, but with function calls where variability is needed. Have subclasses implement these function calls to capture the required variability.*

17.4 CHARACTERISTICS OF DESIGN PATTERNS: VIEWPOINTS, ROLES, AND LEVELS

Design patterns are partially described by class diagrams, but they also can be thought about in two ways: the *static* and *dynamic* viewpoints of the pattern. This section explains these two viewpoints. It also describes the *abstract* and non-abstract (*concrete*) levels of design patterns. Finally, it covers the ways in which design patterns are embedded in applications. The static vs. dynamic viewpoints, abstract vs. concrete levels, and embedding issues are actually characteristic of most designs, and are not limited to design patterns. These characteristics are summarized in Figures 17.14 and 17.15.

- *Viewpoints*–ways to describe patterns
    1. *Static*: class model (building blocks)
    2. *Dynamic*: sequence or state diagram (operation)
- *Levels*–decomposition of patterns
    1. *Abstract* level describes the core of the pattern
    2. *Concrete* (= nonabstract) level describes the particulars of this case
- *Roles*–the "players" in pattern usage
    1. *Application* of the design pattern itself
    2. *Clients* of the design pattern application
    3. *Setup* code initializes and controls

Figure 17.14 Some characteristics of design patterns, 1 of 2

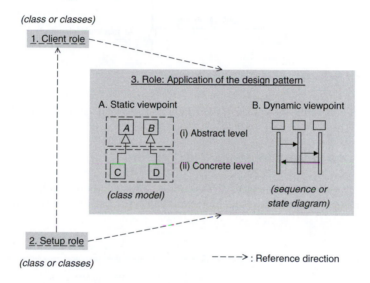

Figure 17.15 Some characteristics of design patterns, 2 of 2

17.4.1 Two Viewpoints for Describing a Pattern: Static and Dynamic

Design patterns are illustrated with class models, showing the classes involved and their mutual relationships; this is a *static* viewpoint of the pattern. The functions of these classes execute in particular sequences, however, which class models do not illustrate. This is the *dynamic* viewpoint of the pattern, and requires appropriate means of expression.

We'll use the KitchenViewer example to illustrate the static and dynamic viewpoints. The static viewpoint was shown in Figure 17.7. This viewpoint does not specify how the design actually works at runtime: what happens first, second, and so on. Figure 17.6 lists the code for *getFloorCabinet()* and *getDoorCabinet()*, and although this code contributes to the dynamic viewpoint of the design pattern application, it is hard to see the whole execution picture. To express the dynamic viewpoint, we often use sequence diagrams, as illustrated in

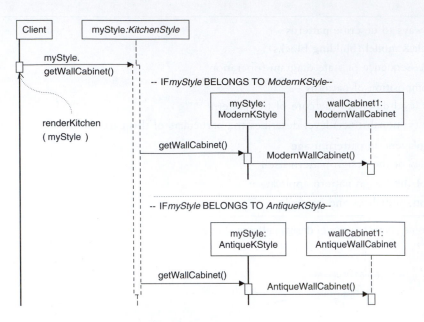

Figure 17.16 Abstract Factory sequence diagram for KitchenViewer

Figure 17.16. It shows the dynamic viewpoint of the KitchenViewer application of the Abstract Factory design pattern.

17.4.2 Two Layers of a Pattern: Abstract and Concrete

Notice that within the KitchenViewer Abstract Factory pattern application, some of the classes are abstract. In conformance with Gamma et al. [1] we will call non-abstract classes "concrete." Figure 17.17

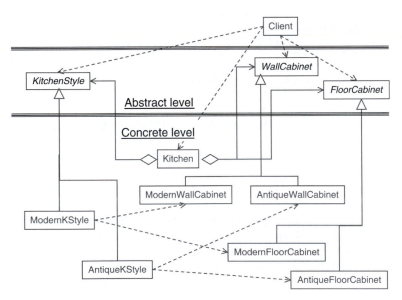

Figure 17.17 Concrete and abstract layers in design patterns

rearranges the physical placement of classes in Figure 17.7 to emphasize the abstract and concrete groupings called *layers*.

The interface of clients with a design pattern application usually needs to be at the abstract layer. This can be seen in the code for *renderKitchen()*, which is written in terms of *KitchenStyle* (and doesn't reference *ModernKStyle* or *AntiqueKStyle*), *WallCabinet* (not *ModernWallCabinet* or *AntiqueWallCabinet*), and so on.

A division into abstract and concrete layers is a often a good design practice, regardless of whether design patterns are being applied, because client code can be written in terms of the more general classes of the abstract layer, making it more versatile.

17.4.3 Three Roles Involved in Pattern Usage: Pattern Application, Client, and Setup

This section explains the three parts—or *roles*—involved in the usage of a design pattern in a design. This discussion is designed to help the student surmount common problems using design patterns. The three roles are as follows:

- The application of the design pattern itself

- The code that utilizes this application (the "client role")

- The code, if required, that initializes or changes the design pattern application (the "setup role")

These three roles are shown in Figure 17.18, and are explained next.

17.4.3.1 The Design Pattern Application Role

A design pattern—the *design pattern application*—involves a specific class model. For example, KitchenViewer, described in this chapter, contains an application of the Abstract Factory design pattern. This is the substance of the design pattern.

17.4.3.2 The Client Role

Many parts of a program can potentially use a design pattern application. We usually refer to these parts as *clients* of the pattern application. Each client is typically a method, but we often regard the method's class as the client. In

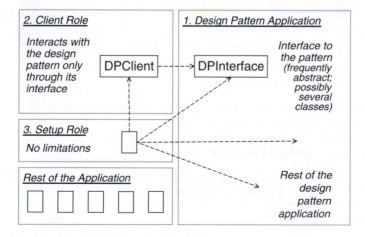

Figure 17.18 The three roles involved in design pattern usage

the KitchenViewer design, for example, the *renderKitchen()* method is a client of the design pattern application. We will use the term *client role* for the community of clients. Typically, the client utilizes the design pattern application only through specified methods of specified classes of the design pattern application. These methods and classes constitute the interface of the pattern application. In the case of the KitchenViewer design, for example, the interface consists of the classes *KitchenStyle*, *Kitchen*, *WallCabinet*, and *FloorCabinet*. Clients may not refer to any other parts of this pattern application, and they generally do not overlap the design pattern application.

17.4.3.3 The Setup Role

The third role involved in the usage of design patterns is not terribly significant, but one can get confused if one does not recognize its presence and necessity. It consists of the code that initializes or changes the design pattern application code at runtime. You can think of this as a janitorial—or housekeeping—role. In the KitchenViewer design, for example, clients specifically do not reference particular styles, such as *Modern-KStyle*. Recall that *renderKitchen()* takes a *KitchenStyle* object as parameter, and deliberately does not reference any subclass of *KitchenStyle*. How are these specific style objects selected and instantiated? This is the task of what we will call the *setup role*. In the KitchenViewer design, it is the code that responds to clicks on the "Style" buttons in Figure 17.4 by instantiating a *KitchenStyle* object and calling *renderKitchen()* with this parameter value.

Setup code needs access to many parts of the application, is normally runtime intensive, and is typically not intended for reuse. This is because it tends to be special to the application and because it depends on too many other classes. One can think of the setup role as not overlapping either the client or the design pattern application, although both are possible.

17.5 SELECTED CREATIONAL DESIGN PATTERNS

This section describes the Singleton and Abstract Factory design patterns as examples of creational design patterns.

17.5.1 Singleton

17.5.1.1 Design Purpose of Singleton

Although a typical class allows the creation of many instances at runtime, we often want a class to have exactly one instance throughout the application, and no more. For example, many applications maintain a profile of the user. Often, there is no need for more than one *User* instance at runtime. In fact, the existence of more than one instance could lead to problems where one part of the application changes the user's profile in one way on one instance, and another part in another way on another instance. This leads to an incorrect implementation. We want a *guarantee* of one and only one *User* instance at runtime. Figure 17.19 summarizes the purpose of Singleton.

Design Purpose

Ensure that there is exactly one instance of a class *S*. Be able to obtain the instance from anywhere in the application.

Design Pattern Summary

Make the constructor of *S* private; define a private static attribute for *S* of type *S*; define a public accessor for it.

Figure 17.19 Design purpose of Singleton

We refer to the desired unique instantiation as the *singleton* of the class, and the class as a *Singleton* class.

17.5.1.2 The Singleton Interface for Clients

As an example, if an application has a *User* class as described above, client methods such as *verifyAccess()* and *sendEmailToUser()* would require a reference to the singleton of *User*. To get the singleton, they would contain a statement such as the following:

```
User user = User.getTheUser();
```

This requires that *getTheUser()* is a static method of *User*. Notice again that a statement such as the following:

```
User user = new User();
```

would create a truly new *User* object, failing to guarantee the requirement that there be only one *User* instance.

17.5.1.3 The *Singleton* Class Model

The first issue is: where do we put the single instance of our class? We will name the class in question *S*. A good place is within *S* itself, as a static variable. So far so good— but the problem is, what's to stop another part of the application from including the following statement?

```
S myVeryOwnInstanceOfS = new S();
```

We prevent this by making the constructor *S()* private. The only remaining issue is a way to obtain the singleton; to do this we include in *S* a public static accessor method.

The Singleton design pattern is actually a special case of Factory in which the object returned is the one and only instance of the class with the Factory method. Singleton is thus in the Delegation form: the method getting the singleton delegates its creation to the constructor. The class model for Singleton is shown in Figure 17.20.

Let's sum up this discussion. Suppose that *S* is a class for which we require one and only one instance. The Singleton design pattern consists of the steps shown in Figure 17.21.

Making the constructor of the class *MyClass* private prevents the creation of *MyClass* objects except by methods of *MyClass* itself. *MyClass* is given a static data member of type *MyClass* that will be the singleton. Let's name this object *singletonOfMyClass*. A public static factory method of *MyClass*, *getSingletonOfMyClass()*, is defined that returns *singletonOfMyClass*. Thus, to get this one and only element of *MyClass*, we merely invoke *MyClass.getSingletonOfMyClass()*.

Our discussion on Singleton does not automatically extend to clients operating in parallel threads, needing access to a singleton object.

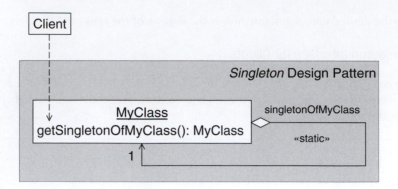

Figure 17.20 *Singleton* class model

---

1. Define a private static member variable of MyClass of type MyClass

   ```
   private static MyClass singletonOfMyClass = new MyClass();
   ```

2. Make the constructor of MyClass private

   ```
   private MyClass() { /* . . . . constructor code . . . . */ };
   ```

3. Define a public static method to access the member

   ```
   public static MyClass getSingletonOfMyClass()
   {
       return singletonOfMyClass;
   }
   ```

Figure 17.21 The Singleton design pattern, applied to *MyClass*

17.5.1.4 Example Singleton Application: "Experiment"

Let's look at the following example:

An application evaluates the results of lab experiments. The application for this phase does no substantive evaluation, takes no input, and always prints the following message to the console:

The analysis shows that the experiment was a resounding success

There is to be exactly one *Experiment* object at runtime, and it can be accessed by any method in the application. Each time the method is called, it displays the following message on the console to verify it was called:

Noting that the Experiment singleton referenced n *times so far*

The output would have the appearance shown in Figure 17.22.
The simple class model for this experiment example is shown in Figure 17.20.

Output

Noting that the Experiment singleton referenced 1 times so far

The analysis shows that the experiment was a resounding success. . . .

Figure 17.22 Output for Singleton *Experiment* example

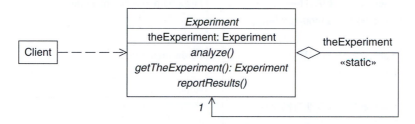

Figure 17.23 Application of Singleton to *Experiment* example

17.5.2 Abstract Factory

Now we turn our attention to the creation of *families* of objects. This kind of problem was discussed in Section 17.1 using the KitchenMaster example.

17.5.2.1 Design Purpose of Abstract Factory

Our design purpose here is to create a family of related objects, chosen at runtime from several possible families. You can often think of a "family" here as a "style" choice. We want to be able to write code that applies to these families without committing to one particular family.

As an example, consider a word processor requirement that allows the user to view a document in several styles. Modern word processors allow users to view documents in a variety of ways: for example, in outline form, showing only the headings. We will simplify this for illustration. Typical input to our primitive word processor is shown in Figure 17.24.

→ Enter title : My Life	→ Enter text: I grew up playing in the woods . . .
→ Enter Heading or "-done": Birth	→ Enter Heading or "-done": Adulthood
→ Enter text: I was born in a small mountain hut	. . . .
	→ Enter Heading or "-done": -done
→ Enter Heading or "-done": Youth	*(continued)*

Figure 17.24 Word processor interaction, 1 of 2—input

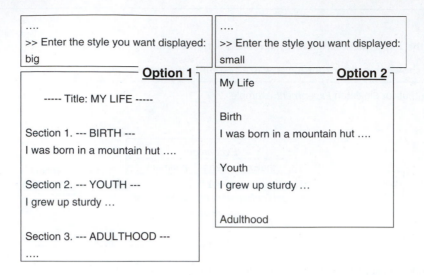

Figure 17.25 Word processor interaction, 2 of 2—output options

The application prints the document in a variety of styles. For simplicity, we will use *small* and *big* styles. In *small* style output, all headings are in left-justified lowercase and end with a colon. In *big* style they are capitalized with section numbering, and so on. The title and the various subheadings appear differently in these two styles. We can assume that more styles will be required in the future. The output for "small" and "big" styles is shown in Figure 17.25.

We want a design with a clean separation into the word manipulation part and the style choice part. We capture the various kinds of headings with classes. In general, a "style" involves a family of classes. For example, *CapitalStyle* involves the classes *CapitalTitle*, *CapitalLevel1Heading*, *CapitalLevel2Heading*, and so on, so the problem is to be able to change the family at run time. The purpose of Abstract Factory, as expressed by Gamma et al., is as shown in Figure 17.26.

The rest of this section explains the pattern that fulfills this purpose.

Design Purpose

"Provide an interface for creating families of
related or dependent objects without specifying
their concrete classes."[1]

Design Pattern

Capture family creation in a class containing a
factory method for each class in the family.

Figure 17.26 Design purpose of Abstract Factory

---

[1]Erich Gamma et al., "Design Patterns, Elements of Renseable Object-Oriented Software," Addison-Wesley, 1995.

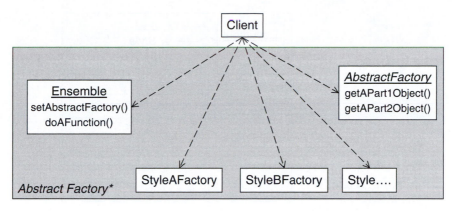

* relationships within pattern application not shown

Figure 17.27 The interface to Abstract Factory

17.5.2.2 The Abstract Factory Interface for Clients

Client code has access to the entity to be constructed with the families. We will name this class *Ensemble* in general. The class *AbstractFactory* encapsulates the style of the *Ensemble* parts. The interface for the client has the appearance of Figure 17.27.

For a discussion on a narrower interface alternative using the Facade design pattern, see Section 17.6.1.1. For our word processor example, the role of *Ensemble* would be held by a class such as *Document*, which supports methods dependent upon *Style* (our Abstract Factory). First the client—or setup code—has to determine the required style, typically depending on user input as in the following.

```
Style currentStyle;
... // interact with the user
currentStyle = new SmallStyle();
... or
currentStyle = new LargeStyle();
...
document.setStyle( currentStyle );
```

Once the style has been set, the client makes calls to *Document* such *document.display()*. A class model for this would have the appearance of Figure 17.28.

But what does a "style" class look like, and how does it achieve our purposes?

17.5.2.3 The *Abstract Factory* Class Model

The Abstract Factory design pattern uses a class to collect coordinated factory methods in one place, one class per "style." In the standard pattern, the base class for these style classes is named *AbstractFactory*. The idea is that each *AbstractFactory* subclass interprets its factory methods to produce objects of a single style. Abstract Factory is in the delegation form, delegating the "getters" of objects to constructors all in the desired style.

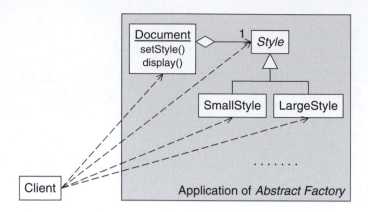

Figure 17.28 The interface of Abstract Factory applied to word processor example

For the sake of simplicity we will illustrate this with just one style to begin with. Let's call the class whose complex objects are to be constructed, *Ensemble*. Figure 17.29 shows how *Ensemble* objects are constructed in a style encapsulated as *StyleA*. *Ensemble* consists of parts: *Part1* objects, *Part2* objects, and so on. The attribute *abstractFactory* of *Ensemble* is instantiated with a *StyleAFactory* object in this case. When a *Part1* object is required, the *getAPart1Object()* method of *abstractFactory* is called. The virtual function property implies that the *getAPart1Object()* method of *StyleAFactory* is actually called, and it returns a *Part1StyleA* object. Similarly, when *getPart2Object()* of *Ensemble* is called, it returns a *Part2StyleA* object. Thus, all of the parts obtained are in the same style. The partial class model is shown in Figure 17.29.

The full *Abstract Factory* class model, with two styles (*AbstractFactory* subclasses) is shown in Figure 17.30.

As discussed in the section above on client interfaces, the client may interface with the *AbstractFactory* and *PartX* classes but specifically not with the *subclasses* of *Part1*, *Part2*, and so on.

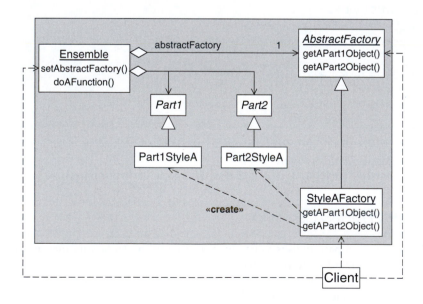

Figure 17.29 The idea of the Factory design pattern

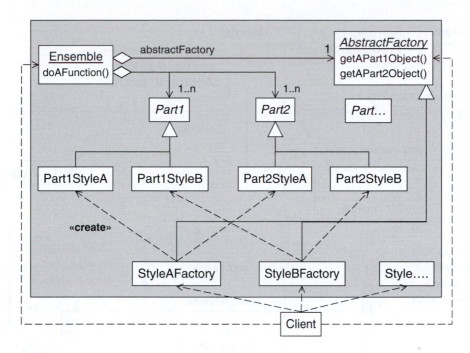

Figure 17.30 *Abstract Factory*

17.5.2.4 The *Abstract Factory* Sequence Diagram

A sequence diagram for *Abstract Factory*, including the setting up of the particular "style" (the *Abstract Factory* object), is shown in Figure 17.31.

17.5.2.5 Example *Abstract Factory* Application: Word Processor

We now show the design of our Word Processor example using the Abstract Factory design pattern. The following use cases describe the application:

View a Document

    Preconditions: none

1. *Application* requests the title of the document

2. *User* provides the title

3. The "Heading/Text" use case (see below) is executed until the user enters "done"

4. *Application* requests a style from a list

5. *User* enters a style from the list

6. *Application* outputs the document to the monitor in the style requested

    The following is the "Heading/Text" use case referenced above.

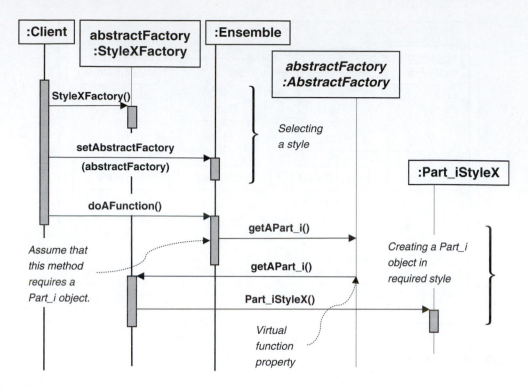

Figure 17.31 Sequence diagram for *Abstract Factory*

Provide Heading/Text

Preconditions: user has provided the title

1. *Application* requests a header
2. *User* provides header text
3. *Application* requests text
4. *User* provides text to fit with the header

The class model is shown in Figure 17.32.
Typical output is shown in Figure 17.33.

17.6 SELECTED STRUCTURAL DESIGN PATTERNS

This section describes the Facade and Adapter design patterns as examples of structural design patterns.

17.6.1 Facade: Interfacing with a Collection of Classes

17.6.1.1 The Design Purpose of Facade

In building applications we parcel out sets of classes to separate developers. This requires the clear modularization of the design. Developers typically require the services of classes that others are responsible

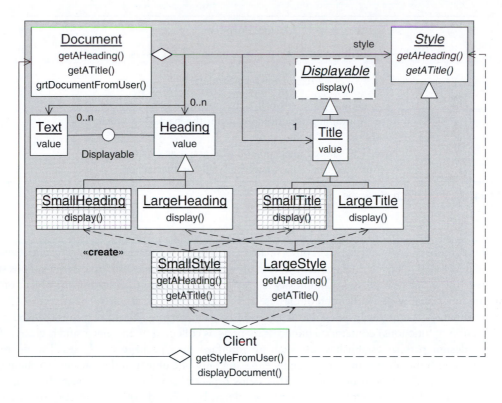

Figure 17.32 *Abstract Factory* applied to word processor

→ Enter the title of your document:
MY LIFE
→ Enter heading or '–done':
Birth
→ Enter the text:
I was born in a mountain hut . . . .
→ Enter heading or '–done':
Youth
→ Enter the text:
I grew up sturdy . . . .
→ Enter heading or '–done':
–done
→ Enter the style you want displayed ('small' or 'large'):
large

——Title: MY LIFE——
Section 1. ——BIRTH——
I was born in a mountain hut . . . .
Section 2. ——Youth——
I grew up sturdy . . . .

Figure 17.33 Interaction for word processor application

Design Purpose

Provide an interface to a package of classes.

Design Pattern Summary

Define a singleton that is the sole means for
obtaining functionality from the package.

Note: The classes need not be organized as a package;
more than one class may be used for the facade.

Figure 17.34 Design purpose of Facade

for developing, so that classes and packages often relate to each other as client and server. The client and server portions are developed relatively independently—the problem is that services are typically in various states of completion as the project progresses. Complexity is greatly reduced when there is just one object providing access to the functionality of a collection of classes.

A component acts effectively as a server when its interface is narrow. "Narrow" means that the interface (i.e., a collection of functions) contains no unnecessary parts, is collected in one place, and is clearly defined. The Facade design pattern establishes just such an interface to a package of classes. Facade regulates communication with the objects in its package by exposing only one object of the package to client code of the package, hiding all of the other classes. This helps organize development because the programmers responsible for a package can publicize the services offered by a Facade object and stub them while the package is under development. ("Stubbing" is temporarily substituting the real content with very simplistic content, or perhaps with none at all.)

Clients of the package have a concrete representation of the package's functionality to use during development. This advantage extends to maintenance. If maintainers can upgrade the way in which functionality is coded without disturbing the façade, they can be assured that all clients of the package are not affected. The Facade object is a typically a singleton. Figure 17.34 summarizes the design purpose and technique of Facade.

17.6.1.2 Interface for Clients of Facade

Suppose that a package contains a collection of classes and that the client code, external to the package, requires a service *myCMethod()* provided by a class C in the package. The client may interface only with the Facade object, which we will call *theFacadeObject*. Thus, the client code calls a method such as *cMethodOfFacade()* of *theFacadeObject* in order to accomplish this purpose.

17.6.1.3 The *Facade* Class Model

The *Facade* class model shows clients interfacing with a single class of a package, but with no others. Actually, there is nothing to stop us from designating more than one class as a *Facade* class. The non-*Facade* classes are not accessible to code external to the package. The *Facade* structure is in the Delegation form since the *Facade* object delegates commands to classes internal to its package. This is illustrated in Figure 17.35.

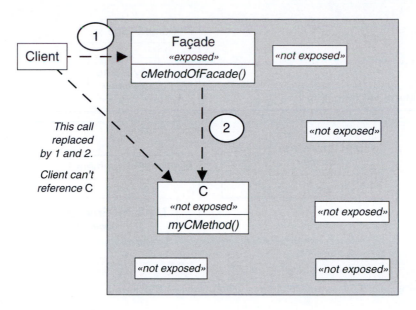

Figure 17.35 Facade design pattern structure

A call that would otherwise refer to an object of a class within the package is replaced by a call to a method of the *Facade* object. This method can then reference the object in question. The sequence diagram is shown in Figure 17.36.

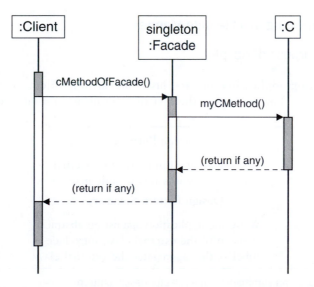

Figure 17.36 Sequence diagram for Facade

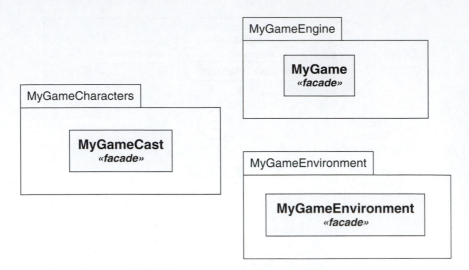

Figure 17.37 Using Facade for the architecture of the Encounter video game

17.6.1.4 Examples of Facade Applications

17.6.1.4.1 Using Facade for a Videogame Architecture

The use of Facade in the architecture of a video game is shown in Figure 17.37. The game's classes are divided into three packages. One pertains to the characters that move about, the second contains the classes that describe the maze, and the third contains the control of the game.

Communication with game characters must occur via the single *MyGameCast* object. Reference to parts of the game's environment must occur through the *MyGameEnvironment* object, and references to the game engine must occur through the *MyGame* object.

17.6.2 Adapter: Interfacing in a Flexible Manner

17.6.2.1 The Design Purpose of Adapter

Suppose that a preexisting application, or even just a preexisting object, provides functionality that our application requires. For example, the existing application could compute the principal

---

Design Purpose

Allow an application to use external
functionality in a retargetable manner.

Design Pattern Summary

Write the application against an abstract
version of the external class; introduce
a subclass that aggregates the external class.

Figure 17.38 Design purpose and summary for the Adapter design pattern

obtained from investing a given amount for a given number of years in a special type of investment, and we want to use this functionality. In using this functionality, however, we want to modify our own application as little as possible. We also want to be able to easily switch to alternative implementations of the required functionality. Figure 17.38 summarizes these purposes and the basic Adapter technique.

17.6.2.2 Interface for Clients of Adapter

The "client" is the application that must use the existing functionality. We create a design in which the client does not directly interface with the existing functionality, however. Instead, it interfaces with an abstract method of an appropriately named abstract class. The latter must be instantiated at runtime with an object of a concrete subclass, as explained next.

Let's call the abstract class *AbstractClass*, and its relevant method we need *standinForRequiredMethod()*. Client code would be something like the following.

```
.....
AbstractClass anAbstractClassObject;
..... // setup code instantiates anAbstractClassObject
....
anAbstractClassObject.clientNameForRequiredMethod(); //use the external functionality
.....
```

Setup code, typically executed at initialization, must instantiate *anAbstractClassObject* at runtime in something like the following manner.

```
.....
if( . . . ) // e.g., from a setup file
{      anAbstractClassObject = new ConcreteSubclassOfAbstractClass();
       . . . .
```

17.6.2.3 The *Adapter* Class Model

The class model for *Adapter* is based on the delegation form because an *Adapter* object delegates the command to the targeted command, as shown in Figure 17.39.

17.6.2.4 The Adapter Sequence Diagram

Adapter works by handing off function calls to *clientNameForRequiredMethod()* as shown in Figure 17.40.

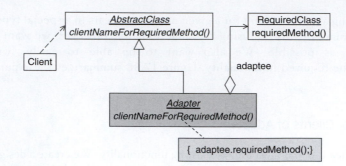

Figure 17.39 The *Adapter* class model

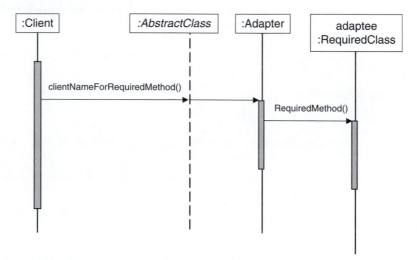

Figure 17.40 Sequence diagram for *Adapter*

17.6.2.5 Example Applications of Adapter

Let's consider a financial application that needs to use the method

```
computeValue( float years, float interest, float amount )
```

of a legacy class *Principle*. We want to be able to easily switch to other implementations of this functionality if necessary. We write our application by giving our own names to the function of interest, and the class/object that owns the function. For example, we can name a method as follows:

```
amount( float originalAmount, float numYears, float intRate )
```

in the class *Financial*. This class is made abstract, as illustrated in Figure 17.41.

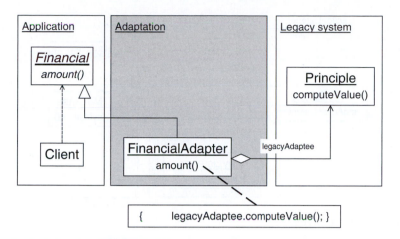

Figure 17.41 An application of the Adapter design pattern

The Adapter design pattern in this case consists of a class, which we will name *FinancialAdapter* here, which inherits from the application's class (*Financial* in our case), and which aggregates the legacy class *Principal*. This could be implemented as follows.

```
class FinancialAdapter extends Financial
{
    Principal legacyAdaptee = null;
    // Constructors go here . . .

    /** This method uses the legacy computeValue() method */
    float amount( float originalAmount, float numYears, float intRate )
    {
        return legacyAdaptee.computeValue
        ( originalAmount, numYears, intRate );
    }
}
```

The new application is *written* against the class *Financial*, but *executed* at runtime with a *FinancialAdapter* object. Setup code instantiates the *Financial* object as a *FinancialAdapter* instance. For example, the client could be written with a method parameterizing *Financial*, such as the following:

```
void executeFinanceApplication( Financial aFinancial );
```

It could then be executed with the following *setup* statement that utilizes the appropriate adapter object.

```
executeFinanceApplication( new FinancialAdapter() );
```

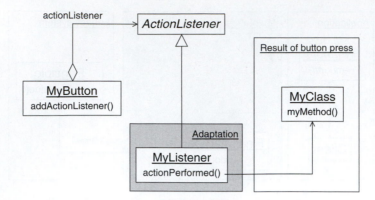

Figure 17.42 Adapter and the Java API

All calls to the *amount()* method of *Financial* are passed to the legacy method *computeValue()*.

It is easy to adapt the application to an implementation of *amount()* in a new class. We would only have to change the code in *FinancialAdapter*. The rest of the application would not be affected. Being able to retarget code by making localized changes like this is valuable for development and maintenance. The alternative is making changes in multiple locations, which is error-prone.

17.6.2.6 Adapter and the Java API

Java *Listeners* are adapters for the following reason. Suppose that we want *myMethod()* in *MyClass* to execute whenever *myButton* is pressed. To do this, we introduce a class *MyListener* that implements the *ActionListener* interface. The class model is shown in Figure 17.42.

The class *MyListener* is the adapter class in this case. At runtime we can instantiate *actionListener* with an *ActionListener* subclass instance such as *MyListener*, according to the effect we require when the button is clicked. The code in *MyButton* references only *ActionListener*, not any particular subclass.

17.6.2.7 Comments on Adapter

- Instead of aggregating *RequiredClass* in Figure 17.39, we could inherit from it, as long as the language allows multiple inheritance. This is shown in Figure 17.43.

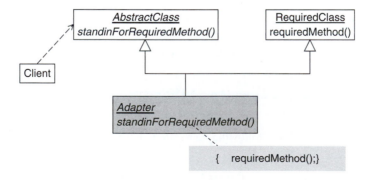

Figure 17.43 Adapter example—inheritance version

We may be satisfied to make *AbstractClass* an Interface if the language does not support multiple inheritance (e.g., Java).

- Adapter is often used when we create an application using library classes, but where we want to retain the flexibility to select other library classes. For example, we might use *Vector* in a Java application to store a collection, but find that it is somewhat awkward for the purpose in question. We could then design and code the application so that it uses an ideal class of our invention to store a collection (e.g., *Automobiles* with methods *storeAuto()* etc.): Then we would incorporate an adapter to fit this to *Vector*. When a more suitable collection management class appears, we could then easily retarget to it, needing to change only the adapter.

- Returning to the financial example, to preserve the option to retarget at runtime, we could retain *FinancialAdapter*, but introduce a new *Adapter* class *FinancialAdapter2*, inheriting from *Financial*. Whenever we want to target the application to the second legacy system, we would execute the application with the following.

```
executeFinanceApplication( new FinancialAdapter2() );
```

17.7 SELECTED BEHAVIORAL DESIGN PATTERNS

This section describes the Interpreter and Observer design patterns as examples of particular behavioral design patterns.

17.7.1 Interpreter: Parsing Expressions

17.7.1.1 Interpreter Design Purposes and Examples

Applications must sometimes deal with *expressions* written in a *grammar*. A compiler, for example, must deal with expressions written in the grammar of a programming language. Compilers are the most common example, but there are many other needs for the interpretation of grammars. The following XML, for example, is an expression, and the grammar (called a *schema*, not explicitly given here) specifies the permissible form for the XML used in this context.

```
<<engineer>>
  <<name>>
      John Q. Doe
  <</name>>
  <<task>>
      Universal payroll Application
  <</task>>
  <<task>>
      Interglactic Web Site Analyzer
  <</task>>
  <<task>>
```

```
      Financial Forecaster
<</task>>
<</engineer>>
```

Our purpose is to design an interpreter for grammars. In the XML example, our interpreter should be able to interpret the following expression as well.

```
<<engineer>>
<<name>>
    Sue W. Smith
<</name>>
<<task>>
    Friendly Server Application
<</task>>
<<task>>
    Intergalactic Web Site Analyzer
<</task>>
<</engineer>>
```

There are two parts relating to the Interpreter design pattern: *parsing* and *interpreting*. Parsing is the process of converting an input—usually a string—into a tree of objects consistent with the class model. In the XML example, this would include picking out individual pieces such as the engineer's name. Interpreting consists of performing useful functionality with the result of the parsing phase. The purpose and basic technique of Interpreter are summarized in Figure 17.44.

17.7.1.2 Interpreter Interfaces for Clients

Once an expression has been parsed and represented using the *Interpreter* class model, clients interface with an *AbstractExpression* object that is the root of the parse tree. The client typically calls an *interpret()* method on this

---

Design Purpose

Interpret expressions written in a formal grammar.

Design Pattern Summary

Represent the grammar using a
recursive design pattern form:

Pass the interpretation to
aggregated objects.

Figure 17.44 Design purpose and summary of Interpreter

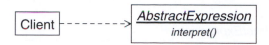

Figure 17.45 Interface to Interpreter design pattern

object. In the above XML example, suppose that the two expressions formed by parsing the two inputs are *johnDoeXML* and *sueSmithXML*. Suppose that the application is intended to convert XML to conversational prose. When the client executes *johnDoeXML.interpret()*, the following might be output.

> *Engineer John Q. Doe is working on the following three projects: Universal Payroll Application, Intergalactic Web Site Analyzer, and Financial Forecaster.*

The class model for the client/design pattern interface looks like Figure 17.45.

17.7.1.3 The *Interpreter* Class Model

The Interpreter design pattern has the Recursive form because expressions can contain further expressions. The class model is shown in Figure 17.46.

AbstractExpression objects are either *TerminalExpression* objects, on which the interpretation function is simple, or *NonTerminalExpression* objects. The latter aggregate *AbstractExpression* objects in turn. The *interpret()* function on a *NonTerminalExpression* object operates by performing required work on the object itself, then essentially commanding each of its aggregated *AbstractExpression* objects to execute its *interpret()* method. This has much in common with the dynamic viewpoint of the Composite design pattern.

17.7.1.4 The *Interpreter* Sequence Diagram

The sequence diagram in Figure 17.47 captures the interpretation process.

17.7.1.5 Example *Interpreter* Application: Network Assembly

As an example of Interpreter, consider an application that handles orders from customers for networked computer systems, and generates installation instructions. For example, consider the order for a network shown in Figure 17.48.

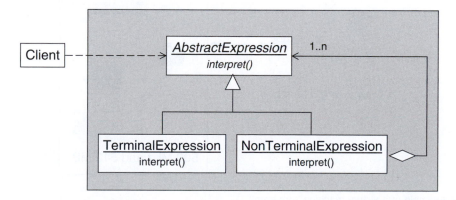

Figure 17.46 The Interpreter design pattern

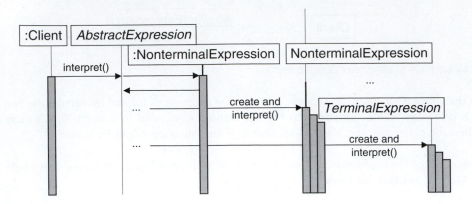

Figure 17.47 The Interpreter sequence diagram

It consists of a 700 Mhz system with 512 MB of RAM connected to a system that consists of the following two connected computers:

a 800Mhz system with 768MB of RAM

a 500Mhz system with 512MB of RAM

This is illustrated in Figure 17.48.
This order can be expressed using the following expression.

```
{ ( 700 512) } { { (800 768 ) } { (500 512) } }
```

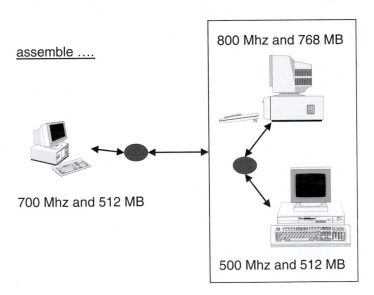

Figure 17.48 Example of a virtual machine "program"

Source: Graphics reproduced with permission from Corel.

The *output* produced by the application would be instructions to the technician, describing how to perform the assembly.

The main use case for this example is as follows. All I/O is to the console.

1. The application prompts the user to enter an order.

2. The application displays the grammar to be used.

3. The application displays an example.

4. The user enters an order.

5. The application echoes the order.

Figure 17.49 specifies the grammar for the orders and shows typical input.

The order example in Figure 17.49 is indeed a legitimate expression in the grammar specified, as the following verifies.

```
component → net system →
{                          component              } { component } →
{ {        component              } { component } } { computer   } →
{ { { component } { component } } { computer   } } { (cpu ram) } →
{ { { computer   } { computer   } } { (cpu ram) } } { (444 44 ) } →
{ { { (cpu ram)   } { (cpu ram)   } } { (333 33 ) } } { (444 44 ) } →
{ { { (111 11)    } { (222 22)    } } { (333 33)  } } { (444 44 ) }
```

The output of the interpretation process—instructions on how to assemble this networking order—are as shown in Figures 17.50, 17.51, and 17.52. In this case, the user selected the example provided by the application.

Our first task is to parse the input and create the corresponding set of aggregated objects. After that, the output is generated in response to a client calling *aNetworkOrder.assemble()*. The method *assemble()* takes the place of *interpret()* in this example. The interpretation of a *primitive* element alone (e.g., a CPU in the example) is

---

Please describe a network on one line using the following grammar for 'component.'
Blank paces are ignored.

component :: = net system | computer
net system:: = { component } { component } | { component }
computer:: = (cpu ram)
cpu:: = integer
ram:: = integer
Example: { { {(400 4)}{ (900 3)} } {(600 3)} } { (750 10) }
An input with a syntactic error will be ignored without comment.

{ { {(111 11)}{ (222 22)} } {(333 33)} } { (444 44) }
You chose { { {(111 11)}{ (222 22)} } {(333 33)} } { (444 44) }

Figure 17.49 Input for network assembly example

Please describe a network on one line using the following grammar for 'component.' Blank paces are ignored. Inputs with syntactic errors will be ignored without comment.

component :: = net system | computer
net system :: = {component} {component} | {component}
computer :: = (cpu ram)|
cpu :: = integer
ram :: = integer

Example: {{{(400 4)}{ (900 3)}}} {(600 3)}} {(750 10)} {{{(400 4)}{ (900 3)}}} {(600 3)}} {(750 10)}

. . . Do some work with the order. . . .

Assemble a network from either one or two parts as follows:

⇒ First Part: Assemble a network, which we will name 'component1', as follows:

Assemble a network, which we will name 'cornponent2', from either one or two parts as follows:
⟶

Assemble a network, which we will name 'component3', from either one or two parts as follows:
⟶

    Build computer component3, from the following parts:
      CPU with specifications 400
   and

Figure 17.50 Output for network assembly example, 1 of 3

simple (see the CPU class in the listing). What remains is to execute an *interpret()* function when applied to a more complex expression.

Applying the Interpreter design pattern to the network order example, we obtain the class diagram shown in Figure 17.53.

For simplicity, we assume that every network consists of just two components, so that each *System* object aggregates two *Component* objects. This can be easily extended to more than two. The source code for the implementation is contained in the accompanying textbook Web site.

17.7.2 Observer

17.7.2.1 The Design Purposes of Observer

Software requirements and design frequently involve a source of data, together with a number of clients that must be updated whenever the data changes. As an example, suppose that the headquarters of International Hamburger Corporation maintains data on its server about hamburger sales throughout the country. Distributed clients for this data include Senior Management, Marketing, and Operations. The data change

RAM with specifications.. . . . 4
second part: →

Assemble a network, which we will name component4, as follows:

Assemble a network, which we will name 'component5', from either one or two parts as follows: →

   Build computer component5, from the following parts:
     CPU with specifications.. . . . 900
  and
     RAM with specifications.. . . . 3

—Now connect cornponent3 with component4 to complete cornponent2—
second part: →

Assemble a network, which we will name component6, as follows:

Assemble a network, which we will name 'cornponent7', from either one or two parts as follows: →

   Build computer component7, from the following parts:
     CPU with specifications.. . . . 600
  and
     RAM with specifications.. . . . 3
     — Now connect cornponent2 with component6 to complete component1—

Figure 17.51 Output for network assembly example, 2 of 3

continually, and each of headquarters' clients needs to update its display according to their various requirements. Let's say, for example, that *Senior Management*'s bar chart must be updated after a 5 percent change has taken place, *Marketing* displays a new pie chart when a change of at least 1 percent has taken place, and *Operations* requires tables to be updated when every change takes place.

⇒ Second part: Now assemble a network, which we will name 'component8', as follows:

Assemble a network, which we will name 'component9', from either one or two parts as follows: →

   Build computer component9, from the following parts:
     CPU with specifications.. . . . 750
  and
     RAM with specifications.. . . . 10

     ====Now connect component1 with component8 to get the resulting network.====
     . . . . . Do more work with the order. . . .

Figure 17.52 Output for network assembly example, 3 of 3

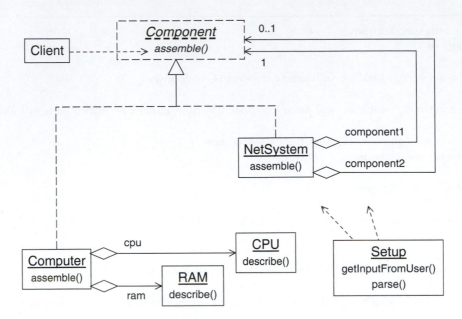

Figure 17.53 Application of Interpreter design pattern

The Observer design pattern is intended to address these requirements. Its purposes and basic technique are summarized in Figure 17.54.

17.7.2.2 Observer Interfaces for Clients

Suppose that the abstract class *Source* is aware of the data source. Whenever a client wants all observers to take notice (typically, of a change in the data), it calls a designated method of *Source*. In the model below, this method is named *notify()*. The client is shielded from the manner in which Observer carries out this process.

17.7.2.3 The *Observer* Class Model

The parties in the Observer design pattern requiring updating are known as *observers*, and are subclasses of a single abstract class, which we will call *Observer*. This pattern is in the Delegation form since *Source* delegates the updating process to the *Observer* objects. The pattern is shown in Figure 17.55.

Design Purpose

Arrange for a set of objects to
be affected by a single object.

Design Pattern Summary

The single object aggregates the set, calling
a method with a fixed name on each member.

Figure 17.54 The design purpose and summary of the Observer pattern

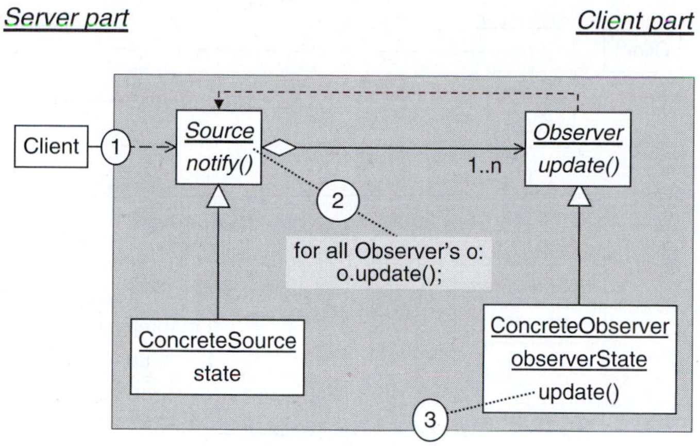

Figure 17.55 The Observer design pattern

We will follow a sequence of steps to show how Observer operates.

Step 1 The client references a known interface object, requesting that the observers be notified. For example, the client could be a process programmed to notice that the data has changed, or it could be a clock-driven task. In the model, this is shown as a *Client* object telling the *Source* object to execute its *notify()* function.

Step 2 The *notify()* method calls the *update()* function on each of *Observer* object that it aggregates.

Step 3 The implementation of *update()* depends on the particular *ConcreteObserver* to which it belongs. Usually, *update()* compares the *ConcreteObserver* object's state (variable values) with that of the central data source on the server, then decides whether or not to change its variable values accordingly. It probably performs other actions such as creating a new display.

The class model tells us that every *Observer* references a *Source* object. In fact, the *ConcreteObservers* will reference the *ConcreteSource* object at runtime. How do the *ConcreteObserver* objects know to reference the ConcreteSource object? We could pass a reference to it in the parameters of *update()*, as is done in the Java API (see Section 17.7.2.5).

17.7.2.4 Example Observer Applications

17.7.2.4.1 ''Hamburgers'' Observer Example
Applying Observer to our International Hamburger Corporation problem, we obtain a model such as that shown in Figure 17.56.

17.7.2.4.2 Mutual Funds Observer Example
We will take as another example application of Observer the updating of mutual fund portfolios. Mutual funds invest in multiple stocks, so that when a particular stock's price changes, it affects the values of all the mutual funds that invest in it. Normally, such changes in a stock's price are transmitted electronically. In our example,

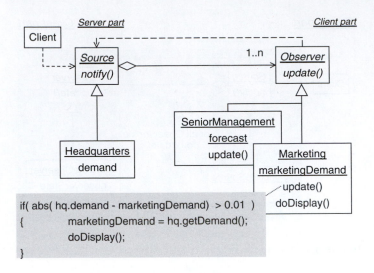

Figure 17.56 Observer applied to International Hamburger Corporation

we will make the change to Awesome Inc.'s stock by hand. The application will then display the resulting changes in the mutual funds carrying Awesome stock. We will use the *Observer/Observable* Java API to carry out this design and implementation.

The main use case is as follows:

1. The application reports the status of mutual funds that invest in Awesome Inc.

2. The following repeats until the user signifies quitting.

    2.1. The application prompts the user to supply a price for Awesome stock.

    2.2. The user enters a price in decimal form.

    2.3. The application reports the status of mutual funds that invest in Awesome Inc.

Figure 17.57 shows a typical scenario.
The class model is shown in Figure 17.58.
This class model uses *Observer* classes in the Java API, which are discussed next.

17.7.2.5 *Observer* in the Java API

Many of the design patterns discussed in this book are present in the Java API. However, one recognizes them by their form rather than by name. Observer is one of the few patterns explicitly called out by name in the Java API. The Java API *Observer* class model is shown in Figure 17.59.

The Java API uses virtually the same terms as Gamma et al. Notice that *update(. . .)* is a callback method in the sense that it provides *Observer* objects a reference to its source, thereby enabling them to compare their data and so on with the *Observable* object in executing *update()*. Because update is implemented as a callback, there is this no need for concrete *Observer* classes to maintain references to the *Observable* object.

Note: HiGrowthMutualFund starts with 3 shares of Awesome, assumes price of 1.0, and has non-Awesome holdings totalling 400.0

Note: MedGrowthMutualFund starts with 2 shares of Awesome, assumes price of 1.0, and has non-Awesome holdings totalling 300.0

Note: LoGrowthMutualFund starts with 1 shares of Awesome, assumes price of 1.0, and has non-Awesome holdings totalling 200.0

Enter 'quit': Any other input to continue.
go on
Enter the current price of Awesome Inc. in decimal form.
32.1
Value of Lo Growth Mutual Fund changed from 201.0 to 232.1
Value of Med Growth Mutual Fund changed from 302.0 to 364.2
Value of Hi Growth Mutual Fund changed from 403.0 to 496.3

Enter 'quit': Any other input to continue.
go on
Enter the current price of Awesome Inc. in decimal form.
21.0
Value of Lo Growth Mutual Fund changed from 232.1 to 221.0
Value of Med Growth Mutual Fund changed from 364.2 to 342.0
Value of Hi Growth Mutual Fund changed from 496.3 to 463.0

Enter 'quit': Any other input to continue.

Figure 17.57 I/O example for mutual fund application

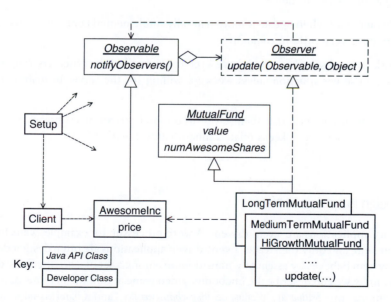

Figure 17.58 *Observer* example class diagram—mutual funds example

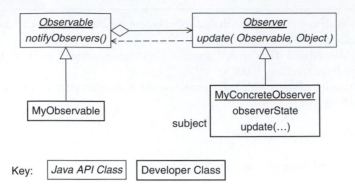

Figure 17.59 *Observer* in the Java API

17.7.2.6 Comments on Observer

• Observer also goes by the widely used name of "Model-View-Controller" (MVC), although there are slight differences in emphasis. The "Model" in MVC is the *Source* in Figure 17.55 (the *Observable* in the Java API). The "Views" are the *Observer* objects, and the "Control" is client and possibly setup code. MVC emphasizes the fact that the model is data and the views are GUIs, whereas Observer is conceived with broader application.

• Observer allows the addition and removal of observers without disrupting existing observer code. Only the loop in *Observable.notify()* must be augmented. Sometimes the process of adding and removing observers is considered part of the pattern (rather than being a "setup" function).

• Observer may be disadvantageous if very few of the observers need to react to changes (in which case the numerous notifications waste resources).

• *Observer* is disadvantageous when update is more naturally implemented centrally, or when update policies among observers have very little in common.

• *Observer* can't work if the observable cannot have a reference to all of the observers. For example, we would not use it in a client/server situation unless we were willing for the server to maintain references to all clients.

• In general, having the observers update themselves (as opposed to external software performing it) is good object-oriented design because it keeps related functionality together.

17.7.3 State

17.7.3.1 The Design Purposes of State

Many contemporary applications are "event-driven." A word processor, for example, waits for the user to click on an icon or menu item, and only then reacts. Event-driven applications are often designed as state-transition systems. When a system behaves by essentially transitioning among a set of *states*, the State design pattern can be helpful. For example, we can describe the Encounter video game at runtime in terms of the state it is in—it could transition among the *Setting-up*, *Waiting*, *Setting-characteristics*, and *Characters-interacting* states, among others. A design should capture this behavior effectively. As the game becomes better defined, the design

---

Design Purpose

Cause an object to behave in a
manner determined by its state.

Design Pattern Summary

Aggregate a *State* object
and delegate behavior to it.

Figure 17.60 The design purpose for the State pattern

should also be capable of gracefully absorbing new states and action handling without disrupting the existing design. Figure 17.60 summarizes the purpose and basic technique of the State design pattern.

17.7.3.2 State Interfaces for Clients

To use the State pattern, the client simply makes a call on a specific method of a specific object. The client is shielded from the various possible effects of calling the method, which depend on the object's state.

17.7.3.3 The *State* Class Model

In general terms, suppose that we want to use a method *doRequest()* of an object *target* of class *Target*, where *doRequest()* can behave in different ways, according to *target*'s state at the time of the call. This is solved by introducing a class, which we will call *TargetState*, and giving *Target* an attribute (we'll call it *targetState*) of type *TargetState*. We ensure that *targetState* properly represents the *Target* object's current state at all times. This is ensured by *targetState* being an object of the appropriate *TargetState* subclass. Figure 17.61 shows this. Note that the State design pattern is in the *Delegation* form.

    The method *doRequest()* calls *targetState.handleRequest()*, so the call to *doRequest()* is translated by the virtual function property into the particular version of *handleRequest()* appropriate to the state of *target*. The client does not need to know the state of *target*. The full class model is shown in Figure 17.62.

17.7.3.4 Example State Applications

The Encounter video game can typically be in a variety of states. When you start to play the game, you may have the opportunity to set your characteristics ("Setting Up" state). When you are in the midst of interacting with other characters, your state is different ("Engaging" state, perhaps). It is reasonable to expect that you can't change your characteristics in the midst of an engagement because the game would not be much fun to

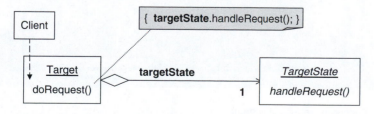

Figure 17.61 The basic structure of the State design pattern

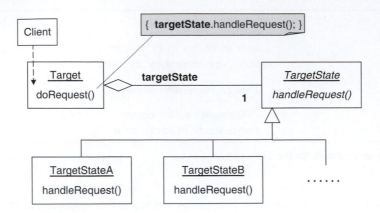

Figure 17.62 The State design pattern: *doRequest()* behaves according to the state of *Target*

play in that case. If the game interface had the appearance in Figure 17.63, the effect of pressing the *Set Characteristics* button would depend on the state of the game at the time.

Figure 17.64 shows how the State design pattern can be used to handle the states and actions of Encounter.

The class *MyGame* has an attribute called *state* of type *MyGameState*. The type of the *state* object (i.e., which subclass of *MyGameState* it belongs to) determines what happens when *setCharacteristics()* is called on a *MyGame* object.

The code for *setCharacteristics()* in *MyGame* passes control to the *handleClick()* function of *state*. Each subclass of *MyGameState* implements *handleClick()* in its own manner. For example, if *MyGame* is in *Waiting* state, then the effect of clicking on the "Set Characteristics" button is that a window appears through which the player can change his characteristics. On the other hand, if *MyGame* is in *SettingQualities* state, then nothing happens because the user is already setting his characteristics.

Figure 17.63 GUI for Encounter role-playing game

Source: Courtesy of Tom VanCourt and Corel.

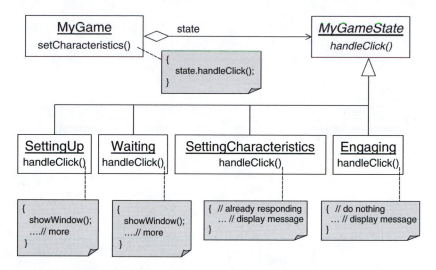

Figure 17.64 The State design pattern applied to the Encounter role-playing game

17.7.3.5 Comments on State

- The State design pattern is particularly beneficial when new states are likely to be needed in the future.

- State does not handle the question of how to set up the successive state (if required) once *handleEvent()* has been performed. Although State does not handle the transition function, it can be a useful framework in which to implement transition. For example, *handleEvent()* can contain code that swaps in the new state. A possible companion to the State design pattern is a state-transition table whose entries indicate what new state the object transitions into for each "current state–event occurrence" pair.

- Whether or not the State design pattern is applied, state-oriented architectures have been used with success for many applications (see, for example, the work of Shlaer and Mellor [2]). Real-time applications tend to benefit especially from the state architecture because they often rely on a state/event perspective.

17.8 DESIGN PATTERN FORMS: DELEGATION AND RECURSION

As the examples of design patterns above illustrate, they occur in a limited number of forms. We could say that there are patterns to the design patterns—meta patterns, if you like. Most design patterns are based on the *delegation* or *recursion* forms, as described in this section.

17.8.1 The Delegation Design Pattern Form

Consider a task that needs doing, the object that initiates it, and an object that does the actual work. *Delegation* is a process by which the initiator employs a third object to get the work done by the doer. An example from real life is the use of a realtor in which the seller (the initiator) wants to sell to a buyer (the doer, in this case). To achieve flexibility, the KitchenViewer design replaces direct code such as

```
new AntiqueWallCabinet(); // applies only to antique style
```

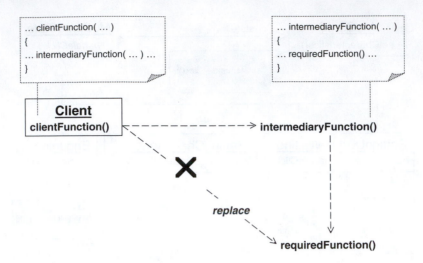

Figure 17.65 The idea of delegation

with a version that delegates construction to an intermediary method

```
myStyle.getWallCabinet(); //applies to whatever style is chosen at runtime
```

The Abstract Factory design pattern replaces several direct method calls (constructor calls, actually) with delegated calls to separate methods, which call the desired methods in turn. The basic idea of delegation is shown in Figure 17.65.

A common way in which design patterns put delegation into practice is through a class that delegates functionality to the methods of an abstract class. When we apply Abstract Factory in Figure 17.7, for example, the work of creating a *WallCabinet* object is delegated to the methods of a *KitchenStyle* object.

A common form of Delegation is illustrated in Figure 17.66, where an abstract class is aggregated and acts as a base class for several concrete subclasses.

The client calls the method *interfaceMethod()* of the interface class *DPInterface*. In turn, *interfaceMethod()* delegates the required functionality to its aggregated *DoerBase* object, *doerObject*. The functionality is carried out by having *doerObject* execute a method that we have named *doIt()*. At runtime *doerObject* is an object of either the class *ConcreteDoer1*, *ConcreteDoer2*, and so on. Since the effect of *doIt()* depends on runtime conditions, so does the effect of *interfaceMethod()*. The class *DPInterface* thus has the following form.

```
class DPInterface
{     DoerBase doerObject;
      .....
      public void interfaceMethod()
      { doerObject.doIt();
      }
}
```

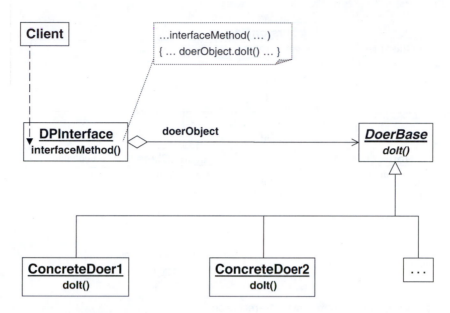

Figure 17.66 Basic design pattern form number 1—delegation

Delegation, implemented using the virtual function property, is the most common form of design patterns. Another common form is Recursion: the use of structures to effectively reference themselves.

17.8.2 The Recursion Design Pattern Form

Several design patterns require recursion—in other words, part of the pattern essentially uses itself. For example, recursion is useful for representing a linked list of objects in which each object of a class aggregates another object of the same class. Another example is constructing a graphical user interface that allows for windows within windows within windows . . . and so on. In this case, the *Window* object aggregates itself.

In a recursive pattern form, a dual inheritance–aggregation relationship exists between a base class and a subclass, as shown in Figure 17.67. Notice that the Recursive form uses the Delegation form—in this case, the delegation doubles back on itself.

From the dynamic viewpoint, in a Recursive form the client calls a method of the interface, which we'll name *doOperation()*. If the object actually belongs to the subclass *RecursiveClass*, then executing its *doOperation()* involves the object(s) of *aggregate*. These objects may once again call *doOperation()*, and so on.

Let's take as an example the case where *RecursionBase* is the class *Employee*, *doOperation()* is the method *printOrganization()*, and *RecursiveClass* is the class *Supervisor*. The idea is to produce a printout of all the employees of an organization. The class model is shown in Figure 17.68.

The method *printOrganization()* in *Supervisor* would be programmed to first print the supervisor's name, then call the *printOrganization()* method in each of the *Employee* objects in *supervisees*. For *Employee* objects of the class *IndividualContributor*, the method *printOrganization()* prints only the name of that employee. For *Employee* objects of the class *Supervisor*, *printOrganization()* prints that supervisor's name and the printing process repeats recursively. This recursive process eventually prints all of the names. The class *Supervisor* thus has the following form.

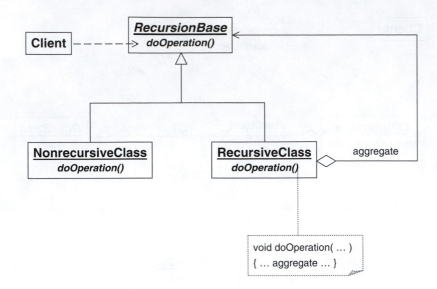

Figure 17.67 Basic design pattern form number 1—recursion

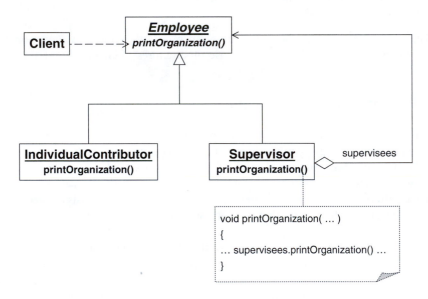

Figure 17.68 The Recursion design pattern form applied to an organizational chart

```
class Supervisor extends Employee
{
    Vector supervisees;
    . . .
    void printOrganization( . . . )
```

```
    {   . . .
        supervisees.printOrganization();        . . .
    }
}
```

17.9 SUMMARY

This chapter introduced design patterns, which are used to satisfy recurring design purposes. A design pattern is a group of classes (the *static* viewpoint) that interact in a recognizable way (the *dynamic* viewpoint). Typically, a design pattern consists of an abstract level of classes and a nonabstract ("concrete") level. Three roles (sets of code) are involved in the use of design patterns: the *application* of the design pattern itself, the code that uses it (the *client* role), and the code that initializes or changes the design pattern application (the *setup* role).

Most design patterns use *delegation*, in which calls to an interface method are handed off to another method to facilitate variation at runtime. Several design patterns also use a form of *recursion*, in which a class references either itself or a base class from which it inherits.

Design patterns can be roughly classified as *creational, structural,* or *behavioral. Creational* patterns create nontrivial object ensembles in a manner determined at runtime. *Structural* patterns are used to represent collections of objects. *Behavioral* patterns deal flexibly with behavior among a set of objects.

This chapter described the following creational design patterns by way of example. The Singleton pattern is used to enforce classes with only a single instance. The Abstract Factory pattern is used when an interrelated family of classes is required but in a variety of "styles." A "style" in this sense is a characteristic applicable to every object in the family.

The following behavioral design patterns were discussed. Facade is a way to treat a group of classes as a unit, by providing its functionality only through a single object. Adapter is a way to switch user object types of given functionality at runtime.

The chapter also discussed the following structural design patterns. Interpreter is used when the situation is viewed as the execution of a language specially designed for the application. Observer is used for designs that separate control from presentation and data. State is used to design application parts best thought of in terms of a set of states.

These points are summarized in Figure 17.69. The reader is referred to Fowler [3] and Vlissides [4] for further explorations of design patterns.

- Design Patterns are **recurring designs** satisfying recurring design purposes
- Described by **Static and Dynamic Viewpoints**
  - Typically class models and sequence diagrams, respectively
- Use of a pattern application is a Client Role
  - Client interface carefully controlled
  - "Setup," typically initialization, a separate role
- Design pattern Forms usually **Delegation** or **Recursion**
- Classified as **Creational, Structural,** or **Behavioral**

Figure 17.69 A summary of this chapter

17.10 EXERCISES

1. Which of the following are applications of design patterns? Explain your conclusions.
   (a) An object-orientated design
   (b) The ability to vary the order in which a *print()* method is applied to the elements of a *Vector*
   (c) Varying the order in which a method is applied to the elements of a collection of objects by introducing a class whose methods include a method like *goToNextElement()*
   (d) Capturing the mutual behavior of a pair of objects of two classes
   (e) Capturing the mutual behavior of a pair of objects of two classes by introducing a third class aggregating the two classes

2. Characterize the following design purpose as *creational, structural,* or *behavioral.* Explain your conclusion clearly.

   We must build an application with 15 different screens involving various combinations of 6 user interface controls (e.g., list boxes) arranged in a simple grid. Performing a mouse action or text entry on a control (e.g., a button) in a screen affects other controls on the same screen. In all other respects the screens are not related and are not similar in appearance. The composition of these screens is very unlikely to change.

3. Characterize the following design purpose as *creational, structural,* or *behavioral.* Explain your conclusion clearly.

   We must build a human resources application dealing with the management structure at a large company. We need to represent the organization chart within the application.

4. Characterize the following design purpose as *creational, structural,* or *behavioral.* Explain your conclusion clearly.

   We must build an application that allows users to build and change their stock portfolio with a various kinds of mutual fund picks from specified subcategories. The mutual fund categories are *technology, old industries, utilities, real estate,* and *mining.* The application allows users to pick categories. It then makes portfolio recommendations depending on the user's choice. For example, the user can ask for a low-risk portfolio of utilities and mining stocks, and the application describes its recommendations within these constraints.

5. Consider the following two statements.
   (a) *Observer* consists of an object of a class that reflects a data source, together with objects of classes that depend on the data source.
   (b) When the data changes value, a method with the name *update()* is called on each observing object.

   Which of these two statements takes a *static* viewpoint and which a *dynamic* viewpoint?

6. The following figure shows the *Observer* design pattern class model. Group the classes to show *abstract* and *concrete* levels. Group the classes to show the three *roles* described in this chapter.

7. (a) What two design pattern *forms* are mentioned in this chapter?

(b) Which of the two forms is more likely to use virtual functions? Explain your answer and give an example.

(c) Which of the two forms is a *linked list of objects* likely to be? Explain your answer.

(d) Which of the two forms is the Observer pattern in Exercise 6?

8. Research the Java Swing software architecture, such as Java Swing, and describe in a few paragraphs how it makes use of the Observer pattern. Draw a class diagram as part of your answer.

9. Research the Java EE platform and describe in a few paragraphs how it makes use of the Facade design pattern. Draw a class diagram as part of your solution.

BIBLIOGRAPHY

1. Gamma, Erich, Richard Helm, Ralph Johnson, and John Vlissides, *"Design Patterns, Elements of Reusable Object-Oriented Software,"* Addison-Wesley, 1995.
2. Shlaer, Sally, and Stephen Mellor. *"Object Lifecycles: Modeling the World in States,"* Yourdon Press, 1991.
3. Fowler, Martin. *"Pattern Hatching: Design Patterns Applied,"* Addison-Wesley, 1998.
4. Vlissides, John M., *"Patterns of Enterprise Application Architecture,"* Addison-Wesley, 2002.

18

Software Architecture

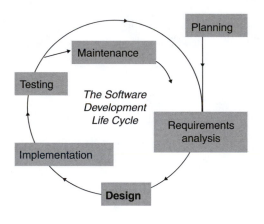

- How do you classify software architectures?

- What are data flow architectures?

- What are three-tier architectures and their generalizations?

- What makes database-centric systems a separate type of architecture?

- What are service-oriented architectures?

- What IEEE standards are there for expressing designs?

- What do real-world architectures look like?

Figure 18.1 The context and learning goals for this chapter

This part of the book, concerned with design, began by describing design goals and principles and then described patterns of design that recur throughout. This chapter describes design at the high level, and the chapter that follows at the detailed level.

A *software architecture* describes the overall components of an application and how they relate to each other. Its design goals, as discussed in Chapter 15, include sufficiency, understandability, modularity, high cohesion, low coupling, robustness, flexibility, reusability, efficiency, and reliability. For a given software

- Dataflow architectures
  - Pipes and filters
  - Batch sequential
- Independent components
  - Client-server systems
  - Parallel communicating processes
  - Event systems
  - Service-oriented (added)
- Virtual machines
  - Interpreters
  - Rule-based systems
- Repository architectures
  - Databases
  - Hypertext systems
  - Blackboards
- Layered architectures

Figure 18.2 Shaw and Garlan's categorization of software architectures

Source: Shaw, M.G. and D. Garlan, "Software Architecture: Perspectives on an Emerging Discipline," Prentice Hall, 1996.

development project, there may be several possible appropriate architectures, and selecting one depends upon the goals that one wants to emphasize.

Flexibility, to choose one of these qualities, is a key goal of many architectures—the ability to accommodate new features. This usually involves introducing abstraction into the process. For example, we might want the architecture for the Encounter video game case study to support not just this particular game, but any role-playing video game.

Attaining one desirable design property may entail a trade-off against others. For example, a designer who uses abstractions to obtain a flexible architecture may make it harder to understand.

18.1 A CATEGORIZATION OF ARCHITECTURES

Shaw and Garlan [1] have classified software architectures in a useful manner. Their classification, somewhat adapted here, is shown in Figure 18.2. Section 18.3 explains these architectures. There is a wide variety of problems requiring software solutions, and there is a wide variety of architectures needed to deal with them. In most cases, the architecture is unique to the problem. Sometimes, one of the architectures identified by Shaw and Garlan matches the problem; in many cases they simply provide ideas on which to base the architecture. This is similar to architecture in house construction, in which classical and standard ideas provide inspiration for great architecture but are not simply copied.

18.2 SOFTWARE ARCHITECTURE ALTERNATIVES AND THEIR CLASS MODELS

The software architect develops a mental model of how the application is meant to work, often with five to seven components. The architect's mental model depends on the application in question, of course, but may benefit from architectures that others have developed in the past, just as a suspension bridge design benefits from the study of previously built suspension bridges. This section elaborates on the architectures classified by Shaw and Garlan. They categorize architectures as data flow, independent components, virtual machines, repository architectures, and layered architectures. Figure 18.2 summarizes these and their subcategories, and the rest of this section explains them. It also adds service-oriented architectures.

18.2.1 Data Flow Architectures

Some applications are best viewed as data flowing among processing units. Data flow diagrams (DFDs) illustrate such views. Each processing unit of the DFD is designed independently of the others. Data

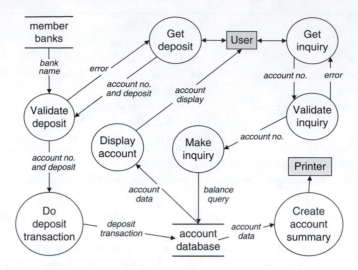

Figure 18.3 Partial data flow diagram for an ATM application

emanates from sources, such as the user, and eventually flows back to users, or into sinks such as account databases. The elements of the DFD notation were explained in Chapter 16. A banking application is shown in Figure 18.3.

Data flow from the user to a "Get deposit" process, which sends the account number and the deposit amount to a process designed to check these data for consistency. If they are consistent, the data may be sent to a process that creates a transaction, and so on. DFDs can be nested. For example, the "Create inquiry transaction" can itself be decomposed into a more detailed data flow diagram.

The functions of a data flow diagram may reside on more than one physical platform. Figure 18.4 shows one possible allocation.

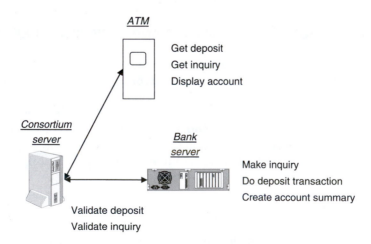

Figure 18.4 Platforms in data flow architectures, and an example

18.2.1.1 Pipe and Filter

One kind of data flow architecture, shown in Figure 18.5, is referred to as the *pipe and filter* architecture. In this kind the processing elements ("filters") accept streams as input (sequences of a uniform data element) at any time, and produce output streams. Each filter must be designed to be independent of the other filters. The architectural feature in Figure 18.5 is implemented by UNIX pipes, for example.

Pipe and filter architectures have the advantage of modularity. An example is shown in Figure 18.6. In it, the application maintains accounts as transactions arrive at random times from communication lines. The architecture includes a step for logging transactions in case of system failure. The withdraw function would have withdrawal input such as *JohnDoeAccountNum12345Amount$3500.00*, or just *JohnDoe12345$3500.00'*—that is, a character stream and bank address input such as *BankNum9876*. The processing elements, shown in ellipses, wait until all of the required input has arrived before performing their operation.

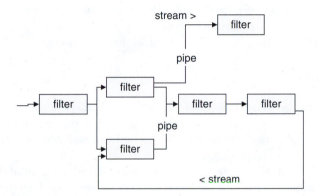

Figure 18.5 Pipe and filter architectures

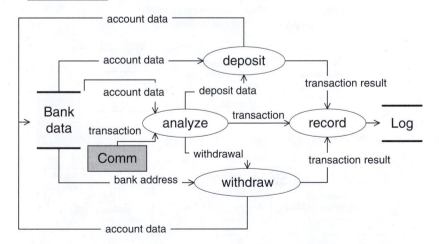

Figure 18.6 Example of a pipe-and-filter architecture, to maintain wired financial transaction

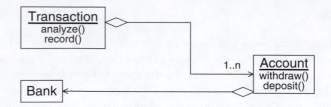

Figure 18.7 Obtaining a class model from a data flow architecture—bank account example

There is no absolutely uniform way to map data flow diagrams (DFDs) onto class models; however, functional units of the DFD can frequently map directly onto methods of classes, as shown in Figure 18.7.

The increasing use of distributed computing is accelerating the application of stream-oriented computing because remote function calling is often implemented by converting the call to a stream of characters. This is done in Web services, for example. These use serialization, which converts objects to XML character streams. In addition, I/O is often implemented using streams, and performing I/O in a language such as Java often amounts to a filtering process of the kind we have discussed.

18.2.1.2 Batch Sequential

In the special case where the processing elements are only given batches of data, the result is a *batch sequential* form of data flow. As an example, consider a banking application that computes the amount of money available for mortgage loans (secured by properties) and the amount available for unsecured loans. A data flow diagram (DFD) is suggested by Figure 18.8.

This DFD is batch sequential because the functions are executed using all of the input data of a given run, taken together. For example, we collect the funds available for mortgage loans by using all of the account data. This is in contrast with the transaction example in Figure 18.6, in which there are many "virtually continuous" transactions, each using selected data from their sources.

Figure 18.9 shows one mapping into a class model in which the functions of the data flow are realized as methods of the *Bank* class. The "batches" of processing are executed by running the relevant methods of this class.

Figure 18.8 Example of a batch-sequential data flow architecture—creating a mortgage pool

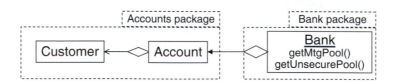

Figure 18.9 Class model for batch sequential data flow—creating a mortgage pool example

For decades, data flow has been the most common way of expressing architectures, and it is bound to be useful for some time to come. Engineers naturally think of data flowing from one processing "station" to the next and of processing taking place at each station. The disadvantages of data flow diagrams include the fact that they do not map very cleanly to code, whether object-oriented or not. An exception to this applies to specific data flow languages (some being actually graphic in nature), which are built around the very concept of data flow. We will use the data flow model once again when we discuss detailed design in Chapter 19.

18.2.2 Independent Components

The *independent components* architecture consists of components operating in parallel (at least in principle) and communicating with each other from time to time. An obvious instance of this can be found on the World Wide Web, where millions of servers and browsers operate continuously in parallel and periodically communicate with each other.

"Components" are portions of software that do not change and that do not require knowledge of the software using them. .NET assemblies and JavaBeans are example component technologies. Components satisfy guidelines aimed at making them self-contained. They use other components by aggregation, and generally interact with other components through events.

The case studies include a discussion of the Eclipse project. Eclipse is a development platform designed to accommodate *plug-ins*. These are independent components that can be created by developers for various purposes, and added to the platform without affecting existing functionality.

18.2.2.1 Tiered and Client-Server Architectures

In a *client-server* architecture, the server component serves the needs of the client upon request. Client-server relationships have the advantage of low coupling between the participating components. When more than one person performs implementation it is natural to parcel out a package of classes to each developer or group of developers, and developers typically require the services of classes for which others are responsible. In other words, developers' packages are often related as client and server. The problem is that these services are typically in varied states of readiness as the application is in the process of being built.

A server component acts more effectively when its interface is narrow. "Narrow" means that the interface (essentially a collection of functions) contains only necessary parts, is collected in one place, and is clearly defined. As explained in Chapter 17, the Facade design pattern establishes just such an interface to a package of classes. Facade regulates communication with the objects in its package by exposing only one object of the package to code using the package, hiding all of the other classes.

Client-server architectures were a steady feature of the 1980s and 1990s. Many of them replaced mainframe/terminal architectures. Client/server architectures have subsequently become more sophisticated and more varied. Some are now designed as three-tier architectures instead of the original two tiers (client and server). The third tier lies between the client and the server, providing a useful level of indirection. A common allocation of function is to design the GUI for the client, the database management system, or procedure management for the middle layer, and assorted application programs and/or the database itself for the third layer. The middle layer can be a common data "bus" that brokers communication. Alternatively, the middle layer can operate via a standard such as Microsoft's .NET *assemblies*. Finally, the World Wide Web can be considered a breed of client/server architecture in which "one server/tens of clients" is replaced by "one server/millions of clients."

18.2.2.2 The Parallel Communicating Processes Architecture

Another type of "independent component" architecture identified by Shaw and Garlan is named *parallel communicating processes*. This architecture is characterized by several processes, or threads, executing at the same time. In his classic book [2], Dijkstra showed that conceiving a process such as the combination of parallel parts can actually simplify designs. An example of this is a simulation of customers in a bank. Traditionally, many such simulations were designed without parallelism by storing and handling the events involved. Such designs can sometimes be simplified, however, if the movement of each customer is a separate process (e.g., a thread object in Java). Such a parallel communicating process design has the advantage that it matches more closely to the activities that it simulates. A good reference to parallel communicating processes in the Java context is [3]. The parallel processes may run on a single platform or on separate platforms, as illustrated in Figure 18.10.

Encounter uses this architectural parallel element by having the foreign character Freddie move independently from area to adjacent area while the game progresses. This thread "communicates" whenever Freddie finds himself in the same area as the player character.

A UML notation that expresses parallelism was discussed in Chapter 16. This notation, used in Figures 18.11 and 18.12, shows an architecture for a banking application designed to handle multiple transactions occurring simultaneously on automated teller machines (ATMs). This particular architecture allows the customer to initiate transactions without having to wait for completion, even when the transaction takes significant time. The application may, for example, inform a customer that funds he deposited will not be immediately available—that is, not wait for the completion of that process before making the announcement.

When customer *n* uses an ATM, an object for customer *n* is created (Step 1 in Figure 18.11). Customer *n* creates *session m* (2). Session *m* then retrieves an *Account* object such as customer *n* checking (3). The retrieval is performed asynchronously, and a thread, or parallel process, is created because it may take time. This allows the customer to carry out other business in the meantime. The method call retrieving the *Account* object is denoted by a stick arrow head indicating that the *Session* object proceeds in parallel with this construction, returning to the customer object. Since we are dealing at an architectural level, we are omitting details here such as showing the thread objects involved and showing how the *Session* objects know that this is its required

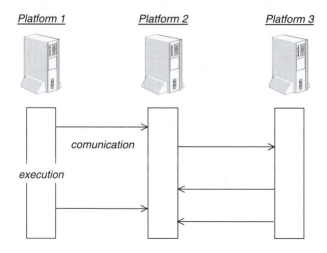

Figure 18.10 Platforms for communicating processors

Requirement: Manage ATM traffic.

Architecture beginning with first session:

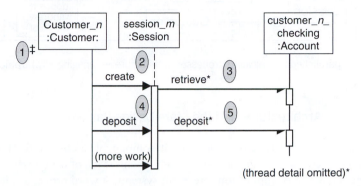

Figure 18.11 Example of parallel communicating processor architecture—managing ATM traffic, fragment of sequence diagram

call. The _Customer_ object immediately performs a deposit transaction by sending a message to the _Session_ object (4). The _Session_ object executes the deposit by sending a deposit message asynchronously to the _Account_ object, spawning a new thread (5). Other work can go on—including by other sessions—while the deposit is processed.

In parallel, other _Customer_ objects such as customer _s_ are creating and operating on other sessions such as session _k_. This is shown in Figure 18.12.

Figure 18.13 shows the beginning of a class model that handles this kind of architecture.

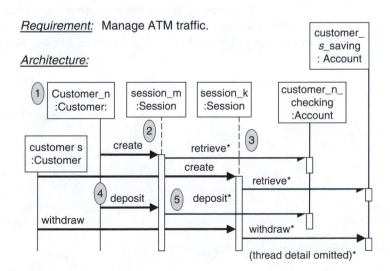

Figure 18.12 Example of parallel communicating processor architecture—managing ATM traffic—sequence diagram

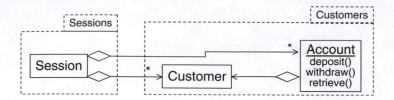

Figure 18.13 Example of parallel communicating processor architecture—managing ATM traffic—class model

18.2.2.3 Event Systems Architectures and the State Design Pattern

Let's turn to *event systems*, the third type of "independent component" architecture classified by Shaw and Garlan. This architecture views applications as a set of components, each of which waits until an event occurs that affects it. Many contemporary applications are event systems. A word processor, for example, waits for the user to click on an icon or menu item. It then reacts accordingly, by storing the file, enlarging fonts, and so on. Event systems are often fulfilled as state transition systems, which were introduced in Chapter 11.

When a system behaves by essentially transitioning among a set of states, the State design pattern should be considered for the design. This design pattern was explained in Chapter 17. For example, we have described the overall requirement for Encounter in terms of the state diagram in Figure 11.26 of Chapter 11. Encounter transitions among the *Setting up*, *Waiting*, *Setting qualities*, *Reporting*, and *Engaging* states, among others. Our design should capture this behavior effectively. It should also be capable of gracefully absorbing new states and action handling as the game becomes more complete, without disrupting the existing design. For these reasons, we will apply the State design pattern described in Chapter 17 to Encounter.

The State pattern solves the problem of how to use an object without having to know its state. In the context of Encounter we want to be able to write controlling code that handles mouse actions but does not reference the possible states that the game can be in, or the specific effects of the mouse actions. This makes it possible to add new game situations without disrupting this controlling code.

Figure 18.14 begins to show how the State design pattern can be used to handle the states and actions of Encounter. The framework class *RPGame* ("Role-playing game") has an attribute called *state*, which is of type *GameState*. The subtype of *state* (i.e., which subclass of *GameState* it belongs to) determines what happens when *handleEvent()* is called on an *RPGame* object. The code for *handleEvent()* in *RPGame* passes control to the *handleEvent()* function of state.

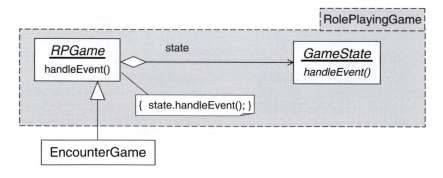

Figure 18.14 Beginning of the State design pattern applied to Encounter

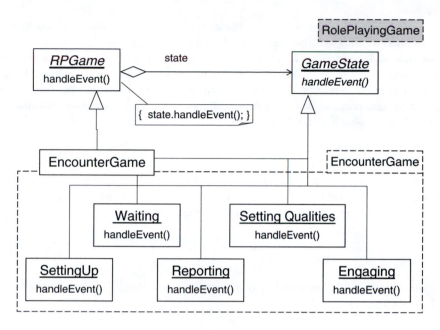

Figure 18.15 State design pattern applied to the Encounter video game

As shown in Figure 18.15, each subclass of *GameState* implements *handleEvent()* in its own manner. For example, if Encounter is in *SettingQualities* state, and the event is the arrival of a foreign character, then the window permitting the setting of character quality values disappears because this is what the method *handleEvent()* in *SettingQualities* is programmed to do. An additional consequence of this particular event/state combination is that Encounter transitions to the *Engaging* state, as required by the state-transition diagram. This transition is implemented by code such as

```
EncounterGame.setState(new Engaging());
```

The next time an event occurs in the game, the *handleEvent()* function of *Engaging* will execute, reflecting the fact that the game is now in the *Engaging* state.

18.2.3 Virtual Machines

A *virtual machine* architecture treats an application as a program written in a special-purpose language. Because an interpreter for such a language has to be built, this architecture pays off only if several "programs" are to be written in the language, generating several applications.

The implementation of a complete virtual machine requires the building of an interpreter. The interpretation requires us to execute an operation—let's call it *interpret()*—on a program written in our language. The interpretation of a primitive element alone (e.g., a CPU in the example of Chapter 17, where the parts of a "CPU" are not relevant) is generally simple (for the example, this could be simply to print "take

CPU out of its box"). The problem is how to execute an *interpret()* function when applied to a more complex "program." To do this, we may use the Interpreter design pattern.

Virtual machine architectures are advantageous if the application consists of the processing of complex entities, and if these entities, such as the orders in the example, are readily describable by a grammar.

An additional example requiring a virtual machine is an application that provides simple user-level programming of a special purpose language. A nonprogrammer user, for example, is capable of writing a script—a simple program—such as the following:

```
Balance checking / add excess to account + subtract deficit from saving;
Save report / c:Reports + standard headings + except replace "Ed''
by "Al'' PrintReport / standard headings
e-mail report to Jayne@xyz.net.
```

A virtual machine architecture parses and interprets such scripts. The idea of such architectures is illustrated in Figure 18.16.

18.2.4 Repository Architectures

An architecture built primarily around data is called a *repository* architecture. The most common of these are systems designed to perform transactions against a database. For example, an electric company maintains a database of customers that includes details about them, such as power usage each month, balance, payment history, repairs, and so on. Typical operations against this database are adding a new customer, crediting a payment, requesting a payment history, requesting a list of all customers more than three months in arrears, and so on. A typical design for this kind of repository architecture is shown in Figure 18.17. This figure mixes the flow of data between entities (solid lines) and control (dashed lines). "Control" means that one of the entities prompts the operation of the other—for example, turns it on and off.

Other examples of applications with repository architectures include interactive development environments (IDEs). IDEs apply processes such as editing and compiling to a database of source and object files.

Our Encounter example in its simplest form does not include a database. If, however, it were to grow into a game with many individual characters, then we might require a database rather than a flat file for storing the characters. This would certainly be true if we wanted to allow the user to call up statistics such as "list the characters with strength under 10," and so on. Structured Query Language (SQL) is a common way to express queries (see, for example, [4]).

Figure 18.16 Virtual machine architectures—leveraging the interpreter concept to facilitate the implementation of multiple applications

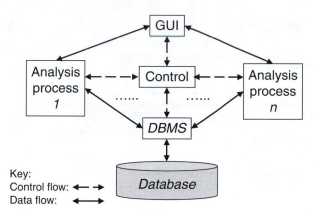

Figure 18.17 A typical repository architecture

Blackboard architectures, developed for artificial intelligence applications, are repositories that behave in accordance with posting rules. The reader is referred to [5] and [6] for a detailed treatment of blackboard architectures.

The final type of repository architectures we mention here is the hypertext architecture. The most common use of hypertext is on the Web. An application that manages the artifacts of a software engineering application is another example.

The word "repository" is often used in industry to denote an application that provides a unified view of a collection of databases (i.e., not just one). This relates to data warehouses. Repositories do not change the structure of these databases, but they allow uniform access to them. This is a special case of repository architectures as defined by Garlan and Shaw.

Repository architectures occupy a significant fraction of applications, since so many architectures make databases their core. When the processing is negligible compared to the formatting of data from the database, repository architectures are appropriate. On the other hand, the presence of a large database can sometimes mask the fact that a large amount of processing may drive the architecture. Ad hoc database programming (e.g., "stored procedures") can easily mushroom into messy applications, which perhaps should be conceived differently from the repository model.

18.2.5 Layered Architectures

An architectural *layer* is a coherent collection of software artifacts, typically a package of classes. In its common form, a layer uses at most one other layer, and is used by at most one other layer. Building applications layer by layer can greatly simplify the process. Some layers, such as frameworks, can serve several applications.

We have already seen the layered approach applied to the Encounter application, where classes in the Encounter packages inherit from classes in the framework packages. This is shown in Figure 18.18. The figure shows how we might organize the use of a 3-D graphics engine as a layer accessible from the Role-Playing Game layer.

Figure 18.19 shows an example of a layered architecture for an Ajax bank printing application. There are four layers in this architecture, and Figure 18.19 shows dependency in the reverse direction compared to Figure 18.18. The application layer, Ajax Bank Printing, has to do with printing and formatting. It is built upon (i.e., uses) the Accounts and the Ajax Bank Common Class layers. The latter are built upon a vendor-supplied layer, which contains general utilities such as sorting and searching. Typically, a layer is realized as a

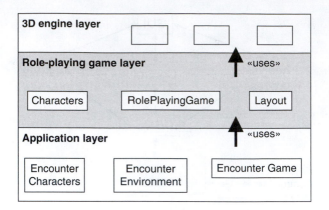

Figure 18.18 Layered architectures, and example of 3D engine and video game

Requirement: Print monthly statements.

Architecture:

"uses"

	Ajax bank printing Layer	
Accounts Layer	Ajax bank common library Layer	
Vendor-supplied Layer		

Figure 18.19 Example of layered architecture for Ajax Bank—highest level view

package of classes. For example, the Ajax common library comprises classes used throughout Ajax applications, and addresses such issues as the bank's logo and its regulations.

The "using" relationship can be inheritance, aggregation, or object reference. In the example, only aggregation is applied between layers, as shown in Figure 18.20.

18.2.6 Service-Oriented Architectures

Service-Oriented Architectures (SOAs) are gaining in usage. They are closely related to the idea of software as a service and cloud computing, and warrant inclusion with those discussed above. SOAs are combinations of *services*: components that provide functionality according to an interface specification. They differ from many other application architectures in that they describe a set of interoperable components that can be dynamically harnessed to create functionality—rather than as a way to create a single application.

SOAs are in the spirit of facade objects, and include Web services as a means of implementation. SOAs are not necessarily object-oriented. In the case of Web services there is no assurance of globally defined classes as we have provided for *Facade* in prior examples. For example, suppose that an SOA is for a business-to-business application concerning *orders*. In an SOA, we would not assume that a unique *Order* class is known to and usable by all service suppliers and consumers. Web services in particular deals with this by defining a schema for an *order* data structure, and referencing the schema when Web services involve orders. This uses a Web service capability known as *Web Service Description Language* and has the effect of making an *Order* class known to clients. This is summarized in Figures 18.21, 18.22, and 18.23.

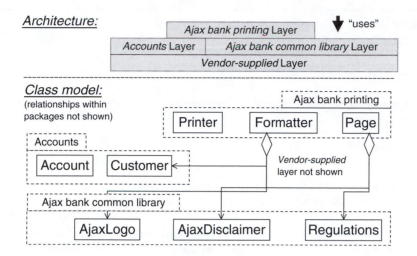

Figure 18.20 Layered architecture example using aggregation

Based on components that provide functionality according to an **interface** spec.
- Principally via Web services
- In the spirit of facade objects
- Not necessarily OO

Example: An application concerning *orders*.
- Wouldn't assume an *Order* class known to all
- Instead: Define an *order* **schema**; reference when Web services involve orders

Figure 18.21 Service-oriented architectures, 1 of 3

Service-oriented architectures envisage a network (mostly an Internet)-dominated environment in which applications (and parts of applications) are not permanently wedded to each other. Rather, SOAs seek to allow dynamic linking of services. For example, suppose that you want to write an application that orders stationery for a company. You would want the application to identify all qualified vendors, check prices and availability, call for bids and terms, select a vendor, and place the order. To do this, the application can't be permanently wedded to a set of vendors. For this reason, SOAs are built around a *registration* system. Figure 18.23 illustrates the four steps involved in publishing and accessing a service. "Querying" is like looking up a business in a telephone book. "Binding" means contacting the service in order to invoke it.

(The reference for Figures 18.21, 18.22, and 18.23 is [7].)

- "Fire and forget"
  - **Stateless** as much as possible
- **Extensible**
  - Additional functionality easily added
- **Discoverable**
- **Account for Quality of Service**
  - For example, security

Figure 18.22 Service-oriented architectures, 2 of 3

- "Fire and forget"
  - **Stateless** as much as possible
- **Extensible**
  - Additional functionality easily added
- **Discoverable**
- **Account for Quality of Service**
  - For example, security

Figure 18.23 Service-oriented architectures, 3 of 3

Service-oriented architectures frequently use a *business process layer*. This defines the components of the business such as the customer data base and business. Credit policies are examples of the latter. The *service interface layer* defines the services available that are based upon the business processes. It specifies functionality such as listing all customers in the database and checking a transaction for conformance to business rules. The *application layer* consists of applications built using the service interface layer. These points are shown in Figure 18.24.

18.2.7 Using Multiple Architectures within an Application

Applications typically use several subsidiary architectures within an overall architecture. Figure 18.25 shows how the framework for role-playing video games could use several of the architecture types listed by Garlan and Shaw. It could make sense, for example, to organize the *Artifacts* package as a database. The game characters could be viewed as parallel communicating processes. We will design the overall control of the game as an event-driven system.

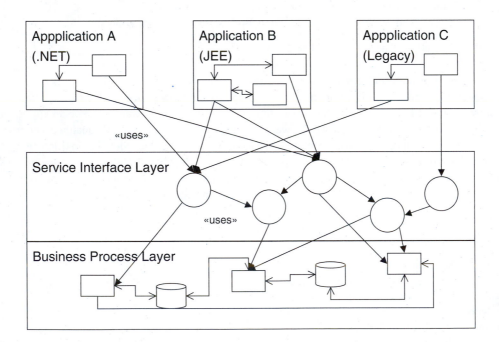

Figure 18.24 Layering for service-oriented architectures

Source: Adapted from Erl, Thomas, "Service-Oriented Architecture: Concepts, Technology, and Design," Prentice Hall, 2006.

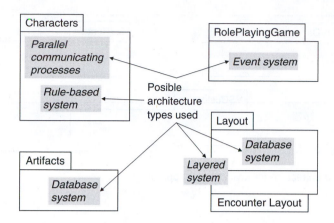

Figure 18.25 Example of the use of multiple subsidiary architectures—Encounter video game extension

18.3 TRADING OFF ARCHITECTURE ALTERNATIVES

Since the choice of a software architecture is so important, it is wise to create more than one alternative for consideration. As an example, we will create and compare two architectures for the video store application.

For the first candidate, we separate the application into three major parts: The "back-end" database, the middle part, which contains the business logic, and the GUIs. This is a *three-tier* architecture. It is often an appropriate choice when some or all of the tiers reside on physically separate platforms. In particular, if the GUIs are all on PCs, the middle layer on a server, and the databases controlled by a database management system, then three-tier architectures map neatly to separate hardware and software units. Note that there is no necessity that hardware decompositions be the same as software architectures; we may want a logical (conceptual) view of an application to be entirely independent of the hardware platforms hosting it. (These are the *physical* view vs. the *logical* view.) Applying three tiers to the video store application, we could obtain the architecture in Figure 18.26.

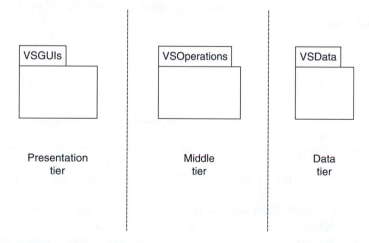

Figure 18.26 Three-tier architecture alternative

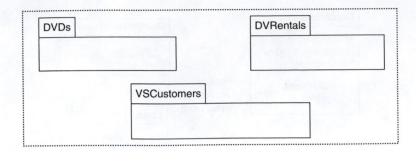

Figure 18.27 Alternative architecture for a video store application

The strength of this architecture is that it's easy to understand. Another strength is that since the GUI part is separate from the rental operations it can be changed without disturbing the latter. One weakness is the coupling between the *GUIs* package and the *VSOperations* package; there may be several GUI classes corresponding to the *Customer* class, for example. There is also coupling between the classes in the *VSData* package and the classes in *VSOperations*. A second architecture candidate is shown in Figure 18.27.

This architecture groups all of the classes pertaining to the videos in a package. The *Rentals* package contains classes that relate videos and customers. The *Customers* package contains the classes pertaining to customers, including associated GUIs. A third option would be to group all displays in a package. Figure 18.28 summarizes one opinion of these architecture alternatives.

18.4 TOOLS FOR ARCHITECTURES

Various computer-aided software engineering (CASE) tools are used to facilitate the software engineering process. Some tools represent classes and their relationships, such as Rational Rose by IBM Corporation. These tools facilitate the drafting of object models, linking them with the corresponding source code and sequence diagrams.

In selecting a modeling tool, a list of the requirements for the tool is drawn up using procedures similar to the requirements analysis process for software application development. Here is an example of some requirements for modeling tools.

- Essential: Facilitate drawing object models and sequence diagrams

- Essential: Create classes quickly

	Three-tier	Alternative
Understandable?	Yes	Yes
Flexible?	Yes: GUI easy to change	Yes: Basic building blocks easy to identify
Reusable?	Not very: Each layer is special to video store rentals	Yes: Easy to generalize to generic rentals
Easy to construct?	Perhaps	Yes: Clear potential to use Facade

Figure 18.28 A comparison of architectures—example

- Essential: Edit classes easily

- Desirable: Should cost no more than $X per user

- Desirable: Zoom into parts of the model

- Desirable: Possible to jump directly from the object model to the source code

- Optional: Reverse engineering available (i.e., create object models from source code)

- Optional: Use color coding for status of class implementation

Tool packages frequently try to span architecture, detailed design, and implementation. Various vendors are developing the capability to hyperlink from source code to documentation and vice versa. Implementation-oriented tools such as Javadoc can sometimes be useful to supplement the design process. Javadoc is useful for navigating packages because it provides an alphabetical listing of classes and the parent hierarchy of each class.

Interactive development environments (IDEs) are delivered with compilers and are widely used as partial modeling tools. Object-Oriented IDEs generally show inheritance in graphical form, and developers are frequently attracted to these tools because of their closeness to the compilation and debugging process. Eclipse, used as a successful software engineering case study itself in this book, is an example of a widely used IDE.

Component assembly tools create applications by dragging and dropping icons that represent processing elements. Java Bean environments are typical of these. Within such environments, beans (Java objects whose classes conform to the Java Beans standard) can be obtained from libraries, customized, and related to each other by means of events. The Java Beans standard was created with the express purpose of facilitating such simple assemblies by means of graphical tools.

A disadvantage of using modeling tools is the project's dependence on a third-party vendor. In addition to the complications of the application and the project itself, engineers must be concerned with the viability of the tool's vendor. Suppose that the vendor goes out of business or tool upgrades become too expensive: How will the project be affected? Despite these issues, the use of design and development tools has increased steadily. The right tools leverage productivity, and economic factors favor their usage.

18.5 IEEE STANDARDS FOR EXPRESSING DESIGNS

The IEEE Software Design Document (SDD) standard 1016-1998 provides guidelines for the documentation of design. The table of contents is shown in Figure 18.29. IEEE guidelines explain how the SDD could be written for various architectural styles, most of which are described above. The case study uses the IEEE standard with a few modifications to account for an emphasis on the object-oriented perspective. As shown in the figure, Sections 1 through 5 can be considered software architecture, and Section 6 can be considered the detailed design, to be covered in the next chapter.

18.6 EFFECTS OF ARCHITECTURE SELECTION ON THE PROJECT PLAN

Once an architecture has been selected, the schedule can be made more specific and more detailed. In particular, the order in which parts are built can be determined. For example, in the case study it makes sense to first develop the *Characters* framework package, followed by the specific *EncounterCharacters* application package. Since these packages will not be completed in the first iteration of the spiral, we name the

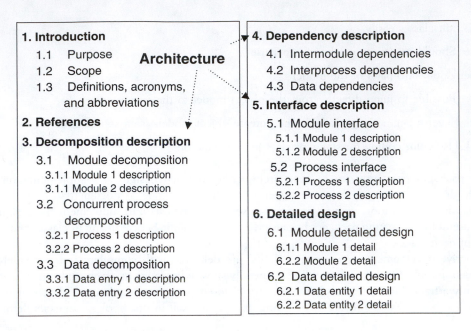

Figure 18.29 The architecture parts of IEEE 1016-1998—SDD table of contents

Source: IEEE Std 1016–1998.

corresponding tasks "Characters I" and "EncounterCharacters I." Arrows indicate dependence of packages on others. For example, "EncounterCharacters I" cannot be completed without the completion of "Characters I," as shown in Figure 18.30. The schedule shows that "Integration and Test I" cannot begin until all of the other tasks in Iteration I have been completed.

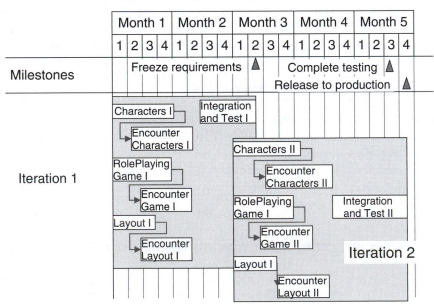

Figure 18.30 Schedule following architecture selection

18.7 CASE STUDY: PREPARING TO DESIGN ENCOUNTER (STUDENT PROJECT GUIDE CONTINUED)

This section describes a scenario of how the Encounter project team may have gone about the creation of the Encounter architecture.

18.7.1 Preparing

In accordance with the SPMP, Karen Peters was the design leader, with Ed Braun backing her up and inspecting all of the design work. Karen aimed to develop two thoroughly prepared alternative architectures for the Encounter project and bring them to the team's preliminary design review. She was determined to avoid unpleasant haggling over architectures that were devised by different engineers. She felt that ego rather than technical issues predominated in such cases. She had even worse memories of architecture "compromises" that were created to reconcile competing architectures. These frequently resulted in poor designs that everyone had to live and work with daily for months, if not years. On the other hand, Karen did not want to produce an architecture in isolation. She decided that she and Ed would select architecture candidates together, research them thoroughly, and present the choices to the team.

18.7.2 Selecting Architectures

Al Pruitt had been thinking about the design of the game application, and he gave Karen a sketch of an ad hoc GUI-driven architecture. He pointed out that it was simple and would be quick to implement. Ed and Karen reviewed Garlan and Shaw's classification of architectures to determine whether Encounter appeared to match any of the architecture alternatives.

They first asked whether Encounter could be described as the flow of data from one processing element to another. The data would have to be the positions of the game characters and/or their quality values. This view did not seem to them to match their conception of the game.

Next, they turned to Garlan and Shaw's "independent components" architectures, the first of which was "parallel communicating processes." To Karen this seemed to be a possible match because each game character could be considered one of the processes. Each could be run on a separate parallel thread, and these threads would communicate whenever the characters encountered each other. They noted this as a candidate architecture.

They considered "client server" next, but it was unclear to them what the "client" and "server" roles would be, so they dismissed this alternative. "Event systems," the next type listed, appeared to be a candidate architecture since the game responded to either user-initiated events, such as the pressing of an area hyperlink to enter an area, or to the arrival of the foreign character in the same area as the player character. They noted this as another candidate architecture.

Next, Ed and Karen considered "virtual machines," asking whether each game execution consisted essentially of the interpretation of a script. This did not appear to them to be the case.

They considered whether the game could be thought of as built around a repository of data (a "repository system"). The data could be the values of the characters and the status of the game. They decided that this might indeed be a possibility if there were many characters and many artifacts, because in that case, the manipulation of large amounts of data might predominate. Since Encounter was not to be data-centric, however, they rejected this candidate.

Finally, they considered a layered architecture. The question here was whether Encounter could be viewed as a series of class groupings with each grouping using one or two of the others. Karen felt that there would indeed be at least two useful layers: one for role-playing games in general, and one for Encounter. They made a note of this candidate architecture, and ended their consideration of Garlan and Shaw's options.

Now they listed the architecture candidates.

Al Pruitt's GUI-driven architecture

Parallel communicating processes

Event systems

Layered

They discussed which of these described the overall architecture and which were subsidiary to the overall architecture. To decide among these candidates they evaluated them in terms of the qualities described in this chapter. Their scheme gave 2 as the highest value and 0 as the lowest. In the case of close scores, the team would have questioned their scores closely. In addition, as they learned more about the application, they understood the need to revisit this table up to the time that they had to commit to architecture. One advantage of the table (Table 18.1) is that it allowed them to more easily reevaluate their reasoning.

Their conclusion was that layering was the primary architectural principle since there was a generic role-playing game layer and the Encounter layer itself. They envisaged the "event systems" architecture as subsidiary to the layers. They postponed a detailed discussion of parallel communicating processes for the game characters. Conceptually,

Table 18.1 Evaluation of architecture candidates by means of design qualities

Candidates	Al Pruitt's	Parallel communicating processes	Event systems	Layered
Qualities				
Sufficiency: handles the requirements	1	1	2	2
Understandability: can be understood by intended audience	0	2	1	2
Modularity: divided into well-defined parts	0	0	1	2
Cohesion: organized so like-minded elements are grouped together	1	0	2	2
Coupling: organized to minimize dependence between elements	0	1	0	1
Robustness: can deal with wide variety of input	1	0	2	1
Flexibility: can be readily modified to handle changes in requirements	1	0	1	1
Reusability: can use parts of the design and implementation in other applications	0	0	1	2
Information hiding: module internals are hidden from others	1	1	2	2
Efficiency: executes within acceptable time and space limits	1	2	0	1
Reliability:	0	1	1	2
TOTALS	6	8	13	18

their main architecture selection is reflected in Figure 18.35

They decided to express the "event systems" architecture by means of states and transitions. Then they debated whether to use the State design pattern or a state/action table to describe the event/transitions, and decided to apply metrics to assist in choosing from the architectures under consideration, including Al Pruitt's.

They used e-mail to try to get agreement on the weighting of criteria for architectures (extension, change, etc.,—see Table 18.1 i.e., "Evaluation of architecture candidates by means of design qualities.") in advance of the meeting, without mentioning the architecture candidates themselves. They then e-mailed Al a draft of the comparison table in advance of the meeting to make sure that they had not missed any aspects of his proposal. Al pointed out that the choice of architecture was heavily dependent on the weighting, but was willing to accept the team's weighting. Karen and Ed drew up the spreadsheet Table 18.1, comparing Al Pruitt's architecture (alternative 2) and two others they had developed, and mailed it to the team members so that they would be prepared for the meeting.

18.7.3 Team Meeting (Preliminary Design Review)

At the meeting, Karen and Ed first confirmed agreement on the weighting of criteria. Because of their use of e-mail prior to the meeting, the team did not take long to iron out the few remaining inconsistencies. No mention was made yet of the architectures themselves. They presented the architecture alternatives to the team, showing the spreadsheet results. After some discussion and modification of their assessments, the team confirmed their selection of the layered architecture and the use of the State design pattern. Karen and Ed's thought process and presentation had been thorough. The team's discussion focused on how to improve the architecture selected. They solicited ideas for refining the architecture, but Karen did not try to rank the ideas or create a single refined version of the architecture at the meeting. She wanted to think through the suggestions offline.

18.7.4 Refining the Architecture

Karen and Ed were now faced with the task of decomposing each layer. They performed this by placing the two additional architectural elements in separate packages. In the role-playing game layer they formed a package for the state machine called *RolePlayingGame*. To handle the game characters, which move around in parallel, they created a *Characters* package. They also created a *GameEnvironment* package to contain classes describing the places in which the characters would move. Finally, they envisaged an *Artifacts* package for the future to describe the miscellaneous items such as shields and swords that would be involved. This package, postponed for future releases, would have a *Repository* architecture.

Their decomposition of the Encounter application layer was analogous since many of its classes had to inherit from the generic game level. They decided to create narrow access paths to the packages of this layer to prevent a situation in which any class could reference any other class. They felt that such unrestricted references would soon become impossible to manage during development and maintenance. To accomplish this narrow access they used the Facade design pattern for each application package. Ed had some reservations about doing this because it increased the amount of code the team would have to create and manage. Methods would not be called directly, he pointed out, but only through special methods of the facade objects, thereby increasing the total number of methods. It also introduced complications in that internal classes could not even be mentioned by objects external to the package (although their generic base classes could be), but Karen convinced him that the price was worth the benefit of having a clear interface for each package.

They obtained approval for their architecture at a subsequent team meeting.

18.7.5 Documenting the Architecture

Ed and Karen used Sections 1 through 5 of the IEEE standard 1016 to express the architecture in a Software Design Document (SDD). Since they had divided the application into two layers, one of which was slated for reuse, they decided to document the framework "role-playing game" layer in a separate SDD.

18.8 CASE STUDY: SOFTWARE DESIGN DOCUMENT FOR THE *ROLE-PLAYING VIDEO GAME* FRAMEWORK

We have two designs to describe. The first is that of the *Role-Playing Video Game* framework; the second is that of the Encounter role-playing game. The SDDs for both designs are split into two parts. The first parts, SDD Sections 1 through 5, shown below, consist of the architectural aspects of the designs. The second part, SDD section six, appearing at the end of Chapter 19, consists of the detailed designs. The dependence of Encounter on the framework is specified in the Encounter case study.

History of versions of this document:

x/yy/zzz K. Peters: initial draft

. . . .

x/yy/zzz K. Peters: revised, incorporating comments by R. Bostwick

x/yy/zzz K. Peters: moved details of classes to Section 3

1. Introduction

1.1 Purpose

This document describes the packages and classes of a framework for role-playing video games.

1.2 Scope

This framework covers essentials of role-playing game classes. Its main intention is to provide an example of a framework for educational purposes. It is not intended as a framework for commercial games since its size is kept small to facilitate learning.

1.3 Definitions, Acronyms, and Abbreviations

Framework: a collection of interrelated classes used, via inheritance or aggregation, to produce families of applications

RPG, Role-playing game: a video game in which characters interact in a manner that depends on their characteristics and their environment

2. References

Software Engineering: An Object-Oriented Perspective, by E. J. Braude (Wiley, 2001).

UML: The Unified Modeling Language User Guide, by G. Booch, J. Rumbaugh, and I. Jacobson (Addison-Wesley.

IEEE standard 1016-1987 (reaffirmed 1993) guidelines for generating a Software Design Document.

3. Decomposition Description

> Note to the Student:
> This section specifies how the framework classes for role-playing video games are to be grouped. This reflects the top-level decomposition: the detailed decomposition into methods, for example, is left for the detailed design (see case study at the end of the next chapter).

3.1 Module Decomposition

> This section shows the decomposition then explains each part in a subsection.

The framework consists of the *RolePlayingGame*, *Characters*, *Artifacts*, and *Layout* packages. These are decomposed into the classes shown in Figure 18.31. The classes in these packages are explained below. Unless otherwise stated, all classes in these packages are public. As indicated by the (UML) italics notation, all of the framework classes are abstract.

3.1.1 *RolePlayingGame* Package

This package is designed as a state-transition machine. The concept is that a role-playing game is always in one of several states. This package makes it possible to describe the possible states of the game and the actions that can take place in response to events. It implements the State design pattern (see [8]). The state of the game is encapsulated

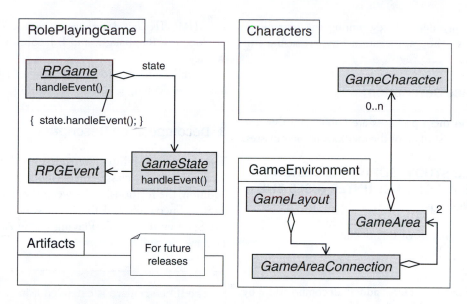

Figure 18.31 RPG framework for role-playing video games

(represented) by the particular *GameState* object aggregated by the (single) *RPGame* object. This aggregated object is named state. In other words, state is an attribute of *RPGame* of type *GameState*.

The function *handleEvent()* of *RPGame* is called to handle each event occurring on the monitor (mouse clicks, etc.). It executes by calling the *handleEvent()* function of state. The applicable version of *handleEvent()* depends on the particular subclass of *GameState* that state belongs to.

3.1.2 Characters Package

> It may seem strange to have a package containing just one class, but most artifacts in software design have a tendency to grow. Even if the packge does not grow, this does not disqualify its usefulness. For another example of a package with just one class, see *java.applet*, whose only class is *Applet* (but it also contains a few interfaces).

This package contains the *GameCharacter* class, which describes the characters of the game.

3.1.3 GameEnvironment Package

This package describes the physical environment of the game. The class *GameLayout* aggregates connection objects. Each connection object aggregates the pair of *GameArea* objects that it connects. This architecture allows for multiple connections between two areas. Each *GameArea* object aggregates the game characters that it contains (if any) and can detect encounters among characters.

3.1.4 Artifacts Package (Not Implemented— for Future Releases)

This package is intended to store elements to be located in areas, such as trees or tables, and entities possessed by characters, such as shields and briefcases.

3.2 Concurrent Process Decomposition

The framework does not involve concurrent processes.

4. Dependency Description

> This section describes all the ways in which the modules depend on each other.

The only dependency among the framework modules is the aggregation by *GameArea* of *GameCharacter*.

5. Interface Description

All classes in these packages are public, and thus the interfaces consist of all of the methods in their classes.

18.9 CASE STUDY: SOFTWARE DESIGN DOCUMENT FOR ENCOUNTER (USES THE FRAMEWORK)

History of versions of this document:

x/yy/zzz K. Peters: initial draft

. . . .

x/yy/zzz K. Peters: added decomposition by use case model and state model

1. Introduction

1.1 Purpose

This document describes the design of the Encounter role-playing game.

1.2 Scope

This design is for the prototype version of Encounter, which is a demonstration of architecture, detailed design, and documentation techniques. The architecture is intended as the basis for interesting versions in the future. This description excludes the framework classes, whose design is provided in the SDD entitled "Role-Playing Game Architecture Framework."

1.3 Definitions, Acronyms, and Abbreviations

None

2. References

"Role-Playing Game Architecture Framework," section in *Software Engineering: An Object-Oriented Perspective*, by E. J. Braude (Wiley, 2001).

UML: The Unified Modeling Language User Guide, by G. Booch, J. Rumbaugh, and I. Jacobson (Addison-Wesley.

IEEE standard 1016-1987 (reaffirmed 1993) guidelines for generating a Software Design Document.

3. Decomposition Description

The Encounter architecture is described using three models: use case, class (object) model, and state. In addition, the relationship between the domain packages of Encounter and the framework described in the SDD entitled "Role-Playing Game Architecture Framework" will be shown.

> The IEEE standard is extended using Sections 3.4 and 3.5 in order to describe these models. Recall that the other possible model is data flow, which we have not considered useful in this case. In the particular case of this video game, we chose to use the state description as part of the requirement as well as the design.

3.1 Module Decomposition (Object Model)

> This section should not duplicate the "detailed design" section described in the next chapter. We do not go into detail here regarding the contents of the packages.

The package architecture for Encounter is shown in Figure 18.32. The three packages are *EncounterGame*, *EncounterCharacters*, and *EncounterEnvironment*. These have facade classes *EncounterGame*, *EncounterCast*, and *EncounterEnvironment* respectively. The facade class of each package has exactly one instantiation, and is an interface through which all dealings with the package take place. The remaining classes are not accessible from outside the package. (See Section 17.7.1 in Chapter 17 and [1] for a complete description of the Facade design pattern.)

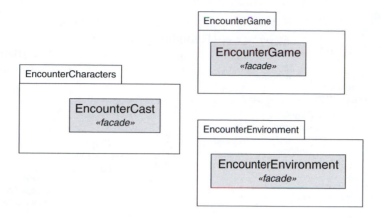

Figure 18.32 Architecture and modularization of Encounter game

3.1.1 EncounterGame Package

The *EncounterGame* package consists of the classes controlling the progress of the game as a whole. The package is designed to react to user actions (events).

3.1.2 EncounterCharacters Package

The *EncounterCharacters* package encompasses the characters involved in the game. These include character(s) under the control of the player together with the foreign characters.

3.1.3 EncounterEnvironment Package

The *EncounterEnvironment* package describes the physical layout of Encounter, including the areas and the connections between them. It does not include moveable items, if any.

3.2 Concurrent Process Decomposition

There are two concurrent processes in Encounter. The first is the main visible action of the game, in which the player manually moves the main character from area to adjacent area. The second consists of the movement of the foreign character from area to adjacent areas.

3.3 Data Decomposition

> Describes the structure of the data within the application

The data structures flowing among the packages are defined by the *Area, EncounterCharacter,* and *EncounterAreaConnection* classes.

3.4 State Model Decomposition

Encounter consists of the states shown in Figure 18.33.

> This state diagram was provided in the SRS, Section 2.1.1, where it was used to describe the requirements for Encounter. The remaining states mentioned in the requirements will be implemented in subsequent releases.

3.5 Use Case Model Decomposition

> This section is added to the IEEE specification, which does not address the use case concept. It has been added at the end of this section so as not to disturb the standard order.

Encounter consists of three use cases: *Initialize, Travel to Adjacent Area,* and *Encounter Foreign Character.* These use cases are explained in detail in the SRS, Section 2.2, and are detailed in sections later in this document.

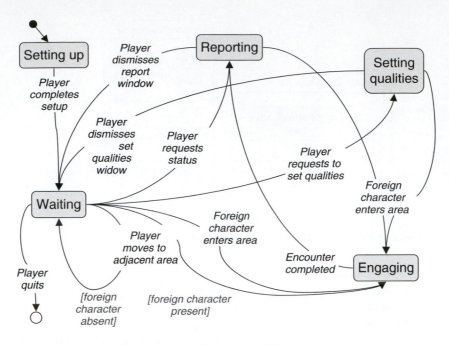

Figure 18.33 State-transition diagram for Encounter video game architecture

Details are given in the "detailed design" section.

There are no significant dependencies among the use cases.

4. Dependency Description

This section describes the dependencies for the various decompositions described in Section 3.

4.1 Intermodule Dependencies (Class Model)

The dependencies among package interfaces are shown in Figure 18.34.

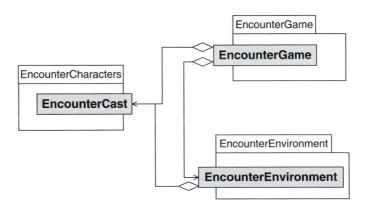

Figure 18.34 Architecture (modularization) of Encounter video game

The *EncounterGame* package depends on all of the other Encounter packages. The *EncounterEnvironment* package is designed to depend on the *Encounter-Characters* package. This is because the game's character interaction takes place only in the context of the environment. In particular, *Area* objects are responsible for determining the presence of the player's character together with the foreign character.

Dependencies among noninterface classes are explained later in this document.

> Such dependencies are detailed design specifications.

4.2 Interprocess Dependencies

When an engagement takes place, the process of moving the main character about and the process controlling the movement of the foreign characters interact.

4.3 Data Dependencies

The data structures flowing among the packages are defined by the classes, whose mutual dependencies are described in Section 6 of this document.

4.4 State Dependencies

Each state is related to the states into which the game can transition from it.

4.5 Layer Dependencies

The Encounter application depends on the *Role-Playing Game* framework as shown in Figure 18.35. Each application package uses exactly one framework package.

5. Interface Description

This section describes the interfaces for the object model. Note that several of the classes described are defined in the design description of the *Role-Playing Game* Framework.

5.1 Module Interfaces

> Describes the interaction among the packages

5.1.1 Interface to the EncounterGame Package

The interface to the *EncounterGame* package is provided by the the *EncounterGame* object of the *Encounter Game* facade class. It consists of the following:

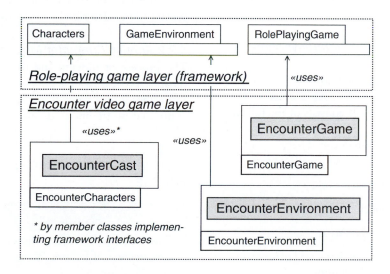

Figure 18.35 Framework-/-application dependencies

1. EncounterGame getTheEncounterGame()//gets the only instance

2. GameState getState()//current state of the *EncounterGame* instance

3. void setState(GameState)//– of the *EncounterGame* instance

4. //Any event affecting the single *EncounterGame* instance:

5. void handleEvent(AWTEvent)

5.1.2 Interface to the EncounterCharacters Package

The interface to the *EncounterCharacters* package is provided by the *theEncounterCast* object of the *EncounterCast* facade class. It consists of the following.

1. EncounterCast getTheEncounterCast()//gets the single instance

2. GameCharacter getThePlayerCharacter()//i.e., the unique character

3. GameCharacter getTheForeignCharacter()//the unique character

4. //Exchange quality values specific to the game area

5. void engagePlayerWithForeignCharacter (GameArea)

5.1.3 Interface to EncounterEnvironment Package

The interface to the *EncounterEnvironment* package is provided by the *EncounterEnvironment* object of *Encounter Environment Facade* class. It consists of the following:

1. EncounterEnvironment getTheEn-counter Environment()//gets the Facade object

2. GameArea getArea(String)

3. GameAreaConnection getAreaConnection(String)

4. void movePlayerTo(Area)

5. void moveForeignCharacterTo(Area) throws AreaNotAdjacentException

6. Image getNeighborhoodAreas(Area)//gets *Area* and areas one or two connections distant

5.2 Process Interface

We stated in Section 3.2 that there are two processes involved in Encounter. There is a significant design decision to be made in regard to the interface to the foreign character movement process, and we describe the result here. One option is to have the foreign character a thread, controlling itself. This has advantages, but requires this character either to know the environment—a disadvantage in terms of changing and expanding the game—or to be able to find out about the environment dynamically, which would be an elegant design but too ambitious for the scope of this case study. The architecture opts for another alternative, which is stated here.

5.2.1 Player Character Movement Process

The interfaces to the process that moves the player's character about the game consist of the graphical user interfaces specified in the SRS. The process reacts to events described in Section 3.4, which are handled by the *EncounterGame* package in accordance with its specifications, described later in this document.

5.2.2 Foreign Character Movement Process

The process of moving the foreign character is a separate process associated with and controlled by the *EncounterGame* singleton object. This process is controlled by the methods inherited from *java.lang. Thread*.

18.10 CASE STUDY: ARCHITECTURE OF ECLIPSE

Note to the Student:
The description that follows describes the architecture of Eclipse in a top-down fashion.

18.10.1 Scope

[This paragraph makes specific the scope of this document (the title "Architecture of Eclipse" seems clear enough until we read in this paragraph that it is qualified).]

As of April 2004, there were three Eclipse releases. We will provide an overall description of the architecture of release 3.

18.10.2 Overview

The Eclipse architecture has been described by Gamma and Beck [9] as shown in Figure 18.36.

> Figure 18.36 has just three parts—a manageable number to comprehend. Eclipse is a large and very complex product, however. Together with the brief explanations below, this decomposition is helpful. One has to search for a while to find a description like this by looking through http://www.eclipse.org.

- The *Platform* is the infrastructure of Eclipse and is independent of languages with which Eclipse can be used and independent of all plug-ins.

- The *Java Development Tools* utilize the *Platform* and is class model for a Java interactive development environment.

- The *Plug-In Development Environment* allows developers to create and add plug-ins. It uses the Java development tools.

18.10.3 Platform Module

The platform decomposes as shown in Figure 18.37. The modules in Figure 18.37 are as follows:

- *Runtime* handles the available plug-ins at runtime.

- *Workspace* manages projects, which consist of files and folders.

- *Standard Widget Toolset* (SWT) provides graphics elements

- *JFace* is a set of UI frameworks using SWT, used for common UIs

- *Workbench* "defines the Eclipse UI paradigm. This involves editors, views, and perspectives."[1]

18.10.4 Java Development Tools

The design philosophy of Eclipse is to e able to build any language environment on top of the *Platform*. The Java Development Tools (JDT) module is the Java environment. It consists of the *Java Core* module. This is shown in Figure 18.38.

> We won't pursue this module or further parts of the Eclipse architecture in this case study.

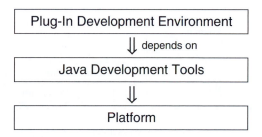

Figure 18.36 Very high-level architecture of Eclipse

Source: Adapted from Gamma, Erich, and Back, Kent. "Contributing to Eclipse: Principles, Patterns, Plug-Ins," Addison-Wesley, 2003, p.5.

---

[1] Gamma and Beck [9], p. 6

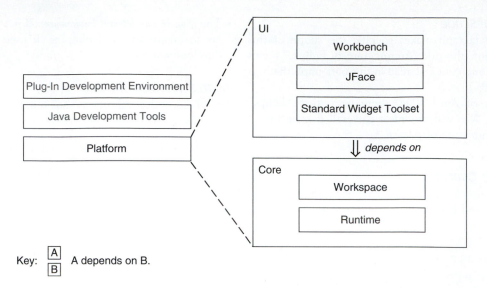

Key: A depends on B.

Figure 18.37 Architecture of Eclipse—platform

Source: Adapted from Gamma, Erich, and Back, Kent. "Contributing to Eclipse: Principles, Patterns, Plug-Ins," Addison-Wesley, 2003, p. 283.

18.11 CASE STUDY: OPENOFFICE ARCHITECTURE

> Note to the Student:
> It is not straightforward to locate the description of the OpenOffice architecture in a single, identifiable place.

The following is a useful white paper that sets out the design methodology used for OpenOffice, and much of this section is adapted or quoted from [10].

The architecture of the *OpenOffice.org* suite is designed to be platform-independent. It consists of four layers, as described in Figure 18.39.

> We will not discuss the *StarOffice* API here. As indicated in Figure 18.39, however, three layers depend on it. The author has made local improvements in the writing of the original. This architecture description is at a very high level.

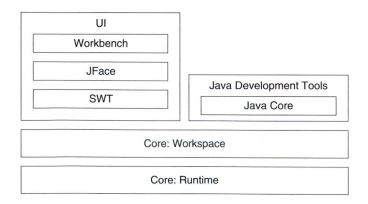

Figure 18.38 Architecture of Eclipse—the Java development tools module

Source: Adapted from Gamma, Erich, and Back, Kent. "Contributing to Eclipse: Principles, Patterns, and Plug-Ins," Addison-Wesley, 2003, p.282.

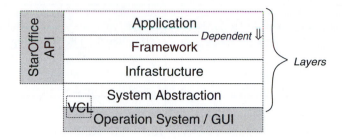

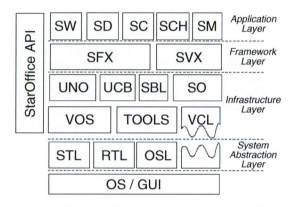

Figure 18.39 The architecture of OpenOffice

Source: Edited from OpenOffice, http://www.openoffice.org/white_papers/tech_overview/tech_overview.html#3.

The System Abstraction layer "encapsulates all system specific APIs and provides a consistent object-oriented API to access system resources in a platform independent manner." It provides a kind of single, virtual operating system on which to build OpenOffice.

The Infrastructure layer is a platform-independent environment for building applications, components and services.

The Framework layer: To allow reuse, this layer provides the environment for applications. It also provides all shared functionality such as common dialogs, file access, and configuration management.

The Application layer: "All *OpenOffice.org* applications are part of this layer. The way these applications interact is based on the lower layers."

The next sections describe these layers in more detail.

18.11.1 System Abstraction Layer

This section is reproduced from [11]. It references Figure 18.39.

Platform-depended implementations take place below the System Abstraction Layer (SAL) or are part of optional modules. "In an ideal world an implementation of the SAL-specific functionality and recompiling the upper layer module will allow you to run the applications. To provide the whole set of functionality, the optional platform specific modules, like telephony support or speech recognition, have to be ported, too." To reduce porting efforts, the SAL functionality is reduced to a minimal set, available on every platform. " . . . for some systems the layer includes some implementations to emulate some functionality or behavior. For example on systems where no native multithreading is supported, the layer can support so called 'user land' threads."

> This description is not very clear. In fact, it is difficult to write meaningfully and clearly at a high level. What follows next, however, is indeed clear and meaningful.

> The last sentence is useful and appropriate at this level. The meaning of "semi platform independent" is unclear. The second sentence is not clear but is presumably explained in the more detailed sections.

As shown in Figure 18.40, the SAL consists of the Operating System Layer (OSL) the Runtime Library (RTL), the Standard Template Library (STL), and the platform-independent part of the Visual Class Library (VCL). These are described next.

18.11.1.1 Operating System Layer

"The operating system layer (OSL) encapsulates all the operating system specific functionality for using and accessing system specific resources like files, memory, sockets, pipes, etc. The OSL is a very thin layer with an object-oriented API. In contrast to the upper layer this object-oriented API is a C-API." The reason for this is to allow easy porting to various platforms using different implementation languages. "For embedded systems or Internet appliances, for example, an assembler language can be used to realize the implementation."

18.11.1.2 Runtime Library

"The runtime library provides all semi platform independent functionality. There is an implementation for string classes provided. Routines for conversion of strings to different character sets are implemented. The memory management functionality resides in this module."

18.11.1.3 Standard Template Library

"As a generic container library the standard template library is used. It supplies implementations for list, queues, stacks, maps, etc."

> The relationship with the Standard Template Library that comes with C++ should be clarified.

18.11.1.4 Visual Class Library

"The VCL encapsulates all access to the different underlying GUI systems. The implementation is separated into two major parts. One is platform-independent and includes an object-oriented 2D graphics API with metafiles, fonts, raster operations and the widget set use by the OpenOffice.org suite. This approach virtually guarantees that all widgets have the same behavior independently of the GUI system used. As a result, the look-and-feel and the functionality of the widgets on all platforms are the same."

> This explains the squiggly lines in Figure 18.39 that separate the two parts of the VCL.

Infrastructure Layer			
System Abstraction Layer			
Operating System Layer (OSL)	Runtime Library (RTL)	Standard Template Library (STL)	Visual Class Library (VCL)
Operation System / GUI			

Figure 18.40 OpenOffice architecture—system abstraction layer

Source: Edited from OpenOffice, http://www.openoffice.org/white_papers/tech_overview/tech_overview.html#3.

The platform-dependent part implements a 2D-graphic drawing canvas that is used by the platform-independent parts. This canvas redirects functionality directly to the underlying GUI system. Currently, there exist implementations for the Win32, X-Windows, OS/2, and Mac. The access to the printing functionality, clipboard and drag-and-drop is also realized inside the VCL."

18.11.2 Infrastructure Layer

The Infrastructure layer consists of the parts shown in Figure 18.41. These are each explained next.

> The figure implies that *Compound Objects* (for example) depends on the *SAL* and that the *Infrastructure* layer depends on it. It implies no dependence between *Compound Objects*, *UCB*, and *SBL*.

18.11.2.1 Virtual Operating System Layer   The purpose of this layer is "to make the usage of system resources like files, threads, sockets, etc. more convenient the virtual operating system layer encapsulates all the functionality of the operating system layer into C++ classes. The C++ classes here offer an easy to use access to all system resources in an object-oriented way."

18.11.2.2 Tools Libraries   "The tool functionality of OpenOffice consists of various small tool libraries. This includes a common implementation for handling date and time related data, an implementation of structured storages, a generic registry, typesafe management, and persistence of property data."

18.11.2.3 Universal Network Objects   *Universal Network Objects* is the component technology used within *OpenOffice.org*. "It . . . is heavily based on multithreading and network communication capabilities."

> This paragraph says something important about the architecture of OpenOffice.

"The system consists of several pieces. An IDL-Compiler, which generates out of the specified definition of an interface a binary representation and the associated C-Header or Java technology files. The binary representation is platform and language independent and is at runtime used to marshal argument for remote function calls or to generate code on the fly for a specific language to access the implementation provided by the interface. This technique reduced the amount of generated code for the different language binding tremendously. The drawback is that not only for every language binding a specific backend for the code generation is needed, it is that for every specific compiler a bridging module is needed at runtime."

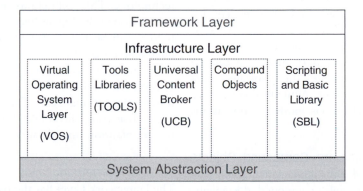

Figure 18.41 OpenOffice architecture—infrastructure layer

Source: Edited from OpenOffice, http://www.openoffice.org/white_papers/tech_overview/tech_overview.html#3.

> This paragraph is not easy to understand but it is at a high level and becomes clearer as one reads more details. It mixes a description of the architecture with a rationale for it. Requirements documents frequently include pieces of rationale.

"Many parts of the UNO technology are implemented as UNO components. This facilitates flexibility and runtime extensions: e.g., providing new bridges or communication protocols. UNO provides transparent access to components locally or over the network. IIOP can be used for network communication. If components are realized as shared libraries, they can be loaded by UNO in to process memory of the application accessed by function calls. This does not require marshalling of arguments as required for remote function calls."

> This paragraph seems to be heralding an ambitious design, consisting of objects available on the network.

18.11.2.4 Universal Content Broker   "The Universal Content Broker allows all upper layers to access different kinds of structure content transparently. The UCB consists of a core and several Universal Content Providers, which are used to integrate different access protocols. The current implementations provides content providers for the HTTP protocol, FTP protocol, WebDAV protocol, and access to the local file system.

The UCB does not only provide access to the content, it also provides the associated meta information to the content. Actually there is synchronous and asynchronous mode for operations supported."

18.11.2.5 OpenOffice.org Compound Objects
"The Compound Object implementation provide the functionality to build compound documents, where for example a spreadsheet is being embedded in a word-processor document." "The implementation provides a platform-independent implementation of this functionality for compound documents and for embedding visual controls such as multimedia players and various viewers. Storage is compatible with the OLE structure storage format. This allows access to OLE compound documents on every platform where OpenOffice.org is available. On Windows the implementation interacts with OLE services and so allows a tight integration of OLE-capable applications."

18.11.2.6 OpenOffice.org Scripting and Basic Library

> "Scripting" refers to the ability to write procedures that cause the application to execute application functions in a desired sequence. For example, *.bat* files in Windows and *.sh* files in Unix are scripting files. Design documents inevitably rely on jargon that the reader must be familiar with.

"The scripting functionality that comes with the OpenOffice.org suite is a BASIC dialect featuring an interpreter that parses the source statements and generates meta instructions. These instructions can be executed directly by the supplied meta-instructions processor or can be made persistent in modules or libraries for later access. All functionality supplied by the upper level application components is accessible via a scripting interface in the component technology. This will help to ensure that new components using the OpenOffice.org component technology can be fully scriptable without spending a huge amount of effort.

The scripting interfaces are also implemented as components that will allow an easy integration of other scripting languages." They provide functionality, such as core reflection and introspection, similar to Java platform functionality.

18.11.3 Framework Layer
The Framework Layer has the parts shown in Figure 18.42.

These parts are described next.

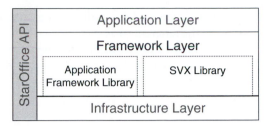

Figure 18.42 OpenOffice architecture—framework layer

Source: OpenOffice, http://www.openoffice.org/white_papers/tech_overview/tech_overview.html#3.

18.11.3.1 The Application Framework Library

See Figure 18.42.

"Functionality shared by all application and not provided by any other layer is realized here. For the framework, every visual application has to provide a shell and can provide several views. The library provides all basic functionality so only the application specific features have to be added."

"The Framework is also responsible for content detection and aggregation." The AFL provides template management and configuration management. It "is in some areas related to the compound documents, because of the functionality for merging or switching menus and toolbars. It also provides the capability for customization of applications."

18.11.3.2 SVX Library

"The SVX library provides shared functionality for all applications which is not related to a framework. So part of the library is a complete object-oriented drawing layer that is used by several applications for graphic editing and output; also a complete 3D-rendering systems is part of the drawing functionality. The common dialogs for font selection, color chooser, etc., are all part of this library. Also the whole database connectivity is realized here."

18.11.4 Application Layer

This layer consists of the actual applications such as the word processor, spreadsheet, presentation, charting, and so on. All these are realized as shared libraries, loaded by the application framework at runtime. The framework provides the environment for these applications and provides the functionality for interaction among them.

> Software architecture descriptions inform the reader, but in a general manner. They are necessarily imprecise about the meaning of the parts. Architectures of nontrival software applications have to be learned over time just as it takes time to learn any complex subject. This process is helped by delving into selected details as needed, perhaps even to the code level, and then re-reading needed architecture and detailed design descriptions. In this book, we omit the detailed design of OpenOffice.

18.12 SUMMARY

A software architecture describes the components of a software system and the way in which they interact with each other. There are many different ways a system can be architected. Garlan and Shaw have classified software architectures into categories such as dataflow, independent components, virtual machines, repository, and layered. Service-oriented architecture is another type of architecture in which various components are combined to provide a service.

Software designs are documented in a software design document (SDD). The IEEE publishes IEEE Std 1016-1998 for such a purpose. The SDD for the Encounter case study uses this as a document template.

For large software projects, it is important to modularize the software design. Modularization facilitates different groups of developers working on the different parts simultaneously. To make this work as efficiently as possible, the Facade design pattern can be used to provide a clean interface for each module. The Facade pattern is typically appropriate when developers are collocated. In distributed environments, Web services can often be used.

Once an architecture is selected, the project schedule is updated to reflect the order in which the parts are to be developed.

18.13 EXERCISES

1. In a paragraph, explain the purpose of a software architecture and how it relates to design.

2. Suppose that you are designing a batch simulation of customers in a bank. Being a batch simulation, the characteristics of the simulation are first set, then the simulation is executed without intervention. How could you describe this as a data flow application? Use a simple skeleton consisting of four parts to the diagram. (Identify your four parts, and then look at how you could describe this application as a state-transition diagram.) Which perspective offers more value in describing the architecture?

3. When designing a client-server architecture, there are generally two alternatives: *thin* and *thick* clients. A thin client implies that client functionality is kept to a minimum; most of the processing is performed via the server. A thick client implies that much of the functionality is contained in the client; the functionality on the server is kept to a minimum. Discuss the one or two major advantages and disadvantages to each of these approaches.

4. Operating systems are frequently designed using a layered architecture. Research the Linux operating system on the Internet, and explain how it utilizes a layered architecture. What are the benefits of such an architecture?

5. Consider a word processing application with which you are familiar. Sketch the software architecture of that program using one of the architectures described in this chapter. Describe the purpose of each of the components of your architecture.

6. Select an alternative software architecture for the word processing application of Exercise 5. Compare both architectures you selected and describe their relative merits.

7. Some design patterns are particularly relevant at the architectural level. Name two of these and explain their relevance.

8. Which software architecture is the best candidate for each of the following applications?
   a. An application for reordering auto parts from hundreds of stores
   b. A real-time application that shows the health of an automobile
   c. An application that provides advice to stock customers. It uses a multi-platform design consisting of several Web sites. One site continually collects and stores prices and other information about stocks; a second site continually collects stock advice from analysts; a third recommends portfolio suggestions to users.
   d. A scientific instrument company builds equipment for analyzing molecular structures. The application you are to design analyzes the structure of DNA molecules, which are very large.

TEAM EXERCISE

Architecture

Develop the architecture for your project. Describe your architecture using the IEEE standard, as in the case study accompanying this chapter. Make it clear what type of architecture and design patterns are being applied. Show at least one other architecture that you considered, and explain why you chose the alternative described. Include the use of metrics. It is not required that you automatically choose the architectures via metrics alone.

Track the time you spend doing this exercise in increments of five minutes, and include a time sheet showing the time spent by individuals and by the team. Use or improved upon the form in Table 18.2 that records the time spent per person on each module. Give your opinion on whether your tracking of time paid off, and whether your time could have been better managed.

Table 18.2 Form showing time spent per module

		Module			
		1	**2**	**3**	**4**
Team member	Smith	10	4		
	Jones		5	12	
	Brown	2			14

BIBLIOGRAPHY

1. Shaw, M. G., and D. Garlan, *"Software Architecture: Perspectives on an Emerging Discipline,"* Prentice Hall, 1996.
2. Dijkstra, E., *A Discipline of Programming*, Prentice Hall, 1976.
3. Lea, D., *Concurrent Programming in Java: Design Principles and Patterns (Java Series)*, Addison-Wesley, 1996.
4. Kaluzniacky, E. K., and V. Kanabar. *Xbase Programming for the True Beginner: An Introduction to the Xbase Language in the Context of dBase Iii+, Iv, 5, Foxpro, and Clipper*, McGraw Hill Professional, 1996.
5. Jagannathan, V., Rajendra Dodhiawala, and Lawrence S. Baum, editors. *Blackboard Architectures and Applications.* Academic Press, 1989.
6. Engelmore, Robert, and Anthony Morgan (Editors), *Blackboard Systems (The Insight Series in Artificial Intelligence), Addison-Wesley,* 1988.
7. Erl, Thomas, *"Service-Oriented Architecture: Concepts, Technology, and Design,"* Prentice Hall, 2006.
8. Gamma, Erich, Richard Helm, Ralph Johnson, and John Vlissides. *Design Patterns: Elements of Reusable Object-Oriented Software*, Addison-Wesley, 1999.
9. Gamma, Erich, and Beck, Kent. *"Contributing to Eclipse: Principles, Patterns, and Plug-Ins,"* Addison-Wesley, 2003.
10. OpenOffice Project, http://www.openoffice.org/white_papers/tech_overview/tech_overview.html#3 [accessed November 29, 2009].

19

Detailed Design

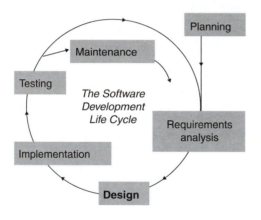

- **Planning**
- **Maintenance**
- **Testing**
- *The Software Development Life Cycle*
- **Requirements analysis**
- **Implementation**
- **Design**

- How do use cases and architectures relate to detailed designs?

- What are useful object-oriented design principles?

- Why design against interfaces?

- What is detailed design for agile processes?

- How do you specify classes, functions, and algorithms, particularly in UML?

- How do you plan for component reuse?

- How does one use standards for expressing detailed design?

- How is detailed design performed for large, real-world projects?

Figure 19.1 The context and learning goals for this chapter

Detailed design is the technical activity that follows architectural selection and covers all remaining aspects of technical creation short of actual code. It addresses major goals of software design (from Chapter 17): sufficiency, understandability, modularity, cohesion, coupling, robustness, flexibility, reusability, information hiding, efficiency, and reliability. This chapter starts by relating the detailed design process to the artifacts that have already been developed by the time we get to this point, especially the use cases of the requirements analysis process and the high-level design—the architecture (Section 19.1).

With regard to sufficiency, detailed design provides enough particulars for developers to implement the requirements of the application. As for understandability and modularity, object-oriented designs specify classes, their attributes, and their methods. Principles of detailed object-oriented designs are introduced in Section 19.3. This form of the application allows us to inspect designs for strong cohesion among grouped components and weak coupling with others. Flexibility, the reuse of components, and information hiding are discussed in Sections 19.4 and 19.6. Detailed design entails the development of sequence diagrams from use cases (Section 19.7), which are principal sources for the specification of classes and methods. The chapter ends with case studies.

The agile method, discussed in Chapter 4, begins coding without a full detailed design, and perhaps without any detailed design at all. This means that the detailed design essentially forms in the minds of the programmers and is generally documented within the code. Nevertheless, detailed design continues to exist for agile developers. We discuss this further in Section 19.8.

19.1 RELATING USE CASES, ARCHITECTURE, AND DETAILED DESIGN

The relationship between use cases, architecture, and detailed design can be understood by analogy with the process of designing a bridge. Use cases would be part of the requirements for the bridge (see the use case example in Figure 19.2). Based on the requirements, engineers would then select an architecture by stepping back, as it were, and looking at the big picture. Usually, more than one architecture suffices. In this case, a suspension architecture was selected. This process is illustrated by Figure 19.2.

Once the architecture has been selected, engineers may develop the detailed design to enable the required use cases with the architecture selected. This is suggested by Figure 19.3.

In the software analogy to the bridge example, each corresponding stage accumulates additional classes, which are shown in Figures 19.2 and 19.3. In Step 1, use cases are specified as part of the requirements. In Step 2, these, together with other sources, are used to identify the domain classes. In Step 3, we develop the software architecture, as described in Chapter 18. In Step 4 we develop the detailed design by defining design classes. We start with the domain classes (e.g., Auto, Road) and add additional design classes (e.g., Guardrail, Cable) to complete the design. We then verify that the architecture and detailed design support the required use cases. For the bridge analogy, we verify that cars can indeed use the bridge design to travel from Green's

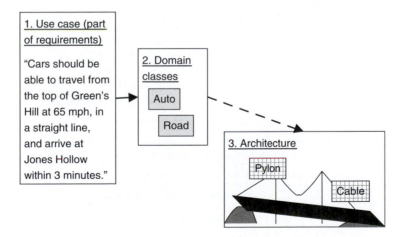

Figure 19.2 The relationship among use cases, architecture, and detailed design—an analogy from bridge building, 1 of 2

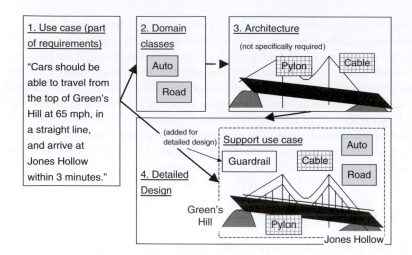

Figure 19.3 The relationship among use cases, architecture, and detailed design—an analogy from bridge building, 2 of 2

Hill to Jones Hollow as specified. For software design, we verify that the classes and methods specified by the detailed design are capable of executing the required use cases.

19.2 A TYPICAL ROAD MAP FOR THE "DETAILED DESIGN" PROCESS

Detailed design starts with the results of the architecture phase and ends with a complete blueprint for the programming phase. Figure 19.4 shows a typical sequence of steps taken to perform detailed design. There is really no universal standard way to go about this process—and, in fact, we frequently cycle back to designing when confronted with the reality of turning a design into reality. The agile process in particular, discussed below in Section 19.8 and in Chapter 4, is an extreme example of this.

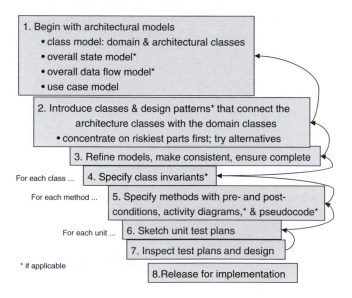

Figure 19.4 A typical road map for creating detailed designs

Step 2 of Figure 19.4 creates the classes that associate the architecture on one hand with the domain classes on the other hand, as illustrated in the previous section. Design patterns may help in doing this for software designs. We often begin the detailed design process with those aspects of the design that must be implemented, come what may, or that present the most risk. For example, in designing Encounter we might consider risky the way in which the classes were modularized (all characters in one package, etc.). This should be settled as soon as possible by specifying the details of the interface methods so that we can get an intimate idea of how this modularization works out. If the use of the State design pattern were perceived as a risk, we would specify its details first.

Step 3 of Figure 19.4 includes checking that we have a complete design. It also includes ensuring that the object model supports the use cases. Step 6 continues the practice of specifying a test as soon as each element is specified.

In test-driven development, often associated with agile development, Steps 6 and 7 are performed prior to some (perhaps all) of Steps 1–5, and their implementations are included in the process. In other words, tests are developed truly as early as possible, and then designs and code created to satisfy them. Regardless of the methodology used, early specification of tests is usually an excellent idea.

19.3 OBJECT-ORIENTED DESIGN PRINCIPLES

Martin [1, 2] identified five principles for class design of object-oriented software that also go hand-in-hand with agile development. These are summarized in Figure 19.5.

These principles are similar to, or follow from several that we have already discussed.

The *Single Responsibility Principle* emphasizes the need for classes to have one clearly understood responsibility such as "represent customer data" or "represent order for camping items," rather than very

---

- **Single-Responsibility** Principle
  - "A class should have only one reason to change."
  - ≡ cohesion
- **Open-Closed** Principle[1]
  - "An artifact should be open for extension but closed for modification in ways that affect its clients."
  - —especially modules, classes, and functions.
  - —a module can be extended without changing its code.
- **Liskov Substitution** Principle[2]
  - "Subclasses should be substitutable for their base classes."
- **Dependency-Inversion** Principle[3]
  - "Depend on abstractions. Do not depend on concretions."
    Both should depend on abstractions.
  - Abstractions should not depend on details.
    Details should depend on abstractions."
- **Interface Segregation** Principle.[4]
  - "Many client specific interfaces are better than one general purpose interface."

Figure 19.5 Some object-oriented design principles

[1] Bertrand Meyer, "Object-Oriented Software Construction," Second Edition, Prentice Hall, 2007.

[2] Barbara Liskov and John Guttag, "Abstraction and Specification in Program Development," MIT-Press, 1986.

[3] Robert Martin, "Agile Software Development: Principles, Patterns, and Practices," Prentice Hall, 2003.

[4] Ibid.

broad topics such as "all there is to know about customers and their habits" or "camping preferences." In other words, classes should exhibit a high level of cohesion. When classes have only one responsibility, they are easier to maintain and reuse.

The *Open-Closed Principle (OCP)* states that modules should be open for extension but closed for modification. That is, if an existing module needs to support additional requirements, then the existing, working code would remain intact. It would not need modification. In other words, new functionality should be implemented with new code. Consider the example shown in Listing 19.1, as described in [1]. The code satisfies the requirement to draw a set of shapes consisting of circles and squares. However, this code violates the OCP because shapes other than circles and squares cannot be drawn without modifying—not simply adding to—the body of the function.

Listing 19.1:   *drawAllShapes()*—adding functionality causes erasures

```
void drawAllShapes( Vector<Shape>someShapes ) {
      for( i=0; i<someShapes.length(); ++i ) {
            if (someShapes.get(i).type() == "circle"
                  drawCircle(someShapes.get(i));
            else if ((someShapes.get(i).type() == "square"
                  drawSquare(someShapes.get(i));
      }
}
```

A common way to avoid modification and conform to the OCP is by utilizing inheritance and polymorphism. Listing 19.2 shows how this is accomplished in a new version of *drawAllShapes()*. In this new version, shapes such as Circles and Squares inherit from the base class Shape. As a Shape is extracted from the vector, its polymorphic *draw()* method is called to draw that shape. This means that each type of shape is responsible for knowing how to draw itself. If new shapes need to be supported, *drawAllShapes()* does not need to be modified—it automatically calls the *draw()* method of that new shape when it is removed from the vector.

Listing 19.2:   *drawAllShapes()* – improved version now open for addition

```
void drawAllShapes( Vector<Shape> someShapes ) {
      for( i=0; i < someShapes.length(); ++i )
            someShapes.get(i).draw();
}
```

The *Liskov Substitution Principle* states that any code referencing an instance of a base class must also work correctly if, instead, it is passed an instance of a derived class. In other words, a derived class must honor the semantics of a base class. If this principle were to be violated, then every time a new derived class is created, code would have to be modified to reference the new class, violating the OCP.

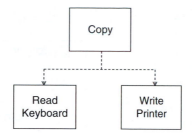

Figure 19.6 Dependency inversion

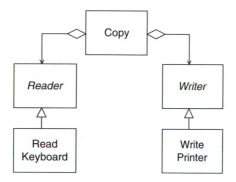

Figure 19.7 Avoiding dependency inversion using abstraction

The *Dependency Inversion Principle (DIP)* is concerned with hiding details. It asks us to design high-level modules in such a way that they do not depend on low-level modules. Instead, each should depend on abstractions. This makes the modules understandable and usable in themselves. Consider the example described by Martin [3].

The Copy module is dependent on the lower level modules–Read Keyboard and Write Printer, making it difficult to reuse as a general purpose copy module. By applying the DIP, we abstract the read and write modules, as shown in Figure 19.7. Now, Copy depends only on the abstract Reader and Writer, making it more flexible and portable. If new types of Readers and Writers are created, Copy is unaffected.

The *Interface Segregation Principle* tells us to collect related methods into separate interfaces rather than mixing unrelated methods (even when needed as a whole group). It draws from lessons of component design (e.g., Microsoft's COM) where we learned to package sets of methods in relatively small, manageable sets. By keeping interfaces small, we increase their cohesion.

19.4 DESIGNING AGAINST INTERFACES

The idea of designing against interfaces is like employing a contract. The program element supplying functionality (e.g., the *Customer* class) guarantees to provide interface functions with specified names, parameter types, and return types (e.g., *void bill(void)* and *boolean printAccounts(String accountType)*). The program elements using the functionality can then be designed without having to know how the functionality is implemented—all they need to know is how to use the interface. We have discussed this concept in the context of design

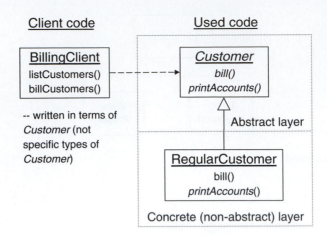

Figure 19.8 Designing against interfaces—an example of designing against *Customer* rather than *RegularCustomer*

patterns where patterns have clients. Also, the Facade design pattern is a way of providing a clean interface to a package of classes.

Designing against interfaces takes many forms. One is the use of abstraction. For example, if code is to be written about *Mammal* objects, then we try to write it so as to mention only *Animal* objects. In other words, we try to use only the *Animal* interface. This allows greater applicability and greater flexibility for our design.

As a further example, suppose that we are writing code about customers. This can be understood as writing against the *Customer* interface. We can actually consider using an abstract class *Customer*, which may have nonabstract subclasses such as *RegularCustomer*, as shown in Figure 19.8. This design is more flexible than writing against a concrete (nonabstract) class *RegularCustomer* because we can easily add other types of customers, such as *SavingsCustomer* objects, with specialized versions of *bill()*, without having to change the code that uses *Customer* objects. The division into an abstract and a concrete layer is characteristic of many design patterns.

For Java in particular, one tries to use Java-specific "Interfaces" for the interface role described above. These specify method signatures (name, return type, and parameters types) only. Unlike Java inheritance, classes can implement any number of interfaces. The UML notation for an interface is a dotted-line rectangle, and a dotted line triangle is used instead of a solid one.

19.5 SPECIFYING CLASSES, FUNCTIONS, AND ALGORITHMS

The goal of complete detailed design is to provide a complete blueprint from which a program can be constructed. A good house blueprint leaves the builder with as few doubts as possible about the intentions of the designer, and the same is true for detailed software design. Figure 19.9 describes typical steps in carrying out detailed design for each class, and the succeeding text explains the steps in detail.

A fully detailed class diagram includes all attribute and operation names, signatures, visibility, return types, and so on. Accessor methods are commonly omitted. It is customary to omit accessor functions (e.g., *getSize()* and *setSize()*), since these can be inferred from the presence of the corresponding attributes (e.g., size). UML tools have the benefit of allowing designers to suppress (i.e., to not show) certain elements of the figure—for example, the "responsibilities" section or the variable types. Many tools allow designers to view only the classes and their relationships, in order to get the big picture.

1. Gather the attributes listed in the SRS.
   - if the SRS is organized by class
2. Add additional attributes required for the design.
3. Name a method corresponding to each of the requirements for this class.
   - easy if the SRS is organized by class
4. Name additional methods required for the design.
5. Show the attributes and methods on the object model.
6. State class invariants.

Figure 19.9 Fully specifying a class

One language-independent manner in which to specify classes is through the CORBA Interface Definition Language (IDL). This is a standard, textual format for specifying the interfaces provided by collections of classes, their attributes, and their functions. For the specification of IDL, see [4].

In some organizations, detailed designs are specified by providing code without function bodies rather than UML. This is sometimes true of agile developers. The advantage of this procedure is that there is no need to translate detailed specifications into code. A disadvantage is that a code form is somewhat less readable than ordinary prose. The functions in the code form are then filled out at implementation time by programmers.

19.5.1 Preconditions, Postconditions, and Invariants

An effective way to specify functions is by means of *preconditions* and *postconditions*. Preconditions specify the relationships among variables and constants that are assumed to exist prior to the function's execution; postconditions specify the required relationships after the function's execution. For example, the function *withdraw(int withdrawalAmountP)* of an *Account* class could be specified as shown in Figure 19.10. Another

Invariant of *withdraw()*:

   $balanceI >= -OVERDRAFT\text{-}MAX$ AND

   $availableFundsI = balanceI + OVERDRAFT\_MAX$

Precondition* :

   $withdrawalAmountP >= 0$ AND

   $balanceI - withdrawalAmountP$

   $>= OVERDRAFT\_MAX$

Postcondition* :

   $balanceI' = balanceI - withdrawalAmountP$

> Conventions used:
> xI denotes an attribute;
> xP denotes a function parameter;
> x' is the value of x after execution;
> X denotes a class constant

*The function invariant is an additional pre- and postcondition

Figure 19.10 Example of specifying functions precisely—specifying *withdraw()* in *Account*

example of a precondition is an *age* parameter that a method assumes is greater than zero. The effects of a method are its *postconditions*. They are the very reason for the method, and must be specified as well. In the experience of the authors, software engineers require significant training in the capacity to specify preconditions and postconditions with precision, as in Figure 19.10.

Invariants of a method are assertions that are both preconditions and postconditions. They are a way to maintain intellectual control over the behavior of functions. They specify relationships that do not change, which is welcome in the environment of an application, where complex change is so often difficult to manage. An example from Encounter is the following possible invariant for the *adjustQuality()* method.

Invariant: the sum of the values of the qualities.

In other words, when the value of one quality is changed with *adjustQuality()*, the values of the remaining qualities change in a way that leaves their sum unchanged.

19.5.2 Expressing Algorithms with Activity Diagrams and Pseudocode

It is helpful to specify nontrivial algorithms at detailed design time. The advantage of doing this is that engineers can inspect the algorithms separately without the intrusion of programming complexities, thereby trapping many important defects before they magnify into code defects. The more critical the method, the more important this activity. Methods with complicated branching are candidates for *activity diagrams* ("advanced flowcharts"). Activity diagrams were described in Chapter 16.

Pseudocode is a means of expressing an algorithm textually without having to specify programming language details. As an example, pseudocode for a hypothetical automated X-ray controller is shown in Figure 19.11. An advantage of pseudocode is that it is easy to understand but can also be made precise enough to express algorithms. Another advantage is that algorithms can be inspected for correctness independently of the clutter of a programming language. A third advantage is that defect rates in pseudocode can be collected and used as a predictor for defect rates in the product, using historical defect data.

Some organizations use inspected pseudocode as annotated comments in the source code listing. Tools are then able to extract the pseudocode from the source. For example, using "//p" to preface pseudocode statements, the code could implement the pseudocode cited above—see Figure 19.12.

Activity diagrams and pseudocode each have the advantages listed in Figures 19.13 and 19.14. The decision whether to use them or not depends on factors particular to the application. Some developers shun activity diagrams as old-fashioned, but activity diagrams and pseudocode can be worth the trouble for selected parts of applications, where they help to produce better quality products.

FOR number of microseconds supplied by operator
    IF number of microseconds exceeds critical value
        Try to get supervisor's approval
        IF no supervisor's approval
           abort with "no supervisor approval
           for unusual duration" message **ENDIF ENDIF**
    IF power level exceeds critical value
        abort with "power level exceeded" message **ENDIF**
    IF (patient properly aligned & shield properly placed & machine self-test passed)
        Apply X-ray at power level p **ENDIF** . . . **ENDFOR**

Figure 19.11 Specifying algorithms with pseudocode—a critical X-ray example

```
//p FOR number of microseconds supplied by operator
for( int i = 0; i < numMicrosecs; ++I ) {
  //p IF number of microseconds exceeds critical value
  if( numMicrosecs >
    XRayPolicies.CRITICAL_NUM_MICROSECS )
      //p Try to get supervisor's approval
      int supervisorMicrosecsApproval=
        getApprovalOfSuperForLongExposure();
      //p IF no supervisor approval
      if( supervisorMicrosecsApproval <= 0 )
        throw ( new SupervisorMicrosecsApprovalException() );
  . . . . . . . . . .
```

Figure 19.12 Pseudocode as extractable comments in source code

- Clarify algorithms in many cases
- Impose increased discipline on the process of documenting detailed design
- Provide additional level at which inspection can be performed
  - Help to trap defects before they become code
  - Increase product reliability
- May decrease overall costs

Figure 19.13 Some advantages of pseudocode and activity diagrams

- Creates an additional level of documentation to maintain
- Introduces error possibilities in translating to code
- May require tool to extract pseudocode and facilitate drawing activity diagrams

Figure 19.14 Some disadvantages of pseudocode and activity diagrams

19.6 REUSING COMPONENTS

Most engineering disciplines (electrical, mechanical, etc.) rely on the use of components that can be procured separately. Bridge designers, for example, try to use standard I-beams. The widespread adoption of object-oriented, object-like, and other component paradigms has helped to promote software reuse. Because of the large number of methods packaged with each class, functionality that we need is often included and is relatively convenient to locate. The use of Microsoft libraries, Visual Basic controls, Microsoft Assemblies, Java Beans, and Java Application Programming Interface classes are examples of code reuse.

Frameworks, discussed in the previous chapter on architecture, are packages of components designed for reuse. We develop frameworks to support application architectures, and so they are effectively reusable. The Java core API is another example of a widely used framework. Java Beans provide reusable components for Java applications. They include graphics beans and "enterprise" beans, which encapsulate corporate tasks such as database access. In addition to the advantages afforded by being classes, beans obey standards that make them capable of manipulation within development environments. Web-based programs (i.e., not components) such as JavaScript and CGI scripts are often reused.

At a different level, the Standard Template Library (STL) provides mix-and-match capability of standard algorithms such as sorting and searching. STL is applicable to a variety of data structures and to objects of virtually any class. In summary, a component marketplace has emerged and is growing continually.

The Encounter video game case study presented at the end of this chapter contains examples of reuse within an enterprise: in this case, a game development business. To be cost-effective—and thus competitive— the company leverages its software as much as possible among projects. For example, rather than invest the resources to develop a class for the character in Encounter alone, it tries to separate the development into a game character class, and use a subclass for Encounter's character. The game character class can be reused for other games. This idea is extended in the case study to a game framework consisting of several related classes, which is the common context for reuse.

Having found an existing component that could possibly be used in an application, *should* it be used? The following factors are typical in making this decision, and they suggest factors that should be accounted for in creating one's own components slated for reuse.

- Is the component documented as thoroughly as the rest of the application? If not, can it be?

- How much customization of the component and/or the application is required?

- Has the component been tested to the same level as, or more extensively than, the rest of the application? If not, can it be?

To decide on reuse of components with significant size, a table comparing the costs can be developed, similar to the one in Chapter 8 where a make vs. buy example was shown.

19.7 SEQUENCE AND DATA FLOW DIAGRAMS FOR DETAILED DESIGN

Some detailed designs are best communicated via detailed sequence diagrams or detailed data flow diagrams. Figures 19.15 and 19.16 provide guidance on what needs to be done with sequence diagrams and data flow diagrams to complete the corresponding detailed design. The text that follows provides details and examples.

1. **Begin** with the **sequence diagrams** constructed for detailed requirements and/or architecture (if any) corresponding to the use cases.
2. Introduce **additional use cases**, if necessary, to describe how parts of the design typically interact with the rest of the application.
3. Provide **sequence diagrams** with **complete details**.
   - be sure that the exact objects and their classes are specified
   - select specific function names in place of natural language
     (calls of one object to another to perform an operation)

Figure 19.15 Refining models for detailed designs, 1 of 2—sequence diagrams

1. **Gather data flow diagrams** (DFDs) constructed for detailed requirements and/or architecture (if any).
2. Introduce **additional DFDs**, if necessary, to explain data and processing flows.
3. Indicate what **part(s)** of the other models the DFDs **correspond to**.
   - for example, "the following DFD is for each *Account* object"
4. Provide all **details on the DFDs**.
   - indicate clearly the nature of the processing at each node
   - indicate clearly the kind of data transmitted
   - expand processing nodes into DFDs if the processing description requires more detail

Figure 19.16 Refining models for detailed designs, 2 of 2—data flow diagrams

19.7.1 Detailed Sequence Diagrams

Recall that use cases can be utilized to express requirements, and that we also use them to determine the key domain classes for the application. For the detailed design phase, we provide classes with the methods referenced in the sequence diagrams.

As an example, the sequence diagram for the "Encounter Foreign Character" is shown in Figure 19.18, showing the messages between objects in the software design. The reasoning behind the functions chosen is as follows:

1. *ForeignCharacter* is to have a display function. We will implement this with a method *display()*. (Since all characters will need to be displayed, we can actually ensure this requirement by giving the base class *GameCharacter* a *display()* method.) The sequence diagram shows *EncounterGame* creating the foreign character (Step 1.2) and also an Engagement object, and then calling *display()*. An engagement is to take place, and a good design is to capture this by creating an *Engagement* object. This is illustrated in Figure 19.17.

2. This step in the use case indicates that we need an *execute()* method in *Engagement*.

   2.1 This step requires that Freddie and the main player character be able to change their quality values. Since this capability is common to all *Encounter* characters, we provide the base *EncounterCharacter* class with a *setQuality()* method.

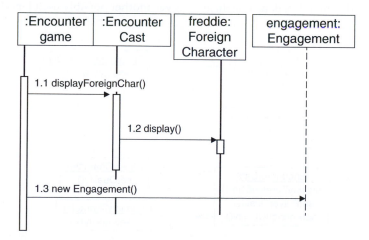

Figure 19.17 Beginning of sequence diagram for *Encounter Foreign Character* use case

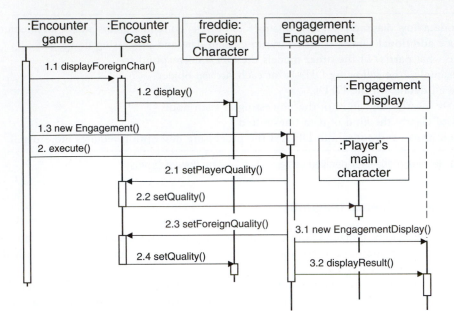

Figure 19.18 Sequence diagram for *Encounter Foreign Character* use case

3. This step requires that the result of the engagement be shown. The following two substeps constitute one way to do this.

3.1 First Engagement creates an *EngagementDisplay* object.

3.2 Now we show the engagement display by calling its *displayResult()* method.

Since the methods required to execute this use case are now known, we can include them on the class model, as in Figure 19.19. Continuing this process, the class model and the use case model (in the form of sequence diagrams) are completed in detail, as shown in the case study. The state model (if applicable) must also be completed in detail. A data flow diagram is yet another possibly useful model, and is discussed next.

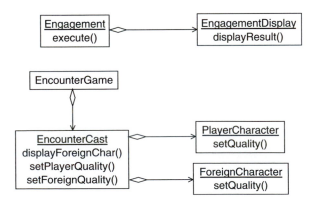

Figure 19.19 Classes for *Encounter Foreign Character* use case

19.7.2 Detailed Data Flow Diagrams

To relate data flow models to classes, we can map each processing element to a method of a class. Figure 19.20 shows a high-level view of a data flow diagram for an ATM banking application. Data flow models can be *telescoped*. For example, Figure 19.21 expands processing elements from the DFD in Figure 19.20.

Telescoping allows us to show a high-level view, followed by successive stages containing as much detail as we wish. This avoids overwhelming the viewer. Each processing element is expanded into a more detailed DFD, and this expansion process is continued until the lowest level processing elements are reached. The latter are typically individual functions, possibly of different classes. For example, the *getDeposit()* function is expanded into three functions (getting the password, verifying it, and making a display). Two of these interact with data stores (a local log of transactions, a list of problem users, and a template for screen displays) that were not shown in the high-level DFD. Note that the data entrances and exits from the detailed expansions match those in the versions from which they are expanded.

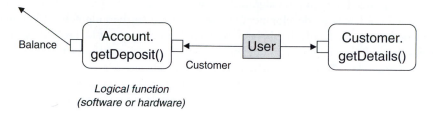

Figure 19.20 Detailed data flow diagram for banking application, 1 of 2—high level

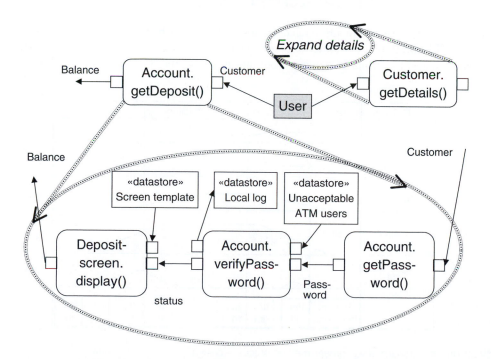

Figure 19.21 Detailed data flow diagram for banking application, 2 of 2—with details

Each processing element is expanded into a more detailed DFD, and this expansion process is continued until the lowest-level processing elements are reached. The latter are typically individual functions, possibly of different classes. For example, the *getDeposit()* function is expanded into three functions (getting the password, verifying it, and making a display). Two of these interact with data stores (a local log of transactions, a list of problem users, and a template for screen displays) that were not shown in the high-level DFD. Note that the data entrances and exits from the detailed expansions match those in the versions from which they are expanded. DFDs are not helpful for all applications. For example, they do not add much to the Encounter case study.

19.8 DETAILED DESIGN AND AGILE PROCESSES

Agile processes, described in Chapter 4 and referred to throughout this book, emphasize working code and place documentation at a lower priority. The latter includes detailed designs. An extreme interpretation of this is that detailed design counts for very little, but a more measured interpretation is that an agile process would create detailed designs for only those parts of applications where the effort to produce them is worth the benefit. An example is a complicated but important algorithm. A non-agile development effort, on the other hand, may document every method. For large development efforts, leaving it to the judgment of hundreds of software engineers as to whether design details should be documented or not may not be favored by project managers.

It is obvious that software engineers should not engage in activities with insufficient benefits. One issue that makes this less than clear, however, is whether one assesses benefits in the short term or the long term. Good, detailed design documentation of a class that supports the code (possibly as comments) would help maintainers. It would also have to be kept up-to-date by maintainers. This is probably a long-term benefit that is not as clear in the short term.

19.9 DESIGN IN THE UNIFIED DEVELOPMENT PROCESS

Recall that the unified development approach of Jacobson et al., described in Chapter 3, groups iterations into the "Inception," "Elaboration," "Construction," and "Transition" categories (see Figure 19.22). Design takes place primarily somewhat during "Elaboration" but mostly during the "Construction" iterations. The idea is

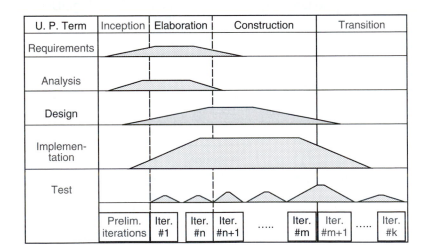

Figure 19.22 Unified software development method process—design

Source: Jacobson, Ivar, J. Rumbaugh, and G. Booch. The Unified Software Development Process, Addison-Wesley, 1999.

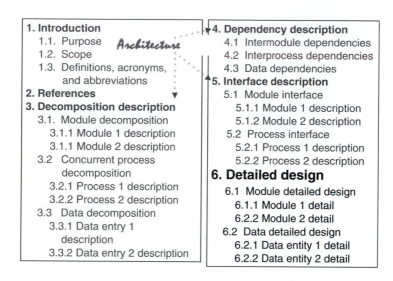

Figure 19.23 IEEE 1016-1998 Software Design Document table of contents, with focus on detailed design section
Source: IEEE 1016-1998.

that most of the requirements will have been gathered by those stages. An "Analysis" phase is frequently identified as part of the waterfall process. Compared with the terminology of this book, the Analysis phase consists partly of requirements analysis and partly of architecture selection.

The unified process encourages three types ("stereotypes") of classes at the analysis level: *entity*, *boundary*, and *control* classes, whereas there is no such restriction on design classes. Entity classes express the essence of the concept, and are unlikely to require change over time or between applications. Boundary classes handle communication with entity objects, and control classes contain methods that pertain to the entity objects but that are typically special to the application in which the entity class is being used. Boundary classes are typically like the *Mediator* object in the Mediator design pattern described in Chapter 16. The unified process promotes visual tools for design. An example of this is the Rational Rose tool sold by IBM.

19.10 IEEE STANDARD 890 FOR DETAILED DESIGN

Recall IEEE standard 1016-1998 for Software Design Documents shown in Chapter 18 on software architecture, as shown in Figure 19.23. This format for the detailed design section of this document consists of specifying a description of each module (package) in turn, with a detailed description of each data part. For OO designs, the latter can be replaced with a detailed description of each class.

19.11 UPDATING A PROJECT WITH DETAILED DESIGN

Once a detailed design is in hand, the project plan can be made more specific in several respects. In particular, cost estimation can be made much more precise, schedules can be broken down into tasks, and tasks can be allocated to individuals. Figure 19.24 includes most of the important updates to be performed once detailed design is complete.

Since we can estimate the number and size of the methods involved in the application using detailed designs, a more precise estimation of the project size is possible. As described in Chapter 8, project costs can then be inferred from the size. Figure 19.25 shows one way of carrying this out.

1. Make sure the SDD reflects latest version of detailed design, as settled on after inspections.
2. Give complete detail to the schedule (SPMP).
3. Allocate precise tasks to team members (SPMP).
4. Improve project cost and time estimates (see below).
5. Update the SCMP to reflect the new parts.
6. Review process by which the detailed design was created, and determine improvements. Include . . .
   - time taken, broken down to include
     - preparation of the designs
     - inspection
     - change
   - defect summary
     - number remaining open, found at detailed design, closed at detailed design
     - where injected; include previous phases and detailed design stages

Figure 19.24 Bringing the project up-to-date after completing detailed design

The COCOMO model can now be used again to refine the estimate of job duration. It is best to use personal data to estimate the LOC for very small, small, and such jobs. In the absence of these data, department, division, or corporate data can be used. Otherwise, Humphrey's table (Figure 19.26) [6] may be usefully applied. Figure 19.26 applies to C++ LOC per method. On the average, Java and C++ require the same number of LOC to implement similar functionality [7, 8].

Calculation methods perform numerical computation; data methods manipulate data (e.g., reformatting); logic methods consist mainly of branching; setup methods initialize situations; text methods manipulate text. Estimates for methods that combine several of these can be computed by averaging. For example, an unexceptional ("medium") method that performs calculations but also has a substantial logic component can be estimated as having $(11.25 + 15.98)/2 = 13.62$ lines of code.

Descriptors such as *Very Small* and *Small* are "fuzzy" in that they describe ranges rather than precise amounts. These ranges can overlap, in which case an average of the corresponding table values can be used. (This is actually a simplification of fuzziness, but adequate for our purpose.) Fuzzy descriptors are practical

1. Start with the list of methods.
   - ensure completeness, otherwise underestimate will result
2. Estimate the lines of code (LOC) for each.
   - classify as *very small, small, medium, large, very large*
     - normally in $\pm$ 7%/24%/38%/24%/7% proportions
   - use personal data to covert to LOC
     - otherwise use Humphrey's table below
3. Sum the LOC.
4. Covert LOC to person-hours.
   - use personal conversion factor, if possible
   - otherwise use published factor
5. Ensure that your estimates of method sizes and time will be compared and saved at project end.

Figure 19.25 Estimating size and time-to-complete from detailed designs

		Category				
		Very small	Small	Medium	Large	Very large
Method type	Calculation	2.34	5.13	11.25	24.66	54.04
	Data	2.60	4.79	8.84	16.31	30.09
	I/O	9.01	12.06	16.15	21.62	28.93
	Logic	7.55	10.98	15.98	23.25	33.83
	Set-up	3.88	5.04	6.56	8.53	11.09
	Text	3.75	8.00	17.07	36.41	77.67

Figure 19.26 Lines of code

Source: Humphrey, Watts S. A Discipline for Software Engineering (SEI Series in Software Engineering), Addison–Wesley, 1995.

because they are easy to understand. They can be made more precise by categorization with the normal distribution, as shown in Figure 19.27.

On the average, about 38 percent of the methods should be classified as "medium," 24 percent "small," and 7 percent "very small," as illustrated in Figure 19.27. These numbers are obtained from the fact that about 38 percent of the values in a normal distribution are within a half of a standard deviation of the mean. In practical terms, if the fraction of methods you estimate as "very large" differs much from 7 percent, for example, then you should be satisfied that your application really does have an unusual number of very large methods. Otherwise, you should revise your estimates.

As an example, let's estimate the size of the *execute()* method of the *Engagement* class. This method involves the recalculation of quality values, which is the essential mechanism of executing the engagement process. For this reason, we could classify the *execute()* method as a "calculation." The size of the *execute()* method is not particularly remarkable, since it consists of a fairly straightforward computation of values, so we'll classify it as "medium." Thus, the estimated contribution of *execute()* is 11.25 LOC.

A level 5 organization (see Chapter 5 on the Capability Maturity Model) would typically plot method size estimates against actual sizes in order to improve this estimation process. In the case study, these estimates are applied to the Encounter video game.

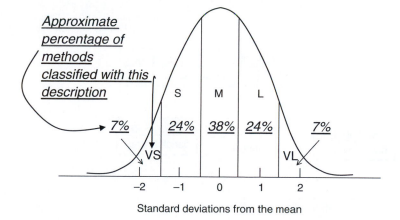

Figure 19.27 Normal distribution of "small," "medium," and "large"

19.12 CASE STUDY: DETAILED DESIGN OF ENCOUNTER

What follows is the detailed design for Encounter, based on the architecture specified earlier in this book, and using the IEEE standard. Each use case is realized as a sequence diagram by deciding, for each use case step, which object should initiate and which should perform the work step involved. The class models should contain the classes that appear in the sequence diagrams.

6. Detailed Design of Role-Playing Game Framework

6.1 Module Detailed Design

Note to the Student:
These sections give all of the nontrivial required details on each of the modules described in Section 3.1 in this SDD for the game framework.

6.1.1 Role-Playing Game Package

All mouse events are listened for by objects of the class *RPGMouseEventListener*, which inherits from *MouseListener* as shown in Figure 19.28. Each object that is sensitive to mouse events asks an *RPGame* object to handle the event. *RPGame* passes control to the *handleEvent()* method of its aggregated *GameState* object. The sequence diagram for this is shown in Figure 19.29. For the current release, the methods are either trivial or are shown in Figure 19.29.

Pseudocode for selected methods within selected classes may be included here. In addition, detailed use cases can be included. Since the methods and their details are still one or two lines in this case, it is sufficient to elaborate on the (barely) nontrivial methods with the notation shown in Figure 19.28.

6.1.2 The Characters Package

This section elaborates on Section 3.1.2 of this SDD. There is one class in the *Character* package: *GameCharacter*.

6.1.2.1 *GameCharacter* Class
Methods of *GameCharacter*

```
setName().
Preconditions: none;
postconditions: none;
  invariants: none
```

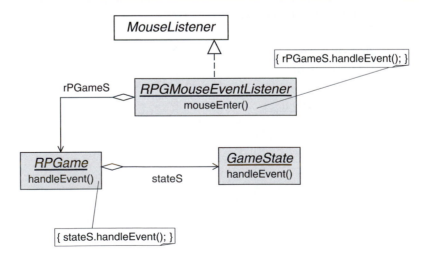

Figure 19.28 Detailed design of *RolePlayingGame* package

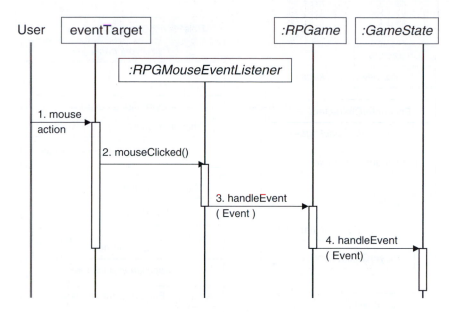

Figure 19.29 Sequence diagram for handling mouse events

Pseudocode:

IF aName parameter **OR**
maxNumCharsInName() make no sense
   Set name to default value and show
   this in system window
ELSE
  IF parameter string too long
    truncate at maxNumCharsInName()
ELSE assign the parameter name

6.1.3 *The GameEnvironment* Package

This package is described completely by Figure 19.31
in Section 3.1 of this SDD (Chapter 18).

6.1.4 *The Artifacts Package*

Not applicable in this iteration.

6. DETAILED DESIGN OF ENCOUNTER

The overall architecture, showing the relationships
among the packages and the domain classes described in this section, is shown in Figure 19.30.

6.1 Module Detailed Design for Encounter

> These sections give all of the required details
> on each of the modules described in Section
> 3.1 in this SDD (i.e., for Encounter).

6.1.1 *The EncounterGame* Package

> This section gives all of the required details on
> Section 3.1.1 in this SDD. It describes com-
> pletely the classes of the *EncounterGame* pack-
> age, and all of their nontrivial behavior. Most
> of this is described by the state transition
> diagram. In the interests of keeping the class
> model free of clutter, we do not show all object
> references.

The state diagram for Encounter is shown in
Section 2.1.1 of the SRS (Figure 11.26 of Chapter 11).
To realize these states and transitions, the *EncounterGame*
package class model is designed as in Figure 19.31.

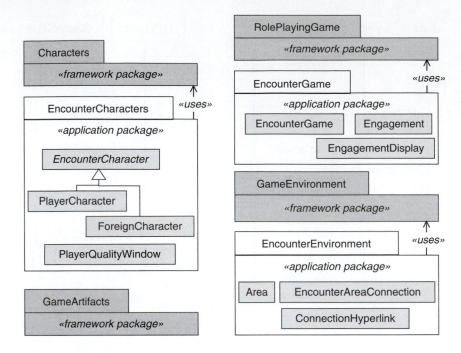

Figure 19.30 Encounter game architecture packages, showing domain classes only

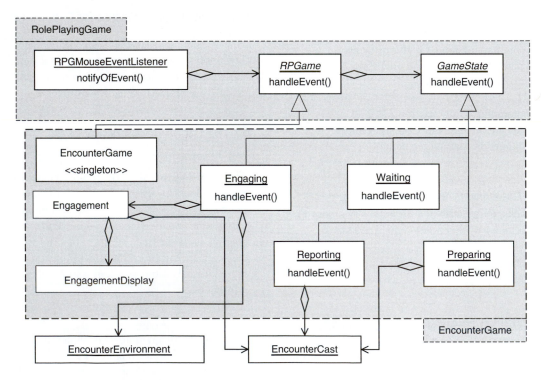

Figure 19.31 Detailed design of *EncounterGame* package

There is exactly one instance of the *EncounterGame* class. The states of this object reflect the states and substates shown in the above state-transition diagram. The *Encountering* state aggregates an *Engagement* object that encapsulates the engagement of the game characters. The *Engagement* class aggregates a display called *EngagementDisplay*. The latter is mouse-sensitive, registering with an *RPGMouseEventListener* object. When the Encounter game is executed, this listener object references the *EncounterGame* object (an *RPGame* object). This enables *EncounterGame* to handle all events according to the game's state, using the State design pattern. The *EncounterGame* package has the responsibility of directing the movement of the foreign character over time. This is performed by methods of the class *Character-Movement*, which is a thread class.

State classes need to reference other packages in order to implement *handleEvent( )*, and this is done through the *Facade* objects *EncounterCast* and *EncounterEnvironment*.

6.1.1.1 The *EncounterGameDisplays* Subpackage of the *EncounterGame* Package Displays corresponding to some of the states are handled by a separate subpackage, *EncounterGameDisplays*, which is shown in Figure 19.32.

QualListDispl is a list box consisting of the qualities of Encounter characters.

QualValueDispl is a read-only text box for displaying the value of a quality.

SetQualValueDispl is an editable text box for setting the value of a quality.

EncounterDisplayItem abstracts the properties and methods of displayable Encounter items such as these.

EngagementDisplay is designed to display the current value of any selected quality.

SetQualityDisplay is designed to enable the player to set the value of any quality.

EncounterDisplay abstracts the properties of these displays, and is a mediator base class.

This document does not provide further details of the design of these classes.

6.1.1.2 Sequence Diagrams for Event Handling

6.1.1.2.1 Player Dismisses Report Window Event Figure 19.33 shows the sequence involved in dismissing the engagement display. (This dismissal event is shown on the state-transition diagram.)

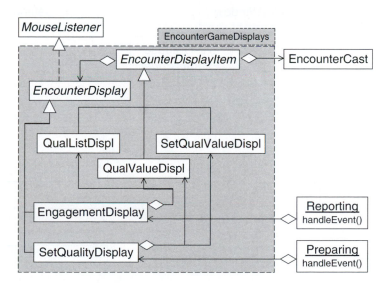

Figure 19.32 Detailed design of *EncounterGameDisplays* subpackage

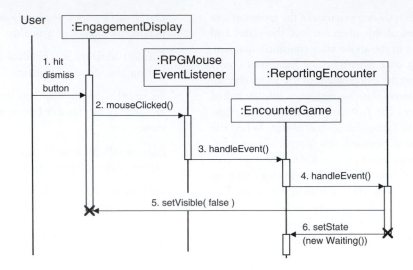

Figure 19.33 Sequence diagram for dismissing engagement display

6.1.1.2.2 Player Completes Setup Event Figure 19.34 shows the sequence involved when the player completes the setup. (This dismissal event is shown on the state-transition diagram.)

6.1.1.2.3 Player Moves to Adjacent Area Event Figure 19.35 shows the sequence when the player moves to an adjacent area by clicking on a connection hyperlink. (This dismissal event is shown on the state-transition diagram.)

6.1.1.2.4 Sequence Diagrams for Remaining Events The remaining events are handled very similarly to those described in Sections 6.1.1.1 through 6.1.1.3.

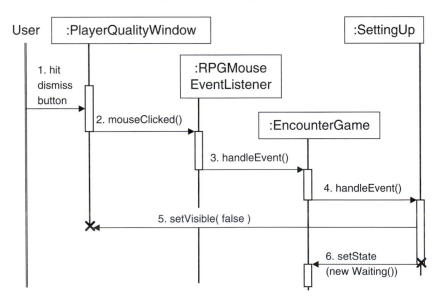

Figure 19.34 Sequence diagram for *Player Completes Setup* use case

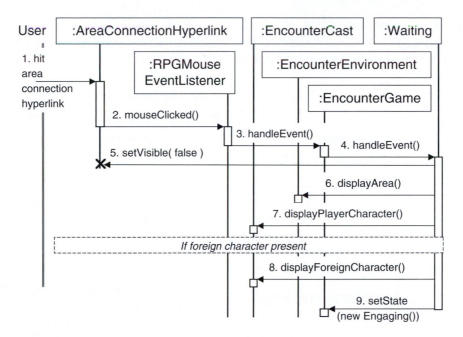

Figure 19.35 Sequence diagram for *Player Moves to Adjacent Area* use case

6.1.1. CM The *CharacterMovement* Class

> As in the SRS, we are using an alphabetical "numbering" scheme to make it easier to find and insert classes. There is also a benefit in being able to trace the requirements to the SRS.

This class controls the movement of the foreign character.

Inheritance
This class inherits from *java.lang*. Thread.

Methods of *CharacterMovement*

`public static EncounterGame run();`

Starts the foreign character in the dungeon. Moves the foreign character from area to area via area connections, changing areas to a randomly selected neighbor, at random times averaging every two seconds.

6.1.2. EG The *EncounterGame* Class This is the facade singleton for the *EncounterGame* package.

Inheritance
This class inherits from *RPGame* in the framework.

Attributes of *EncounterGame*:

`EncounterGame encounterGameS:`

This is the singleton *EncounterGame* object.

Constructors of *EncounterGame*:

`private EncounterGame():`
Preconditions: none
Postconditions: creates an *EncounterGame* instance

Methods of *EncounterGame*

`public static EncounterGame`
`getTheEncounterGame();`
Preconditions: none
Postconditions: *encounterGameS* not null
Returns: *encounterGameS*

6.1.3. EN The *Engagement* Class This class encapsulates engagements between the player's character and the foreign character, and corresponds to requirement 3.2.EN.

Methods

    public void **engage();** //

corresponds to requirement 3.2.EN.3.1

Preconditions: The player's character and the foreign character are in the same area.
Postconditions: The values of the characters' qualities are as required by SRS requirement 3.2.EN.3.1; the player's character and the foreign character are in random but different areas.

6.1.4. ZZ The *Engaging*, *Waiting*, *Preparing*, and *Reporting* Classes

> The "ZZ" numbering is used to collect classes that are not specified individually.

Inheritance
These classes inherit from *GameState* in the framework package.

Each of these classes implements its *handleEvent()* method in accordance with the sequence diagrams of Section 6.1.1.1.

6.1.2 The EncounterCharacters package

> This section elaborates on Section 3.1.2 in this SDD.

The design of the *EncounterCharacters* package is shown in Figure 19.36. It is implemented by the Facade design pattern, with *EncounterCast* as the facade object.

6.1.5. EC The *EncounterCharacter* Class This class encapsulates the requirements for *Encounter* characters that are not covered by *RPGameCharacters*. It satisfies requirements SRS 3.2.EC.
Class invariant: The values of *qualValueI* are nonnegative (see "attributes" below for the definitions of *qualValueI*).

Inheritance
This class inherits from GameCharacter in the framework package.

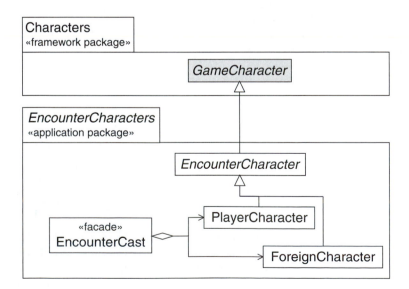

Figure 19.36 Detailed design of *EncounterCharacters* package

<u>Attributes of *EncounterCharacter*</u>

These satisfy requirement SRS 3.2.EC.1

`private static final String[]`
`qualityTypeS`

This represents the qualities that *Encounter* characters possess. These are concentration, stamina, intelligence, patience, and strength.

`private float[] qualValueI`

This is an array containing the values of the qualities.

<u>Constructors of *EncounterCharacter*</u>

These satisfy requirements 3.2.EC.3 of the SRS.
Null constructor

Postcondition: The qualities are all equal fractions of 100.

`protected EncounterCharacter`
`( String nameP )`

Postconditions:

(1) the qualities are all equal fractions of 100.

(2) the character's name is NameP

<u>Methods of *EncounterCharacter*</u>

`public synchronized void`
`  adjustQuality`
`( String qualityP, float`
`  qualityValueP )`

This method satisfies requirement 3.2.EC.3.2.
Invariants: none
Preconditions:

qualityP is in qualityTypesS[]
AND qualityValueP >=0
AND qualityValueP <= the sum of the quality values

Postconditions:

qualityP has the value qualityValueP
AND
the remaining quality values are in the same proportion as
prior to invocation, except that values less than 0.5 are zero.

The following is the pseudocode for the method *adjustQuality()*.

Set the stated quality to the desired amount.

IF the caller adjusts the only nonzero quality value, divide the adjustment amount equally among all other qualities.

ELSE change the remaining qualities, retaining their mutual proportion,

Set each quality whose value is now less than 0.5 to zero.

`public float getQualityValue`
`( String qualityP )`

Preconditions: qualityP is a valid quality string
Returns: the value of qualityP

`public float getTolerance( )`

Returns: the value below which quality values cannot go

`protected int maxNumCharsInName()`

Returns: the maximum number of characters in the names of Encounter characters

`public float sumOfQualities()`

Returns: the sum of the values of the qualities
This method satisfies requirement 3.2.EC.3.2.

`public void showCharacter`
`( Component componentP,`
`Graphics drawP, Point posP, int`
`heightPixP, boolean faceLeftP )`

Displays the character in *componentP*, with center at *posP*, with height *heightPixP*, facing left if *faceLeftP* true

This method satisfies requirements 3.2.PC.1 and 3.2.PQ.1.

`private void setQuality( String`
`qualityP, float valueP )`

Preconditions: *qualityP* is a valid quality string.
Sets the quality indicated by the parameter to *valueP* if the latter is >= 0.5, otherwise sets *valueP* to zero.

This method satisfies requirement 3.2. EC.2 (lower limit on nonzero quality values).

6.1.6. ES The *EncounterCast* Class The method specifications for this singleton, interface class are given in Section 5 of this document.

6.1.7. FC The *ForeignCharacter* Class This class is analogous to *PlayerCharacter*, described next, and is designed to satisfy the SRS 3.2.FC.

6.1.8. PC The *PlayerCharacter* Class This class is designed to satisfy the requirements 3.2.PC.

Inheritance
This class inherits from *EncounterCharacter*.
Attributes:

```
private static final Player
Character playerCharactersS;
```

This is the singleton object representing the player's character.

Methods:

```
public static final Player
Character getPlayerCharacter();
```

This method returns *playerCharactersS*.

6.1.7 *The EncounterEnvironment* Package
The classes of this package describe the environment in which the game takes place. It is shown in Figure 19.37.

6.1.8. AR *Area* Class This class encapsulates the places in which the characters exist, and corresponds to requirement 3.2.AR.

Inheritance
This class inherits from *GameArea*.
Attributes:

```
private String nameI; //
corresponding to requirement
3.2.AR.1.1
private Image imageI; //
corresponding to requirement
3.2.AR.1.2
private String[] qualitiesI; //
corresponding to requirement
3.2.AR.1.3
private Vector connection
HyperlinksI;
```

Methods

```
public void display() //
```
shows the area object's image on the monitor.

```
public static Area getArea
(String areaNameP)
```
returns the area corresponding to *areaNameP* according to requirement 3.2.AR.2.2.

```
public static AreaConnection
getAreaConnection(String   area
ConnectionNameP)
```

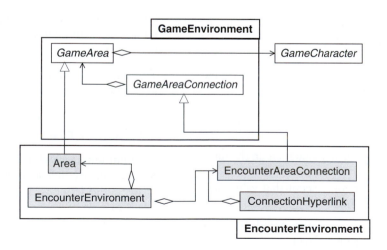

Figure 19.37 *EncounterEnvironment* package

returns the area *Connection* object corresponding to *areaConnectionNameP* according to requirement 3.2.AR.2.2.

6.1.9. CO *EncounterAreaConnection* Class

This class encapsulates the ways to get from areas to adjacent areas. It inherits from *AreaConnection* and corresponds to requirement 3.2.CO.

Inheritance
    This class inherits from *GameAreaConnection* in the framework package.

Attributes:

```
private Area firstAreaI;
//corresponding to requirement 3.2.CO.1.1
private Area secondAreaI;
//corresponding to requirement 3.2.CO.1.1
```

Methods: These are accessors for the attributes above.

6.1.10. EE *EncounterEnvironment* Class This is the facade class for the *EncounterEnvironment* package.

Attributes:

```
private EncounterEnvironment
encounter EnvironmentS;
//the singleton Facade object
//[Area name][Area connection
//name][''North''|''South''
//|''East''|''West'']:
private String[3] layoutS;
```

Methods:

```
public static EncounterEnvironment
getEncounterEnvironment ()
  Returns: encounterEnvironmentS
public static String[3] getLayout()
  Returns: layoutS
```

The remaining methods are specified in Section 5 of this document.

6.1.11. CH *ConnectionHyperlink* Class This class encapsulates the ways to get from areas to adjacent areas. It corresponds to requirement 3.2. CH. This class implements the *MouseListener* interface.

Attributes:

```
private Connection connectionI;//
the corresponding connection
```

Methods:

```
The only meaningful method is
mouseClick().
```

6.2 Data Detailed Design

There are no data structures besides those mentioned as part of the classes in Section 6.1.

19.13 CASE STUDY: DETAILED DESIGN OF ECLIPSE

References: The JavaDoc for Eclipse is at http://www.eclipse.org/documentation/html/plugins/org.eclipse.platform.doc.isv/doc/reference/api/overview-summary.html

> Note to the Student:
> Eclipse is a large project, and this case study does not attempt to describe its design in detail—merely to provide excerpts from a small example of how detailed design is sometimes specified in the case of Eclipse. The complete document would be based on the architecture decomposition described previously. It would have a section on each of the *Platform*, the *Java Development Environment*, and the *Plugin Development Environment*. Within the *Platform* section, it would have a *Workspace* and a *Core* section. Within the *Core* section, it would have a *Runtime* section. Part of the latter is shown next.

Platform.Core.Runtime

> Ideally, this section could be traced to the Eclipse requirements. Although the reader of the Eclipse documentation can understand the trace in general terms, it is not straightforward to locate the exact references to requirements sections.

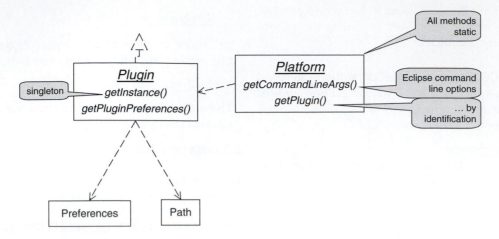

Figure 19.38 Core classes of Eclipse

Platform.Core.Runtime is organized around a small set of core classes, as shown in Figure 19.38.

The classes in Figure 19.38 are described next.

PLATFORM CLASS

> The following is from the Eclipse *javadoc* (as edited by the author). An alternative would be to provide the skeleton of the class itself in the following form.

```
// The central class of the Eclipse Platform
// Runtime
. . .
public final class Platform extends Object
{
public static getInstance(){} ← no content
    . . . .
}
public final class Platform extends Object
```

The central class of the Eclipse Platform Runtime: This class cannot be instantiated or subclassed by clients; all functionality is provided by static methods.

> If a class is to have no instances, all its methods are made static.

Features include:

- the platform registry of installed plug-ins
- the platform adapter manager
- the platform log
- the authorization info management

The platform is in one of two states, *running* or *not running*, at all times. The only ways to start the platform running, or to shut it down, are on the bootstrap *BootLoader* class.

> In other words, the methods that start or shut down the platform are found in the class *BootLoader*.

Code in plug-ins will only observe the platform in the running state. The platform cannot be shut-down from inside (code in plug-ins have no access to *BootLoader*).

    . . . .

public static Plugin **getPlugin**(String id)

Returns the plug-in runtime object for the identified plug-in or null if no such plug-in can be found. If the plug-in is defined but not yet activated, the plug-in will be activated before being returned.

Parameters: id - the unique identifier of the desired plug-in (e.g., "com.example.acme").
Returns: the plug-in runtime object, or null
. . . .

We have provided just a taste of the beginning of the Eclipse design. This example provides a sense of how documentation reads that is generated (via Javadoc) from source code comments. An advantage of using Javadoc is that it tends to remain up-to-date as long as the programmer comments the code according to the standard.

19.14 SUMMARY

Detailed design is an activity in which components such as classes and methods are defined in enough detail so that implementation can commence. We start with the domain classes from requirements analysis and add the necessary design classes to complete the design. Design patterns are introduced as required, to implement any commonly recurring design problems.

During detailed design, interface functions with specified names, parameter types, and return types are defined. The program elements using these functions can then be designed without having to know how the functionality is implemented—all they need to know is how to use the interface. This facilitates the development of each design element separately. The Facade design pattern is one way of providing an interface to a package of classes.

When designing object-oriented software, several well-established design principles help ensure a robust and extensible design: single-responsibility, open-closed, Liskov substitution, dependency-inversion, and interface segregation.

When specifying the details of a class, we start with the domain classes defined during requirements. We gather the attributes already defined and add additional attributes required for design. We also define class and method invariants, and method pre- and postconditions. Pseudocode is written to describe how each method is to be implemented. We then add addition classes necessary to complete the design and draw a class model showing the static relationship between classes. An activity diagram can also be drawn to graphically describe nontrivial algorithms. Some detailed designs are best communicated via detailed sequence diagrams or detailed data flow diagrams. Sequence diagrams show the objects associated with a particular use case, and the messages (i.e., function calls) that flow between them. Data flow diagrams show processing elements (i.e., methods) in a program and the data that flow between them.

The detailed design is documented in a software design specification. We have introduced IEEE standard 1016-1998 for Software Design Documents as an example of such a document.

Detailed design concludes by updating the schedule in the SPMP to reflect the details learned. The process should also be reviewed with respect to the amount of time taken and the number defects discovered. Improvements can be planned based on how these metrics compare against the plan.

19.15 EXERCISES

1. Explain the following:
   (a) The purpose of detailed design (list three benefits)
   (b) How it differs from software architecture
   (c) Why it is generally a questionable idea to go directly from architecture to implementation.

2. Your company produces software that controls a robot arm for manufacturing. Name four classes that would be appropriate members of your company's software framework. Explain your reasoning.

3. Estimate the number of lines of Java code for the following set of methods. The methods are ordered from smallest to largest. Assume that there is nothing unusual about the job *except* as indicated in the information below.

   Method 1: I/O; Method 2: Text; Method 3: Calculation; Method 4: Logic;
   Method 5: Data; Method 6: Calculation; Method 7: Text; Method 8: Data;
   Method 9: Set-up; Method 10: Calculation; Method 11: Text; Method 12: Data

4. Complete the following, explaining under what circumstances you would use the following in detailed design.
   (a) Use activity diagrams when the logic _____.
   (b) Use pseudocode for a method when _____.

5. Define appropriate interfaces that the following class exhibits (or "implements" in Java terms). Assume that additional methods will be required as the application grows. Explain your reasoning. *Hint:* The interfaces indicate what kind of transaction this is.

6. Describe in your own words the advantages of specifying preconditions, postconditions, and invariants. How, specifically, do they help to increase the quality of functions?

7. Perform a design (both architectural and detailed) for a check-balancing application with the following requirements. Fix defects in the requirements if you find them. You can play the role of customer if and when the customer's input is required. Report the time you spent on significant activities to the nearest five minutes.

   1. The system shall display the current balance in the system window.
   2. The system permits the user to record deposits of up to $10,000.
   3. The system permits the user to withdraw any amount from the current balance. An error message "This withdrawal amount exceeds your balance" is displayed when the user attempts to withdraw an amount exceeding the balance.

8. A classic Liskov substitution principle example consists of two classes, Square and Rectangle. Since a square *is-a* rectangle, the relationship between the two can be modeled using inheritance, with *Square* deriving from *Rectangle*. Suppose that Rectangle has methods to set/get the width, and set/get the length. Explain how this relationship between Square and Rectangle violates the Liskov substitution principle.

TEAM EXERCISES

SDD

Provide an SDD for your project. Use, or improve upon the IEEE standard. Please enclose the latest version of your SRS.

Report the time spent by the individuals and the group on the parts of this assignment. Break this down into activities, including architecture, inspection, review, and detailed design. Comment on how the time spent could have been better allocated.

BIBLIOGRAPHY

1. Martin, Robert, *"Agile Software Development: Principles, Patterns, and Practices,"* Prentice Hall, 2003.
2. Martin, Robert, *"Design Principles and Design Patterns,"* 2000, www.objectmentor.com/resources/articles/Principles_and_Patterns.pdf [accessed November 29, 2009].
3. Martin, Robert, *"The Dependency Inversion Principle,"* C++ Report, May 1996, http://www.objectmentor.com/resources/articles/dip.pdf [accessed November 29, 2009].
4. The Object Management Group. www.omg.org (1999).
5. Jurjens, Jan, *"Secure Systems Development with UML,"* Springer, 2005.
6. Humphrey, Watts S., *A Discipline for Software Engineering (SEI Series in Software Engineering)*, Addison-Wesley, 1995.
7. Jones, Capers, *"Applied Software Measurement: Assuring Productivity and Quality,"* 2nd edition, New York: McGraw-Hill, 1996.
8. QSM Function Point Languages Table, (April 2005, Version 3.0) http://www.qsm.com/resources/function-point-languages-table/index.html [access November 29, 2009].
9. Meyer, Bertrand, *"Object-Oriented Software Construction,"* Second Edition, Prentice Hall, 2007.
10. Liskov, Barbara, and John Guttag, *"Abstraction and Specification in Program Development,"* MIT-Press, 1986.

20
Design Quality and Metrics

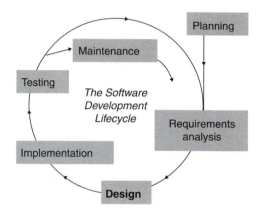

- • How do you assess the degree of understandability in a software design?

- • How do you assess the degree of cohesion and coupling?
  - – degree of sufficiency?
  - – robustness?
  - – flexibility, reusability?
  - – time efficiency, space efficiency?
  - – reliability?
  - – security?

- • How is quality in architecture selection measured?

- • How is the quality of a detailed design measured?

Figure 20.1 The context and learning goals for this chapter

Since a set of requirements can be accommodated by several possible designs, we can compare the *quality* of candidate designs. As explained in Chapter 15, the qualities of a design include *understandability, modularity, cohesion, coupling, sufficiency, robustness, flexibility, reusability, efficiency,* and *reliability*. Project leadership specifies the desired levels of quality in these respects, balanced against the available resources.

Recall that *sufficiency* means that the design accommodates the requirements. Any measure of design quality includes this at a minimum. For example, suppose that the requirements are for an application that manages DVD rentals. A design consisting only of the classes *Manager* and *ManagerGUI* would not be sufficient to accommodate the requirements. This is because there is significant data and functionality specifically associated with the concept of a DVD that is missing. Figures 20.2, 20.3, and 20.4 summarize how design quality can be assessed at a rough level.

The succeeding sections of this chapter elaborate each of the design aspects listed in these Figures.

How . . .

- **understandable** (How cohesive and clear are the parts and how low is the number of connections between parts)

  0: unclear parts and many connections among them

  10: very understandable parts with few interconnections

- **sufficient** (How evidently it accommodates the requirements)

  0: unrelated to the requirements

  10: obviously accommodates every requirement

- **robust**

  0: any input anomaly has serious consequences

  10: every input anomaly accommodated smoothly

Figure 20.2 Qualities of a design—rough metrics, 1 of 3

How . . .

- **flexible**

  0: anticipated additional requirements require extensive change to the design

  10: most anticipated requirements require no change to the design

- **reusable**

  0: no parts of the design can be used in other applications

  10: more than 75% of the classes can be used in other applications

---

Figure 20.3 Qualities of a design—rough metrics, 2 of 3

How . . .

- **efficient**: *Implementation based on this design* . . .

  0: . . . will probably not execute at required speed or use required storage

  10: . . . will execute with as much speed and storage to spare as reasonably conceivable

- **reliable**: *Implementation based on this design* . . .

  0: . . . will probably fail with a clearly unacceptable frequency

  10: . . . will probably fail well within the allowable frequency

- **secure**:

  - *0: . . . will probably exceed the maximum allowable vulnerability limit*

  - *10: . . . will probably have as few vulnerabilities as can be expected*

Figure 20.4 Qualities of a design—rough metrics, 3 of 3

20.1 DEGREE OF UNDERSTANDABILITY, COHESION, AND COUPLING

The main reason for a design is to form an understanding among the software engineers of how the application will actually be coded. It's really a form of communication, and so the quality of a design depends, in part, on its understandability to people. For each part to make clear sense it has to be cohesive. And if the parts are not related by too many relationships, we can tell them apart more easily. This is the concept of low coupling. Thus, the extent to which the cohesion of the modules is high is part of a measure of understandability, and so is the extent to which the coupling between them is low. (The latter is unlikely to be zero, however, otherwise one might as well consider the application to consist of entirely separate ones.)

Fan-in and *fan-out* are measures of the degree of coupling of modules. Fan-in for a component counts the number of components that reference it; fan-out is the number that it references. These definitions can be refined by specializing the nature of the references (e.g., "calling a function of"). Low coupling is reflected by low fan-in and low fan-out.

For more on this, see [1] and [2].

The following is an example of a metric for understandability. It depends on definitions of "strongly cohesive" and "very few," but these can be made precise for a given family of applications.

Understandability metric = ½ × Percentage of strongly cohesive modules
+ ½ × Percentage of modules connected to very few others

Section 20.10.1 describes metrics for connectedness alone.

20.2 DEGREE OF SUFFICIENCY AS A QUALITY GOAL

An essential quality goal is to produce a design that accommodates the requirements. Designs can consist of many parts, but we'll consider a simple example to illustrate degrees of sufficiency. Suppose that our video store application has the following requirements.

Clerks shall be able to check in DVDs

Clerks shall be able to check out DVDs

The *degree of sufficiency* measures the ease with which a design accommodates these requirements. Design 1 in, Figure 20.5, for example, would probably score very low on this quality scale because it fails to capture the DVD, the customer, or the rental in a readily identifiable way. (This design could be *made* to work—it's just not a high-quality design given the requirements.) Design 2, on the other hand, is sufficient to capture the requirements for a realistic video store.

The following is a useful metric measuring sufficiency. It depends on having a thorough set of detailed requirements.

Sufficiency metric = Percentage of detailed requirements clearly accommodated by the design

Increasing the number of classes does not necessarily raise the quality of a design: Redundant classes actually detract from quality. Additional classes may be needed for other quality measures such as flexibility and robustness.

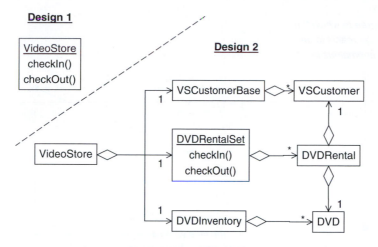

Figure 20.5 Measuring the sufficiency of a design—video store example

20.3 DEGREE OF ROBUSTNESS AS A QUALITY GOAL

A good SRS contains explicit robustness requirements. For example, the video store may require that the application react to the entry of an invalid video name by refreshing the relevant screen with a blank in the *video title* window and popping up a window stating "No such video – Please re-enter." Explicit robustness requirements like this are measured with the "sufficiency" quality metric. If a statement like this is not an explicit requirement, then it is measured with the design robustness metric. Figure 20.6 shows a pair of designs for the video store application.

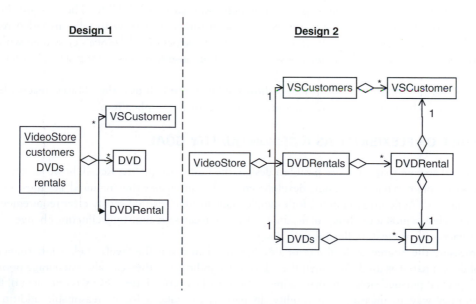

Figure 20.6 Measuring the robustness of a design—video store example

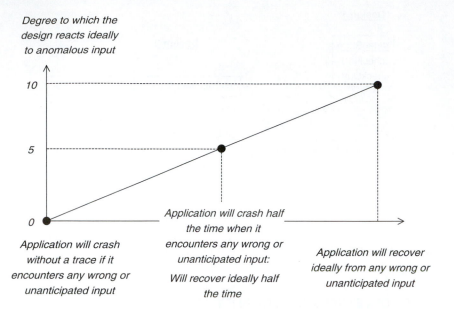

Figure 20.7 A rough robustness metric

In Design 1, the *VideoStore* class contains a collection of *VSCustomer* objects, a collection of *DVD* objects, and a collection of rentals. Each rental can be maintained as a pair consisting of a *Customer* object and a *DVD* object. Design 2 was discussed above. To assess the robustness of Design 1, we think about how to handle anomalous situations such as attempts to enter data for a nonexistent customer. This is more easily accommodated with a class containing all customers—similarly for DVDs. The design should also accommodate erroneous rental entries—for example, a customer forgetting to take his video rental with him from the store. This is more easily accommodated with a separate *DVDRentals* class than with a vector attribute of *VideoStore*, because the latter is less visible and because it occurs among several other, differing attributes.

A metric for the robustness of a design is shown in Figure 20.7. It uses the phrases "reacts ideally" and "recovers ideally." These have to be defined in the context of the application.

20.4 DEGREE OF FLEXIBILITY AS A DESIGN QUALITY GOAL

It is common to assume that the more flexible a design, the higher its quality. Recall, however, that flexibility may come with a price in terms of design, development, and maintenance time required. For these reasons, it is not always pursued. Agile programming, for example, aims for designs that satisfy clear requirements and no more. Nevertheless, a judicious choice of flexibility in a design can save time by facilitating change. Figure 20.8 shows the trade-offs of creating flexibility in designs.

To measure the degree of flexibility of a design, one can count the levels of class inheritance and the number of design patterns used. Although these give some indication, they can also encourage poor qualities in other respects if pursued simply to make a metric become favorable. Extensibility is one facet of flexibility. And so another way to measure extensibility, in part, is to make a list of reasonable additions to the application's requirements and to evaluate the design's ability to extend and cover them.

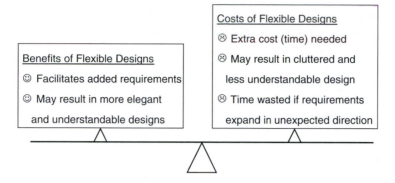

Figure 20.8 Cost-benefit trade-off of design flexibility

20.5 DEGREE OF REUSABILITY AS A DESIGN QUALITY GOAL

Reusability has many benefits but may detract from an application's quality because it is intended to benefit future projects rather than just the current one. For example, some energy is diverted from the current project. However, if the application under design *uses* a reusable component, then this usually benefits its quality because the component is likely to be more reliable than those yet unused.

Let's assume that we want a particular component (e.g., a class) to be reusable. For example, how do we ensure that the *DVD* class can be used in multiple applications? How do we measure the extent to which a particular class is reusable? First, the component must have high quality in the usual sense—be well tested, for example. Interestingly, items can be reusable because they are generic (we use "wood" in many projects) but also because they are specific (we use 1¼ -inch machine screws in many projects). This difference places classes into roughly two reuse categories: those that are useful because they belong in a framework and are reused because they are general; and those that are special to the business at hand, and form part of its toolkit.

Parameterizing a method makes it reusable but too many parameters make it clumsy. Figure 20.9 lists some of the key qualities we want for reusability, and their limitations. (The last point in this figure refers to multiple parameterizations of methods with the same name and similar purposed.) Figure 20.10 indicates how these may be measured.

Listing 20.1 is an example of a class that would rate high on reusability, as explained below. Using the measures of Figure 20.10, we would rate the reusability of this code as follows:

- **Abstract enough to get wide coverage**
  - But too abstract = useless
  - For example, class *RetailArtifact* may have too little content
- **Specific enough to be useful**
  - But not too specific
  - For example, *AcmeNumber6BrownPencil*
- **Parameterized methods**
  - But not more than six parameters
  - Consider f($\times$1) also f($\times$1, $\times$2) also f($\times$1, $\times$2, $\times$3); . . .

Figure 20.9 Attributes of reusability

- **Degree of coverage**
    0 = negligible coverage of different applications
    2 = as wide as can be expected
- **Degree of content**
    0 = negligible content or substance
    2 = very rich content or associations
- **Parameterization of methods—allows method reuse**
    0 = very restrictive methods; very narrow scope
    2 = widely applicable methods

Figure 20.10 Measuring reusability

Degree of coverage: *VideoProduct* covers any video item that a video store could possess, so "coverage" would rate 2.

Degree of content: The complete version of this class does not have extensive content, but nor does it have negligible content, so we can rate this as 1.

Parameterization of methods: The names are about as complete as one can expect so this would rate 2.

Its reusability index is thus 5 out of a possible 6.

Listing 20.1: A detailed design example to be rated for reusability

```
/*
 * Example of a class design highly rated for reuse
 *
 * Intent: Capture all of the properties and functionality of video
   products
 * that companies can deal with.
 *
 * Examples of potential subclasses: DVD, Video
 */
public abstract class VideoProduct
{
        // CONSTANTS ============================================

        private final static int MAXIMUM_TITLE_LENGTH = 100;
        private final static int MAXIMUM_NAME_LENGTH = 100;
        private final static int MAXIMUM_NUM_STARS = 20;

        // METHODS ==============================================

        /************************************************
         * Returns: The copy number
         * Example: 3; if title is "Gone With the Wind," then this would be the
```

```
 * third copy of this video product.
 */
public abstract int getCopyNumber();

/**********************************************
 * Returns: duration of this video product in minutes -- if > 0;
 * otherwise 0
 */
public abstract int getDurationInMinutes();

/**********************************************
 * Returns: Title of this video product in English
 */
public abstract String getEnglishTitle();

/**********************************************
 * Intent: Enter the title of this product in English
 *
 * Preconditions:
 * (1) aTitle != null
 * (2) aTitle has between 1 and MAXIMUM_TITLE_LENGTH characters
 */
public abstract void setEnglishTitle(String aTitle);

/**********************************************
 * Returns: Name of the director of this video product, if known;
 * "unknown" if not
 * Example: Returns "Stanley S. Kubrik IV"
 */
public abstract String getDirector();

/**********************************************
 * Intent: Enter the name of the director of this video product
 * Example: setDirector("Stanley S. Kubrik IV");
 * Preconditions:
 * (1) aDirectorName != null
 * (2) aDirectorName has between 1 and MAXIMUM_NAME_LENGTH
 * characters
 * (3) aDirectorName is the name in the form first/last, first/MI/
 * last,
 * or first/MI/last/suffix
 */
public abstract void setDirector(String aDirectorName);

/**********************************************
 * Intent: Enter the name of the director of this video product
 * Example: setDirector( "Stanley", 'S', "Kubrik", "III" );
 * Preconditions:
```

```
 * (1) aDirectorFirstName != null
 * (2) aDirectorFirstName has between 1 and MAXIMUM_NAME_LENGTH
 * characters
 * (3) aDirectorLastName != null
 * (4) aDirectorLastName has between 1 and MAXIMUM_NAME_LENGTH
 * characters
 * (5) aDirectorSuffix != null
 * (2) aDirectorSuffix has between 1 and MAXIMUM_NAME_LENGTH
 * characters
 */
public abstract void setDirector(
String aDirectorFirstName,
char aDirectorMiddleInitial,
String aDirectorLastName,
String aDirectorSuffix);

/***********************************************
 * Returns: Title of this video product
 */
public abstract String getTitle();

/***********************************************
 * Intent: Enter the title of this product in characters as close as
 * possible to the orginal
 *
 * Preconditions:
 * (1) aTitle != null
 * (2) aTitle has between 1 and MAXIMUM_TITLE_LENGTH characters
 */
public abstract void setTitle(String aTitle);

/***********************************************
 * Returns: Stars of this video product if known; otherwise
 * a single object "unknown"
 */
public abstract String[] getStars();

/***********************************************
 * Intent: Enter the stars of this video product if known; otherwise
 * a single object "unknown"
 *
 * Preconditions:
 * (1) someStars != null
 * (2) someStars has between 1 and MAXIMUM_NUM_STARS objects
 */
public abstract void setStars(String[] someStars);
}
```

20.6 DEGREE OF TIME EFFICIENCY AS A DESIGN QUALITY MEASURE

We inspect designs, and quantify how fast they are likely to execute when built. First, one identifies each operation whose speed of execution is of interest. For example, we could focus on the speed with which the Encounter video game transitions from area to area when a hyperlinked connection is pressed. (If this takes too long, the game loses the player's interest.) This operation is illustrated in Figure 20.11.

To assess the time efficiency of this action, we trace the sequence of method calls that require its execution and examine each of the methods for timing. Figure 20.12 shows the sequence of function calls beginning with the pressing of a hyperlink and ending with the monitor displaying the destination area.

To assess probable time delays, a table like Table 20.1 can be used. It identifies the methods that are potential sources of delay.

We then tackle problem methods one by one. For example, we use double buffering or build a composite image before rendering it on the monitor.

The example in Figure 20.13 contains no parallelism. Its timing is not complicated to calculate as long as one has reliable estimates for the parts of the operation. Recall that sequence diagrams are capable of describing parallel operations, however. In that case, a *timing diagram* would be needed to deal with such issues as differing start times and the need for more than one thread to use a resource that it could alter. To handle this we commonly perform such handling via a method, and we lock all other callers out of calling the method while it is operating. Figure 20.13 is an example in which thread 1 executed method 2, which locks out all other callers such as thread 2. The latter waits until method 3 has completed for thread 1. The estimated elapsed time is measured on the time axis.

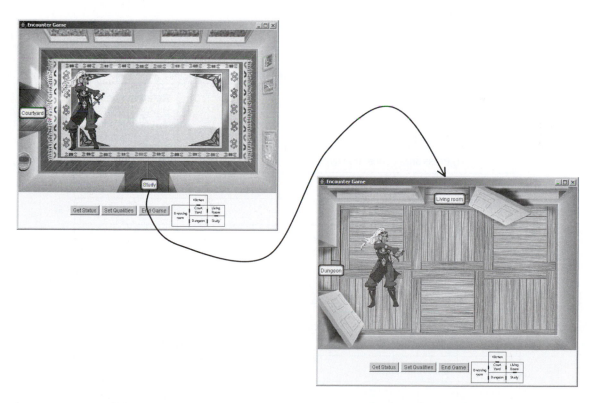

Figure 20.11 Time efficiency example from Encounter video game—time to transition among areas

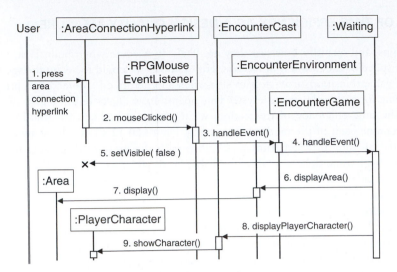

Figure 20.12 Assessing time efficiency—example using a sequence diagram from Encounter video game

Metrics for time efficiency include the following:

Averaged elapsed time for operation X.
Maximum elapsed time for operation X.

Table 20.1 Identifying methods that are highest potential source of delay

Step	Function	Relative speed *0 = negligible* *1 = neither* *2 = significant*
1	Press area connection hyperlink	0
2	mouseClicked()	0
3	handleEvent()	0
4	handleEvent()	0
5	setVisible(false)	1
6	displayArea()	2
7	display()	1
8	displayPlayerCharacter()	2
9	showCharacter()	1
	TOTAL	7/12

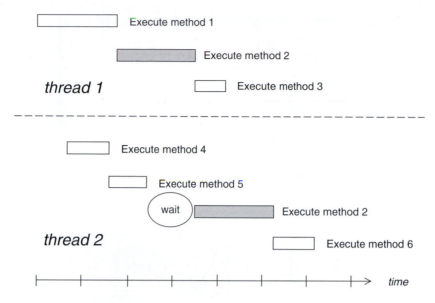

Figure 20.13 Timing diagram for parallel execution

20.7 DEGREE OF SPACE EFFICIENCY AS A DESIGN QUALITY MEASURE

The second major efficiency issue is space usage: secondary (typically, disk) storage, RAM usage, and binary source size. We will discuss secondary storage first.

Analyzing secondary storage usage can be performed by identifying the operations that create storage needs outside RAM. This divides further into temporary data (which is not needed after execution) and permanent data. Table 20.2 is typical of how we might account for this in the case of the video store application.

Table 20.2 Analyzing secondary storage

Source method and class of storage creation or reclamation	Temporary or permanent?	Maximum rate of increase, uncompressed	Minimum rate of decrease, uncompressed	Worst case
Rental: saveRental()	T	514 bytes per minute for 2 days		6 clients; Title 100 bytes; director 30 bytes; stars 4 bytes × 30; length 2. One title every 3 minutes.
Rental: removeRental()	P		0 bytes per minute for 2 days	90% of rentals returned within 2 days
DVDInventory: saveDVD()	. . .	. . .	. . .	. . .
DVDInventory: removeDVD()	. . .	. . .	. . .	. . .

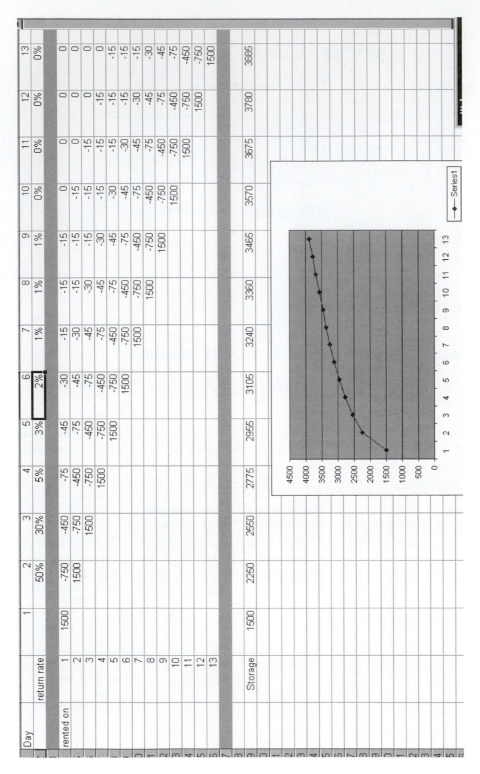

Figure 20.14 Secondary storage needs over time—video store example

Data are often compressed prior to storage (at the expense of speed). In that case the uncompressed storage needs are converted into compressed-form needs. Usually, the key issue in storage is the amount required over the long run—in other words, the accumulation of data. Suppose for simplicity that the 514 maximum bytes are compressed to 100 bytes and that the store is open 15 hours a day. The accumulating needs are shown in the spreadsheet and graph in Figure 20.14, and they suggest the problem that requires resolution.

Storage needs that increase without bound require special consideration. For this reason, designs often involve periodic archiving or purging. In the case of the video store, this could consist of iterating through the database weekly, charging all customers with videos whose fines exceed the DVD's value and archiving those DVD records.

20.8 DEGREE OF RELIABILITY AS A DESIGN QUALITY MEASURE

This section discusses means for ensuring and assessing reliability at design time. To assess reliability in an overall design, we look for points at which the application is most likely to fail. Recall that the UML design models are *use case, class, data flow*, and *state*. We look for a high level for failure likelihood within each of these models. Figure 20.15 indicates places for use cases where failure is typically most likely.

Now let's consider how failures are likely to be evident at the *class* level. Here, we seek parts of the class model that are most likely to harbor failures. Figure 20.16 illustrates two likely types of failure: *choke points* and *deep inheritance*.

- **Data collection**
  - From users
  - From other applications
  - From data communication
- **Steps causing complexity**
  - Use case indicates involved operations
- **Anomalous situations**
  - For example, attempt to rent multiple copies of a movie

Figure 20.15 Identifiable places in use cases where failure is typically most likely to occur

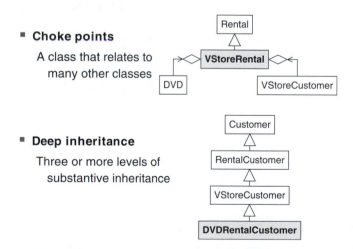

Figure 20.16 Identifiable places in class model where failure is typically most likely to occur—video store example

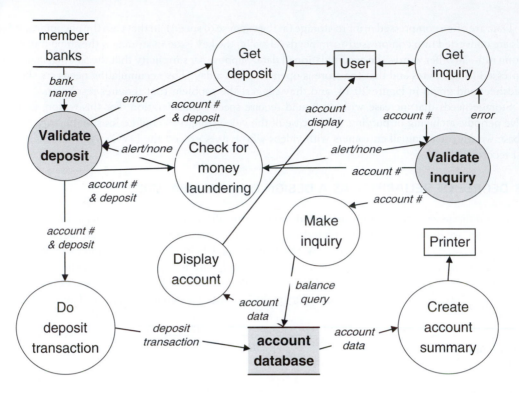

Figure 20.17 Identifiable places in data flow diagrams where failure is typically most likely to occur—banking example

Choke points are potentially problematical because developers tend to make mistakes when the situation is complicated. Deep inheritance can harbor errors because inherited properties are not readily apparent to the developer. The number of types employed should be reduced, or aggregation should be used instead to indicate what qualities are added between types.

Data flow diagrams can expose failure points most readily where multiple streams of data converge. Figure 20.17 shows a partial data flow for an ATM application. The *validate deposit* and *validate inquiry* functions each relate to the most streams. The account database also relates to a relatively higher number of data streams. For these reasons we would investigate these first for reliability. Since use cases control function call sequences in data flow diagrams, we would investigate by checking whether use cases behave clearly at these points. We would ask whether a different decomposition would make this clearer—for example, whether it is advisable to get separate types of inquiries via separate operations.

Choke points can be reduced by introducing additional processing nodes and by decomposing nodes into multiple nodes. For example, we could split *Validate Inquiry* into several validation operations.

The final design model we can inspect for reliability is the *state model*. Figure 20.18 shows the state model for the Encounter video game. The *Waiting* state involves the most transitions, so we would check its reliability first. If time allows, we would then move on to *Engaging*, and so on.

State diagram bottlenecks can be avoided by splitting states into several states or by introducing substates. For example, if *Waiting* state becomes excessively involved, it may be possible to distinguish several modes of waiting.

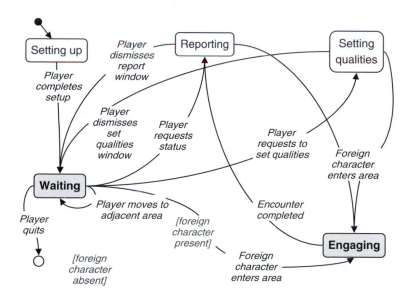

Figure 20.18 Identifiable places in state models where failure is typically most likely to occur—Encounter video game example

20.9 DEGREE OF SECURITY AS A DESIGN QUALITY MEASURE

Security is a special case among metrics because it concerns illegitimate "functionality" of the application that it is capable of but is not specified. It may require a skilled perpetrator to obtain this functionality. An example is "shall be capable of sending customer credit card information to any specified e-mail!"

How can one measure the degree of security of a design? Recognize first that every application must communicate with hardware or software external to itself, otherwise it could not execute. In so doing, however, it acquires some vulnerability. Figure 20.19 illustrates the kinds of artifacts with which an application's object code could make contact. These, in turn, can make contact with other artifacts.

In assessing the degree of security of a design, we are thus obliged to take a systems approach—that is, one that accounts for the vulnerability of our application in the context of the larger system within which it

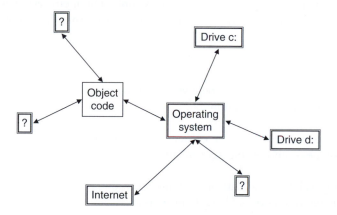

Figure 20.19 Analysis for security quality

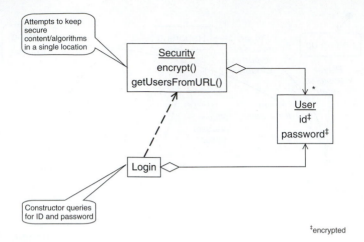

Figure 20.20 Beginning design for simple secure login

must operate. The added dimension here is that we must look not only at the potential of our application for exploitation and damage, but also at its potential to harm artifacts to which it is connected.

Figure 20.20 shows a start for a design of a critical security element of an application. Inspecting it for each security factor in Figures 20.21 and 20.22 provides a framework for assessing its level of security. We need to satisfy ourselves that *an implementation exists* of the class model that satisfies every security factor—the class model by itself does not guarantee any of them.

There are many approaches to measuring the security of a detailed design. We will discuss a few examples. In the first example, we make rough assessments, on a scale of 0 to 10, of the main aspects of security, as introduced in Chapter 18. These are shown in Figures 20.21 and 20.22. Although it is difficult to make these assessments based on a detailed design, this process is better than making a single, overall assessment about the degree of security.

For a second approach example, consider the following metric examples, adapted from [3].

<u>Metric 1</u> Baseline Defenses Coverage: This is a measurement of how well the detailed design enables one to protect the environment of the application against "the most basic information security threats" These require careful definition, but they do include viruses, for example. This metric assumes that security tools will be used such as firewalls and antivirus software. Some vendors claim that the coverage of devices by these

---

- **Confidentiality**
  - Degree to which data passed may become visible to the unauthorized
  - Estimated percentage of data compromises[#]
- **Nonrepudiation**
  - Degree to which parties can prove the existence of agreements
  - Estimated percentage of unprovable agreements
- **Integrity**
  - Extent of ability to validate that data are not altered in transit
  - Estimated percentage of messages alterable in transit

[#]i.e., of a specified severity

Figure 20.21 Property-based security metrics, 1 of 2

- **Authentication**
  - Extent of ability to validate user's identity
  - Estimated percentage of improper authentications
- **Authorization**
  - Degree to which permission to deal with privileged data may be compromised
  - Estimated percentage of unauthorized permissions
- **Availability**
  - Degree to which availability could be compromised; e.g., by denial-of-service attacks
  - Estimated number of availability* compromises per year

*i.e., of given severity

Figure 20.22 Property-based security metrics, 2 of 2

security tools should be "in the range of 94 percent to 98 percent." The meaning of these percentages would require definition too, and backup for claims would be needed.

Metric 2 Patch Latency: This is the time between the identification of a successful security exploit and the development of a patch that renders it impossible. Patches are usually replacement files. Thus, if the detailed design decomposes the application into an appropriate number of well-identified files, patch latency is likely to improve.

Metric 3 Password Strength: This metric measures how hard it is to break (guess at) a password, in some well-defined sense, including finding potential weak spots where systems use default passwords. Breaking passwords is usually performed with the assistance of separate software.

Metric 4 Legitimate Traffic Analysis: This is a family of metrics that measures the extent to which illegitimate traffic could be allowed. It includes incoming and outgoing traffic volume, incoming and outgoing traffic size, and traffic flow with the application.

A third approach is to put the detailed design under a microscope, as it were, and measure the extent to which it is likely to avoid common known security gaps. One example is buffer overflow, in which the bounds of an array are exceeded in order to access data in regions of memory adjacent to it. The content type of these regions is effectively guessed at. Another is SQL injection, which exploits the manner in which database queries are processed. This exploit effectively inserts commands such as "send all credit cards . . ." within an apparently innocuous input data field. Detailed designs can be specified that help guard against many such exploits. Tools are available to check for these types of oversights in code, but designs are less standardized and tools checking for security flaws are rarer.

In reality, we combine elements of all three approaches. A good reference for some of the ideas in this section is Anderson [7].

20.10 ASSESSING QUALITY IN ARCHITECTURE SELECTION

So far, this chapter has based design assessment on the individual qualities that good designs must possess. Now we explore a more holistic view of quality, starting with the high-level view.

20.10.1 Metrics for Architecture Quality

Although most applications can be implemented using one of several possible architectures, some choices are much better than others. Important decisions like architecture selection are made by first developing and comparing alternatives. Proposed architectures are thoroughly examined for defects, because finding a defect at an early development stage has a huge payoff compared with allowing one to persist through the process and then trying to repair it.

As described in Figure 20.23, one simple way to compare architectures is to weight the attributes required and then assign a fuzzy qualifier to each candidate. The kind of procedure described in Figure 20.23 can then be

	Quality weight: 1-10	Architecture alternative		
		1. State design pattern	2. ad hoc GUI-driven	3. State-transition table
Quality		High = 9; Medium = 5; Low = 2		
Extension	9	High	Low	Medium
Change	7	High	Low	Medium
Simplicity	5	Low	High	Medium
Efficiency: speed	5	Medium	High	Medium
Efficiency: storage	2	Low	Low	Medium
TOTAL: (higher = better)		183	126	140

Figure 20.23 A fuzzy method for comparing architectures

used to compare alternatives. For the sake of simplicity, we have omitted some of the design qualities discussed above in this example. One way to weight qualities is to pick the most important one and give it a weight of 10, or 9 (if you want to provide for a quality that may be introduced later). The least significant are assigned 1, and the remaining ones are given weights in between.

Important decisions such as architecture are often made by groups. A group uses a *Delphi* process when the members make individual decisions first, then submit them to the coordinator or leader. Boehm and Farquhar (see, for example, [4]) introduced the "wideband" Delphi process in which the leader plots the results on a chart without attribution to the owners and leads a discussion on the factors involved.

The following metrics from the IEEE [5] can be used to measure the complexity to software designs.

IEEE metric 13. *Number of entries and exits per module* (package). This can be equated with the number of public methods accessible from outside the module. The number of exit points can be counted by the number of public functions that return values to the caller or make changes in the environment external to themselves. The goal is to keep this measure as low as possible to favor narrow interfaces.

IEEE metric 15. *Graph-theoretic complexity for architecture*. The simpler ("static") version of this metric is

(Number of modules in the architecture) −
    (Number of modules having at least one connection between them) + 1

The goal is to keep this number high, since a low number indicates many connections and thus an increased potential for errors.

IEEE metric 25. *Data or information flow complexity*. This measures the information flow of large-scale structures, the procedure and module flow complexity, and the complexity of the interconnections between modules. The reader is referred to metric 4.25 of [5] for the details.

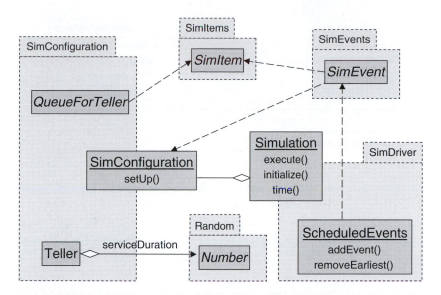

Figure 20.24 An architecture for a simulation

A *connection* between modules A and B is dependence in either direction. As an example, we can apply metric 15 to the architecture of a bank simulation shown in Figure 20.24.

The architecture divides the simulation into the following packages.

SimConfiguration—which describes the way in which the stations are laid out within the bank

SimItems—which describes the entities that move about within the bank (primarily customers)

SimEvents—which handles the present and future simulated events that take place in the bank (e.g., a customer arriving at a teller window)

Simulation—the mechanism that drives the simulation (primarily by selecting the next event to execute, executing it, then orchestrating the consequences, including the generation of resulting events, and queuing them in the *ScheduledEvents* object)

Random—the package that handles the generation of random numbers according to various distributions (for example, producing the duration of service for the next transaction)

This architecture is designed using the Facade design pattern, and we will suppose that the only interfaces between packages are those shown. There are five nodes (packages), and there are five pairs of modules between which there are function calls (either way). Thus, the graph-theoretic architecture complexity is $5 - 5 + 1 = 1$. This suggests an uncomplicated architecture, which is generally good.

Metrics like those listed above provide quantification, but how do we use the resulting numbers? Typically, this has to do with historical data. For example, we can easily tell that the *EncounterGame* package has four public functions at this point (see the case study on the book Web site). Perhaps we can forecast that this number will grow to between 10 and 15. These numbers are compared with the corresponding average numbers for past projects. If the average number is 10 and we have been satisfied with the modularization of past projects, then this value causes no alarm. However, if the average number for past projects is 8 and we are headed toward 15, then a closer look at the architecture and such is needed.

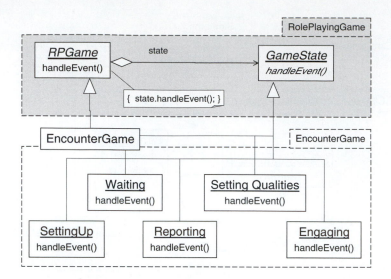

Figure 20.25 An architecture for Encounter: State design pattern applied to the video game

20.10.2 Choosing an Architecture among Alternatives

We resist the urge to commit immediately to one architecture by comparing alternatives. As an example, let's consider the architecture of the Encounter case study.

Alternative 1 for the Encounter case study: State design pattern.

As shown in Figure 20.25, the State design pattern is a possible architecture for Encounter, and we will trade it off against other candidates.

Alternative 2 for the Encounter case study: ad hoc GUI-driven architecture.

A second architecture might dispense with the idea of state altogether and build separate event-handling code into each GUI object that is sensitive to mouse or keyboard actions. Such an architecture is shown in Figure 20.26, where selected methods are included to clarify it.

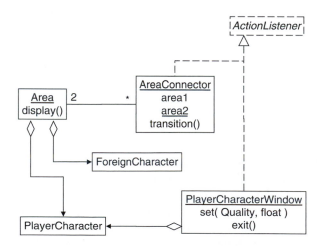

Figure 20.26 A second alternative architecture for Encounter

Key: if this → event occurs while Encounter is in this ↓ state, then perform the corresponding action in the table.	Event				
	Click on exit	**Request quality change**	**Dismiss quality window**	**Foreign character enters**	**Foreign character leaves**
	Go to indicated area	Show quality window	Remove quality window, and Transition to *Waiting* state	Show both characters, and transition to *Engaging* state	
Current State Engaging				(do nothing)	Compute results of engagement, and transition to *Waiting* state
Setting qualities			Transition to *Waiting* state	Transition to *Engaging* state	Transition to *Waiting* state

Figure 20.27 A third alternative architecture for Encounter: table-driven state-transitions

In this architecture the hyperlinks at the exits to areas are (GUI representations of) *AreaConnector* objects; and each has event-handling code. For example, clicking on an exit to the dungeon should cause the screen to display the dungeon area. The resulting design is GUI-driven, somewhat ad hoc, and language-specific. There is no clear connection, however, between the code for this design and the conception of the game as a series of state transitions. As a benefit, however, the class model contains fewer classes.

Alternative 3 for the Encounter case study: state-transition table.

A third architectural alternative is to retain the idea of states, but express the state transitions by means of a table. Table-driven state transitions are emphasized by Shlaer and Mellor [6], for example. Figure 20.27 is an example of such a table. This architecture uses the State concept, but it does not use the State design pattern.

Here is a list of pros and cons contrasting the State design pattern with the table-driven approach. A fuller comparison of the three architectures follows.

Pros of using the State design pattern:

- Can easily add or modify states to accommodate change in game design

- Clarifies what actions can be done in various circumstances

- Classifies all mouse events that can affect Encounter

   Cons of using the State design pattern:

- Class model is more involved and initially more difficult to understand.

- Duplicate data: The state of Encounter could be deduced from variables other than the state object, incurring the possibility of programmer error if these variables and the state object become inconsistent.

Fuzzy method for comparing architectures		Architecture alternative		
		1. *State* design pattern	2. ad hoc GUI-driven	3. State-transition table
Quality	Quality weight: 1-10	High = 9; Medium = 5; Low = 2		
Extension	9	High	Low	Medium
Change	7	High	Low	Medium
Simplicity	5	Low	High	Medium
Efficiency: speed	5	Medium	High	Medium
Efficiency: storage	2	Low	Low	Medium
TOTAL: (higher = better)		183	126	140

Figure 20.28 Fuzzy method for comparing architectures for Encounter

Pros of using a table for describing state:

• The table is easy to understand and the contents are easy to change.

• This architecture can be implemented in a non-object-oriented language.

• Documentation on this approach is available using the Shlaer–Mellor method.

Cons of using a table for describing state:

• It requires a data structure that is virtually global (the table).

• Augmenting the table with new states and actions may disrupt existing code and design.

Figure 20.28 shows a comparison of the three architectures using the pros/cons technique described above. Given the weighting shown, which favors extensibility and change, the architecture based on the State design pattern comes out ahead.

Regardless of the systematic means one uses to evaluate alternatives, engineers also perform "sanity checks," using holistic perspectives and the intuition and experience of team members. This may concern the number of classes involved or even subjective factors such as elegance. If the result disagrees with that of the more objective process we have described, engineers may re-examine the process and the results.

20.10.3 Verifying Architectures

Use cases are developed to express customer requirements. They can't take into account the application's architecture since it will not yet have been determined. Once the architecture has been selected, however, it is essential to revisit the use cases to check that the architecture supports them adequately. For example, the *Engage Foreign Character* use case shown in Chapter 11 must execute upon the architecture we have developed.

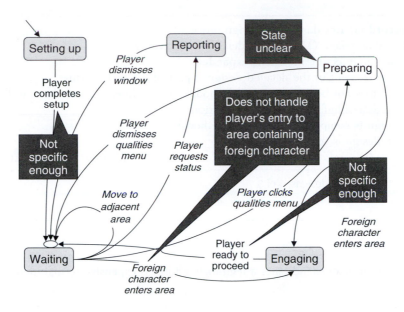

Figure 20.29 Defects in the state-transition diagram for Encounter

Since we retain the domain classes throughout the process, the classes originally referred to in the use case should be present among the classes in the design. Typically, the sequence diagrams for the use cases now involve additional architectural classes (e.g., Facade classes).

Architectures are inspected against requirements. The metrics mentioned above provide a concrete basis for the inspection. For example, inspection of the architectural framework packages for Encounter could lead to the conclusion that there are no requirements yet for game artifacts and that the presence of the *Artifact* package is a defect. Consider the Encounter state-transition diagram shown in Figure 20.29 as an additional example. A perusal of this state diagram could yield the defects noted in the figure. These defects can be removed by clarifying the names and/or descriptions of the events referenced.

20.11 ASSESSING THE QUALITY OF DETAILED DESIGNS

Recall that detailed design consists of all design that is not at the highest, architectural level, but is short of code itself. In this section, we review quantitative measures of effectiveness in detailed design.

20.11.1 Techniques for Assessing the Quality of Detailed Designs

Figures 20.30, 20.31, and 20.32, show steps for ensuring the quality of detailed designs.

Metrics for detailed design are provided in this section that satisfy Step 1 in Figure 20.30. Steps 2, 3, and 4 are checks that the detailed design expands on all of the architecture, and nothing more.

Step 5 ensures that a design is complete. It is easy enough to check that every method of every class is properly specified, but how do we know that we have included all of the classes and methods that are necessary? To do this, we return to the requirements and ensure that the detailed design we have developed accommodates all of the requirements. If we use the requirements organization as in the case study, then we know that every functional requirement corresponds to a specific method. Thus, the functional completeness task is reduced to ensuring that each of these methods can be called at an appropriate point in the execution. Consider, for example, the requirement:

1. **Prepare to record metrics** during the design process.
   - Include (1.1) time taken; (1.2) type of defect; (1.3) severity
2. Ensure that each architecture module is **expanded**.
3. Ensure that each element of the detailed design is **part of the architecture**.
   - If an element does not belong to any such module, the architecture may have to be revised.
4. Ensure that the design fulfills its **required functions**.
5. Ensure that design is **complete** (classes and methods).
6. Ensure that the design is **testable**.[‡]

[‡]See Chapter 5 for inspection procedures.

Figure 20.30 Inspecting detailed designs, 1 of 3

7. Check detailed design for –

- simplicity
  a design that few can understand (after a legitimate effort!) is expensive to maintain, and can result in defects
- generality
  enables design of similar applications?
- expandability
  enables enhancements?
- efficiency
  speed, storage
- portability

Figure 20.31 Inspecting detailed designs, 2 of 3

8. Ensure that all **detail** is **provided**

- Classes
  - Class invariants clear? (required limits on attributes; required relationships among attributes)
- Methods
  - Preconditions
  - Invariants
  - Postconditions
  - Pseudocode

Figure 20.32 Inspecting detailed designs, 3 of 3

3.2.EC.3.2 *Configurability of* Encounter *character quality values*

Whenever an *Encounter* character is alone in an area, the value of any of its qualities may be set. The value chosen must be less than or equal to the sum of the quality values.

We have already ensured that a function to perform this requirement exists, but to verify that our design supports the execution of this function, we have to effectively walk through a fully representative set of function calling sequences, each of which exercises the function. This amounts to developing a set of mental test cases, and the results should be saved for the testing phase. Here is such a set.

Begin game; call up window to set qualities; set quality; set quality again; dismiss window.

Move to area with no foreign character; call up window to set qualities; set quality; dismiss window.

Complete engagement; wait until foreign character departs; call up window to set qualities; set quality; dismiss window.

For each of these scenarios, we verify that the classes and methods do indeed exist to accommodate it. Once we have done this for every functional requirement, we will have verified our design from the functional point of view. We can perform a similar process with our detailed design for every nonfunctional requirement: We can verify mentally, and via calculation (e.g., in the case of timing) that the design supports each of them. Once again, the work we do to create each of these sequences can be used to develop tests that we apply once the implementation has been performed.

Step 6 calls for testability. In other words, is it a reasonable process to test the elements of the design? A design that can't be readily separated into parts tends to be untestable. An effective way to ensure this property is to write tests for each design element as soon as it is specified.

Step 7 concerns the properties that we desire from our detailed designs. We desire all of these properties, but it is usually not possible to have them all. In particular, *simplicity* may be in conflict with *generality* and *expandability*. Design patterns often introduce additional classes, too. Thus, it is best to specify in advance which of these properties we care most about, and then evaluate the design against them. If portability is paramount, we can establish scenarios for implementation on each desired platform.

Step 8 checks that every detail is given, short of code. The orthodox definition of "detail" refers to a complete description of the design short of code itself. Agile methods tend to focus only on key details up front, typically leaving most details until code time. It is common for designers to postpone many details until implementation time because the specification of detail is time consuming. For critical portions of an application, however, this is usually a mistake. There are many issues to consider at implementation time, and so thinking through the details of critical sections beforehand, and inspecting them separately, can pay off handsomely.

20.11.2 Metrics for Detailed Design

Detailed design metrics include counting the number of modules, functions, entry points, and exit points. For object-oriented implementations, this translates into counting the number of packages, the number of classes, the number of methods, the number of parameters, the number of attributes, and so on. When classes are provided with complete class invariants, this increases the chances that the resulting method is of high quality. When preconditions, invariants, and postconditions for a method are all stated in precise terms, chances are that the resulting method is of higher quality than otherwise. These can be measured as follows:

> Percentage of classes supplied with precise class invariants

> Percentage of nontrivial methods supplied with precise preconditions, invariants, and postconditions

A comprehensive, albeit more complicated metric is IEEE metric 19 "design structure" (see [5]), which determines "the simplicity of the detailed design" of a program.

20.11.3 Inspection of Detailed Designs

The overall principles and practice of inspections were expressed in Chapter 5. The inspection of detailed designs consists of inspecting classes, their method prototypes (name, return type, and parameter types), the flowcharts and pseudocode, and the relationships among classes and methods within various models. These models can include the use case models and their associated sequence diagrams, the class model, the state models, and the data flow model.

As with all inspections, data about each defect are noted, including its severity, its type, and the probable source of the defect in the project life cycle. The IEEE standard 1044.1 classifies severity as shown in Figure 20.33.

Designating a defect classification scheme helps to prioritize repair work: However, we avoid using more categories than necessary because time is consumed categorizing defects. The triage classification, shown in Figure 20.34, is fast but provides less information than IEEE 1044.1.

Defect *types* can include those listed below, which have been taken from IEEE standard 1044.1-1995. The types that apply to detailed designs for Javadoc-level inspections are marked "XDOC," and for pseudocode-level inspections are marked "PS".

- Logic problem (forgotten cases or steps; duplicate logic; extreme conditions neglected; unnecessary functions; misinterpretation; missing condition test; checking wrong variable; iterating loop incorrectly, etc.) **PS**

- Computational problem (equation insufficient or incorrect; precision loss; sign convention fault) **PS**

Severity	Description
Urgent	Failure causes system crash, unrecoverable data loss; or jeopardizes personnel
High	Causes impairment of critical system functions, and no workaround solution does exist
Medium	Causes impairment of critical system functions, though a workaround solution does exist
Low	Causes inconvenience or annoyance
None	None of the above

Figure 20.33 IEEE 1044.1 Severity classification

Source: IEEE 1044.1, 1995.

Defect Severity Classification using Triage

Severity	Description
Major	Requirement(s) not satisfied
Medium	Neither major nor trivial
Trivial	A defect that will not affect operation or maintenance

Figure 20.34 Classifying defects by severity using triage

- Interface/Timing problem (interrupts handled incorrectly; I/O timing incorrect; subroutine/module mismatch) **PS**

- Data-handling problem (initialized data incorrectly; accessed or stored data incorrectly; scaling or units of data incorrect; dimension of data incorrect) **XDOC, PS**

- Scope of data incorrect **XDOC, PS**

- Data problem (sensor data incorrect or missing; operator data incorrect or missing; embedded data in tables incorrect or missing; external data incorrect or missing; output data incorrect or missing; input data incorrect or missing) **XDOC, PS**

- Documentation problem (ambiguous description, etc.) **XDOC, PS**

- Document quality problem (applicable standards not met, etc.) **XDOC, PS**

- Enhancement (change in program requirements, etc.) **XDOC, PS**

- Failure caused by a previous fix **XDOC, PS**

- Performance problem (associated with test phase)

- Interoperability problem (not compatible with other software or components) **XDOC, PS**

- Standards conformance problem **XDOC, PS**

- Other (none of the above) **XDOC, PS**

Let's inspect pseudocode examples. The inspection focuses on defects in commission (whether the methods chosen are appropriate) and omission (whether there are other methods that should be included). The pseudocode for a method should be checked against the corresponding requirement in the SRS or in the SDD. For example, the following is an early draft of a D-requirements of Encounter from the SRS:

> "(essential) *Every game character has the same set of qualities. Each quality shall be a non-negative floating point number with at least one decimal of precision. These are all initialized equally so that the sum of their values is 100. For the first release the qualities shall be concentration, stamina, intelligence, patience, and strength. The value of a quality cannot be both greater than zero and less than 0.5.*"

This requirement is implemented by the function *adjustQuality(String aQuality, float aQualityValue)* with the pseudocode to be inspected as shown in Figure 20.35.

An inspection of this pseudocode should expose the following defects.

1. Line 9: method *setQuality()* should be mentioned.

2. Line 10: lacks detail on how to allocate the remaining quality values; also, why always "reduce" (why not sometimes "increase")?

Recall that the inspection process should merely establish that there is a defect in each case. No time should be spent by the inspection team trying to repair this defect during the inspection meeting. The triage severity classification of defect 2 (relating to line 10) is "major" because its interpretation can lead to significant differences in the product. Using the IEEE 1044.1 standard, its classification is "computational."

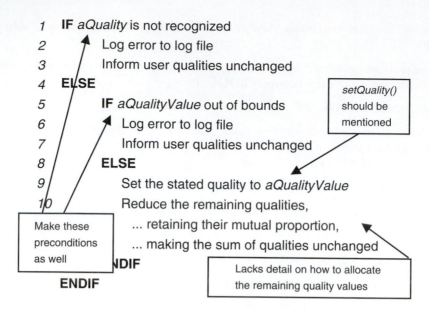

Figure 20.35 Inspecting pseudocode for defects

20.12 SUMMARY

A software design is assessed in terms of design qualities such as *sufficiency*, *robustness*, *flexibility*, *reusability*, *efficiency*, and *reliability*. Metrics are defined, collected, and assessed for each quality. In addition, the IEEE has defined several metrics for assessing the complexity of designs. These include *number of entries and exits per module*, *graph-theoretic complexity for architecture*, and *data or information flow complexity*.

When selecting an appropriate software architecture for an application, we explore several alternatives and compare their relative strengths and weaknesses. Each is measured against several qualities to determine which alternative is the strongest.

The quality of detailed designs is pursued by following steps such as ensuring that each architectural module is expanded, each part of the detailed design maps back to part of the architecture, the design fulfills its requirements, the design is complete and testable, and all the necessary details are provided.

Inspections are used to find design defects. They focus on inspecting classes, their method prototypes (name, return type, and parameter types), the flowcharts and pseudocode, and the relationships among classes and methods within various models, such as use case, class, data flow, and state. Defect types can be classified using the categories specified in IEEE standard 1044.1-1995. These include the following types of problems: logic, computational, interface/timing, data handling, incorrect scope, data, documentation, performance, interoperability, and standards conformance.

20.13 EXERCISES

1. a. List the qualities that designs should possess. In your own words, describe the meaning of each.
   b. Choose three of these qualities. For each, give enough of two different designs for the following application to clearly distinguish one that scores higher than the other in terms of

the quality. The application takes as input the academic record of a high school student and produces as output three careers to which the student appears to be well-suited. An explanation is provided as well.

2. Consider an application that helps manage a fabric store. Assume that the stores sell fabrics and associated items such as buttons and ribbons. Give three to four robustness issues specific to this application. Explain your choices.

3. Below is code for a method *divide()*. Make the method more robust in at least two ways.

```
public double divide( Double aNumerator, Double aDenominator )
{
  return aNumerator.doubleValue() / aDenominator.doubleValue();
}
```

4. Consider a design for a video store application.
   a. Suppose that we use just one class *VideoStore*, which allows the entry and removal of a video name assigned to a customer, stored via a telephone number as key. What exactly is inflexible about this design?
   b. Give an alternative UML class model that would accommodate the inclusion of additional operations.
   c. Which of the classes that you introduced are likely to be reusable in other applications?
   d. How can you make more reusable the classes that reference *Video*?
   e. Which classes are unlikely to be reusable in other applications in any case?

5. Your instructor will pair up student project teams. Conduct an inspection of the other team's software design. Evaluate the classes specified in the design and score them using the list of qualities and metrics described in this chapter. How would you rate the overall design?

BIBLIOGRAPHY

1. Henry, S., and D. Kafura, "Software Structure Metrics Based on Information Flow," *IEEE Transactions on Software Engineering*, Volume *SE-7*, No. *5*, pp. 510–518, September 1981.
2. Shepperd, Martin, "Design metrics: an empirical analysis," *IEEE Software Engineering Journal*, Vol. 5, No. 1, January 1990, pp. 3–10.
3. Berinato, Scott. *"A Few Good Information Security Metrics,"* July 2005, http://www.csoonline.com/article/220462/A_Few_Good_Information_Security_Metrics?page=1) [accessed November 29, 2009].
4. Boehm, Barry, *"Software Engineering Economics,"* Prentice Hall, 1981.
5. "IEEE Std 982.1-2005 IEEE Standard Dictionary of Measures of the Software Aspects of Dependability," IEEE Std 982.1-2005.
6. Shlaer, Sally, and Stephan Mellor, *"Object Lifecycles: Modeling the World in States,"* Prentice Hall, 1992.
7. Anderson, Ross, *"Security Engineering,"* John Wiley & Sons, 2001.

21

Advanced and Emerging Methods in Software Design (Online Chapter)

To access this online chapter please visit www.wiley.com/college/braude.

22

Principles of Implementation

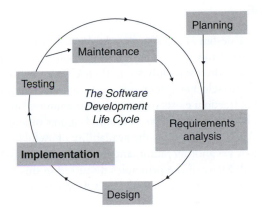

- • How do teams choose programming languages for implementations?

- • How does one define classes? methods?

- • What are standard implementation practices?

- • How do you handle variable naming? Global variables? Function parameters? Initialization? Comments?

- • What is "defensive programming"?

- • How do you handle errors?

- • What does it mean to "enforce intentions?"

- • What are good coding standards?

- • What implementation tools and environments are available for programming?

- • How do software engineers working on large projects go about programming?

- • How should student teams organize for the implementation phase?

Figure 22.1 The context and learning goals for this chapter

Code is created from design, whether the design is expressed in writing or not. In the OO case, this means that many of the classes—and perhaps the methods as well—may already have been identified and defined by the time programming begins. The main goal of the programmer is to translate the design into code that is correct, bug free, and maintainable. Many techniques and guidelines exist to help the programmer achieve these goals, and these are covered in this chapter.

Code listings are provided in Section 22.15 that illustrate several of the precepts discussed in this chapter.

22.1 AGILE AND NON-AGILE APPROACHES TO IMPLEMENTATION

This book has reviewed the idea that agile and non-agile approaches differ but also support each other. If the approach used on a project is agile, then implementation—the subject of this chapter—is begun just as soon as the first user story has been understood. That is very early compared with non-agile approaches. For agile projects, implementation is viewed not only as building the application but also as a process of understanding the requirements. The very act of determining classes and methods is a process of fleshing out a realization of the current user story. There is no other requirements analysis or design or documentation process unless the team feels the need for these in the course of implementing each user story. As the implementation progresses, the process of refactoring (see Chapter 24) is viewed as enabling developers to alter the design and implementation to suit evolving requirements.

On the other hand, if the approach is non-agile, then requirements and a design (though not necessarily of the entire application) are in place when implementation begins.

22.2 CHOOSING A PROGRAMMING LANGUAGE

The programming language selected for implementing a design is usually dictated by the company, the customer, or the environment in which the application must run. For example, if the application is Web-based, some JavaScript may be required. If the company is a Microsoft-only shop, then C# may be the only choice. Given a programming language, it is then necessary to select an interactive development environment such as Eclipse for Java or Visual Studio for C#. When the freedom exists to select a programming language, an identification and weighting of selection criteria can be used to assist the decision. Features of languages needed for the application constitute one set of criteria. Another criterion is the availability of useful libraries. The degree of software engineers' expertise in a language is yet another factor, and its weight is usually high.

As of 2009, most languages used are object-oriented. Many of the principles discussed in this chapter apply, whether the language is object-oriented or not; others make sense only for OO applications.

22.3 IDENTIFYING CLASSES

Let us first look at the origin of classes, which is the basis for an implementation. Each class has one of three origins. *Domain classes* refer back to the corresponding parts of the requirements for their intent; *design classes* refer to the Software Design Document (SDD). Inevitably, additional classes will be needed that were not envisaged in the design. We can call these *implementation classes*. The origins of a class are summarized in Figure 22.2.

A class should have a name that makes sense to its audience. For example, *VideoStoreCustomer* is such a name, whereas *StObsNobKl* probably isn't. Class invariants should be stated and observed by all of the methods of the class. These are concrete statements (e.g., limits on values) about the class attributes and their relationships. The constructors and nonstatic methods of the class are designed to assume but also to enforce the class invariants, thereby making their purpose within the class more explicit and, in consequence, making

- **Domain class**
  - Corresponds to a requirements paragraph
  - Example: *DVD*
- **Design class**
  - Specified in SDD
  - Not a domain class
  - Example: *RentalItem*
- **Implementation class**
  - Too minor to specify in design

Figure 22.2 Where the classes in an OO implementation come from

the class more reliable. The *Rental* class in Listing 22.2 (Section 22.15.1), for example, specifies the following invariant and a method, *checkInvariant()* used for unit testing.

```
/* Class invariant:
EITHER
    the rental is inactive, id == ID_WHEN_RENTAL_NOT_IN_EFFECT,
    rentalCustomer == null, and rentalItem == null
OR
    ID_WHEN_RENTAL_NOT_IN_EFFECT < id < =
        HIGHEST_ALLOWABLE_RENTAL_ID,
    rentalCustomer != null, and rentalItem != null
*/
```

The most important goal of a block of code is for it to satisfy its purpose. We refer to such code as "correct." This means, first, that the programmer knows what that purpose is; second, the programmer writes down that purpose precisely within the comments; third, the code implements the purpose; and fourth, the programmer explains, formally or informally, why the code fulfills the purpose. The *intent/preconditions/postconditions/return/inline comment* format covered in the next section is designed to help realize the goal of correctness.

22.4 DEFINING METHODS

When all is said and done, the work of an application is performed by its methods (also known procedures or functions). For that reason we take special care to state the purpose of each within the code comments. These can be effectively organized under categories such as *intent, precondition, postcondition, return, invariant, exceptions,* and *known issues*. The *intent* and *known issues* are informal, but the rest are precise. They specify completely, couching statements in terms of named variables.

The intent is documentation that programmers usually provide: an informal statement of what the method is intended to do. For example, the method *getNextRentalNumber()* in the class *Rental* of Listing 22.2 has the following:

```
Intent: Get the next available number for assigning a rental
```

This helps a lot in explaining the meaning of the method. Note that it is not a precise or thorough definition. If the method corresponds to a documented detailed requirement or if it is specified in the design, the *intent* statement may simply reference this.

The preconditions define the assumptions that the method makes about the value of variables external to the method, including the parameters. This excludes local variables. The method *setId()* in Listing 22.2, for example, has the following preconditions:

```
anId > RENTAL_ID_WHEN_NOT_IN_EFFECT &&
anId <= HIGHEST_ALLOWABLE_RENTAL_ID
```

In other words, the method's code assumes that *anId* is within the legal bounds. Notice that the specification of preconditions is precise—usually stated in terms of concrete, named variables. For all but the "Intent" section, vague statements lead to ambiguity and should be avoided.

The postconditions specify the method's effects. Every method has a return or a postcondition. This is because methods exist to have effects. There is no reason for their existence otherwise. The effect does not have to be permanent. For example, a method that displays the acknowledgement "DVD Rental Completed" has the following postcondition:

```
"DVD Rental Completed" is present on the monitor.
```

More commonly, postconditions refer to variables whose values could change. The constructor

```
public Rental
    ( int anId, RentalCustomer aRentalCustomer, RentalItem aRentalItem )
throws Exception
```

has the following postconditions:

```
(1) as for postconditions of setId( anId )
(2) RentalCustomer == aRentalCustomer
(3) RentalItem == aRentalItem
```

When a method depends on another method from which preconditions or postconditions are to be repeated, it is preferable not to literally repeat the preconditions, but merely to reference the methods on which it depends. This practice is applied in precondition (1). The benefit of such a reference is that if the preconditions in the called method change, it is not necessary to then update the preconditions in every method using them. The postconditions in this example are pretty much what one would expect for a constructor.

As another example, if we define a method

```
int weirdSum( int addend1, int addend2 )
```

so that *addend2* is assigned the sum of *addend1* and *addend2*, then *addend2* is mentioned in the postconditions as follows:

```
Postcondition: addend2' = addend1 + addend2
```

- *Intent*. **An informal statement of what the method is intended to do**
  - Don't specify the details here: the other categories provide them.
- *Preconditions*. **Conditions on nonlocal variables that the method assumes**
  - Includes parameters.
  - Verification of these conditions not promised in method itself.
- *Postconditions*. **Value of non-local variables after execution**
  - Includes parameters.
  - Notation: x' denotes the value of variable x after execution.

Figure 22.3 Programming conventions—documenting methods, 1 of 2

The notation x' refers to the value of a variable x at the conclusion of a method.

The invariant specifies a relationship among the variables that the method does not alter. This programmer may want to draw attention to an invariant. For example, he may want to stress that the class invariant is honored by the method. Specifying an invariant is equivalent to stating it among the preconditions and the postconditions.

The return specifies the exact nature of what the method is intended to return. Once again, this is specified in precise terms.

Figures 22.3 and 22.4 summarize these points.

Figure 22.5 shows an example. Instead of postcondition 1, we could have specified that the original elements of *gameBoard* are invariant because moves already made should not be changed.

A method is *purely functional* if it has a return, no postconditions, and its preconditions refer only to parameters. In this case, *Return* describes the entire reason for the method's existence. We make methods purely functional unless we want them to participate in an object-oriented design (which is often, however). When there are objects of a class at runtime—which we want in most cases—we need methods that manipulate the attributes of the objects and are thus *not* purely functional. Take, for example the method *area()* in the class *Rectangle*. We could define *area()* purely functionally by passing the length and width, as in

```
class Rectangle { . . .
    public double area( double aLength, double aWidth ) . . . .
}
```

- *Invariant* : **Relationship among nonlocal variables that the method's execution leaves unchanged** (The values of the individual variables may change, however.)
  - Equivalent to inclusion in both pre- and postconditions.
  - There may also be invariants among local variables.
- *Return* :
  - What the method returns.
- *Known issues* :
  - Honest statement of what has to be done, defects that have not been repaired, etc.
- *Exceptions*:
  - These are often thrown when the preconditions are not met because this indicates an abnormality in execution.

Figure 22.4 Programming conventions—documenting methods, 2 of 2

```
/** Intent: Record anOorX at aRow/aCol if aRow/aCol blank; Return 'N' if
* not permitted; return anOorX if full row/column/diagonal
*
* Preconditions: anOorX='O' OR anOorX='X'; 1<=aRow0<=3; 1<=aCol<=3
*
* Postconditions (note use of x and x')
* Post0. All preconditions are met OR Exception thrown
* Post1. gameBoard' contains all non-blank elements of gameBoard
* Post2. gameBoard[aRow-1][aCol-1] = '' OR return = 'N'
* Post3. gameBoard[aRow-1][aCol-1] != '' OR
* gameBoard'[aRow-1][aCol-1] = anOorX
* Post4. There is no full line of anOorX in gameBoard' OR return = anOorX
*/
public static char makeMove( char anOorX, int aRow, int aCol ) throws Exception{
```

Figure 22.5 Example of method documentation—*tic-tac-toe*

This has the property of being independent of the class it belongs to, and we would typically make it *static*. We would invoke this version of *area()* as in

```
. . . Rectangle.area( l, w ) . . . .
```

Alternatively, we could define *area()* with preconditions on the instance variables *length* and *width* of *Rectangle*, as in

```
class Rectangle { . . .
    public double area() . . . . }
```

This leverages the object-oriented nature of *Rectangle*. We would invoke this version of *area()* as in

```
. . . rectangle.area() . . .
```

22.5 IMPLEMENTATION PRACTICES

Figures 22.6, 22.7, and 22.8 summarize good habits for implementing code. They are described in more detail in the following sections, and many of them are put into practice in; Listing 22.2, found in Section 22.15.1; and also applied to the *Rental* class of our video store example.

22.5.1 Use Expressive Naming

When assigning names to variables, parameters, functions, classes, and so on, the most important criteria are that the names are expressive and that they convey meaning. They should not include vague, ambiguous terms. This helps the reader to understand their purpose (recall that our job includes producing maintainable work). Consider the following piece of code:

- **Use expressive naming**: the names of the function, the parameters, and the variables should indicate their purpose
  - . . . *manipulate(float aFloat, int anInt)* ← poor
  - . . . *getBaseRaisedToExponent(float aBase, int anExponent)* ← better
- **Avoid global variables**: consider passing parameters instead
  - . . . *extract(int anEntry) { . . . . . . table = ... }* ← replace?
  - . . . *extract(int anEntry, EmployeeTable anEmployeeTable)* ← better
    But not when the number of parameters exceeds ± 7

Figure 22.6 Good implementation practices, 1 of 3—naming variables; global variables

- **Don't use parameters as method variables**
  myMethod(int i) { . . . . . . for(i=0; . . . ← no!
- **Limit number of parameters** to 6 or 7
- **Give names to numbers**
  for(i = 0; i < 8927; ++i) ← poor: why 8927?
  Instead:
  int NUM_CELLS = 8927;// . . . .
  for(cellCounter = 0; cellCounter < NUM_CELLS; ++cellCounter)
- **Introduce variables near** their first **usage**

Figure 22.7 Good implementation practices, 2 of 3—parameters; no unnamed numbers

- **Initialize all variables**
  - re-initialize where necessary to "reset"
- **Check loop counters, especially for range correctness**
- **Avoid nesting loops more than 3 levels**
  - introduce auxiliary methods to avoid
- **Ensure loop termination**
  - a proof is ideal—in any case, document reasoning

Figure 22.8 Good implementation practices, 3 of 3—initializing variables; handling loops

```
// Example of poor use of naming
int DoIt(int a, int b)
{
  int c;
  c = a * b;
  return c;
}
```

What does this function do? It multiplies the two parameters and returns the result, but what exactly is its purpose? It is hard to tell by the names of the function or the variables—they do not convey any meaning. Now consider this simple function rewritten using expressive names:

```
int ComputeRectangleArea (int length, int width)
{
   int area;
   area = length * width;
   return area;
}
```

Even without comments, the purpose of the function is now clear: it computes the area of a rectangle, using the length and width that are passed as parameters.

22.5.2 Global Variables

Global variables are data accessible from anywhere in a program. Using global variables compromises the principle of *information hiding*, which we discussed in Chapter 15. Instead, we want to minimize their use to reduce the dependence on other parts of the implementation and to hide implementation details.

22.5.3 Function Parameters

Don't use parameters as working variables—this is not their purpose. Parameters should only be used to pass information into and out of a function. If a working variable is needed, it should be declared within the function. Otherwise, unintended errors can be introduced. For example, if an input parameter is used as a working variable, its original value may be modified. Then if the parameter is used later in the function with the assumption that it contains its original value, an error will occur.

Limit the number of parameters to 6 or 7—it is hard to keep track of parameters and use them properly if there are more than 6 or 7. Also, the more parameters are used, the more tightly coupled the calling function is with the called function. If so much data need to be passed, reexamine the design and see whether the coupled functions should be combined, or if they belong in the same class, with the parameters becoming private class members.

22.5.4 Explicit Numbers

It is not good practice to use explicit numbers in code. Consider the following:

```
for( i = 0; i < 8927; ++i )
```

It is not clear what 8927 means. Why loop 8927 times? Using a number like this hides the true meaning of the loop. Now consider the following:

```
const int NUM_CELLS = 8927; // . . . .
   .
   .
   .
for( cellCounter = 0; cellCounter < NUM_CELLS; ++cellCounter )
```

This is much clearer—the program contains cells, there are 8927 of them, and we are looping through all of them.

The other problem with using explicit numbers, especially if used throughout the code, is that they are very difficult to find and change correctly at a later time. Consider the example above, where 8297 is used explicitly in the *for* loop. Suppose 8297 is also used in many other places, and we want to increase the number of cells to 9999. We would then need to locate all occurrences of 8927 and change them to 9999. What if the number 8927 is also used for some other purpose—for example, the number of names in a list? You would have to examine the code to determine whether a particular occurrence of 8927 means the number of cells or the number of names. A better approach is to use a named constant such as NUM_CELLS, as in the example above. Then, in order to change the number of cell to 9999, all that is required is to edit the one statement where NUM_CELLS is defined, and all references to NUM_CELLS will use the new value.

22.5.5 Initialization and Declaration

22.5.5.1 Variable Declaration

It is good practice to declare variables as close to their first use as possible. If you are reading a piece of code you will then be more likely to find and understand the variables it references.

22.5.5.2 Variable Initialization

The reason we initialize variables is to take control of them, avoiding default or garbage values that the system assigns. This avoids potential errors where a variable is used and contains an unexpected value. It is good practice to initialize a variable when it is declared, as in the following example:

```
float balance = 0; // Initialize balance to 0
```

22.5.6 Loops

Loops can be complicated and are common sources of serious failures. They are thus special targets of verification. McConnell [1] suggests the following questions to be answered as guidelines to ensuring loop correctness:

- Is a *while* loop being used instead of a *for* loop?
- Is the loop entered from the top?
- Does the loop body have something in it? Is it nonempty?
- Is the loop short enough to review all at once?
- Have long loop contents been moved into their own function?
- Is the loop limited to at most three levels?
- If the loop is a *for* loop, does the body of the loop avoid modifying the loop index variable?
- Does the loop always terminate?
- If *break* or *continue* are used, are they used correctly?

They are described in more detail in the following sections, and many of them are put into practice in Listing 22.2, found in Section 22.15.1 and applied to the *Rental* class of our video store example.

22.6 DEFENSIVE PROGRAMMING

An effective practice for minimizing bugs is to anticipate potential errors and implement code to handle them. This technique is called *defensive programming*. One of the most common error sources is illegal data, either from a bad value in a function's input parameters, or from an external source such as a file, database, or data communication line. In each case the bad data must be detected and a strategy employed to handle it. There are a number of effective defensive strategies such as ignoring the error, substituting a default value, or if the error is from an external source, waiting for valid data. These are discussed in more detail in the next section.

Exception handling is a mechanism that passes control to error handling code that knows how to respond to the error. Many languages such as Java and C++ have built-in exception-handling facilities. Exception handling is covered in Section 22.6.2.

Other methods of defensive programming include buffer overflow prevention and "enforcing intentions." Each is discussed at the end of this section.

22.6.1 Error Handling

Developers are constantly faced with the issue of what to do with potentially illegal data. An example of illegal data is an account number that does not correspond to an actual bank account. Although we try to make implementations as simple as possible, the real world is not simple. A large fraction of programming goes toward the handling of errors. A disciplined approach is essential: pick an approach, state it, and be sure everyone on the team understands and abides by it.

Given that the possibility of errors must be dealt with, how does one program a method to handle illegal input—for example, a method that gives the balance on an account number when the method's preconditions clearly require that the account parameter be legal? If all of the aspects of the development process have been properly practiced, the method's parameters will always be legal whenever the method is called. But should we program a check of the parameter value in case our design or implementation is flawed? The answer depends on the requirements. For example, suppose there is a system requirement that the continued execution of the application is paramount, even if the execution is degraded or flawed. In this case, the programmer must deal with all inputs, even those that make no sense. Techniques for handling illegal data are described below [1].

Wait for a legal data value. If the illegal data are from an external source such as a user interface, database, or communication device, one possibility is to interact with the data source until the input is changed to a legal one before the processing continues. This is possible for much of user interface programming, where we can often ensure that only legal inputs are permitted. If the only allowable strings that can be entered in a text field are "car," "truck," or "bus," it is easy to prevent the user from continuing until a legal entry is made. A list box is a common way to do this. Even here, however, subtle errors may creep in. For example, the user may enter date of birth as 1/1/80 and age (in 2000) of 30. It is possible to check consistencies, but the onus is on the designer to handle all possible consistency and boundary checks (sometimes called "business rules").

Another example might be when data are transmitted over a faulty communication line. The receiving method may be designed to expect certain data, but the application is often explicitly required to continue execution, even when the data are not legal. Here, the data must be checked and errors processed in accordance with the requirements (e.g., "If the signal is not between 3.6 and 10.9, discard the signal and listen for the next signal . . . ").

Set a default value. Sometimes a default value can replace a bad data value. As an example, consider an application that monitors heart functions and controls an oxygen supply to a patient. Let's suppose that we are coding a method `process(int measurementType, . . . )` where *measurementType* must be positive. Let us assume that this application cannot afford to crash even when an internal method has been given an illegal integer due to a development defect. To deal with this, the code would check the input and set safe default values if possible. If this is not possible, it may place the entire application in a default mode of operation. In either case, some kind of alert would be raised indicating an internal error occurred.

Use the previous result. Some software continuously monitors the value of something—for example, real-time stock quotes. If one time the software reads an illegal value, a possible reaction is to use the last legal value that was read. This a good approach when the data values are read frequently enough that you don't expect much deviation between reads. However, if illegal values are read consecutively, the program may want to raise an alert or log an error to indicate the problem.

Log error. Many software applications implement a logging subsystem to store error information for later use. Log information is typically written to nonvolatile storage such as a file, with data saved including an error description, software function where error occurred, call stack at time of error, register values, and so on.

Throw an exception. Exceptions are a mechanism to handle unexpected program errors, including illegal data values. Languages such as C++ and Java have built-in exception support. Exceptions are covered in more detail in the next section.

Abort. In some applications any bad data are considered fatal and the system is aborted and reset. This is most often the case in applications where safety is a concern and a bad value can cause harm. This can also occur in embedded systems that manage their own memory and detect memory corruption. If logging is available, error information is saved before the software resets.

In some of our previous examples, the action taken in response to illegal data is dictated by the requirements: abort if safety-critical, use the previous result if it is not expected to change, and so on. Now let us consider methods whose exceptional behavior is not determined by the requirements. First, their preconditions must be thoroughly specified so that the conditions under which they are called are clear—but should their parameter values be checked to ensure that the preconditions are met? We distinguish here between execution during development and execution during deployment.

Executing during development allows test and verification code in many parts of an application, and we might well want to insert code that checks preconditions, as in the following:

```
/** precondition: parameters are positive */
int sum( int int1P, int int2P ) {
// verification code for use in development: check parameters positive
. . .
// now do the work
. . . }
```

Executing the delivered product requires a different perspective. If the method is called with negative parameters, this indicates a defect in the application itself. We would like to protect ourselves against our own mistakes, but the cure must be preferable to the illness.

```
/** precondition: parameters are positive */
int sum( int int1P, int int2P ) {
// verification code for deployed application: check parameters
    positive
 // only if we have a clear philosophy of what to do if parameters
    not positive
. . .
// now do the work
. . . }
```

Developers lose control of their application when they apply an arbitrary default whose consequences are not known. This must be balanced against the continued execution of an application with wrong values, however. It may be unethical to distribute, without warning, an application that handles defective development with an incorrect continuation (i.e., a continuation not stated in the requirements). A defect is a mistake, but an arbitrary default not explicitly specified in the requirements is a cover-up. It is often preferable to relaunch an aborted application rather than have it execute incorrectly (think of an application plotting airplane courses). Undisciplined error processing hides defects, and it becomes expensive to find the defect compared with allowing the application to crash (hopefully at test time).

22.6.2 Exception Handling

Exceptions are a mechanism to handle unexpected program errors. Languages such as C++ and Java have built-in support for exceptions. For those languages without explicit support, developers sometimes design and implement their own exception-handling code.

In general, when an error is detected an exception is *thrown*, meaning control is passed to that part of the program that knows how to deal with the error. This is also known as *catching* the exception. As a general rule you should catch those exceptions that you know how to handle. A method handling an exception looks like

```
ReturnType myMethod( . . . ) { . . .
  try{ . . . // call method throwing ExceptionX }
  catch(ExceptionX e) ( . . . // handle it )
  . . . }
```

A method *not* handling an exception (i.e., passing it to callers) looks like the following.

```
ReturnType myMethod( . . . ) throws ExceptionX{ . . . }
```

The following are some guidelines for implementing exceptions:

- If the present method cannot handle the exception, there has to be a handler in an outer scope that can do so.

- If you can handle part of the exception, then handle that part and then rethrow the exception for handling within an outer scope.

- Make reasonable expectations about the ability of callers to handle the exception you are throwing; otherwise, find an alternative design since unhandled exceptions crash applications.

- "If you must choose between throwing an exception and continuing the computation, continue if you can" [2]. The point here is that the continuation of an application can be preferable to shutting it down in cases when the consequences have been thought through.

As an example, the Encounter case study continues to perform with a default name when given a faulty parameter string (e.g., null), since this is preferable to shutting down the game just because a name is illegal. On the other hand, a banking transaction with an illegal amount would not be allowed to continue.

There are differences of opinion concerning the use of exceptions when a method is called and does not satisfy its preconditions. Some believe that this is a legitimate use for exceptions; others disagree, and believe that this is a matter for testing alone. The authors' opinion is that since code is naturally error-prone, a consistent policy for throwing exceptions in such cases is a beneficial practice.

22.6.3 Buffer Overflow Prevention

Some languages, notably C and C++, allow writing to memory that exceeds the space declared in the code. For example, the following C code declares an array within a method:

```
char myCharArray[10];
```

Clearly, we intend to write no more than 10 characters to *myCharArray*. However, the following code will place new bits beyond the memory allocated to *myCharArray* if *someCharArray* happens to be longer than 10 characters:

```
strcpy( myCharArray, someCharArray );
```

The effects of this overwriting can be benign, but they can also be catastrophic for the application; if exploited by a malicious hacker, they can produce a security breach. This can be prevented by checking variable size at key points (e.g., when a user provides input).

22.6.4 "Enforce Intentions"

If you intend something about how the code you are constructing is to be used by other parts of the application, then try to enforce this intention. The authors call this the "Enforce Intentions" principle. It is often evident in user interfaces, where applications try to prevent the user from entering illegal data. We are stressing the "Enforce Intentions" principle for *internal* processing here. The principle is analogous to constructing curbs and islands on roadways to direct traffic along just those paths intended by traffic engineers, and no others. Such enforcement of intentions makes roads safer; it is commonly applied in many engineering disciplines. The following includes examples of the "Enforce Intentions" principle in software engineering:

- Use qualifiers such as *final*, *const* in C++, and *abstract* to enforce the corresponding intentions. *final* classes can't be inherited from; *final* methods can't be overridden in inherited classes; the value of *final* variables can't be changed. If this causes compile-time errors, it means that you do not fully understand your own program yet, and no harm has been done. What we especially seek to avoid are runtime errors.

- Make constants, variables, and classes as local as possible. For example, define loop counters within the loop—don't give them wider scope if this is not your intention.

- Use the Singleton design pattern if there is to be only one instance of a class (see Chapter 17).

- Generally speaking, make members inaccessible if they are not specifically intended to be accessed directly.

- Make attributes protected. Access them through more public accessor functions if required. (In Java, making attributes protected gives objects of subclasses access to members of their base classes, which is often undesirable.)

- Make methods *private* if they are for use only by methods of the same class.

Consider introducing classes to **encapsulate** legal **parameter values** that prevent bad data. For example, if the intention for a method *evaluate()* is to accept only "car," "truck," or "bus" as parameters, then it might be worthwhile not to use *String* as a parameter because it introduces the possibility of illegal parameters. It would be better to define a class such as *SpecializedVehicle* with a private constructor and factory functions:

```
SpecializedVehicle createACar() { . . . }
SpecializedVehicle createATruck() { . . . }
SpecializedVehicle createABus() { . . . }
```

The method in question can then take only a parameter of this type. In other words, instead of

```
evaluate( String vehicle ) . . . // problem with illegal strings
```

use

```
evaluate( SpecializedVehicle vehicle ) . . . // parameter value cannot
   be illegal
```

When the possible parameter values are restricted but infinite, a separate class can still be valuable. For example, a person's age is an integer between 0 and 105, let's say, and so a method

```
getYearOfBirth( int age )
```

may have to deal with errors. In fact, the same error processing would have to be repeated for all methods taking *age* as a parameter. On the other hand, a class *Age* with a private constructor and a public factory method

```
Age getAge( int ageP )
```

would handle erroneous input in a consistent manner, located in the same place as all the other aspects of age. Some options for dealing with this error are described below. The disadvantage of this method is the proliferation of additional classes, and the slight awkwardness of calls such as

```
. . . getYearOfBirth( getAge( n ) ) . . .
```

in place of such simpler calls as

```
. . . getYearOfBirth( n ) . . .
```

22.7 CODING STANDARDS

Applying coding standards across a team improves discipline, code readability, and code portability. We will present one set of standards as an example. Some of these are adapted from Scott Ambler [3]. Other standards can be found at Sun Corporation's Java site. The exact nature of a standard is not nearly as important as the fact that the team uses one.

22.7.1 Naming Conventions

Use a naming convention for variables. Engineers tend to become emotional about their favorite conventions, and true consensus is often impossible. Nevertheless, conventions are necessary. A limited time should be set aside for deciding on conventions and a method for finalizing them. For example, a team member can be designated to draft conventions, e-mail them to the other members for comments, then have the choices finalized by the designated person with the approval of the team leader. There should be guidelines as to when exceptions to conventions are to be allowed.

The following are examples of naming conventions in the Java tradition:

- Name entities with concatenated words as in *lengthCylinder*. These are easy to understand and they conserve space. Exceptions may be permitted at the discretion of the programmer.

- Begin class names with capitals. This distinguishes them from variables. Some tools precede the name of entities with standard letters or combinations of letters, such as C . . . for classes as in *CCustomer*. This is useful when the importance of knowing the types of names exceeds the resulting awkwardness.

- Name variables beginning with lowercase letters. Constants may be excepted.

- Name constants with capitals as in *I_AM_A_CONSTANT* (use static final). *IAMACONSTANT* is hard to read; *IamAConstant* could be confused with a class; *iAmAName* gives no indication that it is a constant.

- Some organizations distinguish between variables local to a method and those of the class ("instance variables"). For example, begin (or end) the name of instance variables of classes with an underscore as in *_timeOfDay* to distinguish them from other variables, since they are global to their object; this is used by Gamma et al. [4] but derided by Ambler [5]. A convention used in the case study is to append the suffix *I* to indicate instance variables, as in *timeOfDayI*. Each instance variable is global to each class instance, and when one is encountered in a block of code, it is useful to know this.

- Consider using a notation to distinguish the static variables of a class. The case study uses the suffix S, as in *numCarsEverBuiltS*. Recall that a static variable is global to a class, and it is helpful to know that a variable encountered in a block of code is one of these.

- Use *get* . . . , *set* . . . , and *is* . . . for accessor methods as in *getName()*, *setName()*, *isBox()* (where the latter returns a boolean value). Alternatively use *name()* and *name(String)*, for attribute name (e.g., in CORBA—see [6]).

- Augment these with standardized additional "getters" and "setters" of collections, for example *insertIntoName()*, *removeFromName()*, *newName()*.

- Consider a convention for parameters. One convention is to use the prefix a, as in *sum(int anInterger1, int anInterger2)*. The case study uses the suffix P, as in *sum(int num1P, int num2P)*.

22.7.2 Other Conventions

Use a consistent standard for separation. Since single blank lines are useful for separating code sections within methods, a consistent standard is to use double blank lines between methods. Within methods, consider standards such as the following:

- Perform only one operation per line.

- Try to keep methods to a single screen.

- Use parentheses within expressions to clarify their meaning, even if the syntax of the language makes them unnecessary. This is an application of "if you know it, show it."

In naming classes, use singular names such as *Customer*, unless the express purpose is to collect objects (in which case *Customers* might be appropriate). To prevent the proliferation of classes, it is sometimes desirable to have a class collect its own instances. This would be done with a static data member of the class.

22.8 COMMENTS

Comments are nonexecuted lines in a program whose purpose is to describe the intent of the program. Effective use of comments is important to understanding code.

Good comments should not simply repeat what is obvious from reading the code. They should provide meaning, explaining how and why a piece of code is doing something. For example,

```
i++; // increment i
```

The comment here provides no additional information regarding what the variable *i* means and why it is being incremented.

Now consider this example, using the function *doIt*() we saw earlier in the chapter.

```
int doIt(int a, int b)
{
   int c;
   c = a * b;
   return c;
}
```

With no comments and poor naming of the function and parameters, the purpose of DoIt is not obvious. By adding comments we can make its purpose clear.

```
// doIt - compute and return the area of rectangle given its length and
      width
// a - length
// b - width
int doIt(int a, int b)
{
   int c;
   c = a * b;
   return c;
}
```

Even though the names of the function and parameters are still unclear, the comments clarify its purpose and the meaning of the parameters.

22.8.1 Documenting Attributes

For each class attribute, state its purpose and provide all applicable invariants. For example, in the class *Triangle*, we would code somewhat like the following:

```
class Triangle {
    private static final double DEFAULT_TRIANGLE_SIDE = Double.MAX_VALUE;
    // Invariant: 0 < len1 <= Double.MAX_VALUE
    protected double len1 = DEFAULT_TRIANGLE_SIDE;
    // Invariant: 0 < len2 <= Double.MAX_VALUE
    protected double len2 = DEFAULT_TRIANGLE_SIDE;
    // Invariant: 0 < len3 <= Double.MAX_VALUE
    protected double len3 = DEFAULT_TRIANGLE_SIDE;
    //Invariant: lenx + leny > lenz for (x, y, z) = (1, 2, 3), (1, 3, 2)
    //and (2, 3, 1)
    . . . .
}
```

for example,

''1 < _age < 130'' or ''36 < _length * _width < 193''.

As a reviewer of this book has noted, one can write a separate private or protected method that is called by other methods when the invariant needs checking.

22.9 TOOLS AND ENVIRONMENTS FOR PROGRAMMING

It has been said often that, as a species, we are toolmakers, and this is no less true of software developers. An increasing number of tools are available that help developers.

Interactive development environments (IDEs) are widely used to enable programmers to produce more code in less time. They include drag-and-drop facilities for forming GUI components, graphical representation of directories, debuggers, "wizards," and refactoring facilities (discussed in Chapter 24).

Profilers such as *JProbe* can be used to accumulate statistics on code such as

- Cumulative CPU and elapsed time

- Time spent by each method

- Cumulative count of objects generated

- Number of calls

- Average method time

Reverse-engineering tools are available that take source code as input and produce limited documentation. An example of a reverse-engineering source code tool is Javadoc. Reverse engineering is discussed more fully in Chapter 24.

Several object-oriented tools (such as Rational Rose, Together/J/C++) generate source code from class models. These forward-engineering tools cannot be expected to generate more than code skeletons within which the programmer must work to produce the eventual implementation. However, as our discussion of MDA in Chapter 21 showed, plans are under way for ambitious code generation capabilities. The same tools also perform reverse engineering by mechanically producing class models from source code (hence the term "round-trip engineering").

The history of tools in other branches of engineering (e.g., CAD/CAM) suggests that, despite a rocky start and several false directions, programming tools will continue to improve significantly, that they will continue to leverage programming skills, and that they will reduce drudgery and mechanical tasks.

22.10 CASE STUDY: ENCOUNTER IMPLEMENTATION

> Note to the Student:
> This section contains implementation notes for the Encounter case study. The source code for Encounter is available online so that the student can inspect the final product.

> Several purely implementation issues need to be documented, as listed next. We include a discussion of *where* these issues should be documented. The sections that follow contain examples of the documentation content.

- *Programming conventions.* These can be provided in the SPMP since they are part of project management to a degree. They could be provided in the SDD although they are not part of the actual design. They could be stated in a separate document, but there are already many documents. They could be provided in a document dedicated to implementation, which would be useful. Finally, they could be included in the SQAP since they are a direct contributor to quality. The Encounter case study selected this option.

- *The implementation model.* This specifies how the physical files are organized (source code, binary, help files, etc.). The SDD is a possible repository for this, although the implementation model is not actually part of the design. A separate document is a possibility. A document on implementation issues alone would be appropriate. Another possibility is the SCMP since it is concerned with configurations and version. The Encounter case study selected this option.

- *Implementation notes.* A document is maintained by individual engineers to describe the current state of their work.

22.10.1 Programming Conventions

> Programming conventions are added to Section 5: Standards, Practices, Conventions, and Metrics, of the Encounter SQAP.

5.2.1 Programming Conventions
(this section has been added to the standard)
   The following conventions will be used.

1. Parts of nonconstant names are delineated by capitalization: for example, *thisIsAName*.

2. Class and interface names begin with a capital: for example, *Account*.

3. Instance variables in classes begin with a lowercase character and end with "I": for example, *balanceI*.

4. Static (class) variables begin with a lowercase character, and end with "S": for example, *interestRateS*.

5. Variables defined in, and global to, a method begin with a lowercase character and end with "M": for example, *interestM*.

6. Parameters begin with a lowercase character and end with "P": for example, *principalP*.

7. Final variables shall be written in capitals and shall use underscores: for example, *BANK_NAME*.

5.2.2 Notation for Showing the Location of Files

We will use UML to describe the implementation [7].

5.2.3 Personal Software Documentation

Each engineer will maintain documentation of his current work, which is referred to as his Personal Software Documentation (PSD). This enables the engineer to report status at all times, and it becomes part of the project's archive. The team or project leader will determine how to organize the PSD of the team. Typically, a personal software document set corresponds to a task that has been allocated to the engineer and consists of a set of classes.

An example of PSD is provided in Section 22.10.3 below.

22.10.2 Implementation Model

A description of the implementation model, which describes how the physical files are organized, is added as an appendix to the Encounter SCMP.

Appendix for *Encounter* SCMP: Implementation Model

A part of the Encounter implementation model is shown in Figure 22.9.

22.10.3 Implementation Notes for Encounter: Part 1 of 2

This document is maintained by individual engineers to describe the current state of their work. It should be complete enough to allow

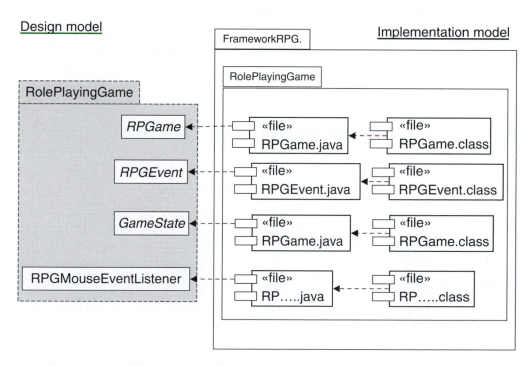

Figure 22.9 Design model and implementation model for the Encounter video game

the engineer to report his or her status at meetings, or to allow another engineer to take over the work in a reasonable amount of time if necessary.

1. Introduction

This document describes the work of John Jones on the class EncounterCharacter. It is under configuration control with the file name PSD_EncounterCharacter. The files referenced here are stored in the directory Encounter\PSD\JJones on the Galaxy system.

2. Defect Recording Log

The log in Figure 22.10 is maintained in file *defectLog*.

3. Time Recording Log

Engineers maintain records of how long it takes them to perform the various activities required by software engineering. These data are essential for the project, and they provide the engineer with a professional "toolkit." Timing data can be collected via written forms or software tools residing on desktop computers, hand-held computers, and so on. Engineers have to develop a common understanding of the degree of precision required by the organization. Note that approximate time measurements can easily become too inconsistent for practical use.

These data are stored in file *Time_Recording_Log* and an example is shown in Figure 22.11.

Date	Number	Type	Phase Injected	Phase Removed	Repair Time (minutes)
6/14/99	142	Interface	Personal detailed design	Personal code review	10
Description: omitted checks on name length in *EncounterCharacter*.					
6/16/99	143	Documentation	Code	Personal code review	4
Description: incorrect Javadoc description of *EncounterCharacter*.					
. . . .	. . . . . .	. . . . . .	. . . . . .	. . . . . .	. . . . . .
This table concludes with defects found during unit test					

Figure 22.10 Example of a defect recording log

Source: Humphrey, Watts S., "Introduction to the Team Software Process," Addison-Wesley, 2000.

Date	Start	Stop	Interruptns.	Time taken	Phase	Comments
6/99	10:04 am	10:25 am	4 + 6	11	Detailed Design	Consulted with V.N.
6/99	1:20 pm	4:34 pm	15 + 20	159	Personal Code review	Defect 14
7/99	. . .					

Figure 22.11 A time recording log

22.10.4 Source Code (without Test Code): *EncounterCharacter*

The reader is referred to Section 22.15.2 for a listing of this code.

22.11 CASE STUDY: ECLIPSE

> Note to the Student:
> The implementation of Eclipse is a large body of code and related artifacts. This section selects just one very small example of standards as an illustration.

Eclipse development standards and resources are listed at [8]. They are quoted from [8] as follows:

Conventions and Guidelines

These cover coding standards, naming conventions, and other guidelines. For example, naming conventions are decomposed as follows:

- Eclipse workspace projects
- Java packages
- Classes and interfaces
- Methods
- Variables
- Plug-ins and extension points . . .

> Next, we give an example of one of the above.

Methods: Methods should be verbs, in mixed case with the first letter lowercase, with the first letter of each internal word capitalized. Examples:

```
run();
runFast();
getBackground();
```

Additional rules: The named of methods should follow common practice for naming getters (*getX()*), setters (*setX()*), and predicates (*isX()*, *hasX()*). . . .

22.12 CASE STUDY: OPENOFFICE

[This section presents examples of *OpenOffice* documentation that relates to implementation.]

22.12.1 OpenOffice Standards

> Note to the Student:
> There are many standards associated with OpenOffice development. We will give one small example.

Each OpenOffice class must begin with the following header from [9].

```
/*******************************
*OpenOffice.org - a multi-platform
*  office productivity suite
*
* $RCSfile: code,v $
*
* $Revision: 1.2 $
*
* last change: $Author: st $ $Date:
* 2005/09/02 16:31:54 $
*
* The Contents of this file are made
*  available subject to the terms of
*  GNU Lesser General Public License
*  Version 2.1.
*
* GNU Lesser General Public License
*  Version 2.1
* ==============================
* Copyright 2005 by Sun Micro-
*  systems, Inc.
* 901 San Antonio Road, Palo Alto, CA
* 94303, USA
*
* This library is free software; you
* can redistribute it and/or modify
* it under the terms of the GNU Lesser
* General Public License version
```

```
* 2.1, as published by the Free
* Software Foundation.
*
* This library is distributed in the
* hope that it will be useful, but
* WITHOUT ANY WARRANTY; without even
* the implied warranty of MERCHANT-
* ABILITY or FITNESS FOR A PARTICULAR
* PURPOSE. See the GNU Lesser General
* Public License for more details.
*
* You should have received a copy of
* the GNU Lesser General Public
* License along with this library; if
* not, write to the Free Software
* Foundation, Inc., 59 Temple Place,
* Suite 330, Boston, MA 02111-1307
* USA
* *****************************/

...
```

22.12.2 Developer's Guide

> The following is quoted from [10]. Notice that the term "guide" is used here instead of "standards." Since many developers contribute to OpenOffice, this is a useful document for unraveling the implementation structure.

"The OpenOffice.org SDK contains now the new Developer's Guide (PDF version). The goal of the guide is to give developers and solution providers the necessary means to use OpenOffice.org as componentware, using it in their own projects and extending it according to their needs. The primary target languages are Java and C++, although the use of OpenOffice.org Basic, CLI (.NET), Python, and MS Automation is treated as well.

The initial version of this guide was a collaboration work of the OOo core developers and two external authors. The developers have collected their detailed knowledge about UNO[1] and the OpenOffice.org API.. . . . . The manual will cover

all important aspects of software development with OpenOffice.org, including the base technology UNO, the programming languages supported by OpenOffice.org, the development of custom components, and of course the office applications Writer, Calc, Draw, Impress, Chart, and Base.

This Developer's Guide should be considered as a growing document where all new API concepts will be described in detail combined with a set of UML diagrams and examples how to use these APIs. This first version is an initial step for an ongoing documentation task and Sun Microsystems will take care of this project for the OpenOffice.org community. . . . "

> The developer's guide title page and URL are shown partially in Figure 22.12

> Section 1 (Reader's Guide) begins to explain the scope of this document. The idea is that to add to OpenOffice, the developer creates components using a set of standards. We continue to quote directly from the Developer's Guide with occasional, minor editing.

1.1 What This Manual Covers

This manual describes how to write programs using the component technology UNO (Universal Network Objects) with OpenOffice.org. Most examples provided are written in Java. As well as Java, the language binding for C++, the UNO access for OpenOffice.org Basic and the OLE Automation bridge that uses OpenOffice.org through Microsoft's component technology COM/DCOM is described.

1.2 How This Book Is Organized

First Steps

The First Steps chapter describes the setting up of a Java UNO development environment to achieve the solutions

---

[1] The component technology UNO (Universal Network Objects)

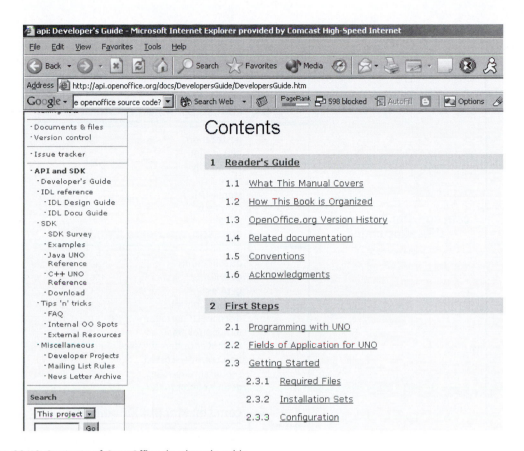

Figure 22.12 Contents of OpenOffice developer's guide

you need. At the end of this chapter, you will be equipped with the essentials required for the following chapters about the OpenOffice.org applications.

. . .

Figure 22.13 is an example of the selected use of UML in this document. It shows the inheritance of a pair of classes and the interfaces (denoted with circles) that each of the two classes implement.

. . .

There is much more to the Developer's Guide, but our sample ends here.

22.12.3 Sample OpenOffice Code

All chapters provide one or more examples that show the use of the API in the current descriptions of this guide. . . .

The following sample, Listing 22.1, is from [11]. The authors' comments are in different type and in bold.

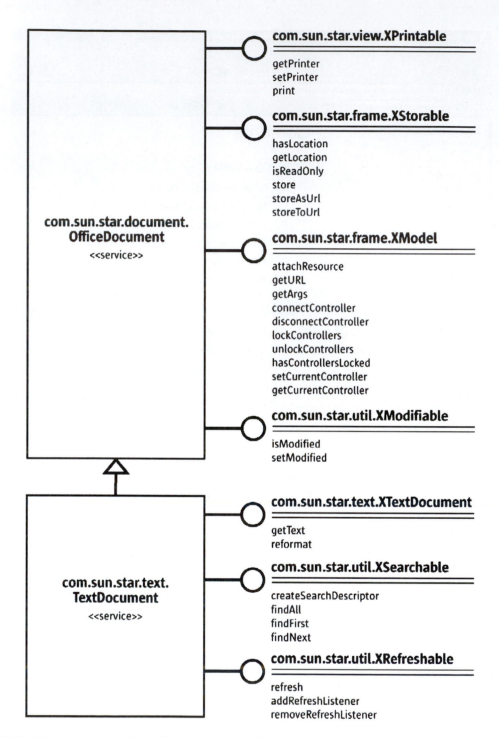

Figure 22.13 UML excerpts from OpenOffice developer's guide

Listing 22.1: Code excerpt from OpenOffice

```
 /***************************
* $RCSfile: ViewSample.java,v $
*
* $Revision: 1.3 $
*
* last change: $Author: hr $ $Date: 2003/06/ 30 15:46:21 $
  //there will be a list of these
* . . .
***************************/

import com.sun.star.uno.UnoRuntime;

//_____implementation_____

/** Create and modify a spreadsheet view.
*/
public class ViewSample extends SpreadsheetDocHelper
{
//_____
public static void main( String args[] )
{
 try
 {
   ViewSample aSample = new View
   Sample( args );
   aSample.doSampleFunction();
 }
catch (Exception ex)
{
  System.out.println("Sample caught exception! " + ex );
  System.exit( 1 );
}
System.out.println("\nSamples done.'' );
System.exit( 0 );
 }
//_____

public ViewSample( String[] args )
{
  super( args );
}
//_____
/** This sample function performs all changes on the view. */
      // informal description
```

```
public void doSampleFunction() throws Exception
{
com.sun.star.sheet.XSpreadsheetDocument xDoc = getDocument();
com.sun.star.frame.XModel xModel = (com.sun.star.frame.XModel)
  UnoRuntime.queryInterface(com.sun.star.frame.XModel.class,
    xDoc);
com.sun.star.frame.XController xController =
  xModel.getCurrentController();

// --- Spreadsheet view ---
// freeze the first column and first two rows
com.sun.star.sheet.XViewFreezable xFreeze = (com.sun.star.sheet.
  XViewFreezable)
  UnoRuntime.queryInterface( com.sun.star.sheet.XViewFreezable.
    class, xController);
if ( null != xFreeze )
  System.out.println( ''got xFreeze'' );
xFreeze.freezeAtPosition( 1, 2 );

// --- View pane ---
// get the cell range shown in the second pane and assign a cell
// background to them
com.sun.star.container.XIndexAccess xIndex =
  UnoRuntime.queryInterface( com.sun.star.container.XIndexAccess.
    class, xController );
Object aPane = xIndex.getByIndex(1);
 . . .
// --- View settings ---
 . . .
// --- Range selection ---
 . . .
synchronized (aListener) // extensive use of synchronize to prevent interruption
{
  aListener.wait(); // wait until the selection is done
}
xRngSel.removeRangeSelectionListener ( aListener );
 . . .
}
// _____

// listener to react on finished selection
private class ExampleRangeListener implements com.sun.star.sheet.
XRangeSelectionListener
{
    public String aResult;
    public void done( com.sun.star.sheet.RangeSelectionEvent aEvent )
```

```
    {
      aResult = aEvent.RangeDescriptor;
      synchronized (this)
      {
        notify();
      }
    }
  public void aborted(com.sun.star.sheet.RangeSelectionEvent aEvent)
  {
    synchronized (this)
    {
      notify();
    }
  }
  public void disposing( com.sun.star.lang.EventObject aObj )
  {
  }
 }
// _____
}
```

The following paragraph invites readers to contribute to the developer's guide. This kind of invitation helps to create a cooperative atmosphere. Developers are less likely to feel constricted by standards and guidelines when they participate in establishing them.

Make a contribution

We would like to invite you to participate in this effort, so as to cover the needs of the community and to bring in the community's experience. Please let us know what you would expect from the Developer's Guide, what might be missing in the current version, which use cases the guide should cover and which extensions you can think of. . . .

12.13 STUDENT TEAM GUIDANCE FOR IMPLEMENTATION

Before commencing with the implementation of your student team project, you should produce the following documentation, using the Encounter case study as an example:

1. Programming conventions

2. Implementation model

3. Integration plan

The *programming conventions* need not be extensive, but should provide enough detail so that code produced by different students exhibit a consistent style.

It is important to document your *implementation model* so the entire team knows where files are to be stored and from where they are to be retrieved.

An *integration plan* is written so you understand the order of implementation and how modules will be tested.

Once you have completed the documentation listed above, use your detailed design as a guide and implement your project. At a minimum you can implement key portions of your application to form a prototype.

22.14 SUMMARY

Program code is created from designs. In the object-oriented paradigm, classes form the basis of the design and implementation. Classes are either *domain* classes, which originate from the requirements, *design* classes, which originate from the SDD, or *implementation* classes, which are created during implementation.

    Defensive programming is an approach to reducing errors. It involves anticipating errors such as illegal data in function parameters and bad data from external sources such as data communication lines. There are several effective strategies for dealing with the illegal data, including ignoring the error, substituting a default value, or waiting for valid data. The philosophy of "enforcing intentions" is fundamental to good, defensive programming.

    There are a number of *best practices* to follow when implementing code, including using expressive naming, avoid using global variables, not using parameters and method variables, limiting the number of function parameters, using named constants, initializing variables, checking loop counters, and ensuring loop termination. Each is intended to reduce the likelihood of introducing errors and make code more maintainable.

    Programming standards are used to improve team discipline, code readability, and code portability. Standards cover all aspects of coding including naming conventions, code layout, use of brackets, and use of parentheses. *Comments*, especially those that observe programming standards, are an important aid to understanding code. They should convey meaning, purpose, and intent, and not repeat what is obvious from reading the code. In particular, a good way to define a method within a class is to explicitly specify in comments its *intent*, *preconditions*, *postconditions*, *invariants*, *exceptions*, and *known issues*. Postconditions define a method's purpose precisely. The result is an increased understanding of the method, which leads to a reduced likelihood of errors.

22.15 CODE LISTINGS REFERRED TO IN THIS CHAPTER

22.15.1 Code Listing for Video Rental Example

The code in Listing 22.2 below illustrates some of the principles discussed in this chapter, applied to the *Rental* class of our video store example.

Listing 22.2: Video store application code—*Rental, RentalItem* classes

```
/**==========================
* Describes a DVD
*/
class DVD extends RentalItem
{
}
/**
* Intent: SDD for Rental Framework: http://.....
*
* Known issues:
* (1) This class is not complete for a first build
* (2) Relies on log() method to log development problems -- not yet
*     created
* (3) Unit test to be moved from main() and upgraded to use JUnit.
*/
```

```
import java.io.*;
abstract class Rental
{
    // CONSTANTS == == == == == == == =
        private final static int HIGHEST_ALLOWABLE_RENTAL_ID = 99999999;
        private final static int ID_WHEN_RENTAL_ NOT_IN_EFFECT = 0;
        private final static int TOLERANCE_ON_RENTAL_ID = 1000;
        private static String FILE_WITH_NEXT_USABLE_RENTAL_NUMBER =
        "RentalNumber.txt'';

// VARIABLES == == == == == == == == == == ==
    protected int id = ID_WHEN_RENTAL_NOT_IN_EFFECT; // rental
        identification
    protected RentalCustomer rentalCustomer = null; // customer rented to
    protected RentalItem rentalItem = null; // item rented

/* Class invariant:
EITHER
    the rental is inactive, id == ID_WHEN_RENTAL_NOT_IN_EFFECT,
    rentalCustomer == null, and rentalItem == null
OR
    ID_WHEN_RENTAL_NOT_IN_EFFECT < id <= HIGHEST_ALLOWABLE_
    RENTAL_ID,
    rentalCustomer != null, and rentalItem != null
*/


// CONSTRUCTORS == == == == == == == == == ==
/************************************
* Intent: Satisfy class invariant with rental not in effect
* Postconditions: id == ID_WHEN_RENTAL_NOT_IN_EFFECT,
* rentalCustomer == null, and rentalItem == null
*/
public Rental()
/************************************/
{
    id = ID_WHEN_RENTAL_NOT_IN_EFFECT;
    rentalCustomer = null;
    rentalItem = null;
}
/************************************
* Intent: Create a specific rental
*
* Preconditions:
* (1) anID > ID_WHEN_RENTAL_NOT_IN_EFFECT
* (2) anID <= HIGHEST_ALLOWABLE_RENTAL_ID
* (3) aRentalCustomer != null
* (4) aRentalItem != null
```

```
 *
 * Postconditions:
 * (1) as for setId( anId )
 * (2) rentalCustomer == aRentalCustomer
 * (3) rentalItem == aRentalItem
 *
 * Known issues:
 * (1) Exception not specific enough
 * (2) No handling of violated preconditions
 *
 */
public Rental
( int anId, RentalCustomer aRentalCustomer, RentalItem aRentalItem )
throws Exception
/*********************************/
{
    setId( anId );
    rentalCustomer = aRentalCustomer;
    rentalItem = aRentalItem;
    checkInvariant();
}
// METHODS ======================
  /***********************************
   * Intent: A check that the class invariant is valid; present for
   * demonstation only. It is possible that this method is not actually
   * used.
   * Exception: Thrown if the class invariant is violated
   * Known issues: Exception not specific enough
   */
public void checkInvariant() throws Exception
/*****************************/
{
    if( ( id == ID_WHEN_RENTAL_NOT_IN_EFFECT ) &&
    ( ( rentalCustomer != null ) || ( rentalItem != null ) ) )
    {
        throw new Exception( "Invariant in 'Rental' violated" );
    }
    if( ( id > ID_WHEN_RENTAL_NOT_IN_EFFECT ) &&
      ( ( id > HIGHEST_ALLOWABLE_RENTAL_ID ) ||
        ( rentalCustomer == null ) || ( rentalItem == null ) ) )
    {
        throw new Exception( "Invariant in 'Rental' "violated" );
    }
}
/*********************************
 * Intent: Get the next available number for assigning a rental
 *
 * Returns: The integer on the only line of the local file
```

```java
* FILE_WITH_NEXT_USABLE_RENTAL_NUMBER
*
* Postcondition: The integer on the local file FILE_WITH_NEXT_
* USABLE_RENTAL_NUMBER has been incremented
*
* Exception that exits the application:
* If the file cannot be accessed or the data is not an integer
*/
private static int getNextRentalNumber()
/**********************************/
{
    String nextRentalNumberString = new String(); //
    String form int nextUsableRentalNumberReturn = -1000;
    BufferedReader reader = null;
    FileReader fileReader = null;
    DataOutputStream writer = null;

    try
    {
      // Prepare to read from the file
      FileReader = new FileReader( FILE_WITH_NEXT_USABLE_RENTAL_NUMBER );
      reader = new BufferedReader( fileReader );
      nextRentalNumberString = reader.readLine();
      System.out.println( nextRentalNumberString );

      // Convert to integer
        nextUsableRentalNumberReturn =
      ( new Integer( nextRentalNumberString ) ).intValue();

      // Increment the next available number for assigning a rental
      int incrementedNumber = 1 + nextUsableRentalNumberReturn;
      Integer integerForm = new Integer( incrementedNumber );
      // and replace the existing record
      writer = new DataOutputStream
      (new FileOutputStream( FILE_WITH_NEXT_USABLE_RENTAL_NUMBER));
      writer.writeBytes( integerForm.toString() );
    }
    catch( Exception e )
    {
        System.out.println( e );
        System.out.println( e.toString() );
    }
    return nextUsableRentalNumberReturn;
    }
/*******************************
```

```java
 * Intent: Self-test of this class
 * Known issue: Not migrated to JUnit
 */
public static void main( String[] args ) throws Exception
/**********************************/
{
   // Create concrete classes because all are abstract
   class RentalTest extends Rental
   {
      public RentalTest() throws Exception
      {    super();
      }
      public RentalTest
      ( int anId, RentalCustomer aRentalCustomer,
        RentalItem aRentalItem )
      throws Exception
      {    super( anId, aRentalCustomer, aRentalItem );
      }
   };

   class ConcreteRentalCustomer extends RentalCustomer{};
   class ConcreteRentalItem extends RentalItem{};

   // Create objects
   ConcreteRentalCustomer concreteRentalCustomer =
   new ConcreteRentalCustomer();
   ConcreteRentalItem concreteRentalItem = new ConcreteRentalItem();

   // Test invariant checker first because it is used in testing
   // - - - - - - - - - - - - -

   RentalTest rentalTest0 = new RentalTest();
   // Test 0.1
   rentalTest0.id = 0;
   rentalTest0.rentalCustomer = null;
   rentalTest0.rentalItem = null;
   try
   {    rentalTest0.checkInvariant();
        System.out.println( ''Test 0.1 succeeded'' );
   }
   catch( Exception e )
   { System.out.println( ''Test 0.1: Should be no exception'' ); }

   // Test 0.2
   rentalTest0.id = 1 + HIGHEST_ALLOWABLE_RENTAL_ID;
```

```java
try
{
        rentalTest0.checkInvariant();
        System.out.println( "Test 0.2 succeeded" );
}
catch( Exception e )
{ System.out.println( "Test 0.2: Exception as expected" ); }

// Test 0.3
rentalTest0.id = 1;
rentalTest0.rentalCustomer = null;
rentalTest0.rentalItem = concreteRentalItem;
try{ rentalTest0.checkInvariant(); System.out.println( "Test 0.3
  succeeded" );   }
catch( Exception e )
{ System.out.println( "Test 0.3: Exception as expected" ); }

// Test 0.4
rentalTest0.id = 1;
rentalTest0.rentalCustomer = concreteRentalCustomer;
rentalTest0.rentalItem = null;
try
{
        rentalTest0.checkInvariant();
        System.out.println( "Test 0.4 succeeded" );
}
catch( Exception e )
{ System.out.println( "Test 0.4: Exception as expected" ); }

// Test constructors
// - - - - - - - - - - - - - - - - -

// Test 1.1: Empty constructor

RentalTest rentalTest1 = new RentalTest();
try
{
      rentalTest1.checkInvariant();
      System.out.println( "Test 1.1 succeeded" );
}
catch( Exception e )
{ System.out.println( "Test 1.1: Should be no exception" );
  }

// Non-empty constructor
// Test 1.2: Legal construction
```

```java
RentalTest rentalTest2 =
new RentalTest( 1, concreteRentalCustomer, concreteRentalItem );
try
{
     rentalTest2.checkInvariant();
     System.out.println( ''Test 1.2 succeeded'' ); }
catch( Exception e )
{ System.out.println( ''Test 1.2: Should be no exception'' );
}
// Test 1.2.1: Legal construction with warning
RentalTest rentalTest2point1 =
new RentalTest( 99999900, concreteRentalCustomer,
               concreteRentalItem );
try
{
     rentalTest2point1.checkInvariant();
     System.out.println( ''Test 1.2 succeeded'' );
     }
catch( Exception e )
{
  System.out.println( ''Test 1.2: Should be no exception'' );
}

// Illegal constructions

// Test 1.3
try
{
     RentalTest rentalTest3 =
     new RentalTest( 0, concreteRentalCustomer,
        concreteRentalItem );
}
catch( Exception e )
{ System.out.println( ''Test 1.3: Exception as expected'' );
}

// Test 1.4
try
{
     RentalTest rentalTest4 =
     new RentalTest( 1 + HIGHEST_ALLOWABLE_RENTAL_ID,
     concreteRentalCustomer, concreteRentalItem );
}
catch( Exception e )
{ System.out.println( ''Test 1.4: Exception as expected'' ); }
```

```java
// Test 1.5
try

{
    RentalTest rentalTest5 =
    new RentalTest( 1, null, concreteRentalItem );
}
catch( Exception e )
{ System.out.println( "Test 1.5: Exception as expected" ); }
// Test 2: of getNextRentalNumber()
System.out.println( "current integer <-->" + getNextRentalNumber() );
}

/***********************************
* Intent: set the id if the parameter is legal; warn if the number
* of rentals is getting close to the maximum.
*
* Precondition:
* anId > RENTAL_ID_WHEN_NOT_IN_EFFECT &&
* anId <= HIGHEST_ALLOWABLE_RENTAL_ID
*
* Postconditions:
* (1) id == anId
* (2) if the rental number is within TOLERANCE_ON_RENTAL_ID of
* HIGHEST_ALLOWABLE_RENTAL_ID, a warning is present on the console.
*
* Exception: if preconditions violated
*
* Known issue: method "log()" to be implemented
*/
private void setId( int anId ) throws Exception
/*****************************/
{
    if( ( ID_WHEN_RENTAL_NOT_IN_EFFECT < anId ) &&
      ( anId <= HIGHEST_ALLOWABLE_RENTAL_ID ) )
    {
        id = anId;
        if( anId > HIGHEST_ALLOWABLE_RENTAL_ID - 1000 )
        { /*tbs:
        Log.log( "setNumber() in 'Rental' set 'id' " +
        "within 1000 of highest allowed id" );
        */
        System.out.println( "WARNING: Rental ID within " +
        TOLERANCE_ON_RENTAL_ID + " of highest allowed value" );
        }
    }
}
```

```
  else // do not change id
  {
     throw new Exception( "setNumber() in Rental tried setting id " +
     "out of bounds: " + anId );
   }
  }


}
/**== == == == == == == == == == == == == == == == ==
* . . . . . . .
*/ abstract class RentalCustomer
{
}


 /**== == == == == == == == == == == == == == == ==
* . . . . . . .
*/
abstract class RentalItem
{
    private String title = "RentalItem title not assigned yet";
    public float length = 0; // 'public' for demo purposes

    // Static constants
    private static final float MAX_RENTAL_ITEM_TITLE_LENGTH = 20;

    /***********************************
    * Intent: Requirement http://tbd.tbd.tbd#3.2.DVD.1.1
    *
    * Postcondition:
    *   If 'aTitle' consists of English alphanumeric characters in lower
    * or upper case, and punctuation marks !, :, ", or ?, then title ==
    * aTitle if length of 'aTitle' <= MAX_DVD_TITLE_LENGTH
    * otherwise title == first MAX_DVD_TITLE_LENGTH characters of
    * 'aTitle'
    */
    private void setTitle( String aTitle )
    /***************************/
    {
// Check that 'aTitle' consists of English alphanumeric characters in
// lower or upper case, or punctuation marks !, :, ', or ?.

        boolean charactersAcceptable = true; // make false when
          unacceptable character found
        char ch = 'x';
        for( int i = 0; i < aTitle.length(); ++i )
        {
```

```
        ch = aTitle.charAt( i ); // temporary name for clarity

  // Make 'charactersAcceptable' false if 'ch' unacceptable
  // true otherwise
          charactersAcceptable = charactersAcceptable &&
          (
          ( ( ch >= 'a' ) && ( ch <= 'z' ) ) ||
          ( ( ch >= 'A' ) && ( ch <= 'Z' ) ) ||
          ch == '!' || ch == ':' || ch == '''' || ch == '?'
          );
  }
  if( charactersAcceptable )
  {
     title = aTitle;
  } // (otherwise leave 'title' unchanged)
  }
}
```

22.15.2 Code Listing for *EncounterCharacter*

Source code for the *EncounterCharacter* class in the Encounter video game (described in Section 22.10) is shown in Listing 22.3. Source code for all of the Encounter case study is available online.

Listing 22.3: Sample code from the Encounter video game implementation

```
package Encounter.EncounterCharacters;

/* Class Name: EncounterCharacter
* Date: 01/13/2000
* Copyright Notice  : copyright (c) 1999-2000 by Eric J. Braude
*/
import java.awt.*;
import java.io.*;
import FrameworkRPG.Characters.*;
import TestUtilities.*;

/** Base class for the characters of the Encounter game. SDD reference:
* 6.2.1
* <p> Invariants: The values of qualValueI[] are >= 0
* @author Eric Braude, Tom VanCourt
* @version 0.2
*/
```

```java
public class EncounterCharacter extends GameCharacter
{
  /** Total quality points at initialization.*/
   private static final float QUAL_TOTAL_INIT = 100.0f;

   // Symbols used when other classes refer to specific qualities.
   /** Symbol for one of a character's qualities */
   public static final String QUAL_CONCENTRATION = ``concentration'';
   /** Symbol for one of a character's qualities */
   public static final String QUAL_INTELLIGENCE = "intelligence'';
   /** Symbol for one of a character's qualities */
   public static final String QUAL_PATIENCE = "patience'';
   /** Symbol for one of a character's qualities */
   public static final String QUAL_STAMINA = "stamina'';
   /** Symbol for one of a character's qualities */
   public static final String QUAL_STRENGTH = "strength''; /** Qualities that
      each Encounter character posesses <p>Req: 3.2.EC.1.2 */

private static final String[] qualityTypeS =
{ QUAL_CONCENTRATION, QUAL_STAMINA, QUAL_INTELLIGENCE, QUAL_PATIENCE,
      QUAL_STRENGTH
}

/* INSTANCE VARIABLES */

/** Values of the qualities <p> Requirement 3.2.EC.1.2 */
private float[] qualValueI = new float[ qualityTypeS.length ];

/** Name of the GIF file containing the character's image.
* The character in this image is assumed to be facing left.
* Select this character's height, relative to heights of other
* characters, by padding the top and bottom with transparent pixels. No
* padding gives the tallest possible character.
*/
private String imageFileNameI = null;

/* CONSTRUCTORS */

/** Allocate initial total quality points equally among the qualities.
* <p> Requirement: 3.2.EC.1.2 (quality value initialization)
*/
protected EncounterCharacter()
{   super();
     for( int i = 0; i < qualityTypeS.length; ++i )
            qualValueI[i] = QUAL_TOTAL_INIT / qualityTypeS.length;
}
```

```
/** Construct a new character using the given name and image file.
* <p> Requirement:    3.2.EC.1.1 (character naming)
* @param   nameP     Printable name for the character.
* @param   imageFileP  Filename, relative to document base, .... for
* character image.
*/
protected EncounterCharacter( String nameP, String imageFileP )
{    this();
    setName( nameP );
    imageFileNameI = imageFileP;
}
/** Construct a new character using the given name.
* <p> Requirement:       3.2.EC.1.1 (character naming)
* @param    nameP       Printable name for the character.
*/
protected EncounterCharacter( String nameP )
{ this( nameP, null );
}
/* METHODS */
/** Requirement 3.2.EC.3.2: "Configurability of Encounter character
* quality values.''
* Synchronization holds qualityValueI constant even with other threads
* running.
* <p> SDD reference: 6.1.2.1.1
* <p> Invariants: see the class invariants
* <p> Preconditions: qualityP is in qualityTypesS[]
*    AND qualityValueP >= 0
*    AND qualityValueP <= the sum of the quality values
* <p> Postconditions: qualityP has the value qualityValueP
*    AND the remaining quality values are in the same proportion as prior
*    to invocation, except that values less than some tolerance are
*    zero.
* @param qualityP Quality whose value is to be adjusted.
* @param qualityValueP The value to set this quality to.
*/ public synchronized void adjustQuality(String qualityP, float qualityValueP)
{
    // Value of the quality to be changed
    float qualityValueM = qualValueI[ indexOf( qualityP ) ];
    // Save the sum of the values
    float originalSumM = sumOfQualities();
    // pc Set the stated quality to the desired amount, adjusted to the
    // threshold value.
    setQuality( qualityP, qualityValueP );
    // pc If the caller adjusts the only non-zero quality value,
    // divide the adjustment amount equally among all other qualities.
```

```java
    if ( originalSumM == qualityValueM )
  {
      float qualityDiffEach = (originalSumM - qualityValueP) / (qualityTypeS.
        length - 1);
        for ( int i = 0; i < qualityTypeS.length; ++i )
          if ( !qualityTypeS[i].equalsIgnoreCase( qualityP ) )
            setQuality( qualityTypeS[i], qualityDiffEach );
  }
else {
  /* Compute factor ("proportionM'') by which all other qualities must
   * change.
   * Example: if the values were 1,3,5 (i.e. sum 9), and the first quality
   * is changed
   * from 1 to 2, then ""3'' and "5'' change from 8/9 of the total to 7/9
   * of the total, so each should be multiplied by 7/8, i.e., by (9-2)/
   * (9-1).
   */
  float proportionM = (originalSumM - qualityValueP) / (originalSumM -
    qualityValueM);
//pc Adjust the remaining qualities, retaining their mutual proportion
  for ( int i = 0; i < qualityTypeS.length; ++i )
    if ( !qualityTypeS[i].equalsIgnoreCase( qualityP ) )
        setQuality( qualityTypeS[i], qualValueI[i] * proportionM );
  }
}
/** Get a copy of the list of names of quality values.
* @return   working copies of name strings representing qualities.
*/
public static String[] getQualityTypes()
{
 String [] returnListM = new String[ qualityTypeS.length ]; // Copy the
   string array.
    for ( int i = 0; i < qualityTypeS.length; i++ )          // Copy each string.
        returnListM[i] = new String( qualityTypeS[i] );
return returnListM;   // Return the copy.
}
/** Returns the value of the specified quality.
* <p>Precondition:      qualityP is a valid member of qualityTypeS[]

* @param   qualityP     The quality we want the value for.
* @return    The value of the specified quality.
*/
public float getQualityValue( String qualityP )
{   return qualValueI[ indexOf( qualityP ) ];
}
```

```java
/** Quality values below this threshold are set to zero to avoid having
 *  the game go on for an indeterminate amount of time.
 * <p>Requirement: e.g. 3.2.EC.1.2 (lower limit on non-zero quality
 *  values)
 * @return      Tolerance value
*/
static final float getTolerance()
{   return 0.5f;
}


/** Returns the index of the specified quality.
* <p> Precondition:      qualityP is in qualityTypeS[], give or take
* capitalization.
* @param              qualityP   The quality we are searching for.
* @return             The quality index.
*/
private static int indexOf( String qualityP )
{
int returnIndexM = -1;          // Default to "missing'' value.
for( int i = 0; i < qualityTypeS.length; ++i )    // Search quality name table.
if( qualityTypeS[ i ].equalsIgnoreCase( qualityP ) )   // Quality name match?
{
returnIndexM = i;          // Note the index value.
  break;
}
return returnIndexM;
}


/** Set default maximum allowable number of characters in names of
* characters.
* <p>Requirement:    3.2.EC.1.1 (limit on character name length)
* @return            Maximum number of characters allowed in a
                     character name
*/
protected int maxNumCharsInName()
{     return 15;
}


/** Set a quality value without regard to the values of other qualities.
* Truncate any value below the threshold value down to zero.
* Synchronization prevents changes to qualityValueI while other
* threads are using it.
* <p>Requirements:  3.2.EC.2 (lower limit on non-zero quality
* values),
* <p>Precondition:      qualityP is a valid member of qualityTypeS[]
```

```
* <p>Postcondition:   Quality values are greater than tolerance
*                     or are 0.
*
* @param   qualityP   The quality to set the value of.
* @param   valueP     The value to set the quality to.
*/
public synchronized void setQuality( String qualityP, float valueP )
{
if( valueP < getTolerance() )
    qualValueI[ indexOf( qualityP ) ] = 0.0f;
else
qualValueI[ indexOf( qualityP ) ] = valueP;
}
/** Display the character
* <p>Requirements: 2.1.2.1 (character displayed in game Area),
*   3.2.PC.1 (character image selection),
*   3.2.PQ.1 (character image in quality update window)
* @param   compP       UI component in which to draw the character
* @param   drawP       Graphics context for doing the drawing.
* @param   posP        Pixel coordinates within compP for the center of
* the image.
* @param   heightPixP  Desired image height, in pixels.
* @param   faceLeftP   <tt>true</tt> if character faces left,
*                      <tt>false if faces right.
*/
public void showCharacter(Component compP, Graphics drawP, Point posP,
int heightPixP, boolean faceLeftP)
{
    if( imageFileNameI == null)
    {  // No image file name. Print the character name instead.
       drawP.setColor(Color.magenta);              // Normally a visible
                                                         color.

       FontMetrics fm = drawP.getFontMetrics();
       drawP.drawString( getName(),              // Print the name, centered
        posP.x - fm.stringWidth(getName()) / 2, // at the character location.
        posP.y - fm.getHeight() / 2 );
}
else    // File name was provided. Draw the image file.
{    Image chImage = compP.getToolkit().getImage( imageFileNameI );
     int imageWidth = chImage.getWidth( compP ); // Raw size of the image.
     int imageHeight = chImage.getHeight( compP );
     int scaledWidth = imageWidth * heightPixP / imageHeight; // Scale width same
                                                                as height.
// Assume that the normal image faces left. Decide whether to reverse
   the image.
```

```
if( faceLeftP )
        drawP.drawImage( chImage,         // Draw the image as given,
        posP.x - scaledWidth/2, posP.y - heightPixP/2, // scaled and centered.
        posP.x + scaledWidth/2, posP.y + heightPixP/2,
        0, 0, imageWidth-1, imageHeight-1, compP );
    else
    drawP.drawImage( chImage, // Draw the image reversed,
      posP.x + scaledWidth/2, posP.y - heightPixP/2, // scaled and centered.
      posP.x - scaledWidth/2, posP.y + heightPixP/2,

        0, 0, imageWidth-1, imageHeight-1, compP );
}
}       // End of showCharacter.
/** Computes the sum of the quality values.
* Synchronization makes sure that another thread won't change
* qualityValueI
* while this thread is part-way through computing the total.
* <p> Requirements:   3.2.EC.3.2 (proportions among quality values)
* @return  The sum of the player's qualities, a value 0 or greater.
*/
public synchronized float sumOfQualities()
{
float sumM = 0.0f;
for( int i = 0; i < qualityTypeS.length; ++i )
    sumM += qualValueI[i];
return sumM;
}
} // end of EncounterCharacter
```

22.16 EXERCISES

1. In your own words, describe what is meant by code being "correct."

2. Suppose that you are about to code a method. What are the major sources describing for you what this method is to do?

3. Provide an example of a domain class, a design class, and an implementation class that might be used in the implementation of a bank ATM application. Explain why you chose each class.

4. Specify the intent, preconditions, and postconditions of a function that computes the square root of an input parameter x.

5. Explain why the use of global variables works against the principle of information hiding. Give an example of when this can lead to program errors.

6. The following function returns the correct value, but violates one of the implementation practices described in this chapter. Which implementation practice is violated, and how might it lead to a problem in the future? How would you fix the problem?

```
// compute amount of interest and return
float computeInterest (float balance, float interestRate)
{
// compute interest earned
balance = balance * interestRate;
return balance;
}
```

7. Describe two to four advantages and one or two disadvantages of enforcing coding standards.

8. For each of the error handling methods described in Section 22.6.1 give an example of when it is sensible to use the method.

9. What does the following function compute? How would you modify the function using comments and more descriptive variable names to make it easier to understand its purpose?

```
int compute (int a )
{
    int result = 1, num = 1;
    while (num <= a) {
result *= 1;
num++;
}
return result;
}
// Intent: Compute the factorial of the input parameter
// Precondition: 0 <= factorialNumber
// Postcondition: Return factorialNumber!
int computeFactorial (int factorialNumber )
{
    int current = 1; factorial = 1;
    while (current <= factorialNumber) {
    factorial *= current;
  current++;
  }
  return factorial;
}
```

10. Describe how the principle of "Enforce Intentions" leads to improved code quality. Provide at least three examples to support your answer.

11. Choose three of the "good practices" listed in this chapter and describe exceptional situations in which they would not apply.

12. Code is rarely perfect. Give three criticisms of the code in the case studies.

TEAM EXERCISE

Implementation

Implement key parts of your application to form a prototype.

BIBLIOGRAPHY

1. McConnell, Steve, *"Code Complete: A Practical Handbook of Software Construction,"* 2nd Ed, Microsoft Press, 2004.
2. Horstmann, Cay. S., *"Practical Object-Oriented Development in C++ and Java,"* John Wiley & Sons, 1997.
3. Ambler, Scott, *"The Object Primer: The Application Developer's Guide to Object Orientation and the UML,"* Cambridge University Press, 2001.
4. Gamma, Erich, Richard Helm, Ralph Johnson, and John Vlissides, *"Design Patterns: Elements of Reusable Object-Oriented Software,"* Addison-Wesley, 1999.
5. Ambler, Scott. www.ambysoft.com (1999) [accessed 12/13/09].
6. Oman P., J. Hagemeister, and D. Ash, "A Definition and Taxonomy for Software Maintainability." University of Idaho, Moscow, Software Engineering Test Laboratory Report #91-08-TR, ID 83843 (1992).
7. Booch, Grady, James Rumbaugh, Ivar Jacobson, *"The Unified Modeling Language User Guide,"* Addison-Wesley Professional, 2005.
8. Eclipse Project. http://www.eclipse.org/eclipse/index.php [accessed 12/13/09].
9. OpenOffice Project. http://www.openoffice.org/dev_docs/source/templates/code [accessed 12/13/09].
10. OpenOffice Developers Guide. http://wiki.services.openoffice.org/wiki/Documentation/DevGuide/OpenOffice.org_Developers_Guide [accessed 12/13/09].
11. OpenOffice Project. http://api.openoffice.org/source/browse/api/odk/examples/DevelopersGuide/Spreadsheet/ViewSample.java?rev=1.3&content-type=text/vnd.viewcvs-markup [accessed 12/13/09].

23

Quality and Metrics in Implementation

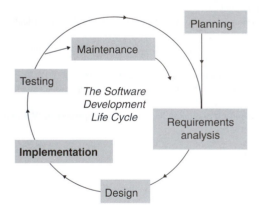

- How do you assess the degree of sufficiency of an implementation?

- How do you measure the degree of robustness?

- What metrics are there for flexibility?

- Reusability metrics? Efficiency? Reliability? Scalability?

- How does one assess the degree of security of an implementation?

- How do code inspections improve code quality? What about code reviews?

- How does pair programming improve code quality?

Figure 23.1 The context and learning goals for this chapter

The quality of an implementation can be measured with attributes similar to those used for assessing a design. The first part of this chapter describes these attributes. The second discusses code inspections—an effective quality process for discovering defects before code is tested. As usual, most metrics described below are meaningful only in the context of comparative data from past projects. In addition, each metric is most effective when used in conjunction with other metrics rather than by itself.

As mentioned in precious chapters, there are two sides to assessing the quality of implementations. One is the *verification* side, in which quality is assessed based on looking at the source code. This chapter discusses the verification side. This includes code inspection, the subject of the second part of this chapter. Included in that part is *pair programming*, a kind of continual inspection favored in agile projects. The other side of implementation quality is an assessment of the completed code. That side is *validation*—essentially, testing—which is the next part of this book.

23.1 QUALITY OF IMPLEMENTATION

The qualities of an implementation can be categorized as shown in Table 23.1. For each category, the two extremes are captured with a rough scale on which 0 indicates low quality and 10 high. More precise measurements for these categories are discussed in this chapter.

Some of these qualities support others, depending on the application. For example, robust code is less sensitive to anomalous conditions, and thus makes application more reliable since they stay operational

Table 23.1 Rough measures of quality of an implementation

Degree of	Rough metric	
. . .	0 . . .	10 (maximum score)
sufficiency	*Fails to implement the corresponding design specification*	
		Satisfies all of the design specifications for this element
robustness	*Will cause crash on any anomalous event*	
		Recovers from all anomalous events as well as can be expected
flexibility	*Will have to be replaced entirely if the design or requirements change*	
		As easily adaptable to reasonable changes as can be expected
reusability	*Cannot be used in other applications*	
		Usable in all reasonably related applications without modification
efficiency	*Fails to satisfy speed or data storage requirement*	
		Satisfies speed or data storage requirement with reasonable margin
reliability	*Obviously won't achieve required mean time between failure*	
		Obviously will achieve required mean time between failure
scalability	*Can't be used as the basis of a larger version*	
		Is an outstanding basis for a version with much larger scope
security	*Security not accounted for at all*	
		No known manner of breaching security is known

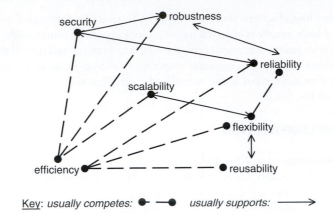

Figure 23.2 Supporting and competing relationships among implementation qualities

longer. On the other hand, some of these goals compete. The goals of reliability and flexibility often compete because flexibility tends to introduce increased opportunity for error. It is difficult, frequently impossible, for a design to enjoy all of these qualities at once. Figure 23.2 shows common support and contradictions among them. Software engineers trade off properties by prioritizing qualities. Agile development, for example, places a lower priority on flexibility and reusability than on sufficiency and reliability.

The sections that follow elaborate upon each of these implementation qualities.

23.1.1 The Sufficiency of an Implementation

The *sufficiency* of an implementation measures the percentage of the requirements and design specifications actually implemented. Although we expect to implement all requirements, time limitations often force us to implement in order of priority, omitting some. The sufficiency of an implementation can be calculated from the following formula (which requires us to have a completely specified list of detailed requirements).

Percentage of detailed requirements *that are implemented.*

If the SDD is detailed, the design specifies classes and methods. Another measure for the sufficiency of an implementation is as follows.

Percentage of methods *specified in the design that are implemented.*

A rougher metric is the following.

Percentage of classes *specified in the design that are implemented.*

A problem with the latter is how to account for classes specified in the SDD that are only partially implemented.

1. Assess **input** to the method
   a. Anomalous parameter values
   b. Anomalous global variables
   c. Anomalous event variables
2. Assess **dependent methods**
   Measure extent of compromise

Figure 23.3 Assessing the robustness of a method

23.1.2 The Robustness of an Implementation

An implementation's *robustness* is the extent to which it handles anomalous input (i.e., input whose form or content is unexpected). In the final analysis, the work of an application is performed by its methods. However, not every method needs to be robust in every way. For example, suppose that a medicine is highly toxic when taken in large quantities. A method that computes doses for it must be as robust as possible. On the other hand, a method that takes input and creates a string for displaying an automobile does not need to be as robust. There are two avenues for assessing the robustness of a method, as listed in Figure 23.3.

To assess the robustness of a method relative to its potential inputs, we investigate the preconditions. First, we assess their completeness. In other words, we ensure that every assumption made by the method is expressed in the preconditions. We then assess whether the method defends against possible violations of each precondition. Consider, for example, the *Rectangle* class in Listing 23.1.

How robust is the method *setArea()*? Let's assume that we do not want to restrict the size of the *float* inputs.

Listing 23.1: A *Rectangle* class

```
/**=======================================
*/
public class Rectangle
{

    // VARIABLES ===================================

    float area = 0;
    float length = 0;
    float width = 0;

    // CONSTRUCTORS ===================================

    /************************************
    */
    public Rectangle()
    /************************************/
    {
    }
```

```
/**************************************
*/ public Rectangle( float aLength, float aWidth )
/**************************************/
{
    length = aLength;
    width = aWidth;
}

// METHODS ========================================

/**************************************
* Preconditions:
* (1) length > = 0
* (2) width > = 0
*
* Postconditions:
* (1) area == length * width
*/
public void setArea()
/**************************************/
{
    area = length * width;
}
}
```

Note 1: The first question is whether the preconditions are complete. In view of the stated desire not to restrict the values of *length* and *width*, the preconditions appear to be adequate. (One is not always correct in one's intentions, but the point is that they are documented and so can be revisited. Undocumented intentions, on the other hand, lead to confusion and greater errors.)

Note 2: Next, we assess whether the method allows a reasonable recovery if the precondition fails. Since there is no provision for this in the code, the method's robustness is compromised. A check on *length* and *width* that leaves *area* unchanged, and that generates reasonable notices, would elevate the method's robustness.

Listing 23.2 is a more robust version of *Rectangle*. It restricts the values of fields to what is intended, a practice that usually makes computing more robust. The objection in Note 2 above is also addressed. Nevertheless, Listing 2 is still subject to criticisms, which are discussed below.

Listing 23.2: A more robust *Rectangle* class

```
/**==========================================
* Rectangle class, including safeguards for limits on area
*
* Known Issues:
* (1) Limits dimensions to floats, not double.
```

```java
* (2) See known issue(s) for individual method(s).
*/
public class MoreRobustRectangle
{

   // VARIABLES ======================================

   // Class invariant (intent: the corresponding area is limited):
   // 0 <= length && 0 <= width && ( length * width <= Float.MAX_VALUE )

   private float area = 0;
   private float length = 0;
   private float width = 0;

   // CONSTRUCTORS ===================================

   /***********************************
   */
   public MoreRobustRectangle()
   /***********************************/
   {
   }


   /***********************************
   * Intent: Robust constructor
   * Postconditions:
   * (1) If the class invariant is true, length == aLength && width == aWidth
   * (2) Otherwise
   *     (i) a message has been logged to the log file described in ErrorUtility
   *         stating that the class invariant was violated and
   *     (ii) the same message appears on the console
   */
   public MoreRobustRectangle( float aLength, float aWidth )
   /***********************************/
   {
      if( classInvariantHolds( aLength, aWidth ) )
      {
         length = aLength;
         width = aWidth;
      }
      else  // Postcondition (2)
      {
         String errorMessage = "Attempt in RobustRectangle(float,float) " +
         "to use values that make the area too large. Ignored";
         ErrorUtility.logAndReportToConsole( errorMessage );
      }
   }
```

```
// METHODS =======================================

/****************************************
* Intent: A single location for checking required class invariant.
*
* Returns: true if the class invariant would be valid after construction
* with length == aLength and width == aWidth; false otherwise
*
* Known issue: Does not deal with aLength > Double.MAX_VALUE or
* aWidth > Double.MAX_VALUE
*/
private boolean classInvariantHolds( float aLength, float aWidth )
/****************************************/
{
      // Create Double form to allow check on product of floats
      double aLengthDouble = ( new Double( aLength ) ).doubleValue();
      double aWidthDouble = ( new Double( aWidth ) ).doubleValue();

      // double form of Float.MAX_VALUE
      double floatMaxValue = ( new Double( Float.MAX_VALUE )).
doubleValue();

      return
      (
      aLength >= 0 &&
      aWidth >= 0 &&
      aLengthDouble * aWidthDouble <= floatMaxValue
      );
}

/****************************************
* Precondition: The class invariant
*
* Postcondition: area == length * width
*/
public void setArea()
/****************************************/
{
   if( classInvariantHolds( length, width ) )
   {
      area = length * width;
   }
   else // Postcondition (2)
   {
      String errorMessage = "Attempt in MoreRobustRectangle.setArea() " +
      "to use out-of-bound value(s). Ignored";
      ErrorUtility.logAndReportToConsole( errorMessage );
```

```java
      }
   }

   /***************************************
   * Precondition: The class invariant
   * Postcondition: length == aLength
   */
   public void setLength( float aLength )
   /****************************************/
   {
      // Safety check on the precondition
      if( classInvariantHolds( aLength, width ) )
      {
         length = aLength;
      }
      else
      {
         String errorMessage = "Attempt in MoreRobustRectangle.setLength()" +
         "to use out-of-bound value for length. Ignored";
         ErrorUtility.logAndReportToConsole( errorMessage );
      }
   }

   /****************************************
   * Precondition: The class invariant
   * Postcondition: width == aWidth
   */
   public void setWidth( float aWidth )
   /****************************************/
   {
      // Safety check on the precondition
      if( classInvariantHolds( length, aWidth ) )
      {
         width = aWidth;
      }
      else
      {
         String errorMessage = "Attempt in MoreRobustRectangle.setWidth()" +
         "to use out-of-bound value for width. Ignored";
         ErrorUtility.logAndReportToConsole( errorMessage );
      }
   }
}
```

<u>A metric for each method</u>: No robustness = 0, some = 0.5, complete = 1

<u>A metric for classes</u>

$$\frac{\sum\limits_{all\ method} (\text{degree of method's robustness on scale of 0 to 1})}{\text{Number of methods}}$$

Figure 23.4 A robustness metric for classes on a scale of 0 to 1

A metric for the robustness of a block of code is shown in Figure 23.4.

Let's calculate the robustness of *MoreRobustRectangle*. This class has six methods (we include constructors). The null constructor is guaranteed to leave all values zero, so it respects the class invariant, and is robust. The *checkInvariant()* method is robust. The rest of the methods check on the preconditions but do nothing if the precondition is not valid. We can give these the score of ½. The formula in Figure 23.4 thus yields the following robustness measure for *RobustRectangle*.

$$(1 + 1 + 1/2 + 1/2 + 1/2 + 1/2)/6 = 67\%$$

It is considerably more robust than *Rectangle*, which has a low score.

23.1.3 The Flexibility of an Implementation

An implementation is *flexible* if it can easily accommodate new or changed requirements. Figures 23.5 and 23.6 list implementation techniques that increase flexibility.

---

1. **Document** precisely and thoroughly
   - Reason: cannot adapt code that you don't understand
2. **Name constants**
   - Reason: understandability
3. **Hide** where possible
   - Variables and methods
   - Reason: reducing complexity increases understanding
4. **Collect** common code
   - As helper methods and classes
   - Reason: reduce complexity

Figure 23.5 Factors in implementation that increase flexibility, 1 of 2

---

5. **Reduce** dependency on **global variables**
   - and on any variables external to the method
   - Parameterize methods
   - Reason: allows method to be used in other contexts
6. Program at a **general level**
   - Reason: applies to more situations
7. Use **understandable** variable and function **names**

Figure 23.6 Factors in implementation that increase flexibility, 2 of 2

We discuss these factors below and subject the code above for *RobustRectangle* to each factor.

1. *Document.* The idea is that the more effectively code is documented, the more easily it can be reused. For example, we can still fault the overall class description in *MoreRobustRectangle* for lacking sufficient description of the purpose of a class. One could possibly fault the "variables" section as lacking a description, although none is needed where obvious.

2. *Name Constants.* When constants are named rather than being stated explicitly, the code becomes more easily targeted to new uses. There are several places in the *MoreRobustRectangle* code where constants would have improved its flexibility— for example, naming *Float.MAX_VALUE* as *MAX_ALLOWABLE_AREA*.
   As another example, instead of the statements

```
private float length = 0;
private float width = 0;
```

   we could state the following:

```
private static final float DEFAULT_LENGTH = 0;
private static final float DEFAULT _WIDTH = 0;

private float length = DEFAULT _LENGTH;
private float width = DEFAULT _WIDTH;
```

3. *Hide Where Possible.* In software engineering, our main adversary is complexity. One useful technique for combating complexity is to hide from view the parts that are not relevant at the time. "Hiding" applies to code that is not available to other code that should not need it. Class members that are not to be accessed by methods of other classes are thus made *private* (or *protected* if inheritance is required). Classes that are not to be accessed by methods of classes outside their package are not made *public*.

4. *Collect Common Code.* When common code is collected into a method, the result is greater flexibility; otherwise the common code would have to be changed in multiple places. *RobustRectangle* does a good job of this by collecting the checking of the invariant in one place: *classInvariantHolds()*. In this respect, then, the code is flexible.

5. *Reduce Dependency on Global Variables.* This means that each method and each class should be self-contained so that they can be mixed and matched.
   Perusing the methods of *RobustRectangle*, we see that the only method referring to an attribute of the class is *setArea()*, which refers to *area*. In principle, we can eliminate *area* as a variable, eliminating *setArea()* and introducing *getArea()* that returns the area. This is an improvement in flexibility, but it could collide with another quality: efficiency. If the application requires very frequent use of *area*, it may be preferable to compute it once and refer to it often.

6. *Program Generically.* Here we ask whether the code is at a sufficiently abstract level to be usable for additional or changed requirements. It is possible to approach this at the design level by using abstract classes, but our focus here is on *implementation* flexibility. Flexibility depends on the direction that an application is taking. For example, if this class is to be part of a 3D application, we may want *area()* to compute the area on the monitor of a rectangle in space, seen at an angle—that is, taking perspective into account. This is a far more generic computation.

7. *Use Understandable Variable and Function Names.* In discussing flexibility, we indicated that variables and methods must be understandable for the code to be flexible. In fact, the very name of a variable or method is an important way of making it understandable. Names should be as explicit as possible without becoming cumbersome. Figure 23.7 shows examples.

Poor	Better	Best
Dose	dailyDosage	maxDailyDosage
mDD		minDailyDosage
		commonDailyDosage

Figure 23.7 Naming variables to improve code quality

Table 23.2 Metrics for various attributes of an implementation

Attribute	Metric
1. Degree of documentation	a) Percentage of comment lines b) Percentage of commented lines
2. Extent of named constants	Percentage of numerals with names (see Note 1)
3. Hide where possible	a) Standard deviation of class size (see Note 2) b) Standard deviation of method size
4. Degree to which common code is collected	Percentage of repeated code paragraphs (see Note 3)
5. Degree of dependency on global variables	a) Percentage of public fields b) Percentage of protected fields c) Percentage of unlabeled fields
6. Degree of generic programming	Percentage of generic classes
7. Use understandable variable and function names	Percentage of names clearly difficult to understand

Metrics for robustness can be based on the attributes of robustness. One can measure them as in Table 23.2, probably using an automated process, or manually by taking random samples from the code base. (Counting all lines manually is usually impractical).

The following elaborates on the indicated points in Table 23.2.

Note 1: One looks for plain numbers in the code and counts those not present in a definition, such as "135" in the following:

```
final int TANK_CAPACITY = 135;
```

Note 2: High standard deviation means high deviation from the average. Measured over a large number of classes, a deviation higher than the usual means an unusual variation in class size. This is not necessarily bad, but it does suggest that the largest and smallest classes should be reviewed, focusing on their size.

Note 3: One considers paragraphs of code, selected at random, and determines the percentage of paragraphs that are repeated at least once (or at least twice, etc.).

Note 4: The higher the percentage of public fields compared with the normal percentage, the more global the variables.

23.1.4 The Reusability of an Implementation

Reusability of code is the capacity for its use in other applications. Making a component more flexible usually makes it more reusable. Reusability is possible at the method, class, and package levels, although the method level is usually too granular. To make a class reusable, the following factors are considered.

Table 23.3 Metrics for reusability

Attribute	Metric
1. The matching of classes to a real-world concept	Percent of classes that clearly match an understandable concept (see Note 1)
2. Level of abstraction	Average number of inheritance levels from a class in the Java library (see Note 2)
3. Degree of description	Percent of classes that are clearly documented (see Note 3)

1. The matching of the class to a **real-world concept** is important, otherwise developers are unlikely to understand it.

2. The **level of abstraction** should be high enough to cover many applications but low enough to allow substance. For example, if a development organization creates insurance industry applications, the level of a class *CadillacEldoradoInsurancePolicy* is probably too low and *Policy* too high, as far as reusability is concerned. An *AutomobilePolicy* class, on the other hand, would be substantive and probably reusable.

3. The **reliability** of code promotes reusability, otherwise no one is likely to reuse the class. It should contain complete *error checking*, for example. In a somewhat circular process, classes that are widely used become trusted and understood, and thus more widely reused.

Metrics for reusability can be based on the attributes of reusability. One can measure them as in Table 23.3, based on an automated process or by manual random samples taken from the code base. (Counting all lines manually is usually impractical).

Note 1: This can be calculated on a random sample by taking a vote among inspectors, for example.

Note 2: The higher this number, the more likely the class can be reused.

Note 3: The better a class is described, the more likely it is to be reusable. Section 23.1.4 described measures of documentation, and those can be used here too.

23.1.5 The Efficiency of an Implementation

Recall that there are two kinds of efficiency: process speed and storage use. Efficiency requirements may or may not be specified in the SRS. For example, suppose that one is specifying the requirements for a calendar application; one should specify time limits such as "the application will reset all calendars with new appointments within ¼ second." When efficiency requirements are not specified, we apply common sense limits as best we can. Neither space nor time is unlimited in practice. For example, a Web site shopping cart application may not specify maximum delays, but it is common sense that the user should not wait more than a minute for a credit card approval, excluding Internet delays.

An appropriate metric for speed efficiency is the fraction of the speed required. For example, if an application is required to process a transaction in at most half a second but actually takes two seconds, we can fairly say that its efficiency measure is ½ /2 =25%. If an application were faster than required, we would still like to be able to measure its speed efficiency. The same formula applies. For example, if the application processes transactions in one quarter second on average, then its efficiency measure would be ½ /¼ = 200%. It has high quality in this respect, with 100% being the success baseline.

An appropriate metric for space efficiency is similar. For example, if an application is required to use no more than 2 MB of disk space but uses 5 MB, then we can fairly say that its space efficiency is 2/5 = 40%. Once again, the formula applies even if usage exceeds requirements. For example, if the application were to use only 1 MB, we would rate its storage use efficiency as 2/1 = 200%.

23.1.6 The Reliability of an Implementation

Reliability is a quality that goes further than sufficiency and robustness. To "rely" on an application is to be sure first that it does what it is supposed to; this includes sufficiency, as described above. Reliability can be considered sometimes to include robustness, where the application behaves appropriately in the presence of anomalous input. An application that is sufficient and robust may still have defects and thus be less than reliable, however. For example, an application may be required to add any pair of integers, each between – 100,000 and 100,000. It can be sufficient in that it does the job required and robust in that it displays an error message for any input not an integer between –100,000 and 100,000. However, if the application crashes after successfully computing additions for an hour (perhaps because of uncontrolled memory use), it is not reliable. Defects affecting reliability are found by inspection and testing.

The most commonly used metric for reliability is the *mean time between failure* (MTBF). To measure MTBF, one first defines "failure." Typically, this means that the application has to be restarted. Run the application several times, for significant durations, and calculate MTBF as follows:

MTBF = (total time up and running)/(number of failures detected in that time)

23.1.7 The Scalability of an Implementation

An implementation is *scalable* if it is sufficient for all reasonably anticipated homogeneous growth (i.e., growth in the same general direction as its current capability). For example, a method that stores data may work well for a data rate of one record per second. If the maximum anticipated data rate is 1,000 records per second, the method's scalability is effectively its adequacy for this growth requirement. We inspect and test the method with this in mind as soon as possible. Inspection and testing for scalability have limitations, however. Scalability can be difficult to assess through inspections; early testing at the required scale can be expensive or even impractical because of the work required to create a scaled-up test structure.

Scalability metrics measure speeds and data storage in these simulated or accelerated environments.

23.1.8 The Degree of Security of an Implementation

Applications often include or are connected to networked parts. The parts may be components of the executing code (as with Web Services, for example), they may consist of distributed data, they may consist of a downloaded Web site, or they may simply be accessible through the Internet or another network. Often, some of the data are confidential. For these reasons, security is a significant consideration. Consider the simple example of logging in. The application checks the user's ID and password before allowing access. We will assume that these data must reside on a file situated remotely from the application. This scenario raises many security questions, as listed in Figure 23.8.

Recall that security considerations can be divided into categories. We can base initial implementation metrics on these, possibly weighted, as shown in Figure 23.9, measured for every unit of code—for example,

---

- Store IDs and passwords without allowing unauthorized access
- Ensure that data go only to authorized requesters
- Design so that security is easily maintained as application evolves
  - Isolate security-affecting classes?

Figure 23.8 Security challenges for *Simple Login* example

- **Confidentiality**: Measure by degree of difficulty; *gaining disallowed access to information*
- **Nonrepudiation**: . . . *repudiating agreement*
- **Integrity**: . . . *altering data in transit, undetected*
- **Authentication**: . . . *verifying identity*
- **Authorization**: . . . *gaining disallowed access to a location*

0 = easy; 1 = not easy but conceivable; 2 = not conceivable

Figure 23.9 Metrics for security—high-level metric using security attributes

on classes and relevant methods. Although this categorization helps, the nontrivial part lies in assessing the liability of the implementation to each kind of security breach.

The difficulty in assessing the degree of security of an implementation is conceiving of breaches. The "not conceivable" category of Figure 23.9 does not necessarily imply that breaches are impossible—merely that the evaluator cannot imagine one.

23.2 CODE INSPECTIONS AND RELATED QUALITY PROCEDURES

The topic of inspecting project artifacts was covered in general in Section 6.3. Now we will describe a specific process for inspecting code.

Code inspections are an effective tool for producing high-quality code. As with other artifacts produced during development, code is reviewed by a team of peers whose goal is to identify as many defects as possible of as high a severity as possible. Inspections are typically conducted after a segment of code is written but before it is unit tested.

Before code is inspected it should be *desk-checked* by its author. This entails the developer reading the code looking for syntax and other obvious errors. There is no point in having others examine your code if you haven't carefully looked through it yourself. The code should compile with no errors or even warnings; if it doesn't, there are obvious errors that need to be fixed before inspection.

Once desk-checking is complete, the inspection process commences. The author distributes the code to a group of reviewers. Sometimes an overview meeting is held before the actual inspection. The goal of this type of meeting is to present an overview of the code, presenting its layout and the overall design. This helps orient the reviewers and provides perspective while they read the code.

The team next prepares for the inspection meeting by having each inspector read the code looking for faults. Their first point of focus is to verify that the code exhibits the qualities listed in Table 23.1, to the extent they are specified in the requirements. In addition, an effective method is to use a *checklist*, which includes specific errors the inspector should be looking for as he or she reads the code. The following is an example list of items found in a code review checklist.

Code Inspection Checklist

1. Variables

   - Do variables have meaningful names?

   - Are hard-coded numbers used instead of named constants?

   - Is a variable value read-only? If so is it declared const or final?

   - Are all variables used?

2. Functions

- Do functions have meaningful names?

- Are all parameters used?

3. Correctness

- Are all parentheses properly matched?

- Are brackets properly matched?

- Does each case in a switch statement terminate with a break? Is there a default case?

4. Initialization

- Are variables initialized before their first use?

5. Loops

- Do all loops successfully terminate?

- If used, do *break* and *continue* statements work correctly?

- Does the body of the loop modify the loop variables?

6. Dynamic Allocation

- Is every dynamically allocated piece of memory properly de-allocated?

7. Pointers

- Can a NULL pointer be de-referenced?

8. Comments

- Is the code properly commented?

- Do the comments accurately describe the corresponding code?

9. Defensive Programming

- Are checks made to prevent errors such as divide by zero or illegal data?

Inspectors should read the code line by line, to fully understand what they are reading. For each line or block of code, skim through the inspection checklist, looking for items that apply. For each applicable item, determine whether the code correctly addresses the item. If not, write this down, as it is a potential defect. This list is brought to the inspection meeting for further review. In order to make efficient use of people's time during the inspection meeting, any syntax or trivial errors discovered can be forwarded to the author prior to the meeting. This way the meeting can focus on more substantial errors.

During the inspection meeting the facilitator leads the group through the code. As a block of code is reached, inspectors raise issues found during their prior code reading. If it is agreed that an issue is indeed a defect, it is duly recorded. An important point is that the fault should only be recorded. It should not be solved, and new code should not be written during the meeting. This is left to the author to execute at a time subsequent to the meeting.

During this and all other inspections, metrics should be collected. Example metrics are as follows:

- Number of defects discovered, by severity and type

- Number of defects discovered by each category of stakeholder inspecting the artifact

- Number of defects per page reviewed

- Review rate (number of pages/hour)

The checklists and data referenced above can be arranged in a form or a GUI for software engineers' use and for data collection.

23.2.1 Code Walkthroughs and Code Reviews

Many teams employ *code walkthroughs* or *code reviews*. The meaning of these terms differs from project to project, but they always involve a meeting—perhaps only a synchronous online meeting. They cover some of the ground of inspections but are less formal. For example, participants may not cover every line of code, and they may not be required to prepare for the meeting. A detailed list of defects may not be compiled. A major difference is that whereas inspections are dedicated to finding defects alone, walkthroughs and reviews are not. In particular, suggesting and discussing alternatives is permitted—sometimes encouraged—at walkthroughs but discouraged for inspections.

23.2.2 Pair Programming

Pair programming is a process by which programming is performed by two software engineers sitting side by side and using a single computer. Typically, one of them enters code while the other inspects continuously—essentially for quality. As a simple example, one engineer types a method for dividing two numbers while the other continually thinks of things that could go wrong (e.g., division by zero) or that the first has missed (e.g., documentation giving the context or limits) or left unclear (e.g., why a standard library is not being used). The pair switches roles periodically. It is clear that the quality of software produced via pair programming will be higher than that produced by a single person. The trade-offs become more complex to assess when one compares pair programming with single-person programming augmented by inspections.

23.3 SUMMARY

In order to assess the quality of an implementation, it is useful to categorize its qualities in the same way as for a design. The qualities we considered in this chapter are sufficiency, robustness, flexibility, reusability, efficiency, reliability, scalability, and security. Various metrics are available to measure the extent of each of these in the application.

Code inspections are a specific type of artifact inspection that is conducted after a piece of code is written but before it is unit tested. The goal is to detect and fix defects in the code as close to their injection point as possible. Checklists are commonly used to guide reviewers to the types of errors they should look for while reading the code.

23.4 EXERCISES

1. List the qualities that implementations should possess. In your own words, describe the meaning of each quality.

2. Explain how *efficiency* and *reusability* can sometimes be competing implementation qualities. Provide an example to support your answer.

3. Describe six factors that increase the flexibility of an implementation, and provide an example of how each contributes to increased flexibility.

4. The code inspection checklist in Section 23.2 is not an exhaustive list. Specify three additional items you think would be useful to add to the checklist, and explain why you have added each.

5. Your instructor will pair up student project teams. Conduct a code inspection of the other team's implementation. Use the code inspection checklist in Section 23.2 to guide your inspection.

6. Chapter 22 contains a code listing for a part of the Encounter video game. Where feasible, apply the informal and formal metrics mentioned in this chapter to measure its robustness. Explain whether the use of a relevant robustness metric is not feasible in this case and describe the reliability of the metrics' use in this case.

7. Chapter 22 contains a code listing for a part of the Encounter video game. Where feasible, apply the informal and formal metrics mentioned in this chapter to assess its flexibility. Explain whether the use of a relevant flexibility metric is not feasible in this case and describe the reliability of the metrics' use in this case.

8. Chapter 22 contains a code listing for a part of the Encounter video game. Where feasible, apply the informal and formal metrics mentioned in this chapter to assess its reusability. Explain whether the use of a relevant reusability metric is not feasible in this case and describe the reliability of the metrics' use in this case.

9. Chapter 22 contains a code listing for a part of the Encounter video game. Where feasible, apply the informal and formal metrics mentioned in this chapter to assess its reliability. Explain whether the use of a relevant reliability metric is not feasible in this case and describe the reliability of the metrics' use in this case.

10. Chapter 22 contains a code listing for a part of the Encounter video game. Where feasible, apply the informal and formal metrics mentioned in this chapter to assess its scalability. Explain if the use of a relevant scalability metric is not feasible in this case and describe the reliability of the metrics' use in this case.

24

Refactoring

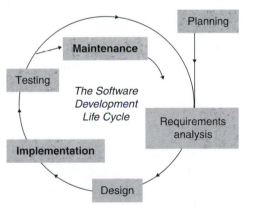

- What is refactoring?

- How does refactoring work at large scales?

- How do you refactor at the method level?

- Can you reorganize classes using refactoring? Reorganize data?

- Can you refactor at the module/package level?

- In what way is refactoring essential for agile projects?

- How is refactoring used in non-agile projects?

- How does refactoring relate to design patterns?

Figure 24.1 The context and learning goals for this chapter

Refactoring is a process of altering source code so as to leave its existing functionality unchanged. Motives for refactoring vary, but a principal one is to improve maintainability, especially enhancement. It is considered as soon as software engineers begin writing code, and is an essential part of most agile approaches. Refactoring was introduced to a wide audience by Fowler in his classic book [1].

All design evolves, and this is especially true for software projects. In the past it has often not been effective to modify code very much as needs evolve. However, object-orientation, improved development environments, and, especially, refactoring, have made this increasingly effective.

Perhaps the simplest illustrative example of refactoring is *renaming*, in which the name of a variable— including a class or package name—can be changed. Most development environments automate renaming, as discussed below. When the name is changed, all references to it except for comments are automatically changed at the same time. Before renaming became available, naming a variable was, in practice, an important decision that became hard to alter once made and used for a time. If he or she wanted a new variable name, the programmer was often obliged to alter so many occurrences of the name in multiple classes that it was seldom worthwhile to carry out for a large program. Naming variables is just as important as in the past, but the ability to rename virtually at will has freed some programmer time and allowed new flexibility.

What follows is a second example that demonstrates the flavor of refactoring. It is called "Promote Attribute to Class," and is used to convert a simple attribute into a class. To accommodate the increased scope of an application, we often need to introduce a new class to replace an attribute. For example, suppose that we already have a class *Automobile* with integer attribute *mileage*.

```
class Automobile
{
  int mileage;
  . . . .
}
```

We may decide later that "mileage" for used automobiles, however, is substantially more involved than a single *int* variable. For example, the auto's motor may be a replacement, resulting in a motor mileage different from a chassis mileage. In addition, if our application is required to account for fraud, the reported "mileage" would have to be modified by other attributes such as whether the car had ever been stolen. For these reasons, we would consider the "Promote Attribute to a Class" refactoring. This would involve introducing a *Mileage* class like

Listing 24.1: *Mileage* class—promotion of *mileage* field

```
class Mileage
{
    int nominalMileageValue = 0;      // shown on odometer
    int chassisMileageValue = 0;      // best estimate
    int engineMileageValue = 0;       // best estimate, accounting for
                                         replacement
    . . . .
    public int computeEffectiveMileage(){ . . . }  // to obtain estimate
    }
    class Automobile
    {
    Mileage mileage;
    . . . .
}
```

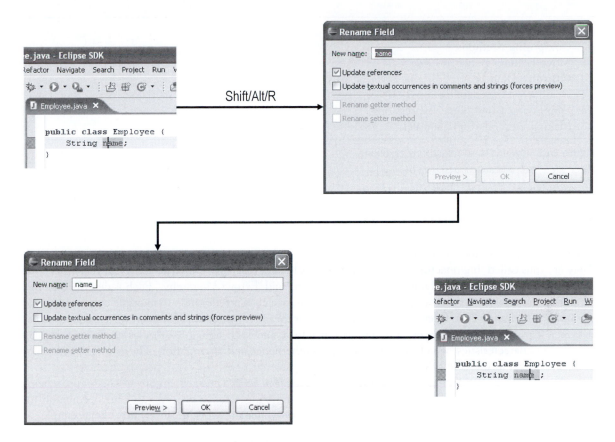

Figure 24.2 Using a refactoring wizard—an Eclipse example

Depending on the progress of this application, even the class *Mileage* could be considered worthy of further refactoring—for example, by extracting some of its properties into separate types of mileage classes. Another direction for refactoring is to extract interfaces for it so that client code (code that uses it) can assume that it possesses a given set of method signatures such as *computeEffectiveMileage()*.

Some refactorings are computer-assisted. This usually takes the form of a wizard that interacts with the programmer. Almost all interactive development environments are equipped with several such refactoring wizards. For example to use *Rename* in Eclipse, one can place the cursor on the variable (in this case *name*) and press Shift/Alt/R. The user is then shown the window seen in Figure 24.2 for the entry of the new name (in this case *name_*). The wizard automatically makes this change throughout the application except within comments.

The rest of this chapter introduces many of the refactorings described by Fowler, as well as an additional one, *Introducing Methods*. IDEs regularly include new refactorings, and it is a good idea to explore these besides the refactorings in [1]. This chapter is intended to give the reader a substantive taste for refactoring and to place it in a software engineering context.

Fowler organizes his refactoring as in Figure 24.3. This chapter does not attempt to explain all of Fowler's refactorings. For example, *Simplifying Conditional Expressions* and *Making Method Calls Simpler* are not elaborated in this book, and the reader is referred to [1].

1. Big Refactorings
2. Composing Methods
3. Move Features between Objects
4. Organize Data
5. Dealing with Generalization
6. Simplifying Conditional Expressions
7. Making methods Calls Simpler

Figure 24.3 Fowler's main refactoring taxonomy

Source: Fowler et al., Refactoring: Improving the Design of Existing Code, Copyright © 1999 by Pearson Education, Inc. Reproduced by permission of Pearson Education, Inc.

24.1 BIG REFACTORINGS

The refactorings described in this section are mainly at the class level and have more of an architectural impact. They are thus called "big refactorings." Fowler describes four: "Tease Apart Inheritance," "Convert Procedural Design to Objects," "Separate Domain from Presentation," and "Extract Hierarchy." Each is described below.

Tease Apart Inheritance can be applied when subclasses of a class proliferate into multiple combinations, as exemplified by Figure 24.4. Effectively, we want to factor the combinations as if converting a product such as 9 (=3x3) classes that describe every combination into a sum such as 6 (=3+3) classes. We do this by identifying characteristics, which we encapsulate via inheritance and aggregation. These are *Employee* types and *Status* types in the case of Figure 24.4.

The next "big" refactoring we'll consider, *Convert Procedural Design to Objects*, is appropriate for use when a design has not fully leveraged object orientation by being unnecessarily procedural. This is common for inexperienced programmers and even for experienced programmers working in a hurry. For example, as

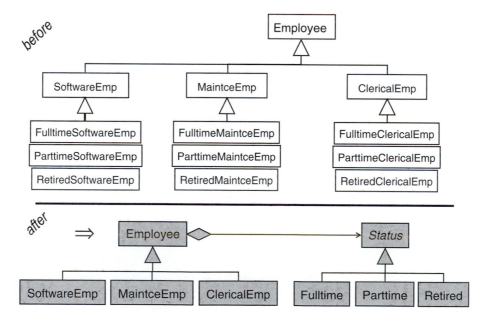

Figure 24.4 Big refactorings, 1 of 4—Tease Apart Inheritance

Source: Fowler et al., Refactoring: Improving the Design of Existing Code, Copyright © 1999 by Pearson Education, Inc. Reproduced by permission of Pearson Education, Inc.

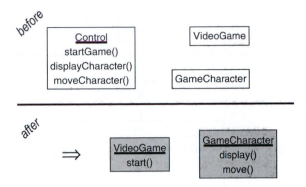

Figure 24.5 Big refactorings, 2 of 4—Convert Procedural Design to Objects

Source: Fowler et al., Refactoring: Improving the Design of Existing Code, Copyright © 1999 by Pearson Education, Inc. Reproduced by permission of Pearson Education, Inc.

shown in Figure 24.5, a designer may use a class such as *Control* to control a video game (i.e., to start and stop various elements of the game). The problem with this is that control classes, when needed, should be used to manage objects only by initiating their methods, not as a replacement for the work that should be performed within an object. When an object is required to control, it should be kept to a minimum: usually a simple, single call to a method in an appropriate object that sets off the entire process. Figure 24.5 shows how elements of what used to be control, such as *move()*, have been relocated to the objects to which they properly apply. The instances of GameCharacter now move themselves. Minimal control may still be needed outside of VideoGame and GameCharacter, but it would initiate the work rather than doing it.

The next "big" refactoring we'll consider, *Separate Domain from Presentation*, is used when a design mixes control with output formats—in particular, when GUI code occurs in the same class as the computational algorithms or the data repository. For example, as shown in Figure 24.6, a designer may use a class such as *Account* to perform computations but also to produce displays. Such a design lacks reusability and conceptual

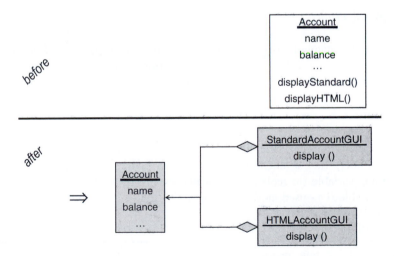

Figure 24.6 Big refactorings, 3 of 4—Separate Domain from Presentation

Source: Fowler et al., Refactoring: Improving the Design of Existing Code, Copyright © 1999 by Pearson Education, Inc. Reproduced by permission of Pearson Education, Inc.

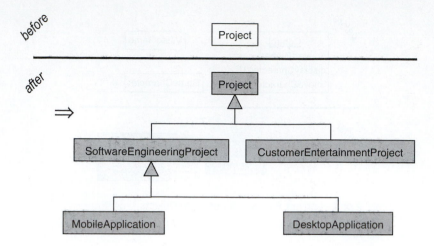

Figure 24.7 Big refactorings''–Extract Hierarchy

Source: Fowler et al., Refactoring: Improving the Design of Existing Code, Copyright © 1999 by Pearson Education, Inc. Reproduced by permission of Pearson Education, Inc.

simplicity. (Consider how complicated it would be to change just the GUI parts or to allow several displays for the same account data.) Figure 24.6 shows how the original design can be decomposed into the core part of *Account*, separated from classes describing various ways to display the account.

Our final example of a ''big'' refactoring, *Extract Hierarchy*, applies when it has become clear that a new or extended hierarchy of classes is needed—in particular, when the classes in the existing hierarchy are not refined enough for the task at hand. For example, as shown in Figure 24.7, a designer may use a class such as *Project* to implement a project management application. We'll presume that the application has become too sophisticated for a generic project. So, for example, quite different functionality is needed by software engineering projects vs. entertainment projects. As shown in Figure 24.7, extracting a hierarchy of classes from the original becomes a needed refactoring.

24.2 COMPOSING METHODS

The ''composing methods'' category of refactorings concerns the process of creating, removing, and combining methods to suit an evolving application. The various types of method composition examined by Fowler are shown in Figure 24.8. They are explained below.

- Extract method
- Inline method
- Inline temp (remove a temporary variable)
- Replace temp with query (i.e., a function)
- Introduce explaining variable (to replace complicated expression)
- Split temporary variable (i.e., used more than once)
- Remove assignment to parameters
- Replace method with method object

Figure 24.8 ''Compose methods'' refactorings

Source: Fowler et al., Refactoring: Improving the Design of Existing Code, Copyright © 1999 by Pearson Education, Inc. Reproduced by permission of Pearson Education, Inc.

Extract Method refers to the process of identifying a block of code and creating a method that serves its purpose. The block of code can then be replaced with a call to that method. One performs such a replacement when the benefit of reducing clutter outweighs the penalty of having to look elsewhere for code details. This depends on the sense of purpose of the code extracted, its relative complexity, its size, and how frequently the functionality involved is needed. As a rough guide, note that the average length of a method in an OO implementation is on the order of 10 lines (i.e., not 100 lines). If several methods call the same block of code, that is strong reason for extracting it to a method. When there are three such calling methods, we very often extract as a matter of course. Most IDEs are instrumented with *Extract Method*.

Inline Method refers to the opposite of *Extract Method*. We replace a call to a method with the actual code from that method. The occasion to consolidate is reflected by the opposite of the justification described in *Extract Method*: when a method is so short or inconsequential that it is simpler to include the code itself instead of the method call. Another case is when the overhead (time or heap space used) of a method call must be avoided.

Inline Temp refers to the process of replacing a temporary variable instead of using the whole expression that it replaces. One considers this very strongly if, for example, the expression is complicated and has more than two terms. An example is replacing $y-(x-z)+x^{**}y$ by a temporary variable in expression (24.1).

$$[x(y + z) - 1]/[y - (x - z) + x^{**}y] \tag{24.1}$$

Replace Temp with Query refers to using a method call instead of a temporary variable. For example, we might want to save expression (24.1) in a temporary variable v and then use v several times; or we might want to dispense with a temporary variable and call the method that evaluates this expression each time we need it. This would make sense if the variable we use takes up a lot of space (true for a large data structure but not for a floating point number like the one above). Another factor to consider here is whether or not the variables in the expression change. The penalty for introducing *Replace Temp with Query* is the time it takes to make the computation.

Introduce Explaining Variable is the opposite of *Replace Temp with Query*. It introduces temporary variables to facilitate working with complicated expressions. Although the hiding quality of *Replace Temp with Query* is usually beneficial, it is counterproductive when there is little to hide.

Split Temporary Variable applies when you use a temporary variable for purposes different from its original one. It consists of introducing one or more additional variables instead. Generally speaking, it is good practice to use a temporary variable only for a single purpose.

Remove Assignment to Parameters fixes the problem of changing the value of a parameter this is not expressly designed to be an *in/out* variable. Generally speaking, it is poor practice to write to a parameter unless the method is specifically designed for this, expecting and using the changed values. In fact, it is usually good practice to make methods parameters *final* (in Java notation) to prevent their use other than for the values they provide.

Replace Method With Method Object is the process of replacing a method such as *doFinancialCalculation*() with a function call on a dedicated object of a specially designed class (*FinancialCalculation*) such as *financialCalculation24.execute*(). The effect of calling *execute*() with object *financialCalculation24* of a separate class gains advantages when the functionality required has too many effects to be handled conveniently by a simple function call alone. Another example is when we need to count the number of times that functionality such as *estimateProfit*() in class *StockHelper* is executed. Instead of simply making *estimateProfit*() a method of *StockHelper*, we create a class *ProfitEstimation* that aggregates *StockHelper*, and we call the method *execute*() of *ProfitEstimation*. A final example is when we want an *undo* capability. If we store the object representing the function, there is a possibility for undoing. Otherwise, we couldn't retrieve the function call that brought us to a current state and would be unable to go back.

24.3 MOVING FEATURES BETWEEN OBJECTS

This category of refactoring concerns changes in the placement of class features. These are summarized in Figures 24.9 and 24.10.

Move Method changes the location of a method from one class to another. For example, we may have classes *Customer*, *Book*, and *Order*, as well as a method that performs ordering. The application could be built with *executeOrder(Book aBook)*, a method of *Customer*. However, this would usually be inappropriate; and *executeOrder()* can be moved with this refactoring to the more appropriate class *Order*.

Move Field is similar to *Move Method*. These refactorings are especially needed when we introduce new classes and recognize better homes for existing variables.

Extract Class allows the software engineer to create a class from a collection of attributes and methods that already exist within a class. We apply *Extract Class* when such a collection makes logical sense together and stands out from its containing class. As an example, an application may be implemented with a *Customer* class containing data about books—perhaps because favorite books were initially understood to be a characteristic of a customer. However, if the application changes to one for which the book notion becomes significant, then we would apply *Extract Class* to create a *Book* class.

Inline Class, the opposite of *Extract Class*, is the incorporation of a class *A*, let's say, into another, *B*, deleting *A* in the process. In other words, there is really no need for *A*.

Hide Delegate is used when a class references classes that are supposed to use it, the effect being to remove these references. Clients of a class need to reference the used class, but the reverse should be avoided. This is expanded upon below.

Remove Middle Man is the opposite of *Hide Delegate*. *Hide Delegate* is accomplished by introducing a separate class, as shown in Figure 24.11; reversing the process amounts to removing this "Middle Man."

Figure 24.11 shows *Hide Delegates* in some detail. Method(s) in *Client* call *method2()* in (server) class *Class2*. However, *method2()* requires the use of *Class1* in a way that forces *Client* to reference *Class1* as well. An example is the following:

- **Move Method**
  - Trades off method holding vs. usage
- **Move Field**
  - Trades off holding vs. usage
- **Extract Class**
  - Encapsulate a set of attributes and methods of a class
- **Inline Class**
  - Opposite of *Extract Class*

Figure 24.9 "Moving Features between Objects" refactorings, 1 of 2

Source: Fowler et al., Refactoring: Improving the Design of Existing Code, Copyright © 1999 by Pearson Education, Inc. Reproduced by permission of Pearson Education, Inc.

- **Hide Delegate** Hide class dependencies from client classes
- **Remove Middle Man**
  - Opposite of *Hide Delegate*

Figure 24.10 "Moving Features between Objects" refactorings, 2 of 2

Source: Fowler et al., Refactoring: Improving the Design of Existing Code, Copyright © 1999 by Pearson Education, Inc. Reproduced by permission of Pearson Education, Inc.

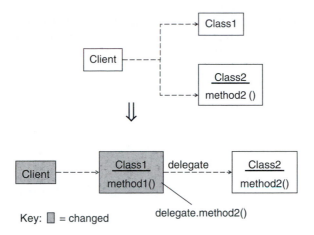

Figure 24.11 "Hide delegates" refactoring

Client. Tax preparation

Class2. Personal profile

Class1. Employer

method2(). Prepare summary tax page

In summary, *Client* has been saddled with unnecessary responsibility. *Hide Delegates* allows *Client* to depend only on *Class2* by aggregating *Class1* to *Class2* (making a *Class1* object an attribute of *Class2*). As a result, *Client* now depends only on *Class2*.

24.4 ORGANIZING DATA

In the refactorings of this section, Fowler lists those having to do with the location of data in a design or implementation.

Self Encapsulate Field changes direct access of an attribute (e.g., `public String name;`) to that via accessors (e.g., `private String name; . . . String getName() . . .`). One would use this refactoring if one forgets to make or postpones making fields private, available only via accessor methods. Using accessors in OO is generally good practice because it allows control such as checking an assigned value to ensure that it is within bounds.

Replace Data Value with Object: As an example, change the attribute `public String name` to `public Name name`. One would apply *Replace Data Value with Object* here when the idea of a name becomes too complex for *String*. An example is when it becomes necessary to track all parts of a name as well as aliases, married names, and former unmarried ones.

Change Value to Reference is used when the value of an object's attribute is better obtained via a function (typically, because obtaining the value is complex) rather than with an explicit instance or with *null*, as in the following example. In the first version below, the attribute *customer* has the value *null*. In the second version, it is a *Customer* object created by a static method of *Customer*. This has the advantage of centralizing the creation of *Customer* objects, which is often desirable. This advantage becomes clear when several different classes need

Customer objects in a standard manner, such as when instantiating a default customer. The undesirable alternative is to repeat the code that creates such objects for each of these classes.

```
class Order { . . .
Customer customer;
. . . .
}
```

. . . replaced by . . .

```
class Order { . . .
Customer customer = Customer.getCustomer( String . . . . );
. . .
}
```

Change Reference to Value is the opposite of the previous refactoring. This would be needed when the machinery of a reference is found to be unnecessary, perhaps because the program turns out to be less complex than anticipated in this respect.

Replace Array with Object: Arrays have the benefit of being standard in form and of having random access. However, they are not as flexible as specially built classes even though both may have essentially the same contents. When the use of an array loses the balance of its advantages, this refactoring makes the conversion. An example is the following.

Change `Company[] companies1 . . . .` to `class Companies{ . . . }`. This refactoring may be beneficial because there are better way to access companies (e.g., why should IBM be `companies1[3]` in particular?), whereas accessing a company by name (e.g., `Companies compa-nies2 . . . companies2.getCompany(''IBM'')`) may be much more appropriate.

The preceding refactorings are summarized in Figure 24.12.

Change Bidirectional Association to Unidirectional: We usually want the relationship between classes C_1 and C_2 to be one-way rather than two-way. For example, C_1 refers to C_2 but C_2 does not also refer to C_1. Otherwise, we cannot use one in another application without the other. Circular references are awkward in any case. *Employee* and *Employer* is an example; if the application is a corporate one, we would probably want *Employer* to reference *Employee*, and there may be no need for the reverse. The result is as follows.

$$Employee \leftarrow Employer.$$

- **Self Encapsulate Field**
  - Change direct access of an attribute to accessor use
- **Replace Data Value with Object**
- **Change Value to Reference**
  - *class Order { Customer customer; . . . .*
  - *class Order { private Customer getCustomer(String . . . .)*
- **Change Reference to Value**
- **Replace Array with Object**

Figure 24.12 "Organizing data" refactorings, 1 of 4

Change Unidirectional Association to Bidirectional is the opposite operation from the preceding refactoring. If there is no clear way to eliminate the dual association direction entirely, we typically try to create a third class to handle the relationship. An example is as follows.

$$Employee \leftarrow EmploymentRelationship \rightarrow Employer.$$

However, if this is not feasible, we apply *Change Unidirectional Association to Bidirectional* by establishing a reference in *Employee* to *Employer*.

Replace "Magic Number" with Symbolic Constant is the process of using symbols for constants within code. An example is NUM_WORKING_MONTHS instead of purely "10." This helps readability, since the reader understands NUM_WORKING_MONTHS but not necessarily just 10. This process also helps with maintenance, since it allows easy changes—for example, changing NUM_WORKING_MONTHS to 11 instead of hunting for all occurrences of 10, checking their context, and changing to 11 where applicable.

Encapsulate Field is the process of changing accessible variables to *private* ones, supplying an accessor method or methods. For convenience, we might intentionally make all variables public when first creating a class and then apply this refactoring.

The preceding set of refactorings is summarized in Figure 24.13.

Replace Record with Data Class is used when we need to encapsulate the data of a class in a database record. In other words, it suits the application better to deal with records as self-contained units. The records become objects with private data fields and accessor methods. This is similar to the *Replace Data Value with Object* refactoring mentioned above.

Replace Type Code with Class is used when a group of attributes of a class essentially specify what type an instance of the class is. For example, in the class *Shoe*, the attributes *countryOf manufacture*, *quality*, and *designerName* would effectively indicate the type as high fashion, intermediate, or low fashion. This refactoring applies when it becomes advisable to call out a specific type class (*ShoeFashionType* with at least three values for the example). Typically, the type class is aggregated with the original class.

Replace Type Code with Subclass: This refactoring implements the same problem as for *Replace Type Code with Class* by using inherited classes, each a different type, as shown in Figure 24.15.

The preceding refactorings are summarized in Figure 24.14.

Replace Type Code with State/Strategy: This refactoring deals with the same type of issue as that described in *Replace Type Code with Class/Subclass* but combines classes into a hierarchy, as shown in Figure 24.15. The result is the aggregation of a type class, such as *AcountType* and inherited subclasses such as *RegularAccountType* and *WholesaleAccountType*. At runtime, the *AcountType* attribute of *Account* is instantiated with an object of type *RegularAccountType* or *WholesaleAccountType*.

- **Change Unidirectional Association to Bidirectional**
  - (Only if necessary); install backpointer
- **Change Bidirectional Association to Unidirectional**
  - Find a way to drop; consider third party.
- **Replace "Magic Number" with Constant**
- **Encapsulate Field**
  - *public* attribute to *private/accessor*

Figure 24.13 "Organizing data" refactorings, 2 of 4

- ▪ **Replace Record with Data Class**
  - o Simplest object with private data field, accessor
- ▪ **Replace Type Code with Class**

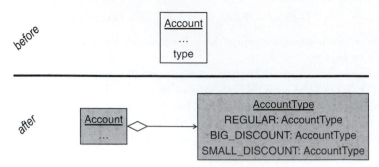

Figure 24.14 ''Organizing data'' refactorings, 3 of 4

Source: Fowler et al., Refactoring: Improving the Design of Existing Code, Copyright © 1999 by Pearson Education, Inc. Reproduced by permission of Pearson Education, Inc.

- ▪ **Replace Type Code with Subclass**

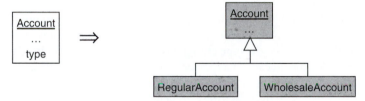

- ▪ **Replace Type Code with State/Strategy**

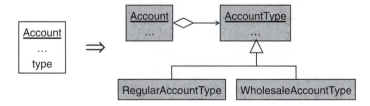

Figure 24.15 ''Organizing data'' refactorings, 4 of 4

Source: Fowler et al., Refactoring: Improving the Design of Existing Code, Copyright © 1999 by Pearson Education, Inc. Reproduced by permission of Pearson Education, Inc.

24.5 GENERALIZATION

The refactorings in this section exploit inheritance to convert a design and code base from one form to another that better suits the situation.

Pull Up Field is used when a field (e.g., *order* in *WholesaleOrder* and in *RetailOrder*) occurs in several subclasses of a class (which we'll call the *base* class). It declares the recurring field in the base class, helping us to extend the functionality of the design since the base class becomes more useful as a result. Figure 24.16 shows an example.

Pull Up Method is the same as *Pull Up Field* except that it refers to recurring methods instead.

Fowler: *Dealing with Generalization 1*

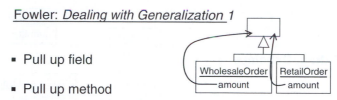

- Pull up field

- Pull up method

- Pull up constructor body

    0 Replace by *super(...)*

- Push Down Method

    0 When base class method not used by most subclasses

- Push Down Field

Figure 24.16 "Dealing with generalization" refactorings, 1 of 5

Source: Fowler et al., Refactoring: Improving the Design of Existing Code, Copyright © 1999 by Pearson Education, Inc. Reproduced by permission of Pearson Education, Inc.

Pull Up Constructor Body is similar to *Pull Up Method*, but here we are referring to a block of code that recurs in the constructors of subclasses. This block is placed in the base class constructor. The derived class constructors must call *super()* in order to effect it. An example in the context of Figure 24.16 is when it becomes clear that there is substantial common code in constructing *WholesaleOrder* and *RetailOrder* objects.

Pull Down Field or Method is the opposite of *Pull Up* . . . . We abolish the field or method in the base class when it is needed only once or twice in derived classes. An example is when we write a *Jewelry* class with the method *estimateTimeToCut()* and realize later that this applies to very few subclasses—such as diamonds and sapphires—and that even they do not have a large amount in common when it comes to this operation.

These refactorings are summarized in Figure 24.16, where the typical motive for each is included.

Extract Subclass is a more extensive version of *Push Down*. Here, we recognize parts of a class that are specialized and are liable to be used together, and so deserve class-hood. The process is exemplified in Figure 24.17, where we recognize the wholesale nature of many orders made to an enterprise.

Extract Superclass is an opposite version of *Pull Up*. Here, we recognize parts of class that can and should be abstracted into a superclass. The process is exemplified in Figure 24.17, where we recognize a generic "employee" aspects of manager and engineer objects. *Extract Sub/Superclass* enable generalization by refining the class model. These two refactorings make it easier to introduce new kinds of capabilities going forward because general concepts are better defined.

Extract Interface arises from asking how a collection of classes would be used by clients. In the example illustrated in Figure 24.18, we ask how a collection of classes, including *Manager* and *Engineer*, would be used. The idea is to collect this information together in a convenient form. In this case, we may come to the conclusion—in the context of the application—that users of these classes need only understand that their functionality is concerned with the concepts of *billability* (for charging customers) and *employment*. Then we create an interface that reflects these concepts.

Collapse Hierarchy applies when we have built an inheritance structure that's unnecessarily refined—that is, it has too many levels. An example from gymnastics is *UnevenBarPerformer* → *Gymnast* → *SportsWoman* → *HSStudent* → *Student* → *Youth* → *Person*. For a small application, this is probably too deep and needs consolidation. For this example, *Collapse Hierarchy* concerns the steps needed to reduce this to the following:

Gymnast → Student → Person

- **Extract Subclass**

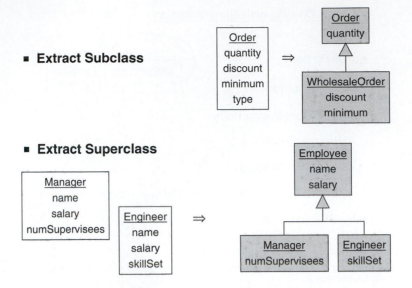

- **Extract Superclass**

Figure 24.17 "Dealing with generalization" refactorings, 2 of 5

Source: Fowler et al., Refactoring: Improving the Design of Existing Code, Copyright © 1999 by Pearson Education, Inc. Reproduced by permission of Pearson Education, Inc.

- **Extract Interface**

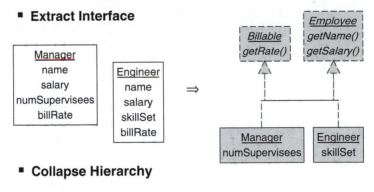

- **Collapse Hierarchy**

  o Inherited class not special enough

Figure 24.18 "Dealing with generalization" refactorings, 3 of 5

Source: Fowler et al., Refactoring: Improving the Design of Existing Code, Copyright © 1999 by Pearson Education, Inc. Reproduced by permission of Pearson Education, Inc.

Form Template Method applies when we notice a skeleton algorithm within a body of code that is common to several algorithms. In effect, we are evolving a design into an application of the Template design pattern. The example in Figure 24.19 shows how the algorithms for *writeBikeInstructions()* and *writeTrikeInstructions()*, which generate assembly instruction manuals depending on parameters, have a common algorithm core. This core consists of parts that can be pulled out as common to both *writeBikeInstructions()* and *writeTrikeInstructions()*: *writePrep()*, *writeSafety()*, *writeWrapUp()*, and *writeManual()*.

Replace Inheritance with Delegation, somewhat self-explanatory, usually effects an improvement on a design. OO languages such as Java do not allow for more than one base class, so that there is an advantage to

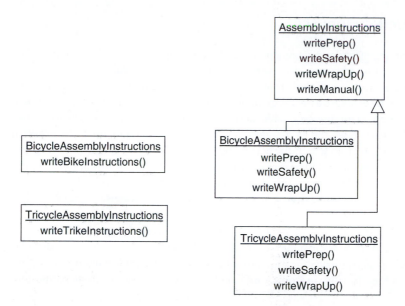

Figure 24.19 "Dealing with generalization" refactorings, 4 of 5, *Form Template Method*

eliminating an inheritance. For the example in Figure 24.20, *Account* can inherit from another class once the refactoring is done, resulting in greater flexibility. The refactoring gives a sequence of steps that ensure a smooth and safe transition from the original form to the refactored form.

Replace Delegation with Inheritance would be appropriate when we want to repair a design in which code becomes understood as having a generalization relationship such as *Employee/Person*. We effect this in code by means of inheritance.

- **Replace Inheritance with Delegation**

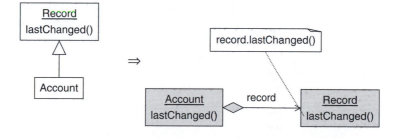

- **Replace Delegation with Inheritance**

Figure 24.20 "Dealing with generalization" refactorings, 5 of 5

24.6 INTRODUCING MODULES

Good design requires modularization: a process of separating its essential elements. Whenever feasible, this should be performed in advance. However, it is very useful to modularize after the fact as well—in other words, to recognize useful modularization as the application grows and transitions into maintenance.

Classes by themselves are a means of modularization, but an application can contain hundreds of classes, and so classes need organizing to enable designers to manage and apply them. A useful way to handle modularity on this scale is via the Facade design pattern. Simplifying matters, the problem can be reduced to that shown in Figure 24.21, in which the design involves classes U, V, and W, where U references (mentions) classes V and W. An example is U=Transaction, V=Customer, and W=Loan pool. Suppose that we want to avoid multiple references like this (think of many classes instead of just the two in this simplification, and you can imagine the resulting complexity). Class U must be modified because it should no longer reference both classes V and W.

The refactoring in Figure 24.21 is simple if U does not need to instantiate V objects or W objects. This is the case when U needs only static methods of V or W. (Example: A transaction needs only a generic customer functionality such as getting average assets of all customers; and the total amount in the loan pool.) In that case, U references functionality in F only, and F does the work of translating such function calls into the static calls on V or W.

The situation may be more involved, however. Suppose that U requires V instances in order to operate (such as is usually the case when a transaction involves a customer). If we want to protect V within a package, then U has to depend on the facade interface F and no longer on V directly. Figure 24.22 shows how this can be dealt with. First, V is provided with an abstract interface VI (Step 1) that abstracts its public methods. The *Extract Interface* refactoring can be used for this. Next, in Step 2, V is enclosed in a module (or package)

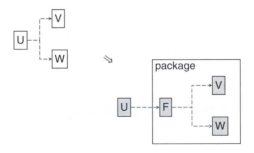

Figure 24.21 Refactoring by introducing facade

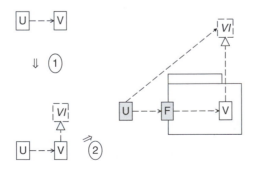

Figure 24.22 ''Introduce module'' refactoring, 1 of 2

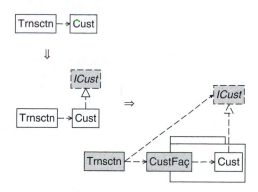

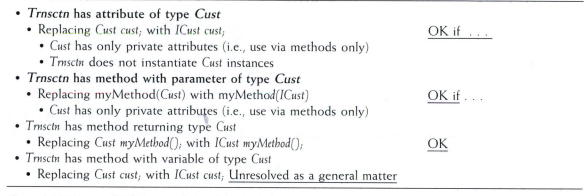

Figure 24.23 "Introduce module" refactoring, 2 of 2

- *Trnsctn* **has attribute of type** *Cust*
  - Replacing *Cust cust;* with *ICust cust;*   OK if . . .
    - *Cust* has only private attributes (i.e., use via methods only)
    - *Trnsctn* does not instantiate *Cust* instances
- *Trnsctn* **has method with parameter of type** *Cust*
  - Replacing myMethod(*Cust*) with myMethod(*ICust*)   OK if . . .
    - *Cust* has only private attributes (i.e., use via methods only)
- *Trnsctn* has method returning type *Cust*
  - Replacing *Cust myMethod();* with *ICust myMethod();*   OK
- *Trnsctn* has method with variable of type *Cust*
  - Replacing *Cust cust;* with *ICust cust;* <u>Unresolved as a general matter</u>

Figure 24.24 Types of references of one class to another

with facade *F*. The class *U* must now be modified so as to reference *VI* and *F* only. It is far less of a problem for a class to reference an interface than to reference a class.

Let's apply this to an example, shown in Figure 24.23, where a transaction object of class *Trnsctn* depends on a customer class *Cust*.

We can introduce interface *ICust*, with *Cust* being unchanged, but we need to deal with the resulting changes needed to *Trnsctn*. The dependence of *Trnsctn* on *Cust* is replaced with dependence on *ICust*. This is a significant improvement because it increases modularity. Think of it as follows: Imagine *Trnsctn* as a bicycle pump. Such a pump would be of little use if it were able to operate only on Ajax tires (not an interface) but would be very useful if it were able to operate on any tire satisfying the standard valve interface. Figure 24.24 lists the implications of this change for *Trnsctn* and introduces remedies for most situations.

24.7 REFACTORING IN PROJECTS

As mentioned at the beginning of this chapter, refactoring can be profitably applied as soon as software engineers begin writing code. Figure 24.25 was introduced in Chapter 4 on agile methods, but with our increased knowledge of refactoring we now have an opportunity to reexamine it. Recall that agile methodologies repeat the waterfall sequence many times but with several differences. Each cycle begins with the (functional) code base. Requirements are usually in the form of user stories. The existing code base

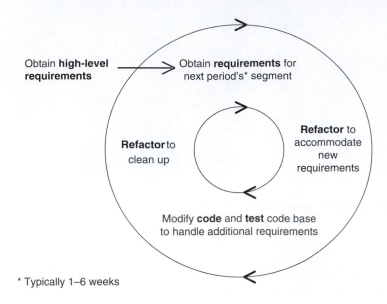

Obtain **high-level requirements**

Obtain **requirements** for next period's* segment

Refactor to clean up

Refactor to accommodate new requirements

Modify **code** and **test** code base to handle additional requirements

* Typically 1–6 weeks

Figure 24.25 Agile methods—cycle of activities

will have been expressly designed for the existing requirements. It is a tenet of most agile methodologies *not* to try to anticipate forthcoming requirements. The existing code base may thus be unsuited to the additional requirements in one or more ways—and refactoring would then be appropriate in order to accommodate them. An example is the user story for a video store application that introduces candy sales (i.e., not just the management of rentals). A new module at the architectural level may be required; and this, in turn, may require pulling control functionality out in order to orchestrate the rental/sales activities.

24.7.1 Refactoring in the Agile Project Life Cycle

Figure 24.25 shows an additional refactoring step—the task of cleanup. Most software addition and modification work leaves a "mess" of one kind and magnitude or other. An example is a set of *displayAccount*() methods, one for an existing account type and two more for added account types. Even if the application does not continue to evolve in this direction, the disorganization described should be cleaned up to make it more reliable and readable. Refactoring is thus an essential part of agile design, implementation, and testing. It is part of the expectation for agile projects.

24.7.2 Refactoring and Design Patterns

Fowler's refactorings, described in [1], stand mostly apart from design patterns—at least in explicit terms. However, refactoring is really an integral part of all design and implementation. In particular, the need for refactoring often points to the need for new design patterns. The classic source for these is [2], in which Kerievsky names most of his patterns in one of the following forms:

"Extract <Design Pattern>"

or

"Extract/Move/Replace <Situation> with/to <Design Pattern>"

Our purpose here is only to draw the reader's attention to this work. Here are some examples.

• Encapsulate Classes with Factory. Helps the software engineer recognize . . .
    . . . when Factory is a better way to construct objects that he or she is dealing with, and how to go about the conversion

• Move Embellishment to Decorator . . .
    . . . when the amount of functionality being added dynamically to objects of a class is extensive enough to require the use of the Decorator design pattern, and how to go about the conversion

• Replace State-Altering Conditionals with State
    . . . when the State design pattern is a better way to handle events that alter the state of the application, and how to make the transition

24.8 SUMMARY

"Refactoring" refers to a discipline of replacing code in such a way as to improve the application but without changing its functionality. The improvement can be of the following kinds:

• A simplification of the design and code (removing unnecessary complexity)

• An increase in its reusability for other parts of the code base for other applications

• Improved preparedness of the design and code for increasing functionality

Refactoring is possible at the architectural level and at the detailed code level. It extends the life of applications because it increases their capacity for modification in response to changing requirements.
    Some refactorings can be done with wizards supplied with development environments.
    Refactoring is essential to agile development. This is because it facilitates the evolution of applications so as to include additional functionality.
    This chapter has cited several classical refactorings. There are many more. An active research community explores new refactorings—see [3], for example.

24.9 EXERCISES

1. One refactoring is to "separate domain from presentation." Explain what this means, and apply it to a calendar application.

2. Write a single that computes the roots of a quadratic equation. Apply "extract method" to it.

3. Describe an application not mentioned in this chapter—or part of an application—in which "Convert Method to Object" would be appropriate.

4. Apply "Extract Class" to the following.

```
class Rental{
    String customer;
    String dvd;
    int customerLicense;
    String director;
Date date;
 . . .
}
```

5. This chapter cites the following class diagram for *Change Bidirectional Association to Unidirectional*:

Employee ⟵——— ⟨⟩ *Employment Relationship* ⟨⟩ ———⟶ *Employer*

(see Section 24.4). Write code consistent with this model that allocates seven employees among two employers and lists them.

6. Give an example in which the addition of a method to a calendar application would cause the software engineer to apply *Pull Up Method*.

7. Explain where *Introduce Facade* was used in the Encounter video game case study.

8. Section 24.7 cited two stages at which refactoring is used in agile projects. Give examples of each in the evolution of a calendar application.

9. The introductory section of this chapter refers to a class *Mileage*. Show how the refactoring of it could progress usefully along the directions suggested there.

BIBLIOGRAPHY

1. Fowler, Martin, *"Refactoring: Improving the Design of Existing Code,"* Addison-Wesley, 1999.
2. Kerievsky, Joshua, *"Refactoring to Patterns,"* Addison-Wesley, 2004.
3. Refactoring. http://www.refactoring.com/ [accessed 12/14/09].

25

Introduction to Software Testing

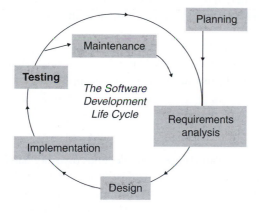

- Why test early? Why often?

- When and why do you retest?

- What is the difference between black box and white box testing?

- What distinguishes unit testing?

- How do you document tests?

- How do you plan for testing?

- How do you know when to stop testing?

- Where does test input come from?

- Who is involved in testing?

- How much effort does it take to test?

Figure 25.1 The context and learning goals for this chapter

Software testing is a validation process. Executing code from the evolving application is provided with input, and the resulting output is compared with the required output. Each discrepancy or unintended side effect indicates a fault, bug, or error in the implementation, design, or requirements. We will use the word *defect* to cover all these terms, defined by the IEEE (IEEE Standard Glossary of Software Engineering

Terminology, IEEE Std 610.121990) as "an incorrect step, process, or data definition in a computer program." "Incorrect" we will understand to mean something that causes a failure to satisfy the requirements in any way. The goal of testing is to uncover as many defects, at the highest level of seriousness, as possible. It is not possible to test an application with every possible input value due to the extraordinarily large number of combinations of input values. For this reason, testing can establish the *presence* of defects but *not their absence* (as so aptly put by Edsgar Dijkstra). In other words, for any practical application, the following is a false statement: "It has been thoroughly tested and therefore has no defects." Thorough testing is nevertheless indispensable.

This chapter describes essential principles of software testing. It also summarizes testing practices so that the reader can understand testing types and their context without getting bogged down in details. Chapters 26 and 27 provide details.

25.1 TESTING EARLY AND OFTEN; AND THE AGILE CONNECTION

Two basic principles of software testing are "test early" and "test often." These precepts have been respected for many years and are a principal feature of agile methodologies.

"Testing early" means testing parts as soon as they are implemented rather than waiting for the completion of the units they are part of. In the video store application, for example, suppose that we are constructing a method that stores rental information using *Video* and *Customer* objects as input parameters. "Testing early" implies testing this method alone as much as possible before constructing additional methods in the class.

"Testing often" means running tests at every reasonable opportunity, including after small additions or changes have been made. For the video store example, suppose that we add functionality to the rental storage method mentioned above. "Testing often" translates here into first rerunning the prior tests and then testing for the new functionality. One reason for testing often is that changes sometimes invalidate code already implemented. We discuss this next.

A goal of modern development methods, and especially of agile methods, is for the application under development to grow only—in other words, not to require any other kind of alteration such as erasures. Accomplishing this (which is not always easy) means that existing tests continue to apply as new elements are developed.

25.2 RETESTING: REGRESSION TESTING

Suppose that we thoroughly test part P of an application. Part P necessarily depends on other parts. (If part P depends on no other parts, it can be treated like a separate application.) Now suppose that we add to or alter part Q of the application. If P depends on Q, then P should be retested. Retesting software to ensure that its capability has not been compromised is called *regression testing*. A regression test is designed to assure us that the code added since the last test has not compromised the functionality that was present before the change(s) were made. Such a test usually consists of a repeat or subset of the tests that were executed on the artifact before changes were made.

As an example, we could find that adding functionality to *DVDRental* to estimate when a customer will return the DVD (mysteriously!) changes the due date. This kind of occurrence is caused by an erroneous addition, a poor design, or an incomplete understanding of the application. Figure 25.2 summarizes this.

A problem in regression testing is assessing whether or not added or changed code affects a given body of already-tested code. Also, we may not always be able to retest every part of an application because this sometimes becomes prohibitively time-consuming (an operating system is such an example). Figure 25.3 explains such situations by considering what regression testing is necessary after code N has been added or changed.

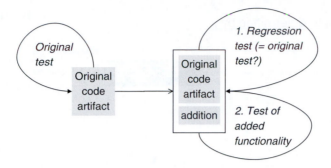

Figure 25.2 The idea of regression testing

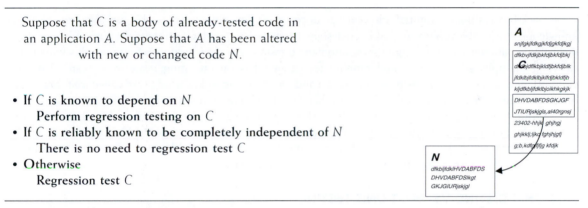

Figure 25.3 Parts to be retested in regression testing

25.3 BLACK BOX AND WHITE BOX TESTING

Suppose that we have built the video store application and we want to test it. We may run the application with data like the following, and then compare the application's behavior with its required behavior.

> *Abel rents "The Matrix" on January 24*
>
> *Barry rents "Gone With the Wind" on January 25*
>
> *Abel returns "The Matrix" on January 30*
>
> . . . .

This type of testing is known as *black box* testing because it does not take into account the manner in which the application was designed or implemented. Black box testing can be performed by someone who needs to know only what the application is required to produce. (He or she does not need to know how the application was built.) This is analogous to building an automobile and then testing it by driving it under various conditions.

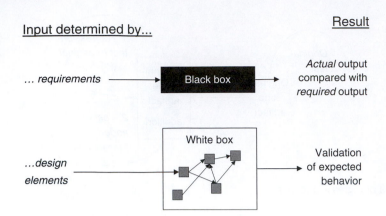

Figure 25.4 Black box and white box testing

Black box testing is essential. However, to uncover as many defects as possible, we also need to utilize knowledge of how the application has been designed and implemented. Continuing the automobile analogy, if the car is built with a new design for its automatic transmission, we would be wise to use this knowledge, stressing multiple gear changes and running tests that focus on changing gears in as many ways and circumstances as possible. Tests based on design and implementation knowledge are called *white box* or *glass box* tests. Figure 25.4 illustrates the difference between black box and white box testing.

White box testing methods are typically performed during unit testing, which is described in Chapter 26. Black box testing is performed both during and after unit testing and is described in Chapters 26 and 28.

Tests that focus substantively on both on the knowledge of how an application is intended to operate as well as how it is constructed are sometimes called *gray box* tests.

25.4 UNIT TESTING VS. POST-UNIT TESTING

Software applications consist of numerous parts. As with all construction, the soundness of the whole depends on the soundness of the parts. This is illustrated by the cantilevered bridge in Figure 25.5.

Because of this dependence, we test software parts thoroughly before assembling them—a process known as *unit testing*. Individual methods are considered *units* for testing purposes, and so are classes. A part as substantial as a grammar checker in a word processor is probably too large to be considered a "unit." At times we inadvertently allow a defect in a unit to remain undetected until the product is complete. In that case, the cost of isolating and repairing the defect is tens or hundreds of times the cost of doing so within the phase during which the defect was created. In other words, there is a very large payoff in detecting defects early—at the unit level.

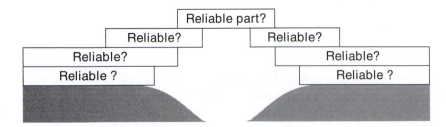

Figure 25.5 A bridge made from parts depends on their individual reliability

- **Interface testing**
  validates functions exposed by modules
- **Integration** . . .
  . . . combinations of modules
- **System**
  whole application
- **Usability**
  user satisfaction
- **Regression**
  changes did not create defects in existing code
- **Acceptance**
  customer agreement that contract satisfied
- **Installation**
  works as specified once installed on required platform

- **Robustness**
  ability to handle anomalies

- **Performance**
  fast enough; uses acceptable amount of memory

Figure 25.6 Some major types of post-unit tests

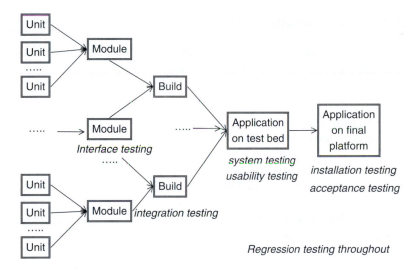

Figure 25.7 Various non-unit test types

Various types of *post-unit* tests are also administered. Figure 25.6 summarizes some of the major types. They are covered in Chapter 28.

Figure 25.7 is a summary of when each of the post-unit testing activities is performed during the process of building an application.

25.5 TESTING OBJECT-ORIENTED IMPLEMENTATIONS

Object-oriented applications, when developed well, benefit from their organization into classes. Like any modularization, this helps with testing because the classes can often be tested separately from—and in addition to—black box functionality. Prior to the advent of OO, modularization tended to be in terms of functional units, decomposed into lower level functional units ("structured programming"). These units can be separately tested but only when cleanly designed. As will be seen in Chapter 26, on unit testing, OO testing includes method, class, and package testing.

25.6 DOCUMENTING TESTS

It requires significant time to decide what to test, how to test, when to do so, and with what data. In addition, test results must be analyzed to determine what defects they uncovered. We therefore treat each test as an item of value. Test procedures, test data, and test records are maintained; tests are reused or modified where possible. Examples of test documentation can be found in Chapters 26 and 27.

25.7 TEST PLANNING

To maximize the effectiveness of resources spent on testing, a systematic approach is required and a plan is devised. Recall that the goal is to detect as many errors as possible at as serious a level as possible with the resources available. Typical planning steps are shown in Figure 25.8 and elaborated in the rest of this section.

25.7.1 Organize "Unit" vs. Non-Unit Tests

The limits of what constitutes a "unit" have to be defined by the development team. For example, do they include the testing of packages, or is this to be considered another type of testing?

---

1. **Define "units" vs. non-units** for testing
2. Determine **what types** of testing will be performed
3. Determine **extent**
   - Do not just "test until time expires"
   - Prioritize, so that important tests are definitely performed
4. **Document**
   - Individual's personal document set included?
   - How/when to incorporate all types of testing?
   - How/when to incorporate in formal documents?
   - How/when to use tools/test utilities?
5. Determine **input sources**
6. Decide **who** will test
   - Individual engineer responsible for some (units)?
   - How/when inspected by QA?
   - How/when designed and performed by third parties?
7. Estimate **resources**
   - Use historical data if available
8. Identify **metrics** to be collected
   - Define, gather, use
   - For example, time, defect count, type, and source

Figure 25.8 A plan for testing

- When tester has **not been able to find** another defect in 5 (10? 30? 100?) minutes of testing
- When all **nominal, boundary and out-of-bounds** test examples show no defect
- When a given **checklist** of test types has been completed
- After completing a series of **targeted coverage** (e.g., branch coverage for unit testing)
- When testing runs out of its scheduled **time**

Figure 25.9 Stopping criteria for testing

For object-oriented development projects, a common sequence of unit testing is to test the methods of each class, then the classes of each package, and then the package as a whole. If we were building a framework, we would test the classes in each framework package first and then move on to the application packages, because the latter depend on the former. Once the "units" and non-unit tests have been identified, they must be organized and saved in a systematic manner.

25.7.2 Determine the Extent of Testing

Since it is impossible to test for every possible situation, the *extent* of testing should be considered and defined in advance. For example, if a banking application consists of withdrawals, deposits, and queries, unit testing could specify that every method should be tested with an equal amount of legal, boundary, and illegal data; or perhaps, due to their sensitivity, withdrawal and deposit methods are tested three times as extensively as query methods, and so on. Test cases are selected both from normal expected operation, as well as from those judged most likely to fail. *Stopping criteria* are established in advance; these are concrete conditions upon which testing stops. Examples are listed in Figure 25.9.

25.7.3 Decide How Tests Will Be Documented

Test documentation consists of test procedures, input data, the code that executes the test, output data, known issues that cannot be attended to yet, and efficiency data. Test drivers and utilities are used to execute unit tests, and these are documented for future use. JUnit is an example of a unit test utility (described in more detail in Chapter 26). JUnit-like and various professional test utilities help developers to retain test documentation. JUnit classes, in particular, tend to be maintained along with the application.

25.7.4 Decide How and Where to Get Test Input

Applications are developed to solve problems in a specific area, and there is often a set of test data special to the application. Examples are as follows:

- Standard test stock market data for a brokerage application

- Standard test chemical reactions for a chemical engineering application

- Standard FDA procedures for the pharmaceutical industry

- Standard test input for a compiler

- Output from previous versions of the application

The procurement process and use of such domain-specific test input must be planned.

25.7.5 Decide Who Will Be Involved in Testing

Unit testing is usually performed by developers in a manner of their own choosing. Testing beyond the unit level is planned and performed by people other than the developer—usually an internal QA organization. Unit tests are made available for inspection and for possible incorporation into higher-level tests. Some post-unit testing requires QA engineers to understand the design, but most organizations do not support this capability, and so they assign QA to higher-level, black box testing only. Some of the independence of QA can be captured by having development engineers unit-test each other's code. It can also be attained by QA assuming an oversight responsibility, ensuring that unit testing is performed thoroughly by developers.

25.7.6 Estimate the Resources Required

Unit testing is often bundled with the development process rather than being called out as a separate budget item. Good leaders foster an attitude that the reliability of units is essential, and they allow developers sufficient time to attain reliable units. Testing beyond the unit level is an identifiably separate item, usually associated with the project's budget but sometimes a part of QA's whole budget. Employing a third party for testing is sometimes used—including offshored resources—and must be budgeted for.

25.7.7 Arrange to Track Metrics

The development organization specifies the form in which engineers record defect counts, defect types, and time spent on testing. The resulting data are used to assess the state of the application, to forecast the job's eventual quality and completion date, and as historical data for future projects. The data also become part of the organization's historical record.

25.8 TESTING TEST SUITES BY FAULT INJECTION

Suites of tests and test plans can be evaluated, and there are ways to improve them. *Mutation testing*, in particular, validates testing suites rather than the code under test itself. Suppose that we have developed a suite of tests for all or part of an application. *Fault injection* is the process of deliberately inserting faults into a program. Mutation testing is a kind of fault injection whereby we change the source code in small, controlled, and deliberately incorrect ways to determine whether the resulting injected errors are detected by the test suite. Examples are changing a *true* to a *false* and a ">" to a ">=". If our tests continue to pass despite fault injections, this exposes weakness in our current test suite. We can infer that the test suite is probably failing to find defects that we did not insert. By working on fault insertion, it is possible to estimate the number of defects that our test suite is failing to find.

Mutation is said to have originated by R. Lipton in a 1971 class. It is computationally intensive, which is one reason it took some time to become active as an area of research and practice.

25.9 SUMMARY

Software testing is a validation process, the purpose of which is to detect as many defects of as high a level of seriousness as possible. Defects are detected when the software under test is provided with input, and the resulting output does not match the expected output.

Two basic principles of software testing are "test early" and "test often." "Test early" means that as soon as a software part is implemented it should be tested. This ensures that defects are detected as close to their introduction as possible, making them easier and cheaper to detect and correct. "Testing often" means running tests at every reasonable opportunity, including after additions or modifications have been made. Updated code may adversely affect the existing code, and the errors should be found and repaired as quickly as possible. The testing for capabilities already attained prior to update is known as regression testing and is performed throughout the testing process.

There are two basic test methodologies: black box and white box. Black box testing does not take into account the manner in which the software is designed or implemented. Test inputs are provided based on the requirements of the application, and outputs are examined to ensure they match what is expected. White box testing takes the design and implementation into consideration, and inputs are devised with these in mind.

Unit testing is performed on the methods and classes of the software. It employs both white box and black box techniques. It ensures that the underlying structure of the software is sound. After some or all units are tested, post-unit tests are run that test the larger system. These include interface, integration, system, usability, regression, acceptance, and installation testing.

25.10 EXERCISES

1. Why not wait for many parts to be built, and then test them together? This seems to kill several birds with one stone.

2. Suppose that you have a developing application, tested so far, to which you add code. Why not, as the next step, test the combined result?

3. Explain why (a) white box testing, by itself, is not enough and (b) black box testing, by itself, is not enough.

4. Why is unit testing most commonly performed by software engineers who program and post-unit testing by QA personnel?

5. Why should test planning be specifically identified as an activity rather than being pursued informally when the time comes?

26

Unit Testing

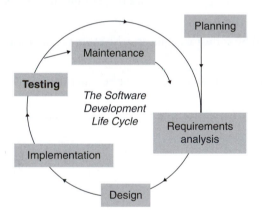

The Software Development Life Cycle

- Planning
- Maintenance
- **Testing**
- Requirements analysis
- Implementation
- Design

- What parts of the code should be subjected to unit testing?

- How do you go about unit testing?

- What is statement coverage? Branch coverage? Path coverage?

- How does equivalence partitioning help in selecting test cases?

- How do you use stubs when the unit under test requires other — but unbuilt — units?

- How do you use JUnit?

- What is test-driven development?

- How is unit testing done in case studies?

Figure 26.1 The context and learning goals for this chapter

Unit testing is the testing of the parts of an application in isolation. Typically these are the methods and classes. Unit testing is conducted by software developers either in parallel with implementation or after a part of the application is coded. In either case both white box and black box methods are employed. White box unit tests focus on the unit's internals such as program logic, branch points, and code paths. Black box unit tests focus on providing inputs based on the particular requirements of the unit, validating that correct outputs are produced. Once they are successfully tested in isolation, units are ready to be integrated and

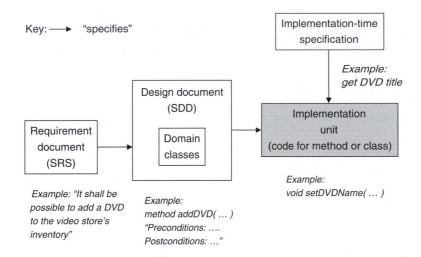

Key: ——→ "specifies"

Figure 26.2 The source of units for unit testing

tested together. This is what we will call *post-unit testing* and is covered in Chapter 27. The rest of this chapter describes specific test methods and strategies employed in unit testing.

26.1 THE SOURCES OF UNITS FOR UNIT TESTING

The first step in unit testing is identifying units and determining what they are intended to do. These are obtained from the SRS or the SDD. They may also be elements too minor to specify in the SDD. Figure 26.2 illustrates this for the video store example.

For units arising from design, we may not possess explicit requirements against which to perform tests. An example is a test for the class *GameCharacter*, introduced for the design of our video game; none of the original requirements specifically involves *GameCharacter* per se. Separate specifications should be written for all design classes once the design is created. When these are not written, as is often the case, test cases have to be devised against the functionality that the class is supposed (by the tester) to possess. Figure 26.3 illustrates unit testing against requirements and against design.

26.2 UNIT TEST METHODS

Both white box and black box methods are utilized during unit testing. Some of the principal techniques are shown in Figure 26.4. As described in Chapter 25, white box testing is conducted with knowledge of the design and implementation of the unit under test. The white box unit tests focus on the internal code structure, testing each program statement, every decision point, and each independent path through the code. Black box methods focus on testing the unit without using its internal structure. Techniques used to conduct black box unit tests include equivalence partitioning and boundary value analysis, topics that are explained in detail below.

There has been, and continues to be, research on the relationship among these testing types since they often overlap and also leave various kinds of gaps. An example of past research is described by S. Rapps and E. J. Weyuker [1], in which paths are selected on the basis of where variables are defined vs. where they are used. Nevertheless, the types discussed form a good starting point and practical basis.

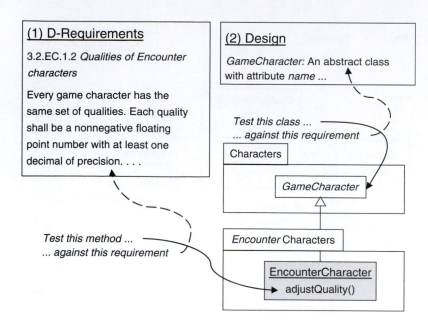

Figure 26.3 Relating tests to requirements and design

26.2.1 Statement Coverage

At a minimum, every statement in a program must be executed at least once during unit testing. If a line of code contains a defect, tests that never execute the line will not detect the defect. Untested statements are thought by many to be a major cause of latent defects.

   Consider the function *computeFine* () **shown in** Listing 26.1. We will use a directed graph, called a *program control graph*, to graphically represent the control paths of the program. Figure 26.5 contains the program control graph of *computeFine()*, where each node in the graph represents an executable line of code, and each

---

White Box Methods

- **Statement coverage**
  Test cases cause every line of code to be executed
- **Branch coverage**
  Test cases cause every decision point to execute
- **Path coverage**
  Test cases cause every independent code path to be executed

Black Box Methods

- **Equivalence partitioning**
  Divide input values into equivalent groups
- **Boundary value analysis**
  Test at boundary conditions

Figure 26.4 Methods for unit testing, categorized by black box and white box types

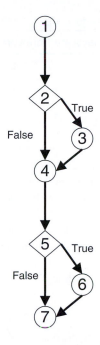

Figure 26.5 Control flow graph of *computeFine()*, with numbers keyed to Listing 26.1

edge represents the transition between lines of code. In the graph we represent decision points such as *if*, *while*, or *for* statements as a diamond, and all other executable statements as a circle.

Listing 26.1: Computing a fine for a late rental

```
  int computeFine(int daysLate, boolean printOn)
  {
1       int MAX_FINE_PERIOD = 21, fine = 0;
2       if (daysLate <= MAX_FINE_PERIOD) {
3               fine = daysLate * DAILY_FINE;
        }
4       logFine(fine);
5       if (printOn == TRUE) {
6               printFine(fine);
        }
7       return fine;
        }
```

In order to satisfy statement coverage, tests are devised with inputs that ensure each line of code is executed at least once. As shown in Table 26.1, only one test is necessary to satisfy statement coverage of *computeFine()* (but not truly complete coverage, as we shall see).

Table 26.1 A test for *computeFine()*

Test Case #	daysLate	printON	Path
1	1	TRUE	1-2-3-4-5-6-7

26.2.2 Branch Coverage

Statement coverage is satisfactory for determining whether a particular line of code has an error, but it will not catch all types of errors by any means. In fact, *computeFine()* does have a defect: the variable *fine* should be initialized to MAX_FINE on line 1, not to 0. The defect will manifest if *daysLate* is input with a value greater than MAX_FINE_PERIOD. This was not detected in the statement coverage test because, although the *if* statement on line 2 was executed, the branch for daysLate > MAX_FINE_PERIOD was not tested.

A stronger form of test coverage, one that includes statement coverage and detects this type of defect, is *branch coverage*, which means that for every decision point in the code, every branch is executed at least once. Listing 26.2 contains an updated *computeFine()* function, with the aforementioned defect repaired—the variable *fine* is now initialized to MAX_FINE on line 1.

Listing 26.2: An updated *computeFine()* function

```
int computeFine(int daysLate, boolean printOn)
{
1       int MAX_FINE_PERIOD = 21, fine = MAX_FINE; // defect fixed
2       if (daysLate <= MAX_FINE_PERIOD) {
3               fine = daysLate * DAILY_FINE;
        }
4       logFine(fine);
5       if (printOn == TRUE) {
6               printFine(fine);
        }
7       return fine;
    }
```

To satisfy branch coverage, one or more tests are run with appropriate inputs to ensure that every statement is executed at least once *and* every branch decision is executed at least once. The two test cases in Table 26.2, for example, satisfy these conditions.

The execution path of each test case is shown in the program control graphs of Figure 26.6, with the bold arrows depicting the control flow.

26.2.3 Path Coverage

An even stronger form of test coverage is *path coverage*, in which all distinct code paths are executed by at least one test case. By distinct code paths we are referring to the complete set of sequences of branches and loop

Table 26.2 Tests sufficient to satisfy branch coverage

Test Case #	daysLate	printON	Path
1	1	TRUE	1-2-3-4-5-6 7
2	60	FALSE	1-2-4-5-7

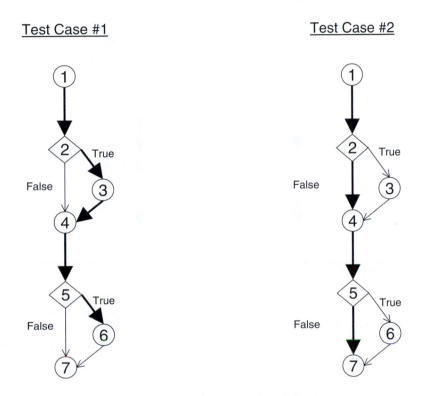

Figure 26.6 Branch coverage of *computeFine*(), with numbers keyed to Listing 26.1

traversals, even if they differ by just one small part of the path. This type of testing detects errors that only occur if a specific path is executed. Path coverage subsumes statement and branch coverage. As an example, *computeFine*() contains two *if* statements, each with two branch decisions: true and false. Therefore *computeFine*() has four distinct paths through the function as illustrated in Figure 26.7.

Four test cases would be required to test all the distinct paths of *computeFine*(), one for each path, as shown in Table 26.3.

As the number of branches and loops increase, the number of distinct paths grows exponentially. It quickly becomes impractical to test them all. For example, if the number of decision points is 30, the number of distinct paths is over 1 billion. It is therefore necessary to limit the number of paths to test. A commonly used method of making the tests viable while gaining significant confidence is to compute the number of linearly independent paths, or *basis paths*, through the code under test. This can be thought of as the minimum number of paths that can be combined to generate every possible path, and is the minimum number of paths that should be tested.

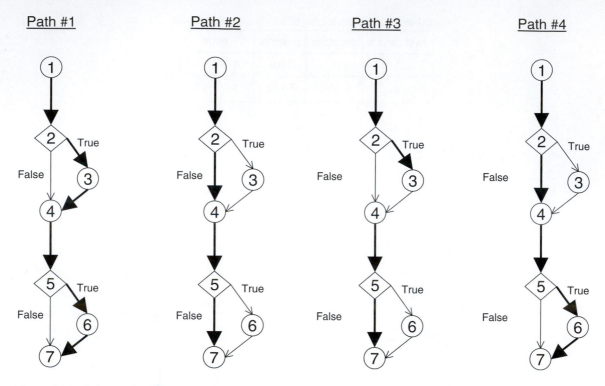

Figure 26.7 Distinct paths of *computerFine*(), with numbers keyed to Listing 26.1

The number of basis paths can be calculated by computing the *cyclomatic complexity* [2], which has its roots in graph theory. The first step in computing the cyclomatic complexity is to represent the code with a program control graph. Then the cyclomatic complexity (CC) is calculated with the following formula:

$$CC = e - n + 2$$

where e = the number of edges, and n = the number of nodes.

As an example, Listing 26.3 contains an updated version of *computeFines*() that has input an array containing the number of days late for a list of DVDs. In order to process the list, a *for* loop is introduced, adding an additional decision point in the function. Figure 26.8 shows the corresponding program control graph for this *computeFines*().

Table 26.3 Test cases for all the distinct paths of *computeFine*()

Test Case #	daysLate	printON	Path
1	1	TRUE	1-2-3-4-5-6 7
2	60	FALSE	1-2-4-5--7
3	1	FALSE	1-2-3-4-5-7
4	60	TRUE	1-2-4-5-6-7

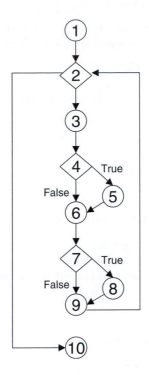

Figure 26.8 Program control graph for *computeFines()*, with numbering keyed to Listing 26.3

Listing 26.3: Updated function—*computeFines()*

```
   int computeFines(int daysLate[], int numDVD, boolean printOn)
   {
 1 int MAX_FINE_PERIOD = 21, int cumFine = 0;
 2 for (i=0; i < numDVD; i++) {
 3          fine = MAX_FINE
 4          if (daysLate[i] <= MAX_FINE_PERIOD) {
 5                 fine = daysLate[i] * DAILY_FINE;
            }
 6          logFine(fine);
 7          if (printOn == TRUE) {
 8                 printFine(fine);
            }
 9          cumFine += fine;
      }
10 return cumFine;
   }
```

To calculate the cyclomatic complexity of *computeFines()*, we refer to the program control graph in Figure 26.8 and note that there are 12 edges and 10 nodes. Therefore, CC is calculated as follows:

$$CC = 12 - 10 + 2 = 4$$

This tells us that there are four basis paths. To generate a specific set of basis paths, the following steps can be followed.

1. Start with the straight path through the code (all conditions true).

2. Set the first condition to false, keeping all the rest true.

3. Reset the first condition to true, set the second condition to false, keeping all the rest true.

4. Continue, setting the next condition false with all the rest true.

5. Stop after the last condition has been set false.

That is, each basis path varies only one of the conditions at a time. Note that the condition nodes in this function are 2, 4, and 7, which are the *for* statement and the two *if* statements. Using this algorithm, the four basis paths for *computeFines()* are as follows:

Basis Path #1: 1-2-3-4-5-6-7-8-9-10 all true

Basis Path #2: 1-2-10 *for* statement false

Basis Path #3: 1-2-3-4-6-7-8-9-10 first *if* statement false

Basis Path #4: 1-2-3-4-5-6-7-9-10 second *if* statement false

The corresponding program control graphs are shown in Figure 26.9.

Four tests are then devised with appropriate inputs to ensure that each basis path is executed once, as shown in Table 26.4.

26.2.4 Equivalence Partitioning

The challenge of testing is the selection of a test set. For example, a function such as *computeFine()*, which takes a simple integer parameter *daysLate*, has all of $2^{32} = 4$ billion possible input values. Any test set is a truly tiny subset of the collection of all possibilities, and so we want it to be as representative as possible.

Equivalence partitioning is a black box test method in which parameter values are divided into nonoverlapping sets that constitute the complete set of possibilities ("partitions"), with the values in each partition expected to produce similar test results. If we can identify such a partitioning, we can have some confidence in a test that selects one value per equivalence partition as test input. Equivalence partitioning is also used in system testing, which is discussed in Chapter 28.

The potential input values for a test can be thought of as points in *parameter space*: an *n*-dimensional space with one dimension per parameter. For example, if we are testing a method intended to compute the area of a rectangle, the parameter space is two-dimensional; each *width/length* pair is a point in two-dimensional space.

As another example, suppose we want to test that the video store function discussed above correctly computes the fine on late movies. Suppose that the store's penalty depends on the number of days late—as usual—but also on whether the movie is a new release, old release, or "one-of-a-kind." The parameter space

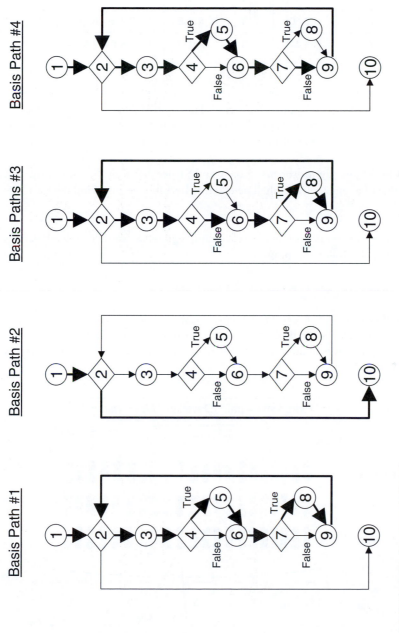

Figure 26.9 Basis paths for *computeFines*()

Table 26.4 Tests that cover all basis paths

Test Case #	daysLate[]	numDVD	printON	Basis Path
1	[1,5,14]	3	TRUE	1-2-3-4-5-6-7-8-9-10
2	[1,5,14]	0	TRUE	1-2-10
3	[1,5,60]	3	TRUE	1-2-3-4-6-7-8-9-10
4	[1,5,14]	3	FALSE	1-2-3-4-5-6-7-9-10

can be thought of as consisting of the points shown in Figure 26.10. The parameter space is not limited to legal values; it includes values that are not permitted. Figure 26.10 suggests the shape of this parameter space.

Suppose that the store's fine calculation requirement is as follows:

The fine shall be $2 per day for the first 5 days and $1 per day after that, up to the value of the movie. The value of all new releases shall be taken to be $20, one-of-a-kind releases $15, and old releases $10.

The parameter space decomposes into corresponding regions such as "new release between 0 and 5 days late," each having the following property.

The application behaves in a similar manner for all values in each region.

These are called *equivalence partitions*, or *equivalence classes*.

Creating equivalence classes can be demanding. To focus on one region in our video store example, we expect that the algorithm behaves in the same way for all of the parameter points in the *new release/6–15 days late* partition shown in Figure 26.11.

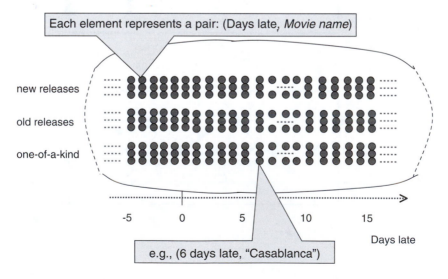

Figure 26.10 Parameter space for *computeFines()*

Figure 26.11 One equivalence partition of *computeFines*()

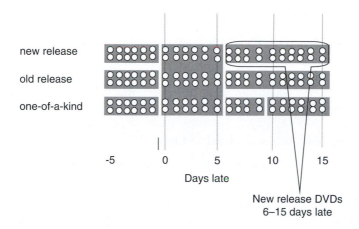

Figure 26.12 Equivalence partitions of *computeFine*() method

A full parameter space equivalence partition for this example is shown in Figure 26.12.

To identify equivalence partitions, determine the limits—or boundaries—on the individual variables or combinations of variables. These limits can be seen either in the code itself or in the requirements that the variables reflect. Often, the relevant requirements are in the form of *business rules*. The fine policy of the video store example is a good example of a rule for doing the business of renting. Once the equivalence partitions have been determined, we create test cases as in Figure 26.13.

26.2.5 Boundary Value Analysis

Many errors occur at the boundaries between equivalence classes. As an example, *computeFine()* contains a boundary between 5 and 6 days late, because at 6 days a fine starts accruing. A common coding error might be

---

Test . . .

- . . . values strictly **within** each region
- . . . values at region **borders**

Notes:

- *Include all illegal regions*
- *Within each constraint, select randomly*
  - *For example, with "new release" input, select lateness days at random between 6 and 15, excluding 6 and 15*

Figure 26.13 Using equivalence partitions to create test cases

to use ">=" instead of "=" when checking for a boundary condition. For example, the code that checks for the *new release/6-15 days late* equivalence class in *computeFine()* should read as follows.

```
if ((numDaysLate > 5) && (numDaysLate <= 15))
```

However, a common error is to write code like the following.

```
if ((numDaysLate >= 5) && (numDaysLate <= 15))
```

If we were to use only a value of 6 to test this equivalence class, the boundary error would not be detected.

Values equal to and on either side of a boundary should be tested. In the example above, we are interested in testing the equivalence class with values in the range [5..15], inclusive. Test cases should be executed that include the following values for *numDaysLate* as input: 4, 5, 6, 10, 14, 15, 16.

In general, one identifies boundaries as follows, the principal sources for unit testing being class invariants and method preconditions.

1. Identify all of the variables involved, global and local.

2. Identify their limits, individually and in combination (example: the condition $2<x+y<7$ identifies 2 and 7 as boundaries for $x+y$).

3. Test for combinations of these variable/combination/values. Testing all combinations is ideal but when this is impractical, we select those that appear most likely to fail or we select combinations at random or both.

Note that 2 being a boundary for $x+y$ implicates the straight line $x+y=2$ in the x-y plane as a boundary.

26.3 TESTING METHODS

Unit testing typically starts by testing the methods of a class. In this section we discuss how to carry this out in an orderly way, incorporating the methodologies covered in the previous section.

26.3.1 Checklist for Testing Methods

Humphrey [3] recommends the checklists in Table 26.5 for performing method tests.

26.3.2 Organizing Test Cases

By now you may be overwhelmed by the sheer number of different types of tests. Several test types overlap. For example, a test with normal inputs may have statement coverage, branch coverage, and path coverage. One way to simplify and organize the unit tests is to list the testing types as in Table 26.6, and to number the individual tests accordingly.

26.3.3 Stubs

A method frequently depends on classes other than the one containing it. This presents no problem if the needed classes have already been built and tested. Otherwise, we use stand-ins with the same name but with

Table 26.5 Humphrey's unit-testing checklist, categorized black box or white box in the context of a method test

Operation	Comment
1. Verify operation at normal parameter values	a black box test based on the unit's requirements
2. Verify operation at limit parameter values	black box
3. Verify operation outside parameter values	black box
4. Ensure that all instructions execute	statement coverage
5. Check all paths, including both sides of all branches	path coverage
6. Check the use of all called objects	white box
7. Verify the handling of all data structures	white box
8. Verify the handling of all files	white box
9. Check normal termination of all loops	white box: part of a correctness proof
10.Check abnormal termination of all loops	white box
11.Check normal termination of all recursions	white box
12. Check abnormal termination of all recursions	white box
13. Verify the handling of all error conditions	gray box
14. Check timing and synchronization	gray box
15. Verify all hardware dependencies	gray box

just enough substance to support the method under test. These are called *stubs*. For example, suppose that we want to test the *rent()* method in the *Rental* class of the video store application framework. It depends on the classes *RentalItem* and *RentalCustomer* as shown in Figure 26.14. We therefore create stubs for these two classes as shown.

Simple stubs like these are not sufficient beyond the method-testing level. As we will describe in Chapter 27, in that case we require artifacts known as "drivers" as well.

26.3.4 Example of a Method-Level Unit Test

As an example of a unit test, we will test for the following detailed requirement for the Encounter case study.

3.2.EC.1.2 Qualities of Encounter characters. Every game character has the same set of qualities. Each quality shall be a nonnegative floating point number with at least one decimal of precision. These are all initialized equally so that the sum of their values is 100. The value of a quality cannot be both greater than zero and less than 0.5. For the first release the qualities shall be *concentration, stamina, intelligence, patience,* and *strength*.

An appropriate test set for a method *adjustQuality(String qualityP, float valueP)* is given next. This method sets the quality named by *qualityP* to *valueP* and adjusts the remaining qualities so that the proportion of the remaining available points remains the same. Within each of the "on range boundaries," "outside range,"

Table 26.6 Checklist for unit tests—an example showing which tests fulfilled each question

Test type	Tests
1. Within bounds?	1, 12, 14, 15
2. On boundary?	12, 3, 5
3. Out of bounds?	6, 3, 4
4. Covers all statements?	9
5. Covers all branches?	1
6. Covers all paths?	1, 10
7. Assertions tested?	12
8. Use all called objects?	6
9. Verifies handling data structures?	8, 7
10. Handles all files?	12
11. Tests all loops with normal terminations?	12
12. Tests loops with abnormal terminations?	7
13. Tests all normal recursions?	N/A
14. Tests all abnormal recursions?	N/A
15. Tests all error conditions?	11
16. Tests all synchronizations?	N/A
17. Tests all hardware dependencies?	N/A

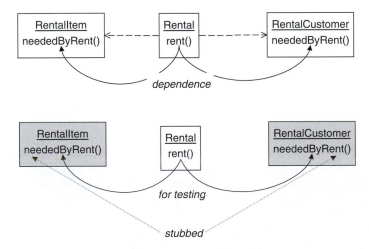

Figure 26.14 Using stubs to test a method

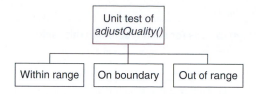

Figure 26.15 Partitioning *adjustQuality*() at the top level

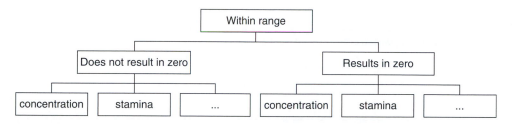

Figure 26.16 Partitioning *adjustQuality*()—''within range''

and "within range" categories, we try to obtain systematic coverage by seeking representatives of each equivalence partition. Figure 26.15 is typical of a systematic decomposition of the input space into equivalence partitions.

The next levels of partitioning are shown in Figures 26.16, 26.17, and 26.18, and the actual test cases are listed below.

A resulting test suite is shown in Table 26.7.

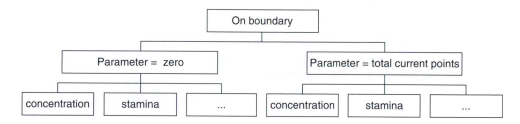

Figure 26.17 Partitioning *adjustQuality*()—''on boundary''

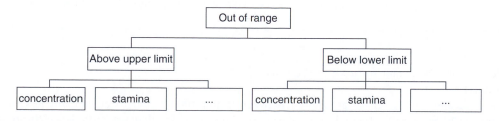

Figure 26.18 Partitioning *adjustQuality*()—''out of range''

Table 26.7 A test suite for *adjustQuality()*

Key to unit tests of *adjustQuality()* (Details for each test follow this table)		
1. Within range		
	1.1 *adjustQuality()* does not result in a zero value	
		1.1.1 *quality* parameter == "concentration" 1.1.2 *quality* parameter == "stamina" . . .
	1.2 *adjustQuality()* does result in a zero value	
		1.2.1 *quality* parameter == "concentration" 1.2.2 *quality* parameter == "stamina" . . .
2. Parameters at range boundaries		
	2.1 zero parameter	
		2.1.1 *quality* parameter == "concentration" 2.1.2 *quality* parameter == "stamina" . . . .
	2.2 parameter value == current total points	
		2.2.1 *quality* parameter == "concentration" 2.2.2 *quality* parameter == "stamina" . . .
3. Parameters outside range		
	3.1 Above upper limit of parameter values	
		3.1.1 *quality* parameter = "concentration"; total points = 100; parameter 101 . . .
	3.2 Below lower limit of parameter values	
		3.2.1 *quality* parameter = "concentration"; total points = 100; parameter -101 . . .

The following are the details for each of the tests.

Test 1.1.1

Input: (Ideally, choose these at random between 0 and 100 to sum to an amount less than 100.) Concentration 20; Stamina 20 [1/4 of the non-"concentration" points]; Intelligence 20; Patience 20; Strength 20;

Execute: adjustQuality("concentration," 10) (Ideally, this value is chosen at random within bounds guaranteed not to result in a zero "concentration" value.)

Expected output: Concentration $20 + 10 = 30$; Stamina $70/4 = 17.5$; (Note: remains 1/4 of the non-"concentration" points); Intelligence $70/4 = 17.5$; Patience $70/4 = 17.5$; Strength $70/4 = 17.5$;

Tests 1.1.2, 1.1.3, . . . are similar, using the other qualities instead of concentration.

Test 1.2.1
Input: Concentration 20; Stamina 20; Intelligence 20; Patience 20; Strength 20;
Execute: *adjustQuality("concentration", 99)*
Expected output: Concentration 99; Stamina 0 (1/4 result replaced by zero); Intelligence 0 (1/4 result replaced by zero);Patience 0 (1/4 result replaced by zero); Strength 0 (1/4 result replaced by zero);

Tests 1.2.2, 1.2.3, . . . are similar, using the other qualities instead of concentration.

Test 2.1.1
Input: Concentration 0; Stamina 25; Intelligence 25; Patience 25; Strength 25;
Execute: *adjustQuality("stamina", 74)*
Expected output: Concentration 0; Stamina 99; Intelligence 0 (result of 1/3 is set to zero); Patience 0 (result of 1/3 is set to zero); Strength 0 (result of 1/3 is set to zero)

Tests 2.1..1.2, 2.1.1.3, . . . are similar

Tests 2.2, 2.3, . . . pertain to other extremes. For example:
2.N *adjustQuality()* called with parameter equaling a current value
Input: Concentration 0; Stamina 25; Intelligence 25; Patience 25; Strength 25;
Execute: *adjustQuality("stamina", -25)*
Expected output: Concentration 0; Stamina 0; Intelligence 33; Patience 33; Strength 33;

Test 3.1.1
Input: Concentration 20; Stamina 20; Intelligence 20; Patience 20; Strength 20;
Execute: *adjustQuality("concentration", 81)*
Expected output: Message to error log stating that *adjustQuality()* was called with out-of-range input; Concentration 100; (20+81 set to 100); Stamina 0; (after concentration is set, there are no remaining quality points to distribute); Intelligence 0; Patience 0; Strength 0

Tests 3.1.2, 3.1.3, . . . are similar

Tests 3.2, 3.3, . . . are similar to test 3.1

Test 3.N.1
Input: Concentration 20; Stamina 20; Intelligence 20; Patience 20; Strength 20;
Execute: *adjustQuality("concentration", -21)*
Expected output: Message to error log stating that *adjustQuality()* was called with out-of-range input; Concentration 0; (20-21 set to zero); Stamina 25; (100/4); Intelligence 25 (100/4); Patience 25 (100/4); Strength 25 (100/4).

The remaining test set is generated in a similar manner.
The relevant parts of the code for *adjustQuality* are part of the class *EncounterCharacter*, given in Listing 26.10 found in Section 5.1.

26.4 TEST-DRIVEN DEVELOPMENT

An effective method for performing unit testing is to conduct testing in parallel with implementation. In fact, an effective way to build quality into an implementation is to specify the tests that an implementation must pass *before* writing the code. After writing such a test, one adds to the implementation until the test succeeds.

This is called *test-driven development* (TDD). TDD is often associated with agile development, but it is useful within any development process. The general steps involved in TDD are as follows:

1. Write a test case for some code that is yet to be implemented.
   Envision what the code is supposed to do. Depending on how thoroughly this part of the code was previously designed, a bit of detailed design may be required. Tests are typically created to test only a relatively small amount of code—as little as several lines.

2. Run the test case to verify it, which fails.
   The first run of the test should always fail, since the code to make it pass has yet to be written. If it does pass, there is a bug in the test case and it needs to be fixed.

3. Write only as much code as necessary to make the test pass.
   In this way a clean implementation emerges with minimal extraneous code.

4. Run the test case.
   If it still fails, go back to Step 3 and fix the problem in the implementation. If it passes, the test case is complete. If there is more implementation to be done, repeat these four steps.

Figure 26.19 summarizes this process.
There are many advantages to TDD, including the following:

Statement coverage—A natural by-product of TDD is that after the tests are written and pass, every line of code is executed by at least one test. Thus statement coverage is satisfied.

Cleaner code—As we mentioned previously, only as much code as necessary is written to make a test pass. This results in an implementation that tends to be clean and contains little extraneous code.

Rapid feedback—Once a section of code is written, it is immediately tested, providing instant feedback as to its correctness. This leads to quicker development time as bugs are easier to identify and correct.

Suite of unit tests—After a test is written and passes, it is saved along with other tests being developed. In this way a suite of unit tests is created and can be used for future testing activities such as regression testing.

It is common to perform TDD within a testing framework such as *JUnit*, which we describe next.

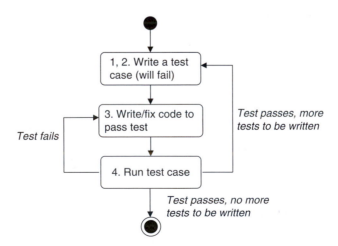

Figure 26.19 Test-drive development—the activities

26.4.1 Using *JUnit* for Unit Testing

JUnit is a public-domain test framework widely used to "write and run repeatable tests" [4]. It is implemented in and used for testing Java programs. It supports unit testing with tools for test result execution, reporting, and error handling.

Suppose, for example, we have a Calculator class and we want to write a test for a yet-to-be coded *subtract* method. If we are using TDD, the first step is to write a unit test for the envisioned method. By convention, when testing a class *X*, tests are placed in a class *TestX* and every method performing a test of method *mmmm()* is labeled *testMmmm()*.

Listing 26.4 is a *TestCalculator* class that contains one test called *testSubtract*.

Listing 26.4: JUnit class for testing *Calculator*

```
import junit.framework.TestCase;
public class TestCalculator extends TestCase
{
    public void testSubtract()
    {
        Calculator c = new Calculator();
        // Test 1: Nominal Case
        double r = c.subtract(2.0000000001, 3.0000000002);
        assertEquals(-1.0000000001, r, 0);
        // Test 2: Corner Case
        r = c.subtract(Double.MAX_VALUE, Double.MAX_VALUE);
        assertEquals(0.0, r, 0);
        . . .
    }
}
```

By examining testSubtract we can imagine the code we must write to pass the test:

1. A subtract method that takes two double arguments and returns a double result.

2. An implementation of a subtract method that subtracts the second argument from the first and returns the result of the subtraction.

To fulfill our envisioned method, we write a subtract method such as in Listing 26.5.

Listing 26.5: Building *subtract()* method for the class *Calculator*

```
package EB.calc;

public class Calculator
{
```

```
    public double subtract(double n1, double n2)
    {
        return n1 - n2;
    }
}
```

Figure 26.20 Output of *JUnit* for a simple test

The result of running TestCalculator in JUnit is the window in Figure 26.20 showing a green bar (for "passed").

To illustrate what happens when a test fails, we will force a defect with a new subtract that erroneously converts to float, as in Listing 26.6.

Listing 26.6: Example of a test that will fail

```
package EB.calc;

public class Calculator
{
    public double subtract(double n1, double n2)
    {
        float subtraction = (float)n1 - (float)n2;
        return subtraction;
    }
}
```

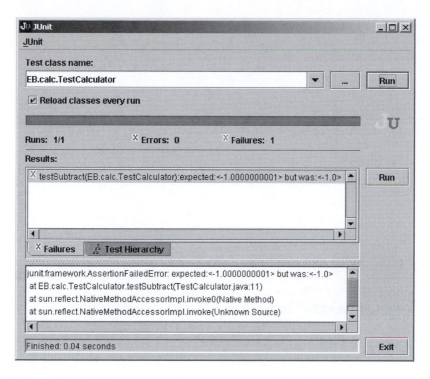

Figure 26.21 JUnit display for a failed test

Re-executing the *testSubtract* **unit test from**
Listing 26.4 results in a JUnit response like that shown in Figure 26.21, with a red bar indicating failure.

In order to run multiple unit tests, JUnit implements the *TestSuite* class. Suppose that in addition to the *TestCalculator/Calculator* pair we also have a *TestConcatenator/Concatenator* pair, as shown in Listings 26.7 and 26.8, respectively. If we run JUnit using the *TestAll* class shown in Listing 26.9, both of these tests will be executed.

Listing 26.7: Test for *Concatenator* class

```
import junit.framework.TestCase;

public class TestConcatenator extends TestCase
{
    public void testconcatenation()
    {
        Concatenator c = new Concatenator();
        String string = c.concatenationOf("abc", "def");
        assertEquals("abcdef", string);
    }
}
```

Listing 26.8: *Concatenator* class

```
public class Concatenator
{
    public String concatenationOf(String aString1,
        String aString2)
    {
        return aString1.concat(aString2);
    }
}
```

Listing 26.9: A *TestSuite* example, combining tests for *Calculator* and *Concatenator*

```
import junit.framework.Test;
import junit.framework.TestSuite;

public class TestAll extends TestSuite
{
    public static Test suite()
    {
    TestSuite testSuite = new TestSuite("A simple test suite example");
      testSuite.addTestSuite(TestCalculator.class); // Add all tests
        from TestCalculator class
      testSuite.addTestSuite(TestConcatenator.class); // Add all
        tests from TestConcatenator class
        return testSuite;

    }
}
```

26.5 CASE STUDY: ENCOUNTER VIDEO GAME

26.5.1 Code Listing for *EncounterCharacter* Class

Listing 26.10 is the class *EncounterCharacter* from the Encounter video game.

Listing 26.10: *EncounterCharacter* class from the Encounter video game

```java
/* Class Name:   EncounterCharacter
* Date:         01/13/2000
* Copyright Notice: copyright (c) 1999-2000 by Eric J. Braude
* Edit history:
*   24 Dec 2003 Eric Braude      Edited to simple stand-alone version
*                                 to show unit test of adjustValue()
*   24 Jul 2000 Tom VanCourt   Cached character image rather than
*                    recreating it on every repaint.
* 13 May 2000 Tom VanCourt    Moved saveQualityValues, getOldValue
*                  and oldValueI from PlayerCharacter
*/
import java.awt.*;
import java.io.*;

/** Base class for the characters of the Encounter game.
* <p> Requirements: SRS 3.2.EC
* <p> Design: SDD 6.2.1
* <p> Invariants: <ol>
* <li> encounterCharacterS contains all objects of this class
* <li> The values of qualValueI[] are >= 0
* </ol>
* <p> Design issues: <ul>
* <li> Character images are switched freely between right- and
* left-handed forms. That means that sword fighters will switch
* hands; scabbards will swing back and forth; scars, tattoos, etc.
* will move around, hair styles will flop back and forth, etc.
* It's good enough for now, though.
* </ul>
* @author Eric Braude, Tom VanCourt
* @version 0.2
*/
public class EncounterCharacter extends GameCharacter
{
/** Total quality points at initialization.
* <p> Requirement 3.2.EC.1.2
*/
public static final float QUAL_TOTAL_INIT = 100.0f;

// Symbols used when other classes refer to specific qualities.

/** Symbol for one of a character's qualities */
public static final String QUAL_CONCENTRATION = "concentration";
```

```java
/** Symbol for one of a character's qualities */
public static final String QUAL_INTELLIGENCE = "intelligence";

/** Symbol for one of a character's qualities */
public static final String QUAL_PATIENCE = "patience";

/** Symbol for one of a character's qualities */
public static final String QUAL_STAMINA = "stamina";
/** Symbol for one of a character's qualities */
public static final String QUAL_STRENGTH = "strength";

/** Qualities that each Encounter character possesses.
* <p>Req: 3.2.EC.1.2
*/
protected static final String[] qualityTypeS =
{  QUAL_CONCENTRATION,   QUAL_STAMINA,
   QUAL_INTELLIGENCE,   QUAL_PATIENCE,
   QUAL_STRENGTH
};

/** Root directory for graphics files. */
static final String FILE_ROOT = "edu/bu/braude/SWEngExample/";

/* INSTANCE VARIABLES */
/** Values of the qualities. <p> Requirement 3.2.EC.1.2 */
protected float[] qualValueI = new float[qualityTypeS.length];

/** Quality values before the last engagement
* <p> Requirement: 3.2.AR.4.6
*/
protected float[] oldValueI = new float[qualValueI.length];

/** Name of GIF file containing the character image.
* The character in this image is assumed to be facing left.
* Select this character's height, relative to heights of other
* characters,
* by padding the top and bottom with transparent pixels. No padding gives
* the tallest possible character.
*/
protected String imageFileNameI = null;

/** Displayable image for the character. Initialized when used. */
private Image chImageI = null;

/* CONSTRUCTORS */
```

```
/** Allocate initial total quality points equally among the qualities.
* <p> Requirement: 3.2.EC.1.2 (quality value initialization)
*/
protected EncounterCharacter()
{  super();
   for(int i = 0; i < qualityTypeS.length; ++i)
     qualValueI[i] = QUAL_TOTAL_INIT / qualityTypeS.length;
   saveQualityValues();
}

/** Construct a new character using the given name.
* <p> Requirement:   3.2.EC.1.1 (character naming)
* @param  nameP       Printable name for the character.
*/
protected EncounterCharacter(String nameP)
{  this(nameP, null);
}

/** Construct a new character using the given name and image file.
* <p> Requirement:   3.2.EC.1.1 (character naming)
* @param   nameP       Printable name for the character.
* @param   imageFileP  Filename, relative to document base,
*             for the character image file.
*/
protected EncounterCharacter(String nameP, String imageFileP)
{  this();
   setName(nameP);
   imageFileNameI = FILE_ROOT + imageFileP;
}
/* METHODS */

/** Adjust quality values, normally retaining a constant total.
* Synchronization holds qualityValueI constant even with other
* threads running.
* <p> Invariants: see the class invariants
* <p> Preconditions: qualityP is in qualityTypesS[]
*  AND qualityValueP >= 0
*  AND qualityValueP <= the sum of the quality values
* <p> Postconditions: qualityP has the value qualityValueP
* AND the remaining quality values are in the same proportion as prior to
* invocation, except that values less than some tolerance are zero.
* <p> SDD: 6.1.2.1.1
* <p> SRS: 3.2.EC.3.2: "Configurability of Encounter character quality
* values."
* @param   qualityP  Quality whose value is to be adjusted.
```

```java
 * @param   qualityValueP    The value to set this quality to.
 */
public synchronized void adjustQuality(String qualityP,
  float qualityValueP)
{  // Value of the quality to be changed
  float qualityValueM = qualValueI[indexOf(qualityP)];

  // Save the sum of the values
  float originalSumM = sumOfQualities();

  // Set the stated quality to the desired amount,
  // adjusted to the threshold value.
  setQuality(qualityP, qualityValueP);

  // If the caller adjusts the only non-zero quality value,
  // divide the adjustment amount equally among all other qualities.
  if(originalSumM == qualityValueM)
  {
    float qualityDiffEach = (originalSumM - qualityValueP)
    / (qualityTypeS.length - 1);
    for(int i = 0; i < qualityTypeS.length; ++i)
      if(!qualityTypeS[i].equalsIgnoreCase(qualityP))
        setQuality(qualityTypeS[i], qualityDiffEach);
  } else {
  /* Compute factor ("proportionM") by which all other qualities must
      change.
   * Example: if the values were 1,3,5 (i.e. sum 9) and the first
   * qualities changed from 1 to 2, then "3" and "5" change from 8/9 of
   * the total to 7/9 of the total, so each should be multiplied by 7/8,
   * i.e., by (9-2)/(9-1).
   */
  float proportionM = (originalSumM - qualityValueP) /
    (originalSumM - qualityValueM);

  //Adjust remaining qualities, retaining their mutual proportion
  for(int i = 0; i < qualityTypeS.length; ++i)
    if(!qualityTypeS[i].equalsIgnoreCase(qualityP))
      setQuality(qualityTypeS[i], qualValueI[i] * proportionM);
  }
}
/** Get a copy of the list of names of quality values.
 * @return     working copies of name strings representing qualities.
 */
public static String[] getQualityTypes()
{
```

```java
    String [] returnListM =      // Copy the string array.
    new String[qualityTypeS.length];
    for(int i = 0; i < qualityTypeS.length; i++) // Copy each string.
        returnListM[i] = new String(qualityTypeS[i]);
    return returnListM;          // Return the copy.
}


/** Returns the value of the specified quality.
 * <p>Precondition:    qualityP is a valid member of qualityTypeS[]
 * @param   qualityP    The quality we want the value for.
 * @return        The value of the specified quality.
 */
public float getQualityValue(String qualityP)
{
    return qualValueI[indexOf(qualityP)];
}


/** Quality values below this threshold are set to zero to
 * avoid having the game go on for an indeterminate amount of time.
 * <p>Requirement: e.g. 3.2.EC.1.2 (lower limit on non-zero quality values)
 * @return        Tolerance value
 */
static final float getTolerance()
{   return 0.5f;
}


/** Returns the index of the the specified quality.
 * <p> Precondition: qualityP is in qualityTypeS[],
 * give or take capitalization.
 * @param   qualityP    The quality we are searching for.
 * @return        The quality index.
 */
protected static int indexOf(String qualityP)
{
//Default to "missing" value.
int returnIndexM = -1;

// Search quality name table and note the index value.
for(int i = 0; i < qualityTypeS.length; ++i)
  if(qualityTypeS[i].equalsIgnoreCase(qualityP)) {
     returnIndexM = i;
      break;
   }
  return returnIndexM;
}
```

```
/** Set default maximum number of characters in names of characters.
 * <p>Requirement:   3.2.EC.1.1 (limit on character name length)
 * @return     Maximum number of characters allowed in a character name
 */
protected int maxNumCharsInName()
{  return 15;
}


/** Preserve the current quality values. */
public synchronized void saveQualityValues()
{
  for (int i = 0; i < qualValueI.length; i++)
    oldValueI[i] = qualValueI[i];
}


/** Set a quality value without regard to the values of other qualities.
 * Truncate any value below the threshold value down to zero.
 * Synchronization prevents changes to qualityValueI while other
 * threads are using it.
 * <p>Requirements:    3.2.EC.2 (lower limit on non-zero quality values),
 * <p>Precondition:   qualityP is a valid member of qualityTypeS[]
 * <p>Postcondition:   Quality values are greater than tolerance or are 0.
 *
 * @param    qualityP    The quality to set the value of.
 * @param    valueP      The value to set the quality to.
 */
public synchronized void setQuality(String qualityP, float valueP)
{
  if(valueP < getTolerance())
    qualValueI[indexOf(qualityP)] = 0.0f;
  else
    qualValueI[indexOf(qualityP)] = valueP;
}


/** Computes the sum of the quality values.
 * Synchronization makes sure that another thread won't change
 * qualityValueI while this thread is part-way through computing the
 * total.
 * <p> Requirements:   3.2.EC.3.2 (proportions among quality values),
 * <br> SRS 3.2.EC.3.1 Living points
 * @return   The sum of the player's qualities, a value 0 or greater.
 */
public synchronized float sumOfQualities()
{
  float sumM = 0.0f;
```

```
    for(int i = 0; i < qualityTypes.length; ++i)
      sumM += qualValueI[i];

    return sumM;
  }

} // end of EncounterCharacter
```

26.5.2 Unit Tests for the *EncounterCharacter* Class

Note to the Student:
The format of this document is derived from the IEEE Standard for Software Test Documentation. This document applies to the testing of one class. JUnit was not used in this case but could have been.

UNIT TEST FOR THE *ENCOUNTERCHARACTER* CLASS

1. Test Design Specification

The unit test for *EncounterCharacter* consists of two public methods as follows.

testEncounterCharacterMethods() tests each of the methods in turn

testEncounterCharacterClass() tests sequences of methods

These methods can be executed by *EncounterCharacter*'s *main()* method or by an external object.

2. Test Case Specification

The test cases for *EncounterCharacter* are built into *testEncounterCharacterMethods()* and *testEncounterCharacterClass()*.

For simplicity, this unit test includes test data with the method. Normally, however, the input data and the expected output are retrieved from a file.

3. Test Procedure Specification

The unit tests for *EncounterCharacter* are initiated by executing the *main()* method of *EncounterCharacter*. The parameter supplied to *main()* specifies the file to which the results are written.

This is a simple procedure. However, the procedure becomes considerably more complex when source files and user interaction are involved. For example, this will be the case in unit testing the class *EncounterGame*.

4. Test Results Documentation

The test results documentation consists of the test log, test incident report, and test summary report.

4.1 Test Log

This is an account of the test's results. See the example below.

This is contained in file *EncounterCharacter_Test_Log_day_month_year.doc*

4.2 Test Incident Report

> This includes any occurrences or noteworthy events that occur during testing. See the example below.

This is contained in file *EncounterCharacter_Test_Incident_day_month_year.doc*

4.3 Test Summary Report

This is contained in file *EncounterCharacter_Test_Summary_Report_day_month_year.doc*

Example of a Test Log (Section 5 of the Personal Software Documentation):
EncounterCharacter_Test_Log_
26_Jul_1999
Method tests:
>>>>GetCharacter Test 1: nominal value <<<<<
querty< – – Obtained
querty< – – Required
>>>>GetCharacter Test 2: Outside parameter values <<<<<
defaultName< – – Obtained
defaultName< – – Required
>>>>EncounterCharacter Test 3: Limit parameter values<<<<<
123456789012345< – – Obtained
123456789012345< – – Required
Expect one name for each character
querty
defaultName
123456789012345
>>>>indexOf() Test 1: valid quality name <<<<<
Actual integer = expected integer.
>>>>indexOf() Test 2: valid quality name <<<<<
Actual integer = expected integer.

>>>>setQuality() Test 1: nominal value <<<<<
Actual float = expected float.
>>>>setQuality() Test 2: nominal value <<<<<
Actual float = expected float.
>>>>adjustQuality() test 0: verify that values add to 100<<<<<
Actual float = expected float.
>>>>adjustQuality() test 1: verify values sum to 100 after adjusting<<<<<
Actual float = expected float.
>>>>adjustQuality() test 2: verify values adjusted as commanded<<<<<
Actual float = expected float.
>>>>adjustQuality() test 3: verify low value reverts to zero<<<<<
Actual float = expected float.
>>>>adjustQuality() test 4: verify values sum to 100 after adjusting<<<<<
Actual float = expected float.
Class test:
>>>>Class test ge-aq-so<<<<<
100.0< – – Obtained
100.0< – – Required
>>>>Class test ge-aq-aq-gq-so: part 1 <<< <<
20.9876< – – Obtained
20.9876< – – Required
>>>>Class test ge-aq-aq-gq-so: part 2 <<< <<
100.0< – – Obtained
100.0< – – Required
>>>>Class test for the invariant '_qualValue [i] >=0'<<<<<
true< – – Obtained
true< – – Required

> The test log example does not show failed tests. These can be detailed in the log, transmitted to a separate file, and can generate monitor text.

Example of a Test Incident Report (Section 4.2 of the Personal Software Documention): *Encounter Character_Test_Incident_26_Jul_1999.doc*

The test was attempted with version 7.2.1 of *EncounterCharacter* using version 2.3 of the *TestUtilities* package. On the first try, the test failed to run. We think that this was due to the fact that we did not really have version 2.3 of *TestUtilities*. When we reloaded this package, the test ran without incident.

> This is a good place to mention mistakes made during testing. These are particularly prevalent when user actions are required, and it is impractical to rerun the entire test.

Example of a Test Summary Report (Section 4.3 of the Personal Software Documentation): *Encounter-Character_Test_Summary_26_Jul_1999.doc*

This test was executed by John Jones at 2:00 P.M. using release 1.1.6 of Sun's virtual machine. Subject to the anomalies in the test incident report, the results were 100 percent pass on the built-in unit test methods. These methods were inserted by E. Braude in version 6.5.2. They are due to be expanded in later versions of *EncounterCharacter*.

Example of Unit Test Source Code:

The following code, for the *EncounterCharacter* class, includes self-test methods.

The class *TestExecution* is used to execute the unit test. It contains a static method *printReportToFile()* whose parameters, in Javadoc notation, are as follows.

- ∗ @param – FileWriter – Destination of report
- ∗ output.
- ∗ @param – String – A description of the test.
- ∗ @param – int – The expected correct result.
- ∗ @param – int – The actual result.
- ∗ @return – void
- ∗ @exception – None

There are no preconditions. The postconditions are that a file has been written to the destination indicated by the *FileWriter* input parameter. It contains the test description input, the expected result, and the actual result, each clearly indicated. The test code is shown in Listing 26.11.

Listing 26.11: Control for testing *EncounterCharacter*

```
/** To test this class
* @param argsP destination of method test log, class test log
* respectively
*/public static void main(String[] argsP)
{
    // Default files on which to write test output & run tests
    String methodOutputFileNameM = "methodOutput.txt";
    String classOutputFileNameM = "classOutput.txt";

    if(argsP != null && argsP.length == 2)  // use defaults if input
      improper
    {   methodOutputFileNameM = argsP[0];
        classOutputFileNameM = argsP[1];
    }


    // 1. EXECUTE TESTS WHICH DO NOT REQUIRE HUMAN INTERVENTION
    // Test methods individually, then test class
    try
    {   testEncounterCharacterMethods(methodOutputFileNameM);
```

```
              testEncounterCharacterClass(classOutputFileNameM);
      }catch(IOException eP)
      {        System.out.println(eP);
      }
        // 2. EXECUTE TESTS WHICH DO REQUIRE HUMAN INTERVENTION
Frame[] imageTests = {                    // Display test cases
      new testCharacterImage(          // Missing image
          new EncounterCharacter("GuyWithNoImage", null)),
      new testCharacterImage(          // Image is present
          new EncounterCharacter("Elena", "elena.gif"))
   };
   for(int i = 0; i < imageTests.length; i++) {//Display each test window
      imageTests[i].setSize(400, 250);//Adequate size for character

      imageTests[i].setVisible(true);
      imageTests[i].show();
   }

   try {                                    // Let user examine windows
        Thread.currentThread().sleep(30*1000);
   } catch(Exception exc) {
   }

   for(int i = 0; i < imageTests.length; i++)    // Shut the windows
     imageTests[i].dispose();

   System.exit(0);
   }
   /** Tests this class by executing its methods in combination
   * @param   destinationP   Location to write results
   * @exception IOException  If there's a problem opening or accessing
   * destinationP
   */
```

Class testing is covered systematically in Chapter 27. It consists largely of testing	combinations of methods. The code testing *EncounterCharacter* is given in the case study there.

26.6 SUMMARY

Unit testing is conducted by software developers either in conjunction with or immediately after implementing a unit of code. Units are typically the methods and classes of the software. Both white box and black box methods are utilized.

The first step in unit testing is identifying units and determining what they are intended to do. This comes from one of several sources: the SRS, the SDD, or else a motivation too minor to specify in the SDD. For methods arising from design, we may not possess explicitly stated requirements against which to perform tests.

A systematic approach is required to effectively implement unit testing. In this way, as many errors as possible at as serious a level as possible can be discovered within a practical time period and using a practical amount of labor. The first step is organizing the testing—typically methods are tested first, followed by classes and packages.

The extent of testing should be considered and defined in advance. Test cases are selected from one or more categories of tests, both from normal expected operation and those judged most likely to fail. Stopping criteria are established in advance; these are concrete conditions at which point this particular testing process will be considered done.

Depending on the problem space of the software, there is often a set of test data that is specific to the application. If applicable, obtaining and using this data must be planned.

Unit testing is typically conducted by developers, as they are the most familiar with the structure and organization of the code under test. However, unit testing is sometimes conducted by a separate organization such as QA because of their objectivity. This requires extra time for the new organization to learn the software design so they can successfully executed the tests.

As with other phases of development, metrics are collected during unit testing. Metrics collected include number of test cases, number of tests per test type, and percentage of failed tests.

There are several different types of white box and black box testing methodologies employed during unit testing. White box methods include statement coverage, branch coverage, and path coverage. Black box methods include equivalence partitioning and boundary value analysis.

When testing the methods of a class, a strategy is required to ensure proper test coverage. Humphrey recommends using a checklist that includes items such as using normal parameters, parameters at their boundaries, illegal values, handling of error conditions, path coverage, loop termination, timing, and hardware dependencies.

After the individual methods of a class are tested, the class as a whole is tested. All of the class methods are tested in combination. This is because the methods of a class are frequently interrelated as they may alter the values of common class attributes. Focus is placed on sequences likely to be commonly used and sequences that appear most likely to contain defects. If an object of a class transitions through several states, state-based testing is employed.

An effective method for performing unit testing, and to build quality into an implementation, is to specify the tests that an implementation must pass *before* writing the code. After writing a test, one adds to the implementation until the test succeeds. This is called *test-driven development* (TDD). TDD is often associated with agile development, but it is useful for any development process.

26.7 EXERCISES

1. In your own words, describe the difference between white box and black box testing. Why is each important and necessary?

2. Why do you think unit testing is usually conducted by the developer who implemented the unit?

3. a. What is equivalence partitioning? Why is it important to partition the test space into equivalence classes? Please use your own words in responding.

   b. For the following function, describe five different test cases and for each describe the type of test case it represents. The application is based on Myers' triangle problem [5]:

```
//x, y and z are the lengths of the sides of a triangle. This function
classifies the

//triangle and returns either ''scalene'' (all sides unequal),
''isosceles'' (two sides

//equal) or ''equilateral'' (all sides equal). If x, y and z don't
form a triangle

//(i.e. either (a) x, y or z is <= zero, or (b) (x+y) < z) the null
string is returned

//Assumption: x, y and z are in ascending order (i.e. x <= y <= z) so you
do not need

//to test for this
char * triangle (int x, int y, int z)

{

    . . .

}
```

4. Explain why testing every line of code for correctness (i.e., 100 percent statement coverage) is generally insufficient for ensuring that a program is bug-free. Give an example of a defect that can go undetected by tests that have 100 percent statement coverage.

5. Why is path coverage a stronger form of testing than statement coverage? Give an example of a defect that would be detected by path coverage but not by statement coverage.

6. Draw a program control graph for the method *adjustQuality()* of Listing 26.4 in this chapter. What is its cyclomatic complexity? Explain your response.

7. Write the code for a class *Account* with attribute *balance*, accessor methods, and method *add()*. Assume that Account has states Sound, Empty, and Arrears, and that these are implemented using the State design pattern. Write a complete set of unit tests for Account, including state-oriented tests.

8. In test-first development, why is it important to execute a unit test to ensure that it fails before the code it is testing is actually written?

9. You intend to implement a *Rectangle* class using test-first development. Suppose the class is defined during design with the following characteristics:

   - Constructor with parameters length and width
   - Methods getLength() and getWidth() to retrieve length and width
   - Method to calculate area of rectangle

   Write a unit test class to test the as yet unwritten class *Rectangle*. Next, write the code to implement the class.

TEAM EXERCISE

Unit Tests

Perform full unit tests on two significant methods of your application. State how long individuals and the whole team spent on developing each part of these tests, and how the process you used could have been improved.

Evaluation criteria:
(1) Degree of clarity of the plan
(2) Extent to which the plan and test include all relevant aspects of the unit tests
(3) Realism of the self-evaluation data and improvement plan

BIBLIOGRAPHY

1. Rapps, Sandra and Elaine. J. Weyuker, "Selecting Software Test Data Using Data Flow Information," *IEEE Transactions on Software Engineering*, Vol. 11, no. 4, 1985, pp. 367–375.
2. McCabe, T. J., "A Complexity Measure," *IEEE Transactions on Software Engineering*, SE-2, no. 4 (1976), pp. 308–320.
3. Humphrey, Watts S., *"Managing the Software Process (SEI Series in Software Engineering),"* Addison-Wesley, 1989.
4. Junit, org. www.junit.org [accessed 12/14/09].
5. Myers, Glenford J., *"The Art of Software Testing,"* John Wiley & Sons, 1979.

27

Module and Integration Testing

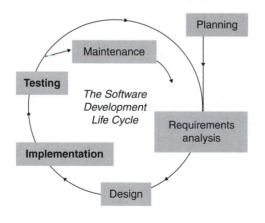

The Software Development Life Cycle

- Planning
- Maintenance
- Testing
- Implementation
- Requirements analysis
- Design

- • How do you test a class?

- • How are stubs and drivers used for testing?

- • What are attribute-oriented tests for a class? Class invariant-oriented tests? State-based tests?

- • What is integration?

- • What is big bang integration? Incremental? Bottom-up? Top down? Continuous?

- • How do daily builds facilitate continuous integration?

- • What is interface testing?

Figure 27.1 The context and learning goals for this chapter

This chapter discusses testing beyond unit testing—to the module level and to the integration of modules. We begin by discussing class testing. Class testing is considered by some to be beyond unit testing and by others not so.

Integration is the process of assembling parts to form a whole. As a physical illustration of this concept, consider Figure 27.2, which illustrates the integration of a suspension bridge. The order of integration and the

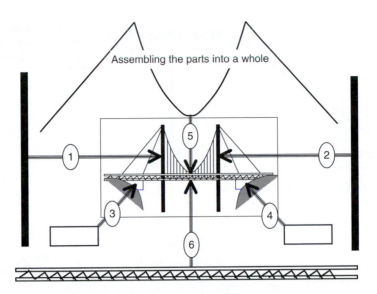

Figure 27.2 The meaning of "integration" —an analogy from bridge-building, steps 1 through 6

manner in which the parts are tested together is critical for the construction of the bridge. For example, assembling it in the wrong order will lead to longer construction times, or worse, a defective bridge. Such issues are equally important for the integration of software systems.

Like all engineering artifacts, software systems must be built from parts. Each part is developed and unit-tested separately. The whole is then assembled. *Integration* is the process of assembling these parts and testing the result to ensure that they work together correctly. A part of a software system to be integrated can consist of several lines of code, a whole method, a class, or an entire subsystem.

Agile methodologies use continuous integration and daily builds as much as possible. We discuss these in this chapter.

An example of a class test is provided in one case study section. In another, an integration plan is described. Both of these apply to the video game example used in this book.

27.1 STUBS AND DRIVERS

Consider the coordination issues associated with integrating the parts of an application shown in Figure 27.3. Several of the parts depend on each other yet must be put together in some order. We use *stubs* and *drivers* for this purpose.

Simple stubs were introduced in Chapter 26. We examine them in more depth here for integration testing, and we also introduce drivers. The left-hand column of Figure 27.4 starts the process by showing the eventual, desired configuration of three items of an application that must be integrated. (The items can be classes or packages of classes.)

If our goal is bottom-up integration (described in detail in Section 27.3.3) then we first create the Item 3 alone in step *BU-A* and test it thoroughly alone. However, a good set of tests tries to reproduce the manner in which the item will be used. For that reason, we create a stub (step *BU-b*), which is substantial enough to exercise Item 1 but is otherwise as modest as possible.

If our goal is top-down integration (described in detail in Section 27.3.4) then we first create stubs in steps *TD-a* and *TD-b*. These are substitutes for the items that are substantial enough for Item 1 to be tested (step *TD-C*) but otherwise require as little effort as possible.

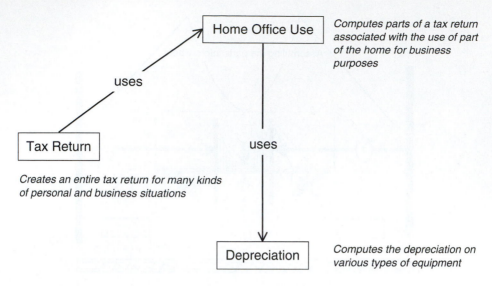

Figure 27.3 Stubs and drivers—motivation from a tax return example

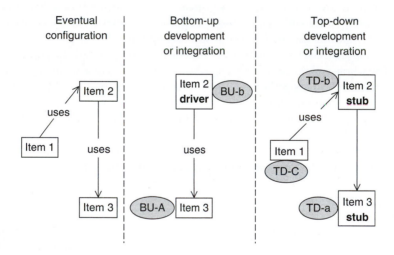

Figure 27.4 Using stubs and drivers for integration and testing

These remarks apply just as much to the development of items in the first place as to their integration and testing.

27.2 TESTING A CLASS

After testing the individual methods of a class, we can move on to testing the class as a whole. This amounts to executing its methods in combination or subjecting objects of the class to events such as mouse action. Recall that the methods of a class are frequently interrelated because they may alter the values of common variables. For example, in an *Account* class, the methods *deposit()* and *withdraw()* would both alter the *balance* variable. If

1. Exercise methods in combination
   - 2–5, typically
   - test most common sequences first
   - include sequences likely to cause defects
2. Focus tests on each attribute
   - initialize, then execute method sequences that affect it
3. Verify that class invariants are unchanged
   - verify invariant true with initial values
   - execute a method sequence
   - verify invariant still true
4. Verify that objects transition among expected states
   - plan the state/transition event
   - set up the object in the initial state by setting variables
   - execute event and check that transition occurred

Figure 27.5 Performing class tests—various focus

deposit() were coded in terms of *float*, for example, but *withdraw*() in terms of *double*, the tester may not notice anything wrong in testing each individually. For this reason, it may not be sufficient to know that each method has been individually unit-tested.

There are several complementary ways of testing classes, as shown in Figure 27.5. Each is discussed in this section, and several are illustrated in the case study.

27.2.1 Example of a Class Test

Each method combination test consists of a sequence of function calls. For the class *EncounterCharacter*, for example, the methods in Table 27.1 would be tested in sequences.

We concentrate our testing resources on the following:

1. Sequences likely to be commonly used

2. Sequences that appear most likely to harbor defects

Table 27.1 Example of a class test—labeling methods for use in combination

Abbreviation	Method prototype
aq	adjustQuality(String qualityP, float qualityValueP)
d	deleteFromEncounterCharacters(EncounterCharacter encounterCharacterP)
ge	EncounterCharacter getEncounterCharacter(String nameP)
gq	float getQualityValue(String qualityP)
gs	float getSumOfQualities()
gt	float getTolerance()
io	int indexOf(String qualityP) throws Exception
ii	InsertIntoEncounterCharacters(EncounterCharacter encounterCharacterP)
m	int maxNumCharsInName()
sq	setQuality(String qualityP, float valueP)

The following sequences are common in playing the game.

ge-aq-gs // get character – adjust qualities – get sum of qualities

ge-sq-aq-gq // get character – set a quality – adjust qualities – get the quality

There are, in fact, infinitely many sequences of methods, because every method can be repeated any number of times. A procedure must be employed to make the number feasible. For example, a triage approach can be useful in identifying common sequences. A given sequence of methods can be categorized as either most likely or least likely to expose a defect. Otherwise, the sequence is consigned to the "neither" category. All of the "most likely" tests are then executed, together with as many of the "neither" category as possible. The "least likely" are executed if there is time.

The process of adjusting quality values in the Encounter video game is relatively complicated. The following is an example of a sequence apparently more likely than many to harbor defects.

ge-sq-aq-sq-aq-gq // get character – set a quality – adjust qualities – set a quality – adjust qualities – get quality

We will assume that the methods have been tested individually, and we'll concentrate on sequences of methods that affect the others. Figure 27.6 shows how the methods in the example chosen relate to each other through their effect on variables. Steps 1 and 2 affect the value of the *concentration* variable. Step 3 affects the value of *strength*. In Step 4, the *stamina* variable is an input to the *adjustQuality()* method, which uses this value (and the current value of *concentration*) to change the value of *concentration*. Thus, each method in the sequence *sq-aq-sq-aq* affects the outcome of a later method. The interaction among seemingly simple methods can be quite complex!

The case study of Chapter 26 shows these tests in action. The sections that follow discuss ways to tame this complexity of choices.

27.2.2 Attribute-Oriented Tests

Attribute-oriented tests focus on variable changes, and create method sequences that effect them. A simple example for an *Account* class is to have the balance grow and shrink to zero. To do this, we could execute the sequence *setBalance(50); addToBalance(70); deductFromBalance(120); getBalance()*. We validate the predicted balance. The example in Figure 27.6 can be designed as an attribute test, focusing on the variable *concentration*.

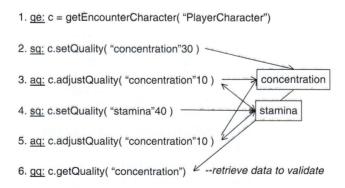

1. <u>ge:</u> c = getEncounterCharacter("PlayerCharacter")

2. <u>sq:</u> c.setQuality("concentration"30)

3. <u>aq:</u> c.adjustQuality("concentration"10)   concentration

4. <u>sq:</u> c.setQuality("stamina"40)   stamina

5. <u>aq:</u> c.adjustQuality("concentration"10)

6. <u>gq:</u> c.getQuality("concentration")   *--retrieve data to validate*

Figure 27.6 Selecting method sequences for unit testing

27.2.3 Testing Class Invariants

As described in Chapter 22, class invariants are constraints among the attributes of the class that must remain true after the execution of every method. A class invariant test consists of executing a sequence of methods and validating that the invariant remains true. For example, suppose that a rule of the bank is that overdrafts are capped at $1,000, including the assets in the customer's savings, and total assets per regular account are capped at $10,000,000. The invariant of the *Account* class would be something like the following.

```
-1000 <= checkBalance + savingsBalance <= 10000000
```

We would initially set the variables to amounts that honor this invariant, such as *checkBalance* $= -3000$ and *savingsBalance* $= 2500$. Then we would execute a sequence of methods such as *deposit*(300); *withdraw*(500); *deposit*(50) and check that the invariant is still true.

Languages such as Eiffel and Java are equipped with functions that test the validity of assertions. An assertion is a statement that can be true or false: for example, "x == y." Assertions are often invariants.

27.2.4 State-Based Tests

As we have seen, the instances of a class can often be usefully thought of as transitioning among states in response to events. We should therefore test such classes in terms of their state. For example, let us test the class *EncounterGame*. Figure 27.7 illustrates the first steps in the testing of the application's state transitions.

The complete state-transition test is shown in Figure 27.8.

The numbered steps denote a typical event sequence for causing a meaningful sequence of events. One test would thus consist of stimulating the system so that it transitions through this sequence. The tester would also introduce events that do not apply for particular states to ensure that indeed they do not affect the application.

To design and execute state-oriented testing requires significant time, especially because extensive user inputs are required. Tools are available that record user interactions with the system and that can reproduce

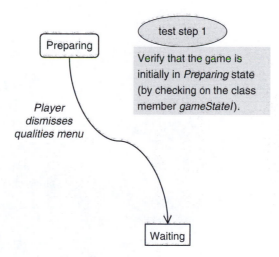

Figure 27.7 State-transition test sequences, 1 of 2

Source: Association for Computing Machinery, http:www.acm.org/~perlman/question.cgi?form=PUTQ

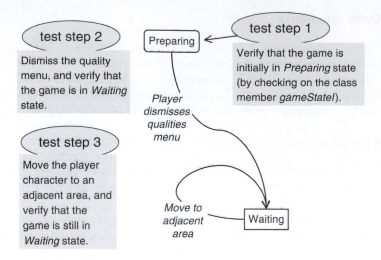

Figure 27.8 State-transition test sequences, 2 of 2

these actions. In addition, assertion checkers can be embedded in the code to verify that the system is in the state it is supposed to be.

27.3 INTEGRATION

This section discusses and compares various types of integration, and is summarized in Figure 27.9. It starts by comparing big bang integration with the incremental style that is generally recommended (when it's possible). The extreme form of incremental integration is *continuous* integration. The last classification discussed is between top-down and bottom-up styles. Projects often mix these integration and testing styles, depending on the nature of the project.

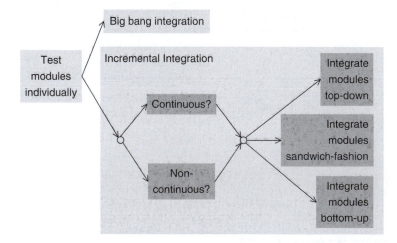

Figure 27.9 Module and integration testing

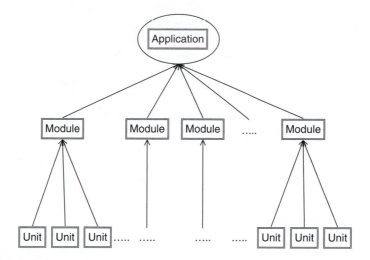

Figure 27.10 Big bang integration

27.3.1 Big Bang Integration

Big bang integration consists of creating modules in parallel and then assembling them in one operation. A form of this is illustrated in Figure 27.10. Although big bang testing reduces or eliminates the need for test drivers and stubs, this benefit is usually far outweighed by the complexity and cost of fault isolation. Since many modules are integrated at once, it is frequently difficult to locate the source of defects.

As an example, consider a system that monitors the health of at-risk patients as they go about their daily lives. As illustrated in Figure 27.11, the application can be thought of as decomposed into a module that

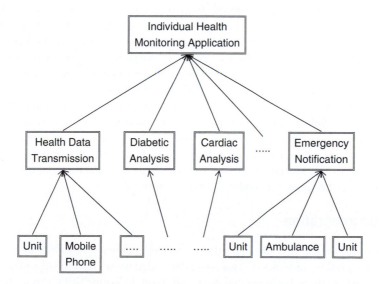

Figure 27.11 Big bang integration of a health monitoring system

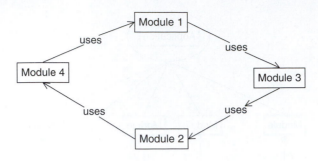

Figure 27.12 Module self-dependency—consider its effect on integration

handles the collection of data from patients, one that analyzes data for specific diseases, one that handles emergency notifications such as calls to the police, and so on. It makes a great deal of sense to develop these modules separately. For example, why not develop the diabetic analysis in an organization specializing in that field, and have emergency notification developed by a company with experience in writing such software reliably? Some modules may be effectively written by skilled teams working anywhere, geographically speaking. Although continual integration, described below, is preferable in general, it may not be practical in a case like this. Each high-level module and its subsidiaries may have to be developed separately, and then integrated in big bang fashion.

The integration and testing of modules illustrates the wisdom of designing so that dependencies are noncyclic. In other words, we try to avoid architectures in which a module depends on itself. Figure 27.12 illustrates such an architecture. We can't fully test any pair of modules alone. Our only choice is to use stubs or to test all of them together, which multiplies the potential for hard-to-find and hard-to-fix defects.

27.3.2 Incremental Integration

Nowadays, software integration typically proceeds in an incremental manner in which software modules are developed and assembled into progressively larger parts of the system. This is known as *incremental integration* [1]. Gradually building the system means complexity increases incrementally, making it easier to isolate integration problems. Incremental integration commences when the first two parts of an application are developed, and continues until all its parts have been integrated into a complete system, at which time system testing commences. Stubs and drivers are employed during this process.

Throughout the integration process, software "builds" may be created that form the emerging system, as illustrated in Figure 27.13. Before adding new modules, integration tests are executed against each build, ensuring that the build works correctly. Figure 27.2 implies that modules are developed and integrated in some order, but does not suggest how the order is determined. We usually determine the integration order by basing it on the design of the system. Two common methods are *bottom-up* and *top-down*, and each must account for dependencies between the modules making up the design.

27.3.3 Bottom-Up Integration

Suppose that an application consists of the modules and dependencies as shown in Figure 27.14.

In bottom-up integration, modules that are most depended on are developed and integrated first. Then the modules that depend on them are integrated next, and so on. In Figure 27.14, this implies that Module 3 is developed first, since it is at the "bottom" of the dependency tree. Modules 1 and 2 are integrated next with

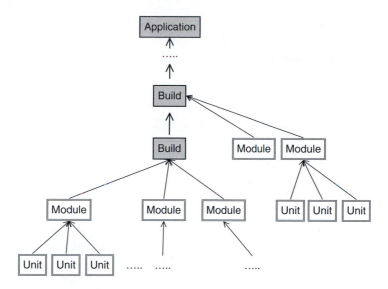

Figure 27.13 Incremental integration with builds

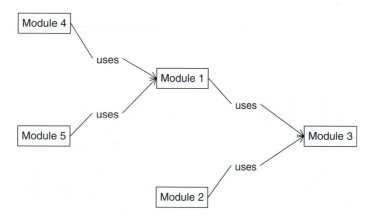

Figure 27.14 Example of module dependencies

Module 3 since they depend on it. Modules 4 and 5 are integrated last. Integrating in this manner is illustrated in Figure 27.15. An advantage to this approach is that it reduces the need for stubs since dependent modules are available when needed for integration.

Let's consider how we might perform bottom-up integration testing on the Encounter video game. Figure 27.16 shows the relationship among the objects of the Encounter architecture.

We have three modules (packages) to integrate, and need to determine which modules depend on which. The direction of the aggregations suggests an appropriate order, as shown in Figure 27.17. Figure 27.18 shows the resulting "using" relationship between the packages.

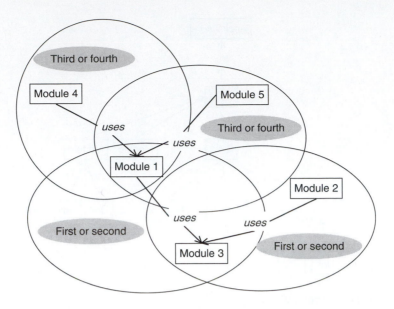

Figure 27.15 Bottom-up integration

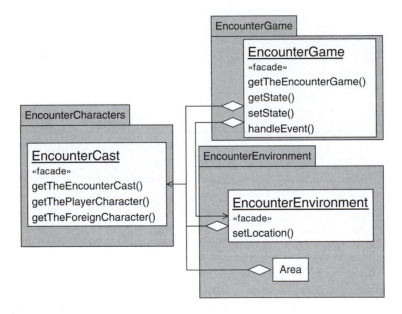

Figure 27.16 Module relationship in Encounter

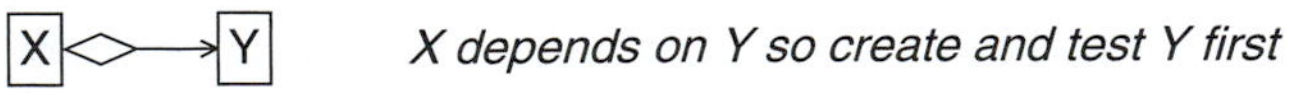

X ◇——▷ Y   *X depends on Y so create and test Y first*

Figure 27.17 Dependence and integration order

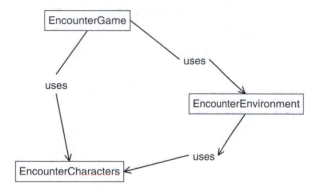

Figure 27.18 Module dependencies in Encounter

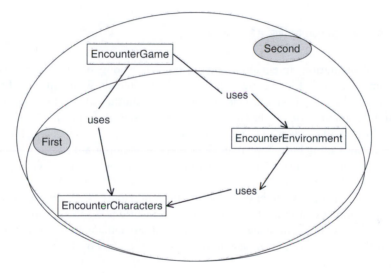

Figure 27.19 Bottom-up integration testing in Encounter

Next, we apply the principle of bottom-up integration to derive an integration order. This tells us to first test the integration of *EncounterEnvironment* with *EncounterCharacters*, and then to integrate *EncounterGame*. This is illustrated in Figure 27.19.

27.3.4 Top-Down Integration

Top-down integration is the opposite of bottom-up: Modules at the top of the dependency tree are developed first, with integration proceeding down the tree. This type of integration requires a considerable use of stubs since dependent modules are not yet ready for integration. The advantage of top-down integration is that modules at the top of the dependency tree are typically higher level functionality of an application, such as user interfaces, and are tested early in the integration cycle. This provides an early feeling for the application, allowing time for important modifications.

Figure 27.20 shows the top-down integration order of Encounter. This tells us to first test the integration of *EncounterGame* with *EncounterEnvironment*, and then to integrate *EncounterCharacters*.

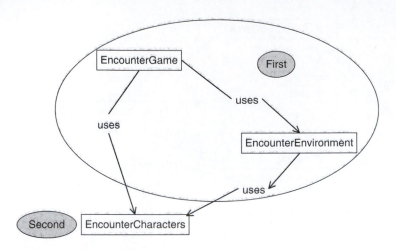

Figure 27.20 Top-down integration testing in Encounter

Top-down implementation, integration, and testing has a long history. In the very early days of computing, programmers reveled in the exciting things they could do with software. Programs tended to explicitly transfer control rapidly from one place in memory to another so that they became very difficult to debug and extend. In a famous letter to the editor of the *Communications of the ACM* [2], Dijkstra suggested the beginnings of what he and others developed into *structured programming*. This called for a hierarchy of functions, with high-level functions calling lower level ones. This remains an important part of what software engineers do. Top-down integration calls for the development of the highest level functions, calling stubbed subsidiary functions.

Returning to the analogy with bridge construction of Figure 27.2, in top-down thinking—and integration—we view and test first in the large ("suspension bridge") and only then begin to fill in the rest in increasing level of detail. Continuing the analogy, we'd test a model of the suspension bridge for wind and simulated load reaction, making gross assumptions about the parts of the bridge (the analog of stubs). Only then would we test the parts.

27.3.5 Sandwich Integration

Sandwich Integration is a process by which one integrates from the bottom and top more or less at the same time, introducing stubs for the intervening classes as one does this. Suppose, for example, that we want to integrate the class *ForeignCharacter*, which is at the lowest level in Encounter, and *EncounterGame*, which is at the highest, without having to worry about the intervening components for now. To have *ForeignCharacter* and *EncounterGame* coexist, we can introduce stubs for the intervening classes. For example, in Figure 27.21, we first have *ForeignCharacter* work with a stub for *EncounterCharacters*, then one for *EncounterEnvironment*, then *EncounterGame*. We don't count the introduction of stubs as true integration, so the only step that's truly integration in this example is the last. It integrates from the top and bottom simultaneously.

27.3.6 Continuous Integration

Continuous integration is a type of incremental integration in which small amounts of code are added to the baseline (the currently state of the application) on a very frequent basis. Intervals are often as frequent as daily (see Section 27.4), and the newly integrated code does not necessarily correspond to a completed method or

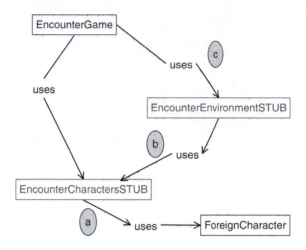

Figure 27.21 Sandwich integration testing in Encounter, in order a, b, c

class but can be smaller. As long as the code is unit-tested and does not introduce errors in the baseline, it can be integrated into the baseline. Continuous integration is one of the twelve practices of Extreme Programming (XP), as we described in Chapter 5. However, it can be utilized even if a non-agile process is being followed.

27.4 DAILY BUILDS

During incremental integration we build the software and regression-test it at regular intervals. Regression testing is designed to ensure that recently added code does not compromise preexisting functionality. Depending on the phase of the project, builds can be created weekly or even as often as daily. Daily builds are often used at the tail end of projects when last-minute additions and changes are required. They are also used during maintenance. Figure 27.22 shows an example schedule of overnight regression testing for an application approaching release.

Figure 27.23 illustrates the daily code integration process. This kind of daily integration and regression test schedule was reported by Cusumano and Selby [3] as being utilized by Microsoft, for example.

Referring to Figure 27.23, a daily code freeze time of, typically, 6 PM is established, after which no new code is accepted for that day. The software system is then built and run, and regression tests are executed on

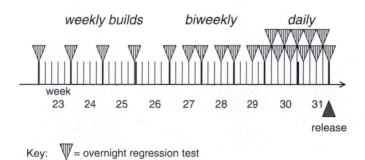

Figure 27.22 Example frequency of overnight regression tests

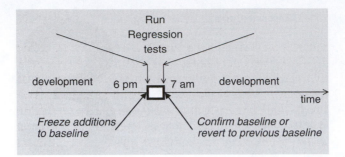

Figure 27.23 Daily builds

the new build between 6 PM and 7 AM. If a problem is found with the new build, it is assumed the defect lies in the code that was checked in during the previous day. This makes the job of problem isolation and resolution easier than if a longer time interval had elapsed between builds.

27.5 INTERFACE TESTING

Interface tests validate the interface of each module from the viewpoint of their usage by a client. These can be conducted, to the extent possible, prior to the integration of a module (with necessary stubs); and then after the integration of the module (with, typically, a reduced set of stubs). The Facade design pattern can be used to facilitate interface testing. A facade object is created for each class or package, providing an implementation of its public interface. Each method in the facade checks its input parameters to ensure they are passed correctly and returns a predetermined response. Thus, the caller can test its interface with a module without knowledge of whether it is using the facade or the real implementation. This makes problem discovery and isolation easier. Let's return to the video store as an example. Figure 27.24 shows the module decomposition for this application.

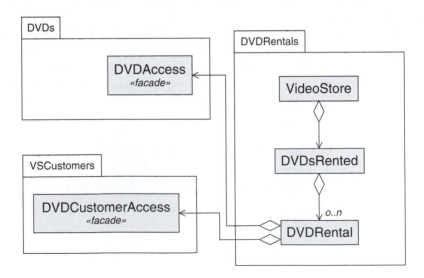

Figure 27.24 Video store module interfaces

Now we will perform an interface test on the *DVDs* module. Its usage by clients (i.e., other parts of the application) can be exercised by means of the facade object only. Thus, the interface tests consist of testing the facade class *DVDAccess*. It exposes methods such as the following:

```
void stockDVD(String aDVDTitle);
RentalItem getDVD(int aDVDID);
RentalItem getDVD(String aDVDTitle);
String describeDVD(int aDVDID);
String describeDVD(String aDVDTitle);
```

Note that the method *getDVD()* returns a *RentalItem* object. The *RentalItem* class is a public framework class, and so is accessible to all objects. The *getDVD()* method cannot return a *DVD* object because the *DVD* class is hidden from clients of the *DVDs* package. The interface test executes interface methods with test cases. An example is the following:

```
DVD gwtw = new DVD( "Gone With the Wind" );

// Get access to the facade object
DVDAccess dVDs = DVDAccess.getTheDVDAccess();

// Now run the tests
dVDs.stockDVD( gwtw );
RentalItem rentalItem = getDVD( "Gone With the Wind" );
// Report discrepancies between strings (assume a "compare()'' test
        utility)
compare( rentalItem.getTitle(),gwtw.getTitle() );
// etc.
```

For the *DVDRentals* package, which does not use *Facade*, the interface is the collection of methods of member classes. For example, the class *DVDRentals* exposes methods such as the following from the *DVDRental* class.

```
DVDRental createDVDRental(RentalCustomer aDVDCustomer, RentalItem
    aDVD)
DVDRental[] getDVDRentals( RentalCustomer aDVDCustomer )
RentalCustomer getDVDRentalCustomer( int aDVDRentalID )
void removeDVDRental( RentalCustomer aDVDCustomer, RentalItem aDVD )
void removeDVDRental( int aDVDRentalID )
float getFine( RentalCustomer aDVDCustomer, RentalItem aDVD )
float getFine( int aDVDRentalID )
```

The interface test is summarized in Figure 27.25.

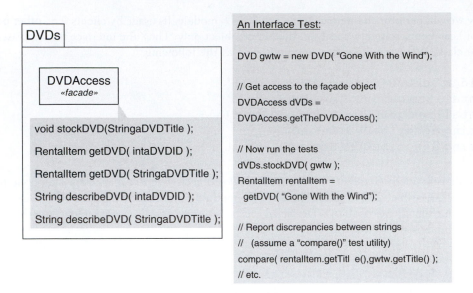

Figure 27.25 Interface tests of DVDs package

27.6 MODULE INTEGRATION

Once interface tests are completed, we can feel confident about the interface between modules. We are then ready to test their interaction more completely with *integration tests*. An integration test focuses on the additional functionality gained by assembling modules.

Now let's integrate fully functional versions of the *DVDs* and *VSCustomers* packages. To perform integration tests, we identify the added functionality that this integration provides—in this case, the additional functionality that the *DVDs* and *VSCustomers* packages provide. In particular, the methods of *DVDRental*, which were using stubbed facade methods in *DVDAccess* and *DVDCustomerAccess*, now use fully functional versions. The methods of *DVDRental* can now be fully tested. The same applies to all classes in *DVDRentals*. Listing 27.1 is an example of a method in *DVDRental* that is part of this integration test.

Listing 27.1: The getDVDRental() method, which becomes more operable after some integration

```
Rental getDVDRental( RentalItem aDVD, RentalCustomer aDVDRental
Customer )
{
  // Check that aDVD is in the inventory
 DVDAccess theDVDAccess = DVDAccess.getTheDVDAccess();
 if( !theDVDAccess.isInInventory( aDVD ) )
    return null; // or some other error indicator
```

```
   // Check that aDVDRentalCustomer is an actual customer
DVDCustomerAccess theDVDCustomerAccess =
     DVDCustomerAccess.getTheDVDCustomerAccess();
if( !theDVDCustomerAccess.verify( aDVDRentalCustomer) )
     return null; // or some other error indicator

  // Check that aDVD is rented to aDVDRentalCustomer
  . . . .

  // Retrieve and return the rental
  . . . .
}
```

27.7 CASE STUDY: CLASS TEST FOR ENCOUNTER

Listing 27. 2, which follows, is a test for the *EncounterCharacter* class and completes the Encounter case study in Chapter 26.

Listing 27.2: Tests for *EncounterCharacter* class

```
public static void testEncounterCharacterClass( String destinationP )
  throws IOException
{
   /* Prepare for the test */
   PrintWriter outM = new PrintWriter(new FileOutputStream(destinationP));
   System.out.println("\nEncounterCharacter class test results on "
      + destinationP + "\n" );
 /*
   * The following methods will be tested in sequences:
   *
   * a. adjustQuality( String qualityP, float qualityValueP )
   * d. deleteFromEncounterCharacters(EncounterCharacter encounterCharacterP )
   * ge. EncounterCharacter getEncounterCharacter( String nameP )
   * gq. float getQualityValue( String qualityP )
   * gt. float getTolerance()
   * io. int indexOf( String qualityP )
   * ii. insertIntoEncounterCharacters(EncounterCharacter encounterCharacterP )
   * m. int maxNumCharsInName()
   * sq. setQuality( String qualityP, float qualityValueP )
   * so. float sumOfQualities()
   *
   *      The following sequences occur commonly:
```

```
 *       ge-aq-so
 *       ge-sq-a-gq
 *       . . . . .
 *       The following sequences have a high potential for defects:
 *       ge-aq-aq-gq-s
 *       . . . . .
 */

   /* Test C1: ge-aq-so */
   EncounterCharacter eC1M = new
      EncounterCharacter( "CharForTestC1" );                    // method "ge"
   eC1M.adjustQuality(QUAL_STRENGTH, 40.0f );                   // aq
   TestExecution.printReportToFile( outM,
         "Class test ge-aq-so", eC1M.sumOfQualities(), 100.0f); // so


   /* Test C2: ge-aq-aq-gq-so */
   EncounterCharacter eC2M = new
        EncounterCharacter( "CharForTestC2" );                  // ge
   eC2M.adjustQuality(QUAL_STRENGTH, 40.0f );                   // aq
   eC2M.adjustQuality(QUAL_STAMINA, 20.9876f );                 // aq
   TestExecution.printReportToFile( outM, "Class test ge-aq-aq-gq-so: part 1",
              eC2M.getQualityValue( QUAL_STAMINA ), 20.9876f ); // gq

TestExecution.printReportToFile( outM, "Class test ge-aq-aq-gq-so: part 2",
              eC2M.sumOfQualities(), 100.0f );                  // so


   /* INVARIANT-ORIENTED TESTS
    * Check for the invariant "qualValueI[i] >=0"
    * -- after executing the sequences of methods executed above
    */
   boolean truthM = true;
   for( int i = 0; i < qualityTypeS.length; ++i )
   {       /* Set truthM false if any entry in eC1M.qualValueI not >= 0 */
           truthM = truthM && ( eC1M.qualValueI[i] >>= 0.0f );
   }
   TestExecution.printReportToFile(outM, "Class test for the
      invariant 'qualValueI[i] >=0'", truthM, true );


/* Conclude */
   outM.close();
   System.out.println( "\nClass tests of EncounterChar class
      concluded." );
} // end of testEncounterCharacterClass


/** Tests all the methods of this class one at a time
```

```java
 * @param       destinationP   Location to write results.
 * @exception   IOException    If there's a problem opening or accessing destinationP
 */
public static void testEncounterCharacterMethods( String destinationP )
    throws IOException
{
    /* Prepare for the test */
    FileWriter outM = new FileWriter( new File( destinationP ) );
    System.out.println("EncounterCharacter method test results on "
        + destinationP + "\n" );

/* Tests for getEncounterCharacter() */
EncounterCharacter eCNorM = new EncounterCharacter( "qwerty" );        // normal
TestExecution.reportToFile( outM,
            "GetCharacter Test 1: nominal value", eCNorM.getName(), "qwerty" );

EncounterCharacter eCNullM = new EncounterCharacter(null);             // null
TestExecution.reportToFile( outM, "GetCharacter Test 2: null parameter",
            eCNullM.getName(), GameCharacter.DEFAULT_NAME );

String tooLongM = "12345678901234567890123456789012345678901234567890";
EncounterCharacter eCTooLongM = new EncounterCharacter(tooLongM);  // too long
TestExecution.reportToFile( outM, "GetCharacter Test 3: Limit parameter values, "
            + "max name len = " + eCTooLongM . maxNumCharsInName(),
            eCTooLongM.getName(),
            tooLongM.substring(0, eCTooLongM.maxNumCharsInName()) );
EncounterCharacter eCZeroM = new EncounterCharacter( "" );             // zero-len
TestExecution.reportToFile( outM, "GetCharacter Test 4: zero-length",
            eCZeroM .getName(), GameCharacter. DEFAULT_NAME );
EncounterCharacter eCPuncM = new EncounterCharacter( "a+b" );          // bad chars
TestExecution.reportToFile( outM, "GetCharacter Test 5: bad char '+' ",
            eCPuncM .getName(), GameCharacter. DEFAULT_NAME );

/* Tests for indexOf() for every valid quality name. */
    for( int i = 0; i < qualityTypeS.length; ++i )
            try { TestExecution.reportToFile( outM,
                "indexOf() Test 1." + i + ": valid name: " + qualityTypeS[i],
                indexOf(qualityTypeS[i]), i );
            } catch( Exception eP )
            {TestExecution.reportToFile(outM,"indexOf()Test1:validname:compare",
                "indexOf('" + qualityTypeS[i] + "')", "with expected " + i );
            }
/* Tests for indexOf() for an invalid quality name. */
    try { TestExecution.reportToFile( outM,
            ''indexOf() Test 2: invalid name: zorch",
            indexOf(''zorch"), --1 );
```

```
        } catch( Exception eP )
        { TestExecution.reportToFile( outM,
                ''indexOf() Test 2: valid name: compare '',
                  ''indexOf(\''zorch\'')'', ''with expected -1'' );
        }

/* Tests for setQuality() */
// Set up for test
        EncounterCharacter hank = new EncounterCharacter( ''Hank'' );

// Nominal value
        hank.setQuality(QUAL_STRENGTH , 10.3f );
        TestExecution.reportToFile(outM,''setQuality()Test1:nominalvalue'',
        hank.getQualityValue( QUAL_STRENGTH ), 10.3f );

// Out of range value
        hank.setQuality( QUAL_PATIENCE, -6.2f );
        TestExecution.reportToFile(outM,''setQuality()Test2:nominalvalue'',
        hank.getQualityValue(QUAL_PATIENCE), 0.0f );

// Value below close-to-zero threshold.
        hank. setQuality(QUAL_STAMINA, getTolerance () * 0.9f);
        TestExecution.reportToFile(outM,''setQuality()Test3:valueclosetozero'',
            hank.getQualityValue(QUAL_STAMINA), 0.0f );

// Tests for adjustQuality().
        // Set up for test and verify: Values should be 20 each.
        EncounterCharacter harvey = new EncounterCharacter(''Harvey'');
        TestExecution.reportToFile( outM, ''adjustQuality() test 0:
          verify that values add to 100'', harvey.sumOfQualities(),
          100.0f );                            // Nominal adjustment
        // strength 30 rest 70/4 each
        harvey.adjustQuality(QUAL_STRENGTH , 30.0f );
        TestExecution.reportToFile(outM, ''adjustQuality() test 1:
          values sum to 100 after adjusting'',
          harvey.sumOfQualities(), 100.0f );
        TestExecution.reportToFile ( outM, ''adjustQuality() test 2:
          values adjusted as commanded'',
          harvey.getQualityValue(QUAL_STRENGTH ), 30.0f );

// Adjustment resulting in a zero value
        harvey.adjustQuality( QUAL_STAMINA, 99.0f );
        TestExecution.reportToFile(outM, ''adjustQuality() test 3:
          verify low value reverts to zero'',
          harvey.getQualityValue( QUAL_STRENGTH ), 0.0f );
```

```java
// Conclude
        outM.close();
        System.out.println( ''\nMethod tests of EncounterCharacter
            class concluded.'' );
}


/** Class to test repainting of characters. Creates a window, which will contain *
 * several copies of the character image.
 */
private static class testCharacterImage extends Frame
{
/** Instance attribute that remembers which character image to
      display. */
private EncounterCharacter characterI;

/** Basic constructor -- create a window for testing some character's image.
 * @param    characterP    Character whose image is to be tested.
 */ testCharacterImage(EncounterCharacter characterP)
{
    super(characterP.getName());       // Do all normal Frame initialization.
    characterI = characterP;           // Remember which character we're testing.
}


/** Repaint the display area of the frame.
 * @param    drawP    Graphics context for drawing the character.
 */


public void paint(Graphics drawP)
{
Dimension frameSizeM = getSize();                   // Size of the window area.
int widthUnitM = frameSizeM.width / 5;              // Convenient divisions of window.
int heightUnitM = frameSizeM.height / 5;
   characterI.showCharacter(this, drawP,      // Drawn small, facing right.
     new Point(widthUnitM, heightUnitM), heightUnitM, false);
   characterI.showCharacter(this, drawP,      // Drawn large, facing left.
     new Point(widthUnitM*4, heightUnitM*3), heightUnitM*2, true);
   characterI.showCharacter(this, drawP,      // Drawn large, facing right.
     new Point(widthUnitM*2, heightUnitM*2), heightUnitM*2, false);
    characterI.showCharacter(this, drawP,     // Drawn small, facing left.
     new Point(widthUnitM*3, heightUnitM*4), heightUnitM, true);
  }
}   // End of testCharacterImage inner class
```

27.8 CASE STUDY: ENCOUNTER INTEGRATION PLAN

APPENDIX FOR ENCOUNTER SCMP: INTEGRATION PLAN

Note to the Student:
We need to describe the order in which the application is to be integrated. The SCMP is an appropriate location for this description, since it describes configurations of the iterations and builds. This could be placed in the SPMP, but it contains design and implementation detail, which are not really project management items. It could be placed in the SDD, but the integration plan is not a design but a way to get to the implementation of the design. A document on implementation issues alone is a possibility. Another possibility is the SCMP, since it is concerned with configurations as the product comes together. The Encounter case study selected this option.

History of versions of this document:

11/1/98 E. Braude: Initial Draft

4/4/99 E. Braude: Revised

8/23/99 R. Bostwick: Documents reviewed and recommendations made

8/24/1999 E. Braude: Recommendations integrated

8/26/1999 E. Braude: Reviewed, comments expanded

1. Introduction

During the integration process, the software for Encounter is constructed in stages or builds. This appendix describes the configuration of the first three builds. Integration testing is based on these builds. The last build is the basis for system testing.

The integration testing associated with this integration plan assumes that the individual classes have been tested (as above).

2. Construction of Integration Baselines

Referring to the various integration techniques discussed above, which one is this? It is largely bottom-up if you take the *uses* relationship for the hierarchy. The *encounterGame* package is then at the top. If the integration process were to be continuous, a description of a daily build process would be provided, perhaps along with some sense of the order of the integration. This is normally associated with an agile process.

The three successive builds for release 1 of Encounter are shown in Figure 27.26. The first build consists of the *GameCharacters* framework package and the *EncounterCharacters* package. The second build uses the first build. It consists of the *EncounterEnvironment* package, its corresponding framework, and the first build. The third build refers to builds 1 and 2. It consists of the *EncounterGame* package, its corresponding framework, build 1, and build 2.

2.1 Integration Build 1

Build 1 is illustrated in Figure 27.27. Build 1 implements the *GameCharacters* framework package and the *EncounterCharacters* package.

Interface testing (see Section 27.5) is performed on this module by identifying all of the methods that its classes make public. (Methods not needed by other modules should be made private to avoid unneeded tests of this kind.) The design is such that these methods are all part of the *EncounterCast* class.

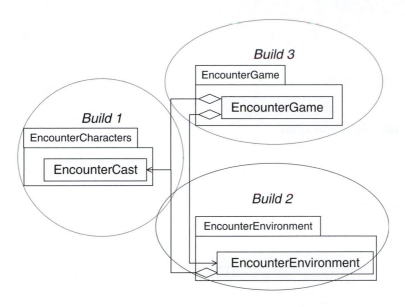

Figure 27.26 Integration plan

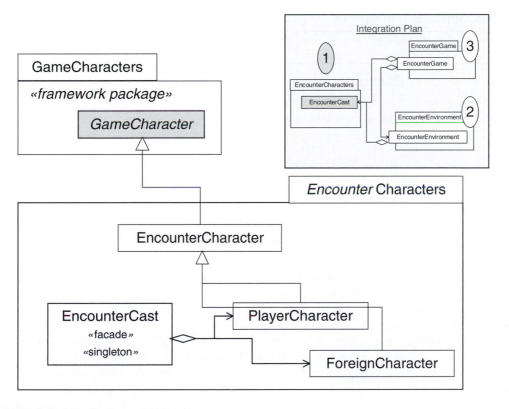

Figure 27.27 Build 1 for the Encounter game

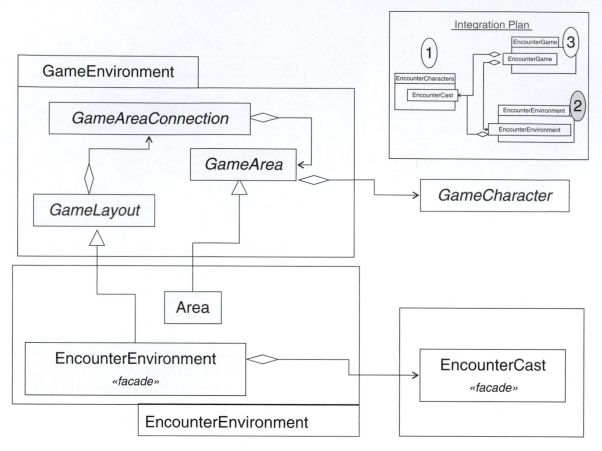

Figure 27.28 Build 2 for the construction of Encounter

2.2 Integration Build 2

Build 2 is shown in Figure 27.28. Build 2 consists of the *EncounterEnvironment* package and the *GameEnvironment* framework package, together with the first build. The *GameEnvironment* and the *EncounterEnvironment* packages use the build 1 *GameCharacter* and *EncounterCast* classes, respectively. Courtyard, dungeon, and living room are examples of areas. Some of these areas are connected. For example, there is a connection between the dressing room and the courtyard.

At the conclusion of build 2, the framework/application decomposition is shown in Figure 27.29. The *EncounterGame* package and its *RolePlayingGame* framework package are not present because they are part of build 3.

2.3 Integration Build 3

The final build, build 3, is illustrated in Figure 27.30. Build 3 consists of the *EncounterGame* package, its *RolePlayingGame* framework package, build 1, and build 2.

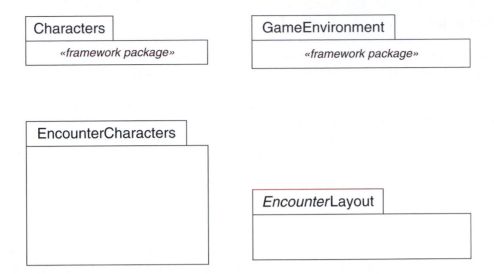

Figure 27.29 Status of Encounter after build 2

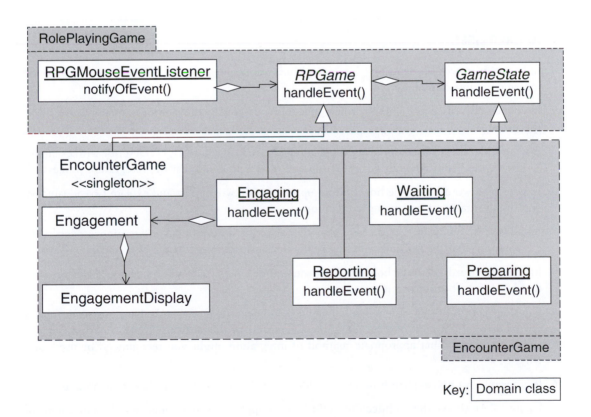

Figure 27.30 Build 3 for Encounter (includes build 1 and build 2, not shown)

27.9 SUMMARY

Integration refers to the process of assembling the parts of an application and testing their interactions to ensure that they work together correctly. The parts that are integrated can be as small as a few lines of code or as large as a subsystem.

Two overall strategies for integrating the parts are *incremental* and *big bang*. In incremental integration, the system is built step by step in relatively small increments. As soon as a part of the application is developed it is integrated into the baseline. In big bang integration, the parts of the system are developed first and then are integrated together in one step. This approach can lead to many problems and is usually avoided if at all possible.

A commonly used technique is to build and test the entire code base on a regular basis. Early in projects the interval can be weekly, but at the tail-end it can be daily. Conducting daily builds ensures that any problems that are uncovered can be isolated to recently added code, simplifying defect isolation and resolution.

The Facade design pattern can be used to facilitate interface testing between modules. A facade stub object is created that implements the public interface of a class or package. Other modules test their interface with that module, and the facade object checks that it is being called correctly and returns a predetermined response. Once the interface is tested, the facade is replaced with the real module and the modules are tested further.

27.10 EXERCISES

1. In your own words, describe incremental integration. Name and explain two benefits of incremental integration.

2. In your own words, explain how a project schedule is affected by the method of integration used on the project.

   2A. Consider the health monitoring application described in Figure 27.11. Describe with examples how you would integrate it bottom-up and how you would test the integration process.

3. In your own words, describe how bottom-up integration works. List and explain two advantages and disadvantages of bottom-up integration.

   3A. The case study in Section 27.8 does not describe a continuous integration process—but suppose that the document did prescribe one instead. What would that document say?

4. In your own words, describe how top-down integration works. List and explain two advantages and disadvantages of top-down integration.

5. Consider a point-of-sale system that is under development. Assume that the hardware platform and device drivers that control it are brand new. The rest of the software is being ported from an existing system. What appropriate method of integration might you recommend be used, and why?

6. In your own words, explain how daily builds facilitate the isolation of defects in a build.

7. Figure 27.31 shows the architecture outline of an application that simulates the movement of customers in a bank. Provide a plan for building and integrating this application.

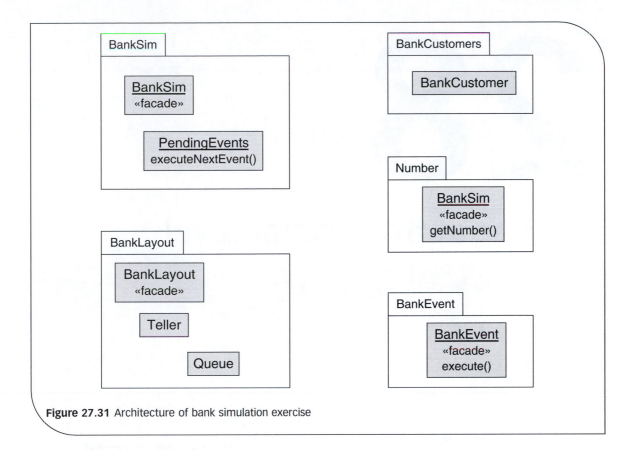

Figure 27.31 Architecture of bank simulation exercise

TEAM EXERCISE

Integration

Obtain project specifications from two other teams in the class. Specify informally a new application that contains significant elements of these applications. Specify an integration plan to build this new application.

Evaluation criteria:

(1) Degree of clarity of the plan

(2) Degree to which the plan contains an appropriate order

BIBLIOGRAPHY

1. Pezzè, Mauro, and Michal Young, *"Software Testing and Analysis: Process, Principles and Techniques,"* John Wiley & Sons, 2008.
2. Dijkstra, Edsger, "Go To Statement Considered Harmful," *Communications of the ACM* Vol. 11, no. 3, 1968, pp. 147–148.
3. Cusumano, M., and R.W. Selby, "How Microsoft Builds Software," *Communications of the ACM*, Vol. 40, no. 6, 1997, pp. 53–61.

28

Testing at the System Level

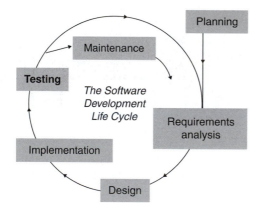

- How do functional and nonfunctional testing differ?

- How do you conduct performance tests?

- What is load / stress event testing? Reliability and availability testing? Recoverability testing?

- How do you test usability?

- How do you validate security?

- How do you test when requirements are sparse or even nonexistent?

- What is acceptance testing?

- How does one test in agile processes?

- What are compatibility, installation, and serviceability testing?

- How do alpha and beta releases relate to testing?

- When is testing automated?

Figure 28.1 The context and learning goals for this chapter

- **Performance** . . .
  Test speed of application
- **Load/Stress** . . .
  Test against heavy event traffic
- **Reliability and Availability** . . .
  Determine percentage up-time
- **Recoverability** . . .
  Test ease with which application recovers from crash
- **Usability** . . .
  Determine degree of user satisfaction.
- **Security** . . .
  Determine susceptibility to intended and unintended breaches
- **Compatibility** . . .
  Application compatible with other systems as required
- **Installability** . . .
  Test ease of installation
- **Serviceability** . . .
  Test ease of keeping up-to-date at customer site

Figure 28.2 Principal system tests

System testing follows integration testing. It consists of black box tests that validate the entire system against its requirements. Once all other system tests are successfully completed, the application is deemed ready for the customer's acceptance testing (Section 28.4.2). These are related to the requirements and to metrics in that each test measures one or more metrics.

System tests are most often conducted by an independent group such as Quality Assurance. During system testing, compliance with both the functional and nonfunctional requirements is validated. Recall from Chapter 10 that functional requirements specify services that an application must provide (e.g., "The application shall compute the value of the user's stock portfolio."). Nonfunctional requirements, on the other hand, describe a quality or behavior an application must possess. Examples of nonfunctional requirements include performance, usability, and compatibility. Figure 28.2 summarizes various types of nonfunctional systems tests. Since system tests ensure that the requirements have been met, they must systematically validate each requirement specified in the SRS, including each of the use cases.

Whenever possible, system tests are performed on the application running in its required environment. This is not terribly complicated for an application that is intended to run on a PC, such as a calendar program, although even for simple platforms we still have to be concerned with complicating issues such as the versions of the operating system. However, many applications cannot be fully tested in their eventual environments. This certainly applies to space-based applications, for example, with sometimes disastrous consequences. The Mars Climate Orbiter spacecraft is a case in point. It veered off course, resulting in a loss of hundreds of millions of dollars. According to Cable Network News, the investigating board's chairman reported that

> the root cause of the loss of the spacecraft was a failed translation of English units into metric units and a segment of ground-based, navigation-related mission software.

Testing for this and other requirements had to take place on a ground-based test bed.

In analogy to the two principal forms of requirements, *functional tests* test the functional requirements of the system, and *nonfunctional tests* the qualities and behavior of the system. The acceptance tests, validating that the requirements have been fulfilled, make up the main functional test set. The main nonfunctional tests are included in the summary of Figure 28.2, and are discussed in the rest of this chapter.

This chapter provides a number of metrics associated with these tests. It also discusses smoke testing (Section 28.7.2), a kind of rough regression test, and testing in the presence of lightweight (incomplete or even nonexistent) requirements.

28.1 FUNCTIONAL TESTING

Functional system tests focus on how customers will use the product in real life. Use cases are a primary source of functional requirements. As an example of testing a use case, recall the following Encounter use case, *Engage Foreign Character*, from the customer requirements.

1. Encounter displays the foreign character in the same area as the player's.

2. Encounter exchanges quality values between the two characters.

3. Encounter displays the results of the engagement.

4. The user hits the "OK" button.

5. Encounter displays player's character in a random area.

To test this, we may begin playing the game until an engagement takes place and is observed, as in Figure 28.3.

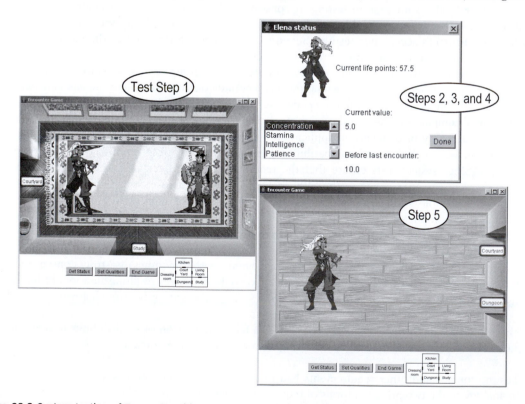

Figure 28.3 System testing of Encounter video game—*Engage Foreign Character use case*

As part of testing this use case, we see that in Step 2 quality values are exchanged. We turn to the detailed requirements for quality values and validate each. The following is an example, taken from the Encounter SRS.

3.2.EC.1.2 QUALITIES OF ENCOUNTER CHARACTERS

Every game character has the same set of qualities. Each quality shall be a nonnegative floating-point number with at least one decimal of precision. These are all initialized equally so that the sum of their values is 100. The value of a quality cannot be both greater than 0 and less than 0.5. For the first release, these qualities will be *concentration, intelligence, patience, stamina,* and *strength.*

This can be decomposed as follows:

3.2.EC.1.2.1 Every game character has the same set of qualities. Each quality shall be a nonnegative floating-point number with at least one decimal of precision.

3.2.EC.1.2.2 These are all initialized equally so that the sum of their values is 100.

3.2.EC.1.2.3 The value of a quality cannot be both greater than 0 and less than 0.5.

3.2.EC.1.2.4 For the first release, these qualities will be *concentration, intelligence, patience, stamina,* and *strength.*

- 3.2.EC.1.2.1 is validated by going through each quality on the *set qualities* window and ensuring that each has a decimal value, as shown in Figure 28.4.
- We validate 3.2.EC.1.2 by checking on Elena's qualities as the game begins.

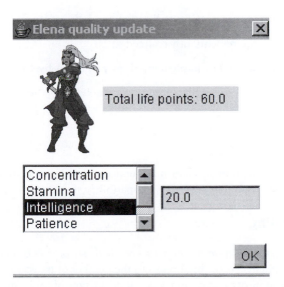

Figure 28.4 System testing of Encounter video game—testing with GUI for setting qualities

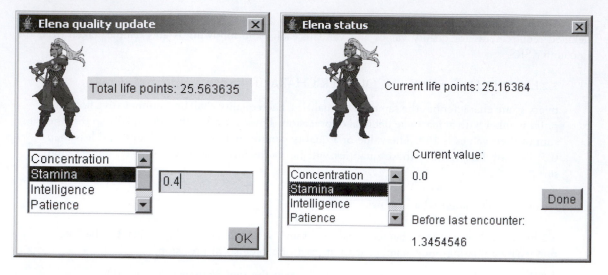

Figure 28.5 System testing of Encounter video game—testing via GUI for setting and viewing qualities

- Validating 3.2.EC.1.3 can be done by reducing Elena's points on a quality to less than 0.5. The result of setting stamina to 0.4 and showing that Encounter actually sets this internally to 0 is seen in Figure 28.5.

- We validate requirement 3.2.EC.1.2.4 by ensuring that all promised qualities are present and that there are no additional qualities. We continue testing in this manner for the rest of the use cases and functional requirements.

Metrics for functional testing are usually based on the requirements, and include the following:

- Number/percent of detailed requirements partially, and not fully realized

- Number/percent of detailed requirements not realized at all

- Number of high-level requirements not implemented, as perceived by the customer

- Number of detailed requirements not implemented, as perceived by the customer

28.2 NONFUNCTIONAL TESTING

This section describes several common types of nonfunctional testing: performance, load/stress, reliability and availability, recoverability, usability, security, compatibility, installation, and serviceability testing.

28.2.1 Performance Testing

Performance testing validates that a system meets its specified performance requirements by observing the throughput, or speed of the system. Throughput refers to the number of transactions that can be processed in a given amount of time. The meaning of a transaction depends on the type of application that is being tested. For our video store application, speed could be measured by the number of video rentals that can be processed per minute.

For a real-time communications system, speed might be measured by the number of data packets that can be processed and forwarded per second. Good requirements will have avoided vague statements about performance such as "customer responses should be acceptably fast." Such vagueness causes problems because the stakeholders can harbor very different interpretations of "fast." For the video store application, a well-written performance requirement is "The application shall be able to successfully handle a load of 1000 rental requests per minute."

Test environments such as Eclipse's Test and Performance Tools Platform (see Section 28.6) identify the packages, classes, and methods with high execution times, as well as those invoked frequently.

Metrics for performance testing are usually based on performance requirements, and include the following:

- Number/percent of speed requirements not satisfied
- Number of memory use requirements not satisfied
- Number of speed requirements not satisfied, as perceived by the customer
- Number of memory use requirements not satisfied, as perceived by the customer

28.2.2 Load/Stress Event Testing

The purpose of load/stress testing is to subject a system to increasing loads and to stress it in various other ways to determine its breaking point. Another way of stating this is "under what load does the system start to break?" Examples of the types of loads used are maximum number of users supported, maximum number of transactions per second, and maximum data transfer rate. Once the points of failure are determined we can understand whether the system meets its load-related requirements. Knowing these limits also allows us to examine the system design to understand those parts of the architecture that are susceptible to stress, and use this for future planning.

A good requirements document specifies the performance of the application under precisely stressed circumstances. As an example, suppose we have the following performance requirement.

The site shall handle customer visits with a maximum of 10 seconds wait time under the following conditions. Visits occur in a Poisson (probability) distribution with an average of 100 per minute. Each order is an average of 2 books, distributed normally with a standard deviation of 1.

An example of a load/stress test based on this requirement is the following.

Visit the site for 10 minutes with an average of 100 customers per minute. Each orders an average of 2 books, with a standard deviation of 1.

Recall that the *Poisson distribution* simulates arrival times at a queue; the *standard deviation* measures the extent to which data varies from the mean. For example, a variance of zero in the orders of the above requirement would mean that exactly 100 customers call every minute. Once we validate the system can handle this load, we increase the number of customer visits per minute to determine the point at which the application exhibits a problem.

In many cases, loads and stress limits are not explicitly specified in a requirements document. In this case, the project manager, QA, or management decides on the targets to be attained based on the following factors.

- User and customer expectations
- Technical limits
- Costs of improvement

- Legal advice

- Market conditions

- Experience with past products

- Comparisons with competitors' products

Tools such as Eclipse's Test and Performance Tools Platform (TPTP—see Section 28.6) provide the number of objects created at runtime and the amount of memory they consume. Various graphical devices are provided that show a "thermometer" reading of memory consumption (min to max) by mousing over a sequence diagram of function invocations. Testers seek maximum and near-maximum readings. The sequence diagram can be generated from the test execution. TPTP shows how many objects referenced a given object at runtime.

Metrics for load/stress testing include the following:

- Number/percent of load/stress requirements not satisfied

- Number/percent of load/stress standards (industry or company) not satisfied

These can be decomposed by types of loads and stresses.

28.2.3 Reliability and Availability Testing

It is an implicit requirement for every application that it be available for use! Sometimes it is acknowledged that the system will have defects or that it will not be able to survive defects in its environment (e.g., the operating system) and will crash at times. *Reliability and availability* assess and measure the extent of this.

Reliability and availability are typically measured by the mean time between failures (MTBF). To obtain MTBF, a definition of "failure" is first specified—for example, a crash of the application that requires its reload. Several different levels of failure may actually be defined and used. To compute the MTBF, a tester starts the application and notes the time. He or she then executes the application using, ideally, random scenarios until the system fails. The elapsed time is computed. This process is performed repeatedly; the MTBF is the average of these times.

Obtaining a very reliable value of MTBF involves hiring people to use the application according to some controlled rules and procedures. Gathering these data for many hours requires significant compensation for testers. Naturally, one tries to gather the data while users are using the application for another purpose. However, the other purpose—or purposes—cannot be permitted to bias the results. A related technique is to have a large body of users exercise the application in advance of its official release (see Section 28.4.3 concerning alpha and beta releases). To obtain an MTBF, it is necessary then to estimate the number of users and the time they spend using the application. As many know, the gathering of this kind of data continues even after a product is shipped, as in the pop-up message "Please send us notification of this failure . . . "

28.2.4 Recoverability Testing

Many otherwise excellent applications crash from time to time: The reasons may be beyond the control of developers, such as power outages. A good SRS specifies what should take place when an application crashes. A common requirement is that, when restarted, the application returns to its state at the time of the crash. This is a *recoverability requirement*. Another common requirement is for a designated log file to contain an explanation of the crash's cause (rather like an airplane's black box). As an example of a recovery technique, consider the "backstop" technique employed by Tom VanCourt on the Encounter video game. The code is shown in Listing 28.1.

Listing 28.1: Recoverability in Encounter video game

```java
public static void main( String[] argv )
{
  try {
      // Create the main application window.
      final GameMain gameFrameM = new GameMain();
      gameFrameM.addWindowListener( new WindowAdapter() {
        public void windowClosed( WindowEvent e )
          { System.exit(0); }
        public void windowClosing( WindowEvent e )
          { gameFrameM.dispose(); }
        }
      );

      // Set frame to a workable size. The size given here is only
      // approximate, since the frame can be resized and the layout
      // manager can adapt the content over a wide range of sizes.
      // Add in approximate amounts for window frames, etc.
      gameFrameM.resize( GAME_AREA_WIDTH + 25,
        GAME_AREA_HEIGHT + THUMBNAIL_HEIGHT + 25 );
      gameFrameM.createGameUI();  // Set up the user interface.
      gameFrameM.show();       // Display the window.
      gameFrameM.validate();   // Display the window contents.
      gameFrameM.toFront();    // Start in front of other windows.
  } catch ( Throwable thrownException ) {
      // Backstop exception handler: Catch any exceptions not already
      // handled elsewhere and try to get debug information from them.
      // RuntimeException objects, in particular, can be thrown by
      // any method without having been declared in a 'throws' clause.
      System.err.println( thrownException.getMessage() );
      thrownException.printStackTrace( System.err );
  }
}
```

The effect of this code is to trap exceptions not handled elsewhere and report them before the application stops. One can test for this at the system level by entering illegal values such as 10^{10} for strength value of a *quality*. Metrics for load/stress testing include the following:

- Number/percent of recoverability requirements not satisfied

- Number/percent of recoverability standards (industry or company) not satisfied

- Mean time to repair (i.e., to regain a given running status)

- Frequency of auto-recovery compared with the desired auto-recovery frequency

- Mean recovery time

- Mean restart time

28.2.5 Usability Testing

Usability testing validates an application's acceptability to its users. The primary goal of usability testing is to ensure that the application satisfies its stated usability requirements. These should be provided in the SRS in quantified terms, together with the manner in which the desired quantities are to be measured. Kit [1] lists the overall criteria in Figure 28.6 as essential for usability testing.

For example, we might require that a random sample of 30 users of our home finance application rate the application on a scale of 0 to 10, as shown in Table 28.1. An inspection of the accessibility results shows that our application scores about 12 percent lower than the industry average—some cause for concern. Our variance is lower than that found in industry, however, which means that the sampled users agreed more on

---

- *Accessibility*
  How easily can users enter, navigate, and exit?
    - For example, measure by average time taken to . . .
- *Responsiveness*
  How ready is the application to allow the user to accomplish specified goals?
    - How often is GUI display accurate (percentage)?
    - How quickly are user actions acknowledged?
    - How often is the application ready for user action?
- *Efficiency*
  Degree to which the number of required steps for selected functionality is minimal
    - "Minimal" calculated theoretically
    - For example, measure by minimal time/average time
- *Comprehensibility*
  How easy is the product to understand and use with documentation and *help?*
    - For example, measure time taken for standard queries

Figure 28.6 Key attributes sought in usability testing

Source: Kit, Edward, Software Testing in the Real World: Improving the Process, Addison-Wesley, 1995.

Table 28.1 An example of usability scores

Quality	Score	Variance	Industry average score	Industry average variance
Accessibility	8.1	2.1	8.2	3.5
Responsiveness	9.3	3.2	5.0	3.0
Efficiency	5.6	2.0	7.2	1.1
Comprehensibility	2.3	0.5	6.0	0.3

this score than users typically agree on the usability of a UI. This tells us that a smaller percentage probably actually dislike using our application than is usual.

The appropriate sample size depends on the desired probability of an erroneous conclusion. If we want a smaller probability of error, we need a larger sample. Usability data can be collected in a controlled or uncontrolled environment. In a controlled environment, subjects are observed and data like the following are obtained:

- Average time for the user to complete designated functions

- The rate of user errors in designated interactions

- Average time taken to learn new functions

- Average time taken to complete designated tasks (e.g., create a letter in a word processor)

- The results are compared with required, company, and industry norms. Users are very sensitive to applications with which their experience deviates much from what they are used to.

In designing usability questionnaires, the challenge is to obtain data that enable engineers to remedy the most serious shortcomings without exceeding the limits of users' time and patience filling out questionnaires. Usability data can be expensive to collect because users often expect compensation for the time and trouble of providing detailed feedback. For example, a client of one of the authors develops software for a device used by physicians. The company provides a free dinner and significant monetary compensation in return for viewing and commenting on screen shots and demonstrations.

Turning now to uncontrolled environments, Figures 28.7 and 28.8 show the beginnings of the Purdue Usability Testing Questionnaire [2], which provides useful data from which to assess the value of and potential improvements in a set of GUIs.

28.2.6 Security Testing

Security testing consists of identifying security defects and measuring the extent of an application's security. Recall that some principal aspects of security are those listed in Figure 28.9. We can base security testing on these. The testing can be performed by using or simulating interception of traffic (called "sniffers"), using software that attempts to break systems, such as scripts that repeatedly try password break-ins, and by using people of varied skill levels to try deliberately breaching the designated security aspects. At the high end of this spectrum of skills are people with experience "hacking." A high level of security clearance is required for them. Using hackers can present major problems when an external consulting company is the only alternative and especially when the experienced people have been involved in unauthorized activities in the past.

The *Open Source Security Testing Methodology Manual* (OSSTMM) is an open standard methodology for performing security tests [3]. OSSTMM focuses on the technical details of which items need to be tested, what to do during a security test, and when different types of security tests should be performed. A checklist for confidentiality testing in information security, partly adapted from OSSTMM, includes the following actions. Some are part of non-security testing as well, as one continues to recognize that many security breaches simply exploit a defect in the software.

- Validate confidential database locations
  - Screen all databases for confidential content

Purdue Usability Testing Questionnaire

Based on: Lin, H.X. Choong, Y-Y., and Salvendy, G. (1997) *A Proposed Index of Usability: A Method for Comparing the Relative Usability of Different Software Systems.* **Behaviour & Information Technology,** 16:4/5, 267-278. Abstract Reproduced by permission. (The ratings of importance are not included in this online version, but could be incorporated into the comments.) About question.cgi

Please rate the usability of the system.

- Try to respond to all the items.
- For items that are not applicable, use: **NA**
- Make sure these fields are filled in: **System:** **Email to:**
- Add a comment about an item by clicking on its 📝 icon, or add comment fields for all items by clicking on **Comment All.**
- To mail in your results, click on: **Mail Data**

System: ▭ **Email to:** ▭

Optionally provide comments and your email address in the box.

[Mail Data] [Comment All] RETURN TO REFERRING PAGE

1. COMPATIBILITY

	1	2	3	4	5	6	7	NA
1. Is the control of cursor compatible with movement? 📝	bad ○	○	○	○	○	○	○ good	○
2. Are the results of control entry compatible with user expectations? 📝	bad ○	○	○	○	○	○	○ good	○
3. Is the control matched to user skill? 📝	bad ○	○	○	○	○	○	○ good	○
4. Are the coding compatible with familiar conventions? 📝	bad ○	○	○	○	○	○	○ good	○
5. Is the wording familiar? 📝	bad ○	○	○	○	○	○	○ good	○

Figure 28.7 Purdue usability questionnaire fragment, 1 of 2

Source: Purdue Usability Testing Questionnaire, http://www.acm.org/~perlman/question.cgi?form=PUTQ.

2. CONSISTENCY

	bad	1	2	3	4	5	6	7	good	NA
6. Is the assignment of colour codes conventional?	bad	○	○	○	○	○	○	○	good	○
7. Is the coding consistent across displays, menu options?	bad	○	○	○	○	○	○	○	good	○
8. Is the cursor placement consistent?	bad	○	○	○	○	○	○	○	good	○
9. Is the display format consistent?	bad	○	○	○	○	○	○	○	good	○
10. Is the feedback consistent?	bad	○	○	○	○	○	○	○	good	○
11. Is the format within data fields consistent?	bad	○	○	○	○	○	○	○	good	○
12. Is the label format consistent?	bad	○	○	○	○	○	○	○	good	○
13. Is the label location consistent?	bad	○	○	○	○	○	○	○	good	○
14. Is the labelling itself consistent?	bad	○	○	○	○	○	○	○	good	○
15. Is the display orientation consistent? -- panning vs. scrolling.	bad	○	○	○	○	○	○	○	good	○
16. Are the user actions required consistent?	bad	○	○	○	○	○	○	○	good	○
17. Is the wording consistent across displays?	bad	○	○	○	○	○	○	○	good	○
18. Is the data display consistent with entry requirements?	bad	○	○	○	○	○	○	○	good	○
19. Is the data display consistent with user conventions?	bad	○	○	○	○	○	○	○	good	○
20. Are symbols for graphic data standard?	bad	○	○	○	○	○	○	○	good	○
21. Is the option wording consistent with command language?	bad	○	○	○	○	○	○	○	good	○
22. Is the wording consistent with user guidance?	bad	○	○	○	○	○	○	○	good	○

Figure 28.8 Purdue usability questionnaire fragment, 2 of 2

Source: Purdue Usability Testing Questionnaire, http://www.acm.org/~perlman/question.cgi?form=PUTQ.

- **Confidentiality**
  - Sniffers validate that data passed not visible to unauthorized parties
  - Hire professional hackers?
- **Nonrepudiation**
  - Experiments to validate
- **Integrity**
  - Alter data and validate consequences
- **Authentication**
  - Hire professional hackers?
- **Authorization**
  - Hire professional hackers?

Figure 28.9 Testing for security

- Validate cookies

  - Content, types, expiration, and encryption

- Check for buffer overflow protection

- Check for memory leaks

- Test for illicit site navigation

- Validate sign-ins

  - Include default IDs and passwords

- Check protection against illegal and out-of-bounds input (not necessarily input that allows breaches)

  Metrics for security testing include the following.

- Number/percent of specific security requirements not satisfied

- Number/percent of security standards (industry or company) not satisfied

- Confidentiality: Average time required to gain disallowed access to information

  - at a specified level of security

  - by testers of a specified degree of training and experience

- Nonrepudiation: Average time required to repudiate agreements

- Integrity: Average time required to alter data in transit, undetected

- Authentication: Average time required to verify identity

- Authorization: Average time required to gain disallowed access to a location

28.2.7 Compatibility Testing

Many applications are designed to work with other applications. For example, a word processor that allows the insertion of a spreadsheet must be compatible with the spreadsheet application. Another example is an application that obtains data from people with mobile devices of various brands. Compatibility testing is similar to integration testing in that it tests the interactions between parts of an application. The difference is that the interfaces are typically developed by different organizations, and developers normally can't change the applications with which they must be compatible.

An important subfield of compatibility testing is assuring that the application operates with designated past versions of software on which it depends. This includes versions of the operating system. An example is an online learning environment, which must work with various versions of Windows as well as with UNIX. Compatibility with future versions can be planned for to some extent, and it is sometimes possible to simulate upcoming changes. Testing must include combinations of versions.

Metrics for compatibility testing include the following:

- Number/percent of specific compatibility requirements not satisfied

- Number/percent of compatibility standards (industry or company) not satisfied

28.2.8 Installation and Installability Testing

An *installation* test validates that an application can indeed be installed. An *installability* test is a more general concept in that it tests via installation test cases whether an application can be installed on a variety of configurations. Installation tests whether an application can be successfully installed on its target systems. These are binary can/can't tests. Many types of errors can occur during installation, especially due to the differences in hardware and software platforms. Applications are often required to execute on multiple hardware and software platforms. Multiple platforms typically require separate tests. For example, if our video store application were required to execute on Windows and Macs with Internet requirements, we would devise tests that ensure the satisfaction of the requirements on each of these platforms. Although we try to develop applications that are platform independent, this has limitations. For example, we may need to test with separate bar code readers for Windows and Mac platforms. Installation tests would be identical for the most part but would contain Windows-specific and Mac-specific parts.

Once we have tested that an application can be installed correctly, we run a second tier, consisting of installability tests that measure the level of difficulty of installing the application. As computer users we are all too familiar with how easy or how hard it is to install an application. Installability tests this process and the aspects of the application that make this easy or difficult.

Metrics for installation and installabilty testing include the following:

- Number/percent of specific installability requirements not satisfied

- Time required to install on designated platform by customers with designated amount of experience or education

- Time required to confirm installation integrity via a standard test sequence

- Number of defects found during installation, with "defects" carefully defined

28.2.9 Serviceability Testing

Servicing an application is the process of repairing or enhancing it. This could include visiting the site and sending a full or partial replacement over the Internet.

An application's *serviceability* refers to the ease or difficulty with which it can be kept operational in the face of changes to its environment. For example, an expert system application relies on its knowledge base, typically in the form of a set of rules, which may be straightforward to modify. Another example is the ease with which an application that runs on one version of an operating system can be made to run on its successor. Serviceability tests execute scenarios such as swapping databases. Serviceability is related to maintainability—the ease or difficulty with which an application can be maintained. The difference is that servicing is a planned, expected, and predictable process.

Metrics for serviceability testing include the following:

- Number/percent of specific serviceability requirements not satisfied

- Number/percent of serviceability standards (industry or company) not satisfied

- Time required to service specified actions on designated platforms

28.3 TESTING WITH LIGHTWEIGHT REQUIREMENTS

This section discusses testing in the context of requirements that range from being not written down at all (Section 28.3.1) to being only partially expressed in writing via the user stories of agile processes (Section 28.3.5).

28.3.1 Testing in the Absence of Requirements

Most of the software engineering literature emphasizes the importance of requirements and the execution of testing against those requirements. Higher CMM levels are bestowed only on those organizations that write down requirements thoroughly (see Chapter 6). However, many real-world applications have incomplete or even nonexistent requirements documents. Our concern in this chapter is how to test such applications.

Even when requirements do exist in written form, they generally cannot provide a very good feeling for the application compared with running code. This is like the difference between drawing detailed plans for a house and living in the house after it is built—they are simply not the same. In fact, if we want to determine whether a house that is already built satisfies needs, it is more useful to ask the occupants than to inspect the architect's drawings. Figure 28.10 summarizes the reasons for testing with little or no reference to a requirements document.

Suppose that you have been asked to test an application for which there is no requirements document. Where do you begin? In the next sections, we'll describe a starting point: a *behavioral model* of the application.

- Provides a "feel" for the application
  Even complete, written requirements do not accomplish this effectively
- The Requirements document omits implicit ones
- The Requirements may –
  - be incomplete
  - be inconsistent with the code
  - be missing
  - never have been written down at all
- You can't access the requirements because the product is from a third party
  Vendor software that you must test before using

Figure 28.10 Reasons to test without basing the tests on written requirements

28.3.2 Models for Software Testing

To test an application in the absence of well-written requirements, the tester needs a sense of how the application is meant to behave and how it actually behaves. This is called *behavioral modeling*. Most of us have already had a behavioral modeling experience in dealing with an unfamiliar application. Although we may read the manual or follow a tutorial, we often simply "play around" with the application. This section concerns disciplined ways to "play around" with the goal of finding as many defects, as serious as possible, in as little time as possible. This is not the black-and-white process of requirements-based testing, and it is sometimes called an "art." Good artists, however, are extremely well-disciplined, and good testers are too.

One approach to forming the concepts of an as-built (already constructed) application is to use the software design models that we covered in Chapter 15. These are the *use case models, class models, data flow models*, and *state models*. These are valuable for creating designs of applications yet unbuilt, but they are less so for modeling already-built applications. Table 28.2 indicates when these design models could apply to behavioral modeling of already-built applications.

This suggests that a different or modified model should be sought, as discussed next.

Table 28.2 Applicability of various design models to black box testing of as-built applications

Design Model	Applicability to As-Built Black Box Testing
Use Case Model	Apply use cases to identify the main, unbranching behavior
Class Model	Typically not especially useful for black-box testing
Data Flow Model	Possible if the tester recognizes principal functions
State Model	Possible if the tester recognizes states that the application transitions through

28.3.3 Constructing Directed Graphs for Black Box Testing

We will use the concept of *directed graphs* in what follows. A directed graph is a figure consisting of nodes, together with arrows between certain nodes, called *edges*, illustrated in Figure 28.11. The meaning of nodes and edges depends on the context in which they are applied.

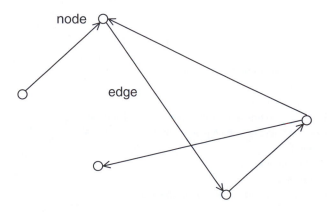

Figure 28.11 Directed graphs

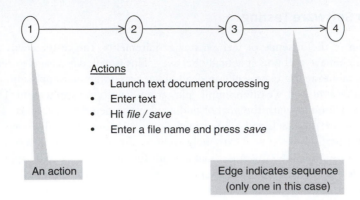

Figure 28.12 Initial directed graph for OpenOffice

One approach to modeling as-built applications is to start from what appears best to be a beginning point of the application, and then keep track of the paths from there in directed graph form. Each node represents an action performed by the user or the application (sometimes a sequence of such actions instead). Each edge leads to the next possible action. Edges are labeled when necessary to distinguish options. This use of nodes and edges is neither data flow nor state/transition. It can be thought of as a control flow in that each node represents a point at which the application is in control.

As an example, let's perform this for the word processor of the open source office suite OpenOffice. Besides serving as a means for black box testing, a directed graph is a means of getting to know the application. Figure 28.12 shows the beginning of a directed graph for executing OpenOffice's "Writer," its word processor.

Since there is no branching in the example of Figure 28.12, there is no need to label the edges to understand the sequence of actions. In Figure 28.13, on the other hand, there is such a need. Branch points are labeled as nodes like any other (which makes these diagrams different from others we have studied in this book). Figure 28.13 shows a continuation of the graphing process. The numbering serves only to label the nodes and does not denote an order. The labels on edges are used to assist in differentiating among branching options.

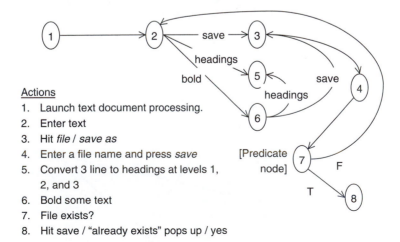

Actions
1. Launch text document processing.
2. Enter text
3. Hit *file / save as*
4. Enter a file name and press *save*
5. Convert 3 line to headings at levels 1, 2, and 3
6. Bold some text
7. File exists?
8. Hit save / "already exists" pops up / yes

Figure 28.13 Example of a directed graph for OpenOffice

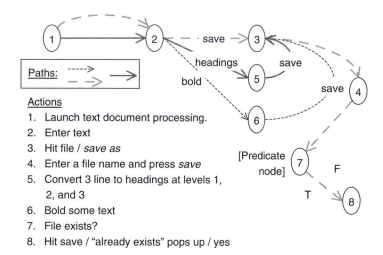

Actions
1. Launch text document processing.
2. Enter text
3. Hit file / *save as*
4. Enter a file name and press *save*
5. Convert 3 line to headings at levels 1, 2, and 3
6. Bold some text
7. File exists?
8. Hit save / "already exists" pops up / yes

Figure 28.14 Using a directed graph for testing—OpenOffice example

---

- The most **expected** paths with **no error** or anomaly conditions
- The most **expected** paths **with error** or anomaly conditions
- The paths **most likely** to yield **defects**

Figure 28.15 Selecting paths in directed graphs for testing

28.3.4 Using Directed Graphs in Testing

Tests are designed via sequences that traverse multiple nodes. A reasonable goal is to create enough of these to cover all nodes. (Attempting to cover all *path combinations* exposes more defects but usually leads to a combinatorial explosion in the number of possibilities.) Figure 28.14 shows three paths that cover all nodes.

The number of sequences made of these paths can be extremely large. The tester can be selective among these as in Figure 28.15, however.

28.3.5 Testing for Agile Processes

As mentioned in previous chapters, continual testing is an integral part of agile processes, especially via utilities such as JUnit and NUnit. Although such tests focus on a method under construction, a growing, cumulative set of unit tests can effectively test large parts of an application as it grows.

A suite of JUnit tests, grown method by method and class by class (as in Chapter 27), may be partly usable for functional testing (i.e., to check that the requirements have been satisfied). However, invariably there will be requirements for which they are not appropriate, such as those that require user interaction.

The following kinds of testing are carried out for agile projects in the same way as for non-agile ones:

- Nonfunctional testing (performance, load/stress, event, recoverability, usability, security, compatibility, installation, serviceability)

- Acceptance testing (a central part of the agile approach)

28.3.6 Qualities of a Good Tester

We have described various techniques for the black box testing of as-built applications. A good tester, however, goes well beyond them in his or her efforts in trying to ferret out defects that could be encountered when many people use the application for a significant time, perhaps in unanticipated ways. He or she should be an independent thinker and should not be part of the team that designed or implemented the application under test. This is because even the most independent person involved in design or implementation develops a vision of the application that, even when excellent, is likely to overlook or misunderstand issues. The following are some of the qualities of a good tester:

- Willingness to learn goals of application

- Willingness to put self in user shoes

- Determined

- Dogged

- Fearless

- Imaginative

- "Outside the box" thinker

- Curious

- Meticulous

Let's translate these qualities into the testing of OpenOffice. To find as many defects as possible within a fixed amount of time, the tester would need sufficient determination to go beyond the obvious ways of using the application. This is because the common procedures will probably have been exercised many times and thus have been debugged. The tester would need doggedness to stay with his or her intuition concerning lurking bugs even when it yields few initial bug finds. In the normal use of an application, users tend to be relatively gentle. For example, they avoid hitting a control-X button while a file is being saved, or pressing many keys in rapid succession, including function keys. A tester, on the other hand, needs the fearlessness to stress the application in such a manner.

There is another sense in which testers need to be dogged: getting action on the defects that they find. Kaner [5] notes that finding *and* obtaining action on discovered defects is significantly more important than simply finding them. His point is that the time spent discovering a defect is wasted if the defect is never repaired. It is certainly the task of QA to ensure that quality is present, and this includes ensuring appropriate action on defects.

Testers need enough imagination to think of many different ways of using the application. They need to "think outside the box" because defects are usually found in execution paths that are not obvious. For example, in testing the OpenOffice word processor, a good tester would pursue sequences very different from the run-of-the-mill *open file/edit/save* sequence. A more demanding sequence is *open file/add 10 lines/set some lines to various heading levels/save in location 1/set some lines to various bullets/save in location 2/retrieve*.

Good testers are curious. They are required to wonder about the limits of the application, repeatedly asking "What if I were to . . . ?" An example is "What if I were to load a non-OpenOffice document, and then . . . ?"

Testers need to be meticulous in that they must keep careful records of the steps followed to discover a defect, and gather detailed information to include in bug reports.

28.4 TESTING SHORTLY BEFORE RELEASE

Every project has a history of testing lasting almost as long as the project itself. However, the period just prior to releasing the application has special testing characteristics, which are described in this section.

28.4.1 Soak Testing

It is common to conduct *soak testing* near the end of the system testing phase. During soak testing the application is executed in an environment that simulates as closely as possible the way a typical customer will use the system under normal load. The soak test is conducted for an extended period of time—for example, two weeks. Test scripts are used so that the testing can continue for the entire duration without interruption. The purpose is to uncover problems such as memory leaks and timing-related issues that only manifest themselves after the system is run for a substantial period of time. The goal of soak testing is to reduce, as much as possible, initial customer complaints about problems—not necessarily serious but annoying ones— encountered when they exercise the application in a manner not exercised before. Ideally, soak tests are run by committed customers, otherwise by QA.

28.4.2 Acceptance Testing

In principle, the customer contracts with the developer to build an application. At some point, the developer claims to have fulfilled his or her part of the contract, the customer validates this, and then pays for the application if satisfied. The customer performs this validation by means of *acceptance tests*. In principle, these are most important for all concerned. Acceptance tests can be executed by the customer, or by the development organization—in some sort of clearly demonstrable manner—on behalf of the customer. Acceptance tests are typically driven by the SRS. A subset of the system tests is selected that validate major functional requirements and selected nonfunctional requirements.

It is a reality of software development that delivered applications contain defects. If a contract were to state that software will not be paid for if a defect is found, very few companies would risk developing software. Defects therefore have to be factored into contracts. There are several ways to deal with this, mostly legal in nature, that relieve the development organization of a degree of responsibility.

Recall that software can meet all its requirements yet not meet the *needs* of the customer. Contracts attempt to navigate the gap between customers, who want applications that are satisfactory to them (written or not), and developers, who need to work with well-defined ends. Acceptance testing is planned and conducted accordingly. Metrics for acceptance testing are a subset of those covered so far in this chapter, by mutual agreement between the customer and developer, made in advance.

28.4.3 Alpha and Beta Releases

This section concerns applications intended for use by a large number of people. A software product version is *released* when it is officially turned over to customers. This usually takes place directly after acceptance tests. Qualified releases may take place prior to the final release. In many cases, internal prospective users, as well as customers, are willing to participate in the system testing process. This process is controlled by *alpha* releases and *beta* releases, as differentiated by Figure 28.16.

Alpha releases are given to in-house users or to a highly selective and trusted group of external users for early prerelease use. The purpose of alpha releases is to provide the development organization feedback and defect information from a group larger than the testers, without affecting the reputation of the unreleased product. Following the dissemination of alpha releases, *beta releases* are given out. These are

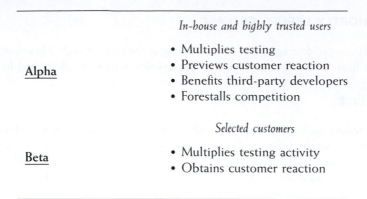

Figure 28.16 Alpha and beta releases

given to part of the customer community with the understanding that they report defects found. Alpha and beta releases are also used to convince potential customers that there really is a product behind the vendor's promises.

A principal motivation to be alpha testers and beta testers is to gain advance knowledge of the product. Developers can gain information about the application (typically its APIs) so that they can begin to develop applications that use it. Users can begin to form decisions about purchasing the application or gain experience using it.

Metrics for alpha and beta testing include the metrics mentioned so far in this chapter, in principle. Alpha and beta testing are generally not focused on particular attributes. Their products are bug reports, which are generally categorized. Metrics include most of those already mentioned in this chapter, as well as those with a simpler categorization such as the following:

- Number of major defects detected within the first x days/weeks/months

- Number of non-major defects detected within the first x days/weeks/months

28.5 CASE STUDY: ENCOUNTER SOFTWARE TEST DOCUMENTATION[1]

Note to the Student:
This document describes the overall testing of Encounter. The document uses the IEEE Standard 829-1998 Software Test Documentation (STD) headings (*introduction, test plan, test design, test cases, test procedures, test item transmittal report, test log, test incident report, test summary*) and refers to the various particular tests (integration tests, system tests, acceptance tests, etc.). These, in turn, are described using the same IEEE STD headings. Those involved in testing appreciate the documentation a

great deal since it improves their ability to make applications more reliable.

History of versions of this document:

11/1/98 E. Braude: Initial Draft

4/4/99 E. Braude: Revised

8/23/99 R. Bostwick: Documents reviewed and recommendations made

---

[1] Reproduced with permission.

8/24/1999 E. Braude: Recommendations integrated

Status: to be completed

game. IEEE standard 829-1998 for Software Testing Documentation is used at every level of testing.

The test philosophy for the Encounter video game is summarized in Figures 28.17 and 28.18.

1. Introduction

This document contains the STD for Encounter and its role-playing game (RPG) framework. The categories of testing addressed in this document include unit, integration, system, acceptance, and installation testing. This document describes the testing required to validate the first three builds of the Encounter video

> Although the SDD is not explicitly a requirements document, it effectively imposes requirements on the implementation. Sometimes these requirements are spelled out in a separate document. The case study in this book does not contain such a separate document.

Test Type	Approach	Corresponding document sections
Unit	White and black box; method and class tests; test against detailed requirements and design.	SRS section(s): 3.2 *Classes/Objects* SDD section(s): 6. *Detailed design*
Integration	Gray box; mostly package-level; oriented to builds (1, 2, and 3); test against architecture and high-level requirements.	SRS section(s): 2. *Overall description*, 3.1 *External interfaces*, validate representative requirements in 3.2 *Classes/Objects* SDD section(s): 3. *Decomposition description*, 4. *Dependency description*, 5. *Interface description*.
System	Black box; all packages; whole system (Build 3); test against nonfunctional requirements, architecture and high-level requirements.	SRS section(s): 2. *Overall description*, 3.1 *External interfaces*, validate representative requirements in 3.2 *Classes/Objects*, 3.3 *Performance requirements*, 3.4 *Design constraints*, 3.5 *Software system attributes*, 3.6 *Other requirements* SDD section(s): 3. *Decomposition description*, 4. *Dependency description*, 5. *Interface description*; validate representative requirements in 6. *Detailed design*.

Figure 28.17 Approaches to system test and their documentation, 1 of 2

Acceptance	Black box; all packages; whole system (Build 3); test against high-level requirements and detailed requirements.	SRS section(s): 2. *Overall description*, 3.2 *Classes/ Objects*
Installation	Black box; all packages; whole system (Builds for customer specific configurations); test against high-level requirements and detailed requirements.	SRS section(s): 2. *Overall description*, 3.2 *Classes/ Objects*

Figure 28.18 Approaches to system test and their documentation, 2 of 2

2. Encounter Video Game Test Documentation

The STD for Encounter and the RPG framework covers test planning, specification, and reporting. There are separate test plans for unit, integration, system, acceptance, and installation testing. Each test plan references its test design, test case, and test procedure specifications. The test reporting documentation consists of the test log, incident report, and summary report.

2.1 Unit Test STD

Refer to the separate unit test document.

> See the case study in Chapter 27.

2.2 Integration Test STD

The STD for integration testing consists of the separate STDs for build 1, build 2, and build 3, as described next. Refer to Appendix A in the SCMP for an explanation of the construction of the build integration baselines. Tests will be identified according to the conventions shown in Figure 28.19.

2.2.1 Build 1 STD

2.2.1.1 Build 1 Test Plan

2.2.1.1.1 Test Plan Identifier Build1_TP

2.2.1.1.2 Introduction This test plan covers the integration test for the *GameCharacters* framework package and the *EncounterCharacters* package. It describes how to verify that the player and foreign characters can be retrieved, modified, and displayed through the singleton *EncounterCast* object.

2.2.1.1.3 Test Items The classes and methods in the *GameCharacters* and *EncounterCharacters* packages are tested through the EncounterCast singleton.

2.2.1.1.4 Features to Be Tested The features tested by the test design specification Build1_TD are based on the requirements within the SRS and SDD, as listed in Figure 28.20.

2.2.1.1.5 Features Not to Be Tested

> Inevitably, infinitely many points simply can't be tested for, but identifying particular issues that will not be tested for sometimes helps to clarify the testing process.

The testing of the features associated with the *EncounterEnvironment* and *EncounterGame* packages and their frameworks is deferred until the build 1 and build 2 integration testing.

2.2.1.1.6 Approach The approach to the verification of build 1 consists of verifying that the characters of the game can be retrieved and displayed through the singleton EncounterCast object. The method and interface tests verify that the required (public) interface methods of the Encounter Characters package are available from the EncounterCast singleton.

Test Document Identifier	
Test Document	**Document Identifier**
Build 1 Test Plan	Build1_TP
Build 1 Test Design Specification	Build1_TD
Build 1 Test Case Specifications	Build1_TC1toBuild1_TC . . .
Build 1 Test Procedure Specifications	Build1_TP1toBuild1_TP . . .
Build 1 Test Logs	Build1_LOG1 to Build1_LOG . . .
Build 1 Test Incident Report	Build1_lnRep1 to BuilcMJnRep . . .
Build 1 Test Summary Report	Build1_SumRep1 to BuildiSumRep . . .

Figure 28.19 Test document file identification

Document	Section	Requirement Title
SRS	2.1.2.2	User interface for setting quality values
	3.1.1.2	User interface for setting quality values
	3.2.EC	Encounter characters
	3.2.FC	Foreign characters
	3.2.P	Player characters
	3.2.PQ	The player quality window
SDD for *RPG* framework	3.1.2	Characters package
	5.0	Interface description
SDD for Encounter	3.1.2	EncounterCharacters package
	4.2	Interprocess dependencies
	5.1.2	Interface to the *EncounterCharacters* package

Figure 28.20 Features to be tested in build 1

2.2.1.1.7 Item Pass/Fail Criteria   Pass/fail criteria are based upon satisfying the corresponding requirements in the SRS and SDD.

2.2.1.1.8 Suspension Criteria and Resumption Requirements   (N/A)

2.2.1.1.9 Test Deliverables   The documents listed in Figure 28.19 are to be delivered to the configuration management group at the completion of the build 1 integration test.

2.2.1.1.10 Testing Tasks   The testing tasks consist of the following steps:

1. Load build 1 and the package Build_1.

2. Execute build 1 test procedures from the main() method of Build_1Test in package Build_1.

3. Write test report documentation in accordance with Section 2.2.1.1.9.

4. Store all test documentation and data in accordance with Section 2.2.1.1.9 under configuration management.

2.2.1.1.11 Environment Needs   Depending upon equipment availability, either an IBM PC, Sun SPARC workstation, or an Apple iMAC hardware configuration can be used. The Eclipse Integrated Development Environment (IDE) should be used for the build 1 testing.

2.2.1.1.12 Responsibilities   Sally Silver and Jose Hernandes from the SQA group are responsible for managing, preparing, and executing the build 1 integration test. In addition, the Encounter development group addresses technical questions and responds to test incident reports. Configuration control stores all test documentation and data.

2.2.1.1.13 Staffing and Training Needs   The SPMP specifies the overall staffing and training needs for integration testing.

2.2.1.1.14 Schedule   The schedule for integration testing is included in the SPMP section 5.5 version 5 and higher. (Section 19.6 discusses the

updating of the SPMP to reflect the architecture selected.)

> The case studies in this book do not include the updated SPMP.

2.2.1.1.15 Risks and Contingencies   If the SQA team is unable to execute tests, or the number of defects causes an unacceptable number of system failures, then Alfred Murray of the Encounter development team will be assigned to the build 1 integration test.

2.2.1.1.16 Approvals   The completion of this test requires the approval of the SQA Manager, the Encounter Development Manager, and the CCB Representative.

2.2.1.2 Build 1 Test Design

2.2.1.2.1 Test Design Specification Identifier   ...

2.2.1.2.2 Features to Be Tested   The test for build 1 will get the *EncounterCast* object and the player and foreign characters, change the values of various qualities, get these values, and then verify their correctness.

2.2.1.2.3 Approach Refinements   ...

2.2.1.3.2 Test Items   The functionality to be tested is contained in the specifications for the following public methods of *EncounterCast*.

> *EncounterCast getTheEncounterCast()*
>
> *GameCharacter getThePlayerCharacter()*
>
> *GameCharacter getTheForeignCharacter()*
>
> *void setPlayerCharacterQuality(String quality, float value)*
>
> *void setForeignCharacterQuality(String quality, float value)*
>
> *float getPlayerCharacterQuality()*
>
> *float getForeignCharacterQuality()*

These are tested in accordance with Figure 28.21.

2.2.1.3.3 Input Specifications: see Figure 28.21

2.2.1.3.4 Output Specifications: see Figure 28.21

2.2.1.3.5 Environmental Needs   This testing is performed with the *GameCharacters* and *EncounterCharacters* packages alone.

	Quality	Player input value	Foreign input value	Other	Action
Integration Test #					
B1.1	N/A	N/A	N/A	Get player character	Verify by name
B1.2	N/A	N/A	N/A	Get foreign character	Verify by name
B1.3	Concentration	30	40	N/A	Verify output values == input values
B1.4	Stamina	30	40	N/A	Verify output values == input values
B1.5	. . . . . .	. . . . . .	. . . . . .	. . . . .	. . . . . .

Figure 28.21 Integration test inputs, outputs, and actions

2.2.1.3.6 Special Procedural Requirements: None

2.2.1.3.7 Interface Dependencies: None

> This section describes the relationships among the various interfaces. This becomes significant for future builds, but is not an issue for build 1.

2.2.1.4 Build 1 Test Procedures

2.2.1.4.1 Test Procedure Specification Identifier

> This identifies the class/method from which the test is executed.

Integration_Tests/Build1_Test in package Tests

2.2.1.4.2 Purpose
To set up a test of build 1 with a minimum of other parts of the application.

2.2.1.4.3 Special Requirements
The test harness in Integration Tests/Build1_Test, consisting of a class with a single method, *main()*, is to be constructed, and tests 1, 2, 3, . . . are to be executed and the results compared.

2.2.1.4.4 Procedure Steps
Populate the file Build1_test_data with input data and expected output values for the qualities in the following format.

<quality name> <input><expected output>

<quality name> <input><expected output>

. . . .

There is no additional beginning or ending text.

2.2.1.5 Build 1 Test Item Transmittal Report . . . . . .

2.2.1.6.3 Activity and Event Entries

> The "defect reference" is the number used by the defect tracking system for this defect.

2.2.1.7 Build 1 Test Incident Report

2.2.1.7.1 Test Incident Report Identifier
Build1_test3

2.2.1.7.2 Summary
see Figure 28.22.

2.2.1.7.3 Incident Description
Ed Blake was distracted during the execution of test 3 by an alarm in the building, and could not record the results. It was decided not to interrupt or repeat the test sequence, and to conduct test 3 as part of the testing for build 2.

	Result	*Defect reference*
Test #	Build 1 Test Log	
1	Passed	N/A
2	Failed	1823
3	Data lost – To be repeated	N/A
4	Lost of precision in returned value	2872
5	. . . . . .	. . . . . .

Figure 28.22 Build 1 test log (summary)

2.2.1.7.4 Impact It was decided that the incident(s) reported above were not serious enough to require a repetition of this test.

2.2.1.8 Build 1 Test Summary Report

2.2.1.8.1 Test Summary Report Identifier . . .

2.2.1.8.2 Summary The build 1 test passed with the exception of the defects noted. This will be handled by the regular defect repair process.

2.2.1.8.3 Variances See build 1 test incident report.

2.2.1.8.4 Comprehensive Assessment . . . .

> Additional remarks supplying details can be placed here.

2.2.1.8.5 Summary of Results . . .

2.2.2 Build 2 STD

> This format is similar to the format in the build 1 STD.

2.2.2.1 Build 2 Test Plan These tests will verify that the areas of the game can be retrieved and displayed through the *EncounterEnvironment* object, and that the connections among them are consistent with the SRS.

2.2.2.2 Build 2 Test Design These tests first will verify that the correct *EncounterEnvironment* object can be obtained, and then will show that the Area objects and *AreaConnection* objects can be retrieved as required.

2.2.2.3 Build 2 Test Case The functionality to be tested is contained in the following public functions of *EncounterEnvironment*.

> *GameArea getTheDressingRoom()*
>
> *GameArea getTheDungeon()*
>
> . . . .
>
> *EncounterEnvironment getTheEncounterEnvironment()*

2.2.2.4 Build 2 Test Procedures: To be supplied
. . . .

2.3 System Test STD

2.3.1 System Test Plan
These tests are performed against the architecture, as described in Figure 28.23.

The tests verify that the effects of game actions in *EncounterGame* correctly manifest themselves as

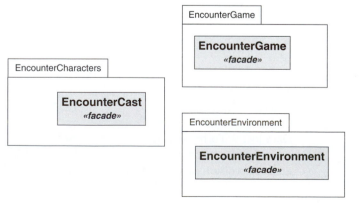

Figure 28.23 Architecture and modularization for Encounter video game

movements of *Encounter* characters within the environment.

2.3.2 System Test Design

These system tests are designed to verify the architecture by executing and verifying sequences of interface methods.

2.3.3 System Test Cases
System Test 1

1. Move player character into dungeon.

2. Move foreign character into courtyard.

3. Move foreign character into dungeon.

4. Execute an encounter in the dungeon.

    System Test 2

    . . .

2.3.4 System Test Procedures

. . . .

2.4 Acceptance Test STD

2.4.1 Acceptance Test Plan

The integration tests verify that the requirements of Encounter, as stated in the SRS, have been satisfied.

The acceptance tests are stored in the *AcceptanceTest* package, and include the use cases.

The Initialize use case is shown in Figure 28.24 and is executed by the *main()* method of the class Initialize in the *AcceptanceTest* package.

The *Encounter Foreign Character* use case is shown in Figure 28.25 and is executed by the *main()* method of the class *AcceptanceTest.Initialize.*

2.4.2 Acceptance Test Design
The use cases indicated in Section 2.4.1 are to be executed in sequence several times, in accordance with the test cases in Section 2.4.3.

2.4.3 Acceptance Test Cases

2.4.3.1 Test Cases for Initialize Use Case

The tests are instances of the Initialize use case, also known as "scenarios."

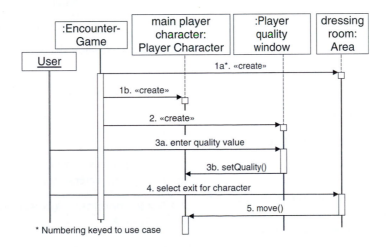

Figure 28.24 Sequence diagram for *Initialize* use case in Encounter

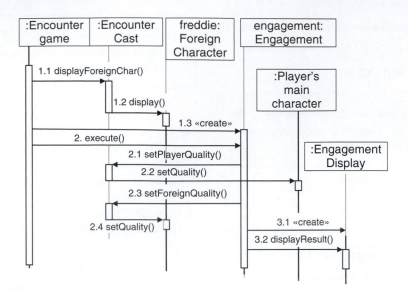

Figure 28.25 Sequence diagram for Encounter Foreign Character use case in Encounter

2.4.3.1.1 Initialize Acceptance Test 1

1. Start up game.

2. Supply main character with the following quality values, in the order shown:
   Strength: 30, then Concentration: 20.

3. Move the main character to the courtyard.

2.4.3.1.2 Initialize Acceptance Test 2

1. Start up game.

2. Supply main character with the following quality values, in the order shown:
   Strength: 30, Concentration: 20, and Patience: 30.

3. Move the main character to the courtyard.

2.4.3.1.3 Initialize Acceptance Test 3

1. Start up game.

2. Supply main character with the following quality values, in the order shown:
   Strength: 30 and Concentration: 20

3. Move the main character to the dungeon.

2.4.3.1.4 Initialize Acceptance Test 4 . . .

2.4.3.2 Test Cases for Encounter Foreign Character Use Case

2.4.3.2.1 Encounter Foreign Character Acceptance Test 1

1. Set the main character's "patience" value to 30.

2. Set the foreign character's "patience" value to 20.

3. Move the main character to the drawing room.

4. Cause the foreign character to enter the drawing room.

5. Verify that an engagement has taken place.

6. Observe the engagement window showing the results.

(The player's patience value should be 40, and the foreign character's 10.)

2.4.3.2.2 Encounter Foreign Character Acceptance Test 2

1. Set the main character's "strength" value to 30.

2. Set the foreign character's "strength" value to 20.

3. Move the main character to the dungeon.

4. Cause the foreign character to enter the dungeon.

5. Verify that an engagement has taken place.

6. Observe the engagement window showing the results.

(The player's strength value should be 40, and the foreign character's 10.)

2.4.3.2.3 Encounter Foreign Character Acceptance Test 3   . . .

2.4.4 Acceptance Test Procedures

Acceptance tests shall be carried out with two designated representatives of the customer present. These representatives shall carry out all testing with the assistance of the vendor. Whenever possible, events should occur as a result of the random processes of the game instead of being stimulated. An example of this is the arrival of the foreign character in an area. A log of all tests shall be maintained by the customer representatives and signed by all parties; any signatory can enter dissenting statements in the log.

2.5 Installation Test STD

These are tests verifying that the application executes correctly in its required hardware and operating system environments.

The installation tests for Encounter consist of executing the system tests on the following hardware configurations.

1. IBM-compatible PC with at least 32 megabytes of RAM and 100 megabytes of disk space.

2. SUN SPARC model mmm with at least 32 megabytes of RAM and 100 megabytes of disk space.

3. Apple iMAC model 1234 or later with 32 megabytes of RAM and 100 megabytes of disk space.

The installation tests shall consist of the acceptance tests conducted on all of the above platforms.

28.6   CASE STUDY: ECLIPSE

We continue to use Eclipse for a case study, as in past chapters. There are many systems for automating tests; and to appreciate the kind of capabilities that they provide, we focus on the Eclipse Test and Performance Tools Platform (TPTP). The following is quoted and adapted from the online documentation for TPTP [6].

TPTP is a suite of "test, trace and monitoring tools." It addresses the "test and performance life cycle, from early testing to production application monitoring, including test editing and execution, monitoring, tracing and profiling, and log analysis capabilities." TPTP addresses many of the issues discusses in this chapter, including the collection of metrics.

The TPTP profiling tool can be used to profile a Web application, including memory use and execution time (the two main performance metrics). The size of the heap as the execution progresses is an example. The profiling process allows the user to select parameters as well as output formats such as graphs.

TPTP can be used to record traffic at a Web application. In particular, it enables loops within which a test engineer can embed a test, test parameters varying from pass to pass. TPTP has built-in facilities for making logs of the test results—for example, a graphical output showing requests that take the longest time.

Several "agents" can be set to monitor various aspects of the execution. These can be thought of as processes acting in parallel with the execution of the application under scrutiny. Besides heap and stack usage data, TPTP can be used to view the usage of objects from various classes. It can account for all of the objects of a class that come into being during execution, allowing a trace into the execution. This can be displayed in the form of parts of a sequence diagram. For example, it may happen that so many instances of the *String* class exist at runtime that the application's performance is compromised.

The key to many analyses is the identification of unusual parts, such as a use of memory by a process that exceeds by far those used by others.

TPTP provides a means for programmers to insert "fragments of Java code that can be invoked at specified points in the Java class . . . " This is called *instrumentation*. It includes monitoring for "method entry, method exit, catch/finally blocks, and class loading." With *static* instrumentation, probes are inserted before execution. These have to be removed—often by hand—before the application can be deployed. This can introduce errors via probes inadvertently left in the code. With *dynamic* instrumentation, modified classes can be substituted for unmodified ones at runtime. This avoids the manual clean-up process, but the application must be executed in a special mode to use it. Listing 28.2 is example output from a class *Order* that has been statically instrumented with method entry and exit probes [7].

Method invocations can be compared, as in Figure 28.26. In this example, display parameters have been chosen so as to avoid displaying methods invoked a negligible number of times [7].

Method execution times can be displayed as in Figure 28.27.

TPTP includes the ability to generate test cases and test procedures from higher-level descriptions, as well as the ability to record GUI interactions. In other words, the application is executed and the user interacts with GUIs. When the application is executed again in *playback* mode, the user's same GUI actions are automatically performed.

Tests are often organized in hierarchies. For example, to test a word processor, we would test "child" tests for file handling capabilities, editing capabilities, display capabilities, and others. The file handling tests break down into subsidiary tests, and so on. Managing tests within such hierarchies is a significant challenge, and tools like TPTP facilitate this.

Listing 28.2: TPTP output trace of entry and exit of *Order* class

```
Entered: Order.main
Start
 Entered: Order.<init>
 Exited: Order.<init>
 Entered: Order.placeOrder
        Entered: Order.getSupplierList
        Exited: Order.getSupplierList
        Entered: Order.connectWithSupplier
        Exited: Order.connectWithSupplier
        Entered: Order.sendOrder
            Entered: Order.constructOrderForm
                Entered: Order.checkProductAvailability
                Exited: Order.checkProductAvailability
            Exited: Order.constructOrderForm
            Exception: Order.sendOrder ! Too many items requested.
        Exited:Order.sendOrder
 Exited:Order.placeOrder
Finish
Exited:Order.main
```

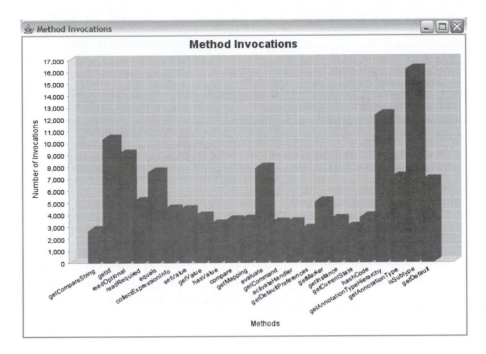

Figure 28.26 A comparison of method invocations in Eclipse

Source: Eclipse Test and Performance Tools Platform Project, reproduced with permission,
http://www.eclipse.org/tptp/platform/documents/probekit/probekit.html.

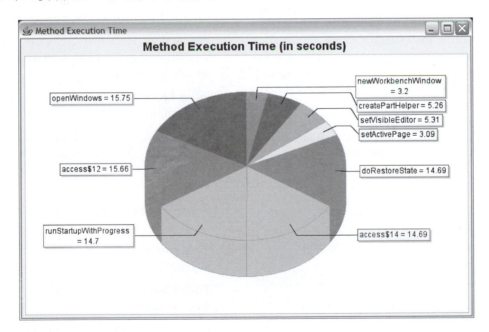

Figure 28.27 Graphical comparison of method execution time in Eclipse

Source: Eclipse Test and Performance Tools Platform Project, reproduced with permission,
http://www.eclipse.org/tptp/platform/documents/probekit/probekit.html.

28.7   CASE STUDY: OPENOFFICE

> Note to the Student:
> QA for open source projects is characterized by user involvement, as exemplified in this case study.

The OpenOffice testing mission statement is at http://qa.openoffice.org/: "To provide an easy way for volunteers to find, update and better define issues, and to define test processes to validate a build of the Office Suite."

28.7.1 Open Contribution to Quality Assurance

Much of this section is quoted or adapted from http://qa.openoffice.org/helping.html.

The latter "describes ways in which anybody can help make OpenOffice.org better, even nondevelopers. Our current focus is on confirming issues that are marked with the flags 'unconfirmed' and 'defect.' Our goal is to respond to new issues posted by users as soon as possible as well as clear out the backlog of unconfirmed issues that currently resides in the *IssueZilla* database.

However, we recognize that there is a lot more to Quality Assurance (QA) than just reviewing and isolating issues. In the future, OpenOffice.org (OOo) QA will involve testing documentation and developing test software. If you are super enthusiastic, feel free to start working on some basic demonstrations of test cases, regression tests, QA specification documentation, or any other idea you think would be valuable to improving the quality of OOo.

> It is indicative of the scale of OpenOffice that settling 100 issues a day (over 36,000 per year) is considered "insignificant."

Every little bit of contribution counts and is invaluable. For example, if we have 100 interested volunteers, and they all work on one issue per day, we would be able to cover 100 issues per day. As insignificant as that may seem when compared to the number of issues that need review, it is positive progress that is essential to keep this project moving forward."

28.7.2 Smoke Tests

> Smoke tests are superficial tests checking that changes to the baseline have not resulted in catastrophic errors. A smoke test is a reduced regression test. "Installation tests" here are not full installation tests.

The following is quoted and edited from the site given at [8].

"Smoke Tests (also called Shakedown tests) validate a build of OOo. These are not fully-fledged test cases, but we may use them to create test cases in the future. Your ideas are welcome." These consist of the following, quoted from the reference.

Installation Tests. Install OOo in both stand-alone and networked environments

File type Test. Test that OOo can open and correctly display specified file types. Can open/execute a Java applet (samples available).

File Actions. Test that OOo can create and save different types of files. Can send mail using an external mail program.

Insert Actions. Test that OOo can insert specified actions into a text document.

Edit Actions. Test that OOo edit actions function as specified with a text document. Test that cut and paste integrate with external editors and OOo.

View Actions. Test that OOo view actions function as specified.

Format Actions. Test that OOo format actions function as specified.

Tools/Options. Test that OOo tools/options function correctly.

Print. Test that OOo prints a text document to a default printer.

Help. Test OOo help contents and functions.

28.7.3 OpenOffice QA Priorities

> The procedure described here is designed to ensure that the most important issues are worked on first. Its somewhat mechanical form is necessary in an open-source environment since no single manager is making continual decisions.

Table 28.3 reflects the OpenOffice QA priorities (taken, with minor editing, from the source given in [9].

QA contributor procedures are given at the source in [10].

28.7.4 Automated Product Source Code QA

> This section describes a test harness for executing OpenOffice tests.

The following is quoted and adapted from [11]. "The *qadevOOo* project provides a test harness to execute test cases written in different programming languages, like C/C++, Java, Python, or Basic. These test cases are responsible for validating the functionality and reliability of specified APIs. The test harness (written in Java) is responsible for setting up, running, and controlling the test processes and threads."

"The test harness and a nearly complete set of Java and Basic test cases for the OpenOffice.org API are at [11] as well as the desired value set for the test runs and a set of test documents used by the test cases."

28.7.5 Automated GUI Testing

"The automated GUI testing provides a test framework with test scripts and an application (*TestTool*) to test almost the whole office application automatically. The *TestTool* scripts are written in BASIC with some additional functions especially for the office. The *TestTool* communicates via TCP/IP with the office application." [8]

Table 28.3 Example of priorities in OpenOffice

Rank	Task	IssueZilla (IZ) Search Tips
1.	New issues posted for the current month or today.	Look at the "Untouched" issues linked at http://qa.openoffice.org/issuelinks.html
		Also try searching IZ with Issue Type set to "Defect" and Status set to "Unconfirmed," where the field(s) is set to "[Issue Creation]" . . .
2.	Follow up on unconfirmed defect issues with the "oooqa" keyword. Ideally, start with the oldest "oooqa" issues and work your way to the most current. If the issue is older than 3 weeks and the issue does not follow the guidelines listed in the "How you can help?" page, leave a comment to the user indicating you are closing the issue for now, but if they can provide more information to help reproduce the issue, they can reopen the issue at their convenience.	Try searching IZ with only the following fields set: Keywords set to "oooqa" . . . Limit the search to a particular time frame. . . .
3.	Close out issues reported against versions of OOo that are no longer current. Do a quick check to see whether the issue is verifable. If the issue cannot be verified, send a message to the user to see whether upgrading to the latest version of OpenOffice.org resolves the issue. If upgrading to the latest version resolves the problem, close the issue. If the upgrade does not resolve the problem follow the OOo QA "How you can help?" guidelines.	Try searching IZ with Issue type set to "Defect," Status set to "Unconfirmed," and the Component and Version fields set to your choice.

28.8 SUMMARY

Once integration testing is completed, the application as a whole is tested. This is known as system testing. System tests are black box tests that validate that the application meets its stated requirements. Both functional and nonfunctional requirements are tested.

Applications are frequently distributed in-house for testing (alpha testing) and to participating customers to try out with a clear understanding of its status as undergoing final testing. The latter is called beta testing.

Acceptance tests are executed by the customer after system tests are successfully completed. Their purpose is to demonstrate to the customer that the application runs satisfactorily on its target hardware and in its intended software environment, such as the operating system. Acceptance tests are usually a subset of the system tests.

Many real-world applications have incomplete or even nonexistent requirements documents. Testing in the absence of well-written requirements requires the tester to obtain a sense of how the application behaves and how it is meant to behave. This is called *behavioral modeling*. An approach to testing in this situation is to start from what appears best to be a beginning point of the application, and then keep track of the functional paths from there. Directed graphs are used to document these paths. Tests are devised to execute a set of paths that attain a kind of coverage.

In order to be effective at finding defects, a good software tester must be determined, dogged, fearless, imaginative, curious, meticulous, and must think "outside the box." The tester's goal is to discover defects that can manifest when an application is used for a significant time by users, perhaps in unanticipated ways.

28.9 EXERCISES

Answer the following exercises in your own words.

1. Why are black box tests (rather than white box tests) used in system testing?

2. What is the purpose of acceptance testing and why is it necessary? Give an example of an application and a defect that could go undetected in system testing yet be caught by acceptance testing.

3. A company is developing an application, and thinks it has discovered a novel way to speed up its testing cycle. It decides to dispense with system testing, and instead deliver the application to customers just after integration testing is completed. The company will therefore rely on its customers to discover problems in the application. What are the advantages and disadvantages of this approach? Be specific and explain your answer.

4. What is the purpose of soak testing? Give an example of a defect this type of testing is likely to uncover.

5. *Load and stress* testing is often conducted on individual units during unit and integration testing. In this testing, units are subjected to high levels of stress to ensure that they do not exhibit any problems. Why is it necessary to conduct system-level stress tests even if all of the unit stress tests are successful?

6. Describe the various levels of testing to which you would subject the application described in Exercise 7 in Chapter 27. Indicate which of the classes and packages (shown in the figure) would be

involved in each. (Many more classes will be involved in building the complete application, but you are not required to show these.)

7. For each of the black box tester qualities listed in Section 28.3.6, give an example of how that quality could be counterproductive if taken to an extreme.

BIBLIOGRAPHY

1. Kit, Edward, *Software Testing in the Real World: Improving the Process*, Addison-Wesley, 1995.
2. Purdue Usability Testing Questionnaire, http://oldwww.acm.org/perlman/question.cgi?form=PUTQ [accessed 12/15/09].
3. Herzog, Peter, OSSTMM – Open Source Security Testing Methodology Manual http://www.isecom.org/projects/osstmm.shtml [accessed 12/15/09].
4. Srinivasan Desikan, and Gopalaswamy Ramesh. Software Testing: Principles and Practices, Pearson Education, 2006.
5. Kaner, Cem, Jack Falk, and Hung Quoc Nguyen, *Testing Computer Software*, John Wiley & Sons, 1999.
6. Eclipse Test & Performance Tools Platform Project. http://www.eclipse.org/tptp/ [accessed 11/11/2009].
7. Eclipse Test & Performance Tools Platform Project. http://www.eclipse.org/tptp/platform/documents/probekit/probekit.html [accessed 11/11/2009].
8. OpenOffice Project. "Shakedown Test Suite." http://qa.openoffice.org/testcase/index.html [accessed 11/11/2009].
9. OpenOffice Project, "OOo QA Issue Review Priorities." http://qa.openoffice.org/priorities.html [accessed 11/11/2009].
10. OpenOffice Project. "A Quick Start Guide to contributing to this project." http://qa.openoffice.org/wwwstaging/tasks/quickstart.html [accessed 11/11/2009].
11. OpenOffice Project. "Automated product source code QA." http://qa.openoffice.org/qadevOOo_doc/index.html [accessed 12/15/09].

29

Software Maintenance

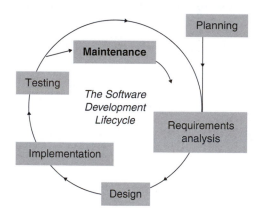

- What are the units of software maintenance?

- What are the differences between corrective, adaptive, perfective, and preventative maintenance?

- What are some management challenges in maintenance? Process challenges?

- What are the main technical issues?

- What is the maintenance process?

- How do patches work?

- What standards are there for software maintenance?

- What is reverse engineering? Reengineering?

- What maintenance metrics are available?

Figure 29.1 The context and learning goals for this chapter

Software systems continue to evolve after their initial release. The *maintenance* of a software system consists of those activities performed upon it after it is released. The IEEE glossary [1] defines software maintenance as follows:

The process of modifying a software system or component after delivery to correct faults, improve performance or other attributes, or adapt to a changed environment.

Maintenance is an activity of truly significant proportions, consuming an estimated 40 to 90 percent of the total life cycle costs of applications (see, for example [2] and [3]). Perhaps the most famous maintenance effort involved the year 2000 (Y2K) problem, for which massive work was performed modifying applications to handle the years of the new millennium. This was maintenance because it ensured that applications already delivered continued to provide their intended functionality.

As software systems evolve over time, they require continuous maintenance in order to remain useful. Lehman ([4] and [5]) claims the existence of several laws of software evolution borne out by extensive experience. The first, *continuing change*, states that if a program is not continually adapted to ongoing needs, it becomes less and less useful over time. According to the second law, *increasing complexity*, as a program is changed over time, its complexity increases unless work is done specifically to alleviate this. An example is a maintenance action that increases coupling between modules. Lehman's two laws are related. As software evolves, it is modified by engineers who may be competent to make each change but may not completely understand the overall design and implementation. This is not surprising, given the sheer magnitude and complexity of many applications. As a result, the application's structure and maintainability decline. It is for these and other reasons that software maintenance of several varieties is necessary.

The addition of new features and functionality to an application is really a kind of development—typically of the application's next release. Nevertheless, the process is sometimes included in the "maintenance" rubric, especially when the new features are very much in the spirit of the application's current functionality and when they are small by comparison. This type of maintenance is explained in this chapter.

In many ways, agile projects can be viewed as being in "maintenance" mode from the beginning. This is because agility relies on adding to a code base—a process that has much in common with maintenance.

29.1 TYPES OF SOFTWARE MAINTENANCE

This section introduces the unit of maintenance. It also names and describes various types of maintenance activities.

29.1.1 Maintenance Requests

Maintenance organizations manage their work by identifying tasks. Ideally, these should be of comparable magnitude (imagine the inappropriateness of a list of chores that includes "buy bananas" and also "build house"). Each such unit of maintenance is called a *Maintenance Request* (MR) in IEEE terminology. We try to size MRs to be of a regular magnitude, but the amount of code needed for each can vary and the impact can vary as well. A physically small code change may have a major effect on an application. One way to keep MRs at comparable effort is to decompose them into child MRs.

An MR is either a *repair* or an *enhancement*. It is a repair when it concerns a defect relative to the existing requirements. An enhancement MR is one of two types. The first introduces a feature not called for in the requirements at delivery time; the second type of enhancement changes the design or implementation, while keeping the functionality unchanged. This is known as refactoring, as introduced in Chapter 24. Refactoring usually improves the design in order to reduce complexity and increase efficiency, and it is a response to Lehman's second law of increasing complexity. Figure 29.2 summarizes these distinctions.

A common categorization of MRs is defined by Lieintz, Swanson, et al. [6], [7], who refine these two types of maintenance into two subcategories, as summarized in Figure 29.3 and explained in the rest of this section.

- **Repair**
  - Fixing defects
    (relative to existing requirements)
- **Enhancement**
  - New requirements
  - Change design or implementation
    (no functional change)

Figure 29.2 Types of maintenance

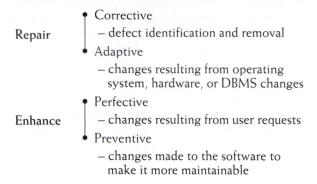

Repair
- Corrective
  – defect identification and removal
- Adaptive
  – changes resulting from operating
    system, hardware, or DBMS changes

Enhance
- Perfective
  – changes resulting from user requests
- Preventive
  – changes made to the software to
    make it more maintainable

Figure 29.3 Types and subtypes of maintenance

Source: Lientz, Bennett P., E. Burton Swanson, and Gerry E. Tompkins, "Characteristics of Applications Software Maintenance," Communications of the ACM (CACM), no. 21, 1978, p. 466–471.

Maintenance Request 78

<u>Problem</u>: When the player changes the value of a quality, the computations are specified to keep the total invariant, but they do not.

<u>Example</u>: If the qualities are

strength $= 10$, *patience* $= 0.8$, and *endurance* $= 0.8$ (sum $= 11.6$), and the player adjusts *strength* to 11, the result is *strength* $= 11$, *patience* $= 0$ and *endurance* $= 0$.

These do not sum to 11.6.

Figure 29.4 Example of corrective maintenance request

29.1.2 Corrective Maintenance

Corrective maintenance is concerned with the repair of defects relative to existing requirements. These defects are typically discovered by customers as they use a software product. Each defect must be analyzed, prioritized, and repaired, and fixes incorporated into new software revisions. As an example defect, consider the MR for the Encounter case study shown in Figure 29.4.

MR 78 requires the maintainer to determine the cause of the defect. One possibility is an error in the code, such as in the method adjustQuality(), which is responsible for adjusting quality values when one of them is changed by the user. Another possibility here is that existing requirements for Encounter characters are defective. Actually, the latter is the case, because the requirements mandate the following:

- The user shall be permitted to set any quality to any value less than or equal to the current sum of the qualities.
- The remaining qualities retain their mutual proportions.
- No quality shall have a value both greater than zero and less than 0.5.
- The sum of the qualities remains invariant.

As can be seen in the example in MR 78, these cannot all be satisfied. Since the defect is in the requirements, it is the customer's prerogative to make or permit the change. One way to do this is to relax the last requirement to the following.

$$|\text{sum of qualities} - 0.5 * (N - 1)| <= (\text{sum of qualities})' => \text{sum of qualities}$$

where N is the number of qualities and x' is the value of x after the adjustment process

This modification keeps the effect of discouraging the player from changing quality values too much or too many times because points may be lost whenever this is done.

29.1.3 Adaptive Maintenance

Adaptive maintenance is concerned with adapting the software to changes in the operating environment such as a new operating system release or a new version of hardware. As software systems evolve, it is inevitable that changes in their external environment will take place. An example is if we were to port our Encounter video game case study to an iPhone. It may seem awkward to classify adaptive maintenance as a kind of repair, but this is appropriate if one views an application as a living entity. In order to remain legitimate, the application must adapt to reasonable changes in its environment.

29.1.4 Perfective Maintenance

Perfective maintenance is the development and implementation of user requests such as new feature enhancements. Recall Lehman's first law—that systems must continually adapt to ongoing needs or become less and less useful.

As an example of a perfective maintenance request, suppose that the marketing department has decided that to make the Encounter video game more attractive and marketable, players require more tangible reward for their skill. They want the entire look of the game to be enhanced whenever the player achieves a new level. The art department will supply the corresponding graphics, and the maintenance organization is tasked with a modification to accommodate this additional requirement, as stated in Figure 29.5. A solution to this MR is discussed later in this chapter.

Maintenance Request 162

Modify Encounter so that the game begins with areas and connections in a coordinated style. When the player achieves level 2 status, all areas and connections are displayed in an enhanced coordinated style, which is special to level 2. The art department will provide the required images.

Figure 29.5 Example of a perfective maintenance request

29.1.5 Preventive Maintenance

Preventive maintenance consists of changing a software application in order to make it easier to maintain. The need for preventive maintenance can be deduced from Lehman's second law. As a program evolves over time, changes made through corrective, adaptive, and perfective maintenance requests cause the system to become increasingly complex unless action is taken to prevent it. Preventive maintenance involves proactively refactoring the system to reduce its complexity. It is always a good idea to perform preventive maintenance on an ongoing basis.

An example of preventive maintenance is to recognize and anticipate industry trends. Suppose, for example, that we sell a Windows-based word processor and that we recognize that word processors are likely to migrate, in part, to the Web. A preventative maintenance action would be to alter the word processor's architecture so that selected parts are more readily moveable to the Web.

Metrics can be used to identify areas that need improvement. For example, by examining defect metrics it may be determined that a certain software module has a high number of defects reported against it. After further investigation it may be determined that many of the defects are a result of changes made while prior defects were repaired. This might lead to a conclusion that the design of that module is too complex, and thus not easily modified. As a result, maintenance work may be performed to redesign the module to make it simpler and more maintainable, without changing its functionality. Subsequently, we would expect fewer defects to be filed against the refactored module.

29.2 ISSUES OF SOFTWARE MAINTENANCE

Software maintenance presents a unique set of challenges. Bennett [8] has categorized them as management (what to do and who will do it), process (what procedures to follow), and technical (design and implementation).

29.2.1 Management Challenges

Senior management tends to focus on delivering new products, which are a source of revenue (or cost saving if internal) and provide a quantifiable return on investment. Funds spent on maintenance, however, are usually not simple to justify. The cost of maintenance is high, and unless the maintenance organization can charge for their services, the return on investment is much less clear than for delivering new products. As a result, maintenance teams can often be understaffed and underfunded, making an already difficult job even harder.

Sooner or later, the need for organized maintenance is recognized by management and resources are allocated to it. Sometimes an individual or a group or is assigned to repair tasks and a separate group to enhancements, incorporated in new updates or releases. As software moves from shrink-wrapped delivery and big-bang integration to online delivery, continuous integration and security updates, the trend has been toward more frequent version updates rather than major releases. The management of more frequent updates is more demanding than that for major releases simply because the act of release is more frequent. This is analogous to the difference between managing a daily newspaper and a monthly magazine.

The management of maintenance involves the assessment of benefits, the calculation of cost, and the allocation of resources, mainly people. Table 29.1 shows examples of costs. MRs are prioritized based on analyses like this. However, maintenance requests are often worked on in groups since maintainers save time by concentrating on related MRs.

Table 29.1 Example of an estimate for implementing a maintenance request

Activity	Estimate (person-days)	Activity	Estimate (person-days)
1. Understand the problem and identify the functions that must be modified or added.	2–5	6. Compile and integrate into baseline.	2–3
2. Design the changes.	1–4	7. Test functionality of changes.	2–4
3. Perform impact analysis.	1–4	8. Perform regression testing.	2–4
4. Implement changes in source code.	1–4	9. Release new baseline and report results.	1
5. Change SRS, SDD, STP, and configuration status.	2–6	TOTAL	14–35

29.2.2 Process Challenges

Process issues—the procedures to be carried out—can also be a challenge. Extensive coordination is required to handle the inflow of MRs. Typically, numerous maintenance requests flow continually through the organization. Some economy of scale can be achieved, reducing the cost of each change, but a stream of maintenance changes places a significant burden on the process. Programmers, testers, and writers have to be coordinated. To take an example, should the SRS be updated as soon as the customer indicates a flaw in a requirement, only after thorough testing, or only when grouped with other maintenance actions? Each of these options leaves the documentation and source code in an inconsistent state for periods of time. Without careful management, these supposedly short-lived inconsistencies can multiply and the documentation gets out of control. The result is that it becomes difficult to know exactly what the application does.

If a single, focused change were the only one we had to handle, then our process problems would be minor. However, source code changes in response to an MR typically cause a ripple effect in the design, documentation, and test plans. An impact analysis (described in Section 20) determines the extent of the ripple effect, and a cost analysis determines the cost of implementation. As an example of a cost analysis, let's imagine that the Navy has informed us (a military contractor) that the algorithm for reconciling three independent sources of shipboard navigation data is flawed. An estimate is needed of the cost of making this repair. Our calculations could be performed as shown in Table 29.1, which shows that the cost of making this change at $400–$800 per day of loaded labor (i.e., including benefits, etc.) is $5,600–$28,000.

29.2.3 Technical Issues

Maintenance can be thought of as a repetition of the development process but with a major additional constraint: that existing required functionality of an existing code base is preserved. This impels us to either add onto the existing design or to redesign the application. Maintenance actions that are repairs usually result in staying with the current design. An exception to this is where the existing design itself is a source of the problem. Adding to an existing design has the advantage of not perturbing what already works but the potential disadvantage of creating an unacceptable overall design. Redesign has the opposite advantages and disadvantages. The redesign-or-not decision differs from project to project and MR to MR.

As an example, suppose that we want to enhance the Encounter video game with the presence of several monsters rather than just one. We would probably keep the current overall design and add to it because the overall game remains the same in spirit and because the current architecture is capable of absorbing the additional capability. On the other hand, if we are required to turn Encounter into a real-time 3D game in which our character engages in various ways with the monster using weapons and they are able to pursue each other within areas and from area to area, we would reexamine—and probably alter—the existing architecture. This is because the combat aspects would dominate the existing state aspects.

Testing is a significant technical issue. Simply focusing tests on changed or added parts takes time enough because special test plans must often be devised for this purpose. But focused testing is not enough. The possibility of ripple effects requires that we execute extensive regression testing to ensure that changes have not compromised the application's preexisting functionality. This is a major factor in the high cost of maintenance.

29.3 MAINTENANCE PROCESS

A *maintenance process* defines the flow of MRs through an organization. Figure 29.6 illustrates a typical maintenance process in a large project, where the thicker lines indicate the nominal path. The additional (thin-lined) paths show other ways in which MRs can be generated and retired.

In the process shown in Figure 29.6, customers provide comments on enhancements and defects through the help desk. These are written up as MRs. Organizations have a limited number of resources to work on MRs, meaning that some of the proposed enhancements and reported defects are either delayed or never implemented. Maintenance engineers must therefore prioritize MRs. A *triage process* is often employed [9] that includes the review of all proposed maintenance requests and the prioritization of their importance to the business and to customers. Triage starts with an official organizational unit, which may be

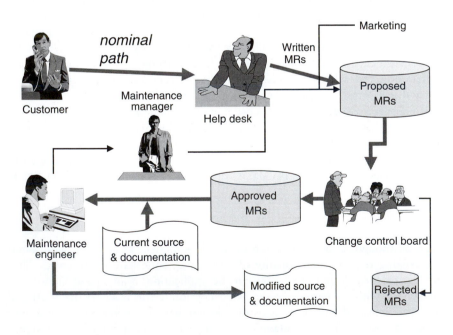

Figure 29.6 A typical maintenance process for a large project

Source: Graphics reproduced with permission from Corel.

a single person or a committee, deciding which MRs will be implemented and assigning them a relative priority. This unit is often referred to as a *Change Control Board* (CCB) [10]. It consists of stakeholders, selected from various organizations such as development, user documentation, marketing, quality assurance (QA), and customer support. Each organization brings its own perspective, and collectively they decide on MR priority.

The group conducts an *impact analysis*, which assesses the scope of the changes to the product's artifacts that are necessary in order to implement the MR. Each group represented by the CCB provides input into the impact analysis. Maintenance engineers prepare an estimate of how long it will take to implement the MR, and its impact on the system, including code and system specifications. The user documentation group determines which user manuals, if any, are affected and require updates. QA determines how much testing is required to validate that the MR is implemented correctly, and also to validate that problems aren't inadvertently introduced into other parts of the system. In the case of repair MRs, customer support may need to determine the impact on customers of the MR and whether there are any possible workarounds that can be employed in lieu of repairing the defect. Using all this information as input, the CCB estimates the number of resources required, the cost, and the risk of implementing the MR. It then decides whether to accept or reject it; and if accepted, assigns it a relative priority. MRs approved by the CCB are then retired by technical maintenance staff. New software versions and documentation are generated and available for customers. For efficiency reasons, multiple MRs are often grouped together and released as part of a single maintenance release.

The number of artifacts affected by the implementation of an MR is variable. Figure 29.7 illustrates two extremes. At one extreme, the defect is in a requirement that requires changes in the SRS, the architecture, and so on, all the way through to the code that makes the system operable in its intended environment. At the other extreme, a defect could be present in the code for a method and the MR could affect that method implementation but nothing else.

The minimal-impact case occurs, for example, when the programmer has failed to follow a standard in naming a local variable, or when an unused variable is removed. In the worst case, however, every part of the process is affected. Even for a defect in the code only, the impact can range from minor to major. A seemingly

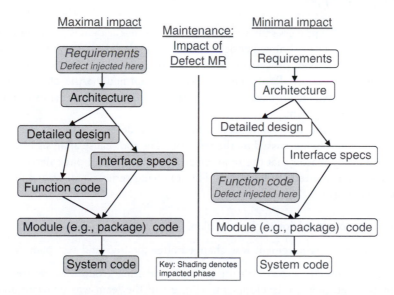

Figure 29.7 The impact of a maintenance request—two extremes

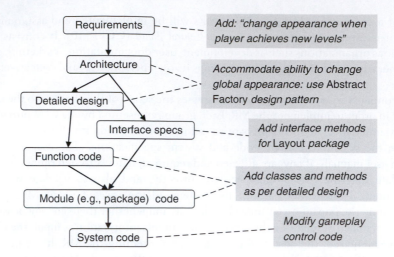

Figure 29.8 The impact of a maintenance request—an example

simple change such as an increase in the size of a compile-time C++ array could have major ripple effects throughout the application.

Maintenance Request 162, described in Figure 29.5, affects every aspect of the process, as shown in Figure 29.8. Recall that this new requirement—the concept of multiple game levels—is a significant addition. It leads to changes in every phase in the process.

When an application is designed with traceability in mind, the documentation of maintenance actions can be manageable. Otherwise, the consequences can be extremely expensive.

29.3.1 Root-Cause Analysis

After a defect MR is repaired, a process sometimes known as *root-cause analysis* is sometimes conducted. This is an iterative, problem-solving process aimed at determining the underlying reason that a defect has occurred. Once the root cause is understood, process or other improvements can be implemented to prevent similar defects from recurring in the future. Root-cause analysis is performed via the change control board or its designee as part of the maintenance process. For each defect, the team asks a series of questions to narrow down the root cause of the problem.

As an example, suppose that after an initial investigation it is determined that the reason for a particular defect is due to a requirement being missed by the test plan. The root-cause analysis process is then invoked to determine the underlying reason that the requirement was missed, and once determined, to ensure that other requirements are not omitted in the future. The following series of questions illustrate the iterative nature of root-cause analysis [9], [11].

1. The requirement is not tested for in the test plan.

2. Why? It appears that the requirement was changed after the SRS and test plans were completed.

3. Why? The customer communicated with the product marketing group their desire for the change, but this was communicated only to development. The rest of the team was unaware and therefore didn't update the SRS and test plan.

4. Why? Product marketing thought this was an isolated change that wouldn't affect product testing, so they communicated it only to development.

5. Why? Product marketing didn't understand that all changes to features must be communicated to the entire team.

Once this root cause is understood, the product marketing department can implement appropriate changes to its process that prevent this type of problem from recurring.

As root causes are determined, metrics are recorded to keep track of them. To provide consistency and make it easier to track and analyze, it is helpful to define a list of root causes from which the team can choose. Rakitin [9] suggests the following list.

1. Function was missing from SRS

2. Function was incorrectly specified in SRS

3. Design problem—design was inadequate or inappropriate

4. Design problem—design review didn't catch it

5. Code problem—code was inadequate

6. Code problem—code review didn't catch it

7. Inadequate unit testing

8. Inadequate system testing

9. Installation/environment/version compatibility issue

A metrics analysis is periodically performed to identify the most common root causes. The results are used to create a plan of action to eliminate these types of defects from recurring. For example, if it is found that many defects are caused by *Code problem—code review didn't catch it*, a review of and improvement to the code review process can be implemented.

29.3.2 Patch Releases

Patches are used in two ways. The first way concerns getting new or replacement software versions or parts to users. The second addresses delays in implementing an MR.

In the first way, patches are permanent replacements of parts of the application. They often take the form of a set of files, sent via the Internet, that replace object code already written. In this case, the challenges are for the customer's organization to ensure that patches are appropriately installed. Many customers conduct their own system tests of patches—that is, in their own environment.

The second way concerns the handling of defect MRs that require significant time to remedy. It also concerns defects that hamper a customer's use of the system and so must be remedied quickly. A rapid fix is not always possible. To take an extreme example, in a military application with which one of the authors was once involved, nine months could elapse between the identification of an MR and its complete implementation and documentation! In these cases patches are modifications or additions to the object code that either fix or work around a defect. Figure 29.9 shows a way in which these patches can be organized within the development organization. It demonstrates the nominal, "official" path taken for a patch—on the

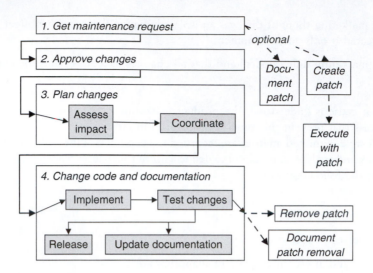

Figure 29.9 Patches in maintenance—workarounds

Advantages	*Disadvantages*

• May be a complete solution to the problem
• Keeps customers satisfied
• Enables continued operation and testing without presence of the defect
• Avoids masking other defects
• Enables test of fix
	• May duplicate work
	   — patch *and* final fix both implemented
	• Temporaries sometimes never replaced
	   — proper fix deferred forever
	• Complicates final fix (where applicable)
	   — must remove
	• Complicates documentation process
	• When tools used for insertion, may compromise code base

Figure 29.10 Advantages and disadvantages of maintenance patches

left—as well as an informal process for getting the patch into the application on a temporary basis—on the right of Figure 29.9.

The advantages and disadvantages of patches include those listed in Figure 29.10.

The comment about "masking" refers to the fact that allowing defects to remain can make it difficult to detect other defects whose effects are hidden by the effects of the nonrepaired defect.

29.3.3 Software Trouble Reports, Maintenance Requests, and Correction Reports

It is simplest when a single test leads to an MR that is worked on as a single action, but the process is often not so simple. Maintenance requests emerge from reports of trouble experienced with the application (often called *software trouble reports*). There may be several pieces of evidence for a single MR or, conversely, several MRs that grow out of a single trouble report. Each part of the work on an MR that is worth documenting is recorded in a so-called *correction report*. To deal with the proliferation of correction reports, we may need to identify a child MR of the MR under consideration. This organization is shown in Figure 29.11.

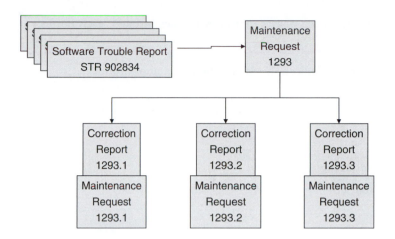

Figure 29.11 Software trouble reports, maintenance requests, and correction reports

29.4 IEEE MAINTENANCE STANDARDS

The IEEE has published standard Std 1219-1998 [12], which describes an iterative process for managing and executing software maintenance activities. It is geared to large projects, but it is instructive to examine this standard as a specific and detailed example of a maintenance process for projects of all sizes. Its table of contents showing the pertinent sections is listed in Figure 29.12.

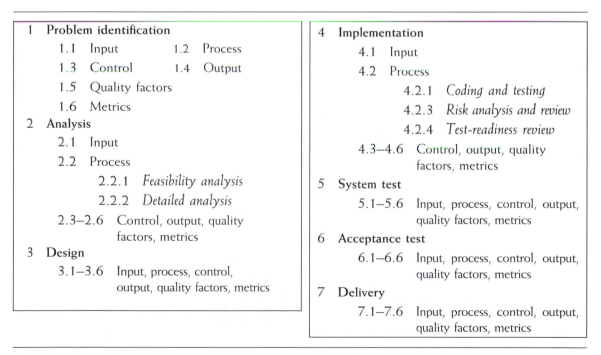

Figure 29.12 IEEE 840-1994 "Software Maintenance" table of contents

Source: IEEE std 840–1994. Reproduced with permission.

The standard defines seven phases that an MR flows through, each corresponding to a section in Figure 29.12, as follows:

1. Problem/modification identification, classification, and prioritization
2. Analysis
3. Design
4. Implementation
5. Regression/system testing
6. Acceptance testing
7. Delivery

Note that these phases are similar to the phases of the development process. Each of the phases has six attributes that describe the actions and data associated with them:

1. Input
2. Process
3. Control
4. Output
5. Quality factors
6. Metrics

Figure 29.13 summarizes the relationship between the phases and attributes. The following sections describe how a maintenance request flows through each phase.

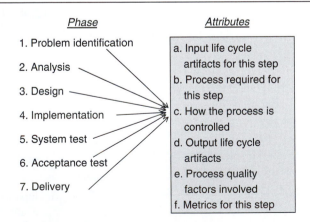

Figure 29.13 Six attributes of each maintenance request phase

Source: IEEE, reproduced with permission.

Table 29.2 IEEE 1219-1998—Maintenance phase 1: problem identification

a. Input	• The Maintenance Request (MR)
b. Process	• Assign change number • Classify by type and severity, etc. • Accept or reject change • Make preliminary cost estimate • Prioritize
c. Control	• Identify MR uniquely • Enter MR into repository
d. Output	• Validated MR
e. Selected quality factors	• Clarity of the MR • Correctness of the MR (e.g., type)
f. Selected metrics	• Number of omissions in the MR • Number of MR submissions to date • Number of duplicate MRs • Time expected to confirm the problem

Source: IEEE std 1219–1998. Reproduced with permission.

This section describes and explains Steps 1–4 in Figure 29.13. Steps 5–7 are similar to the regular testing and delivery process. Testing in particular emphasizes regression testing to ensure that existing functionality has not been compromised.

29.4.1 Maintenance Problem Identification

In this initial phase, MRs are identified, classified, and assigned an initial priority ranking. Table 29.2 summarizes the process for the identification phase of maintenance requests.

"Problem Identification" in the Encounter case study, for example, was performed by the marketing department. They solicited and examined user complaints about the complicated way in which Encounter game characters exchange quality values as a result of engagements.

29.4.2 Maintenance Problem Analysis

Table 29.3 summarizes the analysis phase for maintenance requests.

Maintenance problems range from the simple to the deeply challenging. For example, suppose that we want to provide the Encounter game player with additional image options for the main player. This appears to be a straightforward request; however, the extent of maintenance requests like this is often underestimated. The analysis process is designed to uncover the real work in carrying out modifications and additions. For example, we might determine that the increased number of image options requires a complete reworking of the way in which the images are displayed and chosen.

As an example, let's analyze Maintenance Request #162 for the case study (see Figure 29.5) to estimate the resources required to design and implement it. We will use the Abstract Factory design pattern for the design of this MR, as described in Chapter 17. Modifications to the object model to accommodate these, and the new classes are required. Once these modifications are made, it appears that

Table 29.3 IEEE 1219-1998—Maintenance phase 2: problem analysis

a. Input	• Original project documentation • Validated MR from the identification phase
b. Process	• Study feasibility of the MR • Investigate impact of the MR • Perform detailed analysis of the work required • Refine the MR description

c. Control	• Conduct technical review
	• Verify . . .
	  . . . test strategy appropriate
	  . . . documentation updated
	• Identify safety and security issues

d. Output	• Feasibility report • Detailed analysis report, including impact • Updated requirements • Preliminary modification list • Implementation plan • Test strategy
e. Selected quality factors	• Comprehensibility of the analysis
f. Selected metrics	• Number of requirements that must be changed • Effort (required to analyze the MR) • Elapsed time

Source: IEEE std 1219–1998. Reproduced with permission.

we will need only to replace all Area and AreaConnection references in the client code (the code using the new configuration) such as

```
. . . = new Area(); and
. . . = new Connection();
```

with calls of the form

```
. . . = LevelNBuilder.getArea(); and
. . . = LevelNBuilder.getConnection();
```

and so on

IEEE metrics that quantify these modifications are as follows.

• Number of requirements changes for MR #162: between 140 and 450 as follows.
Since we have organized the requirements by class, we count

  ○ The number of new classes that must be described: 60 to 90 (there are 20 to 30 levels, let's say, and for each of these, Abstract Factory requires a factory class, a subclass of Area, and a subclass of Area-Connection)
  plus

  ○ The number of new methods: (2 to 5) per class * (60 to 90) classes = 120 to 450

- Estimate of effort for MR #162: 2.4 to 9 person-months as follows:

    The effort can be estimated in terms of the number of person-days per requirement, based on these data for the project so far. For example, if the original project has 300 detailed requirements and was completed with 6 person-months, we can use 0.02 person-months per requirement, so that MR #162 should be taken care of with $(120 * 0.02)$ to $(450 * 0.02) = 2.4$ to 9 person-months. The highly repetitive nature of the classes suggests a lower number in this range, perhaps three person-months.

- Elapsed time estimate for MR #162
    The elapsed time estimate can be computed from historical data in a similar manner to the Effort computation.

    To improve on these metrics, apply the following.

a. Use linear regression, in which a set of past data is used to derive a straight-line approximation, and this straight line is used to approximate the result. For example, instead of using simply "300 detailed requirements were completed with 6 person-months $= 0.02$ person-months per requirement," we can use a graph of several different past projects and fit a straight-line relationship to these, as shown in Figure 29.14. This gives a more reliable result: a range of 2.5 to 9.3 person-months. It should be noted that regression methods are also available that fit curved lines.

b. Account for factors such as the nature of the application and the composition of staffing. For example, if the data are available, one can create graphs that use only projects of the same type, or projects whose staff had equivalent experience levels.

c. Include variances with the measures described. (It is useful to know averages, but we are also interested in the extent to which measurements have differed from the averages in the past.)

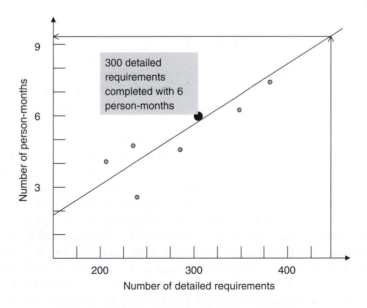

Figure 29.14 Using linear regression to estimate the effort for implementing an MR

Table 29.4 IEEE 1219-1998—Maintenance phase 3: design

a. Input	• Original project documentation • Analysis from the previous phase

b. Process	• Create test cases
	• Revise . . .
	    . . . requirements
	    . . . implementation plan

c. Control	• Verify design • Inspect design and test cases

d. Output	• Revised . . .
	    . . . modification list
	    . . . detailed analysis
	    . . . implementation plan
	• Updated . . .
	    . . . design baseline
	    . . . test plans

e. Selected quality factors	• Flexibility (of the design) • Traceability • Reusability • Comprehensibility
f. Selected metrics	• Effort in person-hours • Elapsed time • Number of applications of the change

Source: IEEE std 1219–1998. Reproduced with permission.

29.4.3 Designing for a Maintenance Request

Table 29.4 describes the design phase for MRs.

A design handling MR #162, for example, follows the Abstract Factory design pattern, which consists of modifying the original *EncounterEnvironment* package. The original documentation for this package is shown in Figure 29.15.

Instead of creating Area and EncounterAreaConnection objects directly, the modified application will do so through methods getArea() and getAreaConnection(). These are methods of a new class, EnvironmentFactory. Client code of the EncounterEnvironment package need have no knowledge of the type of Area and AreaConnection objects being built, because all creation requests are channeled through the particular EnvironmentFactory object aggregated by EncounterEnvironment. In other words, there will be no need to write separate control code for the various levels. At runtime, the client code selects an object of the appropriate EnvironmentFactory subclass. For illustration purposes, the object model in Figure 29.16 shows Area and AreaConnection classes for three game-playing levels only (not for the larger number planned).

A plan is required for migrating from the old design to the new. Figure 29.17 shows such a plan. It integrates the parts in a way that allows their testing, one at a time. We also try to keep existing parts operational while introducing new parts in order to allow the switch only when we have confidence in the new parts.

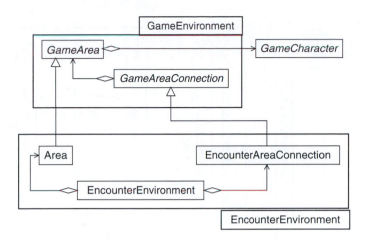

Figure 29.15 *EncounterEnvironment* package (before modification)

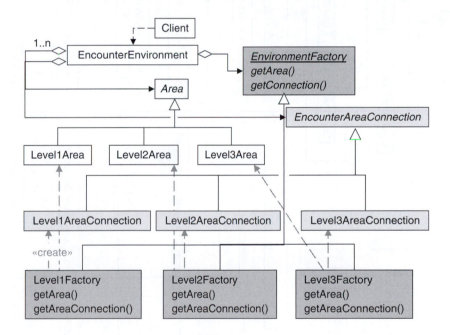

Figure 29.16 *Abstract Factory* applied to Encounter video game

This plan begins with the existing design, then adds and tests parts that do not disrupt the existing implementation such as types of areas and connections. Before the last step, the redesign is ready to execute the Abstract Factory implementation, each of the parts having been thoroughly tested. In the final step, the new creation process is finally "turned on" and tested.

29.4.4 Implementing a Maintenance Request

Table 29.5 shows steps and documentation for the implementation of maintenance requests.

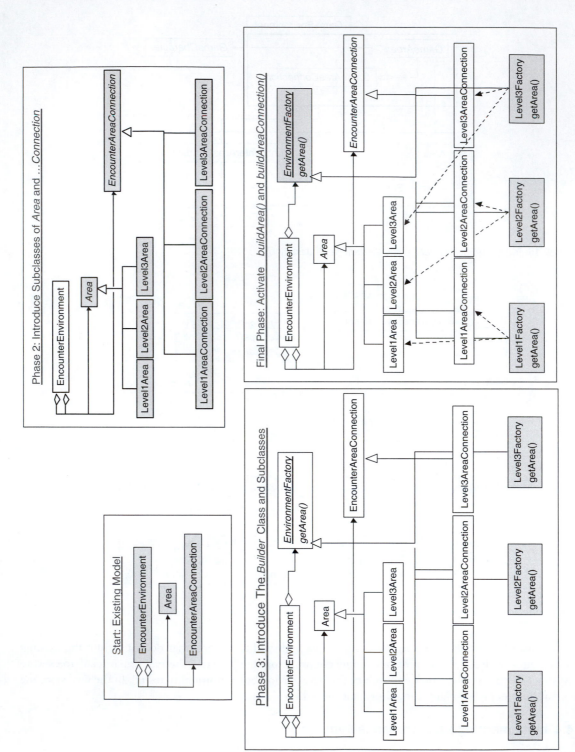

Figure 29.17 Migration plan for level-based graphics

Table 29.5 IEEE 1219-1998—Maintenance phase 4: integration

a. Input	• Original source code • Original project documentation • Detailed design from previous phase
b. Process	• Make code changes and additions • Perform unit tests • Review readiness for system testing

c. Control	• Inspect code
	• Verify . . .
	  . . . CM control of new code
	  . . . Traceability of new code

d. Output	• Updated . . .
	  . . . software
	  . . . unit test reports
	  . . . user documents

e. Selected quality factors	• Flexibility • Traceability • Comprehensibility • Maintainability • Reliability
f. Selected metrics	• Lines of code • Error rate

Source: IEEE std 1219–1998. Reproduced with permission.

The response to maintenance requests can involve a significant amount of development, and this may actually introduce new defects. The *error rate* is the number of defects created by this maintenance effort per unit of effort (e.g., person-month). The measurement methodology for these new defects has to be precisely defined—for example, "the number of defects of medium severity found within three months of deployment." Suppose, for example, that the handling of MR #162 described above consumes twenty person-days and produces ten defects; then the error rate for this MR would be $10/20 = 0.5$ defects per person-day.

The remaining maintenance steps are system testing, acceptance testing, and updating the project documentation. The procedures followed for these are similar to those for regular development.

29.5 SOFTWARE EVOLUTION

Systems that have been maintained for a significant amount of time are referred to as *legacy systems*. This term is often used, more particularly, for systems that most people would like to replace but would be expensive to replace. As previously noted, software systems that are subjected to repeated maintenance activities become larger and more complex, and maintaining them can be a challenge. Some of these challenges are as follows:

• Software complexity due to continuous maintenance—e.g., increased coupling

• Inefficiencies due to older technology

- Lack of accurate documentation

- Original developers who fully understand the systems are no longer available

As the complexity of legacy systems increase, so does the cost of maintaining them. Organizations are faced with the challenge of how to reduce costs by making systems more maintainable. A good approach, especially for systems with little or no documentation or with outdated documentation, is to start with *reverse engineering*. This is a technique in which a system is analyzed to identify its components and their inter-relationships. From this information its design and specifications are recreated. That is, we start with a low level of abstraction (source code) and create a higher level of abstraction (design and documentation). Another common technique is *reengineering*, where the system is restructured in order to improve its design and maintainability. The reengineering process often starts with reverse engineering.

29.5.1 Reverse Engineering

Software products under maintenance have a wide variety of possible histories; many existing applications are poorly or inconsistently documented, and not very well understood. This leads to inefficiencies as maintenance engineers attempt to implement MRs on systems they don't fully understand. Reverse engineering brings such a system to a consistent, documented, understood state. Two components of reverse engineering are *redocumentation* and *design recovery* [13]. Redocumentation is typically the first step in reverse engineering in which documentation describing the system is generated from existing source code. Several commercial tools are available to assist in this purpose, which can, for example, reformat the source code to make it more readable or extract comments to form documents.

Once the necessary documentation is available, the next step is design recovery. This is the process of analyzing the available documentation and knowledge about a system in order to understand its design. Once successfully completed, improvements to the design and the system can be implemented. Tools are available to generate UML class diagrams from source code, for example. This usually produces a very complicated diagram. The diagram can be used to build the key parts of the UML by hand or by erasures. Suppose, for example, that we were to lose track of the UML for the Encounter video game. We could first generate the UML for all of the code. After that we could start with a key class such as EncounterEnvironment, identify all classes that it relates to, select some among those to retain, and then repeat the process with those or start with other known classes.

29.5.2 Reengineering

The short-term goal of maintenance is to fix a problem or install a feature as soon as possible. The long-term goal is to position the changing system so that it continues to work efficiently and with reasonable cost per MR into the future. Due to increasing complexity and the escalation in cost per MR, we periodically take a fresh look at the entire architecture and design of the system. Making changes to the architecture from the top down is the main task of *reengineering*. As defined by Chikofsky and Cross [13], reengineering is the "examination and alteration of a subject system to reconstitute it in a new form and the subsequent implementation of the new form." Sometimes the reengineered system supports new requirements that the older system was unable to implement. The overall goal of reengineering is to create a system that is less complex, and ultimately, easier to maintain and less costly.

As an example of reengineering, suppose that the video store application is required to track the non-video items that customers purchase at the store (candy, paraphernalia, etc.). In the absence of reengineering, we might add variables to the *Customer* class so that when *Customer* objects are stored, these additional data are stored at the same time. In all likelihood, this approach will eventually produce a hard-to-maintain application.

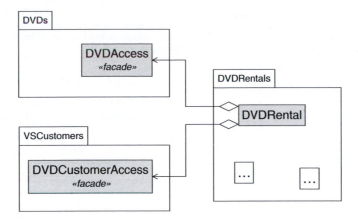

Figure 29.18 Original video store architecture

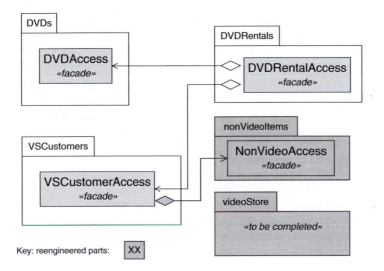

Figure 29.19 Reengineered video store architecture

Now let's consider a reengineering approach. Recall the existing video store architecture, as shown in Figure 29.18.

Tracking non-video purchases does not properly fit into any of the modules shown, and consequently a *nonVideoItems* package is introduced. Since the business of the store now consists of more than rentals, a separate management module is strongly indicated. We will label this module *videoStore*. In addition, it now becomes appropriate to introduce a facade object for the *DVDRentals* package. This results in the reengineered architecture shown in Figure 29.19.

29.6 MAINTENANCE METRICS

Since maintenance consumes a large fraction of life cycle costs, it is particularly important to quantify its costs and benefits. Not all organizations have the same goals in pursuing maintenance. Organizations first determine the maintenance goals for the application, then select or create metrics that measure their degree

Table 29.6 Maintenance metric selection by goal

Goal	Question	Selected Corresponding Metrics (The numbered metrics are from the IEEE)
Maximize customer satisfaction	*How many problems are affecting the customer?*	• Fault density = *[Number of faults found in the application]/KSLoC* "Faults" are defects found during testing or operation. KSLoC = thousands of lines of noncommented source statements • Mean time to failure = *The average time it takes to obtain a failure∗ of the application measured from startup.* • Break/fix ratio = *[Number of defects introduced by maintenance actions]/[Number of defects repaired]*
	How long does it take to fix a problem?	• Fault closure = *Average time required to correct a defect, from start of correction work.* • Fault open duration = *Average time from defect detection to validated correction.*
	Where are the bottlenecks?	• Staff utilization per task type = *Average person-months to (a) detect each defect and (b) repair each defect.* • Computer utilization = *Average time/CPU time per defect.*
Optimize effort and schedule	*Where are resources being used?*	Effort and time spent, per defect and per severity category . . . . . . planning . . . reproducing customer finding . . . reporting error . . . repairing . . . enhancing
Minimize defects	*Where are defects most likely to be found?*	• Number of entries and exits per module • Cyclomatic complexity • Ratio of commented lines/KLoC (KLoC = thousands of lines of source code, including comments)

of success in attaining those goals. Table 29.6, based on a table by Stark and Kern [14], illustrates this by showing how three different goals indicate the use of different metrics.

∗The definition of "failure" for the application under test depends on what the customer perceives as failure, and ranges from application crashes to specific types of problems. For a financial application, for example, any calculation resulting in a discrepancy of a dollar or more could be defined as a failure. In any case, the definitions should be explicit.

Let's consider how metrics can be used to manage a maintenance activity. The fraction of commented lines in the source code helps to predict the relative magnitude of a maintenance effort. For example, suppose that the application being maintained consists of three modules (Accounts Received, Timesheet, and Sick Day Recorder) each with the size and commenting data shown by the respective black and white dots in Figure 29.20.

Compared with the *Accounts received* and *Timesheet* modules, the *Sick Day Recorder* module is liable to produce the biggest maintenance challenge because it is larger and has a larger proportion of uncommented lines of code. The *Accounts Receivable* module is likely to be the least expensive to maintain because it is the smallest and has a higher than average proportion of comments. The proportion of comment lines can be obtained using a utility program or by counting from a random sample of pages of code.

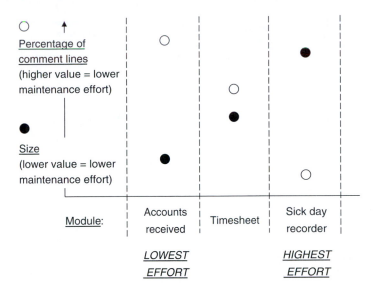

Figure 29.20 Predicting relative maintenance efforts

To manage a maintenance effort, graphs like the one in Figure 29.21 are useful. These show new, open, and closed MRs.

According to the chart in Figure 29.21, a large number of requests for repair and enhancement arrived in the first two years, resulting in a peak backlog during the second year. This backlog was eventually worked off. The profile in Figure 29.21 is a typical one, whether the comparable time scales are years, months, or weeks.

Typically, the maintenance manager tries to account separately for faults and enhancements so that the true cost of the application, as required, can be tracked.

To manage an organization's effectiveness in handling the maintenance workload, a graph such as the one in Figure 29.22 can be used. The graph shows the average number of weeks that a maintenance request (whether

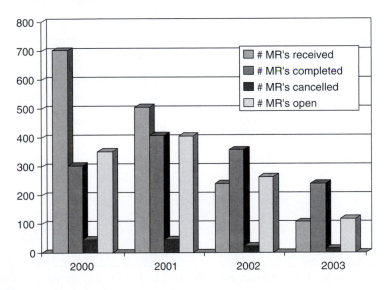

Figure 29.21 Measuring maintenance productivity

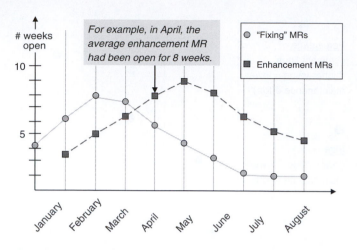

Figure 29.22 Assessing maintenance operations

a repair or an enhancement) has been waiting for resolution, measured from the time it was first reported. It shows a convergence to an average delay of about one week for repairs, and roughly four weeks for enhancements.

29.7 CASE STUDY

The following is an excerpt from the OpenOffice documentation that illustrates a means of handling defects and enhancements.

ISSUE HANDLING AS A QA TECHNIQUE IN OPENOFFICE

The *IssueZilla* (IZ) tool is an accessible list of Open-Office "issues." These include defects and enhancements. OpenOffice publishes guidelines and protocols for dealing with issues. The following is quoted from openoffice.org. Priorities range from P1 (very urgent) to P5 (will be considered when there is time). Here is a general rule of thumb for priorities:

P1–OpenOffice cannot be used for testing or development.

P2–OpenOffice crashes or basic features do not work.

P3–Bugs that usually involve a feature not working as expected.

P4–Bugs that do not affect basic features and usually have workarounds.

P5–Very minor annoying bugs.

ISSUEZILLA STATISTICS

Note to the Student:
Bugzilla allows graphical forms of data, which supplement tables such as that shown below. The core of bug tracking is a history of new, existing, and closed issues over time.

Table 29.7 is an example of the statistics available using IssueZilla [15] during an example time period. It tracks the number of defects in each state (e.g., *reopened*) within each major part (e.g., *spreadsheet*) of OpenOffice.

Table 29.7 Examples of statistics available using *IssueZilla*

Defects

Project	State	Changes	08/02/04	07/26/04	07/19/04	07/12/04	07/05/04	06/28/04	06/21/04	06/14/04	06/07/04	06/01/04
Api	reopened	0	1	1	1	1	1	1	1	1	1	1
Api	started	2	101	99	98	94	97	93	95	100	99	97
Api	unconfirmed	1	15	14	13	14	23	21	15	11	13	13
Api	new	−4	74	78	82	85	70	71	64	59	61	67
api Result			*191*	*192*	*194*	*194*	*191*	*186*	*175*	*171*	*174*	*178*
Chart	reopened	0	0	0	0	0	0	0	0	0	0	0
Chart	started	0	47	47	46	46	42	40	40	38	40	43
Chart	unconfirmed	1	4	3	1	1	1	3	2	2	2	0
Chart	new	0	3	3	3	3	3	3	1	3	2	3
chart Result			*54*	*53*	*50*	*50*	*46*	*46*	*43*	*43*	*44*	*46*
database access	reopened	−1	4	5	6	5	5	5	5	2	2	2
database access	started	−1	30	31	29	29	28	30	30	31	31	31
database access	unconfirmed	6	35	29	27	25	23	22	20	17	23	22
database access	new	−1	72	73	75	74	86	96	96	58	61	59
database access Result			*141*	*138*	*137*	*133*	*142*	*153*	*151*	*108*	*117*	*114*

Table 29.1 shows defect status at a summary level. It is a useful form for project leadership when assessing the maturity of recent MRs. Other forms of the data show defects and features ("issues") grouped according to modules. This enables a developer to work on several related issues at more or less the same time, and it enables a leader to assess the health of a module and the work of teams.

29.8 SUMMARY

Software systems continue to evolve after their initial development and release. Software maintenance consists of those activities that are performed on the system after its release, such as repair of defects, implementation of enhancements, and adaptation to changes in the environment.

The challenges of software maintenance fall into three main areas: management, process, and technical. Management must understand the complexity and value of maintenance and provide adequate support. Implementing an efficient maintenance process helps reduce the complexity. Technical challenges include the design of regression tests to ensure that implemented maintenance requests do not have unintended side effects on other parts of the system.

A typical maintenance process starts with customers providing comments on enhancements and defects through the help desk. These are written up as Maintenance Requests (MRs). MRs are regularly reviewed and prioritized, often by a change control board (CCB). The CCB is composed of stakeholder groups such as development, user documentation, marketing, quality assurance, and customer support.

An impact analysis is performed on incoming MRs that assesses the scope of the changes to product artifacts that are required in order to implement the MR. Each group represented by the CCB provides input.

Root-cause analysis is a process conducted after completing the repair of a defect MR. Its purpose is to determine the underlying reason that a defect has occurred. This information is then used to implement process improvements so that similar defects are prevented from occurring in the future.

IEEE Std 1219-1998 describes an iterative process for managing and executing software maintenance activities. The standard defines seven phases that an MR flows through, similar to the phases that occur during new product development: MR identification and prioritization, analysis, design, implementation, testing, and delivery. Each phase has six attributes associated with it that describe the activities and data for that phase: input, process, control, output, quality factors, and metrics.

As software systems evolve, they become more complex and less understood. Frequently, much of the original documentation is lost or outdated, and many if not all of the original developers are no longer available. Reverse engineering is a process that reconstructs system documentation, such as enhanced, more readable code, or class diagrams, from existing source code. An understanding of software architecture and design is then constructed from the new documentation.

Periodically, organizations take a fresh look at the whole design of a system, with the goal of reducing its complexity, increasing its efficiency, and making it more cost effective to maintain. Changing to the software architecture and design to meet these goals is referred to as reengineering. This is especially needed for older systems whose design has deteriorated over time.

It is common for organizations to define specific maintenance goals and then select or create metrics that measure the organization's degree of success in attaining those goals. For example, if a goal is to minimize defects, metrics would be collected to measure the complexity of the code, with a goal of refactoring those areas that have the highest complexity.

29.9 EXERCISES

1. Define the term "software maintenance" in one sentence.

2. Describe in your own words four types of software maintenance. Is there an example of a maintenance request that might overlap two of the categories?

3. Give examples of corrective, adaptive, perfective, and preventive changes for the Encounter case study.

4. Suppose that a proposal is made to change the length of an array in an application to accommodate requirements that were not previously satisfied. What activity is required before actual changes in the code can be made?

5. Describe a practical scenario in which the rather lengthy maintenance flow illustrated in Figure 29.6 might need to be circumvented?

6. A proposal has been made to implement the following requirement for the Encounter case study, which was initially designated optional.
   PlayerCharacter Requirement [desirable] ("Player character image") The player shall have the option to choose the image representing her main character from at least 4 GIF files

   a. What type of maintenance request (MR) is this?
   b. Provide an impact analysis for this MR.

7. Which of the following would require reengineering. Explain.

   a. Convert a simulation of the operations of a bank into an automated bank security system.
   b. Add to a simulation of the operations of a bank so that it handles the movements of security personnel.
   c. Modify an online tutoring system so that it can to provide multiple-choice quizzes at any time to permit students to assess their understanding of what they are currently reading.

8. There are many commercial reverse engineering tools that automatically generate documentation from source code. Using Internet research, identify two such tools and describe the types of documentation they generate. Explain how the documentation clarifies the source code.

TEAM EXERCISE

Maintenance

(a) Obtain project specifications from two other teams in the class. Propose at least one of each of the following types of modifications: corrective, adaptive, perfective, and preventive.
(b) Another team will have proposed four such modifications to your project. Develop an impact assessment on your project of each of these modifications.

(c) Negotiate with the team proposing modifications to your project to make them reasonable in terms of the resources required, then implement these modifications.

(d) Implement, test, and measure your modifications.

Evaluation criteria:

(1) Degree to which the proposed modifications are of the types specified

(2) Completeness of your impact assessments

(3) Degree to which the modifications have been tested

BIBLIOGRAPHY

1. "IEEE Standard Glossary of Software Engineering Terminology," *IEEE Std 610.12-1990*, December 1990.
2. Foster, J., Cost Factors in Software Maintenance, Ph.D. thesis, University of Durham, NC, Computer Science Dept, 1994, as noted in [9].
3. Pigoski, Thomas M., *Practical Software Maintenance: Best Practices for Managing Your Software Investment*, John Wiley & Sons, 1996.
4. Lehman, M., "Programs, Life Cycles, and the Laws of Software Evolution," *Proceedings IEEE*, No. 19, 1980, pp. 1060–1076.
5. Lehman, M., "Program Evolution Information Processing Management," *Proceedings IEEE*, No. 20, 1984, pp. 19–36.
6. Lientz, Bennett P., and E. Burton Swanson, *"Software Maintenance Management,"* Addison-Wesley, 1980.
7. Lientz, Bennett P., E. Burton Swanson, and Gerry E. Tompkins, "Characteristics of Applications Software Maintenance," *Communications of the ACM (CACM)*, No. 21, 1978, pp. 466–471.
8. Bennett, K.,"Software Maintenance: A Tutorial," Software Engineering, *IEEE Computer Society*, November 1999, as noted in [Dorfman and Thayer, 1999].
9. Rakitin, Steven R., *"Software Verification and Validation for Practitioners and Managers,"* Artech House Publishers, 2001,.
10. McConnell, Steve, *"Rapid Development: Taming Wild Software Schedules,"* Microsoft Press, 1996.
11. Arthur, Lowell J., Improving Software Quality: An Insider's Guide to TQM, John Wiley & Sons, 1993.
12. "IEEE Standard for Software Maintenance," *IEEE Std 1219-1998*, 1998.
13. Chikofsky, Elliott. J., and James H. Cross II, "Reverse Engineering and Design Recovery: A Taxonomy," *IEEE Software*, Vol. 7, no. 1, 1990, pp. 13–17.
14. Stark, George E., and Louise C. Kern, "A Software Metric Set for Program Maintenance Management," *Journal of Systems and Software*, No. 24, 1994, pp. 239–249.
15. OpenOffice. http://qa.openoffice.org/iz_statistic.html [accessed November 18, 2009].

Glossary

Acceptance testing   The process of testing an application on behalf of the customer to enable the customer to validate that the requirements have been met.

Actor   A particular role adopted by the user of an application while participating in a use case.

Agile development processes   Highly iterative processes that emphasize working code and frequent interaction with the customer.

Alpha release   A preliminary version of an application given to highly trusted customers and/or internal users to obtain feedback.

American National Standards Institute (ANSI)   A widely recognized U.S. nonprofit standards and accreditation organization.

Application Programming Interface (API)   A set of classes and member function prototypes provided for the benefit of programmers. The function information consists of its name, parameter types, return types, and exceptions thrown.

Architecture, Software   An overall design of an application, including its decomposition into parts.

Artifact   Any kind of data, source code, or information produced or used by a participant in the development process.

Association for Computing Machinery (ACM)   An organization of professionals involved in the computing enterprise, emphasizing software.

Attribute   A variable of a class as a whole (not a variable local to a method). Also called a *field*.

B-language   A formal, mathematical language for specifying and, in part, implementing an application.

Baseline   A known and documented version, form, configuration, or implementation of an artifact. Subsequent changed versions are compared with it.

Beta release   A preliminary version of an application, given to selected customers to help detect defects, and to obtain feedback.

Black box method   A testing method, applied to implemented code, which takes into account input and output only (i.e., not the internal manner in which the code operates).

Build   A partial implementation of an application.

Business process reengineering (BPR)   A systematic design of a business process, such as purchase order handling, from beginning to end, including human and non-human aspects, typically performed from scratch.

Capability assessment   A process by which the capability of an organization, group, or person to produce software, is measured in a quantitative and objective manner.

Capability Maturity Model (CMM and CMM-I)   A systematic manner of assessing the overall capability of an organization to develop software; developed by the Software Engineering Institute in Pittsburgh, PA. CMM-I is a successor to CMM.

Change control board (CCB)   A committee that decides whether or not a proposed enhancement or repair to an application should be implemented.

Code inspection   A process by which a team inspects a program to find defects.

Coding   Another term for programming.

Commercial off-the-shelf (COTS)   Commercially available software product. In this context, such software is used to work with code built from scratch to create an application.

Common object request broker architecture (CORBA)   A standard under which applications can invoke functions residing on remote platforms, regardless of the language in which they are written.

Computer aided design/Computer aided manufacturing (CAD/CAM)   Graphic-intensive software which assists in the design and manufacturing of electronic, construction, or mechanical products.

Computer-aided software engineering (CASE)   The software engineering process, when assisted by a coordinated set of software tools. These tools are tailored to the various phases of software development.

Configuration item (CI)   An artifact whose versions are specifically tracked from the beginning to the end of a project.

Configuration management (CM)   The process of maintaining and managing the various versions of various artifacts of a software project.

Constraint   A specified limitation.

Constructive Cost Model (COCOMO)   Barry Boehm's formulas for computing the probable labor requirements, in person-months, to build an application, and the probable elapsed time, based on the estimated lines of code.

Critical design review (CDR)   A process of deciding once and for all whether or not to proceed with a proposed design. The process includes, or may consist entirely of, a meeting.

Data base management system (DBMS)   A system for organizing and accessing data.

Data flow diagram (DFD)   A diagram showing how data flows into, within, and out of an application. The data flows among the application's user, the data stores, and internal processing elements of the application.

Defect   A deviation from what is explicitly or implicitly required.

Design pattern   A pattern of commonly occurring classes, relationships among them, and accompanying algorithms.

Detailed requirements   (also "Developer requirements") A form of requirements primarily suitable for developers to work from, but also forming part of the requirements for customers.

Eclipse   An open source software development environment.

Encounter   The video game case study used in this book.

Event   An occurrence affecting an object, initiated externally to the object.

Extreme Programming (XP)   A widely used, early agile process pioneered by Kent Beck.

Formal methods   Rigorous methods for specifying requirements, design, or implementation; mathematical and logical in nature.

Framework   A collection of general classes that forms the basis for several applications. The classes of each application aggregate or inherit from the framework's classes.

Function-oriented organization   A managerial organization built around job functions such as programming and marketing.

Function point (FP)   A measure of an application's complexity.

Functional requirement   A requirement expressing a function which an application must perform. This contrasts with non-functional requirements such as processing speed.

Graphical user interface (GUI)   A graphic display, often interactive, by means of which a user interacts with an application.

Help desk   A facility for providing help to users of an application.

High-level requirements   Requirements stated in a summary form.

Incremental process   An iterative software development process in which each iteration consists of small changes.

Independent verification and validation (IV&V)   The process of performing verification and validation by a third party (i.e., not by the organization performing the development or by the customer).

Institute of Electrical, and Electronics Engineers (IEEE)   An organization of professionals, dedicated to engineering involving electronics, electricity, and software.

Integration   The fusing of application modules to form an application.

Integration testing   The process of testing for the successful fusing of modules.

Interactive development environment (IDE)   A software application that helps developers to create, edit, compile, and execute code.

Interface   An interface for a software system is a specification of a set of functions which the system provides. This includes the names of the functions, their parameter types, return types, and exceptions.

International Standards Organization (ISO)   A widely recognized international body that sets standards such as quality standards.

Invariant   A relationship among variables which, within a specified context, does not change (the values of the individual variables may change, however).

Inverse requirement   A specification which is specifically *not* required of an application.

Iteration   The process of adding requirements, design, implementation, and testing to a partially built application.

Iterative development   A process that repetitively uses the requirements/design/implementation/test sequence of phases.

Legacy application   An application that has been delivered and used.

Legacy systems   Existing computer systems that continue to have value.

Maintenance   The process of repairing and enhancing an application that has been delivered.

Maintenance request (MR)   A request to modify or add to an existing application.

Matrix organization   A way to organize employees in which each manager formally supervises a group with similar skill types (he is their *line manager*). Employees may work on one or more projects involving personnel with different kinds of skill sets. Projects are managed by *project managers*.

Mean time between failures (MTBF)   The quantity (Time an application is in use)/(number of occasions the application failed during that time); a definition of "failure" is made and used consistently.

Mean time to failure (MTTF)   The average time elapsing between starting an application and its first failure.

Meta-process   A process concerning processes.

Metric   A means of measuring (assigning a number to) a software engineering artifact. For example, *lines of code* is a metric for source code.

Model   A view of an application's design from a particular perspective, such as the relationships between its classes, or its event-driven behavior.

Non-comment lines of source code (NCSLOC) A line of source code which is not a comment.

Non-functional requirement A requirement placed upon an application that does not involve any specific functionality. A constraint on memory is an example.

Object-oriented (OO) An organization of designs and code into classes and instances ("objects"). Every object in a given class is provided with a set of functions specified for that class; each object has a copy of a set of variables specified for the class.

Object Management Group (OMG) A non-profit organization of companies, which establishes standards for distributed object computing.

OpenOffice An open source office productivity software suite.

Open Source Project A project to produce a free software application in which the source code is available free and which qualifies individuals to contribute.

Paradigm A way of thinking, such as the object-oriented paradigm.

Personal software documentation (PSD) Documentation that an individual maintains about the current status of his or her code.

Personal Software Process^{SM} **(PSP)** A process, developed by Watts Humphrey at the Software Engineering Institute, for improving and measuring the software engineering capability of individual software engineers.

Phase See *Software development phase.*

Physical configuration audit (PCA) A systematic review of a project's physical artifacts on hand, including the documents, source code, files, tapes, and disks.

Preliminary design review (PDR) A meeting at which an early draft of a design, of all or part of the project, is presented and critiqued by engineers and managers.

Process A "software process" is a sequence of activities or phases in which development activities are performed.

Project management The process of fulfilling the responsibility for the successful completion of a project.

Project-oriented organization A way to organize employees in which each reports to the manager of a project.

Prototype An application that illustrates or demonstrates some aspect(s) of an application that is under construction.

Provably correct program A program written in such a manner that a mathematical and logical proof can be produced which proves that the program satisfies its requirements.

Pseudocode An English-like language which is formal enough to describe an algorithm.

Quality assurance (QA) The process of ensuring that a specified level of quality is being attained in the execution of a project; may also be used to refer to the organization performing this function, rather than the function itself.

Rapid application development (RAD) The process of quickly developing an application, or part thereof, typically sacrificing proper documentation, design, or extensibility.

Reengineering Given an existing application, this is a process of redesigning all or part of it and then modifying the existing application to fit the new design.

Refactoring A process of changing the design and/or code of an application to improve it (e.g., to make it easier to modify) while retaining its functionality.

Regression testing Validating that the addition of code to an application under development, or its alteration, has not diminished the capability it possessed before the changes were made.

Requirements The wants and needs of the customer for a software application; often in the form of a written document.

Requirements analysis The process of obtaining a complete, typically written, statement of what functionality, appearance, performance, and behavior are required of an application.

Reverse engineering The process of deducing the contents of a software development phase from the artifacts of a subsequent phase (for example, deducing the design from the code).

Risk retirement The process of dealing with a perceived threat to the successful execution of a project (a risk), either by finding a way to avoid the risk, or by taking action to eliminate its impact.

Roadmap A list of activities which result in attaining a specified goal.

Robustness The quality of an application in which it responds reasonably to improper input.

Role-playing game (RPG) A game, often a video game, in which the players assume roles and interact with each other in those roles.

Scrum An agile process based on iterations known as *sprints*, developed by Ken Schwaber and others.

Security The property of an application that inhibits malicious exploits on it.

Sequence diagram A diagram involving objects of an application, showing a sequence of function calls between the objects. Sequence diagrams usually elaborate upon use cases.

Software cost estimation The process of estimating the cost to produce an application based on partial information (e.g., the requirements document alone).

Software configuration management plan (SCMP) A document that specifies how the code and documents of a project, and all of their versions, are to be managed.

Software design document (SDD) A document describing the design of a software application.

Software development folder (SDF) A document specifying the current status of the code on which an individual software engineer is working. This includes all details about the unit testing which the engineer has performed to date.

Software development phase An identifiable and related set of activities that is part of the software development process, such as requirements analysis.

Software engineering The discipline for creating software applications.

Software Engineering Institute (SEI) An institute initially founded to improve the quality of U.S. defense software. Its work is used by many non-defense organizations as well.

Software maintenance See *Maintenance*.

Software project management plan (SPMP) A plan stating who will develop what parts of an application, and in what order they will do so.

Software quality The degree to which an application satisfies its explicit and implicit requirements. Sometimes defined as the degree to which an application exceeds requirements.

Software Quality Assurance Plan (SQAP) A document describing the manner in which quality is to be attained in a software project.

Software requirements specification (SRS) A document stating what an application must accomplish.

Software test documentation (STD) A document that specifies all aspects of the testing process for an application.

Software test plan (STP)   Documentation stating what parts of an application will be tested, and the schedule of when testing is to be performed.

Software Verification and Validation Plan (SVVP)   A document describing the manner in which a software project is to be verified and validated.

Spiral Model   An early iterative process, developed by Barry Boehm, in which several of the iterations have identified purposes.

Stakeholder   A person, group, or organization with a stake in the outcome of an application being developed.

State   An object's status; formally defined as set of values of the object's variables. For example, an *Automobile* object can be defined as in "early" state if its *mileage* value is less than 10,000 and in "late" state if greater than 150,000.

System engineering   The process of analyzing and designing an entire system, including the hardware and software.

System testing   The process of testing an entire application (as opposed to testing its parts).

Team Software Process^{SM} (TSP)   A process, developed by Watts Humphrey at the Software Engineering Institute, for assessing and improving the performance of teams developing software.

Testable   An artifact (e.g., a requirement) for which it is possible to write a specific test validating that the product is consistent with the artifact.

Test-driven development (TDD)   A software development process in which each successive part is developed by first creating a set of tests that validate it, then implementing the code that passes these tests.

Traceable   A requirement is traceable if the design and code fragments that implement it can be readily identified; a requirement is not traceable if it is unclear which parts of the design accommodate it, or which parts of the code implement it.

Traceability   The capacity of a software development process to enable developers to track each requirement to the code that implements it and to track each part of the code base back to the corresponding elements of design and requirement.

Transition   (in a state diagram) The process under which an object changes from being in one state to being in another.

TSPi   A version of the Team Software Process® tailored to the restrictions of university student teams.

Unified modeling language (UML)   A graphical notation for expressing object-oriented designs.

Unified Process (UP)   A software development process based on named iterations, developed by Booch, Jacobson, and Rumbaugh and made popular by Rational (and then the IBM) Corporation.

Unified Software Development Process (USDP)   A development process created by Booch, Jacobson, and Rumbaugh, often considered most appropriate for large software projects.

Unit testing   The process of testing a relatively small part of an application such as a method.

Use case   A sequence of actions, some taken by an application and some by the user, which are common in using an application; the user assumes a particular role in this interaction, called an "actor" relative to the use case.

User story   An intended major usage of the application, told from the user's perspective, from beginning to end.

Validation   The process of ensuring that a software application or artifact of the development process performs its intended functions in the manner specified for it.

Verification The process of ensuring that a software application is being built in the manner planned.

Waterfall process A software development process in which requirements are first collected, a design is developed, the design implemented in code, and then the code tested. This is performed in a single sequence, with a small amount of overlap between the successive phases.

White box process A method, typically testing, applied to implemented code, which takes into account the manner in which the code is intended to operate.

Xtreme Programming See *Extreme Programming*.

Z-specifications A mathematical notation for expressing requirements precisely and formally.

Index